Screening China

Critical Interventions, Cinematic
Reconfigurations, and the Transnational
Imaginary in Contemporary Chinese Cinema

Yingjin Zhang

CENTER FOR CHINESE STUDIES
UNIVERSITY OF MICHIGAN ANN ARBOR

MICHIGAN MONOGRAPHS IN CHINESE STUDIES
SERIES ESTABLISHED 1968

Published by
Center for Chinese Studies
The University of Michigan
Ann Arbor, Michigan 48104-1608

Second Printing 2003

Library of Congress Cataloging-in-Publication Data

Zhang, Yingjin.
    Screening China : critical interventions, cinematic reconfigurations,
    and the transnational imaginary in contemporary Chinese cinema /
    Yingjin Zhang.
        p. cm.—(Michigan monographs in Chinese studies ; vol. 92)
    Includes bibliographical references and index.
    ISBN 0-89264-147-9 (cloth : alk. paper)—ISBN 0-89264-158-4
    (paper : alk. paper)
        1. Motion pictures—China. I. Title. II. Michigan monographs in
    Chinese studies ; no. 92.

PN1993.5.C4 Z54 2002
791.43'0951—dc21   2002017516

In memory of my parents:
Zhang Peifen (1921–69) and Guo Jian (1918–99)

Contents

Part I Critical Interventions: History, Politics, Methodology

Part II Cinematic Reconfigurations: Nation, Culture, Agency

Note to the Reader

Except for personal names and bibliographical data, the pinyin system is used throughout the book. The character list also contains all Chinese film titles, studio names, and a selection of technical terms. The index contains all film titles in English with years of release. The reader is advised to locate further information on a particular film (such as its director and studio) in the Filmography, where films are listed chronologically.

The following abbreviations are used throughout the book:

aka = also known as
CCTV = China Central Television (Zhongyang dianshitai), Beijing
CMPC = Central Motion Picture Corporation (Zhongyang dianying gongsi), Taipei

Illustrations

All illustrations courtesy of the China Film Archive (Zhongguo dianying ziliao guan), Beijing.

Acknowledgments

The research and writing of this book spanned over a decade and would not have resulted in the present form without generous fellowships and grants from many agencies and institutions. First, I want to express my gratitude to the Center for Chinese Studies (CCS) at the University of Michigan for a postdoctoral research fellowship in 1995–96, during which time this book initially took shape. As the last year-long fellow at CCS, it is my obligation and honor to publish with Michigan, and I hope this book lives up to the expectations of my colleagues there. I also want to thank the National Endowment for the Humanities (NEH) for a Summer Faculty Stipend in 1999, and to the Pacific Cultural Foundation in Taiwan for a research grant in 1999–2000. To Indiana University I am indebted to the Research and University Graduate School and the College of Arts and Sciences for a research leave supplement in 1995–96, for summer faculty fellowships in 1993, 1995, 1996, 1999, and 2000, as well as for research grants and funds in 1992–2001; to the Office of the Dean of the Faculties for an Outstanding Junior Faculty Award in 1996–97 and a sabbatical research leave in Fall 1999; to the International Programs at Indiana University for two short-term faculty exchanges at Nankai University, China in 1996 and 1999, and an overseas conference travel fund in 2000; and to the Department of East Asian Languages and Cultures for research funds and graduate assistantships in 1996–2001. In addition, I am grateful to the East Asian Studies Center at Indiana University, the American Council of Learned Societies (ACLS), and several research centers and libraries at the University of Chicago, Harvard University, the University of Michigan, and Stanford University for numerous travel grants in 1992–2000.

On the personal side, I would like to acknowledge the encouragement and support from my colleagues and friends on both sides of the Pacific: to Dudley Andrew, Ru-Shou Robert Chen, Chen Mei, Cheng Jihua, Sheldon Hsiao-peng Lu, Paul G. Pickowicz, and Zhiwei Xiao, who have shared my fascination with Chinese cinema; to Michael Curtin, Eugene Chen Eoyang, David Hertz, Sumie Jones, Sue Tuohy, Jeffrey Wasserstrom, and George M. Wilson, who have provided collegiality at

Indiana; to Yi-tsi Mei Feuerwerker, Hans Ulrich Gumbrecht, Jeffrey Kinkley, Wendy Larson, Leo Ou-fan Lee, Shuen-fu Lin, Perry Link, Herbert Lindenberger, David Rolston, Mayfair Yang, and Zhang Longxi, who have endorsed my various research projects at different stages. I also want to thank Noriko Kamachi, Terre Fisher, and Joseph Mooney of CCS Publications for bringing this book through the review, editing, and production process with such efficiency. Last but not least, I appreciate the patience and understanding of my wife Jean Su, my daughter Mimi, and my son Alex, whose interest in watching movies East and West made the writing of this book all the more rewarding to me.

This book is dedicated to my parents, whose life trajectory brought them from a coastal community in southern Fujian, China, to Manila, the Philippines, and through Hong Kong back to Fujian. To them China functioned differently at different times: a native place, a faraway homeland, an occupied country, an exhilarating new society, a paranoiac prison house, a disillusioned world, and a final resting place.

The information regarding previously published portions of this book is indicated in the Copyright Acknowledgments. All earlier publications have been revised and expanded, in most cases extensively, for inclusion in the present book. I am grateful to the editors and publishers of the journals for granting me permission to use my previous publications.

Over the years I presented portions of the earlier drafts of this book at conferences, colloquia, and lectures at various universities. Many thanks go to my hosts, organizers, discussants, and audiences at the University of California at Irvine, Los Angeles, and San Diego, at Indiana University, the University of Iowa, the University of Michigan, the University of North Carolina at Chapel Hill, the University of Notre Dame, the University of Pittsburgh, Rutgers University, the University of Southern California, as well as Beijing University, Nankai University, and Xiamen University in China, the Baptist University, the City University, and Lingnan University in Hong Kong, and Fu Jen University, the National Central University, and the National College of Arts in Taiwan.

Y.Z.

Copyright Acknowledgments

A shorter version of chapter 2 appeared as "Chinese Cinema and Transnational Cultural Politics: Reflections on Film Festivals, Film Productions, and Film Studies" in *Journal of Modern Literature in Chinese* (Hong Kong) 2.1 (July 1998): 105–32. © 1998 Lingnan University, Hong Kong. Reprinted by permission.

A section of chapter 3 appeared as "Review Essay: Screening China—Recent Studies of Chinese Cinema in English" in *Bulletin of Concerned Asian Scholars* 29.3 (July–Sept. 1997): 59–66. Reprinted by permission. © 1997 *Bulletin of Concerned Asian Scholars*, Inc. Reprinted by permission.

A shorter version of chapter 4 appeared as "Rethinking Cross-Cultural Analysis: The Questions of Authority, Power, and Difference in Western Studies of Chinese Films" in *Bulletin of Concerned Asian Scholars* 26.4 (Oct.–Dec. 1994): 44–53. © 1994 *Bulletin of Concerned Asian Scholars*, Inc., all rights reserved. Reprinted by permission.

A section of chapter 5 appeared as "From 'Minority Film' to 'Minority Discourse': Questions of Nationhood and Ethnicity in Chinese Film Studies" in *Cinema Journal* 36.3 (Spring 1997): 73–90. © 1997 University of Texas Press, P.O. Box 7819, Austin, TX 78713-7819. Reprinted by permission.

A section of chapter 6 appeared as "Ideology of the Body in *Red Sorghum*: National Allegory, National Roots, and Third Cinema" in *East-West Film Journal* 4.2 (June 1990): 38–53; anthologized in *Colonialism and Nationalism in Asian Cinema*, edited by Wimal Dissanayake (Indiana University Press, 1994), 30–41. © 1990 The East-West Center, Inc. Reprinted by permission.

Part I

Critical Interventions:
History, Politics, Methodology

Introduction: Screening China at the *Fin de Siècle*

> [T]he film historian may interact with movies on behalf of culture. This is the middle road located somewhere between the highway of socio-economic history and the folk path of personal biography. Along this road lies the varied landscape of culture, a landscape whose ecology features the complex and contradictory interplay of institutions, expressions, and repressions, all subject to the force fields of power.
>
> Dudley Andrew, "Film and History"

Screening China

Since its emergence in international film festivals and its institutionalization in Western academia in the mid-1980s, contemporary Chinese cinema has become part of the "varied landscape of culture" as Dudley Andrew describes above (1998, 187). In China, the Communist government still exercises its repressive power with regard to what images of China are permitted to be produced and screened at home and abroad.[1] In the West, international film festivals select only those "art films" and subversive "underground films" that fit their pre-established visions of China or Chineseness and thereby encourage more production of such films for Western consumption. Meanwhile, Chinese filmmakers, including those in Hong Kong and Taiwan, continue to invent and expand a wide array of cinematic expressions and to redefine and

---

[1] Due to internal political reasons, the Communist government regularly protests the selections made by several international film festivals and from time to time denies filmmakers the right to travel abroad for award ceremonies. In 1997, Zhang Yuan was barred from leaving China to present *East Palace, West Palace* (Donggong xigong, 1997), the first gay feature film in China, at the Cannes International Film Festival, and Zhang Yimou's *Keep Cool* (Youhua haohao shuo, 1997), under pressure from the government, was eventually withdrawn from the festival as a further gesture of protest. In response, however, the Cannes organizers placed an empty chair on the stage to symbolize Zhang Yuan's absence. See Berry 1998b, 84.

reimagine a space of their own vis-à-vis domestic regimes on the one hand and the ever-threatening forces of globalization on the other.

Three sets of problems constitute the core objects of analysis in this book: (1) "Chineseness" as projected and problematized in cinematic and critical discourses; (2) Chinese cinema in relation to Eurocentrism in Western media studies; and (3) negotiations between the local and the global in the production, distribution, exhibition, and consumption of Chinese films around the world.

First, in the age of global consumerism, it is precisely the ethnic and cultural markers in Chinese cinema that appear to be increasingly problematic. As China is screened as cinematic, electronic, and televisual images globally, its very "Chineseness" makes critical scrutiny from a variety of perspectives inevitable. Second, in the course of its institutionalization in Western academia, Chinese cinema is frequently treated as raw material to be processed by the latest "technology" of Western theory, which presumably possesses universal, transhistorical applicability. Questions of difference, power, and authority arise therefore to challenge scholars engaged in cross-cultural representation, further complicating the Eurocentric model of disciplinary, interdisciplinary, or transdisciplinary studies. Finally, in the West there is an "over-riding fear that cultural, ethnic, and racial differences will be continually commodified and offered up as new dishes to enhance the white palate—that the Other will be eaten, consumed, and forgotten" (hooks 1992, 39). In other words, ethnic and cultural differences are now more likely to be consumed as mere glossy images of exotica and eroticism rather than something that matters to the Other. *Eat Drink Man Woman* (Yinshi nannü, 1994), therefore, may be consumed to "enhance the white palate." Similarly, "Western audiences have acculturated themselves to the exotic quality of Hong Kong movies: the Hong Kong cinema is now as universal as Chinese food" (Teo 1997, xi). Thus caught between a seemingly strong demand for ethnic and cultural images from the West and economic and political restrictions at home, Chinese filmmakers must reconsider the very conditions of their existence and survival in the era of transnational capitalism. In this regard, a question Masao Miyoshi raised in the early 1990s still bears relevance today: "How then to balance the transnationalization of economy and politics with the survival of local culture and history—without mummifying them with tourism and in museums?" (1993, 747)[2]

In this book I engage these three sets of problems at two levels: first, Chinese filmmakers' reconfigurations of China and their strategies for positioning their work between the global and the local; and second, critical discourse—especially Western transnational discourse—that screens a limited number of Chinese cinematic texts, purportedly for promoting cross-cultural exchange but most often to demonstrate the power of its theoretical constructs.

Three distinct but interrelated meanings of "screening" may be spelled out at this juncture. First, "screening" refers to "projecting cinematic images," a creative act that pertains directly to cultural production. Second, it carries the sense of concealment, placing a screen in front to conceal something, whether a creative or critical strategy. Third, "screening" means to scrutinize in minute detail, an act most relevant to discursive criticism. To contextualize critical issues in North American academia, where most of the readers of this book may encounter it, I begin my study at the level of critical discourse in Part I, then move on to the primary (or textual) materials in Part II, while keeping an informed dialogue between the two throughout.

My examination of critical discourse on Chinese cinema reveals a number of lenses through which China, otherwise an enormous, complex, and ever-evolving entity, is conveniently broken down, neatly packaged, and brought under close scrutiny. For instance, the Western media pays particular attention to censorship issues and often takes China to be a monolithic political entity, a Communist regime notorious for its hard-line repression of artistic freedom and its repeated violations of basic human rights (see chapters 2 and 8). Similarly, official Communist discourse envisions China as a unitary political entity thriving on the solidarity of its diverse ethnic minorities and their presumed willingness to contribute to and sacrifice for the great nation-state (see chapter 5).

---

[2] Elsewhere, Miyoshi reiterates his warning: "There is always a theoretical possibility that regional cultures everywhere may be obliterated before long" (1998, 259). Anthony Smith argues in a less alarming fashion (1990, 176): "[T]he same telecommunications base will eventually erode cultural differences and create a genuinely 'global culture' based on the properties of the media themselves, to which the 'message' will become increasingly incidental. For the rest, tourism and museology alone will preserve the memory of an earlier era of 'national cultures.'"

On the other hand, China as a singular ethnic marker and Chineseness as an essentialized entity have been critiqued and deconstructed in contemporary scholarly works, especially in anthropology, cultural studies, and history (Ang 1994; Chow 1998c; Chun 1996; Duara, 1995). From the "ruins" of such analyses have emerged, somewhat ironically if not unexpectedly, new concepts of pan-Chinese ethnicity, most recently exemplified in the formulation of "flexible citizenship" (see Ong 1999). Moreover, "cultural China" or "Greater China" as a transnational entity that encompasses (or even unites) all Chinese communities around the world has been posited as a spiritual, civilizing force formidable enough to resist the widespread, all-engulfing material culture of global capitalism (Tu 1991).[3]

At the textual level, Chinese filmmakers have also appropriated China as a cultural and ethnic entity rather than as a political one. The emergence of New Chinese Cinema is in fact a direct outcome of the sustained movement of cultural criticism that fundamentally transformed the Chinese intellectual world of the early 1980s (J. Wang 1996; X. Zhang 1997). In cinematic texts, a kind of "minority discourse" was engaged to challenge the decades-long hegemony of Maoist political culture. Significantly, the ethnic otherness as represented in exotic and esoteric Dai, Mongolian (Menggu), and Tibetan (Zang) cultures provided a space for self-reflection, a reflection of Chinese (Han) culture and history that ultimately aimed to reconstitute and reinscribe individual subjectivity among contemporary Chinese (see chapter 5). The emphasis on the cultural, such as the ideas of searching for one's roots and primitive vitality, and the visual (new film language and new directorial styles) in turn fashioned, consciously or not on the part of filmmakers, a new type of "ethnographic" cinema in the late 1980s and early 1990s (see chapter 6). It is not without irony that the popularity of Chinese films in international film festivals and Western art-theater circuits has provoked severe criticism both in China and overseas. Directors like Chen Kaige and Zhang Yimou have been accused of using China's ethnic otherness as a selling point to cater to and gratify Western audiences' insatiable appetite for cultural exoticism (see chapter 2).

The fact remains, however, that New Chinese Cinema, at least in its most important phase in the mid-1980s, succeeded in creating a hitherto

---

[3] For critiques, see Ang 1998; Callahan, 1993, 67–74; Dirlik, 1995; Harding 1993; Palumbo-Liu 1999, 356–67; Shambaugh 1995. See also Ong and Nonini 1997.

nonexistent discursive space for the formation and transformation of individual identities and subjectivities. These films present China in all its social, historical, political, ethnic, cultural, and economic facets, and provide a stimulating experience for viewers: aesthetic appreciation, emotional release, psychological fulfillment, philosophical meditation, cultural critique, and political intervention, among others (see chapter 6). Given this potential, it is only natural that New Chinese Cinema has been eagerly received by film critics, literary scholars, cultural historians, political scientists, and anthropologists. The rapid growth of academic research in and the teaching of contemporary Chinese cinema in North America over the past two decades, therefore, is itself significant. It not only reconfirms the age-old Western fascination with China as a quintessential Other but also lays bare the sensitive issues in cross-cultural, comparative studies of East and West. Equally important, it foregrounds the issue of the critic's self-reflexivity and self-positioning in relation to the projects of screening China (see chapter 3).

Critical Self-Positioning

A brief detour through an exchange between the critics Rey Chow and Zhang Longxi may help flesh out the problems I mean to address. As early as 1991, Chow admitted that, as an ethnic critic, self-styled as "a 'Westernized' Chinese woman who spent most of her formative years in a British colony and then in the United States," she faced a predicament: "'Western theory' is there, beyond my control; yet in order to speak, I must come to terms with it" (1991b, xv, xvi). For Chow, this process not only involves a total immersion in Western theory, but also aspires to a critique of "the hegemonic status of Western theoretical thinking" (1991b, xii). Yet, in spite of Chow's contention that her "use of 'Western theory' to understand the non-West is . . . a reversal of what happens historically" (1991b, xvi)—the domination of the West over the non-West—such a "reversal" is barely discernible in her review of the Western media coverage of the 1989 Tiananmen pro-democracy movement in Beijing. In her sensationally titled essay "Violence in the Other Country: China as Crisis, Spectacle, and Woman," Chow first acknowledges "the futility of intellectual discourse" in the shock of the Tiananmen crisis, but proceeds to "raise a set of questions that pertain more *closely to us in the U.S.*, where . . . China is . . . a spectacle for the West" (1991a, 82–3, emphasis added). Based on what she sees as the "fetish of the white woman" in the "goddess of liberty" erected by the student demonstrators to symbolize what China "lacks" (freedom and democracy), Chow contends that China-as-spectacle is translatable into China-as-woman, especially in her relation to the West as (male) spectator.[4]

Chow invokes two Hollywood films as "paradigms"—or critical lenses—through which to examine how China-as-woman has been represented in the West. The first paradigm, represented by the film *King Kong* (1933), is "the blatant imperialistic acts of capture and murder that describe the King Kong syndrome" that surfaces in the Western media coverage of the military violence against the students in Beijing. The second paradigm, represented by *Gorillas in the Mist* (1988), is "the lofty spiritual ideal of 'letting the Other live in their place and my love,'" which supposedly characterizes the field of sinology and China studies, where "the authority of the Chinese tradition [is reaffirmed] to the exclusion of other, 'non-Chinese' modes of inquiry" (1991a, 92, 90).[5] Through the metaphor of "ape narratives," Chow extends her personal experience of disillusionment to Chinese literature studies: "I have attended lectures by women sinologists who research well-known classical Chinese texts for their themes on women and who recall with great relish the details of those texts as if they were the details of an exotic jungle. In this case . . . the sinologist 'submits' to the language of the gorillas" (1991a, 90, 94).[6]

---

[4] Chow commits a factual error here, since the Chinese demonstrators specifically named their statue Goddess of Democracy (*Minzhu nüshen*) to distinguish it from the Statue of Liberty (translated as *Ziyou nüshen*) in New York harbor (see Saussy 1999, 151). On another occasion (1991b, 3–33), Chow makes a similar claim on China-as-woman in her reading of *The Last Emperor* (1987).

[5] Chow's interest in the King Kong syndrome is further evident in her essay on the Western coverage of the handover of Hong Kong to China in July 1997 (1998d).

[6] Chow's description of a male "sinologist" elsewhere is even more pointed than her "ape" metaphor. In terms of Freud's analysis of melancholia, she takes note of "a sulking impotence" in Stephen Owen, who appears to be "the abandoned subject" in light of a "reversed" historical situation: "Writers of the 'third world' like Bei Dao now appear not as the oppressed but as oppressors, who aggress against the 'first world' sinologist by robbing him of his love," the tradition of classical Chinese poetry (1993, 4). Owen, to be sure, is by no means a "die-hard" sinologist blind to or ignorant of Western theory; on the contrary, he has published major works on Chinese-Western comparative literature (1989). The occasion of Chow's attack on Owen is the latter's depreciatory review of a contemporary poetry collection by Bei Dao, a dissident, exiled Chinese poet rumored to

In his trenchant criticism of Chow, Zhang Longxi points out the danger of displacing Chinese reality with Western theory: "The problem with such an ingenious use of theory, however, is that the brutal reality of massacre gets lost in the analysis, and that it not only collapses a crucial difference between the reality in China and the fictionality in *King Kong*, but has Chinese reality and its serious, extratextual substance displaced by Hollywood fictionality" (1992, 115). In particular, Zhang questions the arrogance of the Western(ized) critic and the condescending attitude towards the Chinese students, who, in Chow's words, "have been, precisely because of the cultural isolationism implemented by the government at different levels, deprived of the intellectual space that would allow them the kind of critical understanding I am suggesting" (1991a, 87). Chow refers here to the recent deconstruction of notions of "democracy" in Western academia. She deplores the fact that Chinese demonstrators, unaware of this "high" level of critical understanding, were not able to come up with a symbol that would go beyond fetishization of "the white woman." Indeed, in Chow's discursive move, historical contingencies are suspended, and one sees not only a voluntary act of allegiance to Western theory, but also an outright—and surely "imperialist"—demand for the alignment of non-Western thinking to the kind of "critical understanding" originating from and currently in vogue in the West. In cases like this, it is clear that Western theory is not exempt from the charge of "cultural imperialism" (a point to be pursued further in chapter 4).

Not surprisingly, "Chinese reality," a term Zhang Longxi sets up to counter "Western theory," proves difficult, even impossible, to theorize about. Confronted with "the skeptical and sometimes even agnostic attitude characteristic of much of contemporary Western theory," Zhang takes a metaphysical approach: "Chinese reality, not unlike the Chinese philosophical notion of *tao*, exists nowhere and everywhere; nothing contains it in totality but everything bears it in part. . . . It exists, quite simply, in our daily experience of the world and constitutes the circumstances, the physical, social, and cultural environment of our lives, the very condition and substance of our being" (1992, 127–8). Here, I believe, Zhang is calling—although more at an *empirical* than a theoretical

---

have been among the top contenders for the Nobel Prize for Literature (Owen 1990). For a similarly depreciatory view of modern Chinese literature, see McDougall 1993; for criticism of Owen's position, see M. Yeh 1991.

level—for a return of critical attention from the purely theoretical or merely textual to the actual; that is, to the extratextual, historical, material, and psychosomatic.

The critical positions of Rey Chow and Zhang Longxi illustrate the importance of of self-reflexivity in cross-cultural analysis.[7] By aligning Chow with Western theory and himself with Chinese reality, Zhang has, in a sense, mapped out two extreme positions that inform the reception and critique of Chinese cinema and indirectly of China itself. The purpose of my brief intervention in this debate is to argue that we should conceive the screening of China *not* as a *unidirectional* effort, either exclusively from the West to China or vice versa. When Chow describes the efforts of Chinese scholars to introduce Western paradigms such as postmodernism and cultural studies into China as a kind of paranoia in reaction to global modernity, and characterizes them as a series of forever "belated" attempts to catch up with the latest theoretical developments in the West, she is obviously confined by a unidirectional mode of thinking. This thinking categorically denies the possibility that Chinese scholars can creatively transform Western theory in their own cultural, historical context (see chapter 8).

By contrast, a *multidirectional* model in the Chinese-Western exchange allows for negotiations, complications, and transformations on both sides, and in certain Chinese cases may even accommodate "Occidentalism" as a form of "creative misunderstanding" for the benefit of Chinese intellectual and artistic production.[8] What is of ultimate importance, therefore, is not the origin and authenticity of a particular theory or discourse, nor its reputed or "irrefutable" superiority and authority, but what occurs *historically* after this theory or discourse is translated or "travels" to an alien place. In this sense, the key issues Lydia Liu identifies in her study of "translingual practice" in modern China— "the rhetorical strategies, translations, discursive formations, naming practices, legitimizing processes, tropes, and narrative modes that bear

---

[7] Similarly, in modern Chinese literature, these issues are still of crucial importance (see Y. Zhang 1993b).

[8] See X. Chen 1989. My reservation with Chen's use of "misunderstanding" is that it squarely places China on the side of lack or deficiency, always at the receiving end, where the outcome of a "creative" use or misuse of the West usually carries little or no significance to the "originator" of knowledge or theory.

upon the historical conditions of the Chinese experience of the modern"
(1995, xviii)—are all significant to screening China.

While Liu emphasizes modern China, in this book I divide my
attention equally between critical interventions in the West and cinematic
reconfigurations in China. True to the vision of a multidirectional model,
I emphasize how the so-called "native" *returns* the gaze of Western
theory, forcing the West to reexamine its ideological and theoretical
premises, and discursive practices (see chapter 4). Through a survey of
critical problems and methodological issues in Western studies of Chinese
cinema, I aim not only to sketch a history of the institutionalization of
Chinese film studies in North America but also to identify what has been
excluded from such studies and what might account for these exclusions
(see chapter 3). To enhance the historical dimension of the multidirectional model, I also trace the development of early Hollywood
images of China as well as the influence these images might have had on
the (auto)ethnographies of contemporary Chinese filmmakers on the one
hand and on the phenomenal success of Chinese "ethnographic" films in
the West on the other (see chapter 6).

The *Fin de Siècle* Ethos

I evoke the notion of *fin de siècle* for several reasons. For one, the
widespread decadence that characterized the end of the 19th century
resurfaced in the 1990s (Barmé 1999; Zha 1995), and found favorable
treatment in contemporary Chinese cinema. Films such as *Red Rose,
White Rose* (Hong meigui, bai meigui, 1994), *Temptress Moon* (Fengyue,
1995), *Shanghai Triad* (Yao a yao, yaodao waipo qiao, 1995), and *Mahjong*
(Majiang, 1996) are replete with drugs, alcohol, sensual music, and sex,
and together they point to a new *fin de siècle* ethos. Further, if we accept
David Wang's reformulation of decadence as "de-cadence"—both the
falling apart of the established order and the falling together of disparate
voices (1997, 25)—then the decadence in question may be viewed as a
rhetorical strategy deployed by Chinese filmmakers to stage a cinematic
equivalent of Carnival or to reinscribe a textual heteroglossia in Chinese
culture. Both strategies challenge or even temporarily subvert the
hegemonic status of enlightenment discourse and the bluntly elitist stance
many scholars still share.

Moreover, I use *fin de siècle* to indicate filmmakers' acute awareness
of a sea change that is partly reflected in the recurring theme of nostalgia

in contemporary Chinese cinema. This is not simply a nostalgia for the legendary or glorified past, as in *Red Sorghum* (Hong gaoliang, 1987), *Center Stage* (aka *The Actress*, Ruan Lingyu, 1992), *Blush* (Hongfen, 1994), and *In the Heat of the Sun* (Yangguang canlan de rizi, 1995) [Illustration 1]; it is also a nostalgia for the fast-disappearing present, portrayed in *Days of Being Wild* (A Fei zhengzhuan, 1991), *Autumn Moon* (Qiuyue, 1992), and *Yesterday's Wine* (Yu wangshi ganbei, 1995). In the *fin de siècle* of the 1990s, decadence and "nostalgia for the present" often go hand in hand in films with urban settings. Indeed, urban cinema looms large in the convergence of cinematic reconfigurations and critical interventions, where the city becomes a space crisscrossed by competing discourses of new localism, postcolonialism, postmodernism, post-socialism, transnationalism, and globalism (see chapters 7–8).

1. *In the Heat of the Sun* (1995): Nostalgia for the Cultural Revolution

There is little doubt that China, the "Central Kingdom" (*Zhongguo*) just two hundred years ago, is delicately positioned in a "polycentric world" as it enters the new millennium (see Ong and Nonini 1997, 3–33; Y. Zhang 1998, 1–17). How well Chinese cinema will fare in its second century remains to be seen, but one thing is certain: the screening of China will continue. From the perspective of the cultural historian, I believe we are engaged in what Andrew envisions as "a doubly hermeneutic venture": to put into play "the reading of films for their cultural consequences and the reading of culture for the values and moods conveyed in films" (1998, 186). It is with this doubly hermeneutic venture in mind that I begin my investigation of the interrelated critical and textual screening of China in the *fin de siècle*.

Two

Chinese Cinema and Transnational Cultural Politics: Rethinking Film Festivals, Film Productions, and Film Studies

> We ground things, now, on a moving earth. There is no longer any place of overview (mountaintop) from which to map human ways of life, no Archimedian point from which to represent the world. Mountains are in constant motion. So are islands: for one cannot occupy, unambiguously, a bounded cultural world from which to journey out and analyze other cultures. Human ways of life increasingly influence, dominate, parody, translate, and subvert one another. Cultural analysis is always enmeshed in global movements of difference and power.
>
> James Clifford, "Introduction" to *Writing Culture*

One can locate Chinese cinema at three junctures that pertain to transnational cultural politics. The first of these junctures is the impact of international film festivals on Chinese film productions and their reception in the West. The second is the inadequacy of the term "Fifth Generation" and its derivatives to describe Chinese film studies. Third are alternative routes that go beyond current methodological confinement in Western studies of Chinese cinema. By transnational cultural politics I mean the complicated and at times complicit ways in which Chinese films are enmeshed in "a larger process in which popular-cultural technologies, genres, and works are increasingly moving and interacting across national and cultural borders" (During 1997, 808). Designating this process as "transnationalization," Simon During calls on scholars to take up the challenge that commercial cultural production—what he terms "the global popular"—poses to "current cultural studies' welcome to difference, hybridicity [*sic*], and subversion" (1997, 809).

When I completed my first essay on Chinese cinema in the summer of 1989 (Y. Zhang 1990), I could not have predicted the meteoric rise in popularity of Chinese film on the world stage. Despite the fact that *Red*

Sorghum had just won the first Golden Bear for Chinese film at the 1988 Berlin International Film Festival and that, earlier, *Yellow Earth* (Huang tudi, 1984) had attracted critical attention from the West, China's turbulent political situation in 1989 prevented optimistic prediction. Political setbacks notwithstanding, China's economy grew rapidly in the early 1990s, and Chinese film has continued to develop its particular type of global appeal. Today, one is hard-pressed to count all the awards garnered by Chinese films in festivals around the world (see Zhang Junxiang and Cheng 1995, 1433–43). This spectacular global success provides ample opportunity for scholars, but also creates thorny problems in Chinese film studies. In this chapter, I examine some of these issues under the headings "Screening," "Naming" (Section I), "Speaking" (Section II), and "Mapping" (Section III), and reflect on film festivals, film productions, and film studies from the perspective of transnational cultural politics.

I

Screening: Box-Office Boom and Academic Investment

In 1993, Klaus Eder, a program organizer of the Munich International Film Festival, observed: "New Chinese Cinema has dominated many international festivals, most recently Venice in 1992 (*The Story of Qiu Ju*), Berlin in 1993 (*Women from the Lake of Scented Souls*) and Cannes in 1993 (*Farewell My Concubine*). That is a surprising and admirable series of successes, which no other cinema has ever duplicated, at least not within the last two or three decades" (Eder and Rossell 1993, 8). In fact, Eder forgot to mention a Taiwan film, *The Wedding Banquet* (Xiyan, 1992), which shared the Golden Bear at the 1993 Berlin Film Festival. Earlier, a year after *Red Sorghum*'s success, another Taiwan film, *City of Sadness* (Beiqing chengshi, 1989), won the first Golden Lion for Chinese film at the Venice Film Festival. In addition, films by Chen Kaige, Zhang Yimou, and Ang Lee were nominated for the Best Foreign Film category at the Oscars in the early 1990s. Many of their films proved immensely profitable as well. By January 23, 1994, *The Wedding Banquet*, five months after its release, had earned 6.5 million dollars, and *Farewell My Concubine* (Bawang bieji, 1993), three months after its release, took in 4.2 million. (Both figures are from the U.S. commercial circuit alone.) No wonder Hong Kong-based *Asiaweek* included an observation by Jeannette Paulson, director of the Hawaii Film Festival: "This is a time of discovery for films from Asia" (*Asiaweek* 1994, 27).

This "discovery" of Asian film began in the early 1980s. The talents of several of Hong Kong's New Wave directors, such as Allan Fong (Fang Yuping), Ann Hui (Xu Anhua), and Tsui Hark (Xu Ke), were gradually recognized by the Western press, and some of their films were introduced at international festivals (J. Lau 1998, 18). By the mid-1980s, as Paul Fonoroff notes, "The 'wave' turned out to be a mere ripple [in Hong Kong], with many of the young filmmakers absorbed by the commercial movie establishment they had ostensibly sought to transform" (Y. Zhang and Xiao 1998, 42). Nevertheless, a new generation of directors in Taiwan (like Hou Hsiao-hsien and Edward Yang) and mainland China (like Chen Kaige and Tian Zhuangzhuang), carried on the pioneering, avant-garde spirit, and soon became serious contenders for major international film prizes. After what Eder describes as a surprising and admirable series of successes in the early 1990s, Chinese film continued to develop with uninterrupted momentum. In addition to *Eat Drink Man Woman, Shanghai Triad,* and *Temptress Moon,* a number of other films by lesser-known Chinese directors such as He Ping and Zhou Xiaowen, as well as the "Second Wave" directors from Hong Kong and Taiwan, such as Clara Law, Stanley Kwan, Wong Kar-Wai, Stan Lai (Lai Shengchuan), and Tsai Ming-liang (Cai Mingliang) were screened in American art theaters and festival venues (Teo 1997, 162–203; Chiao 1996b). Many of these films have also entered commercial bookstores and video rental stores across the country.

A similar discovery process is also evident in academic publications. Up to 1980, there was only one notable book-length publication in English, by Jay Leyda (1972). From the mid-1980s to the mid-1990s, the situation changed dramatically, as works by Chris Berry (1985, 1991), Paul Clark (1987), George Semsel and his collaborators (1987, 1990, 1993), and Wimal Dissanayake (1988, 1993, 1994) gradually paved the way for serious research on Chinese film in the West. Since the mid-1990s, there have been an ever-increasing number of publications in the U.S.: critical anthologies edited by Nick Browne, Paul Pickowicz, Vivian Sobchack, and Esther Yau (1994; 2001), Linda Erhlich and David Desser (1994), Sheldon Hsiao-peng Lu (1997), myself (1999), Poshek Fu and David Desser (2000), and Esther Yau (2001), as well as individual books by Rey Chow (1995), Ackbar Abbas (1997), Stephen Teo (1997),

Xudong Zhang (1997), Kwok-kan Tam and Wimal Dissanayake (1998), myself and Zhiwei Xiao (1998), David Bordwell (2000a), and Stephanie Donald (2000). This already impressive list of books does not include works in progress or the large number of studies of Chinese film in various academic journals.

Surely, these are the products of a blooming field, a field so new and yet growing so fast that the barely concealed inaccuracy of its key operating terms has been left largely unexamined. One example here will suffice to illustrate the confusion in "naming." In *New Chinese Cinema*, a dossier issued by the National Film Theatre in London, we find under "Biographies of the 5th Generation Directors" such names as Xie Jin, Xie Fei, and Zhang Nuanxin (Eder and Rossell, 1993, 5). Even if this misclassification of one third- and two fourth-generation directors as the fifth generation was an excusable error of editing or proofreading, it likely generated confusion among audiences around the world, as the dossier accompanied a season of Chinese films that opened at the Munich Film Festival (June 1993) and the National Film Theater in London (July-August 1993), and subsequently traveled to the Cinémathèque Suisse, Lausanne (September 1993), the Filmpodium Zürich (September 1993), the São Paulo International Film Festival (October 1993), the Film Society of Lincoln Center, New York (both December 1993), the UCLA Film and Television Archive, Los Angeles (January 1994), the Cinémathèque Ontario (February-March 1994), and the Film Center of the Art Institute of Chicago (April-May 1994). While this confusion in the generational lineup of directors is by no means typical of academic work on Chinese cinema since the mid-1980s, it does betray the problematic nature of naming in Chinese film studies.

Naming, 1: Geopolitical Implications

The business of naming is complex. To begin with, "Chinese cinema" as a general term is often applied to films made in mainland China, Hong Kong, and Taiwan. Yet many Westerners see these regions as three entirely separate and antagonistic "nations" or "countries." Their respective governments, however, view things rather differently. In cultural terms, they see themselves more or less "unified" by their common legacy of Chinese history, culture, and language. One must remember that cultural exchanges between the mainland and Hong Kong had been going on for decades before the return of Hong Kong to China was announced in the Sino-British Joint Declaration in 1984, and after the mid-1980s contacts between the mainland and Taiwan increased dramatically. As far as film circles are concerned, steady flows of investment capital from Taiwan and Hong Kong since the 1980s have resulted in numerous coproductions involving filmmakers from the mainland, Hong Kong, and Taiwan. Without their unified and sustained efforts, the scope and impact of the recent success of Chinese cinema around the world is hard to imagine.

Thus Chiao Hsiung-Ping (Jiao Xiongping), a leading Taiwan film critic, commented on the situation in 1993, "The close cooperation . . . has brought about a trend toward popular unification in advance of political unification" (1993c, 97). As I show later in this chapter, the close cooperation between Chinese directors in the three regions arose in a specific geopolitical and economic context. Still, it is no coincidence that Chiao's playful use of "unification," a politically sensitive word, found an echo in the semi-official, bilingual Taiwan magazine, *Sinorama* (Guanghua), which celebrated the occasion of the Chinese co-winners at the 1993 Berlin Festival with a report bearing this punning title: "Liang'an dianying bai *Xiyan?*" (*The Wedding Banquet* occasioned by films from both sides of the Taiwan Strait?) (Teng 1993).

The unified efforts of film directors from the mainland, Hong Kong, and Taiwan were also praised in 1993 by Zheng Dongtian, a professor and film director at the Beijing Film Academy (Beijing dianying xueyuan). Zheng was particularly excited because a year earlier directors from the three regions had met for the first time in history at a Chinese directors' workshop in Hong Kong. Pleased with a bright future for close cooperation among all Chinese directors across the geopolitical divides, he perceptively observed, "While there are political and cultural, as well as geographical and historical differences between the three places, works by directors from all these places can still validly be described as 'Chinese film'" (1993b, 32). The euphoria of a cinematic "unification" reached a new height with the scholarly contribution that another Beijing Film Academy professor, Huang Shixian, made to a Taipei Golden Horse Film Festival (Jinma jiang) publication in 1994: "Perhaps, Chinese cinema now is at its most vital and most artistic moment in its entire history. A temporary cultural or economic setback will not alter the historical direction of cultural reintegration that Chinese filmmakers in the three geopolitical regions (*liang'an sandi*) are undertaking under the guidance of the holy fire of modern Chinese humanist spirit" (1994, 44).

Huang's use of *liang'an sandi* (literally, "two sides of the Taiwan Strait and three regions"), which I translate as "three geopolitical regions," is in strict conformity with the official rhetoric of the Taiwan government. Although the efforts to include mainland titles for the first time in competition at the 1996 Taipei Golden Horse Film Festival was aborted due to internal politics in Taiwan and the mainland government's withdrawal of its eight entries, *In the Heat of the Sun*, a film coproduced by companies on the mainland, Hong Kong, and Taiwan, eventually won six major awards at the festival and was subsequently approved for commercial release in Taiwan. "It is obvious that the convergence of filmmaking in the three geopolitical regions is an unstoppable trend," concludes a Nationalist government report in Taiwan (Chen Zhikuan 1997, 12). In this regard, Nick Browne's remarks are worth quoting (1994a, 1):

> "China" appears today largely as the consequence of the 1949 Communist revolution, forming an interregional social and economic network defined and sustained by politics. The People's Republic, Taiwan, and Hong Kong and their cinemas are marked as socialist, capitalist, and colonialist, respectively. Yet to exaggerate these differences would be to overlook a common cultural tradition of social, ideological, and aesthetic forms that stands behind and informs Chinese cinema as a whole.

Indeed, this "common cultural tradition" has sustained most of the exchange among filmmakers in the three regions, as is evident from statements presented above. While there is no denying that cultural differences and political tensions abound in all three areas and persist up to the present, it is equally true that some differences may shift categories occasionally, precisely because of the common cultural tradition. As Chiao Hsiung-Ping points out, recent coproductions in the mainland have resulted in visible changes in directors' personal styles. For instance, *My American Grandson* (Shanghai jiaqi, 1991), which had a Hong Kong woman director (Ann Hui), a Taiwan screenwriter (Wu Nien-chen [Wu Nianzhen]), and mainland actors, "looked more like a Taiwan film"; while *Five Girls and a Rope* (Wuge nüzi he yigen shengzi, 1991), which had a Taiwan director (Yeh Hong-wei [Ye Hongwei]), mostly Taiwan actresses, but a mainland screenwriter (Ye Weilin), looked rather like a

Fifth Generation work (Chiao 1993b, 56).[1] On the mainland side, Zhang Yimou acknowledged in 1992 that his award-winning film, *The Story of Qiu Ju* (Qiu Ju da guansi, 1991), was part of an attempt to learn from Taiwan directors (especially Hou Hsiao-hsien) so as to achieve "a concrete delineation of things pertaining to character" and to "make up this deficiency" on the part of mainland directors (Zheng Dongtian 1993b, 32).

The exchange between Taiwan and Hong Kong film industries can be traced to an even earlier period. In the 1960s, Zhang Che, whose *Wind and Cloud on Ali Mountain* (Alishan fengyun, 1949) marked the beginning of Mandarin film (*guopian*) production in Taiwan, left the island for Hong Kong and helped initiate the fashion of new martial arts film with his *One-Armed Swordsman* (Dubi dao, 1967) and *Vengeance* (Baochou, 1970) (Zhang Che 1989). During the same time period, two then-leading Hong Kong directors, King Hu (Hu Jinquan) and Li Hanxiang, temporarily moved to Taiwan and rejuvenated private film studios there.[2] In the early 1980s, Edward Yang, one of the pioneers of new Taiwan cinema, worked on film scripts for Leong Po-chi (Liang Puzhi), whose *Jumping Ash* (Tiaohui, 1976)—codirected with Josephine Siao (Xiao Fangfang)—prefigured the Hong Kong New Wave. As late as 1998, Yang still considered Leong to be his mentor, "a walking film school" for him (Kraicer and Roosen-Runge 1998, 49).

By the early 1990s, Chinese coproductions had made filmmaking in the three regions more complicated, the previously taken-for-granted differences less obvious, and the nationality issue all the more conspicuous. For instance, should we classify *Farewell My Concubine* as a mainland film, according to the original nationality of its director, Chen Kaige, a key figure in the Fifth Generation who nonetheless claims residency both in China and the U.S.? Or ought it be called a Taiwan film, due to the "nationality" of its investor, Hsu Feng (Xu Feng), a veteran actress famous for her screen roles in King Hu's 1970s swordplay films? Or

---

[1] The proximity to the Fifth Generation quality in *Five Girls and a Rope* is further evident in its mainland counterpart, *The Wedding Maidens* (Chujia nü, 1991), which is based on the same story (see chapter 6).

[2] In Taiwan, King Hu first served as production manager for Union Film (Lianbang) and then formed King Hu Film Productions, while Li Hanxiang established his Guolian Film. Both of them produced a number of distinguished films during this period. See Chiao 1993a; Teo 1997, 87–96.

should we designate it a Hong Kong film because of the "nationality" of its registered production company, Tangchen (Tomson Film), through which the Taiwan investment was channeled through strict government regulations?

To avoid unnecessary confusion, we might keep the general term "Chinese cinema" and instruct the reader to bear in mind the problematic nature of China or Chineseness. After all, as Zhang Yimou acknowledged at the 1992 Academy Awards press conference in Hollywood, "Now more and more mainland Chinese realize that China is really three areas: the mainland, Taiwan, and Hong Kong. Among directors, there is a great deal of contact and exchange across these three areas" (M. Yang 1993, 308).

One more example here demonstrates how extensive this type of "reel" contact has been in recent years. Among the eleven Chinese films selected for a special program at the 1994 Taipei Golden Horse Film Festival, the following works by mainland directors are listed as Hong Kong productions: He Ping's *Red Firecracker, Green Firecracker* (Paoda shuangdeng, 1994, Wengshi), Huang Jianxin's *Back to Back, Face to Face* (Bei kao bei, lian dui lian, 1994, Senxin), Wu Ziniu's *Sparkling Fox* (Huohu, 1993, Senxin), and Zhang Yimou's *The Story of Qiu Ju* (Sil-Metropole [Yindu]). In addition to these four "Hong Kong" films, the program features two Taiwan directors (Hou Hsiao-hsien and He Ping's Taiwan namesake) and three Hong Kong directors—Yim Ho (Yan Hao), Stanley Kwan, and Clara Law (the last with three films of her own). These geographic designations or specifications in credit lines, however, do not affect the usefulness of the general term "Chinese cinema," which appears in the title of the program (Golden Horse Film Festival 1994, 140–7).

Naming, 2: Historiographic Complications

Now we can proceed to "New Chinese Cinema" and its confusing relation to "Fifth Generation" films. "New Chinese Cinema," I believe, is a more accurate and more manageable term than "Fifth Generation" when referring to contemporary "art films" or films of high aesthetic value and production quality. The "Fifth Generation" directors are so named because they are all graduates from the Beijing Film Academy in 1982, mainly from the Department of Directing but some from other departments as well. Most notable among them are Chen Kaige, Tian

Zhuangzhuang, Wu Ziniu, Xia Gang, Zhang Junzhao, Zhang Yimou, and their women classmates Hu Mei, Li Shaohong, and Peng Xiaolian. Over the years, other directors of the same age who received advanced training at the Beijing Film Academy but did not earn degrees have also been designated Fifth Generation, including Huang Jianxin, Mi Jiashan, Sun Zhou, Zhang Zeming, and Zhou Xiaowen (Lao Lin 1992; Meng Xianli 1994, 187–90).[3]

This loose designation of the Fifth Generation has caused its share of problems. The first is the incorrect assumption that Fifth Generation films share a homogeneous style. In fact the opposite is true, because these directors exhibit a spectrum of styles in their work. For example, Xia Gang's urban comedies, such as *After Separation* (Da saba, 1992) and *No One Cheers* (Wuren hecai, 1993), have very little in common with either Zhang Yimou's rural myths, such as *Ju Dou* (Ju Dou, 1989) and *Raise the Red Lantern* (Dahong denglong gaogao gua, 1991), or Hu Mei's psychological dramas, such as *Army Nurse* (Nüer lou, 1985) and *Far From the War* (Yuanli zhangzhen de niandai, 1987). Similarly, despite their common urban settings, Zhou Xiaowen's gangster films, such as *Desperation* (Zuihou de fengkuang, 1987) and *The Price of Frenzy* (Fengkuang de daijia, 1988), stand in sharp contrast to both Huang Jianxin's first trilogy of political satires—*Black Cannon Incident* (Heipao shijian, 1985), *Dislocation* (Cuowei, 1986), and *Transmigration* (aka *Samsara*, Lunhui, 1989)—and Zhang Zeming's sentimental tales, such as *Swan Song* (Juexiang, 1985) and *Sunshine and Showers* (Taiyang yu, 1987).

Another problem with the term "Fifth Generation" is that it tends to gloss over the marked differences in any director's work over time. Take Tian Zhuangzhuang for example: after making two exemplary Fifth Generation films, *On the Hunting Ground* (Liechang zhasa, 1985) and *Horse Thief* (Daoma zei, 1986), he produced *Drum Singers* (Gushu yiren, 1987), a film melodrama comparable to the "Xie Jin model," a type of film realism that dominated China from the 1960s to the 1980s (Semsel et al. 1990, 141–8). After *Rock 'n' Roll Kids* (Yaogun qingnian, 1988), a popular entertainment film focusing on contemporary urban youth culture, Tian presented *Li Lianying, the Imperial Eunuch* (Da taijian Li Lianying, 1991), a film funded by Shijia (Skai Film) in Hong Kong and bearing close resemblance, in narrative style and mise-en-scène at least, to

---

[3] Zhang Zeming emigrated to Hong Kong and directed *Foreign Moon* (Yueman Yinglun, 1996) for the Hong Kong-based Media Asia (Huanya).

two previous Hong Kong period dramas of imperial court intrigue, *Burning of the Imperial Palace* (Huoshao Yuanmingyuan, 1983) and *Reign Behind a Curtain* (Chuilian tingzheng, 1983), both directed by Li Hanxiang. Returning from popular genres to a serious engagement with the traumatic experience of the Cultural Revolution (1966–76), Tian directed *The Blue Kite* (Lan fengzheng, 1993), another Hong Kong-financed film, which was immediately banned in the mainland but released to enthusiastic audiences in the West, where it won several prestigious festival awards (Gladney 1995; Lopate 1994; B. Wang 1999; Tam and Dissanayake 1998, 35–46).

A third, more troublesome problem arises from attempts to fix precise dates for the Fifth Generation in Chinese film historiography. The screening of *Yellow Earth* on April 12, 1985, at the Hong Kong International Film Festival is generally considered to be the starting point of the Fifth Generation, while the year 1987, marked by *King of the Children* (Haizi wang), has been noted as a terminal point "when the Fifth Generation dissolved" (Dai Jinhua 1995a, 268).[4] Yet if one accepts these dates, it would then be self-contradictory to regard post-1987 films by Chen Kaige and Tian Zhuangzhuang as belonging to the "Fifth Generation" corpus, and film scholars would face the embarrassing question of why Fifth Generation directors have been making "non-Fifth Generation" works since 1987. This already confusing situation is made even more so by the fact that Zhang Yimou, the most internationally known figure in this group, did not enter the spotlight until 1987. It was also in 1987 that other members of the Fifth Generation saw their first important features released: Peng Xiaolian's *Women's Story* (Nüren de gushi), Sun Zhou's *Put Some Sugar in the Coffee* (Gei kafei jiadian tang), as well as Zhou Xiaowen's *Desperation*.

As a solution and to avoid further confusion, I support the term "New Chinese Cinema" for works of the Fifth Generation, their associates, and other prominent directors since 1980, while keeping the term "Fifth Generation" as a designation for the directors from the 1982 graduating class and their close associates (rather than for their films). Such a distinction ensures a more accurate account of the period from the mid-1980s to the present, when the Fifth Generation directors produced

---

[4] Unlike Dai's unambiguous word, Tony Rayns sees in *King of the Children* the closing of a chapter for the Fifth Generation, thus leaving room for their revival and transformation after 1987 (1989, 55).

films more or less contemporaneously with two other groups active in the mainland. The first group consists of directors from the "Third and Fourth Generations," including Hu Bingliu, Huang Jianzhong, Huang Shuqin, Wang Jin, Wu Tianming, Wu Yigong, Xie Fei, Xie Jin, and Zhang Nuanxin. The second group consists of the post-Fifth Generation directors, including He Ping, Huang Jun, Jiang Wen, Ning Ying, as well as Ah Nian, Guan Hu, He Jianjun (He Yi), Hu Xueyang, Li Xin, Lou Ye, Lu Xuechang, Wang Rui, Wang Xiaoshuai, Wu Di, Zhang Ming, Zhang Yang, Zhang Yuan, and Zhu Feng, several of them known as the so-called "Sixth Generation" in the West.[5] As a single term for all three groups of directors, "New Chinese Cinema" removes the inaccurate and confusing "generational" classification. Moreover, "New Chinese Cinema" is an appropriate term to link art films from the mainland, Hong Kong, and Taiwan over the last two decades, for during this period all three regions saw the emergence of the "New Cinema" or "New Wave" as well as the "Second Wave." Partly due to this linkage, "New Chinese Cinema(s)"—sometimes in the plural—seems to have gained increasing acceptance by film critics and scholars in the West (Chen Kaige and Rayns 1989; Eder and Rossell 1993; Browne et al. 1994; Tam and Dissanayake 1998; X. Zhang 1997).

---

[5] Mostly graduates from the Beijing Film Academy and the Radio and Television Academy (Guangbo xueyuan) in Beijing, this group of directors has been variously termed the "Sixth Generation," the "post-Fifth Generation," and the "New-Born Generation" (*xinsheng dai*). For information, see Berry 1998b; Eder and Rossell 1993, 47; Han Xiaolei 1995; Huang Shixian 1994, 40–43; Lü Xiaoming 1999; Ni Zhen 1999; Zhongguo yinmu 1997; Yin Hong 1998b. The following is a partial list of their representative works up to 1997: Ah Nian's *Urban Love Affair* (Chengshi aiqing, 1997); Guan Hu's *Dirt* (Toufa luanle, 1994) and *Cello in a Cab* (Langman jietou, 1997); He Jianjun's *Red Beads* (Xuanlian, 1993) and *Postman* (Youchai, 1995); Hu Xueyang's *A Lady Left Behind* (Liushou nüshi, 1991) and *The Drowned Youth* (Yanmo de qingchun, 1994); Huang Jun's *Childhood in Ruijin* (Tongnian zai Ruijin, 1990), *The Prostitute and the Raftsmen* (Beilie paibang, 1993), and *Living with You* (Yuni tongzhu, 1994); Li Xin's *Falling in Love* (Tanqing shuoai, 1995); Lou Ye's *Weekend Lovers* (Zhoumo qingren, 1995); Lu Xuechang's *The Making of Steel* (Zhangda chengren, 1997; shot in 1995), aka *How Steel Is Forged* (Gangtie shi zheyang liancheng de); Ning Ying's *For Fun* (Zhaole, 1992) and *On the Beat* (Minjing gushi, 1995); Wang Rui's *No Visit After Divorce* (Lihun le, jiu bie zailai zhaowo, 1997); Wang Xiaoshuai's *The Days* (Dong Chun de rizi, 1993) and *Suicide* (Da youxi, 1994); Wu Di's *Yellow Goldfish* (Huang jinyu, 1995); and Zhang Ming's *Rainclouds Over Wushan* (Wushan yunyu, 1995). Zhang Yuan's films are mentioned separately in this chapter, while some later films by this group will be treated in chapter 8.

Some have objected to "New Chinese Cinema" as a substitute for "Fifth Generation." A leading film critic in mainland China, Shao Mujun, traces the origin of this "inappropriate" substitution to the September 1988 seminar organized by *Film Art* (Dianying yishu), the leading film journal published in Beijing under the supervision of the China Film Association (Zhongguo dianying jia xiehui). He insists that the Fifth Generation cannot take all the credit for the establishment of New Chinese Cinema in the 1980s. Instead, it is the much-neglected Fourth Generation who have contributed most to the revival of Chinese cinema after the devastating decade of the Cultural Revolution. As early as March 1980, a group of directors, among them Ding Yinnan, Huang Jianzhong, Xie Fei, Yang Yanjin, Zhang Nuanxin, and Zheng Dongtian, met in Beijing and founded the Beihai Reading Group. They even drafted a manifesto, which, because authorities quickly moved to investigate the directors to discourage any political motivations they might have had, never saw the light of print. True to Shao's description, the Fourth Generation indeed dominated Chinese filmmaking in the early 1980s, a period when the Fifth Generation was still learning their trade at the Beijing Film Academy. As Shao contends, the Fourth Generation represents "the true nature of the 'New Chinese Cinema'" and that their rightful place in the history of Chinese cinema should therefore be restored (1993, 21–9).

II

Speaking: In the Name of Politics and/or Poetics?

Obviously, much of Shao's objection is directed at Western critics' preference for the Fifth Generation, a group that for him forms only one part of New Chinese Cinema. This objection brings us to the issue of the transnational cultural politics of "speaking": Who speaks for Chinese cinema in the West? To whom do they speak? About what subjects? In whose or what name? And to what effect?

Let us revisit an early moment here. Tracing the rise of Chinese film studies in the U.S. around the mid-1980s, when Fifth Generation directors had just started to attract international attention, William Rothman identifies a kind of political responsibility the West must assume: "We Americans studying Chinese cinema in those years found ourselves envisioning the events sweeping China as a grand historical melodrama" and therefore felt "called upon to play a role" in promoting new Chinese films in the international arena (1993b, 259). By assuming such an urgent moral and political responsibility, Western critics thus see their role as direct participants in the advancement of freedom, democracy, and human rights in post-Mao China.

Indeed, political issues have informed much of Western interest in Chinese cinema. This is evident from the large number of press reports on the notorious cases of Communist censorship. For example, a 1996 report in the *New York Times* bore the title: "In China, Letting a Hundred Films Wither." While the report criticized the Communist party's sponsorship of Xie Jin's *The Opium War* (Yapian zhanzheng)—a film released at the same time as Hong Kong's return to China in July 1997—it also exposed the government's crackdown on Feng Xiaogang's *An Awkward Life* (aka *A Life under Pressure*, Guozhe langbei bukan de shenghuo), a film that had been financed by the popular but controversial writer Wang Shuo (Tyler 1996).[6] Earlier, *The Wall Street Journal* ran an article on the Communist ban on Tian Zhuangzhuang and several defiant "Sixth Generation" directors such as Zhang Yuan and Wu Wenguang (Jaivin 1995). In reports like these, the Western press pays close attention to which Chinese films are suspended in production, ordered for excessive cuts, or banned from release, and which directors are engaged in independent, underground, or subversive filmmaking.

By such political standards, Zhang Yuan, with his independently produced docu-dramas of social prejudice against an autistic child in *Mama* (Mama, 1991), a group of disillusioned rock singers in *Beijing Bastards* (Beijing zazhong, 1993), a documentary of the contrasting official and non-official activities in Beijing in *The Square* (Guangchang, 1995), a study of alcoholism in a dysfunctional family in *Sons* (Erzi, 1996), and a reenactment of the clandestine gay life in *East Palace, West Palace*, has emerged as the most daring and most controversial mainland director to date in the West (Barmé 1999, 189–97; Berry 1996c and 1998; Rayns

---

[6] Wang Shuo's *Papa* (Wo shi ni baba, 1996), a feature production with 3.3 million investment, was reportedly banned by the government, along with *Rice* (Mi, 1996) and *The Soong Sisters* (Songjia san jiemei, 1997). In 2000, *Papa* was illegally smuggled out of China and screened at the Locarno Film Festival, where it won the Golden Leopard. For discussions of Wang Shuo, see Barmé 1999, 62–98; J. Wang 1996, 261–86. For Feng Xiaogang, a close associate of Wang Shuo, see Keane and Tao 1998. I will discuss Feng's popular films in chapter 8.

1996; Reynaud 1997). Indeed, Chris Berry goes so far as to claim, "Given the uneven quality of Zhang Yimou's recent work and Chen Kaige's lapse into the production of *chinoiserie* that out-Bertoluccis Bertolucci, *East Palace, West Palace* stakes a serious claim for Zhang Yuan to be the mainland director who has produced the most consistently interesting body of work so far in the 1990s" (1998, 84).[7] No wonder the majority of mainland directors have been judged by the Western media—and sometimes by Western academics—to be neither interesting nor newsworthy unless caught up in censorship issues.

On the other hand, as far as film audiences are concerned, Western fascination with Chinese cinema may also be explained in so-called "poetic" or "aesthetic" terms. This is evident from reviews in American newspapers and magazines. A *New York Times* review, for instance, piques curiosity with such phrases as "lushly pictorial" scenes, the "unleashed erotic energy," and "sexual ecstasy" to describe *Red Firecracker* (Holden 1995). Phrases like these direct Western audiences to a particular type of ethnic or ethnographic element in Chinese cinema. If we examine those Chinese films that have won major international awards in recent years, we see a narrative pattern gradually taking shape. From Zhang Yimou's *Red Sorghum* and *Ju Dou*, Ang Lee's *The Wedding Banquet* and *Eat Drink Man Woman*, to Chen Kaige's *Farewell My Concubine* and *Temptress Moon*, oriental *ars erotica* as a mythified entity is fixed at the very center of Western fascination (see chapter 6). The fact that such fascination is deliberately cultivated by the Western media is illustrated by one report from Taiwan: "A line in *The Wedding Banquet*, '5,000 years of Chinese sexual repression,' was played up by the British critic Tony Rayns, attracting the attention of people in and outside the film industry." As a result, when the film "was first shown in Berlin, all 2,000 seats of the hall were occupied and when it was over, Ang Lee and the actors had to come out for curtain calls five times" (Teng 1993, 33).

---

[7] However, by the end of 1999, Zhang Yuan seemed to have moved in the opposite direction, at least temporarily, as he sought government approval and succeeded in having his latest feature film released publicly in China (see chapter 8).

Festival-Goers, Post-Tourists, and Cultural Authenticity

In spite of such fanfare, one must not surmise that Western audiences are equally uncritical in their reading of festival catalogues and press reviews. As a regular participant in festival screenings, Bill Nichols offers a self-reflexive account of his festival-going experience and the function international film festivals perform in introducing a continuous succession of "new cinemas" to the West. Influenced by Clifford Geertz, Nichols likens the festival-goer (who is typically "white, Western, middle-class" like himself) to the anthropological fieldworker, or more casually, the tourist, who is engaged in a vivid but imaginary mode of "participatory observation" and who attempts "going native" in the alien land: "There is a reverie in the fascination with the strange, an abiding pleasure in the recognition of differences that persists beyond the moment" (1994a, 18). Two areas of such differences receive most attention in the festival literature—"artistic maturity" that will eventually place an emerging director in an international fraternity of auteurs, and "a distinctive national culture" that marks itself off from the dominant Hollywood styles and themes. As a sensitive critic, Nichols is quick to realize that, like the ethnographer, the festival-goers' pursuit of intimate knowledge and authenticity of an alien culture is only illusory, because the native informants are all too eager to supply evidence that will readily satisfy Western expectations. For most festival-goers, nonetheless, the "dialectic of knowing and forgetting [our limitations] . . . , knowing that they know we know that they calibrate their information to our preexisting assumptions as we watch this process of mutually orchestrated disclosure unfold, becomes a reward in itself" (1994a, 20).

Nichols's self-reflexive account thus places his individual festival-going experience in a larger context of transnational cultural politics. Indeed, Nichols and his fellow "white, Western, middle-class" spectators might belong to what Mike Featherstone describes as a distinct group that consciously positions itself in the contact zones between the global and the local (1995, 98–9):

> [T]here are cosmopolitan intellectuals and cultural intermediaries . . . skilled at packaging and re-presenting the exotica of other cultures and "amazing places" and different traditions to audiences eager for experience. . . . This group can be regarded as post-nostalgic, and can relate to growing audiences in the middle classes who wish to experiment with cultural play, who have

forgone the pursuit of the ultimate authentic and real, who are content to be "post-tourists" and enjoy both the reproduction of the effect of the real, the immersion in it in controlled or playful ways, and the examination of the backstage areas on which it draws.

No longer in pursuit of the "authentic and real" in a given local culture, Western festival-goers are now satisfied with "mutually orchestrated" cultural plays such as to guess what their native informants have guessed they wanted to see in the first place. Films as reproductions of the effect of "authentic" cultures are meant to be enjoyed as a visual feast, if nothing else, but the backstage areas in which such reproductions are planned, packaged, and marketed also hold immense fascination for Western festival-goers, especially critics and scholars.

Stephanie Donald gives another scenario of imagining the "authenticity" of other cultures in her speculation on the appeal of *Beijing Bastards* to the British late-night television audience. Introduced to its U.K. Channel Four screening as "China's first rock and roll movie . . . banned by the Chinese authorities," *Beijing Bastards* thus entered the transnational cultural imaginary, a terrain fraught with profound contradictions and ironies (Donald 1998, 94):

> They had been primed to enjoy familiar music (albeit—they suspected—less subtle than the mature Western varieties of rock), and an anti-Communist, sub-cultural feel-good factor, laced with the peculiarly English self-satisfaction of having sat through a foreign film on a Tuesday night. I want to argue that their expectancy was based on the assumption that Western rock and Western youth have been there before—and that the China factor simply reaffirmed the importance of the Western dominant and subversive relation. The audience expected to be impressed by Chinese temerity in an "authentically" repressive climate, while patting themselves on the back that their youth—imagined, vicarious or actual—provided the template for this musical courage.

What happened in an English sitting room, Donald speculates, was that the screening of this banned Chinese film might give the British audience "a sense of exotic [O]rientalism turned upside down"—upside down because, instead of spectacular Orientalist images of ethnic exoticism found in recent Chinese ethnographic films, what *Beijing Bastards* shows "is all so ordinary, [therefore] it must be interesting, and it cannot help but seem authentic" (1998, 94).

Western Impact on Chinese Film Production and Criticism

Returning to Nichols's observation that the Western festival-goer experiences reward or satisfaction regardless of the status of "authenticity" (real or imagined) of the other culture in question, one may want to look into the *other* side of the transcultural flow. Naturally, many Chinese directors have also felt rewarded by the increasing Western demand for their films, and the seemingly guaranteed success of this genre at festivals around the world has left a visible mark on Chinese film productions. At a September 1993 symposium titled "Western Wonders and Chinese Film Myths," the Beijing-based critic Dai Jinhua pointed out, "Winning such prizes has become a prerequisite for film making; Western culture, artistic tastes, and production standards related to international film festivals now determine our purely national films" (*China Screen* 1994, 29). Dai cited three noted directors from the Xi'an Film Studio as examples. To earn their entrance tickets to international film festivals, they all abandoned their previous explorations of urban subjects and turned to "ethnographic" films centered on China's rural landscape.

Teng Wenji's *Ballad of the Yellow River* (Huanghe yao, 1989), visually reminiscent of *Yellow Earth*, was released in the same year as Zhang Yimou's *Ju Dou* but was overshadowed by the latter's international fame. *The Porter* (Wu Kui, 1993), the mainland release title for Huang Jianxin's only digression to date from urban cinema, carries none of the exotic flavors suggested by its export English title, *The Woodenman's Bride*, and its accompanying Hong Kong title, "Yanshen" (literally, "body inspection"). The film tells of a young bride who is kidnapped by bandits in the wilderness (a tribute to the sequence of rocking the bridal chair in *Red Sorghum*) but is then returned unharmed (that is, her virginity intact) to marry the wooden figure of her deceased husband. She falls in love with a porter, openly defying the social and sexual conventions of a remote desert town (a tribute to the transgression in *Ju Dou*). Although Huang Jianxin's effort failed to win him leading international prizes, Zhou Xiaowen's *Ermo* (Ermo, 1994), a hilarious comedy about a stubborn country-woman's quest for modernity in the reform era—symbolized by her owning the largest television screen in the county—eventually secured him international fame (Rayns 1995). More important, Zhou's artistic success abroad had an immediate political consequence at home. The government censors lifted the ban on *The Black Mountain Road* (Heishan lu, 1990), his earlier film of sexual battles set in a mountain jungle, with its sacrificial ending in which the female protagonist is shot to death by Japanese soldiers and the entire field is set fire (a clear tribute to the ending of *Red Sorghum*).

These films demonstrate that by the early 1990s many Chinese directors were fully aware that a film most likely to satisfy Western expectations (or aesthetic taste) should include formulaic but nonetheless essential or magic ingredients: primitive landscape and its sheer visual beauty (including savage rivers, mountains, forests, deserts); repressed sexuality and its eruption in transgressive moments of eroticism (read "heroism"); gender performance and sexual exhibition (including homo-sexuality, transvestism, adultery, incest) as seen in exotic operas, rituals, or other types of rural custom; and a mythical or cyclical time frame in which the protagonist's fate is predestined. *Red Firecracker* is one such formulaic film that successfully returns the gaze of the West by presenting all that is expected of an ethnography of rural China—and perhaps more than expected, because the film adds a bonus display of spectacular fireworks. Similar films devoted to abnormal or incestuous sexual relations were produced by other Fifth or post-Fifth Generation directors during this period, such as *The Story of Xinghua* (aka *Apricot Blossom*, Xinghua sanyue tian, 1993), *Blush* (1994), and *Family Scandal* (Jiachou, 1994). One must not assume that only younger directors were tempted by international film prizes. Ling Zifeng, a veteran and by official count Third Generation director, won international acclaim for his *Ripples Across Stagnant Water* (Kuang, 1991)—the story of a beautiful woman caught between three men—and successfully entered the film in Western film-festival circuits. (I will analyze some of these films in chapter 6.)

In hindsight, it is rather ironic that not only film directors but film critics as well have yielded to market demand in general and international film festivals in particular. In 1990, Zheng Dongtian judged it unfair that while films depicting rural China and its legendary past had won lots of international prizes, works of the emerging urban cinema had largely flopped abroad. "These new works keep being turned down when festival representatives come to China to select films. . . . Some Western critics even frankly asked: 'Why did you make what we have already made?'" (Zheng Dongtian 1990, 31). Despite such Western arrogance, Zheng still believed at the time that "the emergence of Chinese urban cinema was a step forward which was both necessary and inevitable." For Chinese directors of urban cinema, therefore, "there is no need to feel embarrassed" (1990, 31).[8] Three years later, however, Zheng was alarmed when the news arrived in Beijing that *The Wedding Banquet* had been sold all over Europe and North America, whereas its co-winner of the Golden Bear, *Women from the Lake of Scented Souls*, had barely secured enough renting fees to cover its production costs. Under the pressure of market reform, Zheng issued this new appeal to Chinese filmmakers: "The development of a commodity economy provides people with strategies to survive: Learn to promote yourselves"; and in striking contrast to his position three years earlier, "the first thing for filmmakers to do is to march into the international film market" (1993a, 33).

III

Mapping, 1: Ethnography and the Global/Local

As Zheng's case suggests, while the impact of international film festivals on Chinese film productions is self-evident, its long-term effect on Chinese film studies might not seem as obvious. This deserves closer examination. A review of Western scholarship on Chinese cinema since the early 1980s reveals that research has been shaped in large part by the availability of Chinese films in the market—especially those with English subtitles. With few exceptions, the political melodrama of the 1980s and the aestheticism of the Fifth Generation constitute the dual focuses of critical attention over the past decade (Dissanayake 1993, 9–58, 73–100; Browne et al. 1994, 1–113). Until the late 1990s, scholarly excursions into early Chinese cinema or Hong Kong and Taiwan cinemas have been largely overshadowed by the sheer quantity of publications and conference papers devoted to two preeminent Fifth Generation directors, Chen Kaige and Zhang Yimou.[9]

---

[8] A few Chinese urban films did manage to win top international prizes, such as *Black Snow* (Benming nian, 1989), the winner of a Silver Bear at the 1990 Berlin Film Festival, and *For Fun*, the winner of both a Young Cinema Gold Prize at the Toronto Film Festival and a Golden Balloon at the Nantes Film Festival. However, although they were quite popular among Chinese audiences, Huang Jianxin's second trilogy of urban satires—*Stand Up, Don't Bend Over* (Zhanzhi luo, bie paxia, 1992), *Back to Back, Face to Face* (1994), and *Signal Left, Turn Right* (Hongdeng ting, lüdeng xing, 1995)—did not fare well at international festivals. For studies of some of these new urban films, see X. Tang 1994; White 1997; and Hulsbus 1997.

[9] For Chen Kaige, see An 1994; Berry and Farquhar 1994; Chen and Rayns 1989; Chow 1995, 79–141; Donald 1997; Farquhar 1992; Hitchcock 1992; Kaplan 1997b; Larson

One excellent example of the well-nigh exclusive devotion to the
Fifth Generation is Rey Chow's *Primitive Passions*, which won the 1996
James Russell Lowell Prize by the Modern Language Association in the
U.S. In spite of her declared ambition to "produce a cultural history and
anthropology of modern China" (1995, x), Chow concentrates on half a
dozen films by Chen Kaige and Zhang Yimou—in addition to *Goddess*
(Shennü, 1934) and *Old Well* (Laojing, 1987). She detects in their
cinematic reinvention of ethnic Chinese culture a voluntary confirmation
of China's status as object-of-gaze in cross-cultural representation. In
these directors' willing exhibitionism, China's primitive passions are
displayed in seductive surfaces to the Western audience. Thus, by means
of looking at oneself (China) being looked at by others (the West),
contemporary Chinese cinema seems to ethnographize China (the self)
and becomes, in the end, an "autoethnography" (1995, 180–1).

Undoubtedly, Chow's concept of contemporary Chinese cinema as
autoethnography works perfectly in the context of cinematic exhibitionism in Zhang Yimou and his followers. On closer scrutiny, however,
the autoethnography in question might prove to be not so much a result
of the automatic or voluntary consent from Chinese directors as that of
transnational economic coercion or unequal power relations. After *Ballad
of the Yellow River* had won him the Best Director award at the 1990
Montreal Film Festival, Teng Wenji frankly admitted: "They [foreign
investors] come to look for film directors, and our directors will agree to
go whenever they ask. Just like a court subpoena. This is sad" (China
Screen 1994, 29). This sadness over one's powerless economic position
vis-à-vis transnational forces is echoed by Dai Qing, one of China's
leading dissident journalists. After vehemently denouncing *Raise the Red
Lantern* as being "really shot for the casual pleasures of foreigners . . .
[who] can go on and muddleheadedly satisfy their oriental fetishism," she
immediately adds that "there is something worth our sympathy in the
plight of a serious filmmaker being forced to make a living outside his
own country" (1993, 336–7).

One may very well feel sad and outraged because, in the era of
transnational capitalism, "the 'ethnicity' of contemporary Chinese
cinema—'Chineseness'—is already the sign of a *cross-cultural* commodity
fetishism" (Chow 1995, 59). Such a situation seems to have implicated

1997; J. Lau 1995; H. C. Li 1989; McDougall 1991; Tam and Dissanayake 1998, 11–22;
Yau 1987–8; X. Zhang 1997, 282–305. For Zhang Yimou, see chapter 6, esp. note 7.

contemporary Chinese cinema in a prefixed cycle of transnational commodity production and consumption: favorable reviews at international film festivals lead to production of more "ethnographic" films, and the wide distribution of such films is translated into their availability for classroom use and therefore influences the agenda of film studies, which in turn reinforces the status of these films as a dominant genre. Viewed in this way, a supposedly trend-setting study like Rey Chow's *Primitive Passions*, which aims at critical intervention in "some of the most urgent debates about cross-cultural studies, sexuality, ethnicity, identity, authenticity, and commodity fetishism" (1995, back cover), may turn out to be merely trend-following, for its agenda and scope are shaped by what appears to be a popular cultural product in the market. Studying the popular in this case ironically legitimizes it as the dominant cultural imaginary. What is likely to be glossed over in such trend-setting (or trend-following) scholarship is the historical experience and cultural meaning specific to a nation or region. To quote Nichols' penetrating analysis of the international film-festival phenomenon: "Hovering, like a specter, . . . are those deep structures and thick descriptions that might restore a sense of the particular and local to what we have now recruited to the realm of the global" (1994a, 27).

It is evident that the global and the local are intricately and inseparably connected in the era of transnationalism, but the question remains as to how one can map out the changing relationships between them (a point to be further explored in chapter 7). Here is one such mapping of the "global/local" at the turn of the millenium: "a new world-space of cultural production and national representation which is simultaneously becoming more *globalized* (unified around dynamics of capitalogic moving across borders) and more *localized* (fragmented into contestatory enclaves of difference, coalition, and resistance) in everyday texture and composition" (Wilson and Dissanayake 1996, 1). Here is another, more specific, mapping: "The world has been turning toward all-powerful consumerism in which brand names command recognition and attraction. Everywhere commodities are invented, transported, promoted, day-dreamed over, sold, purchased, consumed, and discarded" (Miyoshi 1993, 747). The "ethnographic" film, no doubt, is one such cultural commodity that is locally produced but globally distributed and con- sumed. Largely due to the workings of transnationalism, theorized since the early 1990s as a dominant force in politics, economy, technology, and culture around the world (Appadurai 1996; Bamyeh 1993; Wilson and Dissanayake 1996), Chen Kaige and Zhang Yimou have become brand names recognizable by consumers in the West.

Mapping, 2: Transnational Cinema and Transregional Cooperation

In view of the shifting configurations of the global/local in the contemporary world, Sheldon Hsiao-peng Lu recommends using "transnational Chinese cinemas" to cover the latest developments not only in mainland China, Hong Kong, and Taiwan, but also elsewhere in diasporic Chinese communities. Transnationalism in the Chinese case, according to Lu, is manifest at four levels: first, the triangulation of competing national/local "Chinese cinemas" in the mainland, Hong Kong, and Taiwan; second, the globalization of the production, marketing, and consumption of Chinese films in the 1990s; third, the cross-examination of "China" and "Chineseness" in filmic discourse itself; and fourth, a revisiting of the history of Chinese "national cinemas" to reveal its "essentially transnational nature" (1997c, 2–3).[10]

While Lu emphasizes the competition among filmmakers in the three regions in his conception of transnationalism, I would like to draw attention to their close *cooperation* as an effective transregional strategy since the late 1980s. Indeed, it is primarily due to their cooperation that a transnational mode of film production and distribution was instituted in the early 1990s. Hong Kong filmmakers, for instance, have increasingly relied on the cheap labor and inexpensive equipment provided by mainland studios. In so doing, they have not only expanded and consolidated their market share in the mainland but have also earned artistic reputation overseas with their prize-winning coproductions such as *The Story of Qiu Ju* and *Farewell My Concubine*.[11] Under pressure of

---

[10] Lu's concept of "transnational cinema" differs from Hamid Naficy's "independent transnational genre." The latter is defined as "(1) belonging to a genre of cine-writing and self-narrativization with specific generic and thematic conventions and (2) products of the particular transnational location of filmmakers in time and place and in social life and cultural difference" (Naficy, 1996, 121).

[11] Hong Kong Film Archive 1997a, 67–8. In 1995, of 143 domestic films, 35 were coproductions (mosly with Hong Kong), representing 24 percent of the total yearly output in mainland China (Zhongguo dianying nianjian 1996, 44–106). The figure for 1996, however, is far from promising: due to China's new policy requiring that most

economic reform, most mainland studios are willing to rent out their equipment and human resources in order to cope with the dramatic decrease in box-office profits as a direct consequence of the popularity of other forms of leisure and entertainment in the 1990s (such as ballroom dances, KTVs, mini-bars, rock concerts, soap operas). To rejuvenate the declining film industry, the mainland government started in October 1994 to import "ten mega films" each year on the basis of splitting box-office revenue with the producers, and *The Fugitive* (Wangming tianya, 1993) and *Forrest Gump* (A Gan zhengzhuan, 1994) were among the first group of imported titles. Significantly, two of those immensely popular mega films are not from Hollywood but from Hong Kong: *Drunken Master, II* (Zuiquan, 1994) and *Rumble in the Bronx* (Hongfan qu, 1994), both featuring Jackie Chan (Cheng Long), a truly transnational film star by 1995 (Chen Zhikuan 1997, 29).

In Taiwan, the transnational/transregional mode of film operation arose in response to a dismal drop in local film output from 215 to thirty-three, and the concomitant decline in movie theaters from 736 in 1981 to 382 in 1992 (Shen 1995b, 10). By 1995, the official figure of Taiwan films screened there was twenty-eight, compared with 133 from Hong Kong and 261 from elsewhere (Government Information Office 1997, 286). The sharp decline in domestic films continued in 1996: only eighteen Taiwan films were screened (down 56 percent), compared with 90 from Hong Kong (down 48 percent) and 253 from elsewhere (Chen Zhikuan 1997, 44). Even a veteran director like Edward Yang had to count on Warner Asia to finance and distribute his urban comedy *A Confucian Confusion* (Duli shidai, 1995). Other new talents have drawn almost exclusively on government subsidies—or "domestic film grants" (*guopian fudao jin*) totaling N.T. $1.85 million in 1995 and $3.7 million in 1996—in their production of a limited number of award-winning films (Government Information Office 1997, 287). Although he himself benefited from such grants, Hou Hsiao-hsien sarcastically likens these subsidized films to "flowers blooming in barren soil" (Wang Fei-yun 1955, 17). Under these circumstances, what the Taiwan government terms "cross-straits collaboration" in filmmaking had become inevitable. After giving the green light to *Five Girls and a Rope* (1991)—the first Taiwan feature film shot in the mainland—a year after its ban, the

---

post-production work be done in the mainland, "the number of co-productions dropped to about ten from forty to fifty in previous years" (Teo 1997, ix).

government decided to allow Taiwan directors to shoot footage on location, or even the entire film in the mainland. One such example of a film shot entirely on the mainland is *Accidental Legend* (Feitian, 1995).

The cooperative relationships between Chinese film industries in the three regions compel us to rethink the concept of transnationalism in the Chinese context, for numerous interregional and intracultural forces are obviously at work in such a transnational operation. In this regard, transnationalism is marked as much by a specific culture, space, and time as by certain transcultural and transregional features. For this reason, while I concur with Sheldon Lu that Chinese cinema has acquired a transnational character over the past decade, I would caution against his pronouncements that "film in China has always been of a transnational character" and that "film has always been a transnational entity" (S. Lu 1997c, 25). For one, "transnationalism" theorized as typical of global capitalism is a period concept rather than a transhistorical one, and as such it differs from both "international trade relations" and "cross-cultural exchanges," which have been going on throughout the century. For another—and more crucial—reason, a replacement of "national cinema" by "transnational cinema" as an overriding term for Chinese film production in the first half of the century runs the risk of erasing the issue of cultural colonialism. We must remember that it is against Hollywood's domination that China launched a national film industry in the late 1920s. To support my modification of Lu's transhistorical claim on transnational Chinese cinema, I turn to Aihwa Ong and Donald Nonini, two anthropologists who consider "modern Chinese transnationalism to be a recent global phenomenon with historical roots in premodern trade systems, European colonialism, and more recent American geopolitical domination of the Pacific" (1997, 12). In short, I believe that we cannot afford to forget hard-won historical lessons about Western colonialism and must, instead, keep transnationalism in proper historical perspective.

Even if we accept that transnational cinema is an apt term for contemporary Chinese film, we must not be blinded by the dazzling display of transnationalism and fail to see a multitude of national, ethnic, regional, and local issues that still exist in contemporary Chinese society. For example, Rey Chow has called on "interested scholars to confront the contradictions of Chineseness as a constructed ethnicity" and to study "other 'Chinese' cultures" such as Tibet, Taiwan, and Hong Kong (1997, 151). But the fact is, except for Tibet, some of the issues suggested by

Chow have been tackled in a number of recent anthologies (Browne et al. 1994, 117–215; S. Lu 1997e, 139–262), although the authors of those essays may not share Chow's particular brand of identity politics. Other areas of contradiction that belie "Chineseness" as a constructed ethnicity, such as the interregional or intracultural relationships between the Han Chinese and ethnic minorities, have also been investigated in Chinese film studies (Clark 1987b; Yau 1989b).

Mapping, 3: The Transnational Imaginary and Site-Oriented Investigation

As a critical concept that simultaneously embraces and questions the transnational, the international, the multinational, and perhaps the intranational or interregional, the "transnational imaginary" involves both a "cognitive mapping" of the global events and "an intensified vision of the local situation" (Wilson and Dissanayake 1996, 5). In the field of cultural studies, film has been given a privileged role in investigating "[t]he image, the imagined, the imaginary—these are all terms which direct us to something critical and new in global cultural processes: *the imagination as a social practice*" (Appadurai 1996, 31). Following Appadurai's reformulation of image-making and imagination as concrete social practices, James Hay proposes "a way of discussing film as a social practice that begins by considering how social relations are spatially organized— through sites of production and consumption—and how film is practiced from and across particular sites and always in relation to other sites" (1997, 216).

The logic of this *site-oriented* investigation entails a number of methodological moves in Chinese film studies. First, we may locate in a film genre a special mapping of various sites of social and/or sexual relations. From this point of view, we can now see clearly that the "ethnographic" film constitutes only a small—albeit much glamorized— genre in Chinese film production, and that this genre is mainly practiced in China's rural landscape, where sexual battles are staged and "primitive passions" are revealed to audiences at home and abroad. Another highly publicized place in film production is the crime world of the Hong Kong gangster film. This fast-paced genre captures political and economic tensions in Hong Kong (or other surrogate sites like Saigon and Tokyo) and parades masculinity as the last trace of heroism (Gallagher 1997; B. Ryan 1995; Sandell 1996; Stringer 1997b; Williams 1997b). Interestingly, as Hollywood became infatuated with the Hong Kong gangster film, the genre was transported to other sites across the Pacific, and its production and distribution are now truly transnational, involving Hong Kong directors and cast such as John Woo (Wu Yusen), Lingo Lam (Lin Lingdong), Tsui Hark, Michelle Yeoh (Yang Ziqiong), and Chow Yun-Fat (Zhou Runfa) in major Hollywood projects while exporting these titles to the vast Asian market and reaping huge profits there.[12]

Second, the site-oriented investigation requires us to map out the changing networks and locations of film production and distribution in or between mainland China, Hong Kong, and Taiwan, as well as their complex relationships with other regions in Asia (especially Japan) and around the world. For instance, apart from some basic facts and film texts themselves, very few research publications to date can tell us what went on behind the scenes in the processes of planning, financing, scripting, shooting, editing, marketing, distributing, and reception of big-budget films such as *Red Cherry* (Hong yingtao, 1995) and *The Emperor's Shadow* (Qinsong, 1996). And the relationships between the declining film industry and the flourishing television and video networks (or the mass media in general) have rarely made it to the top list of research agenda. In this regard, Appadurai's framework for exploring disjunctures and differences in the global cultural economy is also useful to Chinese film studies. For Appadurai, current global cultural flows "occur in and through the growing disjunctures among ethnoscapes, technoscapes, financescapes, mediascapes, and ideoscapes" (1996, 37). Appadurai's mapping makes it clear that to better understand Chinese cinema in the era of transnationalism, we must extend our investigation to include other sites of social, technological, economic, cultural, and political

---

[12] These Hong Kong-affiliated Hollywood titles include John Woo's *Broken Arrow* (Duanjian xingdong, 1996) and *Face/Off* (Duomian shuangxiong, 1997), both shown in mainland China as yearly mega imports; Lingo Lam's *Maximum Risk* (Yingchuang 100% weixian, 1996); Tsui Hark's *Double Team* (Fanji wang, 1997), as well as *Tomorrow Never Dies* (1997) featuring Michelle Yeoh, and *Replacement Killer* (1998), and *Anna and the King* (1999), both featuring Chow Yun-Fat. For discussions of transnational or trans-Pacific operations, see Ciecko 1997; Fore 1999; and Williams 1997a. Additionally, Gu Changwei, a leading cinematographer from the Fifth Generation who collaborated with Chen Kaige, Zhang Yimou, and Jiang Wen on their award-winning films, emigrated to the U.S. in 1994 and has since worked on *The Gingerbread Man* (1998) and other Hollywood pictures through the arrangement of the ICM Agency.

operations, and, more important, the disjunctures within and between these various sites or scapes.

Third, the site-oriented investigation further demands that we be fully aware of our position as film scholars vis-à-vis other sites of current theoretical and methodological debate. Chinese film studies is, after all, a contested site of power and knowledge, and as such is related to other sites of academic production. In view of the current debate on postmodernism in Chinese cultural studies (see chapter 8), I cite a cautionary remark from Jonathan Arac. In his response to the essays in a 1997 special issue of *New Literary History*, "Cultural Studies: China and the West," Arac acknowledges that "in contemporary China there is some degree of postmodernism, as a movement in advanced artistic and intellectual circles," but he immediately cautions that, since modernity is still a dominant discourse, "postmodernity is not the condition of China" and that, "if not China, then not the world" (1997, 144). It is not just a mere coincidence that, in a recent anthropological work, "Chinese transnationalism" is unambiguously defined "as a phenomenon of late modernity"—with "modernities" in the plural to refer to those "cultural forms that are organically produced in relation to other regional forces in the polycentric world of late capitalism" (Ong and Nonini 1997, 14–5).

From my overview of the field in this chapter and my tentative mapping in this final section, it is obvious that neither ethnography (in its close association with the Fifth Generation directors) nor postmodernism (in its varied geocultural manifestations in mainland China, Hong Kong, and Taiwan) can characterize the entire arena of contemporary Chinese cinema. "Screening China" is a complex project that requires our attention to both the textual and critical levels of its many operations. In the chapters that follow, I will, among other things, survey the history of the institutionalization of Chinese film studies in the West (see chapter 3), propose a paradigm of self-reflexive dialogic criticism in lieu of Eurocentrism in cross-cultural analysis (see chapter 4), and study a number of genres—ethnic minority film, war film (both in chapter 5), ethnographic cinema (see chapter 6), nostalgia cinema, and urban cinema (both in chapter 7)—in their specific historical and sociopolitical contexts. Always bearing in mind the question of transnational cultural politics, I will demonstrate that Chinese cinema and Chinese film studies have a significant role to play in the ongoing configurations of the global/local in the field of transnational cultural production.

Three

The Rise of Chinese Film Studies in the West: Contextualizing Issues, Methods, Questions

> Transculturation is a phenomenon of the contact zone. . . . How are metropolitan modes of representation received and appropriated on the periphery? . . . [H]ow does one speak of transculturation from the colonies to the metropolis? . . . [T]he term "contact zone" . . . refer[s] to the space of colonial encounters, the space in which peoples geographically and historically separated come into contact with each other and establish ongoing relations, usually involving conditions of coercion, radical inequality, and intractable conflict.
>
> Mary Louise Pratt, *Imperial Eyes*

As recently as the early 1980s, Chinese cinema barely constituted an academic subject in the West. A number of events in the mid-1980s, however, decisively contributed to its rise. First, on April 12, 1985, *Yellow Earth* showed to high acclaim at the Hong Kong International Film Festival, and the "torrid enthusiasm" of the Hong Kong audience, including many Westerners, was repeated later at the Edinburgh and Locarno festivals, signaling "that Chinese cinema came of age" (Rayns 1989, 1). The international success of *Yellow Earth* soon proved to be the first of a series of spectacular achievements of the New Chinese Cinema, especially works by the Fifth Generation filmmakers. In addition, ground-breaking retrospectives of Chinese films held in Turin, Italy (February 25–March 8, 1982, more than 140 films screened), Beijing (September 1983, more than forty pre-1949 films screened), and Hong Kong (January 1984, mostly films from the 1920s and 1930s screened), also greatly stimulated public interest from the West and helped push China to the center stage of world cinema.[1]

---

[1] The phenomenal Turin retrospective (Ellis 1982), master-minded by Marco Müller, produced two fine Chinese film programs in 1982 (Center for Documentation; Electa). For the Hong Kong retrospective, see Pickowicz 1984; Xianggang Zhongguo dianying.

Second, in the fall of 1983 and spring of 1986, Chinese film scholars Cheng Jihua and Chen Mei came twice to team-teach their "legendary" seminars at the University of California at Los Angeles (UCLA). This marked the formal entry of Chinese cinema into regular university curriculum in the U.S. (Rothman 1993b, 258).[2] As a result of their first UCLA contact, Cheng and Chen initiated a lecture series by American film scholars. Starting in the summer of 1984, several groups of American professors visited Beijing and delivered to enthusiastic Chinese audiences a series of lectures on Western film criticism and film theory. The practice continued with great success in subsequent summers through 1988, with heightened awareness on both sides of each others' filmmaking and film studies.[3]

For the Eastern Horizons retrospective, part of the September 1987 Toronto Festival of Festivals that exhibited films from Hong Kong, Taiwan, South Korea, the Philippines, and Vietnam, see Aufderheide 1987. The National Film Theater in London organized two small Chinese film seasons in 1976 and 1980 (Delmar and Nash 1976–7; Rayns and Meek 1980). A "China Film Week" that toured the U.S. in 1981 is briefly mentioned in Allen 1981. Growing public interest in the West was reflected later in a number of special sections or issues devoted to Chinese and Hong Kong films in journals such as *Film Comment* (1988), *Camera Obscura* (1989), *Jump Cut* (1989, 1998), *Wide Angle* (1989), *Cineaste* (1990), *Modern Chinese Literature* (1993), *Cineaction* (1997), and *Post Script* (1999), as well as regular coverage in *Asian Cinema* and *Cinemaya*.

[2] Later, Cheng Jihua and Chen Mei team-taught courses on Chinese cinema at the University of Iowa and the State University of New York at Stony Brook. In addition, Chen Mei also taught alone at the University of Southern California and served as a Rockefeller Research Fellow at the University of Wisconsin at Madison.

[3] Here is a list of visiting American scholars and their lecture topics: David Bordwell on film theory and practice (1988), Nick Browne on the history of Western film theory (1984) and on ideology (1985), Brian Henderson on narrative theories (1987), Beverle Houston on 1950s melodrama (1984), E. Ann Kaplan on psychoanalysis and woman in contemporary film (1987), Johnathan Kuntz on the history of   television and programming (1988), Janet Neipris on screenwriting (1987) and, with Don Wille, on American film comedy (1987), Bill Nichols on Hitchcock and film interpretation (1986), Robert Rosen on the sociological reading of film language (1984), modernism and modernity (1985), and the aesthetics of sound (1986), George Schaefer on directing and multimedia (1986), Robert Sklar on new film historiography (1988), Vivian Sobchack on the myth and ideology of Hollywood musicals (1986), Janet Staiger on film form and style (1985), Kristin Thompson on contemporary American film (1988), and Richard Walter on screenwriting (1987). In addition to these summer visits, Dudley Andrew was invited to lecture on film hermeneutics (1988). For information presented here I am indebted to Chen Mei, then an editor and translator with *World Cinema*. See also Browne et al. 1985; Hu Ke 1995, 67; Semsel et al. 1993, xxii–xxiii.

Third, as William Rothman testifies, historically, "We Americans studying Chinese cinema in those years found ourselves envisioning the events [of reform and democratization] sweeping China as a grand historical melodrama," and therefore felt "called upon to play a role by championing new Chinese films (1993b, 259).[4] Although the breathtaking events ended in the Tiananmen Incident in the summer of 1989, as captured in the documentary *The Gate of Heavenly Peace* (1995), Chinese cinema has managed to sustain public attention by taking, one by one since the late 1980s, the top prizes awarded by many prestigious international film festivals (Eder and Rossell 1993, 8; Teng 1993, 40; Zhang Junxiang and Cheng 1995, 1433–43). In the meantime, Chinese cinema gradually established itself as a legitimate academic subject. In the new millennium, Chinese cinema is a blooming field, as demonstrated by the number and quality of books and articles published over the past decade. This new field deserves a systematic examination of its achievements thus far and what awaits further research.

This chapter surveys the rise of Chinese film studies in the West from the 1970s through the 1990s. The majority of publications under review here are in English and from critics and scholars based in North America, Europe, and Australia, although a few titles in other European languages are also discussed (for Chinese publications, see Y. Zhang 2000b). I start with a review of major book-length publications (Section I), then move through other representative articles and essays to sort out principal methods and issues in Chinese film studies (Section II), and finally end with comments on some unresolved questions and under-researched topics in this fast-growing field (Section III).

---

[4] Ni Zhen gives an example of the impact of Western critical acclaim on the fate of *Yellow Earth*. The film attracted only a small audience at home when first released in 1984, and a Beijing theater had to refund tickets and replace the film with another program. After the 1985 Hong Kong Film Festival, "when an attempt was made in Shanghai to devote two or three movie houses exclusively to experimental narratives, *Yellow Earth* ran to capacity audiences for a week and had a nationwide impact" (1993a, 31).

I

A Long Road to Recognition: A Glimpse of Pre-1980 Publications

Before "Ombre Electtriche" (Electric shadows), held in Turin in 1982, few in the West knew of China's long history of filmmaking, which began in the early 1900s and maintained a close connection with the West. For example, *Zhuangzi Tests His Wife* (Zhuangzi shiqi, 1913) [Illustration 2], an early Hong Kong short feature, was never released in Hong Kong but was screened in Los Angeles in 1917 instead (Hong Kong Film Archive 1997b, 1: 3; Law Kar 2000).

2. *Zhuangzi Tests His Wife* (1913): An early Hong Kong short feature

Laborer's Love (Laogong zhi aiqing, 1922), aka *Cheng the Fruit Seller* (Zhiguo yuan), now the earliest extant Chinese film, carried both Chinese and English subtitles for export purposes. *Romance of the Western Chamber* (Xixiang ji, 1927), promoted as *Way Down West* to invoke D. W. Griffith's famous *Way Down East* (1920), was actually screened as *La Rose de Pu-shui* (or *The Rose of Pushui*) in Paris in 1928. The artistic quality and emotional impact of early Chinese films were such that some members of the Turin audience were moved to tears. John Ellis thus admits in his 1982 report of the retrospective for the academic journal *Screen*, "The ones that provoked me to cry almost despite myself, are those which draw upon the melodramatic traditions of heroic suffering and sacrifice that were developed in the 1930s and early '40s" (79–80). The critical response to the 1995 Pordenone (Italy) Silent Film Festival, reputedly the largest retrospective of Chinese silents (1922–1938) ever assembled for a Western audience, was no less enthusiastic. "By opening the vault to these historic treasures, many unseen since their first release," concludes a report in the New York-based *Film Comment*, "Pordenone has brought to light a new constellation of auteurs and stars, providing windows to a China seemingly eclipsed by memories of the Cultural Revolution" (Severson 1996, 48).

In his recollection of events before and after the Cultural Revolution, French film historian Régis Bergeron narrates an insider's story of the intermittent film-cultural exchange between China and the West. According to Bergeron, Jean Mitry remembered watching *The Rose of Pushui* at Studio 28, a Paris film theater, in 1928; next year, the film was shown on January 12, 1929, at a Geneva film club, as reported by the Swiss magazine *Close Up*. Earlier, the April 10, 1924 issue of *Mon Cine* had carried a feature article, "The Rise of the Film Industry in China," including photographs and an interview with a Chinese actor who bragged about the accomplishments of the Peacock Film Company (Kongque) in Shanghai. Bergeron's own personal contact with Chinese cinema began in 1955, when *Liang Shanbo and Zhu Yingtai* (Liang Shanbo yu Zhu Yingtai, 1954), a Shanghai opera film that would take the Hong Kong and Taiwan film industries by storm in the 1960s, was shown to a packed house at a private screening organized by André Bazin, George Sadoul, and Jacques Doniol-Valcrose at the Vox, a Cannes theater.

From 1959 to 1961, Bergeron taught French literature at Beijing (Peking) University and communicated with film historians like Sadoul,

Joris Ivens, and Jay Leyda. Bergeron's plan to write a comprehensive history of Chinese cinema, something nonexistent at the time in any language, was greatly encouraged by Cai Chusheng, Cheng Jihua, Shen Fu, Situ Huimin, and Zheng Junli. Among these, Cheng Jihua—in collaboration with Li Shaobai and Xing Zuwen—soon published in 1963 a two-volume history of pre-1949 Chinese cinema. This has since become a standard reference book in the field, but Zheng Junli had published a concise history of early Chinese cinema in 1936, a pioneering work that, for unknown reasons, had been lost and not rediscovered until the late 1980s (Y. Zhang 1999a, 261). Given his long-time China connection (nineteen visits by 1996) and his extensive exposure to leftist film (*zuoyi dianying*) and its leading representatives, it is only natural that Bergeron would acknowledge that his *Le cinéma chinois, 1905–1949* (Chinese cinema), eventually published in 1977, was "inspired by the memory of these prestigious men and this heroic and talented cinema" (1996–7, 124).[5]

Like Bergeron, Jay Leyda, a well-known scholar of Russian-Soviet cinema, had a personal tie with Beijing, where he spent three years (1959–62) cataloguing the collection of foreign films at the China Film Archive (Zhongguo dianying ziliao guan). A Russia specialist, Leyda was disappointed by the intensifying Sino-Soviet ideological conflict at the time and found himself only partially employed after a trip to London (Bergeron 1996–7, 120). As he makes explicit in his foreword, Leyda's *Dianying / Electric Shadows: An Account of Films and the Film Audience in China* (1972) was written in reaction to the official history Cheng Jihua and his associates published in 1963: "As I heard this translation of a history so extremely orthodox in attitude and in structure, I began to imagine another history of Chinese films, looser in both attitude and structure, less anxious to subscribe to habits and taboos, . . . [but yet]

---

[5] For lack of a better designation, I retain "leftist film" in this book as a widely circulated term in Chinese film studies. This term refers to a body of films from the 1930s and 1940s that were directed mostly by the "progressive" filmmakers at the time but were based on scripts by the then underground Communist activists such as Xia Yan and Tian Han and their comrades-in-arm. The slippage of the term is evident in two films Wu Yonggang directed in the mid-1930s. Whereas *Goddess* (1934) was later hailed as a classic example of leftist film, *The Little Angel* (Xiao tianshi, 1935) was an immediate product of the "New Life Movement" (*Xin shenghuo yundong*) launched by the Nationalist government in 1934, since it was based on an prize-winning script endorsed by the Ministry of Education for that movement.

greatly dependent on [Cheng's] data and research" (1972, xiii). Indeed, Leyda's intentionally revisionist history, completed by April 1966 and updated before its publication in 1972, is "loose" in many aspects, not only in organization and interpretation of miscellaneous sources, but in translation of data and documents as well. In spite of the sheer quantity of its material (including direct quotations from print literature, for example) and its chronological scope (1896–1967, including a brief chapter on Hong Kong), the book "unfortunately is marred by errors due to Leyda's unfamiliarity with the Chinese language" (L. Lee 1991b, 18). Lacking a consistent historical vision, Leyda's book is best read as a collection of primary sources arranged in chronological order.

It is worth noting that *Ocherk istorii kitaiskogo kino, 1896–1966* (Essays on the history of Chinese cinema), a book similar to Leyda's in terms of historical coverage, was compiled by Sergei Toroptsev (Tuoluopucaifu), a scholar with the Institute of the Far East at the Soviet Academy of Science, and published in Russian in 1979. The book was translated into Chinese and published in 1982 by the China Film Association for internal circulation. Another noteworthy publication, *Cinema e spettacolo in Cina oggi* (Cinema and performance in today's China), was issued in 1978 for the 14th International Festival of New Cinema in Italy. Published in Italian as catalogue no. 75 of the festival, this collection contains, among other things, a fifty-seven-page survey of Chinese theater from the late 1950s to the late 1970s by Franca Angelini, a ninety-one-page history of Chinese cinema by Ugo Casiraghi, short reflections and "testimonies" by five Europeans (such as Joris Ivens and Régis Bergeron), a speech by Zhou Enlai, a chronology of events from 1895 to 1978, and a total of twenty film synopses. These films range from *From Victory to Victory* (Nanzheng beizhan, 1952); *Dong Cunrui* (Dong Cunrui, 1955); through *Naval Battle of 1894* (Jiawu fengyun, 1962) [Illustration 3]; *Zhang Ga, a Boy Soldier* (Xiaobing Zhang Ga, 1963); to *The Pioneers* (Chuangye, 1974) and *Hai Xia* (Hai Xia, 1975). What is truly impressive is a forty-two-page filmography (in English) of Chinese cinema from 1905 to 1977. Published two years after the Cultural Revolution, *Cinema e spettacolo in Cina oggi* was the most up-to-date publication of its kind in the West by the end of the 1970s.[6]

---

[6] In 1976, Rosalind Delmar and Mark Nash published a critical survey of art and politics in Chinese cinema of the 1970s in *Screen*. The survey included a checklist of seven Chinese films shown at the National Film Theatre in London during the period (1976–

3. *Naval Battle of 1894* (1962): A lesson of defeat in nationalist discourse

77, 83–4). Among them, three movies of "revolutionary model operas or ballets" (*geming yangban xi*)—*Red Detachment of Women* (Hongse niangzi jun, 1970), *The White-Haired Girl* (Baimao nü, 1972), and *Azalea Mountain* (Dujuan shan, 1974)—were produced under close supervision of Jiang Qing, Mao's power-hungry wife, who had been a second-rate film actress in 1930s Shanghai. The rest are representative feature films produced after a hiatus in the late 1960s: *The Pioneers, From Victory to Victory* (1974), *Hong Yu* (Hong Yu, 1975), and *Breaking with Old Ideas* (Juelie, 1975). Out of these seven films, three are remakes of earlier features: *The White-Haired Girl* (1950), *From Victory to Victory* (1952), and *Red Detachment of Women* (1961).

In general, the pre-1980 Western publications on Chinese cinema are of informational (or descriptive) rather than academic (or critical) nature. They supplied basic but then much-needed documents on the cultural and sociopolitical history of modern China. Some of them also came with biographical entries on major directors (as in Leyda) and plot summaries of select films (as in *Cinema e spettacolo in Cina oggi*).

Festival Programs and Film Histories, 1980–87

The 1980s saw an increasing number of publications on Chinese cinema in the West. These fall into three main categories: festival program, film history, and essay volume. In the first category, Tony Rayns and Scott Meek's *Electric Shadows: 45 Years of Chinese Cinema* (1980) tries to imitate the film-festival format of *Cinema e spettacolo in Cina oggi* by featuring a seven-page outline history of the film industry by Meek, a five-page introduction to aesthetics and politics by Rayns, translations of two short articles by Sun Yun and Xia Yan, respectively, as well as film synopses and biographic notes on thirty-four filmmakers. As an early English publication, Rayns and Meek's volume pales in comparison to either *Cinema e spettacolo in Cina oggi* or any other subsequent titles, not only in terms of information presented but also in the quality of typesetting and layout.

Two festival programs grew out of the famous 1982 Turin retrospective: *Ombre elettriche: Saggi e ricerche sul cinema cinese* (Electric shadows: essays and studies on Chinese cinema), published in Milan for the original program sponsored by the Regione Piemonte, and *Ombres électriques: Panorama du cinéma chinois, 1925–1982* (Electric shadows: a panoramic view of Chinese cinema), prepared by the Centre de Documentation sur le Cinéma Chinois for a less ambitious event in Paris in June 1982. In addition to sixty film synopses, *Ombres électriques* presents five essays: He Xiujun on Zhang Shichuan and the Mingxing Film Company (Star); Régis Bergeron on Chinese film and political struggles from 1949 to 1981; Mao Zedong on *The Life of Wu Xun* (Wu Xun zhuan, 1950); Kwok and Marie-Claire Quiquemelle, as well as He Zhengan, on realism in Chinese cinema.

The format of festival program comes near to perfection in *Le cinéma chinois* (1985), coedited by Marie-Claire Quiquemelle and Jean-Loup Passek and issued by the Centre Georges Pompidou in Paris. This large reference book excels its predecessors in all essential features, such as its easy-to-use, thirty-four-page chronological listing of film, political, and cultural events in three columns; 141 film synopses (1922–1984, all titles accompanied by Chinese characters and pinyin romanization); bio- graphical entries (missing in many earlier programs); and an amazing number of quality pictures. It also includes commentaries appended to nearly all synopses. Additionally, the book contains fourteen short articles by Chinese and European scholars: the China Film Archive collective on a brief historical overview; He Xiujun on Zhang Shichuan and the Mingxing Film Company; Lau Shing Hon (Liu Chenghan) on 1930s and post-war films; Li Cheuk-to (Li Zhuotao) on *Spring in a Small Town* (Xiaocheng zhichun, 1948); Sato Tadao on Chinese and Japanese cinemas; Lin Niantong on Chinese film theory and aesthetic tradition; Marco Müller on East-West film relations; an interview with cinematographer Huang Shaofen; Marie-Claire Quiquemelle on Shi Hui's art of acting; Geremie Barmé on methodology; Chris Berry on sexual difference; Régis Bergeron on popular film; Shan Budong on the post-Cultural Revo- lution recovery; and Shu Kei (Shu Qi) on the legend of Ruan Lingyu, a tragic film star. Although the sequence of these articles begs the question, it is interesting to note that Hong Kong scholars had more to contribute here to early Chinese film than their mainland and Taiwan counterparts (the latter with zero representation). With its impressive multilayered presentation, *Le cinéma chinois* had achieved critical depth otherwise absent in festival programs.

In the second category, Jörg Lösel's *Die politische funktion des Spielfilms in der Volsrepublik China zwischen 1949 und 1965* (The political function of feature films in the People's Republic of China between 1949 and 1965), published in 1980, offers a model of political history of Chinese cinema. Film politics (*Filmpolitik*) is given a central role in the structuring of events and texts in Lösel's history, which covers the following key moments: Mao Zedong's "Yan'an talks," the campaign against *The Life of Wu Xun*, the official theory of socialist realism, the "Hundred Flowers," and the "Great Leap Forward." To facilitate further research, Lösel also included a selection of important documents in German translation in the second part of the book. Published in 1984, Bergeron's *Le cinéma chinois, 1949–1983* (Chinese cinema) extends the coverage up to the end of the Cultural Revolution, but with an equally strong emphasis on film politics. Issued in three volumes, Bergeron's new history closely follows prominent political figures (Mao Zedong, Zhou

Enlai, Jiang Qing, and Deng Xiaoping) and uses their names and other political terms (such as "revolutionary romanticism," "class struggle," "anti-spiritual pollution") in his section titles. This method derives from Bergeron's conviction that "a national cinema cannot be studied without taking into account the history of its country of origin" (1996–7, 117).

Despite their obvious restriction by political ideology, both Lösel's and Bergeron's books can be taken as evidence of the considerable achievement of Chinese film studies in the West. This evidence is particularly telling because, by the mid-1980s, mainland China had not been able to produce a film history covering the post-1949 period. An official Chinese version edited by Chen Huangmei—a two-volume set comparable to Cheng Jihua's pre-1949 history—did not come out until 1989.[7] This is why Paul Pickowicz stated in 1984 that "research on Chinese cinema is still in its infancy" (p. 137), an assertion meant to cover the field in China as well as the West.

However, the situation of Chinese film studies in the West changed dramatically with a number of new scholarly publications in the late 1980s. Paul Clark's *Chinese Cinema: Culture and Politics Since 1949* (1987) continued the tradition of political history but brought it to a new level of sophistication. Although Clark intended to address three dominant themes—"the expansion of mass national culture, relations among Party, artists, and audience, and tensions between Yan'an and Shanghai" (p. 2)—his book is mostly structured around the last theme. Through chapter titles such as "Yan'an and Shanghai," "Beyond Shanghai," and "Beyond Yan'an," Clark actually uses these two terms as metaphors for things much larger. In his usage, "Yan'an" (influenced by Moscow) is equated to the Party and politics, whereas "Shanghai" (influenced by Hollywood and the May Fourth tradition) is equated to filmmakers (not necessarily based in Shanghai alone) and artistic creation. The entire history of film from 1949 to 1985 is then reduced to an account of tensions between politics and art, between orthodox ideology and artistic freedom, and between propaganda and individual expression, with the first term in each pair dominating the second most of the time.

Two points of clarification are called for with regard to Clark's schematic history. First, in his interpretation, the audience is virtually a phantom presence, an amorphous something both the Party and artists

---

[7] During the 1950s and 1960s, Chen served as deputy minister of culture and the director of the film bureau.

struggle to define and represent, rather than to serve, not to mention to please or cater to (at least not until the late 1980s). Clark's claim that "film was a battleground for educated, elite heroes seeking access to the rest of society" (p. 183) thus testifies to the relative unimportance of audiences in his account, which leaves little room for intervention, subversion, or resistance on the part of the audience as the third player between Party and artists. Second, bear in mind Clark's own modification: "An emphasis on a great divide between Party and artists can too easily encourage a presumption that each group was more monolithic and united than was the actual case" (p. 182). A case in point is Yuan Muzhi. Already famous in Shanghai as the male lead in *Plunder of Peach and Plum* (Taoli jie, 1934) and as director of *Cityscape* (Dushi fengguan, 1935) and *Street Angel* (Malu tianshi, 1937), Yuan traveled to Yan'an to organize a Communist film team in 1938, studied filmmaking in the Soviet Union during the early 1940s, returned to China in 1946 to establish the Northeast Film Studio (Dongbei), and became the first director of the Film Bureau after 1949. Given the mixture of people like Yuan Muzhi and Xia Yan (the latter representing Shanghai in a high-ranking Party position) in the post-1949 Chinese film industry, it would be interesting to see a series of more subtle interplays between Yan'an-in-Shanghai and Shanghai-in-Yan'an if we want to extend Clark's metaphors.[8]

The Expansion of the Field: Essay Volumes and Other Publications, 1985–91

The most encouraging sign of change in Chinese film studies occurs in the category of essay volume. Chris Berry's edited collection, *Perspectives on Chinese Cinema* (1985), published as number 39 in the Cornell University East Asia Papers series, consists of five articles originally presented to a panel at a 1984 conference on Chinese oral and

---

[8] The head of the underground Communist film team that penetrated the Shanghai film industry in the early 1930s, Xia Yan is credited for leading the leftist film movement to spectacular success. In 1933 alone, Xia contributed screenplays—sometimes in collaboration with others—to Cheng Bugao's *Wild Torrents* (Kuangliu) and *Spring Silkworms* (Chuncan), Zhang Shichuan's *The Market of Beauty* (Zhifen shichang), Li Pingqian's *Children of Our Time* (Shidai de ernü), and Shen Xiling's *Twenty-four Hours in Shanghai* (Shanghai ershisi xiaoshi). Xia later came to assume prominent Party positions such as deputy minister of culture in the 1950s and was influential in setting policies regarding literature and art before the Cultural Revolution.

performing literature, and an additional contribution from Paul Pickowicz. Fully aware that "Chinese cinema is beginning to receive serious attention in Western academic circles for the first time now," Berry anticipates that this emerging field will need "a multidisciplinary approach" (1985, i). For this consideration, Berry's collection includes perspectives from literary history, art criticism, film theory, and history studies.

Writing as a literary historian in "The Tradition of Modern Chinese Cinema: Some Preliminary Explorations and Hypotheses," Leo Ou-fan Lee presents a "central contention that the modern Chinese film grew into a mature art form by virtue of its closer interaction with modern Chinese literature, especially spoken drama (*huaju*)" (1991b, 6). In a "rough scheme" of periodization, Lee charts out this line of development of artistic genres in modern China: the short story dominates the May Fourth period (1917–27), the novel the Nanjing decade (1927–37), the spoken drama the war years (1937–45), and film the post-war period (1945–49). For Lee, the last period also constitutes the "golden age" of Chinese cinema, and "the level of artistic excellence it attained has remained unsurpassed down to the present day" (p. 6).[9] After analyzing the thematic and stylistic features of social realism in Chinese films of the 1940s, Lee further traces the continuation of this tradition in revolutionary films of the 1960s and 1970s as well as in films from the 1980s.

Catherine Woo offers an art-history take in "The Chinese Montage: From Poetry and Painting to the Silver Screen." Proceeding from an "authentic" Daoist outlook that values "the vision of the unity of the human and natural worlds" in traditional Chinese poetry and painting, Woo argues that the "technique of a lyrical montage of simple images filmed with a static camera" enables Chinese filmmakers "to express, visually, the emotional totality of their narratives" (1991, 22). Woo's article, however, suffers from weak evidence from Chinese film texts, and her conclusion that "Chinese painting and poetry have extended their rich conventions to the movie screen, to help in the creation of a truly Chinese cinema" fails to explain by what standards one could define a body of cinema as "truly Chinese" (p. 28). Berry's "Sexual Difference and the Viewing Subject in *Li Shuangshuang* and *The In-laws*" also tries to identify some kind of "Chinese" film aesthetic. In this brief comparison

---

[9] Cf. Stephen Teo, who regards the 1930s as "the golden age" of Chinese cinema (1997, x), a position I would endorse.

of static shots and frame composition in *Li Shuangshuang* (Li Shuang-shuang, 1962) and *The In-laws* (Xi yingmen, 1981) [Illustration 4], Berry discovers "an anti-individualistic aesthetic" in the Chinese convention, something "contrary to the Western paradigm" of the subject-object play (1991c, 38). This Chinese aesthetic, he speculates, may further account for the absence of a discourse centering on gender in Chinese film studies.

4. *Li Shuangshuang* (1962): Viewer positioning and gender construction

The remaining three essays adopt a historical approach. In "The Wan Brothers and Sixty Years of Animated Film in China," Marie-Claire Quiquemelle traces the development, from the early 1920s to the late 1970s, of Chinese animation cinema—"appreciated by the entire world today for its original national style and its high artistic level" (1991, 175)—and the critical contributions from four brothers, Wan Guchan, Wan Laiming, Wan Chaochen, and Wan Dihuan. In "Two Hundred Flowers on China's Screens," Paul Clark compares two historical periods in socialist China, 1956–57 and 1978–81, where the tensions between art and politics are most conspicuous. In "The Limits of Cultural Thaw: Chinese Cinema in the Early 1960s," the longest piece in this edition, Paul Pickowicz uses the concept of "cultural thaw" adopted from the history of Soviet literature and examines a flourishing period in Chinese filmmaking in the wake of the catastrophe of the Great Leap Forward and the Anti-Rightist Campaign. Classifying films into screen images of imperial China, the Republican era (1911–49), and the socialist period, he discusses a variety of genres (such as costume drama, ethnic minority, historical film, comedy, and war film) and themes (like "contradictions among the people"). While the reliance on the traditional theater "satisfied a national emotional need [and] broke away from the Soviet socialist realism model," it nonetheless perpetuated "the tendency to produce caricatures of real people" (1985, 143–4). Pickowicz further argues that films like *Early Spring in February* (Zaochun eryue, 1963) and *Stage Sisters* (Wutai jiemei, 1965) represent attempts to strike out in a new and more independent direction, attempts that were suspended during the Cultural Revolution but were resumed and brought to fruition in the post-Mao era.

In 1991, Berry expanded his collection by including selected essays from the late 1980s, then had the new edition published by the British Film Institute in London, with the Indiana University Press serving as its North American distributor. In terms of historical coverage, the withdrawal of Pickowicz's piece is compensated for by two brief updates on the latest developments: Tony Rayns's "Breakthroughs and Setbacks: The Origins of the New Chinese Cinema" and Berry's "Market Forces: China's 'Fifth Generation' Faces the Bottom Line." The two articles signaled renewed attention to industry research in Chinese film studies, although neither of them is as systematic on this point as compared to John Lent's and George Semsel's work discussed below. This attention is further evidenced by Berry's inclusion of four translated documents dealing with filmmakers' concerns with market factors. Another new feature of Berry's expanded edition is the increased emphasis on film theory, as exemplified in Esther Yau's essay on *Yellow Earth*, Yuejin Wang's on *Red Sorghum*, and E. Ann Kaplan's on cross–cultural analysis (all three to be analyzed in chapter 4). The third noteworthy aspect is Berry's attempt to cover Taiwan and Hong Kong under the rubric of Chinese cinema. On the one hand, Chiao Hsiung-Ping's "The Distinct Taiwanese and Hong Kong Cinemas" seeks to demonstrate, on the basis of entries for the 1987 Golden Horse Film Festival, that "in many ways Taiwanese and Hong Kong films are completely opposite" (1991a, 155) (for example, rural versus urban, feminine versus masculine, nonprofessional cast versus star system, restraint versus excess, long take versus close-up and montage, slow rhythm versus speed, novelty, and fantasy, and lyrical style versus special visual effects).[10] On the other hand, Jenny Lau's "A Cultural Interpretation of the Popular Cinema of China and Hong Kong" tries to develop a model of cultural interpretation partially based on interpretive anthropology and neo-Confucianism, and to establish a cultural linkage between Chinese and Hong Kong films through such indigenous ideas as *li* (principle or reason), *qing* (emotion), and *jing* (cleverness) (1991a, 172–3). A number of other features further facilitate the use of Berry's new edition in research and teaching. Apart from a filmography at the end of each essay, Berry provides biographic notes on major directors, a seven-page chronology of significant events (1894–1989), and a glossary of Chinese characters. Nevertheless, as with his first, Berry's new edition is far from coherent in structure and theme.

Similarly loose in structure and uneven in coverage, George Semsel's edited volume, *Chinese Film: The State of the Art in the People's Republic* (1987), contains chapters on a variety of topics. Semsel's own introduction sketches the institutions and operations of film industry and film

---

[10] Chiao's observation is worth quoting at length: "If one can say Taiwanese films are the products of reflection and nostalgia by intellectuals in their thirties and forties, then Hong Kong films represent the dynamism of people in their early twenties. Because they emphasize introspection and restraint, Taiwanese films have developed a lyrical style based on long takes and a slow rhythm. In contrast, Hong Kong films are a synthesis of chaos and energy, and techniques such as fragmenting extreme close-ups of the body, rapid montage and spatial and temporal disorder are used frequently and indiscriminately" (1991a, 159).

education in contemporary China. Patricia Wilson's "The Founding of the Northeast Film Studio, 1946–1949" offers a historical account of Northeast, the first major studio the Communists controlled after taking over part of the Japanese-run Manchurian Motion Pictures (Manying). Xia Hong's "Film Theory in the People's Republic of China: The New Era" surveys the exciting period of film studies in the 1980s, a period that would become the topic of the next two volumes Semsel edited in collaboration with Xia Hong and other associates of his (reviewed below). Ma Ning's "Notes on the New Filmmakers" provides an excellent critical analysis of some early works of New Chinese Cinema, such as *Narrow Street* (Xiaojie, 1981), *One and Eight* (Yige he bage, 1984), *Yellow Earth*, *Sacrificed Youth*, and *On the Hunting Ground*. Finally, Semsel presents twelve interviews he conducted while working as a foreign expert in the China Film Corporation (Zhongguo dianying gongsi) in Beijing from 1985 to 1986. His interviewees include directors of different generations (Xie Jin, Teng Wenji, Zhang Nuanxin, Tian Zhuangzhuang, Chen Kaige, and Zhang Yimou) as well as actresses, an actor, a screenwriter, an editor, and a composer. Semsel concludes his volume with reflections on the end of an era.

As evident in his selection of interviewees, Semsel's *Chinese Film* does not aim for comprehensive coverage. Because of its scant material on the period 1949–80, Semsel's work is best complemented by Paul Clark's history. Likewise lacking an in-depth study of other active producers of New Chinese Cinema, Semsel's book finds a good supplement in Tony Rayns's more extensive treatment in "Chinese Vocabulary" (1989). Published as a fifty-eight-page introduction to a complete English translation of Chen Kaige's film script of *King of the Children*, Rayns's study—in a more elaborate manner than his television documentary *New Chinese Cinema* (1988)—traces the rise of the new filmmakers and the new film language in the 1980s and conducts close analyses of seven individual directors (Chen Kaige, Huang Jianxi, Hu Mei, Tian Zhuangzhuang, Wu Ziniu, Zhang Yimou, and Zhang Zeming). Like Ma Ning, Rayns approaches films and filmmakers from the cultural and artistic points of view, but his thesis regarding the *zhiqing* mentality or complex (educated youth sent to the countryside) of this group of filmmakers is too biographic in nature to be of much use for a critical study.

Although not entirely devoted to Chinese cinema, two other books also deserve mention here. First, Wimal Dissanayake's edited volume, *Cinema and Cultural Identity: Reflections on Films from Japan, India, and China* (1988) contains four chapters on China. Ma Qiang's "The Chinese Film in the 1980s: Art and Industry" and Shao Mujun's "Chinese Films Amidst the Tide of Reform" are both surveys of the post-Cultural Revolution development in Chinese cinema. In "The Sinification of Cinema: The Foreignness of Film in China," Paul Clark examines the ways Chinese government and filmmakers transform a foreign medium in their construction of a new mass culture in the Communist era. In "The Position of Women in New Chinese Cinema," Tony Rayns analyzes a film each from the three regions—*The Spooky Bunch* (Zhuang daozheng, 1980) from Hong Kong, *Taipei Story* (Qingmei zhuma, 1985) from Taiwan, and *Yellow Earth* from the mainland—and predicts, after defining these films as exceptions to all three industries in their portrayals of women, that "a full feminist consciousness in Chinese cinema is not too far off" (1988, 198). As shown in my discussion of feminist criticism in the next section, Rayns's prediction was far too optimistic and impressionistic, in part because he relied solely on his insider's observations and refused to consult additional sources or to engage in a critical dialogue with other scholars of Chinese cinema.

The film industries in mainland China, Hong Kong, and Taiwan each take a chapter in John Lent's *The Asian Film Industry* (1990). Like Semsel, who actually supplied the chapter on China for Lent's book, Lent relies heavily on interviews and personal observations. With subheadings such as "Introduction," "Historical Background," "Contemporary Scene," and "Notes," Lent classifies material he has gathered from miscellaneous sources but refrains, regrettably, from constructing a coherent narrative or consistent argument for these two chapters on Hong Kong and Taiwan. Another inconvenience for the reader is the absence of a Chinese-English glossary, without which one is often confused as to what English titles or romanized names are given to films, directors, and producers from Hong Kong and Taiwan.[11] Nonetheless, Lent succeeds in drawing attention to some neglected topics in Chinese film studies, such as film distribution and exhibition. With basic information on three Chinese film industries in one volume, Lent's book further points to the

---

[11] One way to solve this confusion is to consult the glossary and indexes of names and titles in Y. Zhang and Xiao 1998, 413–72.

necessity of comparative studies of Chinese cinema in both transregional and transnational contexts.

Whatever limits there are in the publications of the 1980s, it is clear they helped pave the way for the institutionalization of Chinese film studies in the West. The field blossomed in the 1990s, and the new publications have achieved both a higher level of critical interpretation and a wider coverage in historical, geopolitical, and generic terms.

Chinese Cinema: Of Western Melodrama and Traditional Chinese Aesthetics

Wimal Dissanayake's second edited volume, *Melodrama and Asian Cinema* (1993), is based on a 1989 film symposium held at the East-West Center in Hawaii and includes four essays on Chinese cinema. In "Melodrama/Subjectivity/Ideology: The Relevance of Western Melodrama Theories to Recent Chinese Cinema," E. Ann Kaplan takes up the challenge of engaging cross-cultural film studies that avoids defamiliarizing the alien text but at the same time demonstrates the relevance of Western theories of melodrama to recent Chinese cinema. Proceeding with a feminist distinction between the "women's melodrama" ("the story of how man comes to be man"—hence complicitous with the patriarchal order) and the "women's film" (which "raises the question of what it means to be female"—hence resistant to dominant ideology) (p. 13), Kaplan discusses various instances of female subjectivity, sexuality, desire, and transgression in *The Legend of Tianyun Mountain* (Tianyunshan chuanqi, 1980), *A Girl from Hunan* (Xiangnü Xiaoxiao, 1985), *A Good Woman* (Liangjia funü, 1985), and *Army Nurse*.

Ma Ning's "Symbolic Representation and Symbolic Violence: Chinese Family Melodrama of the Early 1980s" starts with conceptions of the Chinese family and then focuses on the issues of family conflict, the power-pleasure nexus, and sexual politics in *The In-Laws, Country Couple* (Xiangyin, 1983), and *In the Wild Mountains* (Yeshan, 1987). Ma asserts that family melodrama of the early 1980s is a site where symbolic violence is staged and where the Chinese peasant's way of life continues. In "*The Goddess*: Reflections on Melodrama East and West," William Rothman approaches an early Chinese masterpiece, *Goddess*, from a comparative, humanistic perspective and analyzes the ways virtue and purity are embodied in the actress Ruan Lingyu [Illustration 5] and are captured—rather than violated—by the camera.

Yuejin Wang presents a creative reading, "Melodrama as Historical Understanding: The Making and Unmaking of Communist History," in which he argues that melodrama is itself a mode of historical understanding because, as in 1989, history presents itself as cinema that commands our melodramatic gaze. Wang then supports his argument with a retake of significant historical events sweeping China and Eastern Europe in 1989.

5. Ruan Lingyu, a tragic film star of the 1930s

The four essays in Dissanayake's volume clearly illustrate the importance of melodrama to Chinese film studies. Informed by multiple theoretical models, the essays offer many interesting—at times insightful—readings of Chinese films, yet leave traces of their struggle to navigate through what Douglas Wilkerson terms "the turbid theoretical verbiage" (1994a, 510). An advocate for area studies, Wilkerson prefers research that demonstrates one's thorough knowledge of other cultures to that restricted by one's chosen discipline.

For an exemplary area studies model, we now turn to Linda Erhlich and David Desser's coedited volume, *Cinematic Landscapes: Observations on the Visual Arts and Cinema of China and Japan* (1994), to which Wilkerson contributed an introduction and translated from Chinese the first two essays in the China section. The five essays on film and visual arts in China cover a wide range of topics, including traditional aesthetics based on Daoist and Zen Buddhist principles, and the influence of traditional Chinese painting, especially the Southern School of landscape (*nanzong*), "with its multiple perspectives, relative flatness, use of blank space, elastic framing, lack of chiaroscuro and sculptural shading, and emphasis on expressive, calligraphic contour lines" (Wilkerson 1994b, 41). Hao Dazheng's "Chinese Visual Representation: Painting and Cinema" is a systematic study of outstanding features of Chinese visual representation, such as dominance of horizontal expanse over depth (hence the use of flat mise-en-scène), interest in communality and totality rather than individuality (hence no need for close-ups), or preference for imaginative over realistic portrayal (hence the use of flat lighting). Ni Zhen's "Classical Chinese Painting and Cinematographic Signification" further discusses specific cases: the ambulatory, panoramic point of view and freely expandable frame in Oriental painting, the manipulation of temporal "blanks" and "empty space" in Chen Kaige's and Hou Hsiao-hsien's films, and the link between the "lyrical film" and the Chinese literati tradition.

Whereas Hao and Ni are thoroughly immersed in Chinese aesthetics, Chris Berry and Mary Ann Farquhar are fully aware of recent debates in the West. Thus they propose, at the beginning of their essay "Post-Socialist Strategies: An Analysis of *Yellow Earth* and *Black Cannon Incident*," to conceptualize the style and strategies of Fifth Generation films as "postsocialist" (a concept to be further elaborated in chapter 8). They then proceed to read *Yellow Earth* in terms of brushwork, ink, and composition—drawing on the Chang'an school of painting in the mid-twentieth century as well as on the concept of yin/yang permutation—and analyze *Black Cannon Incident* in terms of alienation, expressionism/abstractionism, and distanciation. They conclude that the departure of these two films from the socialist-realist tradition in the 1950s and 1960s points to the opening up of postsocialist space, where tradition may be revived for contemporary intervention and Western modern art invoked for Chinese purposes.

As if to illustrate Berry and Farquhar's conclusion on the usefulness of tradition, An Jingfu contends in "The Pain of a Half Taoist: Taoist Principles, Chinese Landscape Painting, and *King of the Children*" that Chen Kaige's recourse to a Daoist aesthetic is not completely successful, and the main character in his *King of the Children* is at best a half Daoist—the other half being Confucian. Finally, Jenny Lau's "*Judou*: An Experiment in Color and Portraiture in Chinese Cinema" takes note of a shift in artists' preoccupation from portraiture to landscape during the Tang dynasty (618–904) and redirects our attention to a neglected genre, the "rich color painting" (*nongcai hua*). In terms of the four basic elements in classical Chinese portraiture, namely posture, facial expression, spacing, and environment, she discusses the characterization and the manipulation of color in *Ju Dou*. She concludes that the film creates meanings new to traditional Chinese cinema, but falls short of specifying exactly what these new meanings are or why they are new in contemporary China.

Technically, *Cinematic Landscapes* is an impressive book, handsomely designed—with many stills and color plates to illustrate the affinities between painting and cinema—and easy to use, with Filmography and Selected Works (but regrettably without a character list). As an attempt to "identify some of the bridges that link both worlds" of film studies and art history and to investigate "how some films cite the visual arts as a reference point" (Erhlich and Desser 1994, 3–4), the anthology is a sure success. It not only helps fill a scholarship gap in the West but also bridges Chinese and Western types of film studies. However, due to its dedication to aesthetic, philosophical, and formal or compositional elements, the China section in this volume (except for Berry and Farquhar's essay) does not fully explain how innovative film styles function in the cultural and political context of contemporary China.

Film Studies in Contemporary China

In his foreword to *Film in Contemporary China: Critical Debates, 1979–1989* (1993), coedited by George Semsel, Chen Xihe, and Xia Hong, which covers the most exciting decade of Chinese film studies in mainland China, often referred to as the "New Era" (*xinshiqi*), John Lent insists that the collection is "important primarily because it allows Chinese film personnel to speak for themselves in their own language, using their own cultural and scholarly traditions" (Semsel et al. 1993, x). Apart from the editors' introductory and concluding remarks, the collection consists of representative Chinese articles in English translation, arranged under five major headings: "The Call for New Social Concepts," "The Issue of Culture," "Yingxi" (shadowplay theory), "The Entertainment Film," and "The Debate on New Chinese Film Theory." The authors represented in the collection include some of the most active in Chinese film studies during the period, ranging from the senior through the middle-age to the young scholars: Zhong Dianfei, Li Shaobai, Ni Zhen, Shao Mujun, Zhong Dafeng, and Dai Jinhua.

According to the editors, works advocating technological development prevailed in the early 1980s, evident in the pursuit of film language, the ontology of film, and other new concepts of film. From the mid-1980s on, Chinese film studies shifted from technical to ideological concerns in an attempt to rethink issues of social function, ideological construction, and the political implications of filmmaking and film criticism. The editors unambiguously attribute the achievements of Chinese film studies in the New Era to the influence of the West. Western film theories, made available for the first time through visiting American scholars and Chinese translations published by the China Film Press (Zhongguo dianying chubanshe) and by such journals as *Contemporary Cinema* (Dangdai dianying), *Film Art* (Dianying yishu), and *World Cinema* (Shijie dianying), provided the necessary discursive means by which Chinese film scholars departed from the official paradigm of the monolithic political criticism of the past and ventured into a new intellectual space.

Presented in a variety of forms, *Film in Contemporary China* exemplifies a type of scholarship markedly different from current Western practice. Whereas film studies, as Rothman laments, had become all but completely "academicized" in the U.S. by the mid-1980s and had lost its valuable "human" dimension, in Chinese film criticism we still see a close tie between filmmaker and critic, and the latter's genuine engagement in—rather than a presumably "disinterested" detachment from—ongoing film production in China (1993b, 259, 267–8).[12] In this sense, the collection is useful to anyone who cares about what film studies meant to Chinese scholars in the 1980s. This is especially so when the collection is supplemented with its companion volume, *Chinese Film Theory: A Guide to the New Era* (1990), coedited by George Semsel, Xia Hong, and Hou Jianping. This earlier volume deals with a number of important debates in the 1980s: the theatricality of film, the literary quality of film, the new concept of film, the nationalization of film, and tradition and innovation in film (especially the Xie Jin model). Like its sequel, *Chinese Film Theory* also includes a selection of representative authors of different generations, several of them active in filmmaking as well, such as Wu Yigong, Xie Fei, Yu Min, Zhang Junxiang, Zhang Nuanxin, and Zheng Dongtian. However, in spite of the attention given to coverage, one cannot but notice visible blemishes in the two collections. For example, inconsistent, incomplete, and sometimes incorrect bibliographic data frustrate the reader and reduce the reliability of the collections as primary information sources.

New Chinese Cinemas: From the Mainland to Taiwan and Hong Kong

In terms of quality research, comprehensive coverage, and rich supplementary materials like illustrations, chronologies, glossary, and bibliography,[13] *New Chinese Cinemas: Forms, Identities, Politics* (1994), coedited by Nick Browne, Paul Pickowicz, Vivian Sobchack, and Esther Yau, was arguably one of the best single-volume publications on contemporary Chinese cinema in English available by the mid-1990s. Based on a conference held at UCLA in January 1990 and published in 1994, it marked the maturation of Chinese film studies in America, a remarkable achievement given the field was only created in the 1980s. In a succinct introduction, Nick Browne, among the first to introduce Chinese film

---

[12] Chinese filmmakers such as Xie Fei, Wu Yigong, and Zhang Nuanxin have also participated in film criticism, while film scholars sometimes joined film production. For instance, Ni Zhen was a screenwriter for *Raise the Red Lantern* and *Blush* (1994).

[13] The reader should further consult the bibliographies compiled by H. C. Li (1993, 1994, 1998, 2000). The journal *Asian Cinema* also contains an ongoing listing of bibliographies of Asian cinema compiled by John Lent.

studies to the U.S., places the anthology in a demanding cross-cultural frame and presents it as an interdisciplinary venture between film studies and Chinese studies. "The challenge is to map the changes of aesthetic form and sensibility upon the resistances and incursions, displacements, and reinscriptions of political power as it seeks to shape the social body." To that end, he reminds the reader, "Western interpretations of these changes . . . must first be historical and cultural" (1994a, 2, 11).

The first two essays in the anthology deal with melodrama. While mapping the manifestation of spatiality and subjectivity in Chinese film melodrama, Ma Ning offers several interesting observations in "Spatiality and Subjectivity in Xie Jin's Film Melodrama of the New Period." For example, the subject position of Chinese narrative discourse is said to be group-oriented, and yin-yang cosmology has reputedly left its mark on screen layout, so that the right-hand side is usually associated with yang/positive and the left-hand side with yin/negative. Clearly influenced by structuralist poetics, some of Ma Ning's observations appear too neatly charted and require further evidence to substantiate their claims to truth. Moving from his conception of Xie Jin's narrative mode as a blending of "history with fiction or legend, the personal with political, in a narrative pattern characterized by a bipolar structure that is typically Chinese" (1994, 15), Ma then discusses spatial dislocation and female subjectivity in *The Legend of Tianyun Mountain* and the construction, in Xie Jin's other films, such as *The Herdsman* (Muma ren, 1982) and *Hibiscus Town* (Furong zhen, 1986), of a coherent social subject at a time of ideological crises.

In "Society and Subjectivity: On the Political Economy of Chinese Melodrama," Nick Browne briefly summarizes Western theories of melodrama and cautiously suggests that Chinese "family melodrama" (as conceived by Ma Ning) is not a true analogy to its Western counterpart. For his own purpose, Browne proposes a concept of "political melodrama" and defines it as "an expression of a mode of injustice whose mise-en-scène is precisely the nexus between public and private life, a mode in which gender as a mark of difference is a limited, mobile term activated by distinctive social powers and historical circumstances" (1994b, 43). Interestingly, he selects basically the same Xie Jin films as analyzed by Ma Ning but offers his own readings of the intricate link between political positions and sexual relations, the tension generated by the expectations of an ethical system (Confucianism) and those of a political system (socialism), a mode of subjectivity at the margin of official discourse, and a concept of the "person" apart from gender per se.

In comparison, Paul Pickowicz's "Huang Jianxin and the Notion of Postsocialism" is theoretically more daring in that it recommends the notion of postsocialism as a more adequate framework from which to comprehend contemporary Chinese culture and society (see chapter 8 for more discussion of postsocialism). He judges modernism to be an abused term and postmodernism to be largely irrelevant to Chinese film studies. Conceiving postsocialism as pertaining to "the domain of popular perception," he claims that "an alienated postsocialist mode of thought and behavior began midway through the Cultural Revolution" and this "negative, dystopian cultural condition" is not restricted to the city alone (1994, 61–3). He regards *Black Cannon Incident* as a postsocialist critique of the Leninist political system, *Dislocation* as a parody that links postsocialism to theater of the absurd, and *Transmigration* as a story of individual resignation and anomie in the postsocialist society.

In "Neither One Thing nor Another: Toward a Study of the Viewing Subject and Chinese Cinema of the 1980s," Chris Berry resumes a study he started earlier but substantially modifies his previous finding that a "nonindividualized, communal subject" is typical of post-1949 "classical mainland Chinese cinema" (1991c). Instead, for films in the 1980s, he proposes "a series of more localized models" of the viewing subject that take into account "a matrix of distinguishing factors, among them gender, distanciation, identification, subjectivity, emulation, and rejection" (1994b, 109). In conclusion, he concedes that the 1980s was an unstable decade, but insists that it is important to try to trace the specificity of its shifts, twists, and turns.

The second part of the anthology focuses on films from Taiwan and Hong Kong. It begins with Fredric Jameson's "Remapping Taipei," an essay on *Terrorizer* (Kongbu fenzi, 1986) and its themes of urban alienation and disillusionment. Jameson refers to a wide range of European modernist works in addition to non-Western texts and suggests that *Terrorizer* assimilates modernization more generally to urbanization than to Westernization as such, that it contains the now-archaic modernist themes of art versus life, the novel and reality, mimesis and irony, and that it articulates the women's situation as fundamentally spatial while presenting the male figures in their temporal destinies. In "The Ideology of Initiation: The Films of Hou Hsiao-hsien," William

Tay employs the notion of initiation to study this world-renowned Taiwan director, and treats *A Time to Live and a Time to Die* (Tongnian wangshi, 1985) and *Dust in the Wind* (Lianlian fengchen, 1987) as cinematic analogues of the *bildungsroman*, which concentrates on its protagonist's maturing process. "But besides the usual psychological inclination to romanticize childhood and to embellish the past," Tay writes, "Hou Hsiao-hsien's unstained and innocent countryside always remains in idealistic opposition to . . . the city, which is usually portrayed as the embodiment of deception, corruption, and exploitation" (1994, 155).

Li Cheuk-to's "The Return of the Father: Hong Kong New Wave and Its Chinese Context in the 1980s" is an informative essay. Conceding that Hong Kong did not produce directors of the caliber of Hou Hsiao-hsien, Edward Yang, Chen Kaige, or Tian Zhuangzhuang, he nevertheless argues that Hong Kong cinema is important in many ways. First, all New Wave directors received formal training in film schools in the West, and technical sophistication, aesthetic stylization, and modern sensibility mark their works. Second, since they were born and grew up in Hong Kong, they exhibit a local Hong Kong consciousness absent from previous generations, who were more concerned with nationalism and Chinese identity. In his reading of Ann Hui and Tsui Hark, Li detects a strategy of allegorization that deals with Hong Kong experience in stories set elsewhere, for instance in Vietnam. The return of Hong Kong to China's sovereignty in 1997 was a shadow that loomed large in the mind of new Hong Kong directors, who sought to articulate the collective anxiety by probing into the China–Hong Kong relationship. According to Li, *Homecoming* (Sishui liunian, 1984) and *Long Arm of the Law* (Shenggang qibing, 1984) constitute "the positive and negative poles of people's perceptions of the mainland in Hong Kong" (1994, 169). Popular violent gangster films became a site where survival and self-interest were paramount, and where a new heroism based on brotherhood was constructed. In the hands of the younger directors in the late 1980s, however, the myth of brotherhood and heroism is refused and the return of the father, who symbolizes Chinese tradition, is staged in films like *Gangs* (Tongdang, 1988).

In "Border Crossing: Mainland China's Presence in Hong Kong Cinema," Esther Yau continues to address the impact of the 1997 anxiety on Hong Kong cinema. She distinguishes between five entities of

China—imperial China, Republican China, socialist China, Taiwan after 1949, and Hong Kong ruled by the British since 1842—and locates a type of colonial-Chinese cultural syncretism in Hong Kong. Like Li Cheuk-to, Yau treats *Homecoming*, which "constructs China as a timeless cultural (read: anthropological) entity that transcends political and social distance and unifies differences," and *Long Arm of the Law*, in which "the 'raping' of Hong Kong is seen from both the rapist's [mainland gangsters] and the rape victim's experience," as two polar expressions, both of which, however, are judged to be equally ambivalent "toward the city's postcolonial future" (1994a, 187, 193, 197).

The final essay, Leo Lee's "Two Films from Hong Kong: Parody and Allegory," examines films representative of popular Hong Kong subgenres—the *gongfu* movie and the romantic comedy—and brings the reader to larger issues of urban culture and postmodern sensibility. Focusing on parody and allegory, Lee starts with Jackie Chan, who appears both serious and comic in his *gongfu*/action films (like *Project A* [A jihua, 1984]). He then concentrates on *Rouge* (Yanzhi kou, 1987) and *Peking Opera Blues* (Daoma dan, 1987). Linking parody further to pastiche, Lee points to "the inevitable theoretical query: Can we regard Hong Kong films as in some way products of a Chinese postmodern culture?" (1994, 212) For him, postmodernity is indeed already present in Hong Kong cinema, and this presence may have something to do with the infrastructure of Hong Kong's urban culture. Although refraining from a thorough investigation of the question of the meaning of postmodernity, Lee nonetheless urges the reader to speculate on how to situate Chinese cinema in the contemporary postcolonial, if not entirely postmodern, world system.

Ethnography, Visuality, and Chinese Cinema

Rey Chow's *Primitive Passions: Visuality, Sexuality, Ethnography, and Contemporary Chinese Cinema* (1995) is one of the most impassioned studies of Chinese cinema and modern Chinese culture to date. Revisiting Lu Xun's well-known story of how he came to write fiction after watching a newsreel about the execution of a Chinese spy by the Japanese,[14] Chow detects signs of a new kind of discourse—that of "technologized visuality"—in the Third World. What she sees as

---

[14] For what Lu Xun might have seen in Japan, see L. Liu 1995, 61–3.

paradoxical in Lu Xun's case is that, while fully aware of the direct and crude power of the new visuality, he nonetheless returned to the "ancient, word-centered culture" in his enlightenment project (p. 10). Drawing on postcolonial discourse, Chow further asserts that, though visuality has been largely marginalized, if not altogether repressed, by modern Chinese intellectuals, "the entry of film represents a moment of an epochal dislocation of the linguistic and literary sign" (p. 18). In her elaborate formulation of "primitive passions," she points to the fantasies of a lost origin and to the strategies of invention and exoticization that structure a way of seeing China as simultaneously victim and empire. After a discussion of the Mao-worship during the Cultural Revolution as "the most enchanting film of the time," she proposes to treat the Fifth Generation directors as "anthropologists and ethnographers," who create a "space where 'China' is exhibited in front of audiences overseas" (pp. 31, 37–8). Their cinematic reinvention of China, Chow insists, must be "seen ultimately as rejoinders to the aspirations of the communist state." To move beyond such "cultural centrism," she calls for decentering the "sign of China" (pp. 43, 48).

Part two of Chow's book consists of four chapters devoted to individual Chinese films. According to Chow, a film like *Old Well* "demonstrates the fundamental nothingness of the labor of social fantasy." Moreover, she claims, "A careful allegorical reading of *Old Well* would demonstrate that the allegory of the 'nation' is, paradoxically, the nation's otherness and nonpresence," a nonpresence "signified by the barrenness of romantic love" (pp. 66, 72). In her reading of *Yellow Earth*, she critiques two positions in current critical thinking about Third World cinema—one "leftist masculinist" (that is, Jameson's "national allegory") and the other "liberal feminist" (that is, E. Ann Kaplan's "heterosexual erotics")—and argues that, in Chen's film, "The image becomes a kind of alibi, with its full signifying power giving way to a significance that is musical in effect" (pp. 89–90). In a radical move, she locates in *King of the Children* a "conception of culture as violence and excrement" and a creation, in the elusive figure of a "mute" cowherd, of "a discourse which counters the institution of education" (pp. 124, 129). As a product of narcissistic male culture, she concludes, "Chen's film offers a fantastic kind of hope—the hope to rewrite culture without woman and all the limitations she embodies" (p. 141). Finally, turning to *Red Sorghum, Ju Dou,* and *Raise the Red Lantern,* she judges these films to be inheritors of the popular Mandarin Duck and Butterfly fictional modes, but admits that Zhang Yimou excedes his precursors in the art of seduction, which involves a self-subalternization and a fetishization of women. She then reviews recent studies of Zhang and objects to interpretations based on *xu/shi* (emptiness/fullness) or on the "repressive hypothesis." For her, "filmic images operate as images, as surfaces whose significance lies in their manner of undoing depth itself" (pp. 158–9).[15] The power of surfaces in Zhang's films, she further contends, comes from their confrontation, from their tactic of returning "the double gaze of the Chinese security state and the world's, especially the West's, orientalism" (p. 170).

In the final part of her book, Chow begins with China's status as object of gaze and claims that this "being-looked-at-ness, rather than the act of looking, constitutes the primary event in cross-cultural representation" (p. 180). By such a twist of looking at oneself being looked at by others (the West), she suggests, contemporary Chinese cinema seeks to ethno- graphize China (the self) and becomes, in the end, an "autoethnography." After a survey of Western translation theories, she reconstructs Chinese cinema as cultural translation, or translation between cultures, and thus concludes her study: "If translation is a form of betrayal, then the translators pay their debt by bringing fame to the ethnic culture. . . . It is in translation's faithlessness that 'China' survives and thrives" (pp. 182, 202).

As "a rejoinder to some of the most urgent debates about cross-cultural studies, sexuality, ethnicity, identity, authenticity, and commodity fetishism" (back cover), *Primitive Passions* is a timely contribution to a new interdisciplinary study of anthropology, film, and literature. However, as "an attempt to produce a cultural history and anthropology of modern China through the technologized visual image" (p. x), Chow's book is far from satisfactory. For one, a project such as she envisions would not be complete without considering other visual genres and forms, such as book illustrations, pictorial magazines, and comic strips, as well as photography, television, advertisement, and architecture.[16] Her

---

[15] It is ironic that Chow herself could not but employ certain "depth models" (such as feminist, psychoanalytic, and postcolonial) to figure out the "depth of meaning" Zhang Yimou's films have supposedly acquired by showcasing "images as surfaces."

[16] For sample works in these areas, see Y. Zhang 2001a and 2001b; see also relevant essays collected in Kuo 2001, and Lent 2001.

restricted use of Chinese sources, which stands in striking contrast to her impressive command of Western critical literature, reduces the persuasiveness of her central arguments. For example, the concept of film as autoethnography is illuminating in regard to Tian Zhuangzhuang's *Horse Thief* but inadequate to his *Rock 'n' Roll Kids* (for the latter's identification with urban youth). Similarly, "primitive passions" are fully present in Zhang Nuanxin's *Sacrificed Youth* but noticeably absent from her *Good Morning, Beijing!* (Beijing nizao, 1990), or from other contemporary urban films such as *The Troubleshooters* (Wanzhu, 1989) and *After Separation*. My remarks here, nevertheless, are not meant to depreciate the value of *Primitive Passions*, which consists at least in the provocative questions it poses, if not in the radical answers it may suggest.

Transnational Chinese Cinemas: Identity, Ethnicity, Nationhood

If Chow prefers depth of analysis to breadth of coverage, Sheldon Lu's edited volume, *Transnational Chinese Cinema: Identity, Nationhood, Gender* (1997), attempts to achieve both. Based on an international conference held at the University of Pittsburgh in September 1994, Lu's volume extends the coverage of Chinese cinema far beyond the boundary of "national cinema" and, by way of including Chinese-American films, he anticipates "the formation of what might be called a new transnational Chinese culture" (1997c, 18). In his "Historical Introduction," Lu argues that, due to its reaction to international domination from the early twentieth century onward, "film in China has always been of a transnational character," and that, given the current fashion of a global screening of China, Hong Kong, and Taiwan, the "study of national cinemas must then transform into transnational film studies" (1997c, 25). While the transnational imaginary and globalization have been of increasing importance to Chinese cinema since the late 1980s (a point to be further developed in chapter 7), I would caution against Lu's transhistorical claim. The present euphoria over global culture cannot gloss over or whitewash the damage done by Western cultural imperialism throughout the twentieth century.

Lu's volume is divided into three parts. Part One charts the development from the national to the transnational. Zhiwei Xiao's historical study, "Anti-Imperialism and Film Censorship During the Nanjing Decade, 1927–1937," documents the Nationalist government's attempts at restricting the negative impact of foreign films on Chinese audiences. In vivid detail, Xiao describes a series of events, such as the Chinese protests against *Welcome Danger* (1929), a film containing negative portrayals of Chinese that resulted in a ban of all Harold Lloyd movies in China; the Nationalist censors' letter to Columbia Pictures requesting cuts from *The Bitter Tea of General Yen* (1933); and a concerted effort by the public and the government to abort the American plan to build an "Oriental Hollywood" in Shanghai. Gina Marchetti's *"Two Stage Sisters*: The Blossoming of a Revolutionary Aesthetic" provides a close reading of Xie Jin's film [Illustration 6].

6. *Stage Sisters* (1965): Revolutionary aesthetic and film realism

Combining theoretical speculation and textual analysis, Marchetti discusses Xie Jin's career development, the theatrical world of Shaoxing opera, Hollywood influence, the possible connection to Brechtian epic theater, and the historical event of the Cultural Revolution, all leaving visible marks in this melodramatic film. My essay "From 'Minority Film' to 'Minority Discourse': Questions of Nationhood and Ethnicity in Chinese Film Studies" contextualizes the concepts of "race," "nation," and "ethnicity," traces the development of nationalism in Chinese cinema, and examines the genre of ethnic minority film from the 1950s to the 1980s (see chapter 5).

Sheldon Lu's "National Cinema, Cultural Critique, Transnational Capital: The Films of Zhang Yimou" brings us to the 1990s by addressing this paradox: "How does one re-create the Third World national allegory, through the cinematic apparatus, in the new transnational setting?" (1997d, 105) Looking through Zhang Yimou's corpus, from *Ju Dou* to *Shanghai Triad*, with special attention to the representation of children, Lu discovers that "the future is at times envisioned as a return to the past, as repetition, cyclicity, circularity, and even total destruction; at other times, there seems to be a glimmer of hope, renewal, and rebirth out of the ashes of the past" (p. 111). In response to the native Chinese critics' charge of a cultural sellout of the Chinese nation in the international film market, Lu offers the apologia, "Given the shrinking domestic film market, the system of film censorship, and the changes in China's film industry, what is termed 'Orientalism,' or the exit to the global cultural market, is also a strategy of survival and renewal for Chinese filmmakers" (p. 132). While Lu insists that filmmakers like Zhang Yimou have continued their cultural critique with the aid of transnational capital, it is not certain whether international audiences are attracted more to the depth (if any) of their intended ideological message or the surfaces of their Orientalist details (a question I explore further in chapter 6).

Part Two of Lu's volume takes up the sensitive issue of identity in Taiwan and Hong Kong. June Yip's "Constructing a Nation: Taiwanese History and the Films of Hou Hsiao-hsien" studies Hou's Taiwan trilogy—*City of Sadness*, *The Puppet Master* (Ximeng rensheng, 1993), and *Good Men, Good Women* (Haonan haonü, 1995). Drawing insights from Walter Benjamin and Jean-François Lyotard, among others, Yip believes Hou is writing a "history from below"—a history "no longer conceived of as a univocal, seamless narrative but as a complex dialogic web of multiple, heterogeneous, and fragmentary stories that by chance touch, intersect, and sometimes contradict each other" (p. 143). Yip's discussion of Hou's representation of the February 28 Incident in *City of Sadness* is persuasive, but her analysis of *Good Men, Good Women* appears much less substantial by comparison. However, she succeeds in demonstrating that recent films like Hou's "have contributed to the reexamination of Taiwanese history from which has emerged an entirely new picture of the Taiwanese 'nation,' one that challenges the Nationalist myth of Chinese consanguinity by revealing the complex multiplicity of heritages that make up contemporary Taiwanese identity" (p. 160).[17]

Yip's conclusion, nevertheless, is indirectly questioned by Jon Kowallis in "The Diaspora in Postmodern Taiwan and Hong Kong Film: Framing Stan Lai's *The Peach Blossom Land* with Allen Fong's *Ah Ying*." By comparing *The Peach Blossom Land* (Anlian taohua yuan, 1993), a Brechtian dramatization of the "radically uprooted" Chinese people in Taiwan, and *Ah Ying* (Banbian ren, 1983), a "realistic" portrayal of a lower-class Hong Kong young woman's "attempt to redefine herself as a member of a larger Chinese community (that is, one that embraces the cultural heritage of Taiwan, the international overseas Chinese community, and, by extension, that of Mainland China as well)," Kowallis points to "the crux of liberation from colonial status: identifying with a larger whole that is beyond the power of one's colonial masters to define" (pp. 178–80) [Illustration 7]. In spite of his implicit endorsement of a "Pan-Chinese consciousness" or a concept of transnational Chinese ethnicity, which runs against Yip's argument, Kowallis does not explain why *Ah Ying*—usually discussed as a "realist" film—is singled out as an example of the "postmodern" Hong Kong film.

Moving further in the transnational direction, Wei Ming Dariotis and Eileen Fung's "Breaking the Soy Sauce Jar: Diasporas and Displacement in the Films of Ang Lee" takes up the director's "father knows best" trilogy—*Pushing Hands* (Tuishou, 1991), *The Wedding Banquet*, and *Eat Drink Man Woman*. The crisis created by the expansion of family boundaries—through both marriage and migration—is resolved in Lee's films, they argue, "by dramatic end moments, or final shots, which both reinscribe normative heterosexual bonds—thus insuring the continuation of the family into the next generation—and simultaneously destabilize these familial relations" (p. 190). In Lee's Hollywood venture, *Sense and Sensibility* (1995), Dariotis and Fung notice the emergence of a

---

[17] For further discussion of the February 28 Incident, see Liao 1993.

transnational sensibility that violates existing boundaries and foregrounds hyphenated identities and hybrid realities.

Anne Ciecko's "Transnational Action: John Woo, Hong Kong, Hollywood" investigates the Hong Kong action genre in a transnational context. Following Woo's trajectory from Hong Kong (with *The Killer* [Diexue shuangxiong, 1989] and *Hard Boiled* [Qiangshen, 1992]) to Hollywood (with *Hard Target* [Zhongji biaoba, 1993] and *Broken Arrow* [1996]), Ciecko discusses issues of transcultural visual pleasure, nostalgia and violence, hyper-realism, hybrid identity, masculinity, and auteurism.

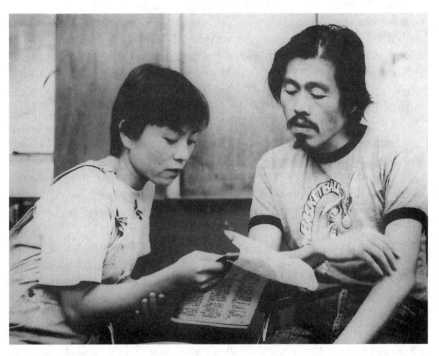

7. *Ah Ying* (1983): Confronting the identity issue in Hong Kong

After pointing out that, in Woo's case, "auteurism almost becomes synonymous with pastiche, parody, and influence/derivation," she hints at a subject in need of further research: "the ways generic and stylistic modes are transformed and complicated by specific local, national, and global industry-based concerns" (pp. 230–1). In a similar transnational context, Steve Fore's "Jackie Chan and the Cultural Dynamics of Global Entertainment" examines the successful strategies New Line Cinema developed in marketing Jackie Chan as a transcultural action hero and in distributing *Rumble in the Bronx* (1994) in North America as something other than a Hollywood entertainment film. Fore concludes that, measured against Hollywood's global hegemony, "the modest success" of Jackie Chan in the U.S. "represents an as yet small-scale but significant revision of the master narrative of global marketing" (1997, 258).

Part Three of Lu's volume addresses gender issues. E. Ann Kaplan's "Reading Formations and Chen Kaige's *Farewell My Concubine*" is the least substantial piece in the volume. Before offering a psychoanalytic reading of the film (in terms of an "abandonment neurotic" and "double transference"), Kaplan refers to her earlier comment on cross-cultural analysis (an issue I confront in chapter 4) and thus insists, "Western critics' dilemmas remained central since that is what I knew something about" (1997b, 266). Even though she pays lip service to Edward Said's work on "traveling theory," Kaplan simply refuses to go anywhere outside her home turf: "It is, thus, in full awareness of the Eurocentric bias of my brief reading of *Farewell My Concubine* that I offer it: Eurocentrism includes ways Western critics are trained to be self-conscious about the emotional impact of a film on the individual spectator and to focus on subjectivity" (266–7). What is intentionally vague in Kaplan's defensive remark is whether or not her individual spectator is a universal entity transcending cultural, historical, geopolitical, sexual, or other kinds of differences.

Kaplan's disappointing piece is followed by two substantial contributions. Kristine Harris's "*The New Woman* Incident: Cinema, Scandal, and Spectacle in 1935 Shanghai" combines textual analysis methods and historical research to reveal the many qualities of *New Woman* (Xin nüxing, 1934). She reads the film against the discourse on the New Woman in Shanghai of the 1920s and 1930s and locates a "split subjectivity" in the female protagonist, Wei Ming (Ruan Lingyu). According to Harris, "Cai constructed the New Woman as equivocally split between word and image, speech and silence, class and gender, subject and trope. These clefts leave open the possibility for alternative, subversive interpretations of the narrative" (1997a, 297). Shuqin Cui's "Gendered Perspective: The Construction and Representation of Subjectivity and Sexuality in *Ju Dou*" also examines the image of "woman" and relies on the method of close reading to unravel the ways Zhang Yimou's film produces gendered meaning. Rather than accepting

Ju Dou (Gong Li) as a victim exposing the oppression of women in China, Cui argues that "behind her entrancing visibility lies the shadow of a patriarchal unconscious" and that "a hidden male subjectivity is projected onto the sexualized heroine of the film" (p. 303). By analyzing three character triangles, Cui leads the reader step by step through a maze of meanings produced by the film's sophisticated use of off-screen sound effects, point-of-view structure, male gaze and female subjectivity, the oedipal plot, the Lacanian concepts of the Imaginary and the Symbolic, as well as color symbolism, the conceptions of yin and yang, and the five cardinal elements in early Chinese cosmology.

Wendy Larson's "The Concubine and the Figure of History: Chen Kaige's *Farewell My Concubine*" returns us to Kaplan's chosen text. (For the sake of transition and coherence, it might have been better for Kaplan's piece to directly precede Larson's.) In Chen Kaige's earlier films, Larson discovers "a split subjectivity" in his male characters: "In each case, the masculine, action-oriented character is feminized" (1997, 335). Situating the "concubine" Cheng Dieyi (Leslie Cheung [Zhang Guorong]) in *Farewell My Concubine*, who "carries both the unification of bodily cultural ecstasy with political purity and loyalty and the morally suspicious posturing of the adorned female," in the global film economy, Larson contends that this necessarily "feminized" concubine "becomes not a unified expression and practice of the cultural nation, but only a disembodied and debased indicator of cultural and historical difference, a kind of local color parading itself before delighted [international] viewers" (pp. 341–2). Yi Zheng's "Narrative Images of the Historical Passion: Those *Other* Women—On the Alterity in the New Wave of Chinese Cinema" engages Rey Chow's arguments in *Primitive Passions* but attempts to direct attention not to the "masculinist" project of cultural critique but to its "alterity," its own "other"—peasants, children, and women. For Zheng, Chow, with her delineation of primitive passions and autoethnography in Chen Kaige and Zhang Yimou, "joins the modern masculinist Chinese intellectuals in their attempt at self-rejuvenation through the relocation of their 'primitives,'" and the result is that "Chow, like Kristeva, has offered the primitive/woman up and reconsigned her as the corporeality of truth . . . in the fabulously constructed transnational world market" (pp. 357–8).

Compared with other edited volumes,[18] Lu's appears to be the most balanced in terms of representation of historical periods, geopolitical regions, and critical issues. The inclusion of a Chinese glossary, filmography, and general bibliography further facilitates the use of the book. Two points become clearer if one places *Transnational Chinese Cinema* (1997) alongside *Perspectives on Chinese Cinema* (1991) and *New Chinese Cinemas* (1994). First, one can see a trend toward a wider critical horizon, beyond mainland China to Hong Kong, Taiwan, and other Chinese diasporas. Second, identity and ethnicity seem to have replaced melodrama as two objects of intense critical scrutiny. Not surprisingly, Rey Chow's *Ethics after Idealism: Theory-Culture-Ethnicity-Reading* (1998) illustrates these two points. Her book contains a chapter each on *M. Butterfly* (1993), a Western film about the China myth that dramatizes the crisis of gender identity; *The Joy Luck Club* (1993), a Hollywood ethnic melodrama from a celebrated Chinese-American director, Wayne Wang (Wang Ying); *To Live* (Huozhe, 1994), a China-Taiwan coproduction about the political oppression in Communist China; and *Rouge*, a Hong Kong nostalgia film comparing the lifestyles of the 1930s and 1980s. In each chapter, Chow extends the discussion of identity and ethnicity in cross-cultural contexts, although she treats cinema more as a "trans-cultural" than a "transnational" enterprise. As she asserts elsewhere, "film has always been, since its inception, a transcultural phenomenon, having as it does the capacity to transcend 'culture'—to create modes of fasci-nation which are readily accessible and which engage audiences in ways independent of their linguistic and cultural specificities" (1998b, 174).

While Chow's assertion signals a rethinking of national cinema in the era of globalization, Xudong Zhang's *Chinese Modernism in the Era of Reforms: Cultural Fever, Avant-garde Fiction, and the New Chinese Cinema* (1997) is in part a critical intervention in this area. Half of Zhang's book is devoted to New Chinese Cinema, which is perceived as "a cinematic articulation of a set of local, national, and transnational issues and politics" (p. 209). First, "the emergence and survival of the Fifth Generation provides a localized interaction between modernism and post-modernism," two categories that seek to appropriate each other in an

---

[18] In addition to the titles discussed in this chapter, Dissanayake has published two other edited volumes. *Colonialism and Nationalism in Asian Cinema* (1994) contains two essays on Chinese cinema: Y. Zhang 1990; Berry 1994a. *Narratives of Agency: Self-Making in China, India, and Japan* (1996) also contains two essays: Yuejin Wang 1996; Yue 1996.

allegorical expression (p. 208). Second, "the Chinese New Wave simultaneously offers itself as a substitute for and a supplement to an emerging national cinema" (p. 205)—a substitute because of the obsolete tradition of socialist realism, and a supplement because it constructs a new mythology of national culture. Third, New Chinese Cinema attempts to "integrate itself into the symbolic, ideological sphere of the global system" by competing at international film festivals and the marketplace of art-house theaters in the West (5). Zhang covers a wide range of topics, such as generational politics, the making of a modern cinematic language (for instance, the interarticulation among landscape, selfhood, and the medium), modernist subjectivity, entertainment film, and international capital. In addition to close readings of *King of the Children* and *Red Sorghum*, Zhang also reconsiders the concept of national cinema and surveys critical positions in the field up to the mid-1990s.

Hong Kong Cinema: Politics, History, and Arts

In addition to Sheldon Lu's volume, two other academic books on Hong Kong cinema were published in 1997, the year the territory was returned to China. Ackbar Abbas's *Hong Kong: Culture and the Politics of Disappearance* (1997) contains one chapter on new Hong Kong cinema and another on its highest-rising star in recent years, Wong Kar-Wai. Like Rey Chow, Abbas draws on postcolonial discourse but focuses more closely on the question of visuality. Defining Hong Kong culture as a space of disappearance, a space dominated by a sense of *déjà disparu* (namely, the feeling that what seems new is always on the verge of disappearing, if not already gone), Abbas locates in the films of Stanley Kwan and Wong Kar-Wai certain techniques of disappearance. For him, these techniques do not pretend to go against disappearance, nor do they aspire to something like "critical strategies of resistance"; rather, they insist on "working with disappearance and taking it elsewhere," or "using disappearance to deal with disappearance" (p. 8). Abbas's hypothesis on the politics of disappearance in Hong Kong is brilliant, but his dependence on just a dozen films to substantiate his large claims—quite similar to Rey Chow's case mentioned above—inevitably raises the question of the theory's credibility and its applicability to the majority of Hong Kong films (a point I take up again in my critique of Abbas in chapter 7).

Stephen Teo's *Hong Kong Cinema: The Extra Dimensions* (1997) is the first book-length study of post-war Hong Kong film history in English. Setting out to strike a balance between information and analysis, in Part One, "Northerners and Southerners," Teo offers a historical overview of Shanghai's influence on the Hong Kong film industry and the revival of Cantonese cinema. He adopts the method of auteurist analysis in Part Two, "Martial Artists"; turns to the film movement (the New Wave and the Second Wave) in Part Three, "Path Breakers"; and differentiates recurring thematic clusters in Part Four, "Characters on the Edge," which includes a chapter each on Hong Kong's China syndrome, ghosts, cadavers, demons, and other hybrids, bad customers and big timers, and, finally, postmodernism and the end of Hong Kong cinema. In part, Teo's book aims to correct "the fallacy that Hong Kong movies are unabashedly 'modern' or 'postmodern,'" a fallacy responsible for fabricating views that "Hong Kong movies were startlingly terse, anti-intellectual, non-historical, non-political and without discourse of whatever shade" (p. xi). Contrary to Abbas, Teo believes that Hong Kong has its own specific identity, an identity evolved through its close interaction with Chinese and Western cultures over a long period of time: "Although Hong Kong is not a country, its residents possessed a form of national identity increasingly identified as Chinese even though artists expressed their Chineseness in ways that were certainly different from the ways artists in China negotiated theirs" (p. 244).

In a sense, Teo answers Leo Lee's earlier question about treating Hong Kong cinema as an example of Chinese postmodern culture. For Teo, from the 1980s onward Hong Kong has displayed many "postmodern" signs described by Western theorists, such as "the random cannibalization of all the styles of the past" (Jameson 1984, 65–6) and "a contradictory phenomenon which uses and abuses, installs and then subverts, the very concepts it challenges" (Hutcheon 1988, 3). However, Teo takes it as his responsibility to describe the specifics of the Hong Kong postmodern, and he does this by contextualizing three manifestations of the postmodern edifice in Hong Kong. The first is Tsui Hark, from whose films one finds that "the postmodern phenomenon grew from a ragbag of causes and effects: New Wave aesthetics mixed with Cinema City-style slapstick, anxiety over 1997 and the China syndrome, the assertion of Hong Kong's own identity as different from China, and a new sexual awakening arising from an increasing awareness of women's human rights and the decriminalisation of homosexuality" (p. 246).[19] The second manifestation is Stephen Chow (aka Stephen Chiau, Zhou Xingchi), whose unique brand of humor—known as *mou lei-tau* (literally, "nonsense")—in a series of box-office record-setting "nonsense come- dies" simultaneously expresses some kind of "witty self-criticism of Hong Kong people's latent prejudices against Mainlanders" and parodies "the can-do attitudes of its entrepreneurial and gambling residents" (p. 246).[20] The third manifestation is the full-swing, by the early 1990s, of nostalgia cinema (*huaijiu dianying*). With its allusions to Cantonese cinema of the 1950s and 1960s (seen by Teo as Hong Kong cinema's incomplete modernity) and its characteristic use of farce, humor, pastiche, and self-parody, "nostalgia cinema has added substance to the idea that there is a postmodernism unique to Hong Kong" (p. 248). Teo's conclusion on the Hong Kong postmodern is worth quoting at length here:

> [C]ontrary to the postmodern use of intertextuality as a random practice of stylistic allusions designed to efface history, there is a genuine attempt to explore history and to acknowledge, even if only grudgingly, Hong Kong's kinship with China's history, both in its glorious and tragic manifestations, while at the same time inscribing a wish to stick one's head in the sand and to efface the history that looms on the horizon by effacing the "real" history of the past. The eclecticism that underpins Hong Kong's type of postmodernism can thus be seen as a sign of a culture caught in the tension between a desire to construct a non-colonial identity by mobilising a sense of the past, and a profound anxiety about the possibility of that very identity being imposed rather than being constructed autonomously. (p. 250)

Teo is a filmmaker and critic who spent years at the office of the Hong Kong International Film Festival and who has remained sensitive to the question of history and the arts. Because of this, his book is less prone to the sweeping theorization that characterizes Abbas's and Chow's

---

[19] Two classic gender-bending films, *Swordsman II* (Dongfang bubai, 1992) and *Swordsman III: The East Is Red* (Fengyun zaiji, 1993), were both produced by Tsui Hark and directed by Ching Siu Tung (Cheng Xiaodong), and both feature Brigitte Lin (Lin Qingxia) as the gorgeous androgynous hero(ine), Asia the Invincible (Dongfang bubai).

[20] Notable among the Stephen Chow vehicles are *All for the Winner* (Dusheng, 1990), *Fight Back to School* (Taoxue weilong, 1991), and *Royal Tramp, I–II* (Luding ji, 1992), the last title taking in a combined gross of 77 million Hong Kong dollars (U.S. $10 million).

work, but it is still much more academic in nature than several other books on Hong Kong cinema released by commercial publishers in Hong Kong, London, and New York (Baker and Russell 1994; Dannen and Long 1997; Fonoroff 1997; Hammond and Wilkins 1996; Logan 1996; Weisser 1997).

Indeed, it is no exaggeration to state at this point that the return of Hong Kong to China actually helped attract academic and commercial investment in Hong Kong film studies during the 1990s. To cite one more example, Poshek Fu and David Desser's edited anthology, *The Cinema of Hong Kong: History, Arts, Identity* (2000), grew out of an international conference held at the University of Illinois at Urbana-Champaign in October 1997. One distinctive feature of this new anthology is its attempt to situate Hong Kong cinema in the entire span of its history. Law Kar's (Luo Ka) "The American Connection in Early Hong Kong Cinema" traces the earliest moments from Benjamin Brodsky's Asia Film Company (Yaxiya) and its short features like *Stealing a Roast Duck* (Tou shaoya, 1909), the first Hong Kong commercial film, to the pioneers of the Hong Kong film industry, Li Minwei (Lai Man-wei), his brothers, and their associates around Minxin Film (China Sun) founded in 1923. According to Law, Grandview Film (Daguan), established by Chiu Shu-sen (Zhao Shusen) and other Chinese diasporas in San Francisco in 1933, played an important role in the development of Hong Kong cinema, especially during the war. Law follows the flow of people and resources between Hong Kong and the U.S. in the ensuing decades and notes in particular the tours of Cantonese opera troupes in North America. Given its specific historical trajectory, Law maintains, Hong Kong cinema has always been pluralistic and open to different ideologies.

Poshek Fu contributes two historical chapters. One of them, "Between Nationalism and Colonialism: Mainland Émigrés, Marginal Culture, and Hong Kong Cinema 1937–1941," focuses on the dilemma of Cantonese cinema during a politically unsettling period. His basic argument is that the confrontation with a "Central Plains syndrome" (*da Zhongyuan xintai*), embodied in wartime émigré Shanghai filmmakers, engendered in Hong Kong an "incipient sense of difference," and the "double marginality" of Hong Kong in the nationalist and colonial discourse further "generated a construction, still tentative, of an ambivalent, hybrid identity that continues to haunt Hong Kong natives

today" (2000a, 199, 201). Fu's historical documentation on the film
industry and film market of the time is impressive, and his observation of
the common rhetoric of the Communists (or Leftists) and the Nationalists
with regard to Hong Kong is quite incisive. However, his criticism of
The March of the Guerrillas (Youji jixing qu, 1938) for lacking "a realistic
and credible appreciation of the Japanese" (2000a, 212) sounds strange,
for the film was produced under difficult circumstances by Shanghai
émigrés for a Cantonese studio. After the censor ordered cuts of 2,000
feet of footage, the film was shelved and not released until 1941 with
additional cuts and a new title, *Song of Retribution* (Zhengqi ge). In spite
of his ideological agenda, Fu does not convince the reader why, instead
of being a byproduct of the nationalist discourse, *Two Southern Sisters*
(Nanguo jiemei hua, 1940), a Cantonese film produced by people
"closely associated with mainland filmmakers," would function
historically as a "valorization of the weak and marginal" and thus might
effect "an ideological subversion of the Central Plains syndrome" (2000a,
218). Obviously, more research is needed to clarify complicated pre-war
film production in Hong Kong.

Fu's other chapter, "The 1960s: Modernity, Youth Culture, and
Hong Kong Cantonese Cinema," takes up youth film as a site of social
contestation. He argues that "a continued tendency to make didactic
statements about social issues" existed in Cantonese cinema side by side
with "a seeming determination to capture the modernity of the city and
its people, strategic images that had been popularized by Mandarin film—
the speed, glamour, energy, crowdedness, overstimulation, and
restlessness of the New Hong Kong" (2000b, 82). His discussion of the
deterioration of Cantonese cinema in the second half of the decade nicely
links his chapter to Stephen Teo's "The 1970s: Movement and
Transition." Two of Teo's assertions are particularly telling. First,
contrary to the death of Cantonese cinema (which came to zero
production in 1972, down from 207 in 1963), Teo believes that Cantonese cinema simply moved into television and had signaled its
comeback—with a vengeance—as early as 1973 with *The House of
Seventy-Two Tenants* (Qishier jia fangke), a popular comedy. Second, the
decade of speaking Mandarin on screen (especially in kung fu films)
ended on an unexpected note: by 1979, "Mandarin was dead in Hong
Kong, killed off by the industry itself as the talent pool diminished and
overproduction made it impossible to continue" (Teo 2000, 108). Teo's

narrative of the reversing fortunes of Mandarin and Cantonese films (including the roles played by the Taiwan film industry and Southeast Asian markets) is intriguing, and his discussion of New Wave directors' formative years in the television industry further advances our understanding of the development of Hong Kong cinema in the transnational context.

A second noteworthy feature of Fu and Desser's anthology is its attention to the reception and impact of Hong Kong cinema in the West. In addition to Law Kar's essay, David Desser's "The Kung Fu Craze: Hong Kong Cinema's First U.S. Reception" enumerates the unprecedented U.S. box-office success of films featuring Bruce Lee (Li Xiaolong) in North America: *Fists of Fury* (aka *The Big Boss*, Tangshan daxiong, 1971) [Illustration 8] and *The Chinese Connection* (Jingwu men, 1972), in the summer of 1973.

8. *Fists of Fury* (1971): Bruce Lee and the kung fu craze in the U.S.

Desser speculates that the increase in American encounters with Asia since World War II accounts for the rising interest in martial arts, with the kung fu craze just one cinematic signifier of post-Vietnam stress disorder on the cultural level. Jenny Lau continues the study of Hong

Kong cinema's reception at the outset of her "Besides Fists and Blood: Michael Hui and Cantonese Comedy." After demonstrating how Hong Kong New Wave directors and the gangster genre were showcased in the U.S. during the 1980s and 1990s, Lau turns to a neglected genre in Hong Kong, the comedy, and its earlier representative, Michael Hui (Xu Guanwen) and his brothers.

The third feature worth noting in Fu and Desser's anthology is the emphasis on genre and auteur criticism. While Lau takes on comedy in a retrospective mode, Tony Williams investigates the gangster film in "Space, Place, and Spectacle: The Crisis Cinema of John Woo" and points to a particular apocalyptic and highly cinematic body of work responsive to a future historical situation—the 1997 handover, perceived and projected as a crisis or catastrophe in Woo's films. After scrutinizing Woo's heroes in *A Better Tomorrow, I–II* (Yingxiong bense, 1986–7) and other titles from a postmodern perspective, Williams asserts that their cinematic survival within different realms of body, space, and place presents one possible solution for a community facing a possible loss of identity and future physical and cinematic diaspora. Likewise attentive to debates on postmodernity, Natalia Chan's "Rewriting History: Hong Kong Nostalgia Cinema and Its Social Practice" studies the function of nostalgia cinema in Hong Kong since the mid-1980s. Always tinged with a certain sadness or melancholy, nostalgia films aim to rewrite history. And to rewrite or reinvent the past in cinematic form, Chan argues, is to reconstruct the collective identities and memories of the social mass.

Operating in a more historical fashion, Ping-kwan Leung (Liang Bingjun) offers a survey of Hong Kong cinema from the 1950s to the 1970s in "Urban Cinema and the Cultural Identity of Hong Kong." He observes that three representations of the city dominated the 1950s: the idealized city, the wicked city, and the satirical city. In the 1960s, Hong Kong was undergoing a structural change, and the cinematic configuration of the city was marked by mixed cultures. Not until the late 1970s did a truly Hong Kong urban cinema emerge, distinguished by its own features and outlook, as exemplified by New Wave directors like Tsui Hark and Allen Fong. Contrary to a clear-cut dichotomy between city and country that is the tradition of leftist film in the mainland, Leung maintains that Hong Kong filmmakers use multi-perspective narrative to explore the ever-changing reality of the city.

Two chapters provide examples of auteur study. In "Richness through Imperfection: King Hu and the Glimpse," David Bordwell offers a detailed analysis—often shot by shot and enhanced by film stills—of King Hu's visual style. After examining the ways "Hu created willed imperfections in the presentation of the action," Bordwell concludes that Hu's "aesthetic of the glimpse" conveys "a sense that extraordinary physical achievement, if caught in a skillfully imperfect way, becomes marvelous" (2000b, 120, 135). In "The Films of Ann Hui," Patricia Brett Erens sketches the entire career of this distinguished Hong Kong woman director, paying particular attention to her dialectical approach and her ongoing negotiation between the traditional values of the East and the modern values of the West.

Gina Marchetti also approaches Wong Kar-Wai as an auteur, but she uses his films to examine the vertiginous bricolage of American pop culture, British colonialism, and Asian commerce. "Commodities create and re-create individual identities," she contends, "not only operating along the axis of sexuality, but moving from the uncertainties of gender and romantic roles to the instabilities of international commerce, American cultural penetration, and the national, ethnic, and linguistic hybridity that is Hong Kong" (2000, 290). For Marchetti, Wong's films are postmodern texts, and like most postmodern texts, their images project a notion of identity as "elusive and equivocal, and, perhaps, ultimately, ambivalent" (2000, 311).

Like Marchetti, Sheldon Lu addresses the issue of identity but investigates it along the China-Hong Kong-overseas trajectory in "Filming Diaspora and Identity: Hong Kong and 1997." Both *Comrades, Almost a Love Story* (Tian mimi, 1996) and *Happy Together* (Chunguang zhaxie, 1997) confront the transnational cultural imaginary by transporting the viewer far away from Hong Kong (to New York City and Buenos Aires, respectively). The ultimate questions these two films seem to pose to the audience, Lu suspects, is this: "Will Hong Kong and China after 1997 be happy together and remain close comrades, and evolve a lasting partnership as sweet as almost a love story?" (2000b, 286).

Early Cinema, Urban Culture, and Cultural History

"The cinema of Hong Kong has until recently been a neglected area of scholarly attention in the West," as Fu and Desser remind us. And they continue to speculate that "[a]lways marginalized both within and without China, the Hong Kong cinema, like Hong Kong itself, seemed to suffer from the same malaise, what Poshek Fu has termed 'the Central Plains syndrome'" (2000, 2). But the return of Hong Kong to China in 1997 has prompted the production of a spate of serious scholarship on Hong Kong cinema, and ironically, it is early Chinese cinema that has long been neglected and marginalized in Western scholarship. For decades, this area has seldom received sustained critical attention in the West, and a number of essays on the subject are scattered in various journals and anthologies.[21] My edited anthology, *Cinema and Urban Culture in Shanghai, 1922–1943* (1999) is an attempt to correct this situation. In "Introduction: Cinema and Urban Culture in Republican Shanghai," I outline the history and historiography of Chinese cinema and highlight different approaches adopted by scholars in mainland China, Hong Kong, and Taiwan over the past decades. I further define the anthology's twofold objective: to reveal cinema as a significant cultural force in Republican China and to link film scholarship to a cultural history of Shanghai.

The nine essays are divided into three parts. Part One, "Screening Romance: Teahouse, Cinema, Spectator," focuses on family romance as a main attraction for urban film audiences from the 1910s to the 1930s. Zhen Zhang's "Teahouse, Shadowplay, Bricolage: *Laborer's Love* and the Question of Early Chinese Cinema" discusses the ways the strong influence of traditional Chinese theater gradually yielded to cinematic and narrative concerns in the 1920s [Illustration 9]. By way of reconstructing the ambience of the teahouse culture, she demonstrates that the shift of attention from theatrical exteriority to narrativized interiority engendered textual tensions that require interpretations in terms of class and gender, and that the whole issue of early Chinese cinema calls for a reexamination from a global perspective in the 1990s. Kristine Harris's "*The Romance of the Western Chamber* and the Classical Subject Film in 1920s Shanghai" unravels, through a close reading of the 1927 film adaptation of a classic Chinese narrative, a complex nexus of intertextual (literature-theater-drama-film) and inter-contextual forces (Shanghai-Europe-Hollywood) at work in Chinese film industry at the time, as well as the rich visual and psychological subtexts created in the film using then cutting-edge

---

[21] Apart from two essays in Sheldon Lu's volume, one can consult the following. For the 1910s and the 1920s, see Zhong et al. 1997. For the 1930s, see Berry 1989; Ma Ning 1989; Pickowicz 1991; Y. Zhang 1994a. For the 1940s, see Fu 1997; Pickowicz 1993b.

techniques and special effects. Rather than dismissing *The Romance of the Western Chamber* as escapism or atavism, Harris contends that popular costume drama was a new film genre that sought to shed the nickelodeon's image of vulgarity, to attract the emerging middle-class audience with its "authentic" representation of the national past, and to secure steady box-office returns that would make it possible for the Chinese film industry to survive the dominance of Hollywood products.

9. *Laborer's Love* (1922): The earliest extant Chinese film

In "The Urban Milieu of Shanghai Cinema, 1930–1940: Some Explorations of Film Audience, Film Culture, and Narrative Conventions," Leo Lee examines the ways urban venues (such as movie theaters, popular magazines, and city guidebooks) promoted movie-going as an indispensable item of the modern urban lifestyle. He demonstrates that the viewing habits of Shanghai audiences at the time might have been shaped by print culture to an extent greater than we previously anticipated. After briefly comparing the narrative modes of Hollywood and Chinese films, he reasons that the Chinese aesthetic of the long-take might be a product not so much of originality as of "stylistic hybridity," marked as it were by slow tempo and theatrical acting on the one hand, and innovative film techniques on the other. Hybrid or not, the emergent film culture contributed its share to the fashioning of a distinct modern sensibility in 1930s Shanghai.

The essays in Part Two, "Imaging Sexuality: Cabaret Girl, Movie Star, Prostitute," study public discourse on the sexuality of three groups of "infamous" urban women and the circulation and manipulation of their on- and off-screen images in Shanghai. Andrew Field's "Selling Souls in Sin City: Shanghai Singing and Dancing Hostesses in Print, Film and Politics, 1920–1949" traces the public perception of cabaret girls in city guidebooks and magazines. Field demonstrates that, though in many ways they were the modern versions of the courtesans of the late Qing and early Republican periods, cabaret girls were not just a new icon in the cultural imagination of Shanghai but were also deeply enmeshed in the political economy of the city. Michael Chang's "The Good, the Bad, and the Beautiful: Movie Actresses and Public Discourse in Shanghai, 1920s–1930s" depicts the emergence of China's earliest three "generations" of movie stars and discerns a striking difference: whereas in the 1920s a negative discourse attempted to delegitimize upwardly mobile actresses, in the 1930s a positive discourse promoted actresses according to its standards of "good girl" and professional training. In my own essay, "Prostitution and Urban Imagination: Negotiating the Public and the Private in Chinese Films of the 1930s," I argue that prostitution used to be a focal point in the urban imagination and that the public presentation of otherwise "unpresentable" figures furnished Chinese filmmakers with a place where the ethico-moral legitimacy claimed by elite intellectuals confronted and sometimes yielded to the epicurean or voyeuristic tendency in mass audiences. With reference to recent Chinese films, I detect a trend that moved from a sympathetic account of the streetwalker's miserable life in the 1920s and 1930s to an ingenious reinvention of the courtesan's glamorous fashion in the 1980s and 1990s.

Part Three, "Constructing Identity: Nationalism, Metropolitanism, Pan-Asianism," explores the question of censorship in terms of what kinds of identities the filmmakers and government regulators sought to construct in the period. Zhiwei Xiao's "Constructing a New National Culture: Film Censorship and the Issues of Cantonese Dialect, Superstition, and Sex in the Nanjing Decade" examines the role of the Nationalist film censorship in constructing a new national culture. Xiao investigates how the new Chinese national identity was measured against and prioritized over the regional (as represented by Cantonese-dialect films), the international (as evident in Hollywood sex scenes), and the traditional (as reflected in age-old Chinese superstition). All these categories were highly contested in the realm of censorship where the government and local interest groups negotiated their deals. In "Metropolitan Sounds: Music in Chinese Films of the 1930s," Sue Tuohy contends that music in Chinese films constituted a heterogeneous space marked by a metropolitan, if not cosmopolitan, quality. She looks at the role of music in the contemporary artistic and intellectual discourse and locates in film music of the time a range of diverse ideas and models (from Chinese folk songs to Hollywood musicals). Finally, in "'Her Traces Are Found Everywhere': Shanghai, Li Xianglan, and the 'Greater East Asia Film Sphere,'" Shelley Stephenson demonstrates that the promotion of Li Xianglan (Yamaguchi Yoshiko), a mysterious but generic Asian actress, in some Shanghai fan magazines closely parallels the discursive function of the ever-absent, ever-moving entity of the ideology of the "Greater East Asia Co-Prosperity Sphere" (*Dadongya gongrong quan*). The discourse on stardom in this case worked for the politics of Pan-Asianism, a Japanese colonialist construct that found a perfect embodiment in Li Xianglan.[22]

As stated earlier, my anthology seeks to direct scholarly attention to a rich tradition in Chinese film culture that unfortunately has long been neglected in the field. With the recent completion of a few dissertations on this crucial, formative period (Harris 1997a; Xiao 1994; Z. Zhang 1998a), the future for early cinema studies looks promising, although much more research is needed, not the least on the 1940s. To be sure, a tremendous amount of information is now available in *Encyclopedia of Chinese Film* (1998) coauthored by myself and Zhiwei Xiao, and the recent publication of English or bilingual filmographies on China and Hong Kong have greatly facilitated further research.[23] Looking back from the beginning of the new millennium, it is certain that Chinese film

---

[22] The summary here is modified from Y. Zhang 1999a, 12–19.

[23] Hong Kong Film Archive 1997b; Fonoroff 1998; Marion 1997. To the best of my knowledge a filmography on Taiwan comparable to these titles does not yet exist, although one may still consult an earlier, outdated synopsis of Hong Kong and Taiwan films of the 1960s (Eberhard 1972).

studies in the West have come a long way since the obscure screening of *Zhuangzi Tests His Wife* in Los Angeles in the 1910s.

II

In this section I attempt to sort out principal methods and issues in Chinese film studies in the West. As Chris Berry rightly anticipated in his 1985 collection, multidisciplinary approaches to Chinese cinema have persisted up to the present. Among scholars active in recent years, we count people trained in film studies proper (Chris Berry, Nick Browne, Steve Fore, E. Ann Kaplan, Jenny Lau, Gina Marchetti, George Semsel, Esther Yau). Yet others also represent a variety of disciplines: anthropology (Mayfair Yang, Dru Gladney), art history (Patricia Wilson, Catherine Woo), Chinese history (Paul Clark, Poshek Fu, Leo Lee, Paul Pickowicz, Zhiwei Xiao), Chinese literature and culture (Mary Ann Farquhar, Kristine Harris, Wendy Larson, Zhen Zhang), communication and media studies (Wimal Dissanayake, Stephanie Donald, John Lent), and comparative literature (Rey Chow, Sheldon Lu, Xudong Zhang, and myself). In addition, the field has benefited considerably from film critics and scholars based in Asia, Europe, and Australia, such as Chiao Hsiung-Ping, Paul Fonoroff, Law Kar, Li Cheuk-to, Tony Rayns, and Stephen Teo. However, it is important to note that methodological differences remain regardless of one's disciplinary training or affiliation (as with Jenny Lau and Esther Yau), and scholars from different disciplines often share interest in certain issues (like gender and sexuality).

Based on the evidence presented in the preceding section, the following methods and issues seem most compelling to scholars of Chinese cinema: historical research, industry research, genre studies, aesthetic criticism, psychoanalytic criticism, feminist criticism, gender studies, and cultural studies. I draw on more individual articles and essays to further contextualize these methods and issues, but the authors and works cited below are intended to be suggestive rather than exhaustive. After a historical survey, this section is intended as a typography of the critical terrain in the field.

Historical Research

Historical research concerns how sociopolitical or cultural events affect film production and reception. Two types of historical research are prominent in Chinese film studies, the first focusing on film politics, the second on film culture. Film histories of socialist China (1950s–1980s) usually fall into the first category, as evident in the works of Régis Bergeron, Paul Clark, and Jörg Lösel. Before his history book (1987), Clark also published "The Film Industry in the 1970s" (1984) and "Two Hundred Flowers on China's Screens" (1985), both examining significant events from the 1950s to the 1980s. Two other essays by Paul Pickowicz further illustrate the usefulness of the historical method. In "Popular Cinema and Political Thought in Post-Mao China: Reflections on Official Pronouncements, Film, and the Film Audience" (1989), Pickowicz uses film to sort out the relationship between what is official and what is popular. He wants the reader "to recognize that in the realm of elite culture there is tension between the official and the unofficial and, second, to consider the ways in which the unofficial political thought of elites interacts with the popular political thought of non-elites" (p. 38). Pickowicz's model here is less rigid than Clark's tripartite division of Party, artists, and audience because each term in Clark's division can easily identify with both the official and the unofficial, thereby complicating and sometimes blurring the line between elites and non-elites. In "Velvet Prisons and the Political Economy of Chinese Filmmaking" (1995), Pickowicz adopts the notion of "velvet prison"—originated by the Hungarian writer Mikló Haraszti—to chart out significant changes in postsocialist China (see also Barmé 1999, 3–10). Citing *The Troubleshooters* and *Obsession* (aka *The Price of Frenzy*, 1988) as two examples of post-Mao urban cinema, Pickowicz seeks to reveal "many underlying and partially hidden structural and psychological dimensions of the Chinese film world that blocked progress" (p. 204). From the perspective of the political economy of filmmaking in the reform era, he arrives at the conclusion that the post-Tiananmen scene is a jumble of contradictions, where quasi-dissident filmmakers like Zhang Yimou and Chen Kaige specialize in reverse Orientalism, Sixth Generation directors like Zhang Yuan and He Yi produce films outside the studio system, and even crude propaganda works subvert state power.

Research on film culture started as early as 1972 with Jay Leyda's historical survey (although there is a long tradition of such publications in Chinese, as in Yang Cun 1954; Gongsun Lu 1977). By presenting miscellaneous print literature such as newspaper and magazine articles, government documents, and filmmakers' biographies and memoirs, Leyda intentionally provides an incoherent or loose account to counter the rigidly structured, politically correct history written by Cheng Jihua and his associates in the 1960s. Interestingly, the film culture approach was largely ignored (if not altogether abandoned, as some short articles in film programs demonstrate an obvious interest in film culture) from the mid-1970s through the early 1990s, and new substantial works on early Chinese film culture did not resurface until the mid-1990s. Zhiwei Xiao's dissertation, "Film Censorship in China, 1927–1937" (1994) is one such example. Otherwise perceived as a political apparatus wielding enormous power over the film industry, censorship is investigated in Xiao's case as a nexus of power in cultural history, a point of convergence between political ideologies and cultural forces of different varieties, ranging from conservative to modern or even radical, but none strictly defined and territorized at the time. The reliance on extensive archival research evident in Xiao is similarly crucial to two other dissertations, Kristine Harris's "Silent Speech: Envisioning the Nation in Early Chinese Cinema" (1997) and Zhen Zhang's "An Amorous History of the Silver Screen" (1998), although both have also integrated techniques of close reading developed specifically in film studies. My anthology, *Cinema and Urban Culture* (1999), articulates a new cultural-history approach to Chinese cinema, and many collected essays, such as Leo Lee's on urban institutions and Michael Chang's on film stardom, map out the vast territory of film culture awaiting further research.

Industry Research

Industry research concerns the institutions and operations of the film industry. John Lent's book and George Semsel's introduction to *Chinese Film* combine to provide an overview of the structures and mechanisms in three Chinese film industries. From a historical perspective, "From *Wenmingxi* (Civilized Play) to *Yingxi* (Shadowplay): The Foundation of Shanghai Film Industry in the 1920s" (1997), coauthored by Zhong Dafeng, Zhen Zhang, and myself, explores the earliest period in Chinese cinema. But industry research on a most important period (1930s–1940s), which marks the transition to sound and the rise of leftist film in the mainland and Cantonese cinema in Hong Kong, respectively, remains basically undeveloped. A long-ignored gap is the Japanese occupation period in Shanghai. Poshek Fu's "The Ambiguity of Entertainment: Chinese Cinema in Japanese-Occupied Shanghai, 1942 to 1945" (1997) provides a detailed account of the negotiations between Zhang Shankun, the Chinese film industry leader of the time, and his Japanese bosses over the production of entertainment films. For Fu, occupation cinema constituted "a site of heterogeneous voices and contested meanings . . . an ambiguous space in which boundaries between heroic and villainous, political and apolitical, private and public were rarely clear and constantly transgressed" (p. 80).

On the other hand, Paul Clark's work paints a clear picture of the socialist period from the 1950s to the mid-1980s, and the post-Cultural Revolution period or New Era has received a great deal of attention, as apparent in Pickowicz's work and Xianggui Wu's dissertation, "The Chinese Film Industry since 1977" (1992). Moreover, Steve Fore's "Golden Harvest Films and the Hong Kong Movie Industry in the Realm of Globalization" (1994) makes a substantial contribution to the study of Hong Kong, although English scholarship on the Taiwan industry remains conspicuously absent in our typography here.[24] A new development in cross-media industry research deserves special attention. In "The Beginning of the Hong Kong New Wave: The Interactive Relationship Between Television and the Film Industry" (1999), Cheuk Pak-Tong documents the close link between television and film industries in the late 1970s that contributed directly to the emergence of the Hong Kong New Wave. In "Industry on Fire: The Cultural Economy of Hong Kong Media" (1999), Michael Curtin examines the situation of the 1990s and brings film and television (including cable and satellite) industries together in his mapping of the mediascape in the metropolis. He suggests that Hong Kong media might benefit from less concentration within particular media and more synergistic relationships across media.

Genre Studies

Genre studies concern the codes and conventions of a particular genre and their manifestations, variations, and ideological functions in individual films. Of all film genres, melodrama has received the closest

---

[24] Unlike in the West, there has been a proliferation of research publications on the Taiwan film industry in Taiwan, especially since the government declared 1993 the "Film Year" (*dianying nian*). See Chiao 1993a; Huang Ren 1994; Li Tianduo 1997; Lu Feiyi 1998.

critical scrutiny, as exemplified by Nick Browne's work on political melodrama, Ma Ning's on family drama, and E. Ann Kaplan's on gender issues in melodrama. In addition, Pickowicz's historical study deserves special attention. In "Melodramatic Representation and the 'May Fourth' Tradition of Chinese Cinema," Pickowicz challenges "the myth that the Communist Party brought the May Fourth movement to the film studios of Shanghai in 1932"—an official view articulated by Cheng Jihua and others and shared by Leo Lee and some Western historians in varying degrees—by arguing that, in spite of their political conviction and ideological infiltration in the industry, leftist filmmakers like Xia Yan "became the prisoners of the film medium," particularly of melodrama, which relies on "rhetorical excess, extravagant representation, and intensity of moral claim" (1993a, 300–1). By reading *Little Toys* (Xiao wanyi, 1933) and *Dream in Paradise* (Tiantang chunmeng, 1947), Pickowicz demonstrates that "leftist" or "Marxist ideas were swallowed up by the melodramatic genre and reduced to stereotypes and caricatures" (p. 312). His analysis of *Hibiscus Town* further illustrates that the melodramatic imagination is deeply rooted in Chinese life.

Another popular genre in Chinese cinema is the martial arts film. From trade books to the Hong Kong International Film Festival programs, numerous publications are devoted to this genre, which is popularly—yet erroneously—perceived in the West as an exclusive Hong Kong genre (Glaessner 1974; Mintz 1978; S. Lau 1980). More recently, some scholars have researched the genre: Kwai-Cheung Lo in "*Once Upon A Time*: Technology Comes to Presence in China" (1993); Mingyu Yang in his dissertation, "China: Once Upon A Time/Hong Kong: 1997: A Critical Study of Contemporary Martial Arts Films" (1995); and Héctor Rodríquez in "Hong Kong Popular Culture as an Interpretive Arena: The Huang Feihong Film Series" (1997). Special mention is due David Bordwell, who devotes considerable space to the genre in *Planet Hong Kong: Popular Cinema and the Art of Entertainment* (2000), and Stephen Teo, whose *Hong Kong Cinema* (1997) has four chapters (out of sixteen) on martial artists, with one chapter each on King Hu, Bruce Lee, and Jackie Chan. Related to martial arts film is the action film, again often conceived as a Hong Kong genre. Most studies of action films, however, lean more toward a particular director or auteur—especially John Woo (Bordwell 2000, 98–114; Ciecko 1997; Williams 1997b)—than toward the genre as a whole.

Other than those devoted to melodrama and martial arts films, genre studies rarely present themselves as such, although over time several other genres have been covered in one way or another. First, literary adaptation, a once-dominant genre in mainland China, is taken up by Lewis Robinson in *"Family*: A Study in Genre Adaptation" (1984), which compares Ba Jin's original novel *Family* (Jia, 1931) with Cao Yu's stage adaptation (1942) and three film adaptations (1941, 1953, 1956) produced in Shanghai and Hong Kong.[25] This genre is further studied in *Lightness of Being in China: Adaptation and Discursive Figuration in Cinema and Theater* (1999) by Harry Kuoshu (Haixin Xu). Second, the comedy, another genre popular in both China and Hong Kong, is respectively investigated by Ma Ning in *"Satisfied or Not*: Desire and Discourse in the Chinese Comedy of the 1960s" (1987), which analyzes *Satisfied or Not* (Manyi bu manyi, 1963), a comic twist to the theme of "serving the people" in socialist China, and by Jenny Lau in "Besides Fists and Blood" (1998), which discusses Michael Hui and his representative films, in particular *Security Unlimited* (Modeng baobiao, 1981).

A third, equally popular genre is urban cinema. Berry's "Chinese Urban Cinema: Hyper-realism Versus Absurdism" (1988) uses *Yamaha Fish Stall* (Yamaha yudang, 1984) and *Juvenile Delinquents* (Shaonian fan, 1985) as examples of "naturalistic realism" and *Black Cannon Incident* and *Dislocation* as examples of absurdism and expressionism. These two polar extremes in cinematic representation of the city, Berry argues, intentionally go against the tradition of socialist realism, "a didactic fusion of classic Hollywood filmmaking and Soviet Stalinist style" (1988a, 76). Xiaobing Tang's "Configuring the Modern Space: Cinematic Representation of Beijing and Its Politics" (1994) differentiates two separate strategies in the cinematic configuration of Beijing: "If we characterize the politics of *Black Snow* as refusal and disengagement by means of a modernist aesthetics of depth, the rhetoric of compromise in *Good Morning, Beijing* necessarily valorizes cultural and political participation, which in turn articulates the legitimating ideology of a growing market economy" (p. 66). In other words, if Xie Fei articulates "a post-Utopian anxiety" by staging the violent, untimely death of Li Huiquan (Jiang Wen), an ex-prisoner in the first film, Zhang Nuanxin works toward a

---

[25] The 1941 version was produced in wartime Shanghai (not Beijing as Lewis indicates), the 1953 version in Hong Kong, and the 1956 version in Shanghai.

compromise by juxtaposing different spatialities and producing some kind of a "collage city" in the second.

In the context of Hong Kong, Ping-kwan Leung leads us through the history of urban cinema from the 1950s to the 1970s, while Natalia Chan confronts a particular Hong Kong subgenre, the nostalgia cinema of the 1980s and 1990s. More research, of course, is needed to assess the full impact of urban cinema (the subject of chapter 7), especially with regard to Taiwan, just as comedy and other genres deserve more attention. For my part, I deal with two other genres specific to mainland China, the ethnic minority film and the war film in chapter 5.

Aesthetic Criticism

Aesthetic criticism concerns film aesthetic in general, aesthetic features of particular directors and films, as well as the influence of traditional aesthetic or regional art forms on film. To varying extents, essays collected in *Cinematic Landscapes* (by Hao Dazheng, Ni Zhen, and others) have touched on the issue of traditional Chinese aesthetic's influence on Chinese cinema. Catherine Woo also traces the influence of traditional Chinese poetry. Another essay, Lin Niantong's "A Study of the Theories of Chinese Cinema in their Relationship to Classical Aesthetics" (1985), provides a glimpse of the author's extensive work on Chinese film aesthetics published mostly in Chinese (see Lin Niantong 1991). Lin regards traditional Chinese film aesthetics (like "the plan sequence of montage" developed in the 1930s and the 1940s) and traditional Chinese art (especially the system built around the concept of *you*) as two major influences on the pursuit of a native art form in post-1949 Chinese cinema. The concept of *you* is illustrated in Zheng Junli's comparison of a particular film technique to the structuring of perspective in traditional Chinese handscroll painting: "What the eye sees as it moves across the long scroll is similar to what the camera shows us with a pan shot" (Lin Niantong 1985, 186). This handscroll structure in Chinese films, like its counterpart in traditional landscape painting, is aimed at releasing the imagination (*shensi*), bringing the viewer to "roam" and "tour" (two meanings of *you*) in a poetic space that encompasses the visible and the invisible, the imaginary and the abstract. Moreover, the concept of *you* also finds expression in film narrative: "Episodes in Chinese film narratives are arranged in chain sequences, which impart a sense of continuous mobility of space and time to the audience. In such a structure of intradiegetic digressions the imagination is allowed to roam freely" (p. 195). The "roaming imagination" (*you*), thus concludes Lin Niantong, is the aesthetic backbone of Chinese cinema, at least during the 1950s and 1960s.

If Lin Niantong proceeds primarily from the Chinese perspective, Héctor Rodríquez furnishes an integral view that reflects the concerns of both Chinese and Western theory in "Questions of Chinese Aesthetics: Film Form and Narrative Space in the Cinema of King Hu" (1998). Rodríquez first recognizes a nostalgic "craving for China" derived from King Hu's experience of exile and cultural rootlessness, his influence by Western auteur theory, which values directorial signature and encourages self-expression, his intense interest in Chinese visual and performing arts, and his concern with the ethical codes of neo-Daoism and Zen Buddhism. With reference to *Dragon Gate Inn* (Longmen kezhan, 1967), *A Touch of Zen* (Xianü, 1970), *Legend of the Mountain* (Shanzhong chuanqi, 1979), and other films, Rodríquez traces in detail Hu's relationship to Beijing opera, landscape painting, and traditional philosophy, all of which contribute to the director's characteristic anti-rationalism, nonattachment, and perspectivism.

Rodríquez's essay shows a deep interest in individual directorial style, a sort of "auteur studies" not widely practiced in Chinese film studies in the West. Besides King Hu, the following directors have received attention, sometimes in terms of aesthetic criticism but more often in connection with other ideological or thematic concerns: Chen Kaige, Hou Hsiao-hsien, Ann Hui, Wong Kar-Wai, John Woo, Xie Jin, and Zhang Yimou.[26] The only attempt to systematically articulate a Chinese film aesthetic in English to date is Chen Xihe's "Shadowplay: Chinese Film Aesthetics and Their Philosophical and Cultural Fundamentals" (1990). Drawing from the Chinese discussion of "shadowplay" (*yingxi*) as a viable branch of indigenous film theory, Chen outlines a comparative framework in which salient features of Chinese film can be better understood. "The basic understanding of the relationship of shadowplay to film," Chen argues, "is that play is the origin of film, but shadow is its means of presentation" (p. 193). The ranking of play (drama, narrative, theme) over shadow (image, technique, structure)

---

[26] In fact, a new introductory book is organized entirely around auteurs, with each of these directors treated in a chapter: Chen Kaige, Zhang Yimou, Tian Zhuangzhuang, Hou Hsiao-hsien, Edward Yang, and Stanley Kwan (Tam and Dissanayake 1998).

strengthens the centrality of the script in Chinese film studies, a centrality first formulated in Hou Yao's theoretical treatise, *Yingxi juben zuofa* (The making of a shadowplay script, 1926). The differences between the Chinese and the Westerners are thus neatly charted: The former emphasize a "synthetic" method, studying "montage and the long take only in the sense of how to present story"; the latter prefer an "analytic" method, taking "the level of image as the key" and that of "story as one element of film" (p. 196). For Chen, shadowplay theory dominated the Chinese screen until the mid-1980s, when "this huge, old, complete system of film aesthetic [was] experiencing a deep crisis" in its collision with Western culture (p. 203).

Psychoanalytic Criticism

Psychoanalytic criticism concerns, among other things, the workings of desire, fantasy, gaze, voyeurism/fetishism, absence/presence, oedipal trajectory, shot/reverse shot, suture, and subjectivity. As a staple of Western film theory, psychoanalysis finds its way into Chinese film studies through Chris Berry's "The Sublimative Text: Sex and Revolution in *Big Road*" (1988) and E. Ann Kaplan's "Problematizing Cross-Cultural Analysis: The Case of Women in the Recent Chinese Cinema" (1989)—two essays I critique in chapter 4 in the context of cross-cultural analysis. A methodology accessible to scholars trained in fields other than film theory, psychoanalysis is also employed in Ban Wang's 1997 study of revolutionary cinema during the 1950s and 1960s. In his reading of *Song of Youth* (Qingchun zhige, 1959) [Illustration 10] and *Nie Er* (Nie Er, 1959), Wang challenges the facile distinction between the individual and the political and contends that Communist culture was attractive precisely because it incorporated sexuality. According to Wang, the revolutionary film "recognizes the importance of the individual's libidinal pleasure" by seducing the viewer into an "imaginary identification" with the mother (the homeland) and then "attempts to orient the released psychic energy" to "the sublime order of the symbolic"—the law of the father, embodied by the supreme leader Mao Zedong (p. 154).

In the context of Hong Kong, David Ing's "Love at Last Site: Waiting for Oedipus in Stanley Kwan's *Rouge*" (1993–94) deals with the unorthodox proposition *Rouge* poses to the normal oedipal scenario: the mobility of woman through both time and space. Ing links women of different social classes—the courtesan Fleur (Anita Mui [Mei Yanfang]), the playboy's mother and her maids—and of different time periods (the 1930s and the 1980s) together through "their common subject position to man: virgin/non-virgin." In so doing, he observes that Ah Chu, the 1987 "career woman . . . portrayed as a putatively liberated postfeminist subject, one who is as independent of Oedipus (Yuan) as traditional woman (Fleur) is dependent on him (Chen Zhenbang) . . . is ultimately reinscribed into a traditional Oedipal scenario of male desire and female discursive submission" (84, 87, 89).

10. *Song of Youth* (1959): The pleasure of viewing the revolution

Without explaining why and how Yuan and Chen, two very different male characters separated by half a century, could simultaneously and unproblematically represent Oedipus, Ing goes on to criticize the film's complicitous relationship with the patriarchal order: "the closing moments of *Rouge* underscore the idea of contiguity between the past, present, and future, and between people, technology, and landscape. Collective memory, collective fantasy, and male privilege all remain intransigently stable within modern gender roles that are fundamental reenactments of the traditional past" (p. 93).

Feminist Criticism

Feminist criticism concerns the dominant cinema's construction of women; it often involves a critique of patriarchal ideologies and a foregrounding of female subjectivity and sexual difference. In "Invisible Women: Contemporary Chinese Cinema and Women's Film" (1995), Dai Jinhua, an outspoken feminist critic in China, offers a concise history of screen images of women in mainland China (from the woman warrior and the suffering mother to object of male desire) and distinguishes three groups of women directors in the industry. The first group, represented by Wang Ping, Wang Haowei, Shi Shujun, and Li Shaohong, assumes male guises and ignores sexual difference, faithfully upholding the socialist myth of gender equality. The second group, represented by Dong Kena and Wang Junzheng, fully acknowledges gender inequality and usually begins a female story by problematizing gender issues, only to "end up adopting another male discourse, which transforms the female narrative into another male formula" (1995a, 273). The third group, represented by Zhang Nuanxin and Hu Mei, foregrounds female consciousness and explores female subjectivity from a specifically female point of view. By Dai Jinhua's standard, very few women's films exist in China, and Huang Shuqin's *Woman, Demon, Human* (Ren gui qing, 1988) is perhaps the sole film in this category. "Since Qiu Yun [the female protagonist] plays a man's role," Dai reasons, "she will never be able to become the woman who is saved, because the only male who can be her savior exists in her own performance" (p. 278). Nevertheless, Huang Shuqin herself admits in an interview with Dai and Mayfair Yang that at the time of filming *Woman, Demon, Human*, she did not really understand feminism. Even after she was invited to participate in the Créteil International Women's Film Festival in France, she still felt uncomfortable with the ways Western feminist films address women's issues. They are, she asserts, "too artificial and unnatural" (Dai and Yang 1995, 796).

If Dai's feminist definition of women's film seems too narrow (only one film qualifies), Chris Berry's 1988 *Camera Obscura* dossier on Chinese "women's cinema" (*nüxing dianying*) provides a broader view of the conditions of women filmmakers in China. Starting with a symposium organized by *Contemporary Cinema* in Beijing in May 1986, Berry summarizes "consensus" views and raises issues such as the connections between subjectivity and female experience, and between female subjectivity and the experience of loss. After asserting that "the archetypal narrative structures of classical Chinese cinema in the People's Republic revolve around separation and reunion," Berry speculates, "If Western ideology seems obsessed with Oedipal experiences, Chinese consensus ideology seems equally obsessed with taking up and deploying the losses involved in the access to subjectivity and the desire for a return to a presubjective state" (1988b, 16). Berry complements his introductory essay with three interviews with Zhang Nuanxin, Peng Xiaolian, and Hu Mei, respectively.[27]

As shown earlier, Rey Chow and E. Ann Kaplan have also provided strong feminist readings of Chinese cinema. In addition, feminist positions are also taken up by Tonglin Lu in "How Do You Tell a Girl from a Boy? Uncertain Sexual Boundaries in *The Price of Frenzy*" (1993) and by Elissa Rashkin in "Rape as Castration as Spectacle: *The Price of Frenzy*'s Politics of Confusion" (1993). Concentrating on *The Price of Frenzy*, both critics discuss the destructive power of the technologies of vision (cameras, binoculars, and the cinematic apparatus) and the director's voluntary identification with masculine authority in his gradual shifting of the blame (the "frenzy" of the title) from the rapist to the victim's sister, Qingqing, who intrudes on the masculine world, symbolized by the police and the mysterious phallic tower (where the hyper-energetic perpetrator hides). In her hysteria and obsession, Qingqing embodies the castration threat to the male world of control, knowledge, and power, and her "frenzy" is diagnosed by Lu as "the symptom par excellence of the potential disappearance of all boundaries, including sexual boundaries" in contemporary Chinese society (T. Lu 1993b, 72).

Echoing Lu's criticism of the "misogynistic attitude" that blames women for men's problems, Shuqin Cui concludes her study of *Ju Dou* with a feminist statement: "From father figure to son and from the past to the future, all men's burdens, desires, and losses are laid on a single woman's shoulders. This is the deep structure and inner voice of the film" (1997, 328). Cui's critique of male subjectivity finds resonance in Stephanie Donald's "Symptoms of Alienation: The Female Body in

---

[27] Berry conducted another interview with Peng Xiaolian after the latter had moved to the U.S. in 1989 to work on her MFA degree at New York University (Berry 1993).

Recent Chinese Film" (1998), which examines *The Days* and *Beijing Bastards*. Donald argues that in both films "male anxiety is displayed from the male onto the female" and that the "'abortion sequence' serves . . . as a narrational device for disguising the empty anarchy of male subjectivity" (97–8). Insofar as the politics of gender representation is concerned, Donald discovers striking "continuities between revolutionary genres and the independent post-revolutionary—or 'sixth generation'—films." As she claims, "Post-socialist heroisms rise out of the politics of translation rather than transformation" (p. 100).

Gender Studies

Gender studies, often integrated into feminist criticism, concern the representation of sexual difference, gender relations, and power structure, as well as issues of femininity, masculinity, and homosexuality. Taking a feminist-psychoanalytic position in "Cultural and Economic Dislocations: Filmic Phantasies of Chinese Women in the 1980s" (1989), Esther Yau examines a fantastic relationship between cinematic representation and contemporary political reality, a line of research later continued in her dissertation, "Filmic Discourse on Women in Chinese Cinema (1949–65): Art, Ideology and Social Relations" (1990). In her 1989 essay, Yau discusses the introspection of cinematic forms in the 1980s, pointing out the dominance of a "humanist" rather than "feminist" perspective, and a cinematic tendency to assume the role of a "selective anthropologist" in the cultural critique. Of particular interest to feminism is what Yau calls the "rhetoric of castration," a Communist rhetoric that denies all forms of male power except those conforming to the Party's. Formulated in the 1950s and carried to a radical extreme during the Cultural Revolution, this rhetoric saw to it that "masculinity . . . was solely subordinated to negative political redefinition," resulting in "a general suppression of power and desire that had more effect on men than on women, since men had occupied the position of power prior to 1949, and indeed after 1949" (1989a, 18). Precisely due to this symbolic castration, rejection of political emasculation of men became a critical issue in the post-Mao period, and several films—from *A Girl from Hunan* to *Red Sorghum*—specifically make ordinary peasant men, and not Party members, desirable sexual partners, thereby signaling a new process of affirmation of masculinity.[28]

My own "Engendering Chinese Filmic Discourse of the 1930s: Configurations of Modern Women in Shanghai in Three Silent Films" (1994) returns to an earlier period when political redefinition of masculinization of both men and women first took place. I unravel the radical changes in discursive strategies of representing the New Woman in Shanghai from *Wild Flower* (Yecao xianhua, 1930) [Illustration 11] to *Three Modern Women* (San'ge modeng nüxing, 1933) and *New Woman*, and argue that these changes anticipate the desexualization or masculinization of women in Chinese films from the 1950s to the 1970s. Yuejing Wang, in "*Red Sorghum*: Mixing Memory and Desire" (1991), negotiates between Chinese cultural tradition and Western critical theory in his study of the Chinese versions of masculinity and femininity constructed in Zhang Yimou's directorial debut.

11. *Wild Flower* (1930): From feminization to masculinization

[28] The political redefinition process Yau delineates here is, of course, subject to other kinds of reading. Later she studies *The White-Haired Girl* in terms of class (1996).

Sheldon Lu's "Chinese Soap Opera: The Transnational Politics of Visuality, Sexuality, and Masculinity" (2000) brings Chinese film and television soap opera into a single, comparative framework. In place of effeminate or femininized male characters in "ethnographic" films by Zhang Yimou and his followers, Lu argues, some recent Chinese films and television serials, such as *Wild Kiss to Russia* (Kuangwen Eluosi, 1995) and *Foreign Babes in Beijing* (Yangniu'er zai Beijing, 1996), insist on staging an absolute victory of Chinese men over their foreign competitors (for instance, Russians and Americans) in claiming white women, thereby reestablishing the centrality of Chinese masculinity in the libidinal economy of the transnational cultural imaginary.

In the context of Hong Kong cinema, Steve Fore's "Tales of Recombinant Femininity: *The Reincarnation of Golden Lotus*, the *Chin P'ing Mei*, and the Politics of Melodrama in Hong Kong" (1993) explores the ways Clara Law constructs a figure of femme fatale in a society dominated by patriarchal ideologies that blend traditional and capitalist value systems. However, Fore realizes that Law's potential "feminist" critique "never reaches the level of the surface text" in *The Reincarnation of Golden Lotus* (Pan Jinlian zhi qianshi jinsheng, 1989). As a result, the film "ultimately does not deconstruct the notion of the femme fatale, opting instead for a more conventionally melodramatic resolution to the story"—namely, Golden Lotus (Joey Wong [Wang Zuxian]) is "fated" to commit suicide in "the film's propulsive, virtually nihilistic drive toward total destruction" (p. 68).

Typically, the question of masculinity in Hong Kong cinema is investigated in relation to the action or gangster film, as in Mark Gallagher's "Masculinity in Translation: Jackie Chan's Trans-cultural Star Text" (1993), Jillian Sandell's "Reinventing Masculinity: The Spectacle of Male Intimacy in the Films of John Woo" (1996), Julian Stringer's "'Your Tender Smiles Give Me Strength': Paradigms of Masculinity in John Woo's *A Better Tomorrow* and *The Killer*" (1997), and Tony Williams's "Space, Place, and Spectacle: The Crisis Cinema of John Woo" (1997). More often than not, action films from the pre-1997 years are read as "metaphorical interpretation of the 1997 Hong Kong annexation to China," a reading Jenny Lau criticizes as "reductionistic": "This '1997 reading' for every contemporary film coming from Hong Kong ran the risk of reducing Hong Kong culture in general, and film in particular, to the narrow spheres of economics and politics" (1998, 21–2).

Homosexuality is a new topic in Chinese film studies. "Sexual DisOrientations: Homosexual Rights, East Asian Films, and Postmodern Postnationalism" (1996) is Chris Berry's attempt to secure a position from which to map out the uncharted terrain. As he sees it, "rendering homosexualities visible on a global scale joins with the other global flows, postcolonial hybridizations, and localized appropriations of an emergent postmodern global order that is simultaneously postnational" (p. 158). He prefers the term "deviationists" to "subaltern" in his description of different sexual communities and groupings, arguing that, "whereas 'deviant' carries a sense of a failure to conform, 'deviationist' implies . . . a more active and positive agency; it incorporates the element of consciousness" (p. 170). He calls for a politics of identity that is post-nationalist and beyond any simplistic reduction to cultural or geographical boundaries. Indeed, visibility continues to be Berry's central concern in "Staging Gay Life in China: *East Palace, West Palace*" (1998). He suggests that Zhang Yuan's cinematic study of homosexuality is "not so much about the way in which identities can be performed differently, which is a major emphasis in the work of Judith Butler and others on performativity, but rather on the whole question of how they can be performed at all" (p. 86).

Cultural Studies

Cultural studies, itself a hard-to-define "field," concerns a broad range of issues such as gender, sexuality, class, race, ethnicity, power, knowledge, and modernity. To varying degrees, Ackbar Abbas and Rey Chow represent the cultural studies approach to Chinese cinema. Both concentrate on the significance of visuality in the cultures of modernity, postmodernity, and postcoloniality, and both move freely and frequently between cinema and other cultural artifacts and discursive practices such as architecture, literature, music, photography, theory, and translation.

Earlier, Peter Hitchcock's "The Aesthetics of Alienation, or China's 'Fifth Generation'" (1992), published in the journal *Cultural Studies*, approached New Chinese Cinema in a highly theoretical manner. Moving between Marx, Althusser, Bourdieu, Lacan, and many other Western theorists, Hitchcock thus defines his objective: "Rather than provide a descriptive history of the 'Fifth Generation' I want to consider their work theoretically along the mutually disarticulating trajectories suggested above ('alienation' as an historically specific Chinese aesthetic practice in the language of contemporary film . . . and the 'metaphor of woman' which figures both a masculinist desire in Chinese cultural relations and a form of cultural imperialism in the international public sphere)" (p. 119). After analyzing *Yellow Earth, Red Sorghum,* and *Women's Story,* Hitchcock concludes: "In many respects these directors' aesthetic attempts to constitute a significant resistance to the homogenizing tendencies of centralized artistic production, yet I think it is clear that they may also reproduce some of the very ideological effects which they often oppose" (p. 136).

Multidisciplinary Approaches

Before leaving this section on methodologies and issues, I offer three observations. First, as in the case of cultural studies, each category above may be further broken down in terms of specific methodology or critical emphasis involved. Under historical research, I have differentiated between film politics and film culture, but one may also distinguish three others: (1) a sociological approach, in which numerical charts and statistics may be crucial to our understanding of the film industry; (2) an empirical approach, where first-hand material is obtained through interviews and personal observations; and (3) an archival approach, which relies on print literature of all kinds, from government documents, industry reports, fan magazines, and film reviews, to biographies, memoirs, diaries, and letters.[29]

Second, a particular scholar can subscribe to different approaches depending on the research subjects at hand. For instance, Chris Berry adopts psychoanalysis in his reading of *Big Road* but switches to industry research in his presentation of the latest developments "Market Forces: China's 'Fifth Generation' Faces the Bottom Line" (1991) and "Outrageous Fortune: China's Film Industry Takes a Roller-Coaster Ride" (1996). Similarly, Esther Yau draws insights from semiotics and structuralism in her "*Yellow Earth*: Western Analysis and a Non-Western Text" (1987–8), but takes a cultural-history approach in "International Fantasy and the 'New Chinese Cinema'" (1993), where she situates the international success of the Fifth Generation directors and the emergence

---

[29] I also cite these as examples: for a sociological approach, see Pickowicz 1989; for an empirical approach, see Leyda 1972; for an archival approach, see Xiao 1994.

of new urban cinema in China against transnational cultural forces and domestic changes in socioeconomic and ideological fronts.

Third, in part due to the above two factors, the field of Chinese film studies in the West is open to multidisciplinary approaches, and none of the methods or issues delineated here dominates, at least for now.

III

In this concluding section I briefly comment on a set of interrelated questions that have been raised in one way or another in the publications reviewed in this chapter. Many of the questions have not been fully resolved, and several are likely to generate further debate. The first and perhaps most sensitive of all concerns the politics of cross-cultural studies, or, more precisely, the unequal relationship between Western theory and Chinese film. Presumably writing against the text-centered approach in the West, Li Tuo, an advocate for the modernization of film language in the early 1980s, recommends that "attention should be paid not only to the [Chinese] film texts themselves, but also to the ways in which Chinese critics interpret these texts and how and in what context their theoretical discourse is produced" (Semsel et al. 1993, xi). Yet, throughout the 1980s, Western theory heavily influenced Chinese discourse. As George Semsel and his collaborators noted,

> Translations of [André] Bazin's *What Is Cinema?* and [Siegfried] Kracauer's *Theory of Film* . . . were quickly followed by studies in semiotics, structuralism, formalism, psychoanalysis, ideological and feminist criticism. . . . The works . . . by [Jean] Mitry, Roland Barthes, Claude Levi-Strauss, [Roman] Jacobson, [Christian] Metz, [Michel] Foucault, [Walter] Benjamin, [Loui] Althusser, Fredric Jameson, [Dudley] Andrew, [David] Bordwell, [Bill] Nichols, Nick Browne, [Laura] Mulvey, and [E.] Ann Kaplan, brought numerous new approaches into the field and, in contrast to the past, heavily influenced Chinese film studies. (1993, 185)

Even more names can be added to this spectacular hit parade of Western masters—Theodor Adorno, Mikhail Bakhtin, Jean Baudrillard, Pierre Bourdieu, Giles Deleuze, Jacques Derrida, Sigmund Freud, Jurgen Habermas, Martin Heidegger, Jacques Lacan, Friedrich Nietzsche, Raymond Williams—as well as a number of new figures in Western discourse such as Homi Bhabha, Stuart Hall, Edward Said, and Gayatri Chakravorty Spivak. And, of course, the list goes on and on.

On the one hand, we may take the presence of Western theorists in Chinese film studies as a sign of the significance of the field and of the level of sophistication it has attained. On the other hand, it may precisely be their presence that is problematic—even to some Western film scholars. In his overview at the end of *Melodrama and Asian Cinema*, William Rothman questions the condition in which Asian cinema becomes accepted as an integral part of academic film study: "For film study in America to accept Asian cinema only as an object to be studied in accordance with already established procedures and doctrines is for the field to deny to Asian films, and to Asians, the status of subjects, subjects capable of thinking for themselves. It is to silence Asian voices, . . . to suppress conversation between and among Americans and Asians" (1993b, 262). Such acts of "silencing" and "suppression" in Western studies of Asian films have been criticized, just as similar charges have been leveled against the "domination" of Western theory in the fields of Chinese and comparative literature (Spivak 1992; Yoshimoto 1991; Y. Zhang 1998, 1–17). Nevertheless, more is at stake in cross-cultural studies (a topic to be further explored in chapter 4), including such a practical thing as the designation "contemporary Chinese cinema" for Western audiences.

This brings us to the second question: How should we respond to contemporary Chinese cinema as ethnography or autoethnography? As is clear from the review above, Rey Chow bases her proposition on a very small number of recent films, most of them set in rural China or in a mythical or cyclical time frame.[30] It is true that, after Zhang Yimou's recent success, Western audiences will have no difficulty recognizing "[o]ppressive feudal practices, ethnic details, myth making, magnificent cinematography, [and] female sexuality" as his trademarks (Chow 1995, 150). However, from a critical point of view, to theorize these individual trademarks as somehow constituting the essential features of contemporary Chinese cinema is, intentionally or not, to disregard its diversity and complexity, to deny its achievements in other categories (say, urban cinema), and ultimately to participate in a new kind of Orientalism.

---

[30] Among the eighteen films she lists in her index, more than half are merely mentioned in the book, and only one, *Goddess*, falls in the category of urban cinema and outside the period of the 1980s and 1990s.

Indeed, Zhang Yimou's exhibitionism is very much a product of Orientalist surveillance exercised by the international film festivals in the West (as indicated in chapter 2). As an immediate result, his model of "visual ethnography" may have become "infinitely reproducible" (Chow 1995, 171, 148–9). It is not an exaggeration, therefore, to state that Chinese film scholars in the West now have two choices: follow the Orientialist trend and perpetuate a myth that reduces China to rural China, to barren landscape, to exotic rituals, to male impotence or castration, to repressed female sexuality—in short, to all that falls under "primitive passions"; or demythify Western fantasies (a task I undertake in chapter 6) and redirect attention to other aspects of Chinese cinema.

A third question I would like to explore further is: how can we better reenvision the directions of critical practice in Chinese film studies? As Chris Berry observed in 1990, "We still lack reliable English-language histories of the Chinese cinema before 1949, the Taiwan cinema and the Hong Kong cinema. . . . [And] individual genres of feature film, documentaries and newsreels remain largely uncharted" (1991b, 4). More than a decade has passed since that observation, but the situation remains basically unchanged as far as documentaries and newsreels are concerned. Other than melodrama and action film, genre studies have barely begun. Moreover, the need for a general film history has not yet been addressed, although work is already underway.[31] What is encouraging is the growing number of discussions of individual auteurs, genres, themes, and films from all periods and geopolitical regions of Chinese cinema as indicated in the previous pages. Just as Hong Kong cinema has enjoyed unprecedented attention as a result of its return to China, so a group of new dissertations has contributed considerably to our knowledge of

---

[31] Two general histories of Chinese cinema are being undertaken by Chris Berry and Mary Ann Farquhar, both for the University of Cambridge Press (according to David Desser, editor of the Cambridge film history series) and by myself for Routledge. For now, a general overview of Chinese film history can be had by reading works of Hill and Gibson 1998, 543–81 (Bérénice Reynaud on China, Stephen Teo and N. K. Leung on Hong Kong, and Kuan-Hsing Chen on Taiwan); Nowell-Smith 1996, 409–12, 693–713 (Chris Berry on pre-1949 China, Esther Yau on post-1949 China, Li Cheuk-to on Hong Kong, and June Yip on Taiwan New Cinema); and Y. Zhang and Xiao 1998, 1–62 (Xiao on China, Paul Fonoroff on Hong Kong, and Robert Chen on Taiwan).

Taiwan cinema, which is so far one of the least-developed areas in Chinese film studies in the West.[32]

Finally, related to the reenvisioning of Chinese film studies is the question of "China" or "Chineseness." In current postcolonial discourse, it is almost imperative to deconstruct the concepts of nation and ethnicity. According to Rey Chow, the ethnic marker "Chinese" connotes a "compliant attitude toward totalitarianism" in the Chinese intelligentsia, as well as their "indifference toward China's imperialism vis-à-vis peoples who are peripheralized, dominated, or colonized by mainland Chinese culture, in places such as Tibet, Taiwan, and Hong Kong" (1995, 51). Indeed, the questions of nationhood and ethnicity are of tremendous importance to Chinese film studies, and as such they require more serious and more systematic study (see chapter 5). Suffice it to say that however "China" or "Chineseness" may be theorized in current critical discourse, we must not and cannot be blind to the historical existence of China as a cultural and political entity, which has had an enormous impact on Chinese cinema throughout the twentieth century. To follow Jameson's distinction, "[e]thnicity is something one is condemned to; neoethnicity is something one decides to reaffirm about oneself" (1994, 120), I conclude this chapter by stating that Chinese cinema is something that exists historically, whereas how that "Chineseness" is theorized is already something after the fact, something metadiscursive. With this historical understanding we may screen China in a more meaningful way; not exclusively in a Western theoretical context, nor merely in one of "authentic" Chinese culture and history, but ultimately in the context of cross-cultural, multiethnic, and transnational aspects of filmmaking, film viewing, and film criticism in the contemporary world.

---

[32] For sample works on Taiwan cinema other than those collected in the edited volumes, see Berry 1994a; Hoare 1993; Kellner 1998; Y. Zhang 1994b. For new dissertations on Taiwan, see R. Chen 1993a; Rodríquez 1995; Shen 1995a; Y. Yeh 1995.

Four

Cross-Cultural Analysis and Eurocentrism: Interrogating Authority, Power, and Difference in Western Critical Discourse

> The "spatially-mobilized visuality" of the I/eye of empire spiraled outward around the globe, creating a visceral, kinetic sense of imperial travel and conquest, transforming European spectators into armchair conquistadors, affirming their sense of power while turning the colonies into spectacle for the metropole's voyeuristic gaze.
>
> Ella Shohat and Robert Stam, *Unthinking Eurocentrism*

After the preceding extensive survey on the rise and institutionalization of Chinese film studies in the West over the past three decades, I concentrate in this chapter on a pair of particularly sensitive issues: cross-cultural analysis and the persistent symptoms of Eurocentrism in Western critical discourse. To contextualize the discussion of Eurocentrism, it is necessary to refer to debates over the question of cultural imperialism (Section I). From there I focus on the late 1980s, a crucial period in the history of Chinese films studies in the West. This period foregrounds the academic equivalent of what Mary Louise Pratt calls the "contact zone"—"the space in which peoples geographically and historically separated come into contact with each other and establish ongoing relations, usually involving conditions of coercion, radical inequality, and intractable conflict" (1992, 4). My critique of three examples of Eurocentric readings of Chinese cinema in this transitional moment calls attention to the discourses that literally "speak" them and, in varying degrees, transfix their subject positions (Section II). Finally, I draw on recent developments in anthropology and cultural studies, working through issues of traveling theory, traveling theorists, and traveling cultures so as to delineate a new paradigm of dialogism and polyphony in Chinese film studies (Section III).

I

Eurocentrism and the Imperial Imaginary

Written "in the passionate belief that an awareness of the intellectually debilitating effects of the Eurocentric legacy is indispensable for comprehending not only contemporary media representation but even contemporary subjectivities," Ella Shohat and Robert Stam's *Unthinking Eurocentrism: Multiculturalism and the Media* (1995) carries a double thrust: to expose the "unthinking" quality of Eurocentrism as "an unacknowledged current" on the one hand, and to "unthink" Eurocentric discourse, "to move beyond it toward a relational theory and practice" on the other (pp. 1, 10). By "Europeans," Shohat and Stam refer not only to the people of Europe per se but also to "the 'neo-Europeans' of the Americas, Australia, and elsewhere" (1), a designation that encom- passes the parameters of what I mean by "the West" and "Western." Shohat and Stam further distinguish between "colonial discourse" ("the historical product of colonial institutions") and "colonialist/imperialist discourse" ("the linguistic and ideological apparatus that justifies, contemporaneously or even retroactively, colonial/imperial practices") (p. 18). Certainly, colonialist/imperialist discourse has informed, sometimes unconsciously, much of contemporary media representation in the West. It is also responsible for the debilitating effects of Eurocentrism in the contact zone.

Significantly, Shohat and Stam point out "the beginnings of cinema coincided with the giddy heights of the imperial project" at the beginning of the twentieth century. Yet, curiously, of all the celebrated "twin beginnings" of cinema and psychoanalysis, cinema and nationalism, cinema and consumerism, this coincidence of cinema with the heights of imperialism has been least explored by film critics and historians (p. 100). Shohat and Stam examine the ways the camera has been used in the West to explore new geographical, ethnographic, and archaeological territories, to register natural and human "wonders" around the world and exhibit them in the metropole, and to map the globe as a space of knowledge production to project the empire and popularize the imperial imaginary. For them, the discourse of empire relies heavily on "tropological operations," such as erotic animalization, exotic vegetalization, infantilization, rape and rescue fantasy—all working to image or imagine the non-West as the virgin land, the terra incognita, the dark continent, the desert, or other "primitive" or "savage" equivalents. "In sum," they contend, "Eurocentrism sanitizes Western history while patronizing and even demonizing the non-West; it thinks of itself in terms of its noblest achievements—science, progress, humanism—but of the non-West in terms of its deficiencies, real or imagined" (p. 3).[1]

Cultural Imperialism and Media Studies

While Shohat and Stam concentrate their efforts on the *discursive* dimensions of Eurocentrism and the counter-strategies from ethnic minorities and the Third World, debates over "cultural imperialism" concern *institutional* practices in the cross-cultural, transnational context. In his meditation on globalization in the late 1990s, Jameson sees the penetration of Hollywood film and television into every corner of the world as evidence of the "violence of American cultural imperialism." This kind of imperialism exports, in addition to screen images, an entirely new way of life, an export that might eventually lead to the "destruction of those traditions" at the receiving ends, regardless of where they are located (1998, 63).

According to Colleen Roach, the concept of cultural imperialism first gained currency in the late 1960s. It was most prominent in Latin America, which produced a host of critics such as Antonio Pasquali, Luis Ramiro Beltrán, Fernando Reyes Matta, and Mario Kaplún. Other influential theorists in the field include Armand Mattelart in Belgium, Herbert Schiller in the U.S., and Dallas Smythe in Canada. "The specific historical period which gave rise to cultural imperialism thinking (the mid-1960s to late 1970s)," Roach observes, "was precisely the years of greatest economic expansion in the South American-based transnational corporations (TNCs)," which coincided with "the extensive exportation of American mass culture and mass media products, as well as communications technology" (1997, 48). Instead of an East-West divide, then, the penetration of the North in the South was at the top of the agenda for earlier critics of cultural imperialism. In spite of the challenge that cultural studies' scholars like John Fiske (with his concepts of "active audience" and "resistance") have posed to the school of cultural imperialism's political economy model (for instance, "dependency

---

[1] For a challenge to the centrality of Eurocentrism and the constructedness of the dominance of Western civilization in human history, see Dussel 1998.

theory") since the mid-1980s, Schiller insisted in 1993 that "Imperialism, understood as a system of exploitative control of people and resources, is alive and well" (p. 103).

In his book-length study of cultural imperialism, John Tomlinson attempts to expand the coverage of the term far beyond media studies. He suggests that, in the postmodern era, "What replaces 'imperialism' is 'globalisation'" (1991, 175). Tomlinson arrives at this suggestion by analyzing four ways of talking about cultural imperialism: as media imperialism, as a discourse of nationality, as critique of global capitalism, and as critique of modernity. For him, it is the final aspect that somehow subsumes all the rest: "the various critiques of cultural imperialism could be thought of as (in some cases inchoate) protests against the spread of (capitalist) modernity" (p. 173). However, Tomlinson's argument against the notion of cultural domination seems rather unwarranted. Reformulating the global spread of modernity as "a process, not of cultural imposition, but of cultural loss," he elides the question of power and difference altogether: "The complaint about cultural imperialism is now the more defensible one of a complaint about the general, global, failure of these [cultural] resources in the condition of modernity" (193–4). From here he goes further: "Capitalist modernity, I argue, is technologically and economically powerful but culturally 'weak'" (p. 174).

The evidence to counter Tomlinson's thesis of Western modernity as culturally weak is found everywhere in Edward Said's *Culture and Imperialism*. In this survey of "a general world-wide pattern of imperial culture" ranging from European literature to contemporary media coverage, Said discovers that "imperialism . . . lingers where it has always been, in a kind of general cultural sphere as well as in specific political, ideological, economic, and social practices" (1994, xii, 9). Moreover, Said believes that "what still remains of imperialism in recent cultural discussion . . . is the residuum of a dense, interesting history that is paradoxically global and local at the same time" (p. 20). The global expansion of capitalism, in other words, does not so much reduce as mask the effects of cultural imperialism, and these effects manifest themselves not only in global economic domination but also in countless local or localized practices, what Said sees as the "imperial attitude," the structuring of academic disciplines (say, anthropology and comparative literature), and the public euphoria about American ascendancy. The following discussion shows clearly that power and difference are two highly contested issues in Western studies of Chinese cinema.

II

The topic of cultural imperialism was formally broached in "Problematizing Cross-Cultural Analysis: The Case of Women in the Recent Chinese Cinema," an article E. Ann Kaplan published in the summer of 1989. Setting her arguments against the backdrop of the increasing film-culture exchange between China and the U.S. since the mid-1980s, Kaplan raises several provocative questions. For example, "What exactly are the different critical paradigms" in the West and in China? "Ought we to think of theory in terms of national/cultural issues?" (pp. 41–2). Fully aware of Chinese scholars' concerns that a Western reading of Chinese film may have nothing to do with "the *Chinese* way of thinking," or, more radically, that "American film theorists are merely enacting a new kind of cultural imperialism when they undertake analyses of Chinese films," Kaplan acknowledges that "Cross-cultural readings are fraught with dangers" (pp. 41, 49).

I contend that dangers in cross-cultural analysis arise every time a Western(ized) critic subjects the "raw material" of a film from another culture to an interpretive "processing" *exclusively* in Western analytic terms. The products of such unilateral processing can be disputed from the native's point of view, which might lead to the issue of cultural colonialism debated in many fields of cross-cultural analysis, including ethnography, film, literature, postcolonial and subaltern studies. Without immediately entering this larger intellectual terrain, I begin by examining two Western studies of Chinese films and locate in them a typical set of strategies that subordinate alien cultural texts under Western film theories. While investigating certain critical concepts that seem to legitimize the critic's arrogant display of interpretive authority and power, I stress at the same time the concealed "powerlessness" in this kind of study. By "powerless" I mean that such critical practice merely reiterates what has already been said in Western critical paradigms, and bear little on the specifics of the other culture. Returning to Kaplan's reading of Chinese women as a third example, I further illustrate that an awareness of the dangers alone is not enough to save the critic from the trap of critical paradigms.

"Pornographic" (Western) Images versus "Silenced" (Chinese) Audience: The Question of Authority

The first example is Chris Berry's essay, "The Sublimative Text: Sex and Revolution in *Big Road*" (1988), a psychoanalytic study of the Chinese silent film. Contrary to his earlier conclusion that cinematic gaze in Chinese film is not restricted to male or female (1985, 32–46), "The Sublimative Text" traces the pattern of alternating gazes in *Big Road* (Dalu, 1934) from male to female and then back to male [Illustration 12]. A passing remark about the female gaze at the male body shows the potential of Berry's perceptive reading,[2] but his elaboration of a particular scene that highlights the relationship between two female protagonists in the film is extremely problematic.

12. *Big Road* (1934): Male body and libidinal/revolutionary energy

---

[2] A sequence in *Big Road*, in which male workers are tortured in the landlord's secret dungeon, may be a good case for a study of the male body in terms of masochistic aesthetic (see Studlar 1989).

The scene in question concerns the "intimate" dialogue between Moli (Li Lili) and Dingxiang (Chen Yanyan). Dingxiang has an accident with the tongs while curling her hair, and Moli rushes to see if she is badly hurt. An intertitle appears in Chinese characters: "*Ni zhenshi! You jiao ren teng! You re ren ai! Suoyi na Xiao Luo lian fan dou buxiang chi na.*" Moli's half-scolding, half-teasing tone here suggests an adult's caring for a naughty, trouble-making child. But Berry's loose English translation intimates something quite different: "You! You really know how to get people's attention! Xiao Luo completely lost his appetite over you just now." Still unsatisfied, Berry works out a "more literal" version—"When you cry out, people feel for you! When you flirt, people fall for you!"— then also explains that "The Chinese for each of these two phrases consists of four characters, the first and the third of which— corresponding to *when* and *people*—are the same in each phrase. This linguistic paralleling emphasizes even more clearly the doubling of Moli and Xiao Luo here" (1988c, 76).

Why should such a parallel—two common four-character phrases in Chinese—necessarily mirror a doubling, and why, if it did, should the doubling be of Moli and Xiao Luo rather than Dingxiang and Xiao Luo, or Moli and Dingxiang, or any other pairs in the film? Without explanation, Berry seizes this perceived linguistic-cum-visual doubling as evidence that Moli is "displaced" in the sequence onto a "male" position and that her displacement reinforces "her propensity for male-associated behavior" (p. 69). Thus delighted by his ingenious discovery, Berry cannot help leaping further by comparing this "transgressive" sequence "to lesbian scenes in Western pornographic movies" (p. 76).

It should be made clear at this point that a *unilateral* imposition of a "lesbian" or "Western pornographic" reading on a scene from an early Chinese film is not so much a matter of potential moral offense—for Berry is fully aware that he may "have already risked the wrath of certain readers" (p. 76)—as it is an issue of *interpretive authority* in cross-cultural analysis. The point in dispute is whether this Western reading in particular is based on a rigorous scrutiny of textual evidence and a sufficient consideration of the sociocultural specificity of the Other. In the case of the latter, Berry refuses to consider a culture-specific phenomenon in China where a close relationship between two females is regarded as common and normal while intimacy between a boy and a girl is traditionally perceived as indecent and improper. The Beijing-based critic Wang Hui, for instance, provides a sociological explanation of the close relationship between Chinese females, which might appear strange or even "perverse" to Western eyes. Against the interpretation of Yaxi as a lesbian in *Sunshine and Showers* (1987), Wang argues that in China the preservation of social hierarchy works to prohibit cultivation of strong emotional attachment to the opposite sex. Thus a specific social phenomenon occurs where the Chinese seek friendship among members of the same sex, a phenomenon not entirely explainable by the Western concept of homosexuality (1989, 17–8).

In the case of textual evidence, I strongly object to Kaplan's verdict that the notion of an erroneous reading can be bracketed off altogether as irrelevant in cross-cultural analysis (1989, 42). Berry's evocation of Western "lesbian" and "pornographic" images, for example, is based precisely on an erroneous understanding of the key word *ai* uttered by the two woman protagonists. His error of translating *jiao* (a causative verb: make someone do something) into "cry" (an action verb: shout, scream) notwithstanding, Berry's rendition of *ai* (meaning both "like" and "love") as "flirt" is indeed misleading. When Moli says that Dingxiang is *re ren ai* (literally, "so lovable" or "so cute"), there is hardly any sexual, not to mention erotic or even homoerotic, implication in the Chinese expression.

This obvious—and perhaps deliberate—distortion of the meaning of *ai* leads Berry further to insist that Moli breaks "more taboos" when she declares in another scene that she "loves" all male workers. Read carefully, Moli's articulation of *ai* (I suggest an equivalent of "like" or "admire") is at once a denial of her emotional attachment to any single male worker and an assertion of her gender identity and female subjectivity: she is the one who actively *ai* (likes or loves), not just *re ren ai* (be "lovable" or "to be loved"). Dingxiang, on the other hand, urges Moli to confess whom she really loves. In an elaborate response, Moli tactfully avoids the emotional/sexual/erotic overtones of the word *ai* by naming the qualities (rather than the persons bearing those qualities) that she "admires/likes"—Jin Ge's courage, Lao Zhang's strength, Zheng Jun's intelligence, Xiao Luo's ambition, Zhang Da's clumsiness, and even Xiao Liuzi's bizarreness. Articulated in this way, *ai* is radically neutralized and stripped of its potential sexual/erotic connotations.

Moli's tactful articulation, paralleled with written dialogue on the screen and a montage of individual male workers, is crucial to the central theme of *Big Road*: what is admirable or likable to Moli is not the individual but the collective. In other words, the film is ideologically framed so that individual qualities are realized only through collective efforts. This ideological framing thus accounts for the recurring scenes of the massive road construction in the film, the cheerful partaking of Dingxiang and Xiao Luo's private romantic moment by their friends, and, as an ultimate expression, the heroic sacrifice at the end of the film, where Moli dies in a Japanese air raid as the only woman among her admiring male compatriots.

Dismissing these scenes of collective activities as irrelevant, Berry concludes that *Big Road* is a sublimative text that "attempts to arouse revolutionary ardor in its audience by the arousal of libidinal drives and their redirection towards the object of revolution" (1988c, 79). This conclusion is unconvincing for a number of reasons. First, it is predicated on the premise that "the film's audience is clearly inscribed in a male position by virtue of physical proximity of the camera to male characters gazing at women" (p. 75). Yet this premise is jeopardized by Berry's earlier finding that the viewing subject in Chinese cinema is often neutral, not assigned exclusively to either male or female. Berry derives this finding from his study of socialist cinema—which he prefers to call "classical Chinese cinema"—from the early 1950s to the late 1970s (1985, 32–6). Even within the diegesis of *Big Road*, Berry finds many instances of the female gaze at the male body, such as Moli's daring act of watching naked male workers bathing in a river. In a later work, Berry admits that his endeavor to construct a paradigm of the viewing subject in Chinese cinema has come to little avail: not only that "the notion of a model is little improvement on the idea of a paradigm," but that he would "prefer to drop the idea of 'models'" altogether and opt for "a series of moments within a dynamic situation" instead (1994b, 109–10).

Second, even though Berry is purportedly concerned with how the film's "cinematic rhetoric works upon the audience to arouse in them a revolutionary spirit" (1988c, 67),[3] nowhere in his essay can one find any serious study of this central concept of *audience*. Compared with the presence of Berry as an eloquent Western critic, the audience in question remains an unknown and undefined entity. If we presume Berry has the

---

[3] It is only in his later work (1994b, 89) that Berry acknowledges the crucial difference between audience (actual viewers) and the "viewing subject" (an ideal viewer constructed by a film).

Chinese audience in mind, his reading of the disputed sequence in the Western pornographic convention is utterly *ahistorical* since there exists an insurmountable gap between the Chinese audience and its putative knowledge of "the lesbian sequence [as] a standard feature of most Western heterosexual pornographic films shot for male pleasure" (1988c, 75). If, more specifically, Berry has in mind the Chinese audience of the 1930s, one has yet to take into account the various—and by no means uniform—effects the film might have had on diverse urban social groups (such as office clerks, college students, and bourgeois ladies) in Republican China.

Third, the Freudian concept of "sublimation" makes sense mostly in a closed system of psychoanalytic theory. A Western critic may indulge in the enjoyment (or *jouissance*, a more exotic term) of working out potential meaning—"narcissistic" or otherwise—within the already constructed paradigms. Once outside the system, nevertheless, he or she often finds the Chinese text too alien for facile Western appropriation. For instance, puzzled by several sequences in *Big Road* that are not immediately explicable in his scheme of sex and revolution, Berry wields his presumed interpretive authority by making irresponsible dismissals: either that a given irrelevant scene "really is just noise in the system" for it "seems to sit uneasily in the film," or simply that "Chinese films of the thirties do not seem particularly unified to me" (1988c, 84).

Such dismissive remarks prove Berry to be fairly trapped within the rigid paradigm of psychoanalysis, rendered virtually blind to the question of film audience. He seems "powerless"—at least momentarily—precisely because of his commitment to an otherwise powerful theory. Berry's failure to address the question of audience can be better understood in terms of what Michael Ryan sees as a major problem in psychoanalytic film theory: namely, an obsessive concern "with the individual viewer's perceptions or with the positioning of individual subjects rather than with collective social processes" (1988, 482). Since film and social discourse are imagined by psychoanalytic theory to be mutually exclusive, Ryan contends "that the psychoanalysis of film cannot be realized fully until it also becomes a sociology of social discourses that permits a more differentiated and situational understanding of how specific films address different audiences and generate different meaning effects in varied contexts" (p. 480). Ryan's observation is worth quoting at length:

Audiences are not univocally "positioned" by films; rather, they either accept or reject cinematic representations of the world, but they do so in accordance with the social codes they inhabit. The specifically cinematic discourse, whereby a film addresses an audience, is determined by broader social discourses, the systems of significance and valorization that determine social subjects as male or female, working class or ruling class, and so on. (p. 480)

Because of his failure to account for the complexity of the audience question as well as the cultural and historical specifics of 1930s China, Berry is naïve to conclude that the audience of *Big Road* invariably responds to the film—despite social, sexual, political, and regional differences—with an arousal of libido and its redirection towards the object of revolution. Before more is known about the Chinese audience of the 1930s, Berry's conclusion on *Big Road* remains an unfounded, albeit theoretically entertaining, speculation. His elegant act of speaking to, or even in the name of, the silent Chinese audience, nevertheless, serves as a case of the domination of Western interpretive authority in cross-cultural analysis.

Two other points need clarification here. First, audience study is admittedly difficult to pursue in early Chinese cinema, but it is *not* an impossible task (see Y. Zhang 1999a). What is puzzling in this case is that, on the basis of her informal discussion with Berry, Kaplan later quickly dismisses the value of audience study altogether, arguing that "relying on audience interviews would not lead anywhere" and that Chinese film reviews are seldom reliable because of their customary lip service to "the establishment party line" (1991, 26). In the absence of research, Kaplan's impatient dismissal of audience study seems even more irresponsible than Berry's.

Second, due to their shared interest in psychoanalysis, Kaplan is eager to endorse Berry's 1980s work: "Those scholars, like Chris Berry, who have lived in China and know the culture and the language, are obviously no longer 'tentative' [in their writings]" (1989, 40). Kaplan's endorsement suggests that interpretive authority attains permanent legitimacy through the critic's physical proximity to another culture. This line of reasoning is similar to one that helped establish participant-observation as a "scientific" mode of practice and the trained ethno-grapher as a "purveyor of truth" in early twentieth-century Western ethnography. In James Clifford's view, participant-observation gave rise to two dominant paradigms of ethnographic writing—experience and interpretation. What invites further investigation in those two paradigms, Clifford argues, is an underlying view of culture as "an assemblage of texts" awaiting a (master) ethnographer to interpret, a disciplinary conception that has been subject to increasing criticism since the mid-1980s (1988, 21–54).

Western Analytic Technology versus Non-Western Raw Material: The Question of Power(lessness)

My second example comes from Esther Yau's "*Yellow Earth*: Western Analysis and a Non-Western Text" (1987–8), acclaimed by Kaplan as exemplary of "different kinds and levels of cross-cultural reading that ideally would all be undertaken" in the space of a single essay (1989, 42). Unlike Berry, Yau's approach is more self-reflexive, as is evident from the binary opposition of Western and non-Western in the title. In this sense, her article is indeed exemplary of the way a certain kind of film criticism proceeds to dissect an alien Chinese text in order to yield a much-desired Western reading. However, as I demonstrate below, Yau's essay comes full circle in an uncanny if not unexpected way and ends up questioning the very basis of its own theoretical conceptualization.

Yau's initial move is, in her own words, to "open up" the text of *Yellow Earth* (1984) "with sets of contemporary western methods of close reading—cine-structuralist, Barthesian post-structuralist, neo-Marxian culturalist, and feminist discursive" (pp. 24–5).[4] Armed with these Western theories, Yau selects from the film "pairs of antinomies such as agriculture/warfare, subsistence/revolution, backwardness/moderniza-tion," "religion/politics," "peasant/soldier," and so on, and maps their interrelationships against a set of pre-given Western paradigms (p. 25). The working of these binaries, therefore, empowers Yau to discuss the film in terms of presence and absence, dominance and subordination.

Yau's essay can also be "opened up" in its own critical terms. From a feminist perspective, Yau sees the woman protagonist in *Yellow Earth*, Cuiqiao, as a victim of three forces: (1) feudal patriarchy, which forces her into a marriage with an older man she barely knows; (2) Communist

---

[4] For other English studies of *Yellow Earth* that rely heavily on Western theories, see Chow 1995, 79–107; Hitchcock 1992.

ideology, which promises liberation but fails to save her life in time; (3) mother nature, as symbolized by the Yellow River that both nourishes and drowns her. Although this interpretation sounds persuasive at first, the way Yau presents her arguments reveals an underlying problem. For example, Yau notices Cuiqiao's "intimacy" with Hanhan and argues that "The prohibition of incest among family members . . . is transferred to prohibition of romantic involvement between Cui Ciao [Cuiqiao] and the soldier" (p. 25). Here, Yau looks not for evidence within the text but a lack thereof. The absence of incest is noted with nearly the same apparent indifference, as when Yau discusses *Yellow Earth*'s use of cinematic gaze: "It frustrates if one looks for phallocentric (or feminist, for that matter) obsessions within an appropriatable space" (p. 27). One wonders whether such an assertion amounts to the critic's frustration if the desired evidence does not surface in a given text—frustration, in other words, when an alien film refuses to be appropriated by Western theory.

Yau's essay emphasizes the problem of sexuality in *Yellow Earth*. As she rightly observes, sexual repression applies to both male and female in the film. In the parting scene, for example, Cuiqiao personally confronts the soldier Gu Qing: "Take . . . me with you" (note the imperative in Cuiqiao's command, after a few moments of hesitation). Though disappointed by Gu's refusal, Cuiqiao expresses her pent-up emotions by singing, apparently to satisfy Gu's previous request and to help him fulfill his assignment in lyrics-collection (see McDougall 1991, 237). As Cuiqiao's voice fills the sound-track, one realizes suddenly that she is, at least in this particular moment, more articulate than Gu. Her unreserved compliments stun Gu, who can do nothing but silently retreat to the mountains. Cuiqiao's failure to be accepted into the Army is "mirrored" in Gu Qing's failure to speak his confused mind. Gu Qing's failure, furthermore, points to the fact that repression of sexuality is not presented in the film as a gender-specific problem.[5] If "an asexual idealization" is standard in most post-1949 Chinese films, as Yau earlier asserted (p. 28), the absence of incest in *Yellow Earth* thus loses much significance.

---

[5] This view is dovetailed by Farquhar's interpretation of *Yellow Earth* in terms of the Daoist notions of yang and yin: "The yang/yin structure of the film is not one of fixed gender configuration, or simple patriarchy, but one of disharmonious relationships" (1992, 156).

Yau's search for feminist-psychoanalytic raw material in *Yellow Earth* (and perhaps her frustration at the lack thereof) is a clear example of the driving "power" of Western theory. Entranced by a pre-established paradigm, the critic searches far and wide for any example that will testify to—but rarely contest—the power of Western theory. Thus interpretive authority is always taken for granted. The text is "opened up"; its "disembodied" parts are sorted out and reconstructed into a "new" meaningful whole. In Yau's case, after her study of the film in "four structurally balanced strands (micro-narratives) on three levels" (that is, "diegetic," "critical," and "discursive"), she concludes her "historicist reading of texts and contexts": *Yellow Earth* is an "avant-gardist" project, "which has focused its criticism only on the patriarchal and feudal ideologies of that culture. Arguably, then, *Yellow Earth*'s modernist power of critique of Chinese culture and history comes from its sub-textual, noncritical proposition of capitalist-democracy as an alternative; it is (also arguably) this grain in the text that attracts the global-intellectual as well" (pp. 25, 31).

Yau's conclusion is debatable on several counts. First, how can she be so sure that *Yellow Earth* directs its criticism "only" at the patriarchal-feudal systems and not at other targets (say, Communist ideology, to which she refers again and again)? Second, by what standard does she define the film's power of critique as "modernist" (as opposed to "traditional," "premodern," or "postmodernist") and further identify it as a "noncritical proposition" (but why noncritical)? Third, does she have any solid textual evidence to support the claim that the film (rather than its director on other occasions) proposes "capitalist-democracy as an alternative" to the Communist-feudal ideologies?[6]

The striking incommensurability between Yau's sweeping conclusion and her otherwise rigorous analysis signals the inherent power(lessness) of Western theory: once outside its frame of reference, such a critical practice will likely find its target completely unaffected by its "penetrating" power. A perfect illustration is the simple Daoist philosophy in *Yellow Earth*, which, Yau admits, "does not yield to an historicist reading" (p. 32). The recurring long and medium shots of the

---

[6] My questioning of the textual evidence of Yau's conclusion does not imply that *Yellow Earth* is not capable of posing a challenge to the hegemony of the Communist ideology. In fact, in the spirit of reform, the film functions precisely as a counter-ideology in contemporary China.

barren Shaanbei land best represent the Daoist concept: "Silent is the Roaring Sound, Formless is the Image Grand." Such a "negative dialectics" (Yau's term) stubbornly refuses to submit to Western theory and stands conspicuously outside its structure. Not without reluctance, Yau brings her essay to a close: "There are many such instances in the film: when the human voice is absent and nobody looks, history and culture are present in these moments of power(lessness) of the text. With this philosophy, perhaps, we may be able to contemplate the power(lessness) of our reading of the text" (p. 32).

Indeed, if meaning is present where words are absent, we are reduced to silence in front of the silver screen while the images of yellow earth refuse to return our gaze. The power of film theory becomes a non-power when the very object it seeks to dominate is wholly unaffected. With such an unexpected twist, Yau's powerful study of *Yellow Earth* seems to come full circle and return to question the very basis of its self-imagined power.

Confrontation, Recognition, Domination: The Question of (In)Difference

The theoretical rationale behind both Berry's and Yau's critical practices must be examined in more detail. On the one hand, knowledge of film theory encourages a "will to power," a will to register the text in one's favorite theoretical constructs. On the other hand, the success of such a will to power depends on a complex linguistic process that both impels and impedes the discursive act of self-empowerment. Mikhail Bakhtin's theory of discourse, in this connection, sheds light on this dilemma (1981, 276):

> The word, directed toward its object, enters a dialogically agitated and tension-filled environment of alien words, value judgments and accents, weaves in and out of complex interrelationships, merges with some, recoils from others, intersects with yet a third group: and all this may crucially shape discourse, may leave a trace in all its semantic layers, may complicate its expression and influence its entire stylistic profile.

The success of a discourse in making its own sense, according to Bakhtin, depends very much on its ability to penetrate into a world of alien meanings. Hence Bakhtin's conceptualization of power as violence:

"The speaker breaks through the alien conceptual horizon of the listener, constructs his own utterance on alien territory." In order to make any sense at all, the writer must be committed to "polemically invading the reader's belief and evaluative system, striving to stun and destroy the apperceptive background of the reader's active understanding" (1981, 282–3).

Bakhtin's will to power has its own target in a specific historical period in the Soviet Union. But his emphasis on the "dialogic" nature of discourse already specifies the limit of a discourse's success in eliminating those conceptual spaces alien to its own.[7] Bakhtin's recognition of "otherness" (or alterity) in discursive practice, unfortunately, is lost in a more radical position articulated by Roland Barthes, who, together with Julia Kristeva, helped introduce Bakhtin to the Western intellectual world. In his highly polemic *Criticism and Truth*, Barthes proclaims that the critical act may have nothing to do with the text: "what controls the critic is not the meaning of the work, it is the meaning of what he says about it" (1987, 81). In other words, engaged in a critical process, "a critic confronts an object which is not the work, but his own language" (1987, 85). Barthes carried his proclamation to an extreme in his inaugural lecture at the Collège de France: "[L]anguage—the performance of a language system—is neither reactionary nor progressive; it is quite simply fascist" (1982, 461). To be fair, the Barthesian formulation of a fascist image should be understood in its own context of language and power. In the same lecture, Barthes argues that "to utter a discourse is not, as is too often repeated, to communicate; it is to subjugate." He further explains that, once he speaks, he is "both master and slave"—a "slave" because he inevitably settles in the servitude of signs (or discourse), but a "master" nonetheless because he asserts his own act of speaking (1982, 460–1).

This fascist image of critical language resonates with Bakhtin's observation on the destructive nature of discourse: both accentuate the "will" to destroy alien conceptual systems in order to build up their own. If, however, one accepts Barthes' intention to reserve a relatively utopian space for "free" discursive play, untainted as it were by other institutional

---

[7] Michael Holquist historicizes the "disruptive" nature of Bakhtin's theory and adds a political dimension to Bakhtin's otherwise formalist arguments (Bakhtin 1984, xiii–xxiii). For elaboration of Bakhtin in relation to other schools of Western critical theory, see Stam 1989, 1–25.

practices, his excessively militant position may have already revealed the inherent "power(lessness)" of critical language vis-à-vis other socio-economic institutions. Seen in this light, although a fascination with one's own language (or critical paradigm) may indeed offer *jouissance* to a critic, a stubborn refusal to engage criticism in dialogue with other discourses betrays the insecurity of one's own defense mechanism.

Returning to the questions of interpretive authority and power(lessness), first, a pure discursive space does not exist in cross-cultural analysis, and, second, any critical act is bound to inflict certain consequences on the culturally specific text and audience. Since this issue of cultural specificity often elicits a response of either recognition or indifference, I turn to the self-conscious way Kaplan confronts it in her "Problematizing Cross-Cultural Analysis."

Kaplan's article consists of four parts: an initial recognition of difference between Western and Chinese paradigms; an analysis of select Chinese films in terms of female desire, sexual difference, and subjectivity; a critique of a reading of *Army Nurse*; and two incompatible conclusions. Proceeding from a "self-conscious perspective of Western feminism, theories of subjectivity and desire, and finally, of the modernism/postmodernism trajectory" (1989, 43), Kaplan emphasizes the cases of eroticism in Chinese films. "Missing from the films," she observes, "are images of female-female bonding of the kind that would rival heterosexual priorities, and representations of the mother" (p. 47). On the basis of these sketchy observations, Kaplan at one point entertains a condescending "postmodernist" view that China might still belong to a "premodern state" (p. 47). She is uncomfortable with director Hu Mei's "alternative analysis," which presents the female situation "as an emblem for *all* Chinese peoples' frustration"—not just women's (p. 48). Informed by "New Age Consciousness," Kaplan thus laments the Chinese belief in "the utopian ideal of submersion of self in the collective," which we in the West "long ago abandoned" (p. 49).

Kaplan's acknowledgement that Hu Mei's reading conforms to Jameson's theory of "national allegory" renders extremely ironic her earlier claim that Jameson's insistence on the ultimate political dimension in a private or libidinal text of Third World culture is arguably "misleading" (p. 43; see also Jameson 1986). Set against Jameson's theory, Kaplan's strategy is clear: she ranks the private and erotic over other dimensions in Chinese films. Kaplan's dilemma is dramatically highlighted in this instance. She is caught between an apparent will to power (in the sense that she wants to register *her* experience of Chinese films exclusively in feminist, postmodernist, and psychoanalytic terms) and the latent powerlessness of the will (in the sense that her discursive space faces an imminent threat of invasion by other discourses).

Two more statements show how Kaplan, though fully aware of the dangers in cross-cultural analysis, is nonetheless entrapped by Western critical paradigms. First, she assumes—tactfully followed by an invitation to rebut—"that the Chinese cinema arises from the same psychoanalytic desire for replacing the lost object; for introjection, displacement, projection, as *we* have theorized, produces the desire for cinema in the West" (p. 43, emphasis added). It is evident from this assumption that after an initial recognition of cultural differences, Kaplan immediately falls back into an attitude of *indifference* to the Other: if Chinese directors are still troubled by easy theoretical questions, then the problems are simply theirs, for we in the West have long ago solved these problems thanks to our advanced theory.[8]

The second statement comes from Kaplan's final reading: "Given the prior phallic order, and given classical Oedipal rivalry with the Father, they [Chinese men] may be harmed even more than women" under the rule of State Communism (p. 50). My objection to this reading is twofold. One, Freud's Oedipal Complex is a Western theoretical hypothesis, not a Chinese cultural given. And, a symbolic order (the phallus in this case) theorized as "prior" to a given culture might not be readily translatable or transportable as equally prior to another culture. By insisting on her interpretive authority and the superiority of Western theory, Kaplan sends a rather mixed message in her 1989 essay. Although confrontation with an alien culture might first necessitate a "benevolent" recognition of difference, the critic could still retreat into indifference to

---

[8] Kaplan's self-positioning here is similar to Rey Chow's vis-à-vis Chinese pro-democracy demonstrators in Tiananmen Square (discussed in chapter 1). It is interesting to note that Chow herself is fully aware of Kaplan's warning of dangers: "One of these dangers is our habit of reading the 'third world' in terms of what, from our point of view, it does not have but wants to have. Once this axis of *possession* is established, our analysis is likely to remain bogged down in a predictable direction, with texts from the 'third world' serving as the latest exotic objects, always confirming what makes sense for us (as subjects) and for us alone" (1995, 83).

the Other by legitimating the "priority" (read "supremacy," and therefore "domination") of Western theory.

III

Decentering, Restructuring, Self-Positioning: The Case of Traveling Theorists

In the above three critiques, my main focus—like Shohat and Stam's in *Unthinking Eurocentrism*—"is less on intentions than on institutional discourses, less on 'goodness' and 'badness' than on historically configured relations of power" (1995, 3). By envisioning a transitional moment in the history of Chinese film studies in the West as a special type of "contact zone," I do not mean to collapse the obvious difference between what Pratt sees as "colonial encounters" that are part of colonial history and the otherwise "enlightened" inter-cultural exchange based on perceived mutual needs in the last decades of the twentieth century. However, what is particularly significant in my case study is that what Pratt conceives of as contact zones—"social spaces where disparate cultures meet, clash, and grapple with each other, often in highly asymmetrical relations of domination and subordination" (p. 4)—proves to be a fitting, indeed almost perfect, description of the critical practice described above. The kind of domination and subordination resulting from the clashing of cultures in the contact zone alerts us to the persistence of Eurocentrism in Western academia. There is no denying that, in her celebration of the superiority of Western theory and her lament for the deplorable state of the "premodern" mentality in contemporary China, Kaplan displays a patronizing attitude toward the non-Western director that is symptomatic of Eurocentrism in general: "[I]t thinks of itself in terms of its noblest achievements . . . but of the non-West in terms of its deficiencies, real or imagined" (Shohat and Stam 1995, 3).

Mike Featherstone further illuminates this Eurocentrism: "It was this confinement of other cultures to past history, to lower stages on the same ladder of history, which enhanced the sense of the threshold-advancing presentness of the European nations, a sense of modernity which in actuality developed out of the occluded spatial encounters with non-Western others" (1995, 153). Because of her pride in the cutting-edge "New Age Consciousness," Kaplan remains blind to the fact that psychoanalytic theory is by no means a universal discourse but only one "dominant particular" among many (that is, a particular theory that happens to claim the status of dominant). As Jameson concedes, "[T]here is a kind of blindness at the center"—the West as the presumed center of global knowledge. "American blindness can be registered, for example, in our tendency to confuse the universal and the cultural" (1998, 59). Kaplan, in spite of her initial awareness of the dangers in cross-cultural analysis, eventually chooses not to confront "the problem of the location of the theorist who necessarily writes from a *particular* place and within a *particular* tradition of discourse which endow him or her with differential power resources not only to be able to speak, but also to be listened to" (Featherstone 1995, 123; emphases added).

In Kaplan's case, the power to speak—and, by extension, the power to refuse to listen to others—thus brings us to Spivak's critique of Kristeva's *About Chinese Women*. Spivak unambiguously argues that "in order to learn enough about Third World women and to develop a different readership, the immense heterogeneity of the field must be appreciated, and the First World feminist must learn to stop feeling privileged *as a woman*" (1988, 136). Unrestrained pride in one's superior theory and enlightened compassion leads one to either indifference to or domination over other cultures. More specifically, Spivak warns against mistaking theoretical speculation for historical fact, especially when it pertains to other cultures, and contends that Kristeva's benevolent prediction about China is a symptom of colonialist benevolence. In later work on subaltern studies, Spivak clearly sees herself within "the current academic theater of cultural imperialism" and thus specifies how difficult it is to attain an unproblematic self: "Nothing can function without us, yet the part [played by a First World critic] is at least historically ironic" (1988, 221).

Spivak's recognition of her ironic position between the West and its Other illustrates what Clifford aptly terms the "predicament of culture." Indeed, a complicated process of "decentering" has been underway since the mid-1980s: as the West is no longer seen as the center of the world, many disciplines have shifted their paradigms to accommodate the emerging "off-centeredness." In the field of ethnography, for instance, those who are marginalized or silenced in the bourgeois West— "natives," women, the poor, and ethnic minorities—have begun to speak back to the "Empire," so much so that "[t]he time is past when privileged authorities could routinely 'give voice' (or history) to others without fear of contradiction" (Clifford 1988, 7).[9] Charting the formation and breakup of ethnographic authority in twentieth-century social anthropology, Clifford concludes that "the West can no longer present itself as the unique purveyor of anthropological knowledge about others" (1988, 22).

The same decentering is also found in the field of history. Many still remember Said's powerful critique of Orientalism, a discursive/institutional practice of cultural colonialism that champions the West as "the spectator, the judge and jury, of every facet of Oriental behavior" (1979, 109). In his survey of Western historiography of modern China, Paul Cohen also notices the dominance of "a Western-centeredness that robs China of its autonomy and makes of it, in the end, an intellectual possession of the West" (1984, 151). Cohen's criticism of the three dominant, parochially Western historiographic paradigms—"the impact-response," "the modernization or tradition-modernity," and "the imperialism"—is worth quoting here: "Like all approaches of a highly teleological nature, they are fundamentally circular in that they end up finding in a vast and complex historical reality precisely what they set out to look for" (1984, 151). Without much modification, Cohen's critique can be equally applied to the three Western studies of Chinese films (in Section II), for all of them proceed from parochially Western paradigms and fail to address the immense complexity and heterogeneity of China's cultural, historical reality. What goes amiss in those Western studies is an attitude of indifference to the experience of China, not that of the West.

My argument here dovetails Berry's 1989 reflection on Western scholarship in Japanese cinema: "What is missing for these pieces on Japanese film is any consideration of what film means to the Japanese themselves. . . . In the politics of criticism, the deployment of a non-Western culture only as a mask of difference by which the West may come to identify itself is an unequal, one might even suggest neo-colonialist, operation" (p. 88). Ironically, this charge can be directed, word for word, at Berry's own practice in "The Sublimative Text," in which he forgets to ask what *Big Road* might actually mean to Chinese audiences, besides "a tantalizing mixture of gratification and deferred gratification" (1988c, 81). Nevertheless, one can take this move as a sign

---

[9] For a critique of the center-periphery paradigm, see Amin 1989. For some related topics, see Ashcroft et al. 1989; Gates 1985; Said 1994; Trinh 1989.

of the increasing awareness among film critics and theorists in the West of the "Eurocentrism trap," as my discussion of other works by Berry and Yau below demonstrates. Indeed, by 1998 Berry had openly admitted he was "in complete agreement with" the argument that "the model of the psychoanalytic subject cannot be assumed to be universal, seamlessly complete, or the only model of subjectivity and agency available or suitable." He continued: "Despite the fact that I have frequently deployed concepts derived from psychoanalytic theory in my work on Chinese cinema, I want to emphasize that I have no interest in privileging that conceptual framework over others" (1998a, 137).

Kaplan, on the other hand, appears reluctant to reposition herself, even though she subsequently devoted an entire book to cross-cultural representation and modified her previous views on the relevance of Jameson's "national allegory" to Chinese cinema.[10] As recently as 1997, she had adopted this defensive position: "It is, thus, in full awareness of the Eurocentric bias of my brief reading of *Farewell My Concubine* that I offer it: Eurocentrism includes ways Western critics are trained to be self-conscious about the emotional impact of a film on the individual spectator and to focus on subjectivity" (1997b, 266–7). In this puzzling statement, Kaplan seems to argue against the abandonment of Eurocentrism on the ground that without it, Western critics could no longer focus on subjectivity, or simply be self-conscious at all. But *whose* subjectivity does Kaplan have in mind? Consider her 1997 statement: "[W]hite subjectivities . . . can also be destabilized when exposed to the gaze of the Other, since this is the gaze to which subjects have not traditionally been subjected" (1997a, xix). Does this imply that Kaplan wants to hold on to Eurocentrism so as to protect "white subjectivities" that are now increasingly under the gaze of the Other?

Kaplan's own unprepared, and thus unwilling exposure to the gaze of the Other is given much space in her book *Looking for the Other* (1997). In his critique of Western studies of Japanese film, Mitsuhiro Yoshimoto cites Kaplan's article on cross-cultural analysis as a new example of cultural imperialism. His statement that "cross-cultural

---

[10] Instead of dismissing Jameson's theory as "misleading," as she did in 1989, Kaplan later conceded, "[T]he allegorical reading that Fredric Jameson theorized as always there in 'Third World' texts would account for both what the Western viewer misses and for a set of meanings that Chinese viewers would have grasped and appreciated. To this extent, Jameson's point is well taken" (1997a, 147).

analysis, which is predicated on the masking of power relations in the production of knowledge, is a newer version of legitimating cultural colonization of the non-West by the West" (1991, 250) is judged by Kaplan to be a most damaging accusation. As she herself has conceived of it, cross-cultural analysis should be "mutually beneficial" to all parties involved (1991, 6). In self-defense, Kaplan is quick to assert, "I was fully aware of the power imbalance in this research. That, however, did not seem sufficient reason not to do it, especially if one was trying to locate oneself as a theorist in the discourse, to examine the position of 'theory' itself and to explore whether or not such research *should be undertaken* by western scholars" (1997a, 151).[11]

As I demonstrated earlier, Kaplan's initial awareness of the power imbalance is not an issue here. What matters is the way she pursues her cross-cultural analysis. Since she enlists Said in her defense, it makes sense to compare Said's notion of "traveling theory" and Kaplan's self-image as a "traveling white theorist." Here is Said's famous passage:

> Like people and schools of criticism, ideas and theories travel—from person to person, from situation to situation, from one period to another. Cultural and intellectual life are usually nourished and often sustained by this circulation of ideas, and whether it takes the form of acknowledged or unconscious influence, creative borrowing, or wholesale appropriation, the movement of ideas and theories from one place to another is both a fact of life and a usefully enabling condition of intellectual activity. (1983, 226)

Said's notion of traveling theory, up to this point, seems an appropriate endorsement of cross-cultural exchange. Yet, as he elaborates, "Such movement into a new environment is never unimpeded. It necessarily involves processes of representation and institutionalization different from those at the point of origin. This complicates any account of the transplantation, transference, circulation, and commerce of theories and ideas" (1983, 226). In other words, in each of the succeeding contact zones, things tend to get more and more complicated, with "too many interruptions, too many distractions, too many irregularities interfering

---

[11] Here, Kaplan seems to echo Berry's argument: "[I]t makes no more sense to refuse to use Western theory than it does to argue that the combustion engine and the computer should not be used in non-Western countries" (1995b, 82).

with the homogeneous space supposedly holding scholars together" (1983, 228).

For Said, "No reading is neutral or innocent, and by the same token every text and every reader is to some extent the product of a theoretical standpoint, however implicit or unconscious such a standpoint may be" (1983, 241). That Kaplan's psychoanalytic reading is a product of a specific theoretical perspective should come as no surprise to the reader by now; but the fact that she defends this perspective in the name of Eurocentrism demands further explication. What is at issue here, I suggest, is the crucial difference between "theory" and what Said perceptively calls "critical consciousness":

> The critical consciousness is awareness of the differences between situations, awareness too of the fact that no system or theory exhausts the situation out of which it emerges or to which it is transported. And, above all, critical consciousness is awareness of the resistances to theory, reactions to it elicited by those concrete experiences or interpretations with which it is in conflict. Indeed I would go so far as saying that it is the critic's job to provide resistance to theory, to open it up toward historical reality, toward society, toward human needs and interests, to point up those concrete instances drawn from everyday reality that lie outside or just beyond the interpretive area necessarily designated in advance and thereafter circumscribed by every theory. (1983, 242)

What is conspicuously absent in Kaplan's 1989 reading of *Army Nurse* is this critical consciousness, without which she is unable—even unwilling—to open psychoanalytic theory toward Chinese reality.

Consider another, more flexible, belief in the intricate connections between cinema and psychoanalysis. In an interview with two clinical psychoanalysts, Bernardo Bertolucci admits, "The only thing I find a bit strange is applying Freudian analysis to other cultures—Confucian, Communist, Marxist, Leninist" (Sklarew et al. 1998, 53). While researching and filming *The Last Emperor* (1987), Bertolucci was fully aware of the huge cultural differences between China and the West: "Really the first thing to accept, and it wasn't easy when I decided to do the movie, is that we are different. That every time we try to read a Chinese event with our mental structure, we are wrong. We are mistaken. Because we always try to interpret their reality with our instrument, which is wrong" (Sklarew et al. 1998, 45). Unlike Kaplan, who dismisses the possibility of erroneous readings, Bertolucci is willing to resist psychoanalytic theory and "ma[k]e the effort of seeing things through Chinese eyes" (Sklarew et al. 1998, 50).

It is not my intention to assess the authenticity or truthfulness of Bertolucci's cinematic representation of China.[12] What is telling is that he at least tried to suspend his "mental structure" in order to comprehend an alien culture from the perspective of the Other. In a sense, Bertolucci has attempted to meet what Trinh Minh-ha specifies as a basic condition of knowing the Other: "The other is never to be known unless one arrives at a *suspension* of language, where the reign of codes yields to a state of constant non-knowledge" (1989, 76). Without such suspension of "master" language or theory, Trinh argues, "No anthropological undertaking can ever open up the other" (1989, 76). And, as Claude Lévi-Stauss says, "Without a doubt, the attempt will remain largely illusory: we shall never know if the other, into whom we cannot, after all, dissolve, fashions from the elements of his social existence a synthesis exactly superimposable on that which we have worked out" (1971, 14).

While reiterating that "cross-cultural analysis is difficult" and "fraught with danger," Kaplan presents two diametrically opposed options that echo Lévi-Stauss's words: "We are either forced to read works produced by the Other through the constraints of our own frameworks/theories/ideologies; or to adopt what we believe to be the position of the Other—to submerge our position in that of the imagined Other" (Kaplan 1991, 6). Since the second option is largely illusory from the West's perspective, Kaplan prefers the first option, and poses this rhetorical question: "Isn't it better that I approach alien texts through cultural constructs that belong to me rather than . . . participating in a cultural 'ventriloquism' which eradicates my own backgrounds, skills, and training?" (1991, 25). In the final analysis, it is exactly this perceived—but historically unjustifiable—threat of "eradication" that compels Kaplan, a "traveling white theorist," to defend her self-described "Eurocentric bias" in an otherwise well-intended project of cross-cultural analysis.

---

[12] For attempts in this direction, see Chow 1991b, 3–33; Loshitzky and Meyuhas 1992; Sklarew et al. 1998, 203–52.

Conclusion: Toward a Dialogic Mode of Cross-Cultural Analysis

Certainly, one problem with Kaplan's "Eurocentric" formulation of cross-cultural analysis is that it traps her in the binary logic of "either/ors"—my knowledge versus their culture, my theories versus their films, my subjectivity versus their "imagined" existence—which all arrive at a seemingly unbridgeable divide: the West (as subject of knowledge) versus the non-West (as object of analysis). Formulated in this way, Kaplan's self-positioning in cross-cultural analysis contrasts sharply with Spivak's subaltern studies. As we have seen, Spivak views her position as feminist theorist between the First and the Third World as profoundly ironic. Another problem with Kaplan's formulation is her hierarchical ranking of "us" versus "them." For correcting this, Said's recommendation is highly valuable: "It is more rewarding—and more difficult—to think concretely and sympathetically, contrapuntally, about others than only about 'us.' But this also means not trying to rule others, not trying to classify them or put them in hierarchies, above all, not constantly reiterating how 'our' culture or country is number one" (1994, 336).

By citing Spivak and Said's critique of Eurocentrism I do not mean to endorse a radical shift from an exclusively Western-centered approach (exemplified by Kaplan, for instance) to what Cohen calls "a more genuinely *other*-centered" one (1984, 7). The problem with a reversed, other-centered paradigm is aptly summed up in Clifford's review of Said's *Orientalism*. First, Clifford shows that Said's work frequently relapses into the same "essentializing" modes it attacks, and then warns that an exclusive dependence on dichotomizing concepts would not save an oppositional critique of Orientalism from falling into "Occidentalism" (1988, 255–76). Instead of either the Eurocentric or the other-centered position, I see more potential in a self-reflexive mode of cross-cultural analysis that favors dialogue and polyphony.

A new formulation of "culture" is needed in order to move beyond cultural essentialism. As Clifford rightly argues, in an off-centered world of many distinct meaning systems, culture can no longer be conceived of as a mere *ensemble* of texts to be packed and then unraveled. Rather, it must be reconceptualized as "concretely, an open-ended, creative dialogue of subcultures, of insiders and outsiders, of diverse factions." In other words, "[W]e should attempt to think of cultures not as organically unified or traditionally continuous but rather as negotiated, present processes" (1988, 46, 273).

"Dialogue" and "negotiation" are two key terms in this new concept of culture. As envisioned by Bakhtin, the outcome of dialogue among discourses is never an absolute hegemony of one—no matter how "fascist," "imperialist," or "colonialist" it might be—over all others, but rather an unstable, competitive, and contested situation in which a discourse "merges with some, recoils from others, intersects with yet a third group" (1981, 276). Negotiation, then, emerges as an appropriate term to describe this complex discursive process, which best captures the dialogic and polyphonic nature of cross-cultural analysis.

The dialogic mode of cross-cultural analysis eases the "anxieties about speaking" felt by traveling white theorists like Kaplan. The issue here is never simply the choice between mastering the skills of "ventriloquism" or eradicating one's subjectivity by encounters with an alien culture. Nor is it a question of either "Can the subaltern speak" or "Can the non-subaltern speak?" Shohat and Stam's reformulation of these questions presents an ideal solution:

> Rather than asking who can speak, then, we should ask about how to speak together, and more important, about how to move the plurilog forward. How might we interweave our voices, whether in chorus, in antiphony, in call and response, or in polyphony? What are the modes of collective speech? While it is dangerous to imagine that one can speak for others (that is, paradigmatically replace them), it is something else again to speak with or alongside others in the sense of forming alliances. (1995, 346)

What is more, Shohat and Stam argue against the notion of a "fixed" identity for the speaker. Instead, they envision "overlapping, polycentric circles of identities" that make it possible for people to "occupy diverse positions, being empowered on one axis (say class) but not on another (say race and gender)" (1995, 346, 343). Rather than a patronizing attitude or "subaltern envy," traveling white theorists can "identify upward or downward," work through strategic "disaffiliation" and "reaffiliation," and ultimately contribute to "a cross-cultural 'mutually illuminating' dialogic approach" to media representation (1995, 343–5, 242).

Shohat and Stam's reformulation resonates with Clifford's idea of "traveling cultures." According to Clifford, the notion of "identity as a politics rather than an inheritance" specifically rejects "all-or-nothing ethnic agendas," for "cultural/political identity is a processual configuration of historically given elements—including race, culture, class, gender, and sexuality—different combinations of which may be featured in different conjunctures" (1992, 116). In the contact zone, therefore, a traveling white theorist does not necessarily encounter what Kaplan imagines as an either/or situation: either speaking for oneself or having one's voice eradicated. On the contrary, a set of alternatives are present in the contact zone, and it is up to the critic or theorist to decide on the best strategy to adopt in cross-cultural analysis.

What I delineate as the new paradigm of dialogism (negotiation) and polyphony (multiplicity and heterogeneity) has been functional in Chinese film studies for some time. As early as 1989, Ma Ning suggested that "Asian cinema criticism in the West as a cross-cultural discipline needs a cross-cultural perspective" (p. 22). In his study of Chinese leftist films of the 1930s, Ma works through both the technicality of Western film theory and the specificity of Chinese film history and locates at least two instances of the Chinese transformation of Western cinematic conventions. First, "The juxtaposition of closed and open POV [point of view] structures . . . is a unique Chinese synthesis of Soviet montage and Hollywood continuity editing." Second, the integration of the "journalistic discourse" (newspaper headlines and historical footage) and "popular discourses" (folk songs, wordplays, magic shows) into the Hollywood melodramatic paradigm is meant to attract attention from both upper- and lower-class viewers in Republican China (pp. 25–6).

Similarly, in a 1991 study, Yuejin Wang reads *Red Sorghum* (1987) against Western theories (including semiotics and psychoanalysis) but pays close attention to the cultural specificity of China and the historical experience of the Chinese people. In a remarkably dialogic mode, Wang interweaves Chinese concepts like yin and yang with Western concepts such as narcissism, pre-oedipal phase, "oceanic self," and "l'hommelette," and brings Chinese scholars like Qu Yuan, Cao Pi, Lin Yutang, and Lu Xun into dialogue with Western theorists and directors such as Bakhtin, Barthes, Mary Ann Doane, Metz, Freud, Jameson, Lacan, Nietzsche, Kaja Silverman, Gaylyn Studlar, D. W. Griffith, and King Vidor. Through this approach Wang arrives at an insightful new reading: "Instead of being afflicted by castration anxiety, the problematic of the lack is quite reversed in the Chinese cultural context. It is the man who lacks. If anything, a femininity complex would be a more appropriate form of the unconscious in the Chinese psyche" (p. 83). As Wang further speculates,

> It is consequently tempting to fix *Red Sorghum* in a Freudian algebra as a narrative about the return of the repressed; or to water down the film into a Lacanian phraseology as the liberation of desire. . . . But there is also a difference. *Red Sorghum* is fundamentally a liberation of repressed collective desire. A lot of psychoanalytic categories, when placed in the Chinese context, cannot be embraced without some reorientation. The patterns of masculinity and femininity, dominance and submission, repression and desire are bound up with other cultural praxes in the Chinese context, and acquire new dimensions. (99–100)

In both Ma's and Wang's system, Chinese films, engaged in dialogue with Western theory, directly speak to and negotiate with an array of Western critical and cinematic constructions. Clearly, if deployed in a dialogic mode, Western theory may prove relevant and illuminating to critical studies of Chinese films. In terms of the dialogic mode of cross-cultural analysis, therefore, the issue is not that Western theory cannot be applied, but that it should not be applied or imposed unilaterally so as to dominate or domesticate an alien cultural text.

A cautionary remark here should be acceptable to critics of various theoretical persuasions. Even Chris Berry argued that "it would be imperialist to impose psychoanalytic theory on non-Western culture as an objective master-code that could be applied *tout court* without taking into account cultural difference" (1995b, 82). At the same time, however, he is all in favor of using Western theory as long as "opening up the frame of reference to make cultural difference present also opens up a reciprocal relation (or, to use psychoanalytic discourse, a counter-transference) that recasts assumptions of universality as culturally and historically specific and points to lacunae and new directions" (1995b, 82). In his psychoanalytic reading of *A Girl from Hunan* and *Red Sorghum*, Berry contextualizes these films in the Chinese categories of genres and themes on the one hand and attempts, on the other, to correct Yuejin Wang's hypothesis on the autonomous female subject and the prevailing maternal discourse in Chinese culture. Although Berry has "argued for a decentering of Mulvey's model of the libidinally engaged sovereign male subject as [E]urocentric and cognate with the structures of industrial capitalism," he still admits that a revisionist notion of patriarchy itself as "fractured," "malleable and polymorphous" is not good news for feminist criticism (1995b, 98).[13] In the spirit of "reciprocity," Berry ends his essay with this diagnosis of a lacuna in psychoanalytic theory: "If acknowl-edgement [of castration] is not enough, does psychoanalysis as it currently exists provide us with useful theories and models to build upon these moments of resistant empathy? I doubt it, and here, I believe, we have reached the limits of the usefulness of psychoanalysis in either a Western or a non-Western context" (1995b, 101).

If Berry represents an effort to advance the dialogic mode of cross-cultural analysis from the standpoint of Western theory, Mary Ann Farquhar's "The 'Hidden' Gender in *Yellow Earth*" (1992) points to the same effort from the other direction. By way of a strategic "reaffiliation" with Chinese culture, Farquhar in a sense begins where Esther Yau leaves off in her evocation of the Daoist concepts of emptiness and silence as hidden meaning in *Yellow Earth*. "In Daoist philosophy," Farquhar explains, "'nothingness' (*wu*) gives birth to the world through 'primitive breath' (*qi*) which forms the two principles yin and yang, the three sources, heaven, earth and man, the four seasons and so on" (p. 162). From this Chinese perspective, Farquhar's "Daoist reading of *Yellow Earth* gives a meaning that is seen and felt directly, a meaning beyond the images and words. . . . Minimalized tone, colour and composition are reminiscent of the restraint of classical Chinese painting. Songs and silence overlay the imagery and evoke the lyricism and elusiveness of traditional Chinese poetry" (p. 14). In Farquhar's 1994 piece with Berry, *Yellow Earth* is further analyzed in terms such as brushwork, ink, and composition, with reference to the so-called "Chang'an school" of

---

[13] Berry commits at least three obvious errors in this essay. First, of his three examples of "fifties films about the sufferings of women" (p. 101)—*The White-Haired Girl* (1950), *New Year's Sacrifice* (Zhufu, 1956), and *Li Shuangshuang* (1962)—the last does not belong to the 1950s. Second, Berry claims that in these early films "the women suffer, but the men . . . do not" (p. 101); yet the suicide of Xier's father (is he necessarily a "patriarchal" figure in Berry's scheme?) at the beginning of *The White-Haired Girl* is meant to end his suffering. This kind of intentional disregard of textual evidence for the purpose of his own theorization makes Berry's claims extremely unconvincing. Third, Berry mistakes Wang's essay on *Red Sorghum* (which I summarized earlier) for a discussion of *Li Shuangshuang*, a film he himself analyzed in terms of the viewing subject (p. 103). Does Berry's Freudian slip here reveal his unconscious desire to possess or appropriate Wang's argument as his own psychoanalytic hypothesis?

regional painting as exemplified by Fang Jizhong's works of the Shaanbei plateau in ink and wash (*shuimo*) (pp. 84–100).

While the chasm between Berry's psychoanalytic criticism and Farquhar's China-centered exercise reveals the spectrum of dialogic modes of cross-cultural analysis, the fact that both successfully collaborated on Chinese film studies sends a positive signal to a field marked by multidisciplinary approaches (see chapter 3). As we have seen, the decentering process and the subsequent restructuring of many disciplines in Western academia have empowered scholars to reposition themselves. For one more example, I turn to two versions of Esther Yau's essay on the cinematic configuration of non-Han women to explain the subtleties of repositioning in cross-cultural analysis.

Yau's "Is China the End of Hermeneutics? Or, Political and Cultural Usage of Non-Han Women in Mainland Chinese Films" was first published in *Discourse* (1989), but it had been thoroughly revised before it was anthologized in *Multiple Voices in Feminist Film Criticism* (1994), edited by Diane Carson and her associates. The first part of the title is a quotation from Barthes's 1975 reflection on the Cultural Revolution, in which he feels that China has defeated the Western hermeneutic system and drifted away from its sphere of knowledge. Sure enough, Barthes figures prominently in Yau's 1989 version, which opens with his long quotation—along with another from Zhang Nuanxin, the woman director of *Sacrificed Youth*, the film under discussion—and Yau's description of the then Western gaze on Red China. According to Yau, her essay "is introverted at first, as this writer, a Han Chinese woman, attempts to come to grips with Chinese racism . . . and the country's obsession with success in the world's power competition" (1989b, 116). In her 1994 version, the two opening long quotations have disappeared, Barthes is relegated to a footnote, and Yau's presence as an outspoken critic is masked by an impersonal voice: "[T]he purpose is to critique the appropriation and subjugation of minority cultures within the national boundary" (1994b, 281).

A similar revision occurs in Yau's concluding remarks. In the 1989 version, she first acknowledges "the slippery nature of inter-cultural representations" suggested by Barthes's reading of the Chinese bodies, Zhang Nuanxin's self-understanding, and Yau's own "problematic silence about the non-Han peoples' historical experiences," and then speculates that "hermeneutics and ethnography in many ways are complicit in their rhetorical violations towards the object(!) of study"—the non-Han women, to be exact (1989b, 135). This has been cut in the 1994 version, which, however, ends on an equally enigmatic note:

> When the relationship of domination and subordination remains unchanged, a better knowledge of the Other can become a form of rhetorical violation toward the Other viewed as an object of study. Thus, there is no consolation except that which is found in self-critical silence. But a silence as refusal to colonize and to be colonized is very different when advanced forms of colonial discourse hardly pause in their benign global advancements in knowledge making. (1994b, 291)

What Yau tries to articulate is that her self-critical silence is different from the silence of the non-Han women she analyzes. Far from her earlier evocation of "silence" in Daoist philosophy, her silence here is invested with ideological significance. With a self-critical gesture, Yau acknowledges her own ironic position as a critic—very much as Spivak does hers—in cross-cultural and intra-cultural representations, a field marked by imbalance of power and uneven developments.[14]

While my discussion of the two versions of Yau's study anticipates issues of nationhood and ethnicity examined in chapter 5, I end this chapter by returning to the new paradigm of dialogism and polyphony in cross-cultural analysis. Indeed, the term "cross-cultural" itself implies a real or imagined boundary line on either side of which critics must negotiate their own positions vis-à-vis other discourses and practices. Through the processes of dialogue, negotiation, self-positioning, and self-fashioning, we can arrive at a new stage of cross-cultural analysis, a stage where Western and non-Western texts may speak to each other as equals, and where scholars may come to better understand not only other cultures but ultimately their own as well.

In conclusion, I believe that cross-cultural analysis stands to benefit from what Clifford calls the new cultural concepts of *writing* ("seen as interactive, open-ended, and processual") as well as *travel* ("practices of crossing and interaction" that rank migrancy over "dwelling," "routes" over "roots") (1997, 3), and—I would add—performance over essence. For Clifford, the new conceptualization of travel naturally results in the increasing importance of "translocal culture" (not global and universal)

---

[14] For an analysis of Yau's shifting positions, see Donald 1995, 332–8.

and "contact" over old terms such as "'acculturation' (with its overly linear trajectory: from culture A to culture B) or 'syncretism' (with its image of two clear systems overlaid)" (1997, 7). What is more, there would be little room for Eurocentrism in this new conceptual space (1997, 7):

> The new paradigms begin with historical contact, with entanglement at intersecting regional, national, and transnational levels. Contact approaches presuppose not sociocultural wholes subsequently brought into relationship, but rather systems already constituted relationally, entering new relations through historical process of displacement.

Clifford's repeated emphasis on the "historical" is crucial to the new paradigms. In Part Two of this book, I investigate the complicated ways different genres of Chinese cinema—the ethnic minority film, the war film, ethnographic cinema, urban cinema, nostalgia cinema—project and problematize historical entanglements, displacements, and reinscriptions of Chinese experiences, all at their intersecting local, regional, national, and transnational levels.

Part II

Cinematic Reconfigurations: Nation, Culture, Agency

From "Minority Film" to "Minority Discourse": Negotiating Nationhood, Ethnicity, and History

> The marginal or "minority" is not the space of a celebratory, or utopian, self-marginalization. It is a much more substantial intervention into those justifications of modernity—progress, homogeneity, cultural organicism, the deep nation, the long past—that rationalize the authoritarian, "normalizing" tendencies within cultures in the name of the national interest or the ethnic prerogative.
>
> Homi Bhabha, *Nation and Narration*

Over the past two decades, cultural critics have returned to the relationship between nationhood and ethnicity with a renewed sense of urgency. This has been in part to critique the established paradigms and *epistemes* (such as the "center-periphery" and the "majority-minority") and, in part, to reconfigure geopolitical and geocultural space in the contemporary world. In this chapter I investigate how a set of critical categories—ethnicity, race, nation-state—as well as their related terms, such as nation-people, nationalism, patriotism, state discourse, cultural hegemony, and subjectivity, functions in Chinese cinema. Proceeding from the "minority film" (*shaoshu minzu dianying*) as a special genre in mainland China to "minority discourse" in New Chinese Cinema,[1] I demonstrate that the categories of nation and ethnicity have been contested in Chinese cinema from the early 1920s to the present. I differentiate two levels of contestation here: filmic discourse (film narrative and narration) and critical discourse (film theory and criticism). I begin with the second level to identify crucial issues (Section I). I then

---

[1] In the system of classification used in mainland China, "minority film" is a special genre of feature films. Other genres under feature films include comedy, film adaptation, historical drama, and revolutionary war; parallel to features are cartoons, films of stage performances, news reels, films of science and education, and sometimes children's features (see Chen Huangmei 1989).

151

return to the first level by reading minority films that illuminate these issues (Section II). Later I take up the war-film genre and examine the ways it is split into two "subgenres." In one subgenre, the mainstream or "leitmotif" (*zhuxuanlü*) films have continued to champion the ideology of the nation-state; in the other, a persistent minority discourse intervenes, interrogating and challenging the hegemony of state nationalism (Section III). Finally, I end the chapter with reflections on cultural nationalism and transnational cultural politics in a world increasingly defined by its multifaceted, hyphenated existence (Section IV).

I

Theoretical Excursions: Race or Ethnicity?

In 1992 Chris Berry published an article in which he equated *minzu*, an ambiguous Chinese term, with "race," an extremely loaded English term. By insisting on equivalents such as "race characteristics" for *minzu tedian*, "race form" for *minzu xingshi*, "race-ization" for *minzuhua*, "race color" for *minzu fengge*, and "racial minority" for *shaoshu minzu*, Berry attempted a deconstructive reading of *minzu* that has resulted in, unfortunately, not so much a clarification as a confusion of several distinct categories in Chinese film studies. While Berry is certainly correct in identifying sinocentrism, which he would rather term "race-centrism," in post-1949 Chinese film, what he sees as "race-ization" (1992, 47)—or "sinification" used elsewhere by Paul Clark (1987a, 69)—refers to, I contend, a politically motivated process of cultural production.[2] This cultural production engenders not just a unified discourse of solidarity among the fifty-six "ethnic minorities" (*shaoshu minzu*) in China, but also an ambivalent filmic discourse on which the dialectic of Self and Other is inevitably predicated.

From the perspective of ambivalent filmic discourse in contemporary China, Berry's formulation is problematic. His indiscriminate use of "race" obscures the difference between "race" and "ethnicity" on the one hand and, on the other, conflates the "state discourse" (which legitimates the Han Chinese cultural hegemony over ethnic minorities)

---

[2] However, "sinification" in Clark's somewhat ambiguous usage (as both *minzuhua* and *guoyouhua*) differs considerably from "sinicization" (*hanhua*) in anthropological and historical literature, a term describing "acculturation to Chinese culture or assimilation by it" (Crossley 1990, 2–5).

and the "politics of nationalism" in Chinese film (which has strategically drawn on minority cultures in the formation of the "Chinese characteristics" [*minzu tedian*]). Consequently, Berry locates in recent Chinese films a fundamental challenge to the discourse of race and "race-ization," yet altogether neglects the possibility that some of these films might have unknowingly reinforced the Han cultural hegemony in their effort to challenge the state discourse.

Before discussing specific representations of ethnic minorities in Chinese cinema, I will review a set of definitions of ethnicity, race, and nation-state in the fields of social sciences as well as literary and cultural studies. Thomas Herberer, for instance, asserts that "China is a multinational state formed from the territorial expansion of the largest nationality (Han) and from a fusion between the Han and different peoples over the course of history" (1989, 10). According to Herberer, the term "minority" in China embraces a group of non-Han people who share distinct characteristics of race, language, religion, customs, morals, traditions, dress, social organization, and so forth (1989, 7; see also Mackerras 1994, 3–45). While Herberer notes that the Chinese language never distinguishes among peoples, nation, nationality, and *ethnos*—all of them lumped together under a single term, *minzu*—he refuses to collapse them into the English term "race."

My objection to equating *minzu* with "race" should not be taken to mean that racial discourse does not exist in modern China. In fact, it has been studied by Frank Dikötter, who argues, among other things, that there were no pervasive differences between the Han Chinese and the Manchus with respect to racial perceptions of outgroups (such as Europeans or Africans). Dikötter's belief in the fundamental similarity among Chinese nationalities in their attitudes toward other races leads him to conclude: "The phenotype of most minorities was not significantly at variance with that of the Han Chinese: there was a physical continuity that precluded the elaboration of racial theories" (1992, x).[3] Based on this conviction, he does not treat inter-ethnic issues in his study.

---

[3] However, as Dikötter later points out, the concept of "race" (as in *zhongzu* or *renzhong*) was instrumental to the discursive formation of nationalism and national identity in modern China, although he does not want to see "a variability of racial narratives . . . be reduced to a single model called 'Chinese racism'" (1994, 411).

The preference of "ethnicity" over "race" as an equivalent of *minzu* in Chinese studies, however, does not deny the usefulness of "race" as a category in Chinese film studies. But we would do better to recognize rather than erase differences in critical categories as they have evolved *historically* in literary and cultural studies.

In the entry on "race" in *Critical Terms for Literary Study*, Kwame Anthony Appiah draws attention to a shocking discovery: "that there is a fairly wide-spread consensus in the sciences of biology and anthropology that the word 'race,' at least as it is used in most unscientific discussions, refers to nothing that science should recognize as real" (Lentricchia and McLaughlin 1990, 277). This discovery is shocking in that references to "race" as a concept of biological heredity have been made in the West historically with such frequency that "race" as a category seems to have been taken for granted, most notably in everyday stereotypes of other peoples, but increasingly in literary scholarship as well. One famous example is Hippolyte-Adolphe Taine's introduction to his *History of English Literature*, which posits "race," "epoch" (or "moment"), and "surroundings" (or "milieu") as three determining factors in the con-stitution of a national literature. Not surprisingly, Chinese literary critics enthusiastically embraced Taine's positivist theory in the 1920s in an attempt to build a national literature in modern China. For that reason it must have exerted a considerable if indirect impact on the subsequent conceptualization of Chinese "national cinema" (*guopian*) in the 1930s.[4] If in the concept of race one can locate a modern understanding of what it is to be a people, then this understanding is intertwined with further understandings of a people as a nation and of the role of culture in the life of nations. In Appiah's words, "the nation is the key middle term in understanding the relations between the concept of race and the idea of literature" (Lentricchia and McLaughlin 1990, 282).

As early as 1882, Ernest Renan pointed out the grave mistake in which "race is confused with nation" (Bhabha 1990, 8). After rejecting one by one a list of "scientific" or "naturalist" categories—race, language, material interest, religious affinities, geography, and military necessity—as inadequate for the creation of a nation, Renan envisions the nation instead as "a soul, a spiritual principle," composed of a rich legacy of

---

[4] See Mao Dun 1979, 187. For the slogan "reviving national films" endorsed by Luo Mingyou, head of Lianhua Film, in December 1929, see Cheng et al. 1981, 1: 148. For modern Chinese literature, see Y. Zhang 1997.

memories of a shared past and a present will to perpetuate the value of the heritage. "A nation is therefore a large-scale solidarity," Renan claimed, a solidarity that transcends the boundaries of race, language, and territory (Bhabha 1990, 19).

Yet how does the will to nationhood articulate itself? In response, Homi Bhabha formulates a theory of "nation as narration"—nation as inscribed in and disseminated through a variety of narratives and discourses. In this light, the category of people (or nation-people) is constructed by means of double-coding: people as "pedagogical objects" in the state discourse (the nation's self-generation in and through its people) and as the "performative subject" that splits Nation into "It/Self," and re-presents it as "a space that is *internally* marked by cultural difference and the heterogeneous histories of contending peoples, antagonistic authorities, and tense cultural locations" (1990, 299). From the perspective of such cultural difference, Renan's vision of the nation as a large-scale solidarity is idealistic and ultimately untenable. On the contrary, Bhabha contends, "The 'locality' of national culture is neither unified nor unitary in relation to itself, nor must it be seen simply as 'other' in relation to what is outside or beyond it" (1990, 4).

Bhabha's speculation on the heterogeneity of national culture dovetails with Prasenjit Duara's deconstructive reading of the Chinese nation in the modern era. Rather than entertaining an accepted view of "the nation as a whole imagining itself to be the unified subject of history," Duara proposes "instead that we view national identity as founded upon fluid relationships" (1993, 1–8). This more flexible position enables him to redefine nationalism as "more appropriately a relationship between a constantly changing Self and Other" (1993, 9). By analyzing what he calls "discursive meaning" and "symbolic meaning" of the nation, Duara concludes with a picture of the Chinese nation as consisting of hard and soft boundaries identifiable on multiple levels—not just the boundaries between ethnic groups, but boundaries between dialects, regions, religions, means of subsistence, and so on.

Bhabha's and Duara's emphasis on *fluid* relations and boundaries in conceptualizing the nation brings us to a similar emphasis in Werner Sollors' definition of "ethnicity." Namely, ethnicity "refers not to a thing-in-itself but to a relationship" (Lentricchia and McLaughlin 1990,

288).[5] Just as the Greek word *ethnos* contains an ambivalence between the inclusive meaning, "people in general," and the dissociative meaning, "other people" (say, "non-Jews" or "non-Christians"), the present meaning of ethnicity carries a sense of "contrast" or "boundary" (Lentricchia and McLaughlin 1990, 288, 299; see also Hutchinson and Smith 1996, 4–5). Representations of ethnicity, therefore, usually involve an impressive array of boundary-constructing devices that tend to stereotype other people, evoking images of the Other only to distance or differentiate it.

Similar to the Greek *ethnos*, *min* in the Chinese term *minzu* refers to "the common people, people at large," while *zu* refers to something as small as a group of people with an acquired sense of kinship or as large as an established, historical people (especially of the Northeast). In this connection, *zu* comes close to what John Hutchinson and Anthony Smith delineate as "ethnie": "a named human population with myths of common ancestry, shared historical memories, one or more elements of common culture, a link with a homeland and a sense of solidarity among at least some of its members" (1996, 6). In the Chinese case, *minzu* was coined around 1895 as the Chinese equivalent of the Japanese neologism *minzoku*, and the new term soon became a powerful concept, frequently used to indicate majority peoples (that is, the Han Chinese) rather than minority peoples (that is, *shaoshu minzu*, a derivative term in subsequent usage). As Pamela Kyle Crossley explains, the Chinese *minzu* is closest to the Russian *narod* (people, nation), with an emphasis upon "popular" (*narodni*) and "nationality" (*narodnost*) (1990, 19–20). Nationhood and ethnicity are thus deeply ingrained and intertwined in the Chinese term *minzu*.

It should be evident by now that in Chinese studies, the term "ethnicity" is less problematic than "race" in dealing with majority (Han)/minority relationships. I follow the same practice in this book, leaving the question of "race" in Chinese cinema for further study. More specifically, I proceed from the "nation"—what Appiah sees as the key middle term—and investigate the historical manifestations of the intricate relationship between nationhood and ethnicity in Chinese cinema. Given the recent "slow contradictory movement from 'nationalism' to 'ethnicity' as a source of identities" (Hall 1987, 46), we might find

---

[5] Sollors elsewhere considers race to be "merely one aspect of ethnicity" (1986, 36).

ethnicity to be a concept as valid—if not more so—as nationalism for the study of contemporary Chinese cinema, insofar as ethnicity is conceived of as a relational (fluid) rather than essentialized (fixed) term. Rey Chow's argument regarding ethnicity in China studies is relevant at this juncture:

> [T]he careful study of texts and media becomes, once again, imperative, even as such study is now ineluctably refracted by the awareness of the unfinished and untotalizable workings of ethnicity. The study of specific texts and media, be they fictional, theoretical, or historical, is now indispensable precisely as a way of charting the myriad ascriptions of ethnicity, together with the cultural, political, and disciplinary purposes to which such ascriptions have typically been put. (1998c, 24)

Thematic Variations: Nationhood and Ethnicity in Chinese Cinema, 1900s–1940s

Two noteworthy events coincided in 1895: the invention of cinema in France and the defeat of China in the first Sino-Japanese war. Since that year, in which the first appearance of *minzu* was detected, "nationalism" (or *minzu zhuyi* in Chinese, literally "ideology of the nation") has become one of the central issues in the political and intellectual history of modern China (Crossley 1990, 19; Townsend 1996). Even at the level of the political unconscious, the question of nationhood never failed to engage the Chinese film circle. This is first of all evident in the name "Western shadowplay" (*xiyang yingxi*) given to movies shown as early as August 1896 in Shanghai's Xu Garden. Arguably, the shadowplay as a traditional Chinese form of entertainment might promise—at least to Chinese scholars initially—some kind of "Chinese" contribution to film as an international art form. Significantly, the first Chinese film, *Conquering Jun Mountain* (Ding Junshan, 1905 and produced by Ren Fengtai in Beijing), was of a Beijing opera performed by the famous actor Tan Xinpei. One may suspect that at the beginning stage of Chinese cinema, an effort had already been made to impose a certain "Chineseness" (here embodied in Beijing opera) on film, which is after all an imported Western technology, despite the phantom "shadows" attached to its Chinese names—first *yingxi* (shadowplay) and then *dianying* (electric shadows).

The assertion of Chineseness as a marker of national identity in the subsequent development of Chinese cinema was made in many different ways. It ranged from the subtle cinematic treatment of ethical problems in family dramas to the radical political protest against the colonialist and imperialist presence in China. For example, we can detect in Zheng Zhengqiu's films of the 1920s an allegorical structure whereby family dramas played out the overarching theme of "national salvation" (*minzu zijiu*). And one can discern in Zhang Shichuan's "escapist" films of romance (also known as Mandarin Ducks and Butterflies stories) and swordsmanship (*wuxia* or knight-errantry) in the same period a fundamental concern with the fate of the nation as a whole (Ma Junxiang 1993). In the political arena, "progressive" (*jinbu*) or "liberal-minded" Chinese film people worked together in the summer of 1932 to defeat the American initiative to build an "Oriental Hollywood" in Shanghai; in June 1936 they protested against the public screening in Shanghai's International Settlement of *The New Land* (Xintu, 1937), a colonialist or "fascist" film coproduced by Japan and Nazi Germany, which called for Japanese nationals to emigrate to Manchuria, their newly conquered territory (Cheng et al. 1981, 1: 187–90, 507–9; Xiao 1997).

Generally speaking, political nationalism was articulated more explicitly in leftist films of the 1930s, which prospered upon growing urban patriotism in the wake of the Japanese invasion of Manchuria in September 1931 and the Japanese attack on Shanghai in January 1932. Films such as *Three Modern Women, Little Toys, Big Road*, and *Children of a Troubled Time* (Fengyu ernü, 1935) reenact in graphic detail the trauma of the Japanese invasions. Needless to say, this type of nationalism has very little to do with the discourse of race internal to the Chinese nation. Rather, it depends on a conceptualization of nationhood that transcends economic, ideological, and political differences. Historically, nationalism in leftist film marks the juncture where Chinese cinema gradually turned from earlier popular genres of romance, swordsmanship, and immortals/ghosts (*shengui*) to the existential crises in modern China (such as draught, flood, famine, war, and so on), although soft-core entertainment films continued to claim their share of the market.[6] When the slogan "cinema of national defense" (*guofang dianying*) was issued in 1936, a year before the full-scale second Sino-Japanese War broke out, there seemed

---

[6] One particular type of entertainment film in the early 1930s was the so-called "soft film" (*ruanxing dianying*), promoted by people like Huang Jiamo and Liu Na'ou, the latter assassinated in 1940 because of his involvement with the pro-Japanese government. For more information, see Chen Bo 1993, 142–4; Luo Yijun 1992, 1: 256–84.

to be no holding back the ever-growing patriotic spirit (Zhongguo shehui kexue yuan 1982, 1: 188-90, 197–201).

During wartime (1937–45), even the Nationalist government sponsored the production of patriotic films. For instance, *Defending Our Land* (Baowei women de tudi, 1938) and *Eight Hundred Heroic Soldiers* (Babai zhuangshi, 1938) were completed in ten months in Wuhan before the city was lost to the Japanese. In the immediate post-war period, it was the evocation of war memories that made two epic films achieve spectacular box-office success: *Spring River Flows East* (Yijiang chushui xiangdong liu, 1947) and *Eight Thousand Li of Clouds and Moon* (Baqianli lu yun he yue, 1947).[7] The nationhood as projected in these films testifies to Renan's observation: "indeed, suffering in common unifies more than joy does. Where national memories are concerned, griefs are of more value than triumphs, for they impose duties, and require a common effort" (Bhabha 1990, 19).

It must be pointed out that the Nationalist government did have its own versions of nationhood to promote, especially in the Nanjing decade (1927–37), although this fact has been largely ignored by the mainland official history of Chinese cinema and is only now being slowly recognized by historians of modern China. Through its own organizations, such as the National Film Censorship Committee established in 1931, the Nationalist government sought to incorporate filmmaking in its nation-building project. Specifically, the government promoted the following as crucial elements of a modern nation: Mandarin as a unified *guoyu* or "national language" (it tried to curtail if not terminate the production of Cantonese-dialect films in southern China); a rational mind (it banned films with explicit superstitious and religious themes); a healthy body (it promoted athletic looks in a new generation of film stars); and neo-Confucian ethics (it frequently ordered sex scenes cut before the films' release).[8] What is historically interesting— and perhaps ironic as well—is that some of the Nationalist agendas on film censorship were enthusiastically endorsed by "progressive" film people, some of them later classified as "leftist." However, this example

---

[7] *Spring River Flows East* was reportedly shown for over three consecutive months and sold 712,874 tickets (Cheng et al. 1981, 2: 222).

[8] The films banned by the Nationalist censors during the period also include Hollywood productions such as *The Ten Commandments* (1923) for allegedly being "superstitious,"and *Top Hat* (1935) for being "sexy" (Xiao 1999).

of common agendas among pro-Nationalist and "progressive" film people illustrates that nationalism, if understood in a broader sense, might become a unifying force in itself, especially at a time when the national existence is perceived to be in jeopardy. This is particularly clear in *Storm on the Border* (Saishang fengyun, 1940), a feature film produced by the Nationalist-controlled China Film Studio (Zhongguo dianying zhipian-chang) in Chongqing. The story of an intricate love-triangle between Mongolians and Han youths and how they eventually overcame ethnic differences in their common fight against Japanese spies, *Storm on the Border* actually foreshadowed some of the recurrent themes (like ethnic solidarity) in later minority films (Cheng et al. 1981, 2: 53–5).

Now, the "nation" in the discourse of nationalism in Chinese cinema could be decoded more accurately. Insofar as film is concerned, it is "nationhood" as constituted by "nation-people" (*minzu*) that was the major concern from the 1920s to the 1940s. As envisioned by film productions and film criticism of this period, a modern nation depends on a strong people who can resist not only foreign military forces but also the cultural infiltration of the West. In the post-1949 Communist era, nevertheless, the idea of "nationhood" had more and more to do with the "nation-state" (*guojia*), which, through its ideological state apparatuses (Althusser 1971, 127–86), brought in "ethnicity" as one of the key categories in its dual project of state-building and nation-building. As James Townsend observes, "State nationalism requires 'nation-building'; creation of a new Chinese nation that incorporates all of its nationalities; concentration of political loyalty on the state; and repudiation of the idea that Chinese history and culture are purely a Han affair" (1996, 18). One may postulate that a nation as envisioned by Renan had finally emerged in socialist China—a nation as "a large scale of solidarity, constituted by the feeling of the sacrifices that one has made in the past and of those that one is prepared to make in the future" (Bhabha 1990, 19). It is in view of precisely such "solidarity" achieved through shared experiences that the minority film was gradually instituted as a unique Chinese film genre in the late 1950s.

II

Minority Films: Homage to the Nation-State, 1950s–1960s

About twenty minority films were produced in the 1950s. The early 1960s saw rapid growth of this new genre, and twenty more minority films were made in a matter of four years (Chen Huangmei 1989, 1: 154–5, 263–9). One of the most popular minority films during this period was *Third Sister Liu* (Liu sanjie, 1960), a musical about a legendary singer of Zhuang minority origin. Set in the Li River area in Guilin, a famous scenic region in southern China, the film invites the audience to participate in an imaginary tour and admire the spectacular beauty of the exotic location [Illustration 13].

13. *Third Sister Liu* (1960): Folk songs and ethnic solidarity

After the initial credits—punctuated by distinctive regional folk music—the film displays in a series of long and medium shots the unique Guilin landscape: the mountain peaks are half-concealed by clouds and mist, the water of the Li River reflects the distant mountains, and green trees and flowering shrubs line the river banks. In a visual style that closely resembles traditional Chinese ink-and-wash painting, this cinematic rendition of the Guilin landscape is accompanied by an off-screen song that fills the soundtrack:

> Cliff flowers spread fragrance down the foot of the hill,
> The river sends its coolness up the bridge.
> Whatever resentment in the mind suppressed
> Erupts like fire in songs from the breast.

For more than four minutes, the images on screen highlight, elaborate, and divert from the song lyrics, and feature among others an arched stone bridge, a tiny bird chirping in its nest, the river seen through the foliage, white birds flying across the screen, a large sailboat being dragged upstream, and an old fisherman and his son Ah Niu (Liu Shilong) in their fishing boat. The woman singer finally appears on a raft with a pole, her face in close-up, and her identity revealed to be Third Sister Liu (Huang Wanqiu), a folk singer famous in the region.

Even in this opening sequence, a noticeable discrepancy between the beautiful images and the sad story narrated in Liu's lyrics slowly emerges. The landlord has driven Third Sister Liu out of her native mountain village, but she survives an attempted murder and drifts to this riverside village. Later, she is welcomed by the villagers and stays with the old fisherman's family. Through her songs she unites the poor in their ongoing struggles against the local landlord, Mo Huairen (literally, "possessing no benevolence"), and together they win a song competition over Mo's hired team of literati. In desperation, Mo has Liu kidnapped and imprisoned in his estate, but Ah Niu and Mo's sympathetic maid servants help her escape in the night. A prolonged chase in the dark follows. The river echoes with song, but none of the singers Mo captures turns out to be Third Sister Liu. As dawn breaks, Liu and Ah Niu are seen together, cheerfully singing love songs to each other under a giant tree on the riverside. Liu expresses her love for Ah Niu by throwing him her hand-made embroidered ball. "Let's pledge our love for one hundred years," they sing. The film ends with the two rowing a small boat down the river, gradually disappearing into the landscape (Loh 1984).

With its picturesque scenery and folk music, *Third Sister Liu* was praised as exemplifying the achievements of "national style" (*minzu fengge*) or "national form" (*minzu xingshi*) in post-1949 Chinese cinema

(Lin Niantong 1985). In his commentary on the film, Paul Clark finds it paradoxical that "one of the most effective ways to make films with 'Chinese' style was to go to the most 'foreign' cultural areas in the nation" (1987b, 25). To be sure, going to the "alien" and "exotic" minority regions did not entail an equal distribution of power in the symbolic structure. On the contrary, the outcome of locating a national style in ethnic cultural practices was never a restoration of minority cultures to a majority status, but always a legitimation of minority peoples as part of the solidarity of the Chinese nation. In the increasingly politicized cultural climate of the 1950s and 1960s—which translated into less artistic freedom for Chinese filmmakers—minority films functioned not so much as coveted exotica to satisfy film audiences' desire for the foreign[9] as an effective means by which the nation-state objectified minorities through stereotypes and co-opted them in the construction of a socialist China.

Objectification and co-optation are better illustrated in *Five Golden Flowers* (Wuduo jinhua, 1959) [Illustration 14], set in the Bai region of Dali in Yunnan and featuring Yang Likun, a famous dancer of Yi minority origin. In this film, Ah Peng (Mo Xingjiang), a Bai youth from Jianchuang, travels through Cangshan and Erhai looking for his beloved Golden Flower, whom he met the year before and with whom he exchanged a love token. But "Golden Flower" turns out to be a popular name in the area, and it is not until Ah Peng has gone through disheartening but comic situations with four other Golden Flowers that his real Golden Flower (Yang Likun), who serves as deputy director of the People's Commune, is united with him in their designated place, Butterfly Pond.

---

[9] Some of Clark's claims with regard to minority films (1987b, 15–6) need more evidence to sustain themselves. First, his thesis that "the tendency to regard films as a source of exotic, usually foreign, images has remained strong," from the first screening of the Lumière brothers' reel in 1896 down to the 1980s, overlooks the entire legacy of mainstream Chinese cinema (especially leftist film of the 1930s and 1940s and socialist realism of the 1950s and 1960s), whose aim was not only to reflect but also to intervene in sociopolitical realities. Second, Clark's remark that "After 1949, with fewer, mostly Soviet, foreign films on Chinese screens, the search for the exotic led Chinese filmmakers and filmgoers to the most non-Chinese parts" also fails to account for the complicity of minority films in the state's project of cultural hegemony.

14. *Five Golden Flowers* (1959): A communal celebration of romantic love

Typical of the genre, minority folk are presented as fond of song and dance, colorfully dressed, decorated with flashy ornaments, and engaged in love affairs. Folk music is an indispensable part of minority films, and the ending of *Five Golden Flowers* is a good example of this. Released from her duty as deputy director, Yang Likun sits by Butterfly Pond and sings of a woman in love waiting for her man. As expected, Ah Peng emerges on the other side of the pond. The lovers are reunited, and, holding their love token, Ah Peng's knife, they sing together. What makes the scene even more painterly is the reflection of the amorous couple in the water, their radiant images surrounded by colorful flowers. From behind the trees, their friends (including two Han cultural workers) watch the intimate exchange with pleasure. Enhancing the atmosphere of communal happiness, four other Golden Flowers and their lovers break into chorus and parade past in pairs. Together they seem to be celebrating not just the couple's reunion but all of their collective achievements, to which Ah Peng serves as witness throughout the film.

Bear in mind, though, that minority films celebrate cultural diversity at a superficial level only. All the display of solidarity and ethnic harmony is actually *staged* as a spectacle mostly for Han viewers, and there is an unmistakably Han-centered viewing position, visually as well as conceptually. Hence, in *Third Sister Liu*, the Zhuang are represented as being identical with the Han in that both of them were oppressed by landlords and both must be united in order to overcome their common class enemy. In *Five Golden Flowers*, minorities are shown as model workers, enthusiastically participating in the socialist reconstruction. This kind of ideological identification of ethnic minorities with the Han confirms both the necessity and the legitimacy of the state discourse in maintaining Han cultural hegemony.

Another example of how ethnic minorities are configured in terms of their alleged ideological identification with the majority Han is found in *Serfs* (Nongnu, 1963), a film about the exploitation of Tibetan (Zang) serfs by their ruthless clansmen and the suppression of the Tibetan uprising by the People's Liberation Army in the late 1950s. Near the end of the film, Jampa (Wangdui), a "mute" Tibetan serf whose life had been saved by a Han soldier in the mountains, returns to his local temple to expose the evil scheme of his master, Namchal, and the living Buddha Thubtan. Jampa is knocked down inside the temple, which is then set fire to cover up the conspiracy and to instigate anger at the Communist troops among a crowd of agitated Tibetans gathering outside. At this critical moment, Jampa emerges from the smoke-filled temple gate carrying a bundle of firearms. He stumbles down the steps, throws the weapons on the ground, and silently points his finger at his master.

The film then cuts to the room where Jampa convalesces in the care of Lamka (Baima Yangjie), his childhood girlfriend. Outside, a public meeting is underway, and slogans like "Long Live Chairman Mao!" are heard. Jampa and Lamka's faces are captured in shots and reverse shots. Lamka opens a window and tells Jampa, "We are liberated. . . . Jampa, please speak up." In response, Jampa sits up—"I'll speak. I've a lot to speak"—and, turning his head, directs his gaze to the portrait of Mao Zedong on the wall. "Chairman Mao . . . ," he slowly utters, seemingly heartfelt but patently scripted—by the Han filmmakers themselves, if not the censors. Jampa's words are accompanied by an audio-visual effect: a melodious song breaks out, and the screen fills with uplifting images of waterfalls, mountains, and clouds.

As Paul Pickowicz comments, "the use of an all-Tibetan cast, the decision to film on location and the care given to photography certainly contribute to [the film's] success. More important, *Serfs* goes much further than other films in detailing the daily humiliations suffered and endured by the common people" (1985, 126). Indeed, *Serfs* contains a distinct measure of realism absent in earlier minority films such as *Five Golden Flowers* and *Third Sister Liu*. However, in terms of ideological configuration and cultural politics, *Serfs* differs very little from other films in the genre, for cinematic representation in minority films works ultimately to contain the alien and potentially subversive elements in the frontier regions. Two other films in this genre further testify to this built-in ideological function. Both *Horseback Merchants Arrive in the Frontier Mountains* (Shanjian lingxiang mabang lai, 1954) and *Visitor on Ice Mountain* (Bingshan shangde laike, 1963) stage a complete victory of Communist soldiers, with the assistance of patriotic minorities, over armed foreign perpetrators in the frontier regions, the former in the Miao area of the Southwest and the latter in the Uygur or Uighur (Weiwuer) area of the Northwest.

The Han cultural hegemony that ensues from the state discourse thus reinforces the existing structure of power and knowledge; secure in the Han-centered position, minority films work symbolically as the *celestial eye* (namely, "I" the Han subject), placing remote alien territories and exotic cultural practices under constant surveillance. The bottom line in such cinematic representation is that the object (in this case ethnic minorities) would never become a full-fledged subject of knowledge. In other words, minorities rarely occupy the subject position in minority films. Instead of acting as agents of change in their own right, they are continually directed to pay homage to the nation-state.

These observations dovetail with Dru Gladney's recent study, which contends that "the objectified portrayal of minorities as exoticized, and even eroticized, is essential to the construction of the Han Chinese majority, the very formulation of the Chinese 'nation' itself" (1994, 94). Following Gladney, one may even speculate that the by-now mandatory staging of romanticized songs and eroticized dances in minority films for consumption mostly by the Han majority bears a "striking resemblance to the 'tribute' offerings of the ancient Chinese empires." Fixed in the state cultural machinery, minority films have in effect participated in a kind of "internal colonialism" and "internal Orientalism"—both proving to be effective discursive means to the establishment of the Han cultural hegemony (1994, 96, 98, 114).

Minority Discourse: Rethinking New Chinese Cinema

Inasmuch as majority/minority relations are concerned, the basic structure of power and knowledge remained unchanged in the mid-1980s, the period when New Chinese Cinema gradually took shape. Even though *Horse Thief*, a documentary-like avant-garde film that purportedly reveals the true Tibetan religious life, may differ radically from previous minority films in its deliberate avoidance of a clearly defined ideological message, there is still no denying that the viewing position is fundamentally Han-centered. In the "primitive" landscape of Tibet, enigmatic religious rituals (such as the sky burial and the ghost dance) are displayed one by one, while the Tibetan protagonist, Norbu (Tseshang Rigzin), a horse thief ostracized by his tribe and exiled to the mountains, is engaged in a fatal struggle for survival. Before a major snow storm arrives, Norbu sends his wife and their baby down the mountains, an act to redeem his sin of horse theft. The film ends with blood stains in the snow, indicating that Norbu has died in the snow-covered wilderness, forgotten altogether by his community.

For Wu Ziniu, an active fellow Fifth Generation director, *Horse Thief* and *On the Hunting Ground*, an earlier film about the equally enigmatic Mongolian hunting codes, depart from previous minority films in that their director, Tian Zhuangzhuang, insists on examining ethnic cultural life "on an equal basis" (*pingshi*). His attempt at "equality" is evidenced by the conspicuous absence of a leading Han character as omniscient narrator (the equivalent of the anthropological fieldworker) in these two films, an absence that seems to return to minority culture an ontological status separable from Han Chinese culture. Wu's contextualization of Tian's efforts in this direction thus highlights the questions of power and knowledge in cultural representation:

The Central Plain culture (*zhongyuan wenhua*) is extremely corrupt and decaying, and yet it has always adopted the policy of exclusion and assimilation vis-à-vis frontier cultures. But frontier cultures themselves are absolutely beyond assimilation. On the contrary, they have repeatedly challenged the Central Plain culture. We have always taken a condescending attitude toward, exoticized, and exhibited frontier cultures of ethnic minorities but have seldom paid attention to the essence of minority cultures. (Liu Weihong 1988, 105)

What is problematic with Tian's seemingly "non-condescending" attitude is that it results in a viewing experience that foregrounds extreme defamiliarization and thereby alienates the majority of his Han viewers. Compelled to defend his position, Tian quickly suspended his interest in ethnic minority cultures and reclaimed the centrality of his own subjectivity. When questioned about the "incomprehensibility" of the film, he unabashedly declared that *Horse Thief* was made for "audiences of the next century to watch" (Yang Ping 1991, 127). Needless to say, the next generation Tian had in mind would be Han rather than Tibetan viewers. Indeed, Tian even admits that *Horse Thief* reflects his "own view of life" in Han society and therefore has very little to do with what religion means to the Tibetan people (Semsel 1987, 132).

In *Sacrificed Youth* one encounters a similar concern with Han society over minority culture [Illustration 15]. During the Cultural Revolution, Li Chun (Li Fengxu), an urban Han girl, was sent to a remote mountain village in the Dai area, where she eventually regained her subjectivity through partial adaptation to the culture of the Other, symbolized by the Dai costumes. In a landscape scene, a group of beautiful Dai girls chase each other to a waterfall, throwing off their sarongs and swimming naked in the stream.[10] Viewing from a distance this Dai practice (in which naked contact with nature is renewed each day), Li Chun is stunned, for she was raised to be ashamed of her own body, not to mention her repressed sexuality. Over time, however, she transforms herself, putting on beautiful Dai costumes that accentuate her figure and, as her own voice-over reveals, learning to swim naked like the Dai girls.

---

[10] In an interview, Zhang Nuanxin admits that she had cut "a scene with the girls washing their hair instead of swimming, with no clothes on" (Semsel 1987, 126).

15. *Sacrificed Youth* (1985): The pleasure of being beautiful and feminine

Taken as a whole, *Sacrificed Youth* is less a film about the Dai people than a narrative about how a Han girl recovers her lost or repressed self. Throughout the film the Dai are presented as the exoticized and eroticized Other, against whom Li Chun redefines her subject position. The nostalgic evocation of Dai culture comes to an end when years later, returning from college in the city, Li Chun discovers that the entire Dai village has been wiped out in a massive landslide. The final scene—a barren landscape—symbolically captures the politics of inter-ethnic representation, for the Han girl remains the only survivor (and hence the sole legitimated subject of knowledge), whereas Dai culture as the Other, despite its idyllic scenery and its exotic customs, has to be wiped out entirely from the surface of the earth, left forever for the Han subject to recall and reconstruct from her fragmented memories.[11]

While criticizing *Sacrificed Youth* as showcasing "a rare bit of soft porn" in the mid-1980s, Gladney finds it noteworthy that the woman director altered the original story, in which the Han girl was sent to a non-minority rural area (1994, 105). Does this alteration automatically implicate the director in a "complicit" relationship with the state discourse, which champions Han cultural hegemony? If so, does the fact that the director is a woman contradict, complicate, or confirm Gladney's set-up of the following discursive parallels: "Minority is to the majority as female is to male, as 'Third' World to 'First,' and as subjectivized is to objectivized identity" (1994, 93)?[12]

The problem with Gladney's rather sweeping statement in this case had already been anticipated by James Clifford's critique of Edward Said's *Orientalism* (which no doubt influenced Gladney's choice of terms above): "Said's work frequently relapses into the essentializing modes it attacks and is ambivalently enmeshed in the totalizing habits of Western humanism." (1988, 271). In other words, what is absent in Said's work—and by extension in Gladney's study—is a "developed theory of culture as a differentiating and expressive ensemble rather than as simply hegemonic and disciplinary" (1988, 263).[13] Seen in this light, what is of equal importance to a study of nationhood and ethnicity—apart from discerning the political hierarchies in majority/minority representation—is a conceptualization of the hegemonic culture not as a self-stabilizing structure, but rather as negotiated, present processes whereby the geopolitical boundaries of centers and margins are periodically redrawn and the localized differences tactfully articulated.

---

[11] Esther Yau thus criticizes Zhang Nuanxin's ethnocentric practice in the film: "Such inability to perceive or act outside one's ideological inscription despite having gained insights from the Others underscores ethnocentrism as a stubborn blind spot of the mind that may generate colonizing moves in cross-cultural encounters" (1994b, 290).

[12] One may of course follow Gladney by arguing in general terms that *Sacrificed Youth* participates in the state discourse of "internal Orientalism"; but this argument alone does not account for the construction of a distinctively female voice in Zhang Nuanxin's film, a rare achievement in the post-Mao era.

[13] However, Gladney seems to have realized the problem at one point when he proposed that "Han-ness" in China be scrutinized in the same critical way as "whiteness" has been recently interrogated in the West (1994, 103). For a study of whiteness in connection with cinema, see Bernardi 1996.

To locate articulations of difference within the hegemonic culture of the nation, I find the concept "minority discourse" more useful than either the "minority film" or "ethnographic cinema" when dealing with New Chinese Cinema. Here I follow Bhabha's formulation. Bhabha's concept, however, should be distinguished from Abdul JanMohamed and David Lloyd's more general use of "minority discourse," which is defined as "a theoretical articulation of the political and cultural structures that connect different minority cultures in their subjugation and opposition to the dominant culture" (1990, ix). JanMohamed and Lloyd aim to construct a theoretical discourse to articulate the relations between various minority discourses already in circulation. Proceeding from this general definition, Rey Chow redefines modern Chinese literature as a "minority discourse" linked to other postcolonial national literatures, all of them being "victimized" and "suppressed" by "the hegemonic discourse of the West" (1993, 100–1). My problem with this more general use of "minority discourse" is that it does not advance our knowledge any further than a mere rephrasing of the already existing terms (such as the West versus the rest, or colonialism/imperialism versus native resistance). To venture on a more relevant topic, one may question whether a designation of Chinese leftist films of the 1930s as a minority discourse in Chow's sense—a body of work doubly victimized and suppressed by the hegemonic discourses of the West (Hollywood dominance) and of the Chinese regimes (the Nationalist and the Communist alike)—would help explain anything specific to the sociopolitical realities of modern China. Bhabha's notion of "minority discourse" as a localized tactic *within* the hegemonic culture, on the other hand, may explain how New Chinese Cinema could have achieved so much in the past two decades by negotiating its way through the fissures and cracks opened by the evolving discourse of the nation-state itself.

Admittedly, films such as *Horse Thief* and *Sacrificed Youth* may conform to ethnographic paradigms in that they usually end up legitimating the power and knowledge of the ethnographer (always a figure of the Han majority) rather than the alien (minority) culture investigated in the remote "jungle fields."[14] Nevertheless, what eventually distinguishes New Chinese Cinema since the mid-1980s is its profound complexity and ambivalence, which not only interrogates at a national

---

[14] Yau discusses "the ethnographic mode" in *Sacrificed Youth* and "Zhang Nuanxin's observation-participation techniques" (1994b, 285, 288).

level the grand myths perpetuated in previous films, but also problematizes at the local level its own position as a knowing subject, an often
individualized subject burdened with reassessing the culture of the nation
and rewriting its history.

Understood in this way, New Chinese Cinema may function as
what Bhabha calls "minority discourse," which emerges "from the
liminal movement of the culture of the nation—at once opened up and
held together," and which "acknowledges the status of national culture—
and the people—as a contentious, performative space of the perplexity of
living in the midst of the pedagogical representations of the fullness of
life" (1990, 305, 307). It is of crucial importance that a minority
discourse take a strategic position of marginality—a reconstructed
marginality that questions and challenges the centrality of the state
discourse. As Bhabha rightly argues,

> The marginal or "minority" is not the space of a celebratory, or utopian,
> self-marginalization. It is a much more substantial intervention into those
> justifications of modernity—progress, homogeneity, cultural organicism, the
> deep nation, the long past—that rationalize the authoritarian, "normalizing"
> tendencies within cultures in the name of the national interest or the ethnic
> prerogative. (1990, 4)

The Big Parade (Da yuebing, 1986) illustrates the workings of a
minority discourse in contemporary China. A film centered on the
military training in preparation for a parade in Beijing on the occasion of
the thirty-fifth anniversary of the People's Republic of China, *The Big
Parade* challenges yet explicitly celebrates the concept of nation in state
discourse. In the film, a team of army soldiers is transported to a remote,
deserted military airport to undergo a rigorous regimen of training.
Though entering the army from different family backgrounds and for
various personal reasons, the soldiers form an apparently inseparable unit,
tolerating unbearable summer heat and marching over a distance of 9,993
kilometers. Near the end of the film, the coach, Sun Fang (Sun Chun),
conducts a farewell ceremony in which those who are dismissed from the
team and those who will stay for the ultimate parade all sign their names
on a red flag. Ritualistically, the soldiers salute to the rising red flag. The
film then restages the spectacular parade in front of Tiananmen, which
Chen had shot on location. In slow motion, ranks of army, navy, air
force, and other soldiers march past, all perfectly synchronized, signifying

the glory, dignity, and pride of the new nation. Indeed, Renan's commentary on the nation-state seems an appropriate description here: "To have common glories in the past and to have a common will in the present; to have performed great deeds together, to wish to perform still more—these are the essential conditions for being a people" (Bhabha 1990, 19).

What is remarkable in *The Big Parade*, nonetheless, is that director Chen Kaige structures a subtext beneath the glorified surface of a national—indeed, nationalist—celebration, a subtext that comes to the fore if one disregards the rhetoric of the state discourse and follows instead the individual participants in the military training. One soldier suffers through a training session with a fever; another misses his mother's funeral to keep his position on the team; yet another questions the necessity of the unbearable, almost irrational reality of military life. By shifting voice-overs from one individual to another, Chen in effect constructs the people as the "performative subject," whose very act of performing in the state-sponsored events inevitably fragments the unified subjectivity (people as "pedagogic object"—the nation-people). *Big Parade* demonstrates that the spectacular display of conformity and discipline in the military parade in front of the square is nothing but a staged event (significantly, Chen originally planned a final shot of the empty training ground instead of the footage of the parade in front of Tiananmen), and that it is the individual soldiers—whose physical and emotional suffering is bracketed off or erased in the state discourse—who ultimately deserve close cinematic attention and empathy.

III

Marginality and Minority Discourse in the War Film

Chen Kaige's attempt at inscribing a minority discourse in New Chinese Cinema occurred earlier than *The Big Parade*. In *Yellow Earth*, he interrogates the myths of the Communist revolution by splitting the two formerly glorified images of the nation-people (namely, the peasant and the soldier) into what Bhabha calls "It/Self"—a fixed pedagogical object and a fluid performing subject. Whereas the figure of the Communist soldier has long been fixed in official representation as the agent of revolutionary change, in his performance in *Yellow Earth* Gu Qing is insufficient with words (that is, persuading peasants and collecting folk songs) and ultimately ineffective in action (bringing change to a poor, remote mountain village). Contrary to the plot of conventional liberation narratives like *The White-Haired Girl* (1950),[15] Gu fails to save the life of Cuiqiao (coded as the suffering peasant woman) and may fail again with Hanhan (coded as the endangered child), as suggested by the film's ambiguous ending—Gu's repeated emergence from the distant horizon. Similarly, whereas poor peasants are customarily imbued with innate or spontaneous class consciousness according to time-honored Communist rhetoric, *Yellow Earth* presents them as blinded by tradition and superstition, suspicious of new ideas, and resistant to any change.

If *Yellow Earth* experiments with conventionally acceptable positive figures in the Communist revolution, *One and Eight*, which like *Yellow Earth* features Zhang Yimou behind the camera, pushes the limits of acceptability even further by including negative characters long marginalized or suppressed in socialist-realist representation [Illustration 16]. Wang Jin (Tao Zeru), a Communist cadre wrongly accused of being a spy, is arrested and imprisoned together with bandits and army deserters. When the Communist escort team is surrounded by Japanese soldiers in a village, Wang persuades the security man Xu Zhi to let him and other prisoners fight against their common enemy. In an unexpected twist, the prisoners prove themselves to be valiant fighters, but the film ends on a rather ambivalent note. Retreating from the battlefield, a Chinese army nurse (the only female character in the film) is cornered by several Japanese soldiers. In the original version, she is shot to death by an old bandit to prevent her from being raped, but the released version works out a much more dignified solution. Hiding behind a rock, the old bandit takes a sip from his bottle of liquor, guns down a Japanese soldier, then rushes forward and kills the rest of the enemies with the nurse's help. The two then retreat into the barren land, becoming two tiny dots on the horizon.

Another group of Chinese survivors is led by Wang Jin, who is injured in the leg but who asks Thick Eyebrows, a former bandit, to carry the wounded Xu Zhi on his shoulders. When the Communist base is close by, Thick Eyebrows puts Xu on the ground, kneels down in front of Wang, lifts his rifle over his head, and asks Wang to let him leave. He then retreats into the barren land in silence, and a revolutionary

---

[15] For critical studies of this "national myth" of the Communist solider liberating a peasant woman, see Meng Yue 1993; Yau 1996.

song is heard offscreen. Suddenly, the bandit stops (in a long shot) and turns around (in a close-up). In an extreme long shot, "The film closes with Wang carrying the wounded security man on his shoulder with the gun for support. As the shot goes gradually out of focus, what remains on the screen is the shape of a tripod, or rather [a graphic equivalent of] *ren*, the Chinese character for humanity" (Ma Ning 1987a, 77). The composition of this final shot is such that the two figures are barely visible against the empty sky, which occupies the upper two-thirds of the frame.

16. *One and Eight* (1984): A challenge to the orthodox vision of history

The visually striking but ideologically ambivalent ending of *One and Eight* foreshadows the increasing significance of primitive landscape and marginalized character in later films by this group of Fifth Generation directors. For example, Zhang Yimou's trademark compositions of earth, human figures, and disproportionately large sky enhance the visual quality of *Yellow Earth*. More than *Yellow Earth*, however, *One and Eight* signifies a radical change in the war film: stripped of the normal mechanism of justification and sublimation in previous war films, images of graphic violence and gruesome death erupt on the screen and directly assault the viewer, driving home powerfully unsettling and lingering effects.

Death, Decapitation, and Desublimation in Wu Ziniu's War Films

In terms of violent death, Wu Ziniu's war films deserve special attention. If the life of an innocent army nurse is saved by the censors in *One and Eight*, Wu's *Secret Decree* (Diexue heigu, 1984) sacrifices two principal female characters caught in the war machine: an underground Communist agent and a patriot, both ruthlessly gunned down by the Nationalist officers. Violence and death are even more graphic and disturbing in the popular *Joyous Heroes* (Huanle yingxiong, 1988) and its sequel, *Between Life and Death* (Yinyang jie, 1988). Near the end of the sequel, three feuding factions of a local community and a Nationalist troop are engaged in a confusing battle, which ends with the deaths of all the leading characters. When Big Head Xu takes over his rivals' village, he rounds the villagers up in the square. Spotting the pregnant wife of his arch enemy, he has her brought to him, pulls out her long jade hairpin, and runs it repeatedly through her belly, simultaneously killing mother and unborn child.[16]

In *The Big Mill* (Da mofang, 1990), Wu's tale of revenge against the local militia's cold-blooded executions of the captives of the Red Army, the young man Qing Guo (Li Yusheng) blackens his face and body and acts as a ghost of retribution by killing eleven perpetrators one by one and piling their bodies on the flat side of a grind stone. When Qing opens the water gate, the giant millstone rolls over the bodies, grinding them to pieces. He then sneaks into the house of Liao Baijun (Tao Zeru), the crippled boss of the evil local militia, strangles him, and sets his house on fire. When Qing brings Jiu Cui (Shen Danping), his former sweetheart but then Liao's pregnant wife, to the mill, she is frightened by his appearance. Qing goes out to open the water gate again and wash himself in the running water. Inside, Jiu screams at the sight of the blood-stained millstone, her eyes in wide-open terror in an extreme close-up.

How should we interpret Wu Ziniu's seeming obsession with blood, violence, and death in the context of Chinese film history? The ending

---

[16] As Wu Ziniu himself sees it, violent deaths in this film may make the viewer rethink that perhaps not all good guys are glorious and not all bad guys are insignificant (see Zhang Xuan 1989).

scenes in *Joyous Heroes* may provide some clues. Cai Laoliu (Tao Zeru), an underground Communist, learns from a friend that the unknown father of his wife Yusuan's daughter is none other than his dissipated, opium-addicted father. Cai secretly returns home and renews his affection for Yusuan, but his father informs the Nationalist officer in exchange for a sum of reward money sufficient to buy him another dose of opium. Cai is captured and beheaded. Doing her best to suppress her emotions under the circumstances, Yusuan brings Cai's head home and places it on the family altar. When Cai's father returns from his opium-smoking, he is shocked into silence by the sight of Cai's head. The close-up shots of the father's staring eyes and trembling lips are intercut with Yusuan's ghostly appearance, seen first through the half-drawn curtain behind the altar and then slowly advancing toward him. Raising his hands as if to ward off the ghost, he drops dead to the floor. Yusuan kneels down and kowtows to Cai's head, her back to the camera. In a frontal shot, she stands up, knocking the candles off the altar. A fire starts and begins to spread, consuming the house. The film ends with Yusuan, still dressed in mourning white, walking slowly into the wilderness in search of her "ghostly" revenge against the Nationalist officer (both of them die in a car accident in the film's sequel).

A comparison of the above scenes in *Joyous Heroes* with the scene of decapitation in *Liu Hulan* (Liu Hulan, 1950) may shed light on the question of sublimation in cinematic representation. A courageous girl who joins the Communist Party at the age of fourteen and is active in the land reform movement in her village, Liu Hulan (Hu Zongwen) is arrested by the Nationalist soldiers and brought to trial. She defies her enemy and refuses to repent. In spite of her young age, the landlord has her beheaded with a *zhandao*, a sharp blade attached to a bench used to chop hay and plant stalks.[17] But the execution is only implied in the film: the shot of Liu walking toward the *zhandao* cuts directly to a battle scene where the murderers are killed. In the semiotics of Communist propaganda, the execution scenes work not only to incriminate the class enemy (the Nationalists in this case) but also—and more importantly—to strengthen the will of the revolutionaries to seek revenge by overthrowing the evil regime. In other words, scenes of violence or death in socialist realism operate almost always as a means of represen-

---

[17] A remake of *Liu Hulan* was released by Shanxi Film Studio in 1996.

tation (a vehicle for political indoctrination), but never as ends in themselves (violence for violence's sake). In contrast, violence and death in Wu Ziniu's films take on lives of their own, repeatedly confronting the viewer with images that appear to have exceeded their intended narrative and ideological functions.

Herbert Marcuse's concept of *desublimation* in literature may help us better comprehend the recurring and seemingly uncontrollable violence in Wu's war films. For Marcuse, desublimation "takes place in the perception of individuals—in their feelings, judgments, thoughts," and functions as "an invalidation of dominant norms, needs, and values" (1978, 7–8). Wu's films, in this reading, contribute to the cinematic rewriting of the history of the Chinese revolution from the perspective of individuals, often those caught at the threshold of life and death or between love and hate. The result of such rewriting is the construction of a new reality that "shatters the reified objectivity of established social relations and opens a new dimension of experience: rebirth of the rebellious subjectivity" (Marcuse 1978, 8).

To a great extent, Wu's desublimation through violence and death evokes a new vision of history in Chinese cinema: *history as the ruin of civilization*. We may borrow Walter Benjamin's words to foreground the rationale for integrating the war film in the project of nation-building in socialist China, a rationale against which Wu's films attempt to rebel by introducing a new subjectivity:

> Hence, empathy with the victor invariably benefits the rulers. . . . Whoever has emerged victorious participates to this day in the triumphal procession in which the present rulers step over those who are lying prostrate. According to traditional practice, the spoils are carried along in the procession. They are called cultural treasures, and a historical materialist views them with cautious detachment. For without exception the cultural treasures he surveys have an origin which he cannot contemplate without horror. They owe their existence not only to the efforts of the great minds and talents who have created them, but also to the anonymous toil of their contemporaries. There is no document of civilization which is not at the same time a document of barbarism. (Benjamin 1969, 256)

To the best of my knowledge, *The Big Mill* provides the most remarkable articulation in Chinese cinema of the Benjaminian vision of history as barbarism and catastrophe. With his haggard face and skeptical glare, Qing Guo the old man (Liu Zhongyuan) appears on the screen like a ghost, taking up the same metadiscursive position as Benjamin's "angel of history," and witnessing the unfolding of revolutionary history with both cautious detachment and utmost horror: "His eyes are staring, his mouth is open, his wings are spread. . . . His face is turned toward the past. Where we perceive a chain of events, he sees one single catastrophe which keeps piling wreckage upon wreckage and hurls it in front of his feet. The angel would like to stay, awaken the dead, and make whole what has been smashed" (Benjamin 1969, 257). The film reenacts such barbarism and catastrophe in the scene in which the giant millstone, itself arguably a symbol of history, literally rolls "over those who are lying prostrate," crushing them. And, like the angel of history, Qing Guo the old man can do nothing but watch from the sideline, visibly tormented but speechless and helpless.

Returning to the symbolism of decapitation in *Joyous Heroes*, we may consider the relevance of David Wang's speculations on the function of decapitation in the literary works of Lu Xun and Shen Congwen. Like Wu Ziniu, both Lu and Shen seem obsessed with the "disconcerting imagery of headlessness and bodily mutilation," and both sometimes present decapitation as "not so much a necessary means of revenge as a decadent game participated in by both the heroes and villains, in search of sadomasochistic pain and pleasure" (D. Wang, 1992, 210, 214). However, Wang detects a crucial difference between the two writers: Lu Xun's "decapitation complex" is derived from his guilty conscience and his moral anxiety "about the primordial loss of origin—meaning and life as symbolized by the head, loss as symbolized by the mutilated body," whereas "In Shen Congwen's lyrical agenda, ugly things are neither erased nor reversed as an offset of the real, but only displaced, as it were, from their roots in order to evoke a dreamlike simulacrum" (1992, 214). In terms of rhetorical strategy, Wu Ziniu comes closer to Shen Congwen in that his films, especially *The Dove Tree* (Gezi shu, 1985), *Evening Bell* (Wanzhong, 1988) [Illustration 17], and *The Big Mill*, manifest "lyrical rhythms by weaving varied sensory images from natural and human environments into a fabric and giving them correspondences to one another" (D. Wang, 1992, 217). Nevertheless, like Lu Xun, Wu Ziniu is keenly aware of the representational power of the body and the head as well as the visual impact of decapitation and bodily mutilation.

17. *Evening Bell* (1988): Wu Ziniu's images of dissent

David Wang's statement that "literally and symbolically, modern China is a 'head'-less country, crowded by spiritually decapitated people whose life is only intensified by watching beheadings or waiting to be beheaded" (1992, 215) brings us to another dimension of Wu Ziniu's war films. Here, Wu's concern with decapitation may be linked on a deeper level to what Dai Jinhua identifies as the Fifth Generation's traumatic experience of the large-scale "patricides" during the Cultural Revolution. Being marginalized figures (due to their family backgrounds) in the irrational patricidal movement, directors like Chen Kaige and Tian Zhuangzhuang are implicated in a predicament.[18] On the one hand, they

---

[18] Chen Kaige's father is Chen Huaiai, a noted film director. Tian Zhuangzhuang's father is Tian Fang, a famous actor and once head of Beijing Film Studio, and his mother Yu Lan, a famous actress turned director of Children's Film Studio based in Beijing. For Wu Ziniu's background, see Jia and Yang 1994; Liu Weihong 1988.

want to interrogate the myths of revolution and to challenge "the Name of the Father" by way of exploring new film language and new narrative modes; on the other hand, they desire to enter the symbolic order by way of reintegrating themselves into the mainstream of cultural representation.

Zhang Yimou's comments on *One and Eight* express their desire to challenge and question the myths of revolution and the name of the father: "Our simplest and most practical aim is to innovate. . . . As the saying goes, 'the son need not look exactly like the father.' Each generation should have its own ideas and aspirations" (Ma Ning 1987a, 74). The immediate results of their renovation in the mid-1980s include narrative segments connected by jump cuts, a large quantity of fixed-camera shots, panoramic views shot from either unusually high or low angles, self-exposing camera movements unrelated to narrative situations, extreme images and frame compositions in which characters are relegated to the corners or margins. All of these are tried out in a process of defamiliarizing the myths of revolutionary history. However, Dai Jinhua argues that the Fifth Generation directors feel obliged to start with the revolutionary myths in order, first of all, to justify the Name of the Father (after the symbolic patricide, or the decapitation of the father) and, second, to "name themselves" (*ziwo mingming*) as "fatherless sons" (*wufu zhizi*), hence fully authorized to rewrite history (1993, 21).

This second move is particularly telling in the mise-en-scène at the end of *One and Eight*. When Thick Eyebrows, the former bandit deserting the Communists, looks over his shoulder, the audience is left to identify with his view of two obscure figures fixed on the horizon. In Dai Jinhua's reading (1993, 22), these figures resemble a tiny wreath, which is dedicated by the new, rebellious generation to the memory of the "father" (the Communist). What is more, the tactic of transferring the right to enunciation from the "father" to the rebellious "son" (here self-identified by the Fifth Generation) in this scene accomplishes two objectives: a rebellion after the self-acknowledged submission to the authorities (Thick Eyebrows kneeling down in front of Wang Jin) and a declaration of independence (Thick Eyebrows walking away by himself) after seeking redemption in revolutionary history.

It is perhaps not mere coincidence that the head placed on the altar in *Joyous Heroes* belongs to an underground Communist. The grotesque image of this decapitation, together with a similar image of a Red Army soldier buried alive under the floor of a peasant's house to dispel the evil spirit that is said to have possessed his daughter in *The Big Mill*, reminds the contemporary viewer of a prior patricidal act. In the absence of the father (that is, a "headless" state), the new generation is fully justified in its rebellious move to claim the right of representation and to project new visions of history different from those of their fathers' generation. Now, to better understand Wu Ziniu and his fellow Fifth Generation directors' new vision, we need to place their war-related films in the framework of the shifting paradigms of the war film in mainland China from the 1950s to the 1990s.

Paradigms of Nationalism, Patriotism, and Heroism in the War Film, 1949–84

As indicated earlier, the discourse of nationalism in Chinese cinema can be traced back to the early 1930s, when a rising tide of patriotism in the wake of Japanese aggression in China changed the ideological orientation of the film industry. A limited number of war films were made during the war, but the genre did not become popular until the 1950s. In fact, the first feature films produced by the Communist studios center on the wars. *Daughters of China* (Zhonghua ernü, 1949), for example, glorifies the sacrifice women soldiers made in defense of their homeland against Japanese invaders in Manchuria. Even the few remaining private studios released war films in an attempt to adopt ideologically safe subjects in a transition period marked by an uncertain political future. *Commander Guan* (Guan Lianzhang, 1951) praises the Communist soldiers' effort to save a group of children trapped in a fierce battle, but its explicit emphasis on a transcending concept of humanism provoked immediate criticism from the authorities and contributed directly to Wenhua Film's "voluntary" decision to merge into the state-controlled Shanghai Film Studio (Y. Zhang and Xiao 1998, 22).

According to one estimate, military and war films accounted for about half of the 200 or so feature films produced during the 1950s and early 1960s. From the mid-1960s to the mid-1970s, when only a select number of feature films were approved for production and release, most of them were related to war. Since the late 1970s, the percentage of war films has dropped to about ten to fifteen. Yet given the overall increased output, they still play a significant role in film production, a role that received the government's renewed emphasis in the 1990s (Hong 1998,

94). Indeed, as far as the first seventeen years of socialist China are concerned, war films are judged to be the most accomplished genre in terms of narrative modes, and the most compelling form in terms of emotional impact (Dai Jinhua 1993, 170). In terms of ideological orientation, nationalism, patriotism, and heroism dominated this period. The battlefield became an indispensable stage on which to celebrate the Communist victory and to reenact heroic human sacrifices, both "performances" readily incorporated into the project of nation-building launched by the government.

Schematically, early war films can be divided into two main categories: Communist hagiographies and military strategies. In addition to *Daughters of China*, Communist martyrs and war heroes were given prominent attention in films like *Zhao Yiman* (Zhao Yiman, 1950), *Shangrao Concentration Camp* (Shangrao jizhong ying, 1951), *Dong Cunrui* (1955), and *Five Martyrs of Wolf-Teeth Mountain* (Langyashan wu zhuangshi, 1958). And the trend continued into the mid-1960s with *Heroic Sons and Daughters* (Yingxiong ernü, 1964) and *Red Crag* (Liehuo zhong yongsheng, 1965). War films about military strategies can be further divided into four sub-groups. First, as in *From Victory to Victory* and *The Shanghai Battle* (Zhan Shanghai, 1959), major military campaigns were restaged to celebrate the Communist victory over the Japanese or Nationalist troops. These films often featured decision making from a high command level, and reached an epic scope in their war scenes. Second, ingenious military stratagems were singled out as evidence of the wisdom of the Communists and were built into the narrative in films such as *Capture Mount Hua by Stratagem* (Zhiqu Huashan, 1953) and *Scouting Across the Yangtze River* (Dujiang zhencha ji, 1954). Third, and closely related to military stratagems, guerilla warfare was used to exemplify Mao Zedong's war strategies, especially during the resistance war against the Japanese. *Guerrillas on the Plain* (Pingyuan youji dui, 1955) [Illustration 18], *Railroad Guerrillas* (Tiedao youji dui, 1956), *Land Mine Warfare* (Dilei zhan, 1962), and *Tunnel Warfare* (Didao zhan, 1965) were among the most popular war films during the 1950s and 1960s. Finally, several war films were specifically targeted at children, such as *Letter with Feather* (Jimao xin, 1954), *Red Children* (Hong haizi, 1958), and *Zhang Ga, a Boy Soldier* (1963).

18. *Guerillas on the Plain* (1955): The paradigm of nationalism and heroism

Several factors, most of them sociohistorical, have been cited to account for the popularity of war films during the 1950s and 1960s (Dai Jinhua 1993, 170–1; Hong 1998, 94–6; see also Zhongguo dianying yishu 1984). What I stress here is that, while the audience might enjoy the relatively high level of artistic achievement in this genre, filmmakers were attracted to it in part because it offered them a comparatively safe subject matter in the increasingly repressive political environment. During the Cultural Revolution, war films were still considered less problematic than other genres, and when film production resumed in the early 1970s after a hiatus, three color remakes of the earlier black-and-white war films were released in 1974 alone: *From Victory to Victory*, *Guerrillas on the Plain*, and *Scouting Across the Yangtze River*. Among other things, war films like these continued to serve the function of sublimation and intensified the myths of the revolutionary past.

From the late 1970s to the early 1980s, the old paradigms of nationalism and patriotism were increasingly revised yet not fundamentally restructured. A number of changes were underway during this time. First, ideologically more tolerant views of the history of the nation made it possible for filmmakers to directly deal with heroes and martyrs who were not Communists, as in *Ji Hongchang* (Ji Hongchang, 1979) and *Xi'an Incident* (Xi'an shibian, 1981). Second, heroes were depicted as much more humanized and less idealized or mythified, not as perfect or god-like as they used to be in earlier war films (Zhou and Zhang 1995, 16–17). Third, romance was no longer a taboo subject and was quickly integrated into films like *Anxious to Return* (Guixin sijian, 1979). Finally, the heightened sense of humanism sometimes contributed to a contemporary intervention in the form of social critique, and this is best exemplified in *Garlands at the Foot of the Mountain* (Gaoshan xiade huahuan, 1984; hereafter *Garlands*).

A war film directed by Xie Jin, the most famous filmmaker during this transition period, *Garlands* merits a closer look. In the unusual position of tackling the sensitive subject of the Sino-Vietnam border war of 1979, *Garlands* at first criticizes the abuse of power by corrupt high-ranking officials, represented by Wu Shuang, who tries to move her son, Zhao Mengsheng (Tang Guoqiang), out of the unit when it is about to enter the war. Zhao decides to stay to allay his comrades' anger, but he is visibly changed in the ensuing battles, which claim the lives of Captain Liang Sanxi (whose wife is about to give birth) and a young soldier nicknamed "Little Beijing" (whose father turns out to be General Lei, the commanding officer in the war). The thrust of Xie's political critique is weakened in the scene in which General Lei and Liang's mother meet in the martyrs' graveyard on the hillside, for the negative (female) image of power earlier embodied by Wu Shuang is now completely negated by the positive (male) image of General Lei as a supreme figure of both heroism and sacrifice (Dai Jinhua 1993, 139–40; Ma Ning 1994, 34–6). A prolonged scene of Liang's wife crying over her husband's grave brings Xie Jin's humanist perspective to a melodramatic climax. The film ends with General Lei saluting to the martyrs' families. This scene is reminiscent of many early war films, and clearly points to the continuity of the paradigms of nationalism and heroism of the early 1980s.

The Sound and the Fury: Wu Ziniu's Images of Dissent

A fundamental challenge to (and, in some instances, deconstruction of) the old paradigms did not come to fruition until the mid-1980s. Whereas veteran directors like Xie Jin used melodramatic elements to highlight the theme of humanism in war films, the Fifth Generation directors seemed to be more interested in constructing images of *dissent* by extending their cameras to those dark areas hitherto concealed or prohibited by the discourse of patriotism and heroism in the earlier paradigms. In an interview, Wu Ziniu developed his argument this way: "We cannot forever stay with the heroism of the past decades, promoting the national spirit and endorsing the invincibility of the Communist Party and its armies. . . . We have too many of this kind of film. Could we add something else? Could we represent war from a higher angle?" (Liu Weihong 1988, 112) The answer to both questions is yes. And the emerging paradigms of humanism, individualism, and sometimes anti-war "internationalism" are characterized by several notable shifts: from a series of tension-filled dramas to a minimalist plot structure; from explicit ideological message (often conveyed in dialogue) to implicit symbolism and allegory (often through silent imagery); from an idealization of heroism to a cultivation of ambivalent moods and pathos; from a pure patriotic spirit to prolonged psychosomatic suffering.

All these aspects of the new paradigm shifts are evident in *Evening Bell*. As in *The Big Mill*, Wu Ziniu turns his attention to the revolutionary past and fixes his camera on the "wreckage" of history. The film opens with a dolorous scene—a sea of white funeral streamers fluttering in the wind over an endless stretch of conical earthen graves— over which the film title is superimposed. A ritualistic recital of their own names and hometowns by a group of Japanese soldiers follows. The track shots of the gasoline poured on the heads of the kneeling soldiers end in a dark, empty frame. Then a white dove appears, a tiny piece of paper tied to its foot. A crane shot of the soldiers lifting their heads cuts to a shot of the dove flying into the distant sky. A machine gun report is heard, and the scene bursts into flame, a conflagration that lasts over a minute in a combination of long and medium shots. Against the setting sun, an old peasant is seen in silhouette chopping at the bottom stake of a Japanese watchtower with an axe. The chopping sounds echo in the empty horizon as the image is repeated in a series of close-up, medium, long, and extreme long shots.

Wu's anti-war message is loud and clear, and his sympathetic portrayal of the mass suicide of the Japanese soldiers is nearly unprecedented in Chinese film history. Certainly, *Evening Bell* has a very simple story line, but Wu's meticulous attention to audio-visual effects makes it a unique war film. For example, in the film, after Japan's surrender in 1945, a team of Communist soldiers is dispatched to clean up the battlefields and bury the dead bodies of their comrades. They come across a group of Japanese soldiers guarding a secret ammunition warehouse inside a mountain cave. The soldiers are starving and near death from hunger. A quick succession of scenes follows. In one, hungry Japanese soldiers fight over food left by the Chinese. An emaciated Chinese woman, her clothes in tatters, suddenly rushes out of the cave and is shot by a Japanese lieutenant. She is rescued, but before her death tells the Chinese platoon leader (Tao Zeru) that the Japanese have cannibalized one of the Chinese laborers in the cave.

The cruelty of cannibalism, though never shown on-screen, is foregrounded by the lieutenant's act of harikari in a headless close-up. Other Japanese soldiers, who have dropped their weapons and lined up to surrender, are shocked when a Chinese soldier suddenly fires his gun into the distance to vent his anger. In the seemingly unbearable silence that follows, a Japanese officer who has gone insane stumbles out of the cave after the warehouse is set on fire. He mumbles a few words, walks straight to a stone wall, bumps his heads twice, and slowly drops down. As the captives are led away, the cave explodes in a spectacular show. The film ends with the repeated image of the old man chopping the stake of the watchtower, but this time the tower gives way and tumbles down in slow motion against the magnificent sunset.

Significantly, Wu Ziniu keeps the characters nameless, thereby suggesting war in general. This allows *Evening Bell* to transcend otherwise unbridgeable political and racial divides. For Wu, the Communist soldiers in the film "must take the responsibility of transcending themselves, embodying the essential meaning of the Chinese nation, the Chinese people, the Chinese soldiers, or even Man in the abstract sense of the word" (quoted in Zhang Xuan 1988). Throughout the film, Wu uses very little dialogue or music. Instead, he concentrates on images, some of which seem to be unrelated to the story but leave striking impressions nonetheless: two widows cry over a grave in a barren landscape; a young blind man scatters pieces of paper money over a hillside graveyard. In most cases, Wu uses natural lighting, and the characters are shown either back- or side-lit. This achieves not only an extra measure of realism but also a veneer of historicity because of the close resemblance between these images and the wood-cut pictures popular during the war (Hung 1994, 93–150).

Compared with earlier war films, *Evening Bell* certainly represents a significant case of dissent. Traces of patriotism are still visible, but nationalism is interrogated, and heroism is presented in an uncanny light. All these acts of dissent serve specific purposes in Wu's cinematic project of rewriting revolutionary history: to depart from the conventional paradigms and to construct a new film language, a new vision of history, and a new concept of humanity. As Dai Jinhua observes, "the Fifth Generation directors look forward to salvation: not only the salvation of themselves, but also the salvation of memory, history, nation, and subsistence. The basic narrative thrust of *Evening Bell* is precisely to bury wars—to bury the corps left behind by an ended war, and perhaps the film also signifies the burial and termination of a tragic but heroic era" (1993, 44).

Evening Bell is unusual in many other ways as well. First, the August First Film Studio (Bayi), officially part of the People's Liberation Army that is widely regarded as a stronghold of conservative ideology in China, held two internal preview meetings to debate the film (one meeting is the norm), with the discussants' views sharply divided. Second, for a film that took less than two months to complete, *Evening Bell* went through two years of screenings at various levels of censorship and four stages of requested revisions, during which time the insiders referred to it as perhaps the last "toll" (*sangzhong*) to the avant-garde films of the Fifth Generation. Third, after it was finally—and by this time unexpectedly—approved for public release by the Film Bureau on March 18, 1988, initial domestic orders in May were nonexistent. This number climbed to one copy later in the year, while Japan alone reportedly ordered seven copies. Finally, *Evening Bell* experienced a complete reversal of its previous fortune when it was named one of the ten best films of 1988, winning several prestigious awards, including a Silver Bear at the 1989 Berlin Film Festival and the Best Director at China's Golden Roosters Awards (Jinji jiang).[19]

---

[19] The Best Director Award was given to Wu Ziniu for three of his films released in 1988: *Evening Bell, Joyous Heroes,* and *Between Life and Death.*

The reference to *Evening Bell* as a "toll" is reminiscent of an earlier censorship problem Wu encountered with *The Dove Tree*, a film dealing with the Sino-Vietnam border war that has remained banned in China since its completion in 1985. In anticipation of *Evening Bell*, *The Dove Tree* conveys a strong anti-war sentiment by foregrounding the unnecessary deaths of innocent men and women on the battlefield. A lyrical sequence in this war film is particularly noteworthy. We see two Chinese soldiers fatally wounded. In the silence that ensues, a thrush sings in the bushes. While dense mist shrouds the scene, the tops of white reeds tremble in the breeze. Smoke rises slowly from the scorched ground and dissolves into the mist. A mysterious sound—possibly footsteps—accompanies the thrush's intermittent song. A slim figure emerges from the mist. It turns out to be a Vietnamese nurse, who begins to treat the wounded. Escaping the gunfire that claimed the lives of his two comrades, another Chinese soldier suddenly appears on the scene. A confrontation with the nurse ensues, and the soldier murders her.

This dramatization of love and hatred, life and death, peace and war best illustrates Wu's concerns in his war films:

> *The Dove Tree* is a tragedy. It describes the conflicts of the human heart in the middle of a cruel war. . . . From there we perceive "duality" and "split subjectivity," as well as the insurmountable "gap," . . . and all these factors are represented and experienced as trauma in literature and art from the partial perspective of the nation. . . . Somebody once described me as "worshiping pain." Yes, I do because pain is the fountain of art. More accurately, I worship humanity, and humanity is the heart of my art. I express pain because I want people to think. (Zhang Xuan 1988)

Indeed, the death of the nurse is meant to make the audience rethink the question of war and feel "pathos over the follies and cruelty of humanity" (D. Wang 1992, 218).

A similar rethinking is evident in Zhou Xiaowen's *In Their Prime* (Tamen zheng nianqing, 1986), another banned Fifth Generation film that directly questions the Sino-Vietnam border war. Rather than showing the human side of the Vietnamese soldiers, Zhou creates a reverse situation in which a Chinese platoon leader, who corners and then releases a Vietnamese mother carrying her baby on her back, is shot to death by her as soon as he turns around to leave. Thematically, by depicting a group of Chinese soldiers guarding a small mountain cave in

Vietnam, *In Their Prime* is a parody of *Shanggan Ridges* (Shangganling, 1956), a heroic film set in the Korean War. The unquestioning devotion to nationalism and heroism that characterizes *Shanggan Ridges* is exactly what is conspicuously absent in Zhou's mock-heroic tale. True, Zhou's soldiers also hold their strategic position, but they do so with complaints, curses, hysterical outbursts, and other sadomasochistic acts—all of them hardly "heroic" according to the old paradigms. When the survivors retreat to China near the end of the film, nothing seems to have been accomplished by the war. This unsettling message binds *In Their Prime* and *The Dove Tree* together, for both function as a direct contradiction to *Garlands* (which glorified nationalism and hence encountered no censorship problem despite the same sensitive subject) and *Shanggan Ridges* (which celebrated heroism at the collective level and was regarded as a classic war film).

Unlike Zhou Xiaowen, who switched to urban cinema in the late 1980s, Wu Ziniu continued his "worship of humanity" by spreading the anti-war message again in *Nanjing Massacre* (aka *Nanjing 1937*, Nanjing da tusha, 1995). As in his earlier work, in this film Wu also stages fierce battles, ruthless massacres, random killings, and rape. Instead of insisting on avant-garde techniques, this time Wu prefers the method of "presentation" (*biaoxian*) to that of "representation" (*zaixian*). The result is a film more accessible to the average viewer (Longxiang gongsi 1995, 143). Furthermore, by featuring among his protagonists a Shanghai refugee family composed of a Chinese doctor and his pregnant Japanese wife, Wu deliberately blurs the human borderline between nations and races, once again placing humanity over nationalism.

Before closing my discussion of Wu Ziniu, I should point out a paradox inherent in his cinematic project of dissent. In order to promote a new concept of humanity that transcends the division of nations, races, and ethnicities, Wu depends almost exclusively on images of violence, death, and decapitation. In this regard, his images of dissent reinforce the Benjaminian vision of history as catastrophe and wreckage, of the history of human civilization as one of barbarism.

A Return to the Mainstream: Epic War Films of the 1990s

With their characteristic images of dissent, the war films of Wu Ziniu and others like him operate at best as minority discourse in contemporary Chinese cinema. Their new paradigms of humanism and individualism may challenge or deconstruct, but never aspire to replace the dominant paradigms of nationalism and heroism. Even in the reform era of the 1980s, the Chinese government did not suspend its financial and ideological investment in the war film, especially those that featured major military campaigns and glorified revolutionary history. Except for a few films that recognize the patriotism and heroism of the Nationalist army fighting against the Japanese invaders, such as *The Battle of Taierzhuang* (Xuezhan Taierzhuang, 1986), most war films tend to celebrate the Communist victory in one way or another.

This tendency gathered more momentum in the early 1990s, when revolutionary epic films received huge subsidies from the government and were produced in series. The most notable example of this kind of newly dubbed "leitmotif film" is *The Decisive Engagements, I–III* (Da juezhan, 1991–92), a collaboration between Yang Guangyuan, Cai Jiwei, Wei Lian, and several others, all under the general direction of Li Jun. The series restages three major military campaigns—the Liaoning-Shenyang Campaign, the Huaihai Campaign, and the Beijing-Tianjin Campaign—that fundamentally changed the balance of power in the civil war and guaranteed the ultimate victory of the Communists over the Nationalists. The series also features a host of historical figures, including most of the top Communist leaders, such as Mao Zedong, Zhou Enlai, Liu Shaoqi, Zhu De, Ye Jianying, Liu Bocheng, and Deng Xiaoping. The success of this first series of major campaigns encouraged the production of other series such as *The Decisive Turning Point, I–II* (Da zhuanzhe, 1996) and *The Decisive Further Advances, I–IV* (Da jinjun, 1996–99).[20] Seen together, these series complete a chapter of the

---

[20] The "success" in question is measured by the fact that *The Decisive Engagements* was voted the Best Film in 1992 at both the semi-official Golden Roosters Awards and the more popular Hundred Flowers Awards (Baihua jiang). In 1997, *The Decisive Turning Point* and *The Decisive Further Advances, II: Pursuing Down to the South* (Da jinjun: nanxian da zhuijian) both made it to the top-ten box-office list of the year, respectively third and tenth (Dianying yishu 1998). In 1998, *The Decisive Further Advances, III: Conquering the Great Southwest* (Da jinjun: xijuan da xinan) received the Best Film, and Yang Guangyuan the Best Director, at the top-level government Huabiao Awards (Huabiao jiang)

revolutionary history during the civil war of 1945–49 that culminated in the founding of the People's Republic of China, an event already narrated in *The Birth of New China* (Kaiguo dadian, 1989).

Several anniversaries from 1991 (the 70th birthday of the Chinese Communist Party) to 1995 (the 50th anniversary of the victory of World War II) were cited by some critics as the direct cause of the growth of the mainstream war film in the 1990s (Hong 1998, 102; Yin 1998a, 7). But I suggest that another crucial link—one with long-term strategic benefits—can be found in the efforts of the Communist regime to reinstill political nationalism in the minds of the young generation after the devastating event of Tiananmen Square. From his inauguration in the leading position in the Party in 1989 to his *Speaking of Politics* (Guanyu jiang zhengzhi) in March 1996, Jiang Zemin consistently advocated tight ideological control by the Communist state apparatuses nationwide. The increasing political pressure resulted in the implementation of a set of concrete policies on literature and the arts, such as the "Five Ones Project" (*wuge yi gongcheng*) launched by the Central Committee's Ministry of Propaganda and the "9550 Project" imposed on filmmakers. Originally stipulating that the Party apparatuses in each province must concentrate their efforts on creating one "excellent" work in each of five categories—film, television drama, literature, stage play, and song—the "Five Ones Project" has been expanded to include other categories (like theoretical work, television programs devoted to theory, and radio plays) and has transformed itself into an elaborate, nationwide competition for special government prizes. In 1999, for instance, over 600 people were involved in the initial round of screening, over 300 experts and government officials participated in the process of selection and validation, and 372 works dated between July 1997 and June 1999 were given special honors in the end, among them twenty-six leitmotif films. Exclusive to the film industry, the "9550 Project" amounts to a new quota system (though not studio specific, hence open to competition) in that it requires the production of ten "excellent quality" (*jingpin*) films each year in the government's ninth five-year plan, which meant a total of fifty from 1996 to 2000 (Yin 1998a, 5–10, 125). Although these two projects of "souls-engineering" may sound absurd to critics of China in

---

ceremonies jointly presented in Beijing by the Ministry of Radio, Film, and Television, the Ministry of Propaganda, and the CCTV. For an interview with a director of these films, see Wei Lian 1997.

the West, one should not underestimate the long-term effects of such centrally planned regulations and programs. In spite of its repressive political climate, China experienced a rapid economic development in the early 1990s, and a corresponding new surge of patriotism and nationalism, best manifest in the controversial but immensely popular book *China Can Say No* (Zhongguo keyi shuo bu, 1996), coauthored by Song Qiang and others (Chow 1997; X. Zhang, 1998).[21] Placed in this new ideological context, the epic war film deserves further investigation.

Describing the revival of war films as "both a setback and a progress" in 1998, Junhao Hong is disappointed on the one hand because films are "once again functioning chiefly as an ideological or political instrument," but feels elated on the other hand because the new trend "meant the maturity of China's film," since the new films "have been more entertaining and less ideological or political," and are judged to be "much more objective, bold, and open when reflecting history" (1998, 102–3). The problem with Hong's sociological assessment of the new situation is evident in his indiscriminate use of words such as "maturity," "objective," and "reflecting," but more puzzling yet are his two other assertions. First is "the 1990s' military movies seem to have had a win-win situation: both the Party leaders and the audience are satisfied with the revolutionary epic movies." Second, "China has only had real military movies since these changes [in the early 1990s]" (1998, 104). My objection to Hong's first statement is twofold: an endorsement of certain films by the authorities does not necessarily mean the "progress" or "maturity" of filmmaking in China, and the relatively high box-office returns of these war films might have derived more from the tickets given free of charge by government units to their employees or from the required viewing for urban school students than from the audience's desire for war images. Hong's second statement is even more untenable: what does he mean by "real military movies"? By what standards could one dismiss pre-1990 films like *Garlands* and *Evening Bell* as "unreal"?

---

[21] A video compact disk (VCD), "The Chinese Say No Today" (Zhongguo ren jintian shuo bu), issued by the Fujian Dragon Film and TV Company, features on its cover an angry Jiang Zemin holding a loudspeaker in his left hand while raising his right in a tight fist, against a red background of the Chinese national flag. The disk contains many fighting songs from the Sino-Japan War and Korean War eras, including footage of at least two war films, *Shanggan Ridges* and *Heroic Sons and Daughters*, as well as the popular theme song from the former.

And how could one prove *The Decisive Engagements* to be any more "real" and "objective" than *The Battle of Taierzhuang?*

The danger of Hong's uncritical celebration of a largely misconceived "win-win situation" of the 1990s is only too obvious, for it reduces our study of the war film in China to a mere explanation of what the government intends to achieve. Writing in the early 1990s, Berry was already suspicious of the new cinematic investment in nationalism. For him, the massive production of epic war films signaled not only a policy shift in the post-Tiananmen period but also a "hysterical" compensation for damages done to the sacred image of a unitary Chinese nation: "This return to revolutionary history is an attempt to reunite precisely those fragments . . . the People's Republic is shattered into by the shock of Tiananmen" (1994a, 45). Critical of the new war epics as leitmotif films, Berry identifies two of their "conservative" objectives: "denying difference and blocking change" (1994a, 49). Seen from this critical perspective, the new mainstream war films represent not progress but a setback from the 1980s trend toward desublimation, marginalization, and hybridization, a trend best exemplified in the minority discourse of the Fifth Generation, especially in Wu Ziniu's images of dissent.

The Commercial Packaging of Art and Politics in War Films

At this point, we should remind ourselves that there is no permanently fixed position in the shifting political landscape of filmmaking in contemporary China. With *The National Anthem* (Guoge, 1999), Wu Ziniu seems to have chosen a radically different path for his career. A film depicting a key figure in China's leftist film movement— screenwriter Tian Han—as a great national hero in the turbulent years of the early 1930s, *The National Anthem* was buttressed by substantial government subsidies (with a budget of 20 million yuan, compared to the average of 2.5 to 4 million per feature; hereafter all figures in Chinese currency) and was designated as one of the "must-see" titles during the September-October season celebrating the fiftieth anniversary of the People's Republic of China in 1999. In spite of its handsome budget and its potentially fascinating subject, *The National Anthem* generated mixed critical response and little popular enthusiasm. In general, the public tended to see it as yet another piece of propaganda in leitmotif films, even though Wu admitted it was his first-ever attempt in the category. In academic circles, some critics enumerated examples of Wu's "unfaithful" or "unwise" historical representation, while others criticized his lack of imagination and his overt preference for grand-scale mise-en-scène over characterization and dramatic conflict (Dangdai dianying 1999a).

What is even more unsettling to many critics, I suspect, is Wu's apparently all-too-willing identification with official ideology and mainstream filmmaking by 1999. Leitmotif films should not be misunderstood as "shallow, vulgar works merely illustrating government policies," he argues; instead, he intended *The National Anthem* to be a new kind of "mainstream film" (*zhuliu dianying*) that would engage its audience in a celebration of "patriotism and the national spirit," something that had long been marvellously achieved in certain "excellent" mega imports, themselves essentially "leitmotif films" in the West (1999b, 5).[22] *The National Anthem*, Wu continues, was thus dedicated as "a monument to the national spirit, to the Chinese nation, and to outstanding Chinese people like Tian Han" (1999b, 5). Renouncing his earlier position of transnational, transracial humanity, Wu now opted to embrace the ideology of nationalism and believed that "some education in humiliation and hatred is still necessary for the nation that has suffered so much" in modern history (1999b, 6). "I think that the gene of patriotism must reside in the thick blood of the Chinese people," Wu says, and "I want to tell the audience that they must love their nation, or otherwise they would have no individual existence at all" (1999a, 6). It is rather disheartening, therefore, to take note of the eventual retreat of Wu Ziniu, formerly a conscientious (and at times even solitary) explorer in the marginal space of minority discourse in contemporary Chinese cinema, into the mainstream of state-sponsored leitmotif films.[23]

A more noteworthy development in recent Chinese cinema, on the other hand, is the war film that aims at a high level of artistic quality in addition to guaranteed commercial returns. The release of *Red Cherry*, a high-budget coproduction (27 million) of the Youth Film Studio in

---

[22] Specifically, Wu cites *Forrest Gump* and *Saving Private Ryan* (Zhengjiu dabing Leien, 1998), since both work to promote "the American spirit" and "various American public opinions and ideologies" (1999a, 4).

[23] The exploratory quality of Wu Ziniu's art film is best exemplified in his *Sparkling Fox*, a coproduction with Hong Kong that relies on a minimalist use of plot and props to investigate the existential crisis of an urban dweller.

Beijing and the Gorky Film Studio in Moscow, is significant in many ways [Illustration 19].[24]

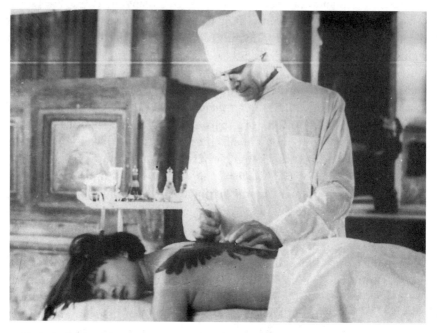

19. *Red Cherry* (1995): Commercial packaging of art and memory

First, the film symbolically as well as psychologically returns the Chinese audience to its pre-Cultural Revolution familiarity with Soviet films, a cinematic tradition lost or suppressed for some time. Shot on location in Russia under difficult circumstances (Ye Daying 1996), *Red Cherry* tells the tragic story of two Chinese orphans who suffer through the devastation of World War II. While in Moscow, Chuchu, one of the orphans, recounts how she was forced to witness the Nationalist agents' brutal execution of her father, an underground Communist who, despite having been cut in two through the waist by a *zhandao*, was still able to look at her in his final moments. Second, more than *Nanjing Massacre*, a coproduction with Taiwan released in the same year, *Red Cherry* turned

---

[24] Ye Daying graduated from the Directing Department of the Beijing Film Academy in 1986, technically a couple of years before noted members of the emerging "Sixth Generation," such as Wang Xiaoshuai and Zhang Yuan. For a critical forum on *Red Cherry*, see Dianying yishu 1996a; for the investment figures, see Pan 1996.

out to be an immense commercial success, setting a domestic box-office record of 50 million in spite of the fact that the majority of its dialogue is in Russian (with Chinese and English subtitles).[25] The unprecedented success of *Red Cherry* and, to a lesser extent, *Fierce Battles: True Records of the Korean War* (Jiaoliang: kang Mei yuan Chao zhanzheng shilu, 1996; a documentary of war footage), convinced many industry watchers and investors of the market potential of Chinese productions, even those in the category of war film.[26] Finally, *Red Cherry* beat *Kong Fansen* (Kong Fansen, 1996)—a government-sponsored leitmotif film that glorifies a self-sacrificing Han Communist model cadre in Tibet—to win Best Film at the 1996 Golden Roosters Awards. This achievement testified to the strong appeal of *Red Cherry* among the more educated members of the audience. What is more, winning domestic and international awards quickly translates into additional revenues: *Red Cherry* generated about 1.5 million in award monies alone.

Similar to *Red Cherry*, Feng Xiaoning's *Grief Over the Yellow River* (Huanghe juelian, 1999; hereafter *Grief*) was a daring film in the 1999 National Day season. It distinguished itself as a unique war film by maintaining a delicate balance of political correctness, high artistic value, and aggressive commercial interest. Like *Red Cherry*, *Grief* portrays the war as utterly inhuman, but it does so with a great deal more graphic violence, including bombing, rape, mass murder, infanticide, and decapitation.[27] Unlike *Red Cherry*, however, *Grief* provides the viewer

---

[25] In the top-ten domestic box-office hits of 1995, *Red Cherry* came first, beating *Shanghai Triad* and *Blush*, the latter a winner of a Silver Lion at the Berlin Festival (see *Dianying yishu* 1996b).

[26] Contrary to conventional wisdom, in 1995 *Fierce Battle* generated higher box-office returns (510,000 Chinese yuan) than several Hollywood mega imports, including *Lion King* (Shizi wang, 1994; earning only 190,000 yuan), in the city of Guangzhou (Canton). It is worth noting that Guangzhou is a commercial city close to Hong Kong and Macau, and innovative marketing strategies were credited for the unusual success of *Fierce Battle* (see Qi 1997). Interestingly, the calligraphy of the film's title was done by Jiang Zemin, as in the case of *The Decisive Engagements*, signaling government support at the top level.

[27] Intertextual references to other war films abound here, including those to Feng's two previous films, *The Medium of War* (Zhangzhen ziwu xian, 1990) and *Red River Valley* (Honghe gu, 1997), both of which contain an abundance of graphic scenes of violence and death. A summer box-office hit in China, *Red River Valley* might have functioned as a state-sponsored project that deliberately aimed to correct the "distorting representation"—as the Chinese government saw it—of modern Tibetan history in two 1997 Hollywood films, *Seven Years in Tibet* and *Kundun*. In 1997, *Red River Valley* was the second-highest

with effective means of sublimation: conceptually through its condemnation of brutal war crimes committed by Japanese soldiers; visually through scenes of the Yellow River and its surrounding landscape; and, most important of all, psychologically through its unraveling of a transnational, interracial romance between An Jie (Ning Jing), a Communist army nurse, and Irving (Paul Curci, Ning's off-screen American husband), an American reconnaissance pilot whose injured plane drifts over a portion of the Great Wall and crashes into a Japanese watch tower in a remote mountain area. Narrated in English (with Chinese and English subtitles) through Irving's melancholy voice-overs, *Grief* is a war film punctuated with nostalgia for lost love and bygone heroism. In spite of its abundant violence, the film confirms from a Western perspective that China is an honorable country with an ancient culture, and Chinese people are legendary, self-sacrificing heroes.

As a war film, *Grief* is remarkable in its integration of diverse visual and narrative elements, and its rich intertextual references to previous films—often with ironic twists—call for further scrutiny. As a 1982 graduate from the Department of Art and Design at the Beijing Film Academy (Feng Xiaoning 1997), the director Feng Xiaoning is particularly fond of references to *Yellow Earth*. Like *Yellow Earth*, *Grief* offers a series of breathtaking scenes of the surging Yellow River and the oddly shaped "yellow" landscape of the region (geologically called the Loess Plateau). But Feng's artistic sensibility is such that he includes new scenic spots as well: for example, a mountain cliff from which Irving climbs out of his plane before it drops to the bottom and explodes; a winding section of the Great Wall along the mountain ridge on which a unit of Communist soldiers escort Irving to their faraway base; and a wooded valley where red maple leaves shine under the autumn sun and An Jie appears even more like an "angel" to Irving.

What is most intriguing in *Grief* is the creative transformation Feng makes of the characters taken from *Yellow Earth*. Hanhan, the silent peasant son from *Yellow Earth*, reappears in almost the same clothing as the stupid-looking boy in *Grief*. But instead of rushing toward the Communist soldier as in the end of *Yellow Earth*, the peasant boy in *Grief* rescues Irving by throwing a piece of rope to him down the cliff, only to

grossing domestic film, losing only to *The Opium War* (Dianying yishu 1998). As recently as October 1999, *Red River Valley* was still being shown in the 4 Star Theater in San Francisco together with *Xiu Xiu: The Sent Down Girl* (Tianyu, 1999).

be killed in a subsequent Japanese bombing. Similarly, the peasant father from *Yellow Earth* reappears in *Grief*. But instead of insisting on traditions and refusing any change as in *Yellow Earth*, this time the adult male peasant is reincarnated as Grandpa who sacrifices his life in support of the Communists' anti-Japanese operations.

The most radical character changes in *Grief* occur in the Communist soldier and the rural woman. Unlike Gu Qing, an inarticulate and inefficient song-collector in *Yellow Earth*, Zhao Heizi, leader of the Communist escort unit in *Grief*, is a man of action. He risks his life several times to save Irving, and he convinces the head of a rival local militia to fight against the Japanese as their common enemy. Eventually, Heizi uses his own body to block a Japanese soldier's machine gun so that Irving can swim across the Yellow River with An Jie and Huahua, Heizi's young daughter. Likewise, An Jie appears far different from Cuiqiao, a suffering peasant woman in *Yellow Earth* who escapes her arranged marriage but drowns while attempting to cross the Yellow River to join the Communists. The daughter of a village head, An Jie is actually more "urban" than rural (having attended a city school and thus speaking English), and she is much more resourceful and romantic than Cuiqiao. Wounded in the battle, An Jie is dragged along with Huahua by Irving against the torrents of the Yellow River, all of them supported by a string of empty gourds tied around their waists, an ingenious device invented by Grandpa. Since she does not know how to swim, An Jie realizes that Irving cannot drag both her and Huahua across the river, so she cuts her length of rope and is swallowed by the rapids. "She gave herself to the mother river," reminisces the aging Irving, who revisits the scene with his daughter and, in a solemn ritual, floats the photos of An Jie, Huahua, Grandpa, and others down the river one by one.

Although framed by Irving's return to the Yellow River, thus making public history part of private memory, *Grief* successfully restores the iconic figures of the heroic Communist soldier and the self-sacrificing peasant, two figures whose historical accuracy and narrative efficacy have been challenged by the minority discourse I discussed earlier. The official endorsement of *Grief*, therefore, should come as no surprise. Feng's skillful rewriting—in fact, rewriting of some previous revisionist or deconstructive rewritings—of the history of the Communist revolution thus points to a new stage in the development of war films in China, a stage in which the commercialized production of artistic titles coexists with war epics of a more propagandist nature (like *The Decisive Further Advances, IV,* released in 1999). In its self-conscious effort to distance itself from minority discourse as exemplified in Wu Ziniu's earlier war films, *Grief* no longer questions the legitimacy of the Communist vision of history. And with its commercial packaging of a fated transnational romance, *Grief* also distinguishes itself from epic war films by heavily investing in the emotional and psychological impact of its narrative. The presence of Irving as a love-sick Westerner eager to trace his Chinese "roots" does not bother the Communist censors, for the vision projected by *Grief* does not challenge the official ideology, although it certainly competes with war epics in the commercial realm.

Given this new development in war films in China, the question that remains is the future of minority discourse as defined in this chapter. Even with the obvious—and at times embarrassing—evidence of Chinese filmmakers' complicity with the Communist propaganda machinery, it would be too early to conclude that leitmotif films have completely wiped out the space formerly occupied by minority discourse. While it is true that the commercial packaging of art and politics may constitute a new, alternative paradigm in war films in China, one must not forget that, no matter what ideological message new war films like *Grief* seem to transmit through their narratives, certain visual images from these films stand outside the narrative, haunting the viewer and leaving profoundly unsettling effects.

An analysis of the decapitation scene in *Grief* illustrates the power of such disturbing visual images. On their way to a Yellow River ferry, Zhao Heizi, An Jie, and Irving are arrested on Japanese orders by the militia of the An village. It turns out that An Jie is the only daughter of the village head, who lost his wife in a fight between the feuding An and Zhao clans years ago—a reference to *Old Well* (1987) and *Life on a String* (Bianzou bianchang, 1991). In a dream experienced by An's father, Heizi is brought under a *zhandao* (in a low-angle, close-up shot) and decapitated (off screen) in a public meeting guarded by Japanese soldiers. An Jie rushes to the scene and is shot to death by a Japanese officer. An's father wakes up from his dream, but he still brings Heizi to a public trial. The gruesome decapitation scene is staged once again, but this time An Jie rushes to the scene, threatens to blow herself up with a grenade tied around her waist, and rescues Heizi and Irving because no Japanese soldiers are present and An's father does not want his only daughter dead.

The incomplete decapitation scene thus ends with Heizi, An Jie, and Irving riding on horseback and disappearing into the barren landscape.

Although the mechanism of moving from death and decapitation to desublimation is clearly in place in the narrative of *Grief*, the powerful images of the incomplete decapitation invite critical interpretation along the lines of an imaginary "head-less" state and the unconscious act of "patricide" elaborated earlier. True, *Grief* does not interrogate the Communist vision of the Chinese revolution at its narrative level, but by its tragic end all Communists and their supporters are dead, except for Huahua, whose whereabouts cannot be verified in Irving's nostalgic narrative. As with *The Big Parade*, it is still possible to locate traces of minority discourse in the subtexts established by certain sequences of unsettling visuals in *Grief*. In brief, I would contend that subtle challenges to official ideology are still present in certain war films that possess rich, potentially disturbing subtexts, and that what makes the late 1990s markedly different from the late 1980s is that such challenges may not always come directly from a marginal space of confrontation or opposition, but may instead emerge from the very cracks and fissures in mainstream contemporary Chinese cinema.

IV

Cultural Nationalism and New Chinese Cinema

The recent surge of nationalism—in either politically blunt or commercially disguised form—in Chinese war films brings us back to Berry's 1992 formulation of "race-ization" in Chinese cinema. While he is perceptive in warning us against the dangers of nationalism, we are now in a better position to understand why Berry has overstated the case when he takes certain works of New Chinese Cinema as posing a radical challenge not only to "sino-centrism" but also to "the very assumption of a fundamental duality separating the Han Chinese and the foreign" (p. 51). As demonstrated earlier, *Horse Thief* and *Sacrificed Youth* are still deeply anchored in a Han-centered position. Indeed, Berry's insistence on a "rupture" between recent Chinese films and classical mainland Chinese cinema of the 1950s and 1960s might be potentially contradicted by his 1994 essay on nationhood, which demonstrates the continuity of the "classical" mode in epic war films. The latest development of leitmotif films in the 1990s once again cautions us against a premature celebration of ruptures or fissures in the dominant paradigms.

What Berry overlooks in his 1992 essay, I suggest with historical hindsight, is the idea that New Chinese Cinema may be a trend toward *cultural nationalism* in the history of modern China. In this regard, Gladney's observation is more pointed than Berry's because the former reveals a fundamental connection in the two periods of the ethnic minority genre: "Just as the singing and dancing, squeaky-clean minorities of an earlier genre failed to convince audiences that these people really were 'liberated' by the party, . . . so Tian's minority films disappointed audiences: they both break with earlier representations of minorities and simultaneously reconstitute them" (1995, 169).

The question of cultural nationalism deserves further elaboration. For John Hutchinson, "there are two quite different types of nationalism—cultural and political—that must not be conflated": whereas the latter embodies "a cosmopolitan rationalist conception of the nation that looks forward ultimately to a common humanity transcending cultural difference," the former seeks to locate "the essence of a nation [in] its distinctive civilization, which is the product of its unique history, culture and geographical profile" (Hutchinson and Smith 1994, 122). According to Hutchinson, among chief proponents of cultural nationalism are historical scholars, "myth-making" intellectuals, and, above all, artists, all of whom attempt to "recover this creative force [of the nation] in all its dimensions with verisimilitude and project it to the members of the nation" (Hutchinson and Smith 1994, 123). As should be apparent from the numerous films discussed in this chapter, Chinese filmmakers are one group of such cultural nationalists-cum-artists actively engaged in the recovery and projecting of certain kinds of Chinese cultural myths and symbols, especially in the post-Mao era. This is so because the post-Mao era presents a perfect condition for the (re)emergence of cultural nationalism, which, in Kosaku Yoshino's view, "aims to regenerate the national community by creating, preserving or strengthening a people's cultural identity when it is felt to be lacking, inadequate or threatened" (1992, 1; see also Sakai 1997).

Cultural nationalism, as Harumi Befu writes on the context of East Asia, "focuses on the creation, crystallization, and expression of the cultural identity of the nation" (1993, 2). In the process of defining a national identity, cultural nationalism "asserts the claim of certain cultural characteristics and traditions, almost always containing a strong primor-dialist element" (D. Buck 1994, 6). The fact that New Chinese Cinema has in varying degrees participated in reshaping cultural nationalism in contemporary China is evident in its typical fascination with an entire repertoire of recognizable cultural symbols, myths, and traditions of the Chinese nation: the Loess Plateau and the Yellow River, as in *Yellow Earth*, *Ballad of the Yellow River*, and *Grief*; traditional operas, as in *Woman, Demon, Human*, *The True Hearted* (Xinxiang, 1992), and *Farewell My Concubine*; indigenous folk music or art, as in *Swan Song*, *Drum Singers*, and *The King of Masks* (Bianlian, 1995); local marriage customs, as in *Red Sorghum*, *Raise the Red Lantern*, and *Bloody Morning* (Xuese qingchen, 1990); various funeral proceedings, as in *Ju Dou*, *The Big Mill*, and *A Yunnan Story* (Yunnan gushi, 1993).

Few would dispute the fact that New Chinese Cinema has helped rekindle public interest in national identity in the post-Mao era. However, viewing enticing images from the above films, one gets the impression that it is the filmmakers' consistent exploration (in their self-appointed role as both artist and historian in Hutchinson's sense) of the seemingly "unfathomable" depths of national culture—or the culture of the "Chinese nation" broadly defined, including its customs, legends, myths, and rituals—that has secured an international reputation for New Chinese Cinema since the mid-1980s. Indeed, one of the greatest successes of New Chinese Cinema might be its "cultural exhibitionism," the repackaging of what is generally believed to be Chinese national culture and its redistribution to the international film market.[28]

Transnational Cultural Politics in a Hyphenated World

For many Chinese viewers, it is precisely what Western audiences might mistake as authentically "Chinese" in recent successful Chinese films that has provoked indignation and criticism. Dai Qing, for one, was not at all impressed by *Raise the Red Lantern*, despite "its international cachet seemingly enhanced by the involvement of producers and financing from Hong Kong, Taiwan, Japan, and other countries." She sees clearly that "this kind of film is really shot for the casual pleasures of

---

[28] As Yau puts it, "In the Western critics' fascinated and approving gaze, then, the young Chinese directors saw themselves as 'worthy of love,' and pride in 'national' cultural products grew as verified by international exchange" (1993, 96).

foreigners . . . [who] can go on and muddleheadedly satisfy their oriental fetishisms" (1993, 333–6). As a native Chinese, Dai is not to be cheated "by half-baked new fashions and trends." To prove her case, she compiles a long list of "false notes" (or "inauthenticities") in Zhang Yimou's filmic representation of Chinese culture, such as his invented rituals of foot-massage and raising the red lantern, both significantly absent in the original story (Su Tong 1993, 11–99).

What is interesting in Dai's case is that, ironically, she sees the trendy practice of cultural nationalism in New Chinese Cinema as being complicit with Orientalist discourse in the West. Such complicity can be better understood in terms of Anthony Smith's comments: "Standarized, commercialized mass commodities will nevertheless draw for their contents upon revivals of traditional, folk or national motifs and styles in fashions, furnishings, music and the arts, lifted out of their original contexts and anaesthetized" (1990, 176). Sure enough, many recent Chinese films, especially those by Chen Kaige and Zhang Yimou, have been generously financed by foreign capital and have continued to attract Western attention. Seen from this perspective, cultural nationalism in contemporary China is deeply implicated in the cultural economy of transnational capitalism (see also chapter 2).

To conclude my investigation of the relationship between nationhood and ethnicity, hegemony and minority discourse, center and margin, national glories and individual sufferings, cultural nationalism and transnational capitalism, I point out that, increasingly, we find ourselves at a crossroads in our continued efforts to redefine or remap our *fin-de-siècle* world. That the products of cultural nationalism in New Chinese Cinema have not only met with international approval but have also attracted transnational capital is itself a comment on the currently hard-to-define geopolitical world. Whether labeled as "postmodern," "postcolonial," "post-imperialist," "post-Orientalist," "postsocialist," "postnational," "post-ethnic," "post-historical," "post-contemporary," "post-future," or even "posthuman," our present-day world seems to have but a hyphen-ated existence.[29] Again, Bhabha's words nicely articulate our deep-seated

---

[29] I survey discussions of Chinese postmodernism and postsocialism in chapter 8. For a critique of postcolonial discourse, see Dirlik 1994. For the "post-imperialist," see King 1990. For post-Orientalism, see Rogers 1994. For the "postnational," see Matustik 1993. For the "post-ethnic," see Hollinger 1995. For the "post-historical," see Fukuyama 1992, 276–84. The term "post-contemporary" is used in a book series, "Post-Contemporary

anxiety: "Our existence today is marked by a tenebrous sense of survival, living on the borderline of the 'present,' from which there seems to be no proper name other than the current and controversial shiftiness of the prefix 'post'" (1994, 1). We are, indeed, overwhelmed by what Jameson calls "an untotalizable totality" (Jameson and Miyoshi 1998, xii).

Yet, whatever happens, as Hutchinson and Smith argue, "Given the longevity and ubiquity of ethnic ties and sentiments throughout history, it would be rash to make predictions about the early transcendence of ethnicity or to imagine that a world of so many overlapping but intense affiliations and loyalties is likely to be able to abolish ethnic conflicts" (1996, 14)—or cultural difference and national identity, I would add. It is imperative that the seeming crisis in *epistemes* alone not prevent us from keeping track of the constantly shifting geopolitical and geocultural configurations of power and difference. In the next two chapters, I investigate two dimensions in the projects of screening China, one located in ethnographic cinema, the other in urban cinema.

Interventions," coedited by Stanley Fish and Fredric Jameson and published by Duke University Press. The term "post-future" is found in Gaines and Lahusen 1995. And the term "posthuman" is used in Hayles 1999. To the best of my knowledge, Berry is the first to use "postnational" in Chinese film studies (1994a, 45).

Six

Seductions of the Body: Fashioning Ethnographic Cinema in Contemporary China

> If ethnographic texts are a means by which Europeans represent to themselves their (usually subjugated) others, authoethnographic texts are those the others construct in response to or in dialogue with those metropolitan representations. . . . Autoethnographic texts are not, then, what are usually thought of as "authentic" or autochthonous forms of self-representation. . . . Rather autoethnography involves partial collaboration with and appropriation of the idioms of the conqueror.
>
> Mary Louise Pratt, *Imperial Eyes*

My discussion of mainstream films and minority discourse in contemporary Chinese cinema in chapter 5 reveals two mechanisms by which nationhood, ethnicity, and history are constructed in film. On the one hand, a mythified, unitary vision of China—based on reputedly shared experiences of glories and miseries—was imposed by the Communist regime in the early 1950s and has continued to be projected in Chinese films over the past half century. On the other hand, a minority discourse emerged around the mid-1980s and has worked between the interstices of the dominant paradigms by opening up and questioning the grand notions of people, civilization, and revolution, among others. What happened in the minority discourse of the late 1980s, however, was that in its efforts to break free of the strictures of Communist ideology through critical reflection on Chinese culture and its pre-revolutionary history, it has played an unexpected role in promoting a new kind of cultural nationalism, one that makes it "rebellious" (as the self-imaged "patricidal" son) on the domestic front but "complicit" (as the eager collaborator with transnational capitalism) in the international arena. To use Dai Jinhua's apt metaphors, the Fifth Generation directors like Zhang Yimou "are trapped—or more

207

accurately, have entrapped themselves—in the net" of the global market economy (1993, 80).

In this chapter I first pursue a close reading of *Red Sorghum*—one of the most significant transition films in contemporary Chinese cinema—in terms of an emerging ideology of the body in the 1980s (Section I). The international success of this film made ethnographic cinema an entirely new genre in mainland China. But ethnographic cinema may be better understood as "autoethnography" in that it conscientiously seeks to exhibit all conceivable aspects of the "body" and the embodied meanings of "ethnic" Chinese culture in exotic and often erotic forms (Section II). The significance accorded the body and landscape (with their fascinating and enigmatic contours and shapes) in some works of ethnographic cinema requires further examination of two separate realms of geocultural production: Hollywood's images of China during the 1930s and 1940s (in a distinct ethnographic mode) and the characteristic devotion to the native soil (*xiangtu*) in New Taiwan Cinema during the 1980s and 1990s, the latter arguably constituting another kind of ethnography or autoethnography (Section III). Finally, I place my investigation of ethnographic cinema in a larger framework of transnational cultural politics, thereby setting the stage for a view into the relationship between globalization and Chinese urban cinema in chapter 7.

I

"National Allegory" in Third World Culture

In his seminal essay, "Third-World Literature in the Era of Multinational Capitalism" (first published in *Social Text* in 1986 and later changed to "World Literature in an Age of Multinational Capitalism" in a 1987 anthology), Fredric Jameson postulates a theory of "national allegory" for Third World texts. The primacy of national allegory is, he claims, a remarkable feature apparently common to all Third World cultural productions and radically distinguishable from analogous cultural forms in the First World. "Those [Third World] texts, even those narratives which are seemingly private and invested with a properly libidinal dynamic, necessarily project a political dimension in the form of national allegory: the story of the private individual destiny is always an allegory of the embattled situation of the public Third World culture and society" (1987, 142). Jameson's theory is based on his observation of "a radical split between the private and the public, between the poetic and the political" (or "Freud versus Marx") that characterized much of capitalist culture, "the culture of the Western realist and modernist novel" (1987, 141). Third World culture, on the contrary, is "necessarily" allegorical in that "the telling of the individual story and the individual experience cannot but ultimately involve the whole laborious telling of the experience of the collectivity itself" (1987, 158).

Given his mapping of Third World cultural "totality"—in complement with another mapping of the contemporary Western, postmodern world (Jameson 1991)—Jameson's theory of "national allegory" has obvious relevance to the study of Third World literature and cinema, even though the theory itself did not go without an immediate challenge from the Third World (Ahmad 1987). My reason for invoking Jameson's theory here, however, is not to critique its hypothetical nature or its obvious disregard of the vast differences among Third World countries, but rather to see how its theoretical insights, such as the interplay between the private and the public, the libidinal and the sublimated, the poetic and the political, can better inform our reading of contemporary Chinese cinema. With this in mind, I now turn to *Red Sorghum*, the first Chinese film to win the Golden Bear at the Berlin Film Festival. My discussion necessarily takes into account the problem of "national roots," partly because the film itself is incorporated into director Zhang Yimou's broader project to search for the distinctive features of the Chinese people and culture.

The Body: Images of Violence and Obscenity

What impresses the viewer first in *Red Sorghum* is the exuberance of its initial celebratory mood, conveyed by the sedan-chair dance that is coded as typically Chinese. As the film opens, against a setting of barren yellow land, eight shirtless male sedan carriers dance with a red sedan chair, hoarsely chanting a vulgar and obscene song, and rocking and shaking the young bride helplessly confined within (Gong Li, enunciated in the male voice-over as "My Grandma"). For nearly ten minutes, we are treated to a feast of color and movement, accompanied by exotic regional music and lurid remarks. We are only later reminded of Grandma's impending fate: she is being forced by her greedy father to marry the fifty-year-old leprous owner of a sorghum-wine distillery in exchange for a small mule.

Several repeated shots in this scene deserve closer attention. From within the sedan, Grandma, though disturbed, anxiously peeks through the curtains, only to have her view obstructed by the sweat- and dirt-covered bodies of the sedan carriers. In spite of their warnings about her soon-to-be husband, Gong Li seems to be fascinated with the muscular carriers. This idea of fascination is further strengthened in another scene when the sedan carriers overpower and beat to death a masked bandit who tries to kidnap Grandma with a fake pistol.

In terms of this repressed fascination with muscles, or more precisely, with the human body, Grandma's "willing" submission in a later scene to abduction and "rape" (Canby 1988) by the chief sedan carrier (Jiang Wen, as "My Grandpa") would be more understandable to a Western audience. In fact, the rape scene (or rather the "love-making," as many Chinese critics prefer) is portrayed poetically and solemnly. After chasing Gong Li through the underbrush and revealing his identity to her when he captures her, Grandpa stamps out a space amid the sorghum stalks, a round circle much like a place of sacrifice. Grandma lies motionless on the ground, her eyes closed, while Grandpa kneels, his face turned to the sky. Arguably, this is intended as a solemn moment: a moment of deification, a moment of returning the human to its natural elements, and a moment of triumph of the primitive "body," in all its violence and life force, over the repressive tradition of the Chinese patriarchal society.[1]

Another scene with equal emphasis on the body is set in the wine distillery after the mysterious murder of the leprous owner (suggested off-screen as the target of Grandma's scissors). The male workers, again shirtless, perspire by the wine distiller. Grandma, now the sole owner of the distillery, is invited to see the fruits of wine making: the pouring out of new wine, which visually suggests male potency. All partake of the moment of joy and fulfillment as they taste the new wine. The festive mood, however, is disrupted by the arrival of Grandpa, who had been driven out of the winery after drunkenly insulting Grandma with obscene references to their love-making in the field. This time, however, he is sober and determined. He shows off his strength and contempt by lifting and carrying big pots of new wine, placing them in a row, and urinating into each of them. In spite of such a blasphemous affront (which later

---

[1] Zhong Chengxiang considers this "love-making" scene as a celebration of "man's freedom" and as such is "a classic scene" in Chinese film history (1988, 44–50).

miraculously turns out to be a "blessing" in disguise because the wine proves better than before), the sheer presence of his muscular body intimidates the other male workers and, significantly, "intoxicates" Grandma into a trance-like state. With a triumphant air, Grandpa hoists Grandma under his arms—the primitive act of the cave man—and strides directly into her bedroom. As typical of all legends of romance, they live together happily, and Grandpa's position is later legitimated by the birth of their son.

From the violence, vulgarism, indecency, and abusive language highlighted in these scenes, all closely linked to the human body, we can see clearly that in *Red Sorghum* the images of the body are deliberately exaggerated, primitivized, and projected so as to fulfill a special ideological function, which can be better interpreted in light of Mikhail Bakhtin's theory of carnivalism.

Carnival: The Private Returned to the Public

In *Rabelais and His World*, Bakhtin offers an exhaustive examination of what he calls the "popular-festive forms" (for example, eating, drinking, and cursing) and "the grotesque images of the body" (such as sex, defecation, pregnancy, birth, and death). For Bakhtin, all forms of "degradation" in carnival are not just "entertainment" in the negative sense of the word; rather, "with all its images, indecencies, and curses," carnival "affirms the people's immortal, indestructible character" (1984, 256).

Bakhtin arrived at this positive view of carnival in a dialectic way through his recognition of the original—and by now almost lost or forgotten—meaning of the human body in Western culture. In the Middle Ages and up to the Renaissance, there was little question as to the unifying forces within the human body. According to Bakhtin, two characteristic tendencies existed in Renaissance philosophy: "First is the tendency to find in man the entire universe with all its elements and forces, with its higher and lower stratum; second is the tendency to think of the human body as drawing together the most remote phenomena and forces of the cosmos" (1984, 365). The human body, seen in this light, is a unity of heaven and earth, of the public and the private, and even of death and rebirth. This primordial unity, however, was lost in the subsequent development of human (especially bourgeois) societies. As Bakhtin puts it, "in the modern image of the individual body, sexual life, eating, drinking, and defecation have radically changed their meaning:

they have been transferred to the private and psychological level" (1984, 321). In other words, the previously public features of the human body have been transformed and confined exclusively to a private, psychologized space. From this observation, one can see that Bakhtin's theory of carnival carries with it an important historical mission: to return the human body from its now private and psychological status to its original public domain.

Red Sorghum may be read as an attempt in the same direction. In the film, the private spaces are continually transgressed or even destroyed. For instance, Grandma's closed space in the sedan chair is first metaphorically "penetrated" by obscene words and then literally violated by the bandit. Similarly, the privacy of Grandma's wedding room is destroyed by Grandpa, whose macho behavior seems to have placed her completely under his spell. Private acts, such as urinating and perspiring, are performed unabashedly in public. The implication of these private-turned-public moments, I contend, is that they emphasize precisely the interconnectedness of all human bodies. To quote Bakhtin: "The individual feels that he is an indissoluble part of the collectivity, a member of the people's mass body. In this whole the individual body ceases to a certain extent to be itself; it is possible, so to say, to exchange bodies, to be renewed. . . . At the same time the people become aware of their sensual, material bodily unity and community" (1984, 255). Given the original unity within the human body, the dominance of the bodily images in *Red Sorghum* functions as a visual index to the reconceptualization of a reunion of the private and the public, a reunion crystallized in the central object of the film, red sorghum wine.

Wine: A Shared Poetic Spirit

Because of the carnivalesque nature of *Red Sorghum*, where images of the body dominate the screen, wine invites interpretation on at least three levels. First, on a popular level, wine accompanies festivity and is consumed in celebrations of all kind. It is both the product of collective labor and the reward for the worker. Drinking wine is, therefore, "not a biological, animal act but a social event" (Bakhtin 1984, 281). The winery workers' drinking and chanting to the wine god are good examples of this. In the film's two praying scenes, drinking is not only done as a social event but is specifically performed as a ritual, where it acquires a mythic dimension that outweighs any individual concerns.

Second, on a less obvious level, wine (or liquor) is a poetic image deeply rooted in Chinese culture. It is, for one, a well-known way for a solitary poet to escape his or her immediate realities. It is also a spirit that inspires a poet's artistic visions (for example, Li Bai's solitary drinking to the moon and to his own dancing shadows on the ground) and further sustains his or her independent, often secluded life. Wine, seen from the perspective of this cultural tradition, symbolizes a worldly passion for an intoxicated, ecstatic life (rather than a mediocre, repressed one)—a passion for a unique vision of life with all of its essential meanings, such as vitality, productivity, and creativity.

Third, on a more specific level, wine in *Red Sorghum* refers to a special type of sorghum wine that is brewed by collective labor, magically "finished" with Grandpa's urine, given the name "Shibalihong" (red over eighteen miles) by Grandma, consumed by the workers in the ritual scenes, and finally deployed as the dynamite to destroy a truckload of Japanese soldiers. It is not difficult to identify several individual elements in the wine, for it is a strange mixture of many things. Nor is it surprising to see that it becomes near the end of the film an object dedicated to the collective memory of Luohan, who has left the winery to join the Communist army and is later captured by Japanese soldiers and skinned alive in front of the Chinese laborers. Sorghum wine, as a locus of the unified private and public, encompasses the cycle of life, death, and rebirth, serving as witness to the glory of collective work and the tragedy of lost freedom and independence in the wake of the Japanese invasion.

Wine, then, is a powerful unifying force. As such, it immediately evokes another image in the Western tradition—that of Dionysus, the Greek god of wine. In *Red Sorghum*, the viewer is often touched—or intoxicated—by scenes similar to what Friedrich Nietzsche so enthusiastically eulogizes in *The Birth of Tragedy*: "Not only does the bond between man and man come to be forged once more by the magic of the Dionysiac rite, but nature itself, long alienated or subjugated, rises again to celebrate the reconciliation with her prodigal son, man" (1971, 637). The love-making scene in the sorghum field is one such magic moment, as are the two wine-praying ritual scenes. As if all intoxicated by the Dionysian spirit, the characters in *Red Sorghum* often express themselves, in Nietzsche's words, "through song and dance as the member[s] of a higher community," and their collective power is manifest "to the glorious satisfaction of the primordial One"—an ultimate unity (1971, 638).

To further illustrate how an individual can lose him or herself in the public or communal, I would make two points here. First, in *Red Sorghum*, wine, from its initial production to its ultimate use as a destroyer, is closely associated with Grandma. Second, Grandma is virtually the only one in the film endowed consistently with clairvoyance. At the beginning of the film, she feels (and thus shows us) her fascination with muscles; in the middle, she realizes the importance of collective work and leads the winery to spectacular business success; in the end, she senses the moral obligation to avenge the death of Luohan and brings the story to a tragic-heroic closure. From this particular angle offered by the symbolism of wine, *Red Sorghum* could well be seen as Grandma's story— a story about her individual vision shared and realized by the public.

The idea of such a shared vision is effectively demonstrated in the final ritual scene. Before setting out for combat, the male workers line up in front of a portrait of the wine god to perform their ritual prayers while drinking wine. "Drinking our wine," they chant, "we won't kowtow to the emperor." The idea of fighting originates with Grandma and is readily adopted by the collective without question. Significantly, Grandma sees the importance of fighting not in terms of Communist ideology but simply in terms of the loyalty an individual must demonstrate to his or her own community. Their self-sacrifice, in other words, is performed exclusively by and for themselves, not for illustrating abstract concepts such as nationalism, patriotism, and anti-imperialism. The conspicuous absence of the dominant ideology in the film brings us to the question of cinematic narration in *Red Sorghum*.

An Innocent Narrator: The Politics of Depoliticized Narration

The final scene of *Red Sorghum* is of Grandpa and his nine-year-old son (enunciated as "My Father") standing in the midst of a bombed-out sorghum field. Grandma's bullet-ridden body lies nearby. A folk song fills the soundtrack. Then the narrator (Grandson) tells of his father's vision of a solar eclipse and a blood-stained world. This voice-over, which has been heard on and off throughout the film, finally pulls the viewer back to a perspective of the late 1980s.

A striking contrast, then, exists in *Red Sorghum* between the visual events and the narration. While one actually sees the winery workers' lives, one also listens to the voice that attempts to encode their lives in more overtly political terminology. For example, at one moment the narrator says that "Uncle Luohan tried to mobilize local armed bandits into anti-Japanese forces"—an announcement beyond the comprehension of the winery workers within the film's diegesis. Such a contrast amounts to an embarrassing confession that the "innocent" narrator, speaking on behalf of the present generation, knows very little of the richness of the narrated story. The narrator's lack of knowledge at once foregrounds his limited perspective at a fully politicized present and evokes an ever-increasing yearning for the "lost" meaning of that primitive life.

From the narrative point of view, therefore, we are confronted with a strange ideological phenomenon in *Red Sorghum*: the entire story is presented in such a way as to reduce its political overtones to a minimum. This deliberately *depoliticized* narration is "strange" and non-canonical in the overall cultural and political context, where Communist policy dictates that literature and art serve politics.[2] Yet this phenomenon is not so strange if one takes into consideration the 1980s trend in Chinese literature and art toward depoliticization in narration, a trend exemplified by the Fifth Generation directors in cinema and by the roots-searching and avant-garde fiction writers—including, not surprisingly, Mo Yan, the original author of *Red Sorghum*.[3]

It must be evident by now that *Red Sorghum* belongs outside mainstream ideology. The marginality of the film is particularly telling in a number of obvious omissions in the text. First, the setting of the story—in a remote wine distillery—indicates a deliberate absence of the historically agricultural mode of production in Chinese society, what Jameson calls "the great bureaucratic imperial systems" (1987, 140). Its celebratory presentation of another mode of production, that of "primitive, or tribal society" (Jameson's term), with all its backwardness, vulgarism, and blasphemy, places the film in direct opposition to traditional values of Chinese culture and civilization. Second, the depoliticized narration in *Red Sorghum* brings about a complete disregard

---

[2] This party line was originally laid down by Mao Zedong in the early 1940s and has been kept consistently ever since, though the present version—literature and art must serve socialism, one with Chinese characteristics—is comparatively mild in tone (see McDougall 1980).

[3] For Chinese avant-garde writers, see J. Wang 1996; X. Zhang 1997, 101–200. For Mo Yan, see Duke 1993; T. Lu 1995, 129–54; Zhu Ling 1993.

for class distinctions (such as master-servant) and political consciousness (like the cliché of self-conscious patriotism) in the film. Luohan, the only character with a political vision, is given little narrative function in the film; even worse, he is portrayed as a helpless victim of Japanese brutality. The gruesome scene of Luohan being publicly skinned alive shows that, historically, Zhang Yimou has joined Wu Ziniu in a cinematic project of desublimation by projecting scenes of decapitation and violent death (see chapter 5). Third, the primitive, communal life-style poeticized in the film poses a fundamental challenge to traditional moral values. Instead of exemplary virtuous women in mainstream films, *Red Sorghum* endorses the transgressive behaviors of Grandpa and Grandma, both of whom are significantly deprived of proper names. True, Grandma at one point insists that her workers call her Jiu'er (literally, "the ninth birth"), but that is actually her nickname and does not signify her social status as a widow in patriarchy. By strategically denying its protagonists their proper names, *Red Sorghum* aspires to a mythic representation of the primitive life, which thrives only on unrestrained passions. Invigorated by wine and regenerated by sorghum fields, such primitive passions give poetic expression to an emerging ideology of the body in Chinese cinema.

The depoliticized narration in *Red Sorghum* thus testifies fully to the subversive or rebellious nature of its chosen marginality. The film's self-positioning outside mainstream Chinese filmmaking and dominant Communist ideology enables—actually compels—the viewer to reflect critically on larger social and cultural issues in contemporary China.

Ideology of the Body: The Search for Cultural Roots

The depoliticized narration in *Red Sorghum*, I would argue, is in part achieved through a process of "degradation" of what used to be the gentle (in human behavior), the decent (in human speech), the moral (in human relations), and the honorable (in social interaction). The purpose of degradation, as Bakhtin points out, is "the lowering of all that is high, spiritual, ideal, abstract" (1984, 19). By a radical twist, the civilized becomes uncivilized, the indecent glorified, and the blasphemous blessed. And the result of such a degradation is, unavoidably, a restructuring of the existing concepts of world order.

This is exactly what Bakhtin so enthusiastically embraces in his concept of carnival: "[Carnival] is outside of and contrary to all existing forms of the coercive socioeconomic and political organization, which is suspended for the time of festivity" (1984, 255). "Carnival was the true feast of time," he continues, "the feast of becoming, change and renewal. It was hostile to all that was immortalized and completed. . . . Carnival celebrates the destruction of the old and the birth of the new world" (1984, 10, 410). Just as the subversive and destructive force is true and real in Bakhtin's formulation of carnival, so is it in an ideology of the body—an ideology not only articulated in *Red Sorghum* with much fanfare but also ascertainable in varying degrees in the works of Chinese cinema, literature, and literary theory in the 1980s.

The essential principle of the ideology of the body is to return the body to its primitive origin. The image of the body can be a human body, thus returning it to its most basic biological needs, such as eating, drinking, defecating, love-making, child bearing and rearing—themes or motifs that are consistently explored in *A Girl from Hunan* [Illustration 20], *Horse Thief,* and *Old Well.*

20. *A Girl from Hunan* (1985): Female sexuality and primitive passions

The image of the body can also be the body, in an abstract sense, of one's ontological status, thus returning the long-forbidden topic of subjectivity to the Chinese intellectual millieu, as in Liu Zaifu's aesthetic projects of literary subjectivity (1985–86 and 1986; see also J. Wang 1996, 196–206). The image of the body can be extended much further, even to that of the entire nation, thus returning Chinese culture to its original cradle, the Loess Plateau, as is clearly the case in *Yellow Earth* and *Ballad of the Yellow River.*

A much-studied Chinese cultural phenomenon of the 1980s, "the search for cultural roots" (*xungen*), can also be meaningfully discussed in terms of the emerging ideology of the body (Ji Hongzheng 1989; J. Wang 1996, 213–24). As in the case of an ideology of the body, the search for cultural roots in China entails a conceptually "downward" movement, exploring the most fundamental elements of human life. Not surprisingly, what is considered most "national" or "Chinese" is often rediscovered in rituals, folk customs, and religious ceremonies, all invariably and significantly set in locales remote from China's contemporary cultural and political centers. The search for roots, therefore, is frequently executed in the form of myth, with all its emphases on legend, ritual, and even superstition.

What Nietzsche says at the end of *The Birth of Tragedy* is illuminating in this connection: "Man today, stripped of myths, stands famished among all his pasts and must dig frantically for roots, be it among the most remote antiquities" (1971, 641). It is as if the "modern man," having lost his vital ties with history and nature, can only move backward and downward to search for his lost origins—the mythic home (or womb?). In the context of 1980s China, it is as if only by moving away from the interfering forces of political dogma and doctrine—a movement indicative, nonetheless, of the powerful workings of the politics of absence and marginality—can a new ideology be fully established, an ideology that reunites the high and the low, the far and the near, all in a truly material, tangible, and hence comprehensible self, the body.

One of *Red Sorghum*'s messages is clear: it eulogizes the life of a nameless couple whose unabashed confrontation with their own bodies creates for us a new ideology of the body. The body in question, to borrow Bakhtin's apt expression, is not "the biological body, which merely repeats itself in the new generations, but precisely the historic, progressing body of mankind" (1984, 367). From here I would contend, following Bakhtin further, that an ideology of the body is "not abstract thought about the future but the living sense that each man belongs to the immortal people who create history" (1984, 367). Indeed, it is the body of the people, not dogmas and doctrines, that is immortal, and it is this immortality that Zhang Yimou worships in *Red Sorghum*.[4]

Liberation: Third World Allegory and Third Cinema

The final tragic scene in *Red Sorghum* conforms, in a sense, to what Jameson calls the Third World's "life-and-death struggle" with First World imperialism (1987, 140). Such a struggle, by its very definition, must be a political struggle. Jameson's insistence on the political nature of the allegory form in Third World culture may find support in the discussion of Third Cinema in the West. Initially proposed by Fernando Solanas and Octavio Getino in a manifesto in 1969, "Third Cinema" now refers to "a cinema of decolonization and for liberation" (Gabriel 1982, 1; see also Solanas and Getino 1976; Pines and Willemen 1989). Given the political agenda built into the proposition of Third Cinema, it is no surprise that its style must be subversive and revolutionary, "full of the imagery of guerilla combat" (Armes 1987, 99).

Judging from this political criterion, *Red Sorghum* does not fit perfectly into the category of Third Cinema. While there is no denying that recent Chinese films also make use of major themes in Third Cinema—class, culture, religion, sexism, armed struggle—to varying degrees (Gabriel 1982, 15–20), the concept of Third Cinema may be more usefully applied to a study of Chinese leftist films in the 1930s, which are marked by a heavy ideological emphasis on anti-colonization and anti-imperialism (Berry 1989). The apparent discrepancy between the revolutionary politics explicit in Third Cinema and the seemingly depoliticized narration of *Red Sorghum* (and other recent Chinese films) presents an obvious problem.

However, this discrepancy alone does not rule out other grounds for comparison. The central tenet of "liberation" in Third Cinema, for instance, is still eminently evident in *Red Sorghum*. What needs to be differentiated at this point are the various levels at which the concept of liberation is applied. At the top level, that of nationhood, the liberation

---

[4] One Chinese critic goes so far as to call Zhang Yimou "the Dionysus of today's China" (Chen Xiaoxin 1989, 30).

of the country from the Japanese imperialists is overtly set as the background of the story. At a lower level, that of the individual, the liberation of women from patriarchal oppression is touched on in the film. Yet these two kinds of liberation constitute only a small part of the film. *Red Sorghum* visually proclaims a total liberation and triumph of the body. It is this ideology of the body that undermines other political concerns in the film. By endorsing a primitive way of living and the simple nature of the Chinese people—free from any form of political indoctrination or repression—*Red Sorghum* aspires to a liberation of the human body, a liberation that returns the Chinese people from their uniform lifestyle and sterile ways of thinking to their nurturing, regenerating origins. Indeed, the fast pace and celebratory mood of *Red Sorghum* are meant to awaken and return Chinese viewers to their lost vitality, thus rejuvenating (the body of) the whole nation.

Red Sorghum is, therefore, not a story of any individual. Its poeticized narration, no matter how depoliticized it appears, is ultimately political in nature. In the final analysis, the aspiration to liberate thought from political indoctrination, to subvert the seemingly insurmountable authority of the dominant ideology, and, in short, to advocate a new ideology of the body in contemporary China, is, and must be, a political aspiration in itself. It is in this sense that Jameson's theory of national allegory can be meaningfully applied to *Red Sorghum*. The individual experience of archetypal Grandpa and Grandma, narrated in a seemingly depoliticized way, is ultimately an allegory of China, an allegory involving the experience of the whole Chinese nation—the experience, this time, not of liberating the country from colonization or imperialist invasion, but of liberating its own body. Given the contemporary Chinese situation, the new task of liberation, as assumed by the ideology of the body, is as political in nature as the earlier ones.

II

Ethnographic Cinema: The Consequences of Marching to the World

In his reflections on the question of Third Cinema, Paul Willemen argues that, in the Third World, "any discourse of national-cultural identity is always and from the outset oppositional, although not necessarily conducive to progressive positions" (1989, 18). Three options are available to Third World intellectuals and artists. First, "to identify with the dominant and dominating culture, which is easy for the metropolitan intelligentsia"; second, "to develop the antagonistic sense of national identity by seeking to reconnect with traditions that got lost or were displaced or distorted"; third, "particular aspects of some cultures are selected and elevated into essentialized symbols of the national identity: the local answer to imperialism's stereotypes" (1989, 18). As analyzed above, *Red Sorghum* chooses the second option and, in its second half, launches an apparently antagonistic move against Japanese imperialism. Nevertheless, as Willemen perceptively points out,

> this [second] option presents considerable difficulties and dangers. The main ones derive from the need to reinvent traditions, to conjure up an image of pre-colonial innocence and authenticity. . . . The result is mostly a nostalgia for a pre-colonial society which in fact never existed, full of idyllic villages and communities peopled by "authentic" (read folkloric) innocents in touch with the "real" values perverted by imperialism or, in the most naive versions, perverted by technology. (1989, 18)

Precisely due to an urgent need to reinvent tradition, a practice more evident in his subsequent films such as *Ju Dou* and *Raise the Red Lantern* (see Clark 1989), Zhang Yimou proceeded quickly from the second option to the third, and the result was the immediate popularity of ethnographic cinema in mainland China during the early 1990s.

Bear in mind that "ethnographic cinema" discussed here refers to a particular kind of fictional film, not ethnographic documentary.[5] By definition, ethnographic cinema involves the "writing" (that is, construction and projection) of aspects of *ethnos*—ethnic or national culture, language, religion, and so on—in the cinematic medium. Like other types of writing, ethnography relies on textual strategies of differentiation, classification, selection, exclusion, and reorganization. The agency of such ethnographic writing and the questions of power and representation, therefore, have been particularly sensitive to all parties involved. According to Mary Louise Pratt, whereas "ethnographic texts

---

[5] Ethnographic documentary has never been a major film practice in mainland China. Indeed, ethnography or anthropology has never been fully developed as an academic discipline there. For an overview of recent ethnographic films in China, see Liu Debin 1997. For sample studies of ethnographic film in the West, see MacDougall 1998; Rony 1996.

are a means by which Europeans represent to themselves their (usually subjugated) others, authoethnographic texts are those the others construct in response to or in dialogue with those metropolitan representations" (1992, 7). While it is true that Pratt bases her differentiation of these two modes of ethnographic writing on her study of European travel writings of the eighteenth and nineteenth centuries, what happens in the cultural arena of transnational capitalism in the late twentieth century, I would argue, is that the power structure of domination (the West) and subordination (the non-West) has remained fundamentally unchanged since the earlier periods of colonization and imperialism.

In her critical work on primitive passions, Rey Chow insists on approaching contemporary Chinese cinema "as a kind of postmodern *self*-writing or *auto*ethnography," which is first and foremost exhibited for the gaze of the West and which, therefore, constitutes a special type of "the Oriental's orientalism" in its "self-subalternizing, self-exoticizing visual gestures" (1995, xi, 171). As I argued in chapters 2 and 4, to classify all of contemporary Chinese cinema as autoethnography is surely an overstatement, and the label "postmodern" also calls for further quali-fication and contextualization (see chapter 8). However, "autoeth-nography," as a new kind of ethnography Chow identifies in Zhang Yimou's early films, does appear to be a perfect designation for his cinematic project. As Chow rightly states,

> Zhang's films have become a spectacular and accessible form of imaginative writing about a "China" that is supposedly past but whose ideological power still lingers. While many of the ethnic customs and practices in Zhang's films are invented, the import of such details lies not in their authenticity but in their mode of signification. Such import makes up the second major element of the newness of Zhang's ethnography: the use of things, characters, and narratives not for themselves but for their collective, hallucinatory signification of "ethnicity." (1995, 143–4)

We should remember here that what Chow sees as the "hallucinatory" or "seductive" power of signification in Zhang's films relates more to the Western than to the Chinese audience. Largely, Zhang's strategic move from the second to the third option in Willemen's scenario represents a specific "local answer" or response (hence, autoethnography as a second-order event) to "imperialism's stereotypes" (as in ethnography, a first-order event). I have more to say in

Section III about an earlier phase of cinematic "ethnography" in Hollywood's imaging of China, but before that we must account for Zhang Yimou's switch from the antagonist and subversive (as mentioned in Section I) to the submissive, complicit position in just a few years.

Dai Jinhua has furnished an interesting reading of Zhang Yimou's early cinematic project. For her, the cultural-reflection movement of the 1980s was plagued by a profound contradiction. On the one hand, it aspired to reconnect with the May Fourth spirit and clear away the obstacles to modernization by negating traditional Chinese culture. On the other hand, it relied on the process of roots-searching to bridge the cultural gaps (*liegu*) created by revolution and to return to the origins of national culture. "This inherent contradiction," Dai speculates, "determines that the art of the Fifth Generation directors has only built a 'broken bridge' (*duanqiao*)." In other words, theirs was an incomplete project that ended with *King of the Children*, which features Lao Gan (Xie Yuan), a stubborn, "rebellious son," with his imaginative but doomed message of "anti-heroism, anti-patriarchy, anti-history" (1993, 16, 29).

According to Dai, *Red Sorghum* charts a new path with the return of formidable archetypal images of the hero, patriarch, and history. This return simultaneously completes the belated "initiation rite" (*chengren shi*) for the Fifth Generation and their "ritual of pardoning" (*shemian shi*), which pardoned them above all because from then on they would be willing to address "My Grandpa" in "a submissive attitude" (*chenfu zitai*) (1993, 29–30, 41). Moving gracefully from the revolutionary history to the myths of a timeless China, Zhang has transformed, with *Ju Dou*, an Oriental story of repression, abuse, and patricide into a beautiful legend subjected to the intense gaze of the Western audience. Similarly, with *Raise the Red Lantern*, he has fossilized Chinese history and culture and displayed it like a gorgeous specimen in a museum exhibit. In this way, concludes Dai, "Zhang Yimou has provided us with a typical postcolonial cultural model" (1993, 86), a conclusion shared by several other Chinese critics (Wang Ning 1995; Zhang Yiwu 1993).

Like Dai, Chen Xiaoming also believes that "*Red Sorghum* marks both an end and a beginning" (1997, 130): that is, an end to the critical mode of cultural reflection and the beginning of an exhibitionist mode of visualizing China. To see how Zhang Yimou abandoned his earlier posture of antagonism (as reflected in the emerging but short-lived ideology of the body) after its spectacular international success and quickly took up a complicit position vis-à-vis dominant transnational cultural imaginaries in the West, we should take a closer look at his dialectic of subversion and submission as well as some of the textual strategies he employed and transmitted to his fellow filmmakers in mainland China.

Seductions of the Female Body: Dialectic of Subversion and Submission in the Films of Zhang Yimou

In *Red Sorghum*, despite its impressive staging of subversive acts (such as the murder of two contenders for the "Name of the Father"—the leper [patriarchy] and Luohan [Communism]), Dai Jinhua sees a disturbing sign of submission to the Father signified by the male narrator's repeated references to "My Grandpa." What is more disturbing to Dai is "the necessity of returning the 'Father's Woman,' of sacrificing woman and female images to the altar of history" (1993, 41). According to this narrative logic, Grandma is twice sacrificed. The first time, she lies in the field wearing red clothes (indicating desire), eagerly sacrificing herself to the altar of male desire and male initiation. The second time, she runs with open arms in slow motion (suggesting ecstasy) yet falls dead to the ground wearing white (indicating sacrificial rites), a victim offered to the altar of history.

If, in *Red Sorghum*, the dominant images of the male body somehow conceal a victimization-of-woman subtext, in subsequent films, Zhang Yimou effects a complete reversal of his cinematic attention from the male to the *female body*, an apparently "aesthetic" move with far-reaching ideological implications. As Lydia Liu observes in the context of modern Chinese literature, "Compared with the male body, the female body signifies a woman's lack of control over her destiny, not so much because sexual desire is an animal instinct as because patriarchy determines the meaning of desire and chastity and hence the female body serves the interest of men" (1995, 205). This is exactly what Zhang has attempted to show in his films from *Ju Dou* all the way to *The Story of Qiu Ju* and *Shanghai Triad*: the female body serves the interest of men regardless of a particular film's spatial, geographic, and temporal setting. As in several other films of the mid-1980s such as *A Girl from Hunan* and *A Good Woman*, Zhang's concerns have switched to a cinematic exhibition of "the impasse a woman faces in human society: the patriarchy desires her body, demands her chastity, and punishes her for transgressive acts" (L. Liu 1995, 206).

Much has been written about Zhang's films, and several critics have chosen to discuss his ambivalent treatment of female oppression as an apparent victimization discourse.[6] Rey Chow, for instance, argues that "even though Zhang's interest is not inherently in women's problems themselves, he relies for his culture-writing on a focalization, a 'zoom-in' on the women characters" (1995, 147). The result is "a fetishization of women that can . . . be more accurately described as a *self-exoticization* through the tactics of visuality" (1995, 148). The play with visuality further leads Chow to surmise that "[w]hat Zhang 'fetishizes' is primarily cinematography itself" (1995, 149). The combined effect of Zhang's double fetishization is his art of seduction:

> [T]he seduction of Zhang's films—the appeal of his visual ethnography—is that they keep crossing boundaries and shifting into new spheres of circulation. The wish to "liberate" Chinese women . . . shifts into the liberation of "China," which shifts into the liberation of the "image" of China on film, which shifts into the liberation of "China" on film in the international culture market, and so on. (1995, 149)

Parallel to Zhang's fetishization of women is his reliance on "Oedipalization," a "modernist" conceptual method that necessitates the use of narrative ingredients such as incest and patricide, as well as the physical impotence and symbolic castration of his male characters. All these, Chow asserts, "constitute a reading of China's modernity and 'ethnicity' that is a *self-subalternization*: we are made to feel that, being fatherless, China is deprived of power; China is a subaltern in the world of modern nations" (1995, 148). From the initial defiance and subversion in *Red Sorghum*, Zhang quickly retreats into the safety of his cinematic art, a space in which he performs his self-acknowledged submission to traditional Chinese culture on the one hand and to the globalizing power of Western culture on the other.

---

[6] Apart from critics mentioned in this chapter, see Callahan 1993; Chen Mo 1995; Cinemaya 1995; Cui 1997; Dai Qing 1993; Fong 1995; Kong 1996–7; J. Lau 1991b and 1994; J. Lee 1996; H. C. Li 1989; S. Lu 1997d; Tam and Dissanayake 1998, 23–34; Y. Wang 1991; M. Yang 1993; M. Yue 1996; X. Zhang 1997, 306–28; Zhongguo dianying chubanshe 1994.

As early as 1991, Ma Junxiang had noticed the impact of international fame—or, more precisely, the repositioning in global
capitalism—on Zhang Yimou's subsequent films. If *Red Sorghum* aims to
deconstruct the discourse of revolutionary history (the theme of class
struggle included) by simultaneously staging acts of patricide and
reimagining a "new patriarch" in the pre-Communist period, in *Ju Dou*
Zhang reexamines the theme of patricide from an essentially
"conformist" perspective,[7] and the overall mood changes from a
carnivalesque celebration to desperation and fatalism. Contrary to the
imaginary classless world of *Red Sorghum*, in *Ju Dou* all the characters are
squarely situated in the preexisting patriarchal order as husband and wife,
uncle and nephew, father and son, elder brother and younger brother. Its
setting, a secluded family-run dye factory, further suggests the oppressive
nature of the patriarchal society, which exercises its power by
legitimating and perpetuating the "Name of the Father" (pronounced in
the film as "the ancestors' rules" that could never be altered). Unlike the
primitive acts of taking the patriarch's woman and claiming her son in
Red Sorghum, in *Ju Dou* the acts of sexual and moral transgression are
committed clandestinely (including peep-hole voyeurism) and with an
overwhelming sense of guilt. Tianqing (Li Baotian), the biological father
of Tianbai, can never muster enough courage to claim his son, even after
Ju Dou (Gong Li) announces the fact to Tianbai. To be sure, Tianbai
twice commits patricide in the film, but Zhang presents these patricidal
acts not as a direct challenge to patriarchy but as part of a natural cycle
through which patriarchy perpetuates itself. After staging the final
triumph of the "Law of the Father," Zhang abandons his patricidal
fantasies, and, as Ma Junxiang believed, "the game was over" (1991, 132).

Yet the game was far from over. Since *Ju Dou*, Zhang has been
engaged in an entirely different set of games, best exemplified in *Raise the
Red Lantern*, which is set in a large, old rural family compound. Five
wives take to the stage by turn; each acts out her desires and fantasies,
"virtues" and rewards, transgressions and punishments, all predetermined
by age-old family rules and scripted to serve only the interest of the
patriarch (whose face, significantly, is never fully shown). Dai Jinhua
interprets the family compound this way: in addition to its resemblance

---

[7] Zhang Yimou admits that, to effect a change from the transgressive characters in *Red
Sorghum*, he tried to depict Tianqing more as a conformist in *Ju Dou*, one who represents
the repressed psyche and the duality of human nature (Ye Tan 1998, 57).

to an ethnographic museum located in the native land, it also evokes the architectural structure of Michel Foucault's famous panopticon, the prison with a central surveillance tower. From a Foucauldian perspective, the five wives appear to be no better than prison inmates whose fates are sealed and whose performance of any subversive act is but a futile gesture against the repressive, invisible, but all-pervasive power. *Raise the Red Lantern*, Dai suggests, thus completes a double displacement of the initial heroic efforts of the Fifth Generation. First, the representation of "unrepresentable" Chinese history and culture (because of its "unfathomable" depths) is displaced by the exhibition of the surfaces of Chinese history; second, the surfaces of Chinese history are further displaced as pure exotica to the Western gaze (1993, 85).

The nature of the exotica is clearly illustrated in Wendy Larson's chart of characterization changes in three of Zhang's early films. Each film follows a similar narrative movement centering on erotic desire and its fulfillment or punishment: "The female character played by Gong Li is positioned between two men, one an older man who is diseased, perverted, or cruel, . . . and the other a younger man who . . . is attracted to her erotically" (Laron 1995, 215). From *Red Sorghum* to *Ju Dou* and *Raise the Red Lantern*, the female character's power to challenge patriarchy becomes progressively weaker, and the young male character loses his earlier ability to fight for revolutionary change. Conversely, the old male character gets stronger and stronger, to the point of being omnipresent and, indeed, omnipotent in *Raise the Red Lantern*. Corresponding to the ideological shift from subversion to submission, Zhang changes the settings in his later films from the liberating outer space of primitive nature to the claustrophobic inner space of traditional culture. As Larson observes:

> The man's world of *Red Sorghum*—a place of direction, earth, and power—has been replaced by the woman's world of *Red Lanterns* [*sic*]—a place of games, rooms, and form. The vast countryside has shrunk . . . into a simple complex of rooms, and the markers of the outside world and the progression of historical time have almost disappeared. Through Grandpa, Tianqing, and the phantom homosexual lover, the alternative possibility of remasculinization through a strong body and a firm mind diminishes, while the conservative, orthodox power of the past increases. (1995, 223)

Sadly, Zhang seems to be submissive not only to the conservative power of the past but also to the repressive regime of his present ruler. In *To Live*, a film about the political repression and persecution in the Communist revolution that would otherwise demand a critical, if not oppositional, stance (as embodied in *The Blue Kite* as well as numerous films from the 1980s, such as *Hibiscus Town* and *China, My Sorrow* [Niupeng, 1989]), one encounters everywhere acts of submission, conformity, and complicity, which are miraculously elevated to the level of being true "virtues" of the Chinese people. In the words of one critic, Fugui (Ge You) and Jiazhen (Gong Li) deserve praise for representing "ordinary folks in a great country with five thousand years of civilization." Moreover, the fact that they have endured and survived hardships of every conceivable kind is itself a testimony: "If Chinese culture and the Chinese people can ever stand firmly in the world, it all depends on [the will power of] its ordinary folks to live" and endure (P. Cheng 1994, 99).

Nevertheless, in her reading of *To Live*, Rey Chow criticizes precisely this time-honored "Chinese" philosophy of life:

> In Zhang's film, the conventional notion of endurance as a strength is not simply reproduced but consciously staged, and it is through such staging, such dramatization or melodramatization, that a crucial fantasy which props up "China"—whether as a culture, a nation, a family, or a common person—is revealed. "We, the Chinese, are the oldest culture, the oldest people in the world," this fantasy says. "The trick of our success is the ability to stick it out—to absorb every external difficulty into ourselves, to incorporate even our enemies into our culture. We endure, therefore we are." (1998a, 128)

Although Zhang's *To Live* may have revealed what Chow describes as a "remarkable" insight, namely, that "China is governed, managed, and fantasized as a collective by the self-fulfilling, self-perpetuating ideology of endurance and survival—by an ethical insistence on accommodating, on staying alive at all costs," I would rather dispute Chow's reading of a "fundamental critique of Chinese society in Zhang's film" simply because, as Chow herself admits, even with little Youqing's small rebellious acts and Chunsheng's enigmatic final gesture, there is at best only "a glimpse of the possibility of an alternative mode of self-governance and political culture" in the film (1998, 129–30, 132).

According to Zhang, *To Live* is first and foremost a dramatization of a uniquely "Chinese" quality: "the attitude of just taking what comes and living on" (Larson 1999, 189).

Reproduction of "Art": The Flourishing of Ethnographic Cinema

Insomuch as Chinese film history is concerned, the dialectic of subversion and submission in Zhang's films may carry far less significance than what his attention to ethnic or ethnographic details has engendered in subsequent Chinese film productions. To the wedding and wine-drinking rituals in *Red Sorghum*, Zhang has added, among other things, the rituals of naming the new-born son and blocking the patriarch's coffin forty-nine times in the funeral procession in *Ju Dou*, and the rituals of raising the red lantern, the foot massage, and operatic singing in *Raise the Red Lantern*. "Ritual, it can be said, embodied the unity and the diversity of China—Chineseness in all its complexity" (Sutton 1994, 32). It is understandable that after Zhang's unprecedented success in the international film market, many Chinese filmmakers would compete in restaging and reinventing exotic, erotic rituals and other ethnic cultural elements, and together they fashioned a new type of ethnographic cinema from the late 1980s to the mid-1990s. Tales of all-pervasive patriarchal oppression, insatiable female desire, sexual seduction, illicit or incestuous affairs, outrageous moral transgression, graphic corporal punishment, male impotence and castration, even patricide and infanticide were released one after another. What Berry reports as the Communist government's new policy of tightened ideological control after the Tiananmen event in 1989 (1994a, 44–5) seemed to have no immediate effect on the production of ethnographic cinema in China, at least not until the late 1990s, when the number of coproductions with Hong Kong and Taiwan dropped considerably under increasing official pressure.

It is significant that most of the ethnographic films mentioned above were financed—at least partially—by transnational capital and billed as "art films." Of course, except for those who firmly believe in cultural authenticity, few would expect all rituals and ethnic details in these films to be historically accurate. For ethnographic filmmakers, a more pressing question is how to generate a heightened effect of "the real" by means of intriguing narratives and spectacular visuals. Jean Baudrillard's theory may be useful for us to measure the "artistic" dimension in Chinese ethnographic cinema: "A possible definition of the real is: *that for which it is possible to provide an equivalent representation.*" Accordingly, "the work of art redoubled itself as a manipulation of the signs of art," and "art entered the phase of its own indefinite *reproduction*" (1988, 145, 147). Indeed, from rituals and folk custom to regional landscapes and narrative formulae, many ethnographic elements in recent Chinese films may be indefinitely reproducible, hence I focus only on certain elements in the following discussion.

As suggested in Larson's study, the narrative formula most common to ethnographic cinema is the triangular relationship between a youthful, sexually active woman and her two men—that is, two husbands or lovers who stand for opposing terms in the categories of class, power, legitimacy, personality, age, physical strength, and sexual potency. What is foregrounded in such narrative triangulation is the enigmatic, unpredictable, even "perverse" nature of female desire and sexuality. An early case in point is *Savage Land* (Yuanye, 1981). As in *Ju Dou* and *The Black Mountain Road*, *Savage Land* was initially banned from domestic release by the censors because of its emphasis on sexual transgression, graphic violence, and utter irrationality. In spite of the critical acclaim it received at the 1983 Venice Film Festival, the film was not given the green light in China until 1988, when it went on to claim Best Film and Best Actress (Liu Xiaoqing) at the Hundred Flowers Awards.

Based on Cao Yu's 1936 play of revenge and retribution, *Savage Land* depicts two "savage" characters, the escaped convict Qiu Hu (Yang Zaibao) and his former sweetheart Jin Zi (Liu Xiaoqing). Qiu sneaks back to his hometown to seek revenge on the landlord Jiao, who murdered his father, raped his sister, and took over their land years ago. But Jiao is dead now, and Jin Zi is married to Jiao's effeminate son, a childhood friend of Qiu. With her bitter speech and flirting manner, Jin Zi defies the traditional ideals of virtuous wife and caring mother. She despises her husband, flaunts her sexuality, and readily accepts Qiu in her bedroom. The torturous psycho-drama of passionate love, fated friendship, and rampant hatred reaches its climax one night when Qiu kills Jiao's son with a knife, Jiao's blind mother clubs her grandson to death by mistake, and Jin Zi, showing no feeling over the deaths of her husband and son, escapes with Qiu into the wilderness. At the end of the film, the two lovers are cornered by the police, and after instructing Jin Zi to tell their unborn child about his heroic deeds, Qiu commits suicide in defiance.

A leading female star whose controversial sexual life was closely scrutinized by the public during the 1980s (Liu Xiaoqing 1995), Liu Xiaoqing appears in another film as an equally aggressive, strong-willed woman character, albeit this time in an urban setting. In *A Woman for Two* (Chuntao, 1988), an adaptation of Xu Dishan's 1934 story set in Old Beijing, Liu plays Chuntao, a hard-working scrap-paper collector who lives with Liu Xianggao (Jiang Wen) in common-law marriage. One day, Chuntao runs into her long-lost husband, who, crippled in the warlord army, is reduced to a pitiable beggar who drags himself along by his hands. Chuntao brings him to her room, where the three share the same bed. Although the film may not work out the same kind of "idealization of a woman . . . on a conception of her as clean and untouched by sexuality" as the original story does,[8] *A Woman for Two* is heavily invested in moral issues and thus appears to be much less ethnographic than the director's other literary adaptations such as *Border Town* (Biancheng, 1984) and *Ripples Across Stagnant Water* (1991; hereafter *Ripples*).

In *Ripples*, female desire is given a crucial role in the narrative, and the *ménage à trois* in *A Woman for Two* is expanded to an even more complicated situation of a young mother caught between three competing men. Sister Cai (Xu Qing) is married to an incapable, mildly retarded husband. When her affection for Luo, her husband's manly cousin, grows deeper over time, Luo's enemy, Gu, accuses them of being Boxer sympathizers. Cai's husband's shop is ransacked by imperial soldiers, the husband is arrested and imprisoned, and Luo goes into hiding. At the end of the film, Cai agrees to Gu's proposal for marriage, but she insists on dictating her own terms in the marriage contract, which include her former husband's immediate release from prison and her freedom to meet her lover Luo at will. As implied in the Chinese title (*kuang* meaning "mad" or "uninhibited"), Sister Cai appears to be a "madwoman" who manipulates men around her with her "uninhibited" sexuality and who, as an initiator, stirs up "ripples" in the "stagnant" male world as suggested by the English title. Yet, contrary to *Savage Land*, where sex and violence are somehow justified by class hatred, *Ripples* brackets off class issues and, instead, zooms in on the female body as a site where male battles for sexual possession and legal ownership are constantly waged.

---

[8] See Rey Chow's analysis of the story, translated as "Big Sister Liu" (1991b, 145–50).

It must be evident by now that the *ménage à trois* formula involving an aggressive female character was not invented by Zhang Yimou (who must be credited correctly, though, as the most influential practitioner, rather than the sole originator, of Chinese ethnographic cinema). Nonetheless, in the wake of Zhang's spectacular success, this "local" formula has become one of the most important "global" signatures in Chinese ethnographic cinema since the early 1990s. A classic example is *Red Firecracker, Green Firecracker* (1994; hereafter *Red Firecracker*), which features Chunzhi (Ning Jing) as a cross-dressing heroine who is brought up as a boy (for lack of a male child) to run the family-owned fireworks business after the death of the patriarch. Her repressed sexual feelings are aroused by the arrival of Niu Bao (Wu Gang), a poor but arrogant itinerant artist hired to paint door gods who cares very little about the age-old rules of this wealthy family. Against the warnings and evil schemes of the foreman (Zhao Xiaorui), Chunzhi pursues Niu across the Yellow River and, to the astonishment of her clan members, starts to wear woman's clothes after her sexual adventure.

A competition over the ownership of her body is held between Niu and the foreman, two equally masculine characters (thus a variation on Zhang's emasculated or impotent men as one of the sexual triangles). A display of male courage follows when Niu and the foreman take turns playing with firecrackers in their bare hands, feet, and mouths. As engrossed spectators watch, a powerful firecracker suddenly explodes when Niu tries to launch it from between his legs. Inevitably, castration results, and the wounded Niu is carried away. The ironic meaning in the metaphor of sexual explosion in the Chinese title then becomes clear: "Paoda shuangdeng" literally means "the twin lamps exploded by the firecracker," the lamps symbolizing the testicles, which in turn are intended by the director to symbolize "a revitalizing force" in the otherwise "repressed life of the Chinese" (Dai Jinhua 1995b, 289–95). In spite of Niu's tragedy, the film manages to end on an optimistic note: Chunzhi is pregnant but determined to raise her illegitimate child. We are once more shown the prison-like enclosures of the Cai compound that incarcerate Chunzhi as a mere puppet, although she is dressed in women's clothes this time.

Red Firecracker offers three types of Oriental ethnic spectacles in addition to the display of repressed female desire.[9] First, the architecture of the traditional Chinese family compound (borrowed directly from *Raise the Red Lantern*) represents the self-stabilizing system of oppressive patriarchy, which, speaking in the name of ancestry, dictates the fate of Chunzhi regardless of her status as the nominal head of the Cai family. Comparing the Cai compound to Lu Xun's metaphoric "iron house," Dai Jinhua notices a revision here, since Niu, as a rejuvenating outsider (a lone romantic hero), has penetrated into the suffocating interior and effected a permanent change in Chunzhi (from the asexual head of the family to an expectant mother) (1995b, 289–95). Second, exotic items of folk culture are woven into the narrative to enhance the ethnographic atmosphere. Apart from paintings of door gods, the film stages two all-male folk-religious dances. The first is performed by monks with painted faces outside of Chunzhi's bedroom as a ritual to drive away the evil spirit that supposedly has taken possession of her, and the second by men wearing demon masks (a reference to a similar scene in *Horse Thief*) who dance around the two contestants right before the firecracker competition, while a crowd of onlookers cheer. Finally, the sheer power of the river landscape (captured from more dramatic angles than those in *Yellow Earth*) adds to this tale of seduction and transgression in a timeless China. As Dai points out, the location shootings in two officially classified "nationally protected key cultural relics"—an ancient mountain town in Shanxi and a ferry bordering Shanxi and Shaanxi provinces—are absolutely necessary for the spectacularization of this Oriental tale for the gaze of Western culture (1995b, 295). It is probably not an exaggeration to say that not only are erotic sexual desire, exotic folk custom, and traditional architecture reproduced for the Western gaze, but even the natural landscape along the Yellow River is "fossilized" by cinematic techniques into some kind of permanent display item in the global cultural museum for the gratification of Western viewers as adventurous "post-tourists" (see chapter 2).

---

[9] An internationally successful ethnographic film, *Red Firecracker* won the grand prize at the 1994 Hawaii Film Festival, among others, and made it into art-house theaters in the U. S. It was even popular enough to become available at major bookstore and video-store chains.

From Savage Landscape to Decadent Cityscape: Variations in Ethnographic Cinema

Love triangles and primitive passions in a savage landscape are also a feature in many other ethnographic films of the late 1980s to the mid-1990s. For example, in *Ballad of the Yellow River*, the concubine of a bandit chief escapes and falls in love with Danggui, an itinerant worker wandering along the barren landscape of the Yellow River playing sorrowful tunes on his *suona* (a trumpet-like instrument). But she is soon recaptured, and the bandit chief fixes an iron ring permanently on Danggui's collarbone as punishment. Decades later, the aging Danggui encounters the bandit chief and learns that the concubine has died. The film ends with Danggui singing a ballad while disappearing into the wilderness. Apparently, *Ballad of the Yellow River* incorporates narrative and audio-visual elements of *Yellow Earth* and *Red Sorghum* in order to highlight its ethnographic nature.

The Black Mountain Road is the story of a savage woman who lives with an old one-eyed man and a fierce-looking dog; together they operate a makeshift inn in an abandoned church in the jungle. One day, a bandit wearing a mask blocks a merchant band led by Brother Gong (Zhao Xiaorui). During the fight, Gong is injured in the leg, and the bandit, who has been killed in the fight, turns out to be the one-eyed man. Gong returns to claim "Woman" (as she is called throughout the film), but she goes her own way, eventually seducing a younger man (Xie Yuan). The sexual tension is resolved in a subsequent fight with Japanese troops. "Woman" is shot to death, and Gong and Woman's young lover dash into the fray seeking revenge. Seen from an ethnographic point of view, *The Black Mountain Road* contains a collage of ingredients from earlier films such as *Red Sorghum* and *Ju Dou*.

In another film of triangles and passion, *The Woodenman's Bride*, a young bride is kidnapped by bandits on her wedding day but is rescued by a porter named Wukui. The groom, however, dies in an explosion in his family compound. The groom's chaste mother, Liu, seeking to prove the bride's virginity, conducts a sexual examination in which the naked bride squats over a pan of ashes. If she sneezes without disturbing the ashes, her maidenhood is proved. An elaborate funeral for the groom doubles as a wedding, and the bride is married to a wooden figure of her deceased husband (a symbol of male castration). Predictably, the bride develops a sexual relationship with Wukui. When their affair is exposed, her Achilles tendons are severed, and she is chained to the wooden figure. Wukui is beaten and driven out of town. A year later, Wukui returns as the new bandit chief and claims the disabled bride as his own. Widow Liu is coerced into hanging herself, and an arch of virtues (*zhenjie paifang*) is later erected in her memory. Apart from obvious nods to *Red Sorghum* and *Ju Dou*, *The Woodenman's Bride* also represents a revisionist response to Huang Jianzhong's *Two Virtuous Women* (Zhennü, 1987), an investigation of the tragic lives behind the grandiose facade of the fifteen arches of virtue in a rural town during the late imperial era.[10]

An interesting feature of these ethnographic films is an assumption that the man from the lower classes—or at least from a lower rank of the power hierarchy—is always sexually attracted to the female lead, who motivates him through their sexual liaisons to rebel against or even temporarily subvert the patriarchal order. Yet in all these films, rebellion or subversion is usually achieved at the expense of the death of or severe bodily injury to the female lead, just as in Zhang Yimou's early films. Again, with Zhang, subversive elements in these films are quickly absorbed in or glossed over by the spectacular exhibition of repressed female desire against the labyrinthine architecture of the traditional family compound on the one hand and, on the other, picturesque landscapes of rivers, ravines, mountains, jungles, and deserts.

The absorption of subversive elements through ethnographic exhibition is equally functional in Wang Jin's women trilogy. Reputedly the first mainland title of the 1980s to be billed as "adult only," *Widow Village* (Guafu cun, 1988) is an ethnographic investigation into a peculiar sexual practice in a Southeastern coastal village. According to the tradition, the newly wed wife may only visit her husband on three festival days each year, but they are forbidden to have sex for the first three years. After that, the wife may move to her husband's house only if she gets pregnant on one of the three festival days. If she fails to conceive, she becomes the laughing stock of the village. This set of ancient rules keeps three sisters from consummating their marriages.

---

[10] For two other films dealing with the arch of virtues, see a Taiwan production, *The Arch of Virtues* (Zhenjie paifang, 1966), and a Hong Kong production, *The Arch* (Dong furen, 1970). Like *Two Virtuous Women*, these two films also dwell excessively on human sacrifices dictated by the repressive patriarchal society. Yet *The Arch*, directed by a woman, manages to impart a strong female consciousness.

One night, the Nationalist troops descend and conscript all able-bodied men from the village and ship them to Taiwan. The town becomes a village of widows. The first sister drowns herself, and the second sister misses her husband with whom she refused to have sex earlier. Only the third sister manages to break the rules and become pregnant before her husband is taken away. Near the end of the film, she brings her new baby and joins the second sister in mourning the first sister and praying for a reunion with their husbands. Shot with such ethnographic interest, *Widow Village* exoticizes regional sexual culture.

In *The Wedding Maidens*, all conceivable situations suffered by young wives—from arranged marriage at an early age, physical and psychological abuse, and punishment for adultery, to life-threatening childbirth and endless household chores—are presented one by one to five village girls aged sixteen to nineteen, who then realize what a misery married life will be for them. Prompted by a witch who believes the soul of a virgin girl will soar like a white bird to the heavenly garden if she hangs herself before the wedding, the five girls decide to commit group suicide. They dress themselves in red, gather in a deserted house outside the village, and hang themselves on a piece of long white cloth. The sole witness to this tragedy is an idiot who utters something unintelligible as the house crumbles, and a flock of white birds flies over the river in alarm. Compared with *Five Girls and a Rope*, a Taiwan production based on the same story but set in Northern China (see chapter 2), *The Wedding Maidens* reveals Wang's preference for poetic landscapes in Southern China and his tendency toward aestheticization. Moreover, these two films, made in the same year but in different locations, also suggest that an ethnography of women's suffering and confinement in the patriarchal tradition tends to transcend geographical as well as temporal boundaries (hence, the recurring images of the "timeless China"—a geographically unspecified village or town in an undetermined historical period).

Also set in Southern China, *Women Flowers* (Nüren hua, 1994) examines another local sexual practice in the Pearl River Delta around Guangzhou. The object of study is the society of "self-combed sisters" (*zishu nü*), single women who wear their hair in a bun and who have renounced sex. If any member breaks the rules, she is punished by drowning. *Women Flowers* presents two cases of transgression. One woman commits suicide because of her pregnancy, but another is rescued from the river by her lover. Shang Meiju, head of the local self-combed sisters, is portrayed as a negative character not only because she enforces the regulations without mercy but also because she turns out to be a lesbian. Moreover, to support herself, Shang adopts young girls, brings them up as "sister flowers" who are sexually attractive and skilled in music and singing, and then sells them to officials and merchants as concubines. Near the end of the film, one of the sister flowers realizes that she is merely a commodity and kills herself in front of her buyer. Shang goes insane, and the film thus passes judgement on the "insanity" of the self-combed sisters' collective resistance to patriarchy.

What is missing in Wang Jin's women trilogy and other works of ethnographic cinema discussed in this chapter is, as in many ethnographic works, "a sharp critique of a classic quest—exoticist, anthropological, orientalist—for pure traditions and discrete cultural differences" (Clifford 1997, 5). Under the pretext of an anthropological study of pure traditions and cultural differences, ethnographic cinema tends to indulge in intriguing elements of ethnic culture, thus diluting the tone of its ideological critique. In Wang's case, each of his three films may be regarded as a critique of patriarchal ideology (especially its equation of woman to a reproductive machine, a piece of exchangeable commodity, and a source of cheap labor). But Wang's critique is itself marked by a fundamentally *male* perspective. Accordingly, *Widow Village* and *Women Flowers* give expression to a yearning for male potency and male salvation, while *The Wedding Maidens* offers up five virgin girls as sacrificial items to the altar of patriarchy in such a fatalistic manner as to imply that there is absolutely no other way out for young women in rural China.

Among recent films bearing visible ethnographic signatures, I have found two exceptions to the dominance of male perspective, and both are set in contemporary China and are related to the theme of economic reform.[11] Like many ethnographic titles, *The Story of Xinghua* foregrounds sexual productivity and effeminacy in two male characters who compete for the affection of Xinghua. A rich entrepreneur in a mountain village, Wanglai purchases his pretty wife Xinghua with 5,000 yuan, but grows worried when after two years she fails to conceive. He abuses her at home and has an affair with another woman, a mother of three, hoping

---

[11] Another film that challenges the dominance of male perspective is *Women's Story*. While following three country women into the city during the reform era, this film is not ethnographic in nature but is rather critical of the persistence of patriarchal values in contemporary China.

she will give him an heir. In the meantime, Xinghua falls in love with
Fulin, an educated youth who has started a small tree farm. When
Xinghua announces her pregnancy to Wanglai and discloses Fulin as the
real father, Wanglai is enraged and destroys Fulin's trees. Fulin cannot
overcome his financial loss, and Wanglai dies in an accident when he
ignores warnings and tries to dig up a legendary gold toad under a watch
tower in a section of the Great Wall not far from the village. The film
ends with the pregnant Xinghua leaving her weeping lover and her
husband's property behind, determined to start her life anew.

In a sense, *Ermo* begins where *The Story of Xinghua* leaves off. As the
sole bread-winner in the family, Ermo (Alia) toils at night making
noodles and during the day goes to market to sell them. At the suggestion
of her neighbor Xiazi (literally, "Blindman"), who has gotten rich driving
a run-down truck to transport goods between the mountain village and
the nearby towns, Ermo leaves her old, incapacitated husband (a former
village chief) and her young son at home and starts her adventure in the
city. Her goal is to earn enough money to buy the biggest television in
the county. Gradually, she develops a sexual relationship with Xiazi, but
she angrily breaks it off when she learns that he has been subsidizing her
restaurant wages. An aggressive, self-determined, and often stubborn
woman, Ermo is a fresh departure from the oppressed, obedient, and self-
sacrificing women who populate most ethnographic films.

As Anne Ciecko and Sheldon Lu observe, by means of a trademark
"self-orientalizing, ethnographic approach," *Ermo* "participates in the
marketing of consumable symbols of rural 'Third World' China through
the reworking of images of regionalism, primitivism, and exoticism
which have become paradigmatic and symptomatic of the Fifth
Generation—and intrinsic to global conceptions and receptions of
Chinese art cinema" (1998, 78). Indeed, *Ermo* is replete with
ethnographic details, ranging from the highly charged, erotic shots of
Ermo kneading noodle dough with her bare feet, to scenes of wild
mountains, against which Xiazi's truck zigzags along the dirt-covered
road with a full load of baskets, Ermo screaming atop the driver's cab.
The consistent use of heavily-accented local dialect invites comparison

with *The Story of Qiu Ju*, and the adultery of the strong-minded, enterprising Ermo is reminiscent of *Women from the Lake of Scented Souls*.[12]

Moreover, Ermo's adventure in the city suggests that the kind of autoethnography characterized by self-exhibitionism and self-orientalization may take place in urban milieux as well, especially in ancient "cultured" cities and towns in Southern China, which provide settings for *Blush*, *Family Scandal*, and *Temptress Moon*. If *Temptress Moon* is an expression of nostalgia for lost childhood innocence (see chapter 7), then *Enchanted by Her Long Braid* (Da bianzi de youhuo, 1995; hereafter *Enchanted*), a coproduction of Pearl River and the Cai brothers in Macau, articulates a nostalgia for the colonial years in the Portugese colony.

The film opens with Atoshinto on his way to a party. He is enchanted by a leading player in the Chinese lion dance, who turns out to be a charming woman with a long braid. He pursues her to the Chinese quarter and there falls madly in love with her. However, their liaison disturbs both the Chinese community and Atoshinto's aristocratic family, and both of them are driven out to live in poverty. At one point, Ah Ling (Ning Jing) almost sells her long braid, which is fetishized as a sexual object, a natural extension of her exoticized body. Through hard work and his own sincerity, Atoshinto eventually convinces Ah Ling's adoptive mother of his commitment to the marriage. The film ends with a celebration of the birth of Ah Ling's child and the acceptance of the interracial couple into the Chinese community. Narrated exclusively from the perspective of Atoshinto as a romantic Western male adventurer in the Orient—a narrative device that became trendy in the late 1990s (see chapter 8), the film highlights Atoshinto's male potency and his incredible survival skills among the subjugated natives.[13] A "benevolent" colonizer, Atoshinto represents the gaze of the imperial eye.

---

[12] Like many other ethnographic films, *Women from the Lake of Scented Souls* features a lame husband and his idiot son, who are placed in sharp contrast to the strong-willed female lead (Siqin Gaowa).

[13] Another rare example of male potency in the 1990s is *The Emperor's Shadow*, in which a rape magically "cures" the disability of the princess, who has been crippled for years.

III

From the Metropole: Hollywood's Images of China, 1930s–1960s

Not surprisingly, *Enchanted* illustrates what Pratt describes as a general pattern of cross-cultural practice in the colonial situation: "Autoethnographic texts are not, then, what are usually thought of as 'authentic' or autochthonous forms of self-representation. . . . Rather autoethnography involves partial collaboration with and appropriation of the idioms of the conqueror" (1992, 7). Arguably, *Enchanted* caters both to the local Chinese audience fascinated with Western culture (as symbolized by the grand mansion, the ballroom dance, and the cocktail party) and to the Western audience fascinated with "authentic" Chinese culture (as exemplified by the lion dance and the barefoot girl with the long braid and charming smile). In fact, the Western fascination with authentic Chinese culture has a long history, as implied in the French term *chinoiserie*. Inasmuch as Hollywood is concerned, films like *Love Is a Many-Splendored Thing* (1955) and *The World of Suzie Wong* (1960, produced by Paramount British Pictures), both set in the British colony of Hong Kong, tend to present a "white knight" like Atoshinto who travels to the exotic land and rediscovers himself through sexual relations with a Chinese or Eurasian woman (Marchetti 1993, 109-24). Both films include numerous ethnographic sequences of exotic urbanscapes of Chinese communities in the colony. The parallels in narrative structure and visual detail between these Hollywood productions and *Enchanted* point clearly to the extent to which recent Chinese ethnographic cinema, as autoethnography in the transnational context, has collaborated with and appropriated the cinematic tradition from the metropole in the West.

Another example of such collaboration and appropriation is the similarity between the dual fascination with the barren landscape and the primitive passions of Chinese women in Chinese ethnographic cinema on the one hand, and, on the other, Hollywood's wartime image of China as a resilient people desperately trying to survive in a savage land. In many ways, *The Good Earth* (1937), based on Pearl Buck's best-selling novel of the same title, stands as a perfect example of this enduring Hollywood image of China (P. Buck 1951; Conn 1996). As one historian puts it, all of us "can be challenged to compare the China which Buck invented with the Chinas invented by others, . . . even with the Chinas in recent movies [such] as *Yellow Earth* or *Red Sorghum*" (Hayford 1998, 7).

A milestone in the Hollywood production of images of China, *The Good Earth* marks a radical departure from previous screen stereotypes of the Chinese. These include Chinese men as pathetic extras (opium eater, thief), comic figures (laundryman, cook), or diabolical villains (Fu Manchu and "Ming the Merciless," two icons produced by the "Yellow Perils" discourse). For women, the stereotypes include the "Lotus Blossom Baby" (the China Doll, a passive, feminine, sexual-romantic object) or the "Dragon Lady" (embodied by Anna May Wong [Huang Liushuang] in her performance as the scheming Mongol slave in *The Thief of Bagdad* [1924]).[14] Contrary to these demeaning and derogatory images, *The Good Earth* presents a poor but spirited Chinese peasant woman, O-Lan (Luise Rainer, winner of an Oscar for Best Actress for this role), who defies all odds, leading her family through one disaster after another. Historically, the radical change in screen images of China from the predominantly negative to the more sympathetic owes much to the wartime situation in East Asia, where Japan became the aggressor and was depicted as such by Hollywood. In terms of cultural influence, however, *The Good Earth* achieves something unexpected: an enduring image of the Chinese peasants (though, in many cases, "farmers" is a more accurate word), who "love the earth with a passion perhaps unknown in the Western countries, but understandable in 'primitive' China" (Oehling 1980, 196).

This passion for the land is most evident in the scene where O-Lan, who just gave birth to a still-born child, tries to dissuade her husband Wang (Paul Muni) from selling their land during a severe drought and famine. "The land is our life," she says in a quiet but determined voice. "It is better to go south or die walking—than to give [the land] for nothing." Throughout the film, O-Lan is portrayed as deeply attached to the land and to everything the land stands for. At the beginning of the film, Wang brings his new bride home on their wedding day, and O-Lan picks up the pit of a peach Wang just ate and plants it near their house. By the end of the film, the peach tree is shown bearing abundant fruits, and after O-Lan dies of old age, Wang looks out of the window and says, with religious solemnity, "O-Lan, you are the earth."

---

[14] For overviews of Hollywood images of Asians and Asian-Americans, see Choy 1978; Brownlow 1990, 320–53; Marchetti 1993; Oehling 1980; Stromgren 1990; Tajima 1989; E. F. Wong 1978; as well as relevant chapters in Bernardi 1996; Bernstein and Studlar 1997; Friedman 1991.

As embodiment of the land, O-Lan represents all its virtues, in particular fertility and resilience. It is interesting to note that three out of four "outstanding" scenes Laurence Stallings locates in *The Good Earth* are closely related to the land, and two of these are exclusively devoted to O-Lan. In the first scene, O-Lan gives birth to her first child "in a profusion of camera force, the chief effect of images being that of hailstones and rain which mottle a landscape of bursting wheatstalks" (Brownlow 1989, 86-7). In the second, after Wang fails to muster enough courage, O-Lan proceeds to kill a starving bullock in "a heartbreaking scene" shot in silence in the middle of night. Another scene related to the land is that of swarms of locusts descending from the sky. Guided by their educated son, the Wang family instructs the villagers to set fires in precise spots in the fields to drive the locusts away.

As Richard Oehling points out, "*The Good Earth* set out to make real and likable the Chinese peasants; it succeeded so well that it set the pattern for the treatment of the Chinese peasant in the war films which would flood the screen in the early 1940s" (1980, 195). In many of these wartime films, Oehling continues, "the Chinese appeared as industrious, persevering, smiling, happy allies, indomitable in the face of all kinds of adversity. One American remarked in *Thirty Seconds Over Tokyo*—and he could have been speaking for all the new Chinese image films—'You're our kind of people.' That was the highest compliment the filmmakers could have made to the Chinese" (1980, 197).

Based on this new perception of the Chinese peasant, *Dragon Seed* (1944) dramatizes the Chinese passion for the land and their willingness to fight and die for it. A peaceful village is devastated when the Japanese troops arrive, and to save themselves the villagers agree to set fire to their crops and property. The female protagonist Jade (Katherine Hepburn) and her husband decide to join the guerilla fighters and entrust their son (the titular "dragon seed") to the grandparents, who are on their way to the hinterland but who instruct their sons to reclaim their land when the war is over.

Like *The Good Earth*, *Dragon Seed* is also based on a novel by Pearl Buck, and the emphasis on the peasants' passion for the land acquires a strong religious overtone in both films. Yet the religion in question is not Buddhism or Daoism but Christianity, and this is only natural because Pearl Buck grew up in an American missionary family in China. If, in *The Good Earth* and *Dragon Seed*, passion for the land only indirectly stands for religious belief, *The Inn of the Sixth Happiness* (1958; hereafter *The Inn*) foregrounds missionary discourse in its depiction of China as a savage land. Gladys Aylward (Ingrid Bergman), an English maid determined to become a missionary, journeys far from home to a remote mountainous region of China. One of the earliest experiences she has in China is as a witness to a public decapitation. Such a shocking scene seems to prove that China, indeed, is a backward place in urgent need of spiritual salvation. With her religious compassion and medical knowledge, Gladys launches a crusade to end foot-binding for young girls. Among her other accomplishments (including converting a powerful local mandarin to Christianity), the greatest feat she achieves is to lead one hundred homeless children on foot through Japanese-held terrain in the mountains. At the end of the film, she delivers the dirty, weary children to their destination, singing a Christian song in chorus as they enter the town, while the townspeople line up and cheer. This is truly a scene of the "reincarnated" shepherd and her new-found "lambs" in a foreign land.

Unlike other Hollywood films in which missionary discourse may be interpreted in an ambivalent if not altogether negative light, such as *The Bitter Tea of General Yen* and *The Sand Pebbles* (1966),[15] *The Inn* continues the tradition of *The Good Earth* and perpetuates the myth of the Chinese as singularly defined by their land. Although shot on location in Wales (hence greatly weakening the film's claim to geographic and ethnographic "authenticity"), *The Inn*'s construction of China confirms and reinforces a prevalent Western perception of China as essentially a timeless, primitive land populated by poverty-stricken but hard-working peasants on the one hand and, on the other, by opium-smoking mandarins living comfortably in their refined, antique-filled compounds.

After this brief detour through a number of select Hollywood productions from the 1930s to the 1960s, we may contemplate a new—which is in fact old—factor in the success of Chinese ethnographic cinema in the West since the late 1980s. *Yellow Earth*, for instance, dwells excessively on the hard-working peasants and their primitive—almost incomprehensible—passion for the land. Likewise, *Red Sorghum* depicts a

---

[15] In *The Bitter Tea of General Yen*, it is not clear whether Megan, a missionary woman, converts the ruthless warlord General Yen, or the other way around. In *The Sand Pebbles*, Chinese students in a missionary school revolt against their imperialist masters, and a gunboat is dispatched to save the endangered missionaries.

rural community that can be described with the same adjectives Oehling uses for Hollywood's wartime images of the Chinese ("industrious, persevering, smiling, and happy"), and Zhang Yimou's legendary heroes appear "indomitable in the face of all kinds of adversity," including the skinning of their compatriots by Japanese soldiers. *Raise the Red Lantern*, furthermore, presents the exotic sexual practice of concubinage familiar to Western viewers from such films as *The Good Earth* (in which O-Lan agrees to let Wang take a concubine) and *The Inn*. Indeed, even the stubbornness of the single-minded "peasant" woman like Qiu Ju or Ermo appears more comprehensible if considered side by side with O-Lan of *The Good Earth* or Jade of *Dragon Seed*. As recently as the mid-1990s, when Chinese audiences showed little interest in *A Mongolian Tale* (Hei junma, 1995), the film was praised at some international film festivals for its portrayal of a Mongolian woman whose body is explicitly likened to fertile soil (Lent 1996–97)—as we saw in *The Good Earth*.

What I am suggesting here is not a case of direct cause-and-effect cinematic influences. Most likely, the depiction of rural China and its suffering women in Chinese ethnographic cinema taps the fountain of cultural memory in the West at an unconscious level and produces an uncanny feeling in the Western audience. From *Yellow Earth* and *Red Sorghum* to *Ermo* and *A Mongolian Tale*, the majority of Chinese ethnographic films reconfirm the dominant images of China and the perceived meaning of Chineseness in the West. As Pratt remarks: "Autoethnographic texts are typically heterogeneous on the reception end as well, usually addressed both to metropolitan readers and to literate sectors of the speaker's own social group, and bound to be received very differently by each" (1992, 7). The striking difference at each end thus explains why many Chinese critics denounce ethnographic films as "cultural sell-outs" when these same films are enthusiastically received in the West as "authentic" and beautiful portrayals of Chinese life.

Passions for the Native Soil: New Taiwan Cinema and (Auto)ethnography

Before concluding my study of Chinese ethnographic cinema, I want to pursue a different line of investigation with regard to cinematic images of the native soil in Taiwan. It is generally acknowledged that New Taiwan Cinema, which emerged in the early 1980s, is indebted to nativist literature (*xiangtu wenxue*) in Taiwan. This literature provides a critical examination—most often through the bewildered eyes of innocent villagers or town folks—of the devastating effects of commercialization, industrialization, and urbanization on their local communities (Hoare 1993; see also S. Y. Chang 1993). For instance, all three segments in the omnibus work *Sandwich Man* (Erzi de da wan'ou, 1983) are adapted from stories by Hwang Chun-ming, an outspoken nativist writer, by the screenwriter Wu Nien-chen, himself a noted fiction writer. Each of these segments directly tackles the Taiwanese people's painful experience at the threshold of modernity, and the directors' critical stance is clearly demonstrated in their consistent use of Taiwanese dialect in addition to Mandarin (officially labeled the "national language" or *guoyu*) and, occasionally, English. Similarly, *In Our Time* (Guangyin de gushi, 1982), another omnibus work of four segments, follows the lives of a school boy, a teenage girl, a college athlete, and a married office clerk in a progressively alienating society. Together, *In Our Time* and *Sandwich Man* inaugurated a film movement known as New Taiwan Cinema, which has fundamentally changed the direction of filmmaking in Taiwan.[16]

Three distinctive themes characterize New Taiwan Cinema of the 1980s: growing up in a village or a small rural town, urban alienation and corruption, and the life-long suffering of women. Except for the second theme, which is most notable in the cinematic oeuvres of Edward Yang and which has become central to the new directors in the 1990s (see chapter 7), the other two fall neatly within the parameters of ethnographic cinema charted in the previous pages. For instance, *Osmanthus Alley* (Guihua xiang, 1987) traces the life of Ti-hung (Lu Xiaofeng) from when she was an orphan to when she was the aging matriarch in an influential family (Y. Zhang 1994b). Elements of local ethnic culture abound in the film, and range from folk-religious ceremonies to regional operatic performance. Like many ethnographic films in mainland China, *Osmanthus Alley* foregrounds the absence of dominant male figures: Ti-hung's father dies when she is twelve, and her husband passes away shortly after the birth of their son. Like its mainland counterparts, *Osmanthus Alley* explores female sexuality at great length. At one point, Ti-hung develops an intimate relationship with an actress who plays male characters on stage. At another point, Ti-hung has sex with a

---

[16] For New Taiwan Cinema, see R. Chen 1993a and 1993b; Chiao 1988; Huang Jianye 1990, 49–164; Kellner 1998; Li Youxin 1986a, 37–136.

handsome man who is hired to serve her opium regularly. When she gets pregnant, her filial son brings her to Japan, and her newborn child is given up for adoption by a Japanese couple. The film ends with Ti-hung in old age sitting in an armchair, contemplating her fate as a lonely woman in the world.

Also starring Lu Xiaofen, *Passion in Late Spring* (Wanchun qingshi, 1989) features the narrative situation of "a woman for two" typical of ethnographic cinema. A newly widowed woman, Chunyan obeys her mother and remarries into a rich family as young master Chang's second wife. Treated brutally by Chang as a mere sex object and a reproductive machine, Chunyan falls in love with a neighbor from a lower class. But their plan to elope together is aborted by the Chang family, who secretly settle the case by forcing the man to leave town and incarcerating Chunyan in a dark room for three months. Miraculously, Chunyan, although treated like a caged animal, repents her "sins" and completely represses her primitive passions. She reemerges as a dutiful wife, courteously smiling to husband, in-laws, and family guests.

In spite of their close resemblance to ethnographic cinema and their unmistakable signs of exhibitionism and autoethnography, neither *Osmanthus Alley* nor *Passion in Late Spring* has been labeled an ethnographic film. A pressing question remains as to why New Taiwan Cinema has rarely been studied in terms of ethnographic cinema. An easy answer may be that films like *Osmanthus Alley* and *Passion in Late Spring* never make it to international film festival circles, and are therefore not subject to the Western gaze to which an autoethnographic work usually positions itself.

But what about Hou Hsiao-hsien's films? It is interesting to note that, before *Osmanthus Alley*, Chen Kun-hou had directed at least two "growing up" films—*Growing Up* (Xiao Bi de gushi, 1983) and *Little Daddy's Sky* (Xiao baba de tiankong, 1984)—in collaboration with Hou Hsiao-hsien as one of the two screenwriters (the other being Chu Tien-wen [Zhu Tianwen], a woman fiction writer who has contributed to most of Hou's films to date). And Hou Hsiao-hsien is internationally known for his "poetics of landscape," by means of which his passion for the native soil finds expression in a distinct cinematic style (Browne 1996). Moreover, ethnographic elements are visible everywhere in Hou's reconstruction of ordinary life in Taiwan, especially in the island's earlier historical periods. After casting his favorite Taiwanese-speaking actor Li

Tien-lu (Li Tianlu), a noted puppet master, in several of his major films, such as *Dust in the Wind* and *City of Sadness* [Illustration 21], Hou devotes long sequences to Li in *The Puppet Master*, where Li talks directly to the camera about his life experience during the Japanese occupation. In cases like these, "autoethnographic" seems to be an appropriate term for Li's oral history. Yet, what is it that precludes Hou from the category of ethnographic cinema?[17]

21. *City of Sadness* (1989): The power of silence in Taiwan history

[17] For discussions of Hou Hsiao-hsien, see Browne 1996; Cheshire 1993; Chiao 1991b, 36–59; Li Youxin 1986b, 121–69; Tam and Dissanayake 1998, 46–59; Tay 1994; Yip 1997.

To answer this question would involve an investigation of the distinctive style in which Hou approaches his otherwise ethnographic subject matter. Douglas Kellner describes some of these distinct features in a 1998 study (105):

> New Taiwan Cinema favors outdoor locations over studio ones. It utilizes natural rather than artificial lighting as it explores ordinary people's real living and working spaces. Long takes and deep focus shots allow viewers to explore the details in unfamiliar social environments, ones cinema rarely depicted before. Often the directors cast non-professional actors and script dialogue in a way in which the characters' dialects point to their specific region and class. Problems of the underclass, women, youth, and other marginalized and oppressed groups take on a new dramatic importance.

Following Kellner's definition of New Taiwan Cinema as "a political cinema" that tends to "combine social realist with modernist aesthetics,"[18] we could argue that Hou's preference for documentary techniques (as in the case of Li Tien-lu in *The Puppet Master*) and non-spectacular modes of presentation (like long takes and long shots, instead of fast edits and close-ups) is precisely what challenges the commercial type of scopophilia (pleasure of viewing) and precludes most of Hou's films from the category of ethnographic cinema.

If Hou's distinctive style is one deciding factor, another, more significant, factor would be his unflagging attention to the specifics of Taiwan history. Unlike the majority of ethnographic cinema in mainland China, which typically blurs spatial and temporal references, Hou always situates his films in a clearly demarcated frame of space and time. The historical dimension thus contextualizes ethnographic elements in his films and demythifies the grand notion of a unified Chinese culture. Hou's insistence on historical specificity is echoed in other Taiwan films from the 1980s to the 1990s. In tales of women's life-long suffering, such as *Rapeseed Woman* (Youma caizi, 1983) and *Kuei-mei, a Woman* (Wo zheyang guole yisheng, 1985), a straightforward notation of the lapse of historical time (like the civil war in the mainland and the Nationalist

---

[18] According to Kellner, "modernist aesthetic innovations include sound and image juxtapositions, fragmented narratives, flashbacks and temporal dislocations, and open-ended, often puzzling endings" (1998, 105).

government's retreat to Taiwan) prevents these films from becoming mere legends or myths. Similarly, in historical films like *The Hills of No Return* (Wuyan de shanqiu, 1992) and *A Borrowed Life* (Duosang, 1993), markers of history and geography—especially the presence of Japanese nationals and the use of the Japanese language in dialogue—hold sway over ethnographic details and primitive passions for the native soil.

It appears that a postcolonial, critical, and self-reflexive consciousness in New Taiwan Cinema has produced a particular vision of multi-layered history and heterogeneous culture as well as a distinctive style with which to interrogate and reconstruct memory, hybridity, and grass-roots politics. Ironically, it is with the notion of "postcoloniality" that postmodern critics in mainland China have proceeded to denounce ethnographic cinema as a purely cultural sell-out, for it has developed since the early 1990s into a mature genre in which cultural authenticity is reproduced as art and is exhibited as such in the West. One may wonder whether such different receptions of mainland and Taiwan films have originated from an entrenched Western view that an authentic culture is not to be expected from Taiwan because of its colonial history, its geopolitical complexities, and its multi-lingual, multi-ethnic population.

Transcultural Fantasies, Post-tourists, and Postnostalgic Productions

To conclude this chapter, I would like to consider a statement by Arjun Appadurai: "The past is now not a land to return to in a simple politics of memory. It has become a synchronic warehouse of cultural scenarios, a kind of temporal central casting" (1996, 30). Indeed, Chinese ethnographic cinema as discussed in this chapter has supplied an impressive list of exotic cultural scenarios. Defamiliarized from con-ventional realist codes in Chinese film production and distantiated from their original narrative space and time, these scenarios appear at first to have enacted a simple politics of memory, retapping "forgotten" legends of primitive passions and repressed sexuality in the local context, while retrieving earlier Hollywood images of China as an essentially agrarian society in a transnational context. However, their masquerade as scenarios of the "authentic" Other to the West must be examined from a contemporary global perspective. As Appadurai suggests,

[T]he apparent increasing substitutability of whole periods and postures for one another . . . is tied to larger global forces, which have done much to show Americans that the past is usually another country. If your present is their future (as in much modernization theory and in many self-satisfied tourist fantasies), and their future is your past . . . , then your own past can be made to appear as a normalized modality of your present. Thus, . . . postindustrial cultural productions have entered a postnostalgic phase. (1996, 31)

From this perspective of transnational cultural production and consumption, I would speculate that the recent popularity of Chinese ethnographic cinema in the West can be attributed in part to the extent to which this genre has successfully satisfied a demand in the global market by feeding "self-satisfied tourist fantasies" dominant for decades and still currently prevalent in the West. In the "postnostalgic" age, then, Western film audiences may very well be what Mike Featherstone calls "post-tourists," people who are willing to accept the substitutability of screen images (as simulacra, that is, reproductions of the "real" without origins) for "authentic" experience obtainable through the participation-observation modes of field work and can therefore satisfy their desire to tread the globe and taste ethnic difference without ever leaving the comfort of their home (1995, 99).

Paul Ricoeur anticipated this distinctively "postmodern" scenario as early as 1965 (278):

When we discover that there are several cultures instead of just one . . . we are threatened with destruction by our own discovery. Suddenly it becomes possible that there are just *others*, that we ourselves are an "other" among others. All meaning and every goal having disappeared, it becomes possible to wander through civilizations as if through vestiges and ruins. The whole of mankind becomes an imaginary museum: where shall we go this weekend—visit the Angkor ruins or take a stroll in the Tivoli of Copenhagen?

It would not be an exaggeration to assert that for the "postnostalgic" post-tourists in the West, Chinese ethnographic cinema has become a priced and prided item in the global imaginary museum, promising a simulated experience of time-travel to the past and an ecstatic encounter with that much-coveted, fantasized Oriental exotica or erotica.

In his study of global image consumption, Bill Nichols also connects the museum, the tourist, and the international film festivals where most ethnographic films from the Third World are "discovered" by seasoned festival patrons in the West. Suspicious of any claim on authenticity, Nichols lays bare the processes in which imaginary identities and virtual cultures are constructed in the global context and projected onto local products. "Though made locally, film production is always a site at which the global penetrates the local, the traditional, the national," so he concludes, but is quick to point out, "Local films need not, however, be made with an eye toward escape from this global net of capital, technology, and style" (1994b, 77). Drawing on James Clifford's work, Nichols refers to a "contestatory strategy of exhibition," one that questions the existing power hierarchy and celebrates "a more diffuse, carnivalesque spirit of potential subversion" (1994b, 73, 81). To see how local films could reposition themselves and renegotiate with transnational capital, technology, and other forces of globalization, I turn to the cinematic projection of what I call the "glocal city" in the next chapter.

Seven

The Glocal City of the Transnational Imaginary: Plotting Disappearance and Reinscription in Chinese Urban Cinema

> The world we live in now seems rhizomic, even schizophrenic, calling for theories of rootlessness, alienation and psychological distance between individuals and groups on the one hand, and fantasies (or nightmares) of electronic propinquity on the other.
>
> Arjun Appadurai, *Modernity at Large*

In this chapter I investigate new visions and cityscapes in contemporary Chinese urban cinema, a cinema that at once projects and problematizes new boundaries and desires in the era of globalization. While acknowledging the importance of the transnational imaginary in creating and sustaining these shifting visions and cityscapes on the global scale, I draw attention to local cultural forces that seize every opportunity to negotiate their own transregional, translocal, transcultural, translingual, or transindividual operations against the hegemonic power of the "new American semiotic empire." As Wimal Dissanayake sees it, this empire engages in "promoting a voracious scopic consumption of images and inserting American-created visualities into circuits of multiple discourse and generating a transnationalized memory" around the world (1996a, 102). More specifically, I analyze a number of recent cinematic configurations of Hong Kong, Shanghai, and Taipei and extend the concept of the "global city" by placing an emphasis on the "glocal" as Roland Robertson formulates, or the "global/local" as Rob Wilson and Wimal Dissanayake prefer. It is my contention that this new critical concept envisions—indeed, enables—a double conceptual move in contemporary Chinese urban cinema. In addition to documenting the processes of the "disappearance" of the local in the age of post-colonialism, postmodernism, and postsocialism, the "glocal city" promises possibilities of retrieving images, information, and memory of the past and of reimagining, reconstructing, and reinscribing new identities, subjectivities, and ethnicities.

I

The Glocal City

As Robertson points out, the term "glocal" is derived from *dochakuka*, a Japanese marketing neologism from the 1980s. Although a "less-than-elegant" term (King 1997, x), "glocalization," Robertson believes, in some sense better conveys much of what he has theorized about "globalization," which is defined as a process that "has involved the simultaneity and the interpenetration of what are conventionally called the global and the local, or—in a more abstract vein—the universal and the particular" (1995, 30). Conceived in a similar way, the "glocal city" not only recognizes the forces of globalization that have come to play an increasingly important role in a given city, but also attends to what Robertson describes as "the reconstruction, in a sense the production, of 'home,' 'community,' and 'locality'" in the same process (1995, 38). Further, the concept of the glocal city possesses what Robertson attributes to "glocalization"—"the definite advantage of making the concern with space as important as the focus upon temporal issues" (1995, 41). As such, the glocal city contains within itself the same problematics of time-space and homogeneity-heterogeneity as "glocalization" does.

In their study, which tends to favor the term "transnationalization" over "globalization," Rob Wilson and Wimal Dissanayake construe the "global/local" as a synergy, a "fast imploding heteroglossic interface" that is undoing the nation-state as an "imagined community" on the one hand and activating "multiple lines of social invention, contestation, mobility, reimagining, coalition, and flight" on the other (1996, 2–3).[1] What they term the "global/local nexus" or "global/local linkage," therefore, highlights a spatial dialectic at work in the "global city," a critical concept Saskia Sassen uses to designate a new type of city. For Sassen, "the combination of spatial dispersal and global integration has

---

[1] For some reason (perhaps to form an alliance with the Marxian tradition?), Wilson and Dissanayake chose not to engage Robertson's theory of globalization even though Jameson describes Robertson as "surely one of the most ambitious theorists of the matter" (Jameson and Miyoshi 1998, xi). See Robertson 1992; Waters 1995. For the distinction between the Marxian and the non-Marxian tradition, see Buell 1994, 265–324.

created a new strategic role for major cities" since the early 1980s (1991, 3), and the result is the emergence of global cities like New York, London, or Tokyo (and, by the same standards, I would add Hong Kong, Taipei, or Shanghai since the 1990s). Sassen cites four new functions of these global cities: They are now highly concentrated command points; key locations for finance and for specialized service industries; sites of production (including innovations); and markets for the products and innovations produced. In spite of her primarily economic interest in these functions, Sassen is nonetheless sensitive to issues concerning the integration of local and global processes. She poses these challenging questions: "What happens to the relationship between state and city under conditions of a strong articulation between city and the world economy? . . . how does the historical, political, economic, and social specificity of a particular city resist, facilitate, remain untouched by incorporation into the world economy?" (1991, 14–5).

More than the "global city," then, the "glocal city"—the term I prefer—seems to better capture the integration of local and global processes and, at the same time, their fluid boundaries. To better contextualize the glocal city, one can refer to Arjun Appadurai's framework for remapping the global cultural economy. This framework includes "(a) ethnoscapes; (b) mediascapes; (c) technoscapes; (d) finance-scapes; and (e) ideoscapes" (1996, 33). With his emphasis on the fluid, irregular shapes of these landscapes, Appadurai's framework, in Frederick Buell's assessment, "presents us with, first, with the most complete picture to date of a global system composed . . . of a multitude of deterritorialized globalist-localisms that operate above and below the level of the nation-state," and secondly, "describes a world system that is no longer unitary, but rather both one and many . . . systems at the same time" (1994, 316). Appadurai's framework, therefore, enables us to examine the glocal city in the proper perspective. In what follows, I pay special attention to the projection and problematization of "ethnoscapes" (the flow of people, especially immigrants and tourists), "mediascapes" (the flows of images, narratives, and information), and "ideoscapes" (the flow of ideas and ideologies) in Chinese urban cinema.

Hong Kong: A Culture of Disappearance?

Let us start with Hong Kong, a glocal city of migrants and "transients" whose culture, according to Ackbar Abbas, is "a culture of disappearance, whose appearance is posited on the imminence of its disappearance" (1997a, 7). To be sure, Abbas explains, "disappearance here does not imply nonappearance, absence, or lack of presence. It is not even nonrecognition—it is more a question of misrecognition, of recognizing a thing as something else" (1997a, 7). Drawing on Freud's concept of "negative hallucination," Abbas specifies this "misrecognition" as "reverse hallucination . . . [that] means *not* seeing what *is* there" (1997a, 6).

Two questions arise with regard to Abbas's argument. First, what is out there that is not seen or not properly recognized? Second, who is the subject or agent of such (mis)recognition? While evasive on the second question, Abbas is quite straightforward with the first: it is the Hong Kong culture's status as a space of disappearance that has not been properly acknowledged. Cultural critics and historians generally agree that Margaret Thatcher's 1982 visit to China, which culminated in the 1984 Sino-British Joint Declaration announcing the return of Hong Kong to China's sovereignty in 1997, marked the beginning of a period of intense anxiety and identity crisis in Hong Kong and therefore heightened the sense of disappearance in question.[2] As a consequence, New Hong Kong Cinema (or the Hong Kong New Wave), which emerged in the late 1970s, has found Hong Kong itself as a subject—"a worthy subject" in Abbas's judgment—and has succeeded in articulating an uncanny feeling of what he calls "the *déjà disparu*": "the feeling that what is new and unique about the situation is always already gone, and we are left holding a handful of clichés, or a cluster of memories of what has never been" (1997a, 25).

For Abbas, while the feeling of *déjà disparu* has also been articulated by some Hong Kong writers such as Leung Ping-kwan (Liang Bingjun, pen name Ye Si), the process of disappearance is even more apparent in the realm of architecture, where Hong Kong turns out to be "a peculiar kind of 'invisible city'—it appears in the moment of disappearance (first sense), and it disappears in appearance/representation (second sense)" (1997a, 73). Here, Abbas refers to disappearance in a double sense: disappearance not only through misrecognition or misrepresentation (for example, Hong Kong as "a cultural desert") but also through constant

---

[2] See Chow 1998a, 149–88; Yau 1994a. Jenny Lau, on the other hand, has questioned the tendency to read all recent Hong Kong films as containing an allegorical reference to the 1997 anxiety (1998, 21–2).

media representation (Hong Kong as a popular tourist destiny, as a financial center in Asia, as the last colony of any political significance to the British Empire).

To return to the question of the subject of (mis)recognition, it is difficult to address the concept of agency in relation to the dominant trope of disappearance. From Abbas's point of view, both the global and the local seem to have misrecognized Hong Kong and have long been ignorant of the process of disappearance. It is therefore the responsibility of the cultural critic to expose instances of such misrecognition inside and outside Hong Kong. Thus theorizing exclusively from the transcendent standpoint of a "global cosmopolitan,"[3] Abbas, who teaches comparative literature and cultural studies at the University of Hong Kong, is criticized by Gordon Matthews of the Chinese University of Hong Kong for neglecting local Hong Kong experience. For Matthews, Abbas's "generalizations have an expatriate feel to it; he does not describe Hong Kong, or Hong Kong cinema, architecture, and literature as experienced by most Hong Kong people" (1998, 1113). Indeed, for Matthews, "Abbas's method is in a sense a literary version of dependency theory: Hong Kong cultural 'raw materials' are analyzed and refined via Western cultural theory, leaving no space for Hong Kong commentators' own interpretations of Hong Kong culture. The book's bibliographic notes contain remarkably few references to Hong Kong, and no references at all in Chinese" (1998, 1112).

To be fair, Abbas's interest does not lie in collecting or transcribing the experience of *nameless* Hong Kong people. For him, it is ostensibly the fate of a majority of them to live in a type of built space he terms "the Anonymous"—"all those nondescript commercial and residential blocks that seem to replicate themselves endlessly . . . [and] may not inspire a second look" (1997a, 82).[4]

---

[3] For a discussion of Ulf Hannerz's portrayal of "global cosmopolitans, who represent a new breed of identities based on mobility," such as intellectuals, bureaucrats, politicians, business people, journalists, and diplomats, among others, see Buell 1994, 291–2. Abbas himself, nevertheless, does not like Hannerz's model of cosmopolitanism (1997a, 13–4).

[4] The other two types of built space in Hong Kong are described by Abbas as "the Merely Local" (traditional Chinese or colonial-style buildings that belong to another historical era) and "the Placeless" (all those impressive multinational hotels and office buildings with no local memories).

Instead, what inspires Abbas is the politics of disappearance in colonial Hong Kong, as his book's title suggests. With its focus on space (as a theoretical construct) rather than people (as agents of construction), Abbas's notion of the *déjà disparu* drastically limits the *agency* of the local subject. Of course, from his point of view, the "postcolonial subject" has yet to emerge, and "one essential condition" for such emergence is this: "It must learn how to survive a culture of disappearance by adopting strategies of disappearance as its own" (1997a, 15). In other words, the Hong Kong subject would not be able to survive the "disappearing present" (Hong Kong as a British colony) without "strategically" using "disappearance" (some sort of representation or self-representation) to deal with "disappearance" (a historical or geopolitical reality). Thus pronounced "survivors" at best, who are imprisoned by a circular logic of one disappearance contingent upon a prior disappearance, the yet-to-emerge Hong Kong subjects are imagined by Abbas as implicated in a perpetual dilemma. On the one hand, they are charged with the urgent task of "cultural self-reinvention . . . in a space of disappearance." On the other hand, they are informed by Abbas that the best kind of reinvention they could aspire to might be "systematic irresolutions" as projected for example in Wong Kar-Wai's films—irresolutions that are unequivocally judged by Abbas to be "the most political of all" strategies in dealing with *déjà disparu* in Hong Kong (1997a, 1, 49).

What is problematic in Abbas's argument, I should clarify here, is not so much his reduction of agency as the particular type of "agency" (which appears to be always self-contradictory or self-negating) he proposes for the postcolonial Hong Kong subject. Fascinated with Paul Virilio's connection of speed to disappearance and Henri Lefebvre's concept of "concrete abstraction," Abbas is delighted to locate in Wong's films "an excess of light and movement . . . a kind of abstract expressionism or action painting" (1997a, 9–10, 59). Here, as elsewhere in his book, Abbas reveals his rather elitist preference for the space of abstraction (the purely visual or, better still, something beyond the visual) over other types of private and public spaces, enumerated as "the erotic spaces of pleasure and encounter, the heterotopic spaces of contestation, [and] the liminal spaces of transition and change," all of which he finds either lacking or "somewhat ambiguous" in Hong Kong culture, and therefore less deserving of his critical attention (1997a, 86).

Arguably, it is Abbas's preference for the abstract (or theoretical, hence "universal" or "global") over the quotidian (or everyday, hence particular or local) that provoked Matthews to criticize him for neglecting local Hong Kong experience. Indeed, Abbas's self-confident diagnosis of "misrecognition" or "reverse hallucination" in Hong Kong denies validity to other types of local recognitions that differ from his vision of Hong Kong culture as a space of disappearance. This does not mean that Abbas is blind to everything local. Rather, he is interested only in a particular kind of the local, what he defines as "the new localism," one that "investigates the dislocation of the local, where the local is something unstable that mutates right in front of our eyes" (1997a, 28). Ideally, the new localism should enhance the agency of the Hong Kong subject and, as Abbas foresees, to develop a new Hong Kong subjectivity. However, if the sole objective of this new localism is to produce nothing but an endless visual or verbal play or replay of mutations and dislocations of the local, or to fabricate a series of "systematic irresolutions" without ever moving to a self-defined position, the new subjectivity Abbas imagines would then verge on non-subjectivity, and his brand of agency a matter of non-agency. Furthermore, without the possibility of constructing a new subjectivity, the reader would be hard pressed to accept Abbas's assertion that "disappearance is not only a threat—it is also an opportunity" (1997a, 14).

But exactly what types of opportunity does Abbas envision for his readers? In the Coda to his book, he envisages the post-1997 future by redefining Hong Kong culture as a "postculture" (1997a, 145):

> [I]t is a culture that has developed in a situation where the available models of culture no longer work. . . . A postculture, therefore, is not posmodernist culture, or post-Marxist culture, or post-Cultural Revolution culture, or even postcolonial culture, insofar as each of these has a set of established themes and an alternative orthodoxy. In a postculture, on the other hand, culture itself is experienced as a field of instabilities.

Rhetorical gesturing aside, Abbas's reformulation of Hong Kong culture as a postculture is hardly convincing on several counts. First, it makes little sense to define postculture exclusively in terms of its "field of instabilities" because all other "post" cultures in Abbas's list are similarly characterized by instabilities (chapters 5–6 examine just a few of such instabilities in the post-Cultural Revolution or postsocialist, if not quite post-Marxist China). Second, to accept Abbas's implied argument that Hong Kong culture, for whatever reasons (mostly economic and political according to him), has failed to develop its own "established themes" and alternative visions, one would have to disregard or deny the existence of historical evidence of decades of cultural production in Hong Kong. Indeed, such disregard or denial would contradict Abbas's own assessment of the achievement of Hong Kong cinema and architecture: "We get a better sense of the history of Hong Kong through its new cinema (and architecture) than is currently available in any history book" (1997a, 27).[5] Third, if Abbas's postculture refers to Hong Kong culture *after* (that is, "post") its predicted "disappearance" in 1997, one must determine in the first place whether or not there was a sea change—a definitive rupture—immediately after the July 1997 "disappearance."[6] If the signs or symptoms of disappearance and the feeling of the *déjà disparu* persist in Hong Kong in the post-1997 era, then Abbas's apocalyptic vision needs correction, and the question of disappearance deserves a reexamination from a comparative, transcultural perspective.

Rather than continuing to debate Abbas's terms such as "culture of disappearance" or "postculture" in relation to Hong Kong, I suggest we go back to the concepts of culture itself and try to figure out what aspects of a local culture in this glocal city might be threatened with disappearance in the age of globalization.

Territorial Culture Versus Translocal Culture

In his study of globalization as hybridization, Jan Nederveen Pieterse distinguishes two concepts of culture. The first "views culture as essentially territorial . . . [and] assumes that culture stems from a learning

---

[5] Rey Chow criticizes Abbas for using a binary opposition between lack and compensation to explain a "paradoxical phenomenon of doom and boom" in Hong Kong: "Hong Kong thrives economically *only* because it is lacking in political autonomy and self-determination" (1998a, 170).

[6] To give one striking example here: the prediction by many pundits around the world that the Chinese Communist government would no longer permit the annual commemoration of Tiananmen after the handover in July 1, 1997 has proven entirely wrong. In June 1998, the commemoration was held in Victoria Park in Hong Kong and "managed to draw a crowd of 40,000 despite a thunderstorm" (Fore 1998, 45). In June 1999, thousands of Hong Kong demonstrators took to the streets in commemoration of the tenth anniversary of Tiananmen.

process that is, in the main, localized," whereas the second sees culture as "a translocal process" that "involves an *outward-looking* sense of place" (1995, 61). Two lists of opposing terms are assigned to these two assumptions of culture (1995, 61):

Territorial culture	*Translocal culture*
endogenous	exogenous
orthogenetic	heterogenetic
societies, nations, empires	diasporas, migrations
locales, regions	crossroads, borders, interstices
community-based	networks, brokers, strangers
organic, unitary	diffusion, heterogeneity
authenticity	translation
. . .	. . .

From Pieterse's description, it is apparent that Hong Kong culture is a translocal culture, exogenous, diffused, and heterogenetic in nature, characterized by movements of diasporas and migrations, and replete with images of crossroads, borders, interstices, networks, brokers, and strangers. On the other hand, mainland Chinese culture is by and large a territorial culture, endogenous and orthogenetic in nature, seemingly organic and unitary, and extremely proud of its authenticity and its long history as an empire and a civilization. Instead of pursuing cultural hegemony and autonomy (discussed in chapter 5) as in a territorial culture, a translocal culture seeks pluralism and interculturalism, favors cultural flows in space, and tends to produce syncretism, synthesis, hybridity, and possibly even third cultures.

To a certain extent, we may also regard Hong Kong culture as a kind of third culture. As Mike Featherstone proposes,

[W]e can point to the existence of a global culture in the restricted sense of "third cultures": sets of practices, bodies of knowledge, conventions and lifestyles that have developed in ways which have become increasingly independent of nation-states. In effect there are a number of trans-societal institutions, cultures and cultural producers who cannot be understood as merely agents and representatives of their nation-states. (1995, 114)

As is well known, Hong Kong culture is not subsumed by any nation-state (Great Britain or China), nor has it been homogenized—at least not yet—by colonization, decolonization, or globalization. Precisely due to the decades-long interpenetration and cross-fertilization of cultures and trans-societal institutions, local cultures continue to exist in Hong Kong alongside regional, "national," and global cultures.

Given Hong Kong's distinctive features of syncretism, plurality, and hybridity—one is reminded of Esther Yau's characterization of Hong Kong culture as a "colonial-Chinese cultural syncretism" (1994a, 185)—Abbas's vision of Hong Kong culture as a singular space of disappearance, albeit theoretically intriguing, is far from accurate. "Disappearance" as an epistemological construct formulated by Abbas, therefore, does not and cannot dictate the fate of disappearance to all local cultures. In fact, if examined from a longer historical perspective, disappearance turns out to be something that has occurred in earlier periods, long before the onset of globalization and postmodernity, and these other kinds of disappearance as reflected in Chinese cinema have attracted critical attention elsewhere (Jameson 1994).

The dialectic relationship between what Anthony Giddens conceptualizes as "disembedding" and "reembedding" can further assist us here. Giddens defines the former as "the 'lifting out' of social relations from local contexts of interaction and their restructuring across indefinite spans of time-space" (1990, 21). As such, the process of disembedding always engenders a complementary move, that of *reembedding*, defined as "the reappropriation or recasting of disembedded social relations so as to pin them down (however partially or transitorily) to local conditions of time and place" (1990, 79–80). Adopting Giddens's framework, we may treat Abbas's notion of disappearance as a special form of displacement and attend to what Giddens sees as "the intersection of estrangement and familiarity" that points to a dialectic of "displacement and reembedding" (1990, 140). For my purposes in this chapter, I use "reinscription" to refer to an individual act or tactic that contributes, directly or indirectly, to the larger process of reembedding.

It should be evident by now that the politics of disappearance or displacement is not confined to Hong Kong culture alone, nor to that period between 1982 and 1997, however anxiety-ridden it might have been or how far-reaching its historical significance. Instead, I would suggest that we contextualize disappearance in a specific geopolitical

locale at a specific time. Rather than feeling apprehensive about disappearance in an abstract sense, as Abbas does in his depiction of Hong
Kong culture as a postculture, we may now proceed to locate tactics of
reinscription as they are emplotted in a broad range of narratives of
disappearance in contemporary Chinese urban cinema. To facilitate
discussion, I devote a section each to Hong Kong, Shanghai, and Taipei,
and a concluding section to further explore the ramifications of the glocal
perspective. Given space limitations, however, I leave the complicated
geopolitical relationships between these three glocal cities for further
research (Shih 1998).

II

Disappearance and Reinscription in *Chungking Express*

After winning the Best Director award at the 1997 Cannes
International Film Festival for his *Happy Together* (1997), Wong Kar-Wai
has become a world renowned avant-garde director—some even say "a
true postmodernist auteur" (C. Tsui 1995, 93). Experimenting with
several commercial genres such as the gangster film in *As Tears Go By*
(Wangjiao kamen, 1988), melodrama in *Days of Being Wild*, martial arts in
Ashes of Time (Dongxie xidu, 1994), comedy in *Chungking Express*
(Chongqing senlin, 1994), and film noir in *Fallen Angels* (Duoluo tianshi,
1995), Wong has added new dimensions of meaning to each. With their
distinct signature, all of Wong's films are thematically linked "with their
meditations on memory and identity, turmoils of the human heart, time
and space, the local and the cosmopolitan" (C. Tsui 1995, 93).[7] His films
thus provide us with the best access to what Abbas sees as "techniques of
disappearance" deployed in Hong Kong new cinema—techniques of
"using disappearance to deal with disappearance" and therefore to
develop a subjectivity "out of a space of disappearance" (1997a, 8, 11).

In *Chungking Express*, for instance, we meet two ordinary
policemen, one obsessed with an expiration date (a sure sign of
disappearance), and the other blinded by reverse hallucination. In the first
half of the film, "Cop 223," or He Qiwu, yearns for an ex-girlfriend
named May. Every day he buys a can of pineapple printed with the same

---

[7] For sample discussions of Wong's films, see Abbas 1997a, 33–6, 48–62; Luo Feng 1995,
37–59; Stephens 1996b; Y. Yeh 1999; J. H. Zhou 1998.

expiration date (May 1, 1994, his birthday), in the hope that May might suddenly appear and rejoin him. Tortured by feelings of frustration and loneliness, he talks by turns to himself and his dog, and makes random phone calls to former schoolmates he has not spoken with in years. By midnight of April 30 May has not returned. Bitterly disillusioned, Cop 223 eats all thirty cans of pineapple, then throws up. The episode ends on a somewhat hopeful note when he receives a happy birthday message on his beeper. The message is apparently from a mysterious woman (Brigitte Lin)—perpetually cloaked in brown wig, sunglasses, and raincoat—he met the night before in a bar but whose true identity he never learned. (She is a Hong Kong drug smuggler who deals with multinationals, including Indians and Caucasians.)

The second half of *Chungking Express* concerns Cop 663 (Tony Leung Chiu-Wai [Liang Chaowei]), who is also recovering from the disappearance of his ex-girlfriend, a flight attendant who returns his apartment-door key to Midnight Express, a fast-food deli shop he frequently visits. Growing curious about 663, deli-worker Faye (Faye Wong [Wang Jinwen]) steals into his apartment with the unclaimed key. Hiding out in 663's apartment, Faye notices how much he misses his ex-girlfriend and how he fetishizes her personal items and speaks to inanimate objects such as a bar of soap, a can of food, and a large stuffed animal. Little by little, Faye rearranges the apartment, replacing the soap, the canned food, the stuffed animal, and the bedding with items of different brands. Particularly comic is that 663 never notices the changes—hence, his reverse hallucination of not seeing what is there—until one day when he discovers Faye in his apartment. A romance buds. Yet, ironically, Faye misses their first date, at a restaurant called "California," by flying to California, the real place, alone. She leaves 663 an envelope containing a handwritten airplane boarding pass, dated exactly a year later but without a pre-set destination. A year later, 663 has quit his post and become the new owner of Midnight Express, listening to Faye's favorite song, "California Dreamin'," at a deafeningly high volume. Faye returns, dressed in a flight attendant uniform, and the film ends with dialogue about the missing destination: "Where do you want to go?" "Doesn't matter. Wherever you want to go."

Chungking Express makes extensive use of doubling to intensify the effect of character and spatial mutation in the matrix of the local and the global: May, the absent ex-girlfriend of Cop 223, and another deli-worker named May who waits for him but eventually goes on a date with someone else (hence, both Mays are figures of disappearance); the ex-girlfriend of 663, the unnamed flight attendant (a figure of the global, the migrant, the transitory) and Faye who becomes a flight attendant (a figure of the glocal, the local-turned-global who may choose to remain a local); California as a restaurant (the local) and California as an off-screen "dream land" (the global from the perspective of Hong Kong) that Faye visits and discovers is not as attractive as the song "California Dreamin'" depicts. What emerges from such mutations in *Chungking Express*, then, is not just a fatalistic vision of disappearance or even destruction (as in *Days of Being Wild*, where the male protagonist is murdered on a train, away from "home"), but a space of new possibilities (to stay or leave by oneself, or to stay or leave together) for the locals, no matter how dislocated they are at present.

What deserves further consideration in Wong's mutations in *Chungking Express* are the gender implications in his plotting of dislocations of the local. While the two policemen are trapped physically, psychologically, and emotionally by the locale (symbolized by their cramped apartments), the female characters seem to enjoy the freedom of movement, disappearing and reappearing whenever they prefer. Admittedly, the "disappearance of woman"—most noticeably a femme fatale—is a familiar trope in urban narratives ranging from film noir to Italo Calvino's *Invisible Cities*. These tend to project male desire and fix the enigmatic figure in a labyrinthine urban space, from time to time dwelling on the pathos of its ultimate failure.[8] Viewed from this angle, *Chungking Express* not only configures woman as what Elizabeth Wilson calls "the Sphinx in the city" but also uses this figure to project male anxiety over the new kinds of dislocation and disorder engendered in the glocal city by transnational and transcultural forces.[9]

As a study of disillusionment and disappearance, *Chungking Express* thus brings us to Appadurai's vision: "The world we live in now seems

---

[8] For tales of urban desires, see Calvino 1972; de Laurentis 1984, 12–4. For sample discussions of woman and the film noir, see Dick 1995; Kaplan 1980; Maxfield 1996.

[9] Wilson's comment is worth quoting in more detail: "at the 'commonsense' level of our deepest philosophical and emotional assumptions, . . . it is the male-female dichotomy that has so damagingly translated itself into a conception of city culture as pertaining to men. Consequently, women have become an irruption in the city, a symptom of disorder, and a problem: the Sphinx in the city" (1991, 9).

rhizomic, even schizophrenic, calling for theories of rootlessness, alienation and psychological distance between individuals and group on the one hand, and fantasies (or nightmares) of electronic propinquity on the other" (1996, 29). This vision is particularly relevant when we consider images of modern technology in Wong's films. More often than not, the telephone does not function as a vehicle of communication between characters. On the contrary, it frequently adds to their distance, as when the continual telephone ringing signifies the absence of an intended receiver in *Days of Being Wild*.

As indicated above, there are signs in *Chungking Express* that point to Wong's suggestion of new possibilities in the glocal city. The message from the brown-wigged woman shows her concern for a local policeman, and Faye's return from California and her visit to the new owner of Midnight Express may symbolize her confidence in, if not commitment to, the local. What is more, Faye's earlier acts of rearranging and renegotiating Cop 663's personal space serve as an unmistakable index to a tactic of reinscription in the glocal city. As Curtis Tsui observes, by showing Cop 663 as "an individual who can accept and work with alternations in his life, and see them as possibilities rather than disasters," Sending a positive message to Hong Kong audiences Wong notes, "They can acknowledge and influence changes, rather than view them in an apocalyptic fashion, so that those alternations can work in their favor. They can build a new sense of self out of their previous existences, and create their own, clearly defined Hong Kong" (1995, 122–3).

Tactics of Reinscription in *Autumn Moon*

Another film that pursues a new sense of self and searches for new tactics of reinscription is Clara Law's *Autumn Moon*, which won the Golden Leopard at the 1992 Locarno Film Festival. Similar to Wong, Law emerged as a notable director in Hong Kong after successfully experimenting with several commercial genres, among them comedy in *The Other Half and the Other Half* (Wo ai taikong ren, 1988), melodrama in *The Reincarnation of Golden Lotus* (1989), and costume drama in *The Temptation of a Monk* (Youseng, 1993). Her distinctive female vision and the highly sensual quality of her films landed her an opportunity to contribute a short entry, "Wonton Soup," to the four-part feminist portmanteau film *Erotique* (1994), a multinational venture with three

other directors from the U.S., Germany, and Brazil. Over the years, Law
has incorporated her personal experience of space, place, and home into
many of her films, and it is her sensitive examination of the politics of
migration, identity, gender, and sexuality that has secured her an
international reputation.[10]

Autumn Moon is the second film in Law's migration trilogy, which
also includes *Farewell, China* (Aizai biexiang de jijie, 1990), a study of
mainland Chinese diasporas in New York City, and *Floating Life*
(Fusheng, 1996), a film produced in Australia. Set in Hong Kong,
Autumn Moon follows two young urbanites struggling to redefine their
identities. Tokio (Masatoshi Nagase), a jaded, twenty-something Japanese
tourist, arrives in the glocal city in search of authentic cuisine and sex.
Initially, he is not satisfied with what he finds, which is appropriately
displayed to the audience through the view-finder of his camcorder: the
shining glass windows, bathed in eerie blue light, of what Abbas has
described as the "placeless" multinational hotels and office buildings of
Hong Kong; nameless people walking in the streets; their bodies,
especially women's bodies and legs; and a smiling, naked young Hong
Kong woman washing her face in the bathroom of his hotel room. One
morning, fishing by the pedestrian promenade near Tsim Sha Tsui,
Tokio meets Wai (Wai Wong), a fifteen-year-old local girl whose parents
and brother have emigrated to Canada. They use broken English to
communicate, but each continues to rely on Japanese or Cantonese in
asides and voice-overs. An unlikely friendship develops, and they soon
start to share their feelings of displacement and frustration.

Autumn Moon shows tactics of reinscription through at least the
following three interconnected channels: memory and recollection of
one's past experience, understanding of the Other, and reconnection with
one's own cultural tradition. First, the power of memory and recollection
in restoring one's sense of self is demonstrated in Tokio's meetings with
Miki, who works for a transnational corporation in Hong Kong and who
is the elder sister of one of his former girl friends. At first, a chance
encounter on the street ends in casual sex in Tokio's hotel room. Later in

---

[10] Law was born in the Portuguese colony of Macao, received education at the University
of Hong Kong and at the National Film School in England, and worked at Radio and TV
Hong Kong before moving into the film industry. She emigrated from Hong Kong and
now lives in Melbourne, Australia with her scriptwriter-director husband Eddie Fong
(Fang Lingzheng). For sample analyses of Law's films, see Fore 1993 and 1998.

the film, Tokio visits Miki at her place, and the two come to a better understanding of themselves and of each other by reactivating repressed memories through mundane questions such as "What's your favorite ice cream?" and "What's your favorite film?" Not surprisingly, in Tokio's case, the answers to these questions involve recollections of time he spent with his father and grandfather in his early childhood. Second, Tokio's fascination with Wai's grandmother, who prepares for him in her small kitchen authentic Chinese cuisine, illustrates the positive impact of understanding the Other. Since he does not know Cantonese, Tokio can only observe Grandma in her daily routines. An enigmatic icon of the Other, Grandma is symbolically "a living repository of historical tradition and memory" to Tokio (Fore 1998, 36), who becomes so fascinated with her and with what she represents that he volunteers to take care of her in the hospital when she is sick. Finally, the best example of reconnection with one's own cultural tradition occurs near the end of the film, when Tokio and Wai celebrate the Autumn Moon Festival in a deserted fishing village. They light lanterns and set off fireworks according to the Chinese tradition, and Tokio also makes tiny wood-and-paper boats and sails them into the open sea in accordance with the Japanese holiday of Obon.

As Steve Fore points out, "the characters in *Autumn Moon* maintain a degree of agency—they are shown to be capable of acting in relation to, not just within, their environment" (1998, 38). Like Cop 663 and Faye in *Chungking Express*, both Tokio and Wai are in transitional moments in their lives, but both succeed in finding tactics of everyday practice that help reinscribe their sense of self and place in relation to a sea of nameless people and "placeless" buildings in the glocal city. As defined by Michel de Certeau, a "tactic" refers to "a calculated action determined by the absence of a proper locus." Unlike a strategy, which involves "the calculation (or manipulation) of power relationships" on a grand scale, as typical of modern science, politics, and military operations, a tactic "must play on and with a terrain imposed on it and organized by the law of a foreign power" (1984, 35–7). Deployed against the dominance superimposed by the "strategies" of globalization and transnational capitalism at a high level of command and control (beautifully captured in *Autumn Moon* by the aerial view of the cityscapes shot from a helicopter), "tactics" consist of those discrete, dispersed acts that nonetheless articulate the individualized, localized experience of the local (like Grandma), the translocal (like Wai, who will soon emigrate to Canada), and even the cosmopolitan (like Tokio, who moves between the glocal cities).

Thanks to its attention to the question of agency as exemplified in tactics of reinscription, *Autumn Moon* does more than merely catalogue images of disappearance in Hong Kong. It projects a new vision of space, place, and home in the glocal city by interrogating the theory of globalization as homogenization. As Featherstone cautions, "One of the dangers of the 'no sense of place' type of arguments is that they seem to point to processes that are assumed to be universal in their impact and which do not vary historically" (1995, 94). What *Autumn Moon* does so admirably is not just reinscribe a sense of place in a space of disappearance; it also reintroduces historical experience to the process of negotiation between the global and the local. By injecting her childhood experience, for instance, Wai transforms a local McDonald's restaurant into an endearing place closer to her "home" (the place where she used to celebrate her birthdays), when it would otherwise be a mere replica of a multinational chain found all over the world.

"A sense of home," Featherstone writes, "is sustained by collective memory which itself depends upon ritual performances, bodily practices and commemorative ceremonies" (1995, 94). Sure enough, by the end of *Autumn Moon*, both Tokio and Wai have acquired a new sense of home through their ritual performances and celebration of Chinese and Japanese cultures. In particular, at the end of the film Wai recites some verses from a poem her grandfather taught her years ago:

> When will the spring flower and autumn moon fade?
> How much of the past do we know?
> At my home last night, the east wind blew . . . .

Unable to continue, Wai murmurs "I don't remember" and stops abruptly. The film ends with a shot of Wai and Tokio smiling, their innocent faces lit by fireworks.

Although the poem is not identified in the film, viewers familiar with traditional Chinese literature will readily recognize the verse that Wai recites as lines taken from a nostalgic *ci* poem, "The Beautiful Lady Yu" (Yu meiren), composed by the Southern Tang Emperor Li Yu while in prison.[11] Wai's inability to remember the entire poem, therefore, foregrounds the film's ambivalent ideological position and invites further interpretation. On the one hand, it may be argued that, perhaps too young to understand the full impact of the "loss" of Hong Kong, Wai has *unconsciously* deleted from her memory the rest of Li Yu's poem, which elaborates the emperor's grief over his "lost country" (*guguo*). The autumn moon, taken out of the original context, where it bears witness to the emperor's sorrows, is used as the film's title and is evoked as a common symbol of (or a yearning for) family reunion during the Autumn Moon Festival. Wai's recitation of the poem, therefore, may serve a specific purpose in the film: to establish a new sense of home in her future life of migration by reinscribing herself, however temporarily, in an age-old Chinese cultural tradition. She might not be able to remember Li Yu's poem in its entirety at that particular moment, but her effort to recite it is itself a sign of agency, an exercise against memory loss, an homage to her ancestry.

On the other hand, it may be argued that Wai *purposefully* deletes from her memory the rest of the poem simply because it symbolizes Chinese culture, something her grandfather had wanted her to identify as her heritage. Her lapse of memory, in this reading, would then become an act of resistance against the power of ideological interpellation: she evokes a symbol of Chinese culture only to renounce it, to leave it in fragments and ruins. This tactic is further exemplified in the film's ending sequences, where the traditional fishing village is shown in ruins, forgotten by the global city of multinational buildings projected in the opening sequences. By saying "I don't remember" to her grandfather's legacy, Wai not only releases herself from her previous cultural

---

[11] Eugene Eoyang's translation of the poem is quoted in full below (see W. Liu and Lo 1975, 305–6):

Spring blooms, autumn moon, when will they end?
How many yesterdays have passed?
Last night, at my little pavilion, the east wind again!
Oh, lost country, when the moon is bright, I can't bear to look back.

Carved balustrades, marmorean stairs no doubt will stand;
Only the once bright faces have changed.
Ask the sum of grief there's to bear,
It's just a river in full spring flood flowing east to the sea.

obligations but also reasserts her subjectivity and her agency in choosing her own present or future identity.

Clara Law, I believe, intentionally leaves *Autumn Moon* with an ambivalent ending. Whichever interpretation the viewer may prefer, one thing is clear by the end of the film: the threat of disappearance (as in the case of the lost homeland or the renounced cultural legacy) does not necessarily produce only an apocalyptic vision. Rather, it might enrich one's life if one could use the experience of migrancy and diaspora *positively* to acquire a new sense of self, a new sense of one's place vis-à-vis various cultures, regions, and nations in the world.

In his study of old and new identities in the age of globalization, Stuart Hall contends that "identities are never completed, never finished; that they are always as subjectivity itself is, in process" (1997b, 47). From this perspective, it would not make sense to expect Wai to have secured a "completed" identity by the end of *Autumn Moon*, which she could then pack with her other belongings and bring with her to Canada. What is important in the film is that, by deploying tactics of reinscription, Wai has arrived at a new understanding of her identity (or, more precisely, her old and new identities). "What is more is that identity is always in part a narrative, always in part a kind of representation" (Hall 1997b, 49).

Old and New Ethnicities in *Comrades, Almost a Love Story*

Peter Chan's *Comrades, Almost a Love Story* (hereafter *Comrades*) is another Hong Kong film that confronts the 1997 anxiety with questions of identity and ethnicity. "A film that started out innocently as a story about two immigrants from China," Chan says in an interview, "turned out to be my story, my friends' story and most probably the story of a large proportion of the Chinese people" (A. Tsui 1997, 26). The film's built-in allegorical structure works to convey Chan's twin realizations: "I was really talking about the rootlessness of the Chinese as a people, and of their continuing search for a new home . . . [and] the story is also a reflection on the lives of the Hong Kong natives of my generation, people like me who are trying to cope with a deadline called 1997" (A. Tsui 1997, 26).

Chan's emphasis on the rootlessness of the Chinese people reminds us of what Law asserts elsewhere in reference to both mainland Chinese and Hong Kong Chinese: "The fact that we don't have a home strongly affects us . . . [and] weighs heavily on our minds" (Tan et al. 1994–5, 20).

Unlike Law or Wong Kar-Wai (the latter was born in Shanghai and emigrated to Hong Kong at the age of five), Peter Chan is a Hong Kong native. But like both Law and Wong, Chan himself underwent quite a bit of dislocation: he moved to Thailand with his family at the age of twelve, emigrated to the U.S. at eighteen, and returned to Hong Kong at twenty-one to work for Golden Harvest Films. Probably best known for his popular romantic comedies such as *He's a Woman, She's a Man* (Jinzhi yuye, 1994) and *Who's the Woman, Who's the Man* (Jinzhi yuye 2, 1996), Chan in fact tackled the diaspora issues in his directorial debut, *Alan and Eric: Between Hello and Goodbye* (Shuangcheng gushi, 1991), the story of an immigrant in San Francisco who returns to Hong Kong to renew his friendship with his closest childhood friend.[12]

Naturally, questions of identity and ethnicity interest Chan, who admits that he is "Chinese by ethnicity but not by nationality" (A. Tsui 1997, 26). However, his tactics of reinscription differ significantly from the standard Hong Kong filmic strategies of viewing China in bipolar terms: either positively as the lost homeland—represented by *Homecoming*—or negatively as the threatening invader—represented by *Long Arm of the Law*.[13] In fact, the so-called "China factor" in Hong Kong cinema can be traced to even earlier periods. According to Leung Noong-kong, there are three main stages in the development of Hong Kong cinema in relation to mainland China. First, the period up to 1966 (in my opinion too long a time to be treated as homogeneous) was characterized by a "sinicized subjectivity" that viewed Hong Kong as a peripheral place to be abandoned without regrets. This is exemplified in Cai Chusheng's wartime patriotic feature, *Ten Thousand Li Ahead* (Qiancheng wanli, 1940), where the characters march off to defend China against the Japanese invasion. Second, from 1966 to 1979, Hong Kong cinema reached what Lacan calls the "mirror stage," since the film industry was obsessed with its own narcissistic images of affluence, pleasure, and power, entirely oblivious to the "Law of the Father." Third, in the early 1980s, Hong Kong cinema entered the "post-1997 consciousness stage," where it must face "the pain and melancholia"

---

[12] Like other Hong Kong film talents, Chan moved on to Hollywood and directed *The Love Letter* (1999).

[13] See Yau 1994a; Li Cheuk-to 1994. Steve Fore furthers the argument by adding class and genre as two other factors that contribute to the polarized images of China in these two films (1998, 35).

engendered by the 1997 issue (Leung Noong-kong 1997, 72–3; see also Ng Ho 1997). For Leung, *Homecoming* testifies to the experience of a return to China as the imaginary "homeland," whereas Tang Shuxuan's *China Behind* (Zaijian Zhongguo), produced in 1974 but banned for nearly fifteen years by the Hong Kong censors, points to the opposite direction, that of a bitter farewell to—indeed a desperate flight from—China, a terrible and terrifying Other incapable of evoking any feeling of nostalgia.

In a sense, Peter Chan's *Comrades* revisits China (*zaijian*, "see again," as used in Tang's Chinese title) by plotting a story of farewell similar to that of *China Behind*, but one governed by a different emotional register. Instead of constructing the mainland Chinese as the Other, who merely a decade before appeared, in Chan's own words, "more alien to me than people of a different race" (A. Tsui 1997, 26), *Comrades* transcends the entrenched Hong Kong viewing position and portrays Hong Kong (the nominal self) as the Other—an alien and alienating glocal city—from the point of view of two new mainland immigrants who struggle to make a living first in Hong Kong and then in New York City. Moreover, by featuring as a unifying thematic and musical structure the popular songs of Deng Lijun (Teresa Teng), a Taiwan woman singer famous in Chinese communities around the world, *Comrades* foregrounds the interconnectedness and the multidimensionality of geocultural and geopolitical differences in China, Hong Kong, and Taiwan, as well as Chinese diasporas (Gold 1993).

In its black-and-white prelude (replayed at the end) set in 1986, the film shows Xiaojun (Leon Lai [Li Ming], a Hong Kong pop singer who grew up in Beijing) and Li Qiao (Maggie Cheung [Zhang Manyu], a leading Hong Kong star) on a train from the mainland, sitting close to each other while dozing off. Though physically close to each other, they depart from the station without making each others' acquaintance. Interestingly, it is in a McDonald's restaurant, where Li Qiao works part time, that the two meet again, and this time they formally introduce each other. Knowing Xiaojun to be a newcomer to the city, Li helps him enroll in an English class, yet takes advantage of him by getting him to run errands for her. Xiaojun gladly helps Li, openly admiring her intelligence, such as her shrewdness in stock-market speculation. Originally from Guangzhou (Canton) and a fluent speaker of Cantonese, Li passes as a Hong Kong native and at first shows contempt at Xiaojun's awkward mainland manners. In spite of their regional differences, the two are forced to face cultural differences in Hong Kong when their joint venture in selling recordings of Deng Lijun's songs in a local fair proves financially disastrous.

A romantic melodrama, *Comrades* does not delve much into issues of identity and ethnicity. Without actually developing the geocultural and geopolitical conflicts between mainland China and Hong Kong—other than such clichés as playing the Chinese national anthem when Xiaojun is seen delivering food on his bicycle in the streets of Hong Kong—the film moves quickly to the sexual relationship between Xiaojun and Li. By the time Xiaojun's fiancée joins him from the mainland in 1990, Li has become sexually involved with Baoge, a triad boss who is soon pursued by the local police and has to flee Hong Kong. The remainder of the film is set in the U.S., where Baoge is killed in a street fight, and both Li and Xiaojun are immigrants working in New York City. They do not meet until May 8, 1995, when the news of Deng Lijun's death brings them together at a window display outside an electronic equipment store. They watch Deng on the TV screen and listen to the bittersweet song of her "Tian mimi" (the film's Chinese title, literally, "honey sweet").

In his overview of 1996 Hong Kong film productions, Li Cheuk-to judges *Comrades* to be a "mature work . . . appealing to both the more and the less cultured of film audience," but he immediately qualifies his judgment by labeling the film as "somewhat too conceptualized" for an immigrant film (1997b, 11). Rather than "too conceptualized," I would argue that *Comrades* is actually not conceptualized enough, at least not clearly conceptualized as far as its vision of ethnicity is concerned. As a result, the film is highly ambivalent in its treatment of the immigration theme. Although *Comrades* fared better at the box office in Hong Kong than either *Farewell, China* or *Crossings* (Cuoai, 1994), Peter Chan's depiction of New York resembles very much the tourist guidebook: pointing out urban landmarks and scenic spots while bypassing ethnic and racial issues. As an immigrant film, *Comrades* pales in comparison not only to *Farewell, China* and *Crossings* (the latter a thriller about a pregnant Hong Kong woman illegally traveling to New York City in search of her lover, only to be murdered in a subway station), but also to earlier films like *An Autumn's Tale* (Qiutian de tonghua, 1987) and *Full Moon in New York* (San'ge nüren de gushi, aka Ren zai Niuyue, 1989), the latter a study of three Chinese women (respectively from China, Hong Kong, and Taiwan) and their struggles and friendship, or *Pushing Hands* (1991) and *The Wedding Banquet* (1992), both set in New York. (Parenthetically, it is worth mentioning that, with its fractured identities and hybridized ethnicities, its multilingualism and multiculturalism, its synchronicity of past, present, and future, its contrast between wealth and poverty, its magnificent skyscrapers and back-alley filth, present-day New York has been frequently projected in recent Hong Kong cinema as an uncanny Other, though a much less glamorous Other than Old Shanghai, as we shall see below.)

It is my contention that, by treating New York merely as a setting, Hong Kong as a port of transit (Abbas 1997a, 4; Chow 1998a, 176), and mainland China as a singular point of reference, *Comrades* does not fully utilize the advantage offered by a new vision of the glocal city as the simultaneously fascinating and frustrating Other, nor does it adequately explore the troubling question of old and new identities, or old and new ethnicities for that matter. First, unlike *Autumn Moon*, where Wai, a Hong Kong local, manages to develop a global sense of place by conscientiously preparing herself for her upcoming emigration to Canada, *Comrades* presents Xiaojun's and Li Qiao's immigration to the U.S. as an accident, as something that just happens. Second, unlike *Chungking Express*, where Faye and Cop 663, two Hong Kong locals who are willing to work out alternatives of living in the glocal city from their localized experience, *Comrades* portrays Xiaojun and Li Qiao as essentially two outsiders, two migrant workers who lack commitment to the places they pass through. Finally, unlike *Homecoming* and *Song of the Exile* (Ketu qiuhen, 1990),[14] *Comrades* evokes China as a faraway off-screen space in which regional difference is almost inconsequential from the Hong Kong point of view. This blindness to or ignorance of significant regional differences in China is particularly telling when the film's subtitles (in Chinese and English) refer to Xiaojun's hometown as Wuxi (a cultural city in the Yangtze delta) while the characters refer to it as Tianjin (an industrialized coastal metropolis near Beijing).[15]

Perhaps Peter Chan was so intent on telling a story of the root-lessness of Chinese people around the world that he chose to emphasize

---

[14] For sample studies of *Song of the Exile*, see Keng 1998; Williams 1998. For Ann Hui's other films, see Erens 2000; Ho 1999.

[15] For large cultural differences between Northern and Southern China, see Y. Zhang 1996, 3–27.

their *sameness* rather than their difference. But the problem with *Comrades*, I suggest, lies in its overindulgence in melodrama, in a romantic narrative whose initial attention to issues of identity and ethnicity is carried away or taken over by the overwhelming melody of Deng Lijun's songs. Consequently, the film revels in an excess of nostalgia. As a structure of feeling that surfaced in many Hong Kong films since the mid-1980s, nostalgia points to something of special significance, something that deserves more consideration in the transcultural and transregional context of the glocal city.

Nostalgia Cinema and Hong Kong's Marginality in History

My critical analysis of three Hong Kong films in the preceding pages is meant to demonstrate that, set against the trope of disappearance, tactics of reinscription deployed by individual films are highly ideological in nature, ideological in the Althusserian sense of "interpellating" characters to certain subject positions.[16] If one direction of such ideological reinscriptions is looking outward to the global flows in the ethnoscapes, mediascapes, and ideoscapes, as exemplified in *Chungking Express, Autumn Moon* and *Comrades*, another direction is looking inward or backward to earlier periods in local, translocal, and transregional history, as in the case of contemporary nostalgia cinema in Hong Kong.

According to Li Cheuk-to, *Rouge* (1987), which juxtaposes the contrasting lifestyles of the Hong Kong of the glamorized 1930s and the rationalized 1980s, marked the onset of a craze for nostalgia films in Hong Kong (1993, 3). For Chiao Hsiung-Ping, however, it is *Love in a Fallen City* (Qingcheng zhilian, 1984), which contrasts Hong Kong and Shanghai of the early 1940s, that initially set the nostalgic trend in Hong Kong film production (1987, 193). Regardless of its pioneering texts, Blanche Chu reminds us, nostalgia cinema did not enjoy full popularity until its commercialization in two subgenres: the "biographical nostalgia film" such as *Lee Rock* (Wuyi tanzhang Lei Luo, 1991) and *To Be Number One* (Bohao, 1991), and "nostalgia comedies" such as *92 Legendary La Rose Noire* (92 hei meigui dui hei meigui, 1992) and *He Ain't Heavy, He's My Father* (Xin nanxiong nandi, 1993; hereafter *He's My Father*). Some nostalgia films hark back to the period between the 1920s and 1940s, to

---

[16] Althusser 1971, 127–86. For a sample Althusserian reading of subjectivity in post-Mao China, see Y. Zhang 1993a.

either Hong Kong or Shanghai (and sometimes both), for example *Hong Kong 1941* (Dengdai liming, 1984), *Shanghai Blues* (Shanghai zhiye, 1984), *Rouge, Shanghai 1920* (Shanghai jiaofu, 1991), *Center Stage*, and *Red Rose, White Rose*. But the majority of Hong Kong nostalgia films prefer Hong Kong of the 1950s and 1960s. This preference, in Natalia Chan's opinion, arises from the fact that the period of the 1950s and 1960s is generally seen as the beginning of the history of Hong Kong as a modern city. Seen as the golden age of the colonial period, this era is characterized by the government's policy of non-interference as well as by self-determination, free speech, and prosperity (Chan 2000; P. Leung 2000). In retrospect, especially against the fast-approaching 1997 deadline, local history—hitherto a blank page in the colony's middle-school history textbooks (Luo Feng 1995, 65)—has fascinated Hong Kong filmmakers since the mid-1980s.

Nostalgia, Abbas writes, "is not the return of past memory: it is the return of memory to the past" (1997a, 83). Nostalgia, therefore, is never an entirely passive act, a kind of "involuntary memory" accidentally triggered by an object from the past.[17] Rather, it is an *active* investment in affectivity, an emotional expenditure through acts of remembrance and reminiscence—often in these films enhanced by a subjective voice-over—that "reproduces" a particular type of past, one that is fantasized, sentimentalized, and romanticized as more heroic, more glamorous, and more memorable than the present. Conceived in this way, nostalgia is, as Rey Chow observes in her analysis of *Rouge*, "most acutely felt not as an attempt to return to the past as such, but as an effect of temporal dislocation—of something having been displaced in time" (1998a, 147).

Such temporal dislocation turns out to be a structuring principle in many Hong Kong nostalgia films. As in *Rouge* and *Center Stage*, the juxtaposition of past and present occurs in *He's My Father*, where Chu Yuan (Tony Leung Chiu-Wai), a contemporary Hong Kong youth, jumps into a dry well one night and time-travels back to the 1960s. He finds his father, Chu Fan (Tony Leung Ka-Fai [Liang Jiahui]), who emerged as a folk hero defending the rights of his fellow tenants in crowded old houses along Memory Lane. Another strategy typical of nostalgia cinema is the transplanting and recycling, often in the form of parody or pastiche, of the well-known titles, names, and episodes from

---

[17] For a discussion of involuntary memory, or Proust's *mémoire involontaire*, see Benjamin 1969, 202–3.

previous Hong Kong films. The Chinese title of *He's My Father*—"Xin nanxiong nandi" (literally, "a new version of brothers in trouble")— refers to a much earlier Hong Kong film, *Brothers* (Nanxiong nandi, 1934). Yet the story of *He's My Father* has very little to do with the original film but instead alludes to Chor Yuen's (Chu Yuan) 1973 Cantonese comedy *The House of Seventy-Two Tenants*, which dramatized housing problems in Hong Kong. The theme, in fact, can be traced to an even earlier Hong Kong production, *In the Face of Demolition* (Weilou chunxiao, 1953). In addition to featuring Chor Yuen's namesake as its protagonist (Chu Yuan), *He's My Father* names the father Chu Fan after Ng Cho-fan (Wu Chufan), a famous Hong Kong actor who appeared in over 250 features from 1933 to 1966.

Likewise, the Chinese title of *C'est la vie, mon chéri* (Xin buliao qing, 1993) refers to *Love Without End* (Buliao qing, 1961), but the film relocates the story of romantic love and explores the lives of those in Hong Kong's lower social strata in the 1990s, away from the central icons of modernity and postmodernity. To intensify its nostalgic ambience, *C'est la vie, mon chéri* even enlists Fung Bobo (Feng Baobao), the former "Hong Kong Shirley Temple" and child star of the 1960s. Fung's melancholic, impressive performance of Cantonese opera in the film gives local audiences a bittersweet rendition of one of their own neglected cultural traditions. In films such as these, Blanche Chu observes, "The specific object of nostalgia is the 'auratic' local Cantonese film industry of the 50's and 60's in terms of mannerisms, habits, customs, fashion, names or nicknames, the unique image of well-known Cantonese stars, or all-too-familiar filmic style, punchlines, [and] ethical relationships portrayed in old Cantonese films" (1998, 43–4). What is remarkable in cases like these is that, while confronting the threat of imminent disappearance or disintegration, nostalgia cinema resorts to tactics of reinscription and successfully carves out a recognizable space in which to flaunt an excess of *localized* cultural icons and products, at least for the duration of the film.

But nostalgia cinema does more than simply invoke history and affectivity. Derived from the Greek *nostos* (to return home) and *algia* (a painful condition), nostalgia denotes "a painful yearning to return home" (F. Davis 1979, 1). The etymology of the term thus nicely captures the tension between disappearance (imaged as a forever lost past or a faraway homeland) and reinscription (exemplified by the effort to make sense of oneself in relation to the past, present, and future), a tension that surfaces in most of the films examined in this chapter. As Davis speculates, "nostalgia (like memory, like reminiscence, like daydreaming) is deeply implicated in the sense of who we are, what we are about, and . . . whither we go. In short, nostalgia is one of the means—or, better, one of the more readily accessible psychological lenses—we employ in the never ending work of constructing, maintaining, and reconstructing our identities" (1979, 31). Seen in this light, nostalgia cinema itself constitutes an attempt at reinscription of identity in Hong Kong's ongoing negotiation with its fate of disappearance.

The question remains, nevertheless, as to what kind of identities nostalgia cinema seeks to (re)construct for Hong Kong audiences. As Blanche Chu suggests, "The sentiment of nostalgia flourishing in Hong Kong popular culture in recent years should be understood as a pursuit of identity which is not targeted at the rediscovery of a native past. It is not directed at recovering a 'pre-colonized' or 'original' identity of Hong Kong people" (1998, 43). Instead, nostalgia cinema's invocation of either Hong Kong or China in different historical periods reveals "the Janus-faced nature of 'Hong Kong identity'" (1998, 48). In her critical reading of the representation of the "unrepresentable" in *Center Stage*—be it the legend of the tragic actress Ruan Lingyu, Shanghai film culture of the 1930s, or history as such—Chu detects "a self-imaging of Hong Kong, its sense of inferiority, by positioning the self as an outsider of history who is incapable of intervening in history" (1998, 52–3).[18] However, Chu contends, it is precisely such "critical distance" from history—or marginality in history, I would argue—that allows Hong Kong citizens to embrace "pessimism as empowerment" and to effect "an affirmation of passivity through deriving from an aesthetic level a self-justificatory narrative of being a passive, mechanistic 'imitator' or teller of history" (1998, 53).

In light of de Certeau's theory, what is noteworthy in Chu's argument is her affirmation of the value of "tactics" as they are developed from the margin of history and her deployment of these tactics against the "strategy" of the master narrative superimposed on the margin by the center. Chu's acknowledgement of passivity and pessimism, in this sense, does not equate to an abandonment of the concepts of agency and subjectivity. Although Hong Kong, as a city living "on borrowed time in

[18] For other discussions of *Center Stage*, see Abbas 1997a, 44–7; Cui 2000; Stringer 1997a.

a borrowed place" (Han Suyin's description, quoted in Abbas 1997a, 142), is never located at the center of history and has long been denied the privilege of writing its own history, it could still imagine from the margins those "alternative times and alternative values" (Chow 1998a, 147) that are best captured in nostalgia cinema. The term "alternative" is crucial here: alternative to the center of geopolitical power (the nation-state, cultural hegemony), to the master narrative of modernity (progress, revolution, rationality), and to the forces of transnational capitalism (globalization, homogenization, cosmopolitanism). Such alternatives, furthermore, both depend on and contribute to the discursive power of marginality.

Marginality, as Stuart Hall envisions it, "is a space of weak power but it is a space of power, nonetheless" (1997a, 34). Similarly, de Certeau concedes that "a tactic is an art of the weak," and his description of the discrete operations of a tactic illuminates the ways nostalgia cinema approaches Hong Kong's identity and history (1984, 37):

> It takes advantage of "opportunities" and depends on them, being without any base where it could stockpile its winnings, build up its own position, and plan raids. What it wins it cannot keep. . . . [It] must accept the chance offerings of the moment. . . . It must vigilantly make use of the cracks that particular conjunctions open in the surveillance of the proprietary powers. It poaches in them. It creates surprises in them. It can be where it is least expected. It is a guileful ruse.

III

From Hong Kong to Shanghai:
Eileen Chang, Transregional Romance, Interpreted Nostalgia

Let us pause here to consider *Love in a Fallen City*, Ann Hui's 1984 film adaptation of Eileen Chang's (Zhang Ailing) story that reputedly started the nostalgia cinema craze in Hong Kong. In terms of self-positioned marginality, discrete tactics, and alternative values, we can easily discern an uncanny resemblance between Chang's female protagonist, Chang the writer herself, and recent Hong Kong nostalgia cinema. Published in 1943, Chang's original story—its Chinese title, "Qingcheng zhilian," also meaning "a love that topples the city"—features Bai Liusu, a cunning modern divorcée who escapes the traditional household of her parents' family in Shanghai to date a

Westernized businessman in Hong Kong. Her desperate attempt to secure herself in a decent marriage does not come to fruition until the ultimately "unexpected" event (from the characters' point of view) occurs: the Japanese invasion of Hong Kong. Ann Hui's film ends with Liusu (Miao Qianren), who, after the announcement of her lover Fan Liuyuan (Chow Yun-Fat) that they are already "married," wakes up alone in bed from nightmarish visions of gunshots, bombings, and dead bodies. Against the backdrop of the devastated urban ruins (surely a dramatization of the 1997 anxiety in Hong Kong), Eileen Chang's words appear on the screen, capturing the "guileful ruse" attributed to her female character: "Hong Kong's defeat had given her victory. But in this unreasonable world, who can say which was the cause, and which the result? Who knows? Maybe it was in order to vindicate her that an entire city fell. . . . Liusu did not feel that her place in history was anything remarkable" (E. Chang 1996, 92).[19]

With reference to de Certeau's theorization, I would suggest that, just as Bai Liusu seizes the "chance offerings of the moment" (the fall of Hong Kong) and "poaches" in the field of "the proprietary powers" (as manifest in the constant surveillance of female virtues in the repressive patriarchal society), so did Eileen Chang take advantage of historical "opportunities"—the Japanese occupation of Shanghai and the voluntary or involuntary silence of most veteran writers there during war time—and created "surprises" by articulating her alternative voices and visions when they were "least expected" in the history of modern Chinese writing.[20] Using her fictional character to dismiss, at least symbolically, "that her place in history was anything remarkable," Eileen Chang expressed her profound dissatisfaction with the center, master narrative, and historical monumentality. Instead, she opted to embrace marginality, concrete imagery, and an apocalyptic vision of civilization, thereby setting a discursive precedent for contemporary Hong Kong nostalgia cinema. In retrospect, Chang's fiction about the two preeminent colonial cities in modern China—Old Shanghai and Hong Kong—has become a cherished, if not yet fully fetishized, object of nostalgia.

---

[19] For sample analyses of the story, see Chow 1991b, 112–20; L. Lee 1999b, 41–52; Gunn 1980, 214–8; Y. Zhang 1996, 242–9.

[20] For the uncanny resemblance between Chang and her character Liusu, see Ke Ling's article in Xiao Nan 1995, 1–19.

This fetishization of Old Shanghai and Hong Kong as objects of nostalgia is integral to Leo Lee's "interpretative reconstruction" of a tale of two cities, a textual reconstruction itself unraveled in an ambience of deeply felt nostalgia (L. Lee 1999c, 341; see also his 1998–9). In the epilogue to his *Shanghai Modern* (which begins and ends with quotations from Eileen Chang), Lee reflects on the dual processes of what I would call the "transregional romance" between these two cities: Hong Kong as the "Other" of Shanghai (most evident in Shanghai modernist writing of the 1930s and 1940s) and Shanghai as the "Other" of Hong Kong (as in the case of contemporary Hong Kong nostalgia films). Lee's catalogue of the cultural trafficking, real or imaginary transactions, and symbolic linkages between these two cities from the late 1930s to the 1990s adds further evidence to the importance of Hong Kong and Shanghai in a cultural history of modern China. As many scholars have demonstrated, the "reel" contact between Hong Kong and Shanghai dates back to the early decades of the twentieth century and persisted up to the recent *fin de siècle* (Teo 1997, 3–39; Law Kar 1994; Z. Zhang 1998b). A perceptive cultural historian, Lee points further to an interesting contrast in Eileen Chang's fictional world: "Hong Kong is too blatant, too vulgar and flamboyant in its Western imitation, . . . too eager to 'prostitute' itself to the desires of its colonial master," whereas "Shanghai for all its foreignness is still Chinese" (1999c, 327–8).

Writing in a nostalgic mode, Lee does not clarify his (or Chang's) idea of "Chineseness" and instead hastens to enumerate what happened in Shanghai and Hong Kong during and after the war (including what he terms the "Shanghainization" of Hong Kong in the 1950s). But two recent nostalgia films, one of them financed by Hong Kong's Tomson Film, seem to question what Lee posits above as an "obvious" contrast between Hong Kong and Shanghai. By restaging the Hollywood-style cabaret songs and dances, *Shanghai Triad* demonstrates that Old Shanghai was equally willing—if no more "eager" than Old Hong Kong—to "prostitute" itself to colonial demands. In contrast to the promiscuity, decadence, and violence of urban life, Zhang Yimou has his characters retreat in the second half of the film to an isolated island far from the madding city. There, his vision of Chineseness finds embodiment in the idyllic rural setting and is further evoked by a nostalgic children's song, "Row the Boat to Grandma's Bridge" (hence, the film's Chinese title, "Yao a yao, yaodao waipo qiao"). What is worse, in *Temptress Moon*, even the rural setting, symbolized by the traditional lifestyle and rigid patriarchal order in the Pang family compound, is inevitably corrupted by Western culture, and the heroine Ruyi (Gong Li) is willing to "prostitute" her "Chineseness," which is cinematically encoded as her demure manners and virginity, to the colonizing forces of Shanghai.

That Old Shanghai is imagined as Western, foreign, exotic, erotic, feminine, sexually impure, or morally suspect, has long been a cliché in the cultural imagination of modern China (Y. Zhang 1996, 117–231). In her reading of the seductions of homecoming in *Temptress Moon*, Rey Chow identifies a strong feeling of nostalgia articulated through the image of uncorrupted children. Ironically, this film of moral corruption and sexual degradation ends with the innocent faces of Ruyi, Zhongliang (Leslie Cheung), and Duanwu as children, all three gazing directly at the camera, as if puzzled by the unthinkable events that would soon ruin their adult lives. For Chow, this ending constructs a utopia, a non-place, and the idealism projected in the film only leads to homesickness, which in turn feeds idealism, thereby forming the "vicious circle of a cultural complex" (1998f, 14–5).[21]

Chow's reference to homesickness thus brings us back to the question of nostalgia. According to Fred Davis, "nostalgia" was a word invented by the Swiss physician Johnannes Hofer in the 1680s to designate a "condition of extreme homesickness among Swiss mercenaries fighting far from their native land." It referred to an imaginary "disease" whose "symptoms" were said to be "despondency, melancholia, lability of emotion, including profound bouts of weeping, anorexia, a generalized 'wasting away,' and, not infrequently, attempts at suicide" (1979, 1–2). (For readers familiar with Eileen Chang, these symptoms could be diagnosed in many of her fictional characters and even Chang's own reclusive life in the U.S. later on [see Ji Ji and Guan 1996; Tang Wenbiao 1976 and 1982; Xiao Nan 1995].) By the 1950s,

---

[21] In a review of Chow's *Ethics after Idealism*, Eric Hayot correctly observes that Chow's book "theorizes, somewhat paradoxically, a nostalgics of nostalgia, in which nostalgia itself is remembered, or put back together, via the construction of a particular history that shows us how we must always repeat and reenact its various inflections. In such a scenario, it is the struggle against idealism's inevitability—of knowing that each new reading must construct its ethics retrospectively out of the ghost of its past—that defines Chow's own ethics of reading" (1999, 225). Chow's work, in other words, may also be seen as an example of "interpreted nostalgia," though of a rather different nature from Leo Lee's, the latter verging on a wholesale endorsement of nostalgia.

however, the word "nostalgia" had entered the popular parlance and been fully "demilitarized" and "demedicalized." In its contemporary usage, nostalgia tends to idealize or romanticize the past, infusing it with beauty, pleasure, joy, satisfaction, goodness, happiness, love, and the like. Yet it also carries an implied judgment of the present as bleak, grim, wretched, ugly, deprivational, unfulfilling, frightening, or at least cold, gray, unpromising, unengaging, and uninspiring. Furthermore, Davis differentiates three orders of nostalgic reaction—simple nostalgia, reflexive nostalgia, and interpreted nostalgia—and states that none of them should be considered better than or exclusive of the others.

Davis's distinction between reflexive nostalgia (which questions the historical accuracy of simple nostalgia) and interpreted nostalgia (which further questions the reflexive response) sheds new light on nostalgia cinema and its critical reception. If a nostalgia film like *Temptress Moon* or *Center Stage* contains "reflexive nostalgia" (for, in the name of investigating the object of nostalgia, such a film inevitably reproduces and intensifies the appeal of nostalgia itself), then a certain kind of critical study of nostalgia may resemble "interpreted nostalgia" in that, despite its apparent rhetorical gesture and "impartial" historical evidence, it perpetuates the belief that there is something authentic or mysterious about the object of nostalgia in the first place.

As suggested above, Leo Lee's approach to nostalgia cinema is a case in point. In his discussion of *Center Stage*, for instance, Lee endorses Stanley Kwan's creative use of film as a medium not only to re-present the past for the present (the reenacted scenes where Maggie Cheung poses as Ruan Lingyu) but also to bring the past (the extant film footage of Ruan Lingyu herself) literally into the present. Ruan's "haunting presence thus becomes a reminder . . . of the haunting mystery of Shanghai itself that continues to hold Hong Kong audiences spellbound" (1999c, 336–7). On the other hand, Lee judges Kwan's adaptation of Eileen Chang's *Red Rose, White Rose*, which "is so faithful that even quotations of Chang's prose are inscribed on the screen as 'subheadings,'" to be largely a failure, "because in my view Kwan simply cannot reproduce Chang's unique (meta)narrative voice" (1999b, 54).[22] Similarly,

---

[22] However, as Liu Chi-hui convincingly argues, Kwan has deliberately altered Eileen Chang's voice in order to stage a challenge to—if not subversion of—Chang's language-heavy original film (1996, 125–38). For an overview of Kwan's films, see Tam and Dissanayake 1998, 72–82.

even though Ann Hui directed *Love in a Fallen City* and has "obviously done meticulous research on the decor and milieu of old Shanghai" for her new adaptation of Chang's *Eighteen Springs* (Bansheng yuan, aka Shiba chun, 1997), Lee suspects that "if Chang were watching it, . . . she would say that the story still suffers because the characters on the 'foreground' are not exactly right—not because they all speak Cantonese, not Shanghainese, but because the modern actors and actresses from Hong Kong and Taiwan no longer have the authentic 'look' of her fictional characters" (1999b, 55).

What is problematic in Lee's approach to nostalgia cinema is less his hypothetical self-positioning as a legitimate spokesman for Eileen Chang ("she would say . . .") than his insistence on Chang's "unique voice" and the "authentic look" of her characters from Old Shanghai. For Lee, after fifty years, "it is inevitable that the 'look' of [Chang's] characters already takes on a certain historical, even mythological, layer: in other words, they are part of the myth and . . . 'mythology' of old Shanghai itself" (1999b, 56). One may question here whether all writings half a century old are equally capable of evoking nostalgia. Evidently, Lee's use of "old Shanghai itself" as a mythological reference (à la Roland Barthes) is crucial to his version of "interpreted nostalgia," a third order of nostalgia Fred Davis considers to be "the framing of the nostalgic response . . . [that] adds yet another dimension to the experience" (1979, 25).

After all, Lee confesses that he is a fan of Chang's fiction or "Chang-fan" (*Zhang mi* in Chinese), though not a "full-fledged" one at that. It is only expected, therefore, that Eileen Chang appears to him and other Chang-fans like a legendary movie-star, not just with a national reputation (like Ruan Lingyu, who is read as coterminous with Old Shanghai in *Center Stage*), but with an international one (like Greta Garbo). Typical of nostalgia's muting of the negative, for Chang-fans, Chang's self-confessed egotism and her unsavory relationship with Hu Lancheng, a notorious womanizer and pro-Japanese traitor during the war (Ji Ji and Guan 1996, 72–124), no longer raise eyebrows; instead, they have added further appeal to her legendary life. In his attempt to answer "what constitutes Eileen Chang's legend?" Lee dismisses *Red Dust* (Gungun hongchen, 1990), which is based on a screenplay by the legendary Taiwan woman writer San Mao, as a mere "glamorized version of Eileen Chang's life." In its place, Lee recommends Chang's last book, *An Album of Mutual Reflections* (Duizhao ji), a narcissistic account of reading her old photographs, as one that contains a series of "'still shots' for a never-to-be-made movie" (1999b, 56–9).

That Leo Lee has added a new layer of subjective feelings—in addition to a new interpretive framework, namely, Hollywood screwball comedy as Stanley Cavell interprets it—to the current nostalgia for Eileen Chang and Old Shanghai should come as no surprise by now. Using "authenticity" as almost a magic term, Lee not only announces the impossibility of ever capturing the unique "look" of Eileen Chang's Old Shanghai in film adaptations but also, and significantly, judges Chang's post-Shanghai writings to be less "authentic" (especially in their treatment of Hong Kong) and less satisfactory than her earlier romances in fiction and film. More specifically, Lee considers the screenplays Chang wrote for the Motion Picture & General Investment (MP&GI or Dianmao) in Hong Kong between 1952 (her arrival in Hong Kong) and 1964 (the end of her first decade in the United States) to be "intentionally vulgar," and some to be rather "flat and formulaic," which indicates her "crisis of creativity caused by dislocation and exile from her familiar environment in her beloved city, Shanghai" (1999b, 53).[23]

Lee's diagnosis of Chang's crisis of creativity notwithstanding, we are still faced with an intriguing question: What purpose does an interpreted nostalgia serve? Two basic points Fred Davis raises may help us in this connection: "(1) the nostalgic evocation of some past state of affairs always occurs in the context of present fears, discontents, anxieties, or uncertainties, even though they may not be in the forefront of awareness, and (2) it is these emotions and cognitive states that pose the threat of identity discontinuity . . . that nostalgia seeks . . . to abort or, at the very least, deflect" (1979, 34). The 1997 anxiety, as discussed in the preceding section, is a contributing factor to the nostalgia cinema craze in Hong Kong. In Leo Lee's case of interpreted nostalgia, however, it is amply evident that his interest lies more in the identity of Old Shanghai than

---

[23] The screenplays Chang wrote in her post-Shanghai period include *Courtship Is Like a Battlefield* (Qingchang ru zhangchang, 1957), *June Bride* (Liuyue xinniang, 1960), *The Greatest Wedding on Earth* (Nanbei yijia qin, 1962), *Father Takes a Bride* (Xiao ernü, 1962), and *The Greatest Love Affair on Earth* (Nanbei xi xiangfeng, 1964) (see L. Lee 1999b, 52). Earlier, Chang contributed three successful screenplays to Shanghai's Wenhua Film Company, *Lingering Passion* (Buliao qing, 1947), *Long Live the Mistress!* (Taitai wansui, 1947), and *Sorrows and Joys of a Middle-Aged Man* (Aile zhongnian, 1949), all directed by Sang Hu.

that of present-day Hong Kong. In spite of—or because of—an increasing nostalgia for Old Shanghai in both Hong Kong and Shanghai, Lee is keenly aware that the old charm has faded or dissipated, if not entirely disappeared. In response, he draws our attention to what Fred Davis sees as "nostalgia's propensity to fasten on what was offbeat, marginal, odd, different, secret, and privatized about our former selves" (1979, 41)—and, I would add, about an earlier, presumably "lost" period of our culture. Given nostalgia's function to abort or deflect discontents and uncertainties, it is only appropriate that Lee concludes his *Shanghai Modern* with an enigmatic figure described by Eileen Chang in 1947—a Daoist priest utterly lost in the hustling streets of Shanghai. As Lee speculates, Chang herself would choose to assume the allegorical role of a Daoist if she were to be reincarnated in "the new metropolis of Shanghai in post-socialist China half a century later" (1999c, 341).

Shanghai Fever, Anti-Nostalgia, and the Chaos of Simultaneity and Multiplicity

Given the recent vogue of nostalgia for the "good old days" in both Shanghai and Hong Kong, it would be interesting to see how contemporary Chinese filmmakers relate themselves to certain tropes, such as transnational flows of capital and eros and the spatialization of time and desire, that were fully functional in Chinese literature and film in earlier periods (L. Lee 1999c, 153–303; Shih 1996; Y. Zhang 1996). *Shanghai Fever* (Gufeng, 1993), a China–Hong Kong coproduction, serves as a good illustration. An analysis of this urban comedy, which problematizes value systems in postsocialist China, will not only put in context the popular nostalgia for Old Shanghai occasioned, as it were, by the loss of its "authenticity" or the disappearance of its genuine "look" (as indicated by Leo Lee), but will also connect us to new conceptions of space and place.

Shanghai Fever follows Ah Lun (Lau Ching-wan [Liu Qingyun]), a love-sick Hong Kong stockbroker who chases his former girlfriend to Shanghai. When he arrives, he is persuaded to begin speculating in the market with the help of Fan Li (Pan Hong), a local bus conductor. Working together, the two realize huge financial gains. Fan soon becomes a local investment celebrity, and her neighbors and co-workers entrust their savings to her. After leading viewers through a quick succession of comic, farcical, and melodramatic situations, the film reaches its climactic scene. Fan's husband Xu Ang, an architect who has lost all of a friend's 20,000 yuan in the stock market, leaves a suicide note and ascends to the top of a high-rise hotel to jump. Fan rushes to the scene with her daughter and tearfully pleads with Xu, to no avail.

The scene takes a dramatic turn when Ah Lun climbs to the top and reveals his own "miserable" life: orphaned at the age of four, he is now unemployed and has no place to live when he returns to Hong Kong. Speaking in heavily accented Mandarin, Ah Lun confronts Xu: "You're a legitimate Chinese [tangtang de Zhongguo ren]. Who am I? I'm only a Hong Kongese. I have no identity, no nationality. No country wants to take me if I want to emigrate. If they accept me, I'll be a second-class citizen." The film cuts to Ah Lun's girlfriend, who finds an engagement ring Ah Lun has apparently bought for her. She hurries to the scene, where Ah Lun switches to Cantonese: "And my beloved girlfriend left me. Now I have nothing." With these words he rushes to the edge and almost jumps, only to be rescued by Xu.

As expected of a comedy, *Shanghai Fever* brings about the reunion of Fan and Xu, the reconciliation of Ah Lun and his girlfriend, and, to complete happiness for all, a celebration when Fan's neighborhood investment group realize that they did not lose all their money in the stock market after all. The film ends with Fan's family moving to a new apartment, the news of the birth of Ah Lun's son in Hong Kong, and a character's comment on the skyrocketing real estate value of the development zone east of the Huangpu River (*pudong*): "Shanghai is a land of gold."

Two things merit our attention. First, given the fact that Pan Hong (one of the most famous actresses in China) is credited for cowriting the screenplay, *Shanghai Fever* unequivocally establishes mainland China as the political center and Hong Kong as a colony soon to be returned to its motherland.[24] Even though he is investing in Shanghai and lives in a luxurious hotel, Ah Lun's character is scripted to confess his past experience as an orphan and his current state of "homelessness" in Hong Kong. This is exactly the kind of mainland "superiority complex" or chauvinism that Rey Chow critiques as "political idealism" taking "the form of rescue": "Hong Kong is *in need* of a mother: she is longing to be reunited with China; her 'real' source of identification is mainland China,

---

[24] For critical discussions of Hong Kong's return to China's sovereignty in 1997, see Abbas 1997b; Chow 1998d; Wu Hung 1997.

and so forth" (1998a, 172). This complex is all the more conspicuous in the film when Shanghai is staged as a place where a love-sick, "unemployed" Hong Kong broker can fulfill his emotional, libidinal, and financial needs all at once.

Second, Shanghai is used as a metonymy for the stock market; hence, the Chinese title "gufeng" (literally, "stock fever") is translated as "Shanghai fever" in the English title. Thus equating Shanghai to money, the film celebrates—in an almost carnivalesque fashion—what Lydia Liu describes as the emerging "ideology of entrepreneurship" (*qiye jia*) in the era of reform. According to Liu, in the same year when *Shanghai Fever* was released, between eight- and nine-hundred million viewers watched *Beijing Sojourners in New York* (Beijing ren zai Niuyue), a television serial codirected by Feng Xiaogang and Zheng Xiaolong and aired on CCTV in October 1993 (1999, 763; see also Barmé 1999, 255–80; M. Yang 1997, 304–8). Liu places this television serial, which dramatizes a Beijing musician's quest for financial success, social status, and Chinese nationalistic pride in New York City, in a transnational context, one that is defined by the postsocialist official discourse on the one end and the mainstream American media on the other. Although her "tentative conclusion" that "*postsocialism produces transnationalism just as much as transnationalism produces postsocialism*" (1999, 792) may seem rather far-fetched on first reading, it does highlight the complicit relationship between two otherwise conflicting value systems—Chinese postsocialism and Western capitalism.

Evidence of the complicity between postsocialism and transnational capitalism is also discernible in *Shanghai Fever*, where the new ideology of entrepreneurship is enthusiastically embraced by ordinary folks in the city's back alleys (*lilong*), and a new chapter of transregional romance between Shanghai and Hong Kong—this time centered in the financial sector—is being written. The ideological reorientation of *Shanghai Fever* comes to the fore when we compare the film to *Crows and Sparrows* (Wuya yu maque, 1949), a classic leftist film from the pre-Communist period. In *Crows and Sparrows*, the Xiaos (Zhao Dan and Wu Yin), two street vendors, join thousands of small-time speculators outside the Shanghai Stock Exchange one night. When dawn breaks, however, their dream of making a fortune through stock speculation is literally crushed by the frenetic crowd which, instigated by gang members, beats them up and throws them out. By comparison, the crowd outside the stock exchange in *Shanghai Fever* is smaller, but individual speculators like Fan are no less determined to make money. Fan camps out by the entrance overnight and, early next morning, defends her position against a group of line-cutters who use a malodorous night-soil cart to block the entrance. In this scene, scatological humor reaches its height.

What emerges from this comparison is fundamentally ironic. Not only is the critique of money as a principal source of evil—a theme persisting from early leftist films through *Crows and Sparrows* to numerous films during the Mao years[25]—completely nonexistent in *Shanghai Fever*, but *Shanghai Fever* simply presents its characters as a community of speculators as feverish as, if no more frenetic than, their counterparts in *Crows and Sparrows*. In a single stroke, *Shanghai Fever* seems to wipe out forty years' worth of Communist propaganda. Money has become almost the only thing people care about, and the importance of human emotions, which fluctuate like stocks, is not reestablished until the scene of the attempted suicide near the end of the film. This scene reestablishes Shanghai as a site of emotional fulfillment and a place of financial success. Nevertheless, the plot line here is so contrived, the dialogue so exaggerated, the emotions so cheap, and the narrative resolution so absurd that *Shanghai Fever*, as an urban text, can hardly offer the charm and aesthetic pleasure one expects from Eileen Chang's Old Shanghai tales. In this sense, *Shanghai Fever* may be taken as a film of *anti-nostalgia*, a film that intentionally ridicules such notions as taste, decency, propriety, and authenticity. Instead of offering a legendary urban romance, the film forces its viewers to recognize and confront the comic, the farcical, the absurd, and the irrational in a rapidly changing glocal city.[26]

In view of the ideological thrust of anti-nostalgia in *Shanghai Fever* (and many other urban films, as we shall see), one can now better

---

[25] See, for example, *New Woman* (1934), *Myriad of Lights* (Wanjia denghuo, 1948), *City Without Night* (Buye cheng, 1957), and *Sentinels Under the Neon Lights* (Nihongdeng xiade shaobing, 1964).

[26] What is significant about *Shanghai Fever* is that, though billed as a comedy, both the government and audiences took it rather seriously. The film earned the lead actress Pan Hong the rare triple crowns in 1994: the title of Best Actress from the Golden Roosters Awards, the Hundred Flowers Awards, and the Ministry of Radio, Film, and Television. The popularity of *Shanghai Fever* owes as much to Pan's outstanding performance as to the film's subject matter, for there are other films dealing with stock speculation, among them *Romance of the Stock Exchange* (Gushi hunlian, 1993), that did not do as well at the box office.

comprehend why Leo Lee's assertion, based on his cursory remark on *Shanghai Triad*, that "half a century of revolution has indeed destroyed in toto China's urban culture, together with its cosmopolitan sensibilities" (1999c, 338) is rather dubious. The question here is not just the possibility (historical as well as theoretical) of preserving China's urban culture "intact" for half a century, with or without the destructive forces of the Communist revolution, for one can hardly imagine such a continuity even in Hong Kong, despite its colonial government's preservation efforts (Abbas 1997a, 63–90). The question has more to do with the lenses through which one perceives the kaleidoscopic picture of urban culture in postsocialist China. Admittedly, nostalgia is one such lens, but it is an uncritical one and as such is incapable of penetrating an anti-nostalgia text.

For an urban film ideologically akin to *Shanghai Fever*, we now turn to *The Troubleshooters* (1988), one of four films adapted from Wang Shuo's novellas in late 1988 and early 1989. Together they constitute a "Wang Shuo Fever" or "Wang Shuo phenomenon" in Chinese film production.[27] As Esther Yau shows in her analysis, *The Troubleshooters* displays a profound ideological ambivalence. On the one hand, it playfully "subverts" the hegemony of Maoist ideology by combining comedy, farce, cross-talk, black and scatological humor, cynicism, absurdity, profanity, even obscenity. On the other hand, it embraces—somewhat reluctantly—a new "consumption myth" engineered by the postsocialist regime without hinting at any other alternatives (1993, 101–5). Such ideological ambivalence is best demonstrated in a fashion show the director Mi Jiashan added to Wang Shuo's original story (Mi Jiashan 1998, 10). One Chinese reviewer of *The Troubleshooters* describes the fashion scene in this way (Barmé 1999, 76):

> [P]airs of opposites from throughout Chinese history are thrown together on stage: an imperial plenipotentiary with a near-naked female weight lifter; a landlord and a poor peasant; the Red and White armies; the PLA and

---

[27] *The Troubleshooters* has also been referred to as *The Operators*, *The Playboys*, or *The Wise Guys* (Rosen 1998, 3). The other three films based on Wang Shuo's work are *Transmigration* (1989), *Out of Breath* (Da chuanqi, 1988), and *Half Flame, Half Brine* (1989). Wang Shuo is also credited for coauthoring the screenplay for *No Regrets* (Qingchun wuhui, 1991). For a discussion of Wang Shuo films, see Meng Xianli 1994, 174–84. For sample studies of *Transmigration*, see Pickowicz 1994; Y. Wang 1996. For *Dislocation*, see Kaldis 1999.

Chiang Kai-shek bandits; a Red Guard and a Capitalist Roader . . . all disco dancing on the same stage. It is a historically important collage, a miniaturization of Chinese society itself, one in which numerous ideologies are trapped discoing on the same stage.

The result of the blurring or collapse of ideological, temporal, and geopolitical differences in the same scene, intensified by the swirling lights and pounding beat, is an acute sense of the chaos of simultaneity and multiplicity.

A consideration of new concepts of space and place here will help us understand new urban configurations in postsocialist China. In her brilliant study, Doreen Massey launches a critique of the "view of place as bounded, as in various ways a site of an authenticity, as singular, fixed and unproblematic in its identity." This is a view, in short, of "space as stasis" that accounts for "a continuation of the tendency to identify 'places' as necessarily sites of nostalgia" both within academic literature and in society as a whole (1994, 4–5). To the question of why "place *is* so frequently characterized as bounded, as enclosure," and is so rigidly defined through "the counterposition of one identity *against* another" (for our purpose, say, Old Shanghai against Hong Kong), Massey responds that "the need for the security of boundaries, the requirement for such a defensive and counterpositional definition of identity, is culturally masculine" (1994, 7). For her, it is not merely that, as critics, "we need to have the courage to abandon such defensive—yet designed for dominance—means of definition," and to rethink "any possibility of claims to internal histories or to timeless identities." It is Massey's contention that we must view the spatial "as constructed out of the multiplicity of social relations across all spatial scales," and, as a corollary, that we must view a place "as a particular articulation of those relations, a particular moment in those networks of social relations and understandings," including, importantly, "relations which stretch beyond—the global as part of what constitutes the local, the outside as part of the inside" (1994, 4–5).[28]

Massey's statement that "the identities of place are always unfixed, contested and multiple" returns us to the tactics of reinscription many

---

[28] Massey's remark dovetails Pieterse's observation: "What globalization means in structural terms, then, is the *increase in the available modes of organization*: transnational, international, macro-regional, national, micro-regional, municipal, local" (1995, 50).

filmmakers in postsocialist China invent or improvise in order to articulate their individual understandings of "an ever-shifting geometry of power and signification" in an entirely new urban world (1994, 3–5). As evident in my brief analysis of *Shanghai Fever* and *The Troubleshooters* above, this new world is marked by the chaos of simultaneity and multiplicity, by contending ideologies and lifestyles, by constant movement across all spatial scales between the global and the local, by overlapping boundaries and ever-changing relationships, as well as by cracks and fissures in the existing system that promise new freedom and new opportunities. "Shanghai" stock fever, in this sense, may easily be a "Beijing fever" as well, and the desecration of language so typical of Wang Shuo's new Beijing argot (as captured in *The Troubleshooters*) can be assimilated into other subversive discourses and practices in cities across mainland China. To quote Geremie Barmé: "As the spirit of commercialized socialism spread in the 1990s, the language of Wang Shuo, itself a refined artistic articulation of nonmainstream social and cultural forces, gave many people a means with which to deal with the schizophrenic realities of the nation" (1999, 96).

The Female Body, Spatialized Desire, and the Transnational Imaginary in *Yesterday's Wine*

In light of Massey's theory of the spatial as multiple articulations, *Shanghai Fever* represents only one mode of representation vis-à-vis the changing social relations in contemporary China. Contrary to Hong Kong's nostalgia for Old Shanghai, which has been read as a "back-to-the-future syndrome" (Daisy Ng's formulation, quoted in L. Lee 1999c, 332), *Shanghai Fever* takes an anti-nostalgic stance and thus projects a specific view of the present: a present devoid of fond memories of the past (be it Communist China or Old Shanghai), a present crisscrossed by conflicting interests and fraught with existential crises, and a present from which the future could be bought or secured through financial speculation more than sociopolitical networking. However, even a present-oriented, market-driven society cannot preclude retrospective modes of articulation. Barmé has documented a widespread "totalitarian nostalgia" in China of the 1990s (1999, 316–44; see also Dai Jinhua 1997), and nostalgia has found its way into Chinese urban cinema as well. In this connection, Xia Gang's *Yesterday's Wine* deserves close attention not just because it may articulate a new type of nostalgia—"nostalgia for the present" (Jameson 1991, 279–96)—but also because it conscientiously participates in the construction of a broader vision, "a Chinese transnational imaginary world order" (M. Yang 1997, 288).

Like Huang Jianxin (albeit not as famous), Xia Gang is known for his urban films and has adapted Wang Shuo's work in *Half Flame, Half Brine* (Yiban shi huoyan, yiban shi haishui, 1989). Rather than Huang's trenchant political satires, such as *Stand Up, Don't Bend Over* and *Back to Back, Face to Face*, Xia prefers mild humor, subtle irony, and compulsive self-mockery. His *Unexpected Passion* (Zaoyu jiqing, 1991), *After Separation*, and *No One Cheers* (screenplay coauthored by Wang Shuo) feature the Wang Shuo type of urban characters as well as the garrulous, wisecracking dialogue typical of them. These characters have been variously referred to as *wanzhu* ("a master of fooling around," as used in the Chinese title of *The Troubleshooters*), *pizi* ("ruffian" or "riffraff"), or simply *liumang* (an untranslatable term loosely meaning, for John Minford, "loafer, hoodlum, hobo, bum, punk") (Barmé 1999, 64, 73–4). In *After Separation*, Xia has already configured the Shanghai international airport as a transnational space, best exemplified by the beginning and the end of the film, in which Gu Yan (Ge You) bids farewell first to his wife and then to his closest girlfriend, both bound for North America.[29] But it is not until *Yesterday's Wine* (though not explicitly set in Shanghai) that Xia Gang successfully engages the transnational imaginary, exploring a new film style and projecting a new urban vision in the process.

What immediately distinguishes *Yesterday's Wine* from Xia's earlier films is its female voice-over, which ponders over a network of socio-sexual relations that confine the female protagonist Xiao Mengmeng (Liu Yan) throughout the film. Narrated in a sentimental, even melancholy tone, the voice-over uses an ornate literary language similar to that of Qiong Yao, a popular Taiwan woman writer whose tales of adolescent romance and bittersweet love triangles exerted a considerable influence on Taiwan cinema during the 1960s and 1970s.[30] The opening lines, "I

---

[29] *After Separation* set the box-office record of the year and won Xia Gang the Best Director at the 1993 Golden Roosters Awards in China. Xia's later films include *Accompany You to the Dawn* (Banni dao liming, 1996) and *Life on a Tune* (Shengming ruge, 1997). For an analysis of *After Separation*, see Meng Xianli 1994, 214–21.

[30] From 1965 to 1983, approximately fifty-one of Qiong Yao's works were adopted for screen in Taiwan and Hong Kong, some by top directors (see Government Information Office 1997, 383; Zhang Junxiang and Cheng 1995, 774–5). These include *The Silent*

have been remembering ever since my birth; I have never stopped remembering" cast the film in a sorrowful retrospective mood. From the beginning, then, *Yesterday's Wine* takes on a strong subjective shade. Seen through a definite feminine point of view, the film is imbued with a reflexive nostalgia that constantly questions whether the past in recollection was really more fulfilling than the present.

Four pairs of socio-sexual relationships stand out in Mengmeng's recollection: a close tie to her mother, a close relation with her female classmate Jiani, an illicit affair with her middle-aged neighbor Dr. Song, and an initially ecstatic, yet eventually tragic liaison with Lao Ba (Shao Bing). Mengmeng has been traumatized by her abusive, alcoholic father throughout her childhood. After her parents' divorce, she spends her adolescent life in the peaceful courtyard of a deserted warehouse within a shaded alley, where she and her mother live with a neighboring family, Dr. Song and his wife. The long summer days drag on as Mengmeng prepares for the college entrance examinations. Jiani, who cares little about the rumors of her "lesbian" relationship with Mengmeng, commits suicide after her parents' divorce. Mengmeng's secret yearning for paternal love is satisfied one night when she throws herself into the arms of Dr. Song. Their affair ends when Mengmeng moves with her mother into a new apartment in a high-rise. After graduation from college, Mengmeng meets a Chinese-American tourist, Lao Ba, falls in love with him, and flies over to join him in Los Angeles. Before their wedding, however, Mengmeng discovers that Lao Ba is none other than Dr. Song's long-lost son from a previous marriage, and her feelings of guilt and shame, as we shall see, bring her back to China.

Of the four pairs of socio-sexual relations, Mengmeng's close tie with her mother may imply a pseudo-feminist preference for a natural rather than patriarchal order. The scene in which Mengmeng rejects her father's claim—"I'm your father!"—on the street clearly conveys the younger generation's disillusionment with (or even repudiation of) the socialist legacy, which has practically nothing to offer as far as Mengmeng

---

Wife (Yaqi, 1965), *Whose Belongings?* (Hualuo shuijia, 1966), *Deserted Courtyard* (Tingyuan shenshen, 1970), and *Outside the Window* (Chuanwai, 1973). Qiong Yao established her own film companies, Fire Bird (Huoniao) and Superstar (Juxing), and produced more than a dozen adaptations of her novels between 1966 and 1983. Her works were also adopted in mainland China in the 1980s; one example is a remake of *Deserted Courtyard* (1989).

remembers. The suicide of Jiani, itself a protest against her parents' irresponsibility, alludes to the lack of a social space in urban China where a female-female bonding, not to mention a homoerotic relationship, can be nurtured. The figure of Dr. Song, admittedly, is the most enigmatic of all in the film. On the one hand, he stands for a necessary discursive site against which Mengmeng measures her female subjectivity. On the other hand, presenting Mengmeng's initiation into adulthood as contingent upon a benevolent father figure—a caring doctor who nurtures Mengmeng's mind and body—ineluctably softens the film's critique of patriarchal values. Furthermore, the film's insistence on Mengmeng's uncontrollable desire for Lao Ba weakens the female subjectivity the film seeks so hard to construct.

In *Yesterday's Wine*, I would argue, Mengmeng's body is projected as a fluid and highly libidinalized site, and in spite of the female voice-over, the narrative boils down to a rivalry between a Chinese father and his long-lost American son over the possession of her body, a body invested with male symbolism. A closer look at the scenes that cement Mengmeng's relations with these two men reveals the film's fundamental ambivalence in gender configuration. When Dr. Song sees Mengmeng sitting under a tree in the courtyard, rain-soaked and distressed by Jiani's suicide, he takes her to his room and hands her a dry bath towel. Quietly but stubbornly, Mengmeng holds onto his hand until he embraces her and admits his secret desire. Mengmeng unbuttons her shirt, and a close-up shot of Song's hand gently touching the curve of her naked back follows, accompanied by Song's metaphoric expression—"My angel, my child . . . . You're like a perfect field. I'm a good farmer. I won't hurt you. I'll protect that field." The sequence ends with Song resting his head on Mengmeng's bosom.

The exact same gesture is repeated four years later, but this time it is Lao Ba who falls in love with Mengmeng when the two meet in a seaside resort. He has come to China looking for the "hometown" (*guxiang*) he lost long ago, and he is delighted to have found Mengmeng and his metaphoric hometown in and through her. The two lie down on a rock, listening to the sound of waves. With his head on her bosom, Lao Ba murmurs, "This is my hometown." As if the connection between the female body and the hometown is not clear enough, Mengmeng later reminisces that, after their separation, Lao Ba kept sending her letters expressing how much he missed her and his hometown.

Mengmeng confesses that there is something mysterious in Lao Ba that attracts her—something other than his childlikeness, innocence, and sincerity. When she identifies Lao Ba's relation to Dr. Song from a photo album in Lao Ba's house, Mengmeng panics: "A sense of having committed incest penetrated my entire body. I suddenly realized I had projected another man onto this boy's body." After declaring that the new world, impressive as it is, does not belong to her, she tearfully bids farewell to Lao Ba, who later dies in a car crash. Thus framed in "incestuous" relationships in an all-too-apparent Oedipal tale, the circulation of Mengmeng's body between Dr. Song and Lao Ba testifies to the continuation of patriarchal values in the film, even though Xia Gang may have earnestly tried to renegotiate a space for femininity in the cultural economy of the newly emerging transnational imaginary.

Three points need further elaboration. First, Mengmeng and Lao Ba's transnational romance is a sure indication of the increasing cosmopolitanism and the emergence of transnational subjectivity in contemporary China. As Mayfair Yang observes, an identification with overseas Chinese others and an imaginary trip with mobile Chinese subjects in other lands are two mechanisms in the mainland mass media that have contributed to the disembedding of Chinese identity out of the confines of the state and to the construction of a transnational Chinese imaginary. Both mechanisms are operational in *Yesterday's Wine*. Apart from the film's resemblance to Qiong Yao's fiction in terms of narrative voice and its characters' willing "insertion into a discourse of love and sexuality" (M. Yang 1997, 301), we may now realize that Mengmeng's brief sojourn in Los Angeles—an icon of the global, with all the luxuries imaginable from a localized Chinese point of view (a convertible car, a seaside house, lavish interior design and furnishings, private yachts, walks along the beach)—is meant to satisfy a domestic demand for refined cosmopolitan sensibilities in media representation.

Second, if we treat Lao Ba and, to a lesser extent, Mengmeng as figures of the new Chinese cosmopolitans, what should we make of the untimely death of the former and the homecoming of the latter? True, *Yesterday's Wine* makes no recourse to place as a haven from the global world (say, the courtyard as a quintessential, uncontaminated "Chinese" place, an example of "the rural in the urban" [*dushi lide cunzhuang*] so typical of many Chinese urban films) (Ni Zhen 1993b), but a yearning for home is palpable throughout the film. Moreover, the manifestation of this yearning is split along the gender line. On a superficial level, Lao Ba satisfies his desire for the lost home by equating Mengmeng's body to his hometown or motherland. (Mengmeng tells him that he kept calling her Mommy when making love to her.) In this sense, Lao Ba can only expect a tragic end because, as the embodiment of homeland, Mengmeng must return to China. On a deeper level, Mengmeng herself is yearning for her lost home—an empty space temporarily filled by Dr. Song, a man she admits is old enough to be her father. Significantly, Mengmeng's yearning for home, intertwined with her adolescent sexual awakening, is articulated through spatialized desire. In other words, Mengmeng's desire follows a trajectory that cuts across several spaces in an ascending scale from the local to the global, only to be abruptly suspended and returned to its starting point, to its origin as a lack, a lacuna, an immense emptiness. As suggested by a shot of a broken fish bowl before Mengmeng's departure for Los Angeles, Mengmeng is like the fish out of water, stranded in a claustrophobic environment, desperately desiring something. In spite of its apparent outward look to the global, the end of *Yesterday's Wine* thus highlights its rather conservative position on China as the absolute point of departure and return.

Mengmeng's unfulfilled desire brings us to a final point: can we possibly locate something like "nostalgia for the present" in *Yesterday's Wine*? For Jameson, postmodern nostalgia films in the U.S. are characterized by "dual symptoms": "they show a collective unconscious in the process of trying to identify its own present at the same time that they illuminate the failure of this attempt, which seems to reduce itself to the recombination of various stereotypes of the past" (1991, 296). To be sure, *Yesterday's Wine* recycles stereotypes of the past, such as the alcoholic, abusive father, the romantic, tragic young lovers, and the agrarian metaphor of the female body as a perfect field. Like many recent Western films, it also seeks to grasp the present at the same time that it repeatedly confesses in the voice-over that the present is forever slipping through its grasp, through its inadequate interpretive grid. By means of induced and interjected memories, sentimentalized narration, and glossy images of global/local ethnoscapes and ideoscapes, *Yesterday's Wine* articulates an uncontrollable yearning for a present that threatens to disappear, to vanish like smoke, in a blink of the eye (illustrated in the ending sequence of Mengmeng's hallucinations, where Dr. Song and Lao Ba in turn appear and disappear before her). The film may be viewed, alternatively, as a collective wish-fulfillment, an expression of emerging cosmopolitan sensibilities (including a yearning for the global), or as a nightmare, an expression of deep, unconscious, collective fears about the uncertainty of evolving social realities in the era of postsocialism and transnational capitalism.

IV

Hybridity, Global Mélange, and Edward Yang's Remapping of Taipei

As Pieterse suggests, "we can construct a *continuum of hybridities*: on one end, an assimilationist hybridity that leans over towards the center, adopts the canon and mimics the hegemony, and, at the other end, a destabilizing hybridity that blurs the canon, reverses the current, subverts the center" (1995, 56–7). Inasmuch as the ideology of entrepreneurship and its attendant celebration of money and bourgeois lifestyle are concerned, *Shanghai Fever* and *Yesterday's Wine* seem to align themselves with the discourse of assimilationist hybridity. Regardless of their respective comic-hilarious or nostalgic-sentimental modes of representation, both films lean toward the center (as embodied in glocal cities such as Hong Kong and Los Angeles), adopt the values of the transnational (as represented by traveling cosmopolitans like Ah Lun and Lao Ba), and mimic the hegemony of the global over the local (as exemplified in the disappearance of the traditional space of urban living). Although a lingering sense of local pride (for instance, Shanghai's real estate value and China as a diaspora's imaginary hometown) may still be detected, both films project the global as a new point of identification for local audiences.

To look for examples of a destabilizing hybridity, we now turn to Edward Yang's cinematic remapping of Taipei, another glocal city in the Chinese transnational imaginary. As well known by now, Yang and his friend Hou Hsiao-hsien share the honor of having led New Taiwan Cinema in the 1980s (see chapter 6). Unlike Hou, who concentrates on the ethnic-cultural makeup of rural Taiwan society and its traumatic local history in his representative films, Yang has made the metropolis of

Taipei the foundation of his films.[31] *That Day on the Beach* (Haitan de yitian, 1983; hereafter *That Day*), Yang's solo directorial debut, established his reputation as a modernist auteur. As in *Yesterday's Wine*, a consistent female voice-over runs through *That Day*, thus weaving "the texture of women's lives" and endowing Yang's film with a strong sense of female subjectivity.[32] Yet, unlike *Yesterday's Wine*, Yang's retrospective narrative—punctuated by frequent flashbacks and fragmentary reminiscences from various characters—does not lead to a nostalgia for the past. Rather, it offers a promising end, where Lin Jiali (Sylvia Chang [Zhang Aijia]), formerly a tormented housewife, has been transformed into a strong-willed career woman by the unsolved mystery of her husband's disappearance one day on the beach.

That Day distinguishes several urban spaces, among them the domestic (associated with the ennui of a bourgeois housewife), the commercial (characterized by moral corruption and sexual degradation), and the transnational (represented by Jiali's childhood friend, an internationally renowned woman pianist visiting from Europe). Instead of celebrating the global money economy, however, Yang situates his female protagonist firmly in the local, following her life trajectory from a Japanese-style house in a rural town to a modern apartment in the glocal city. If *That Day* is still restricted to the bourgeois spaces in Taipei, Yang expands his urban vision by including spaces of the lower classes in *Taipei Story* [Illustration 22]. Although they grew up together in two closely related families, Ah Lung (Hou Hsiao-hsien) and Ah Zhen drift apart due to their connections to two diametrically different urban spaces: the former managing a traditional fabric store in the old Ximending and the latter finding her way through modern establishments in the eastern district (Lin Wenchi 1998, 110–1). Yang further extends his camera to the underworld (that is, the otherwise "invisible" criminal space) of Taipei in *Terrorizer* (1986), where White Chick, a teenage Eurasian streetwalker, stands simultaneously for the unintelligibility of the city and for the violence that threatens to erupt at any moment from anywhere in the urban landscape.

---

[31] For discussions of Edward Yang, see Chiao 1991b, 60–80; Huang Jianye 1995; Jameson 1994; Li Youxin 1986b, 72–120; Tam and Dissanayake 1998, 60–71.

[32] The phrase is quoted from Yang's objection to *Raise the Red Lantern*: "In China, . . . the texture of women's lives . . . is far more interesting than how they are exploited by men" (Kraicer and Roosen-Runge 1998, 55).

22. *Taipei Story* (1985): A tale of urban alienation

In Jameson's assessment, "*Terrorizer* is indeed very much a film about urban space in general" (1992, 153). In fact, Jameson is so impressed by Yang's attention to relationships between individual spaces (especially boxed dwelling spaces) and the city as a whole that he expresses his admiration for Yang's successful arrangement of "these two powerful interpretive temptations—the modern and the postmodern, subjectivity and textuality—to neutralize each other, to . . . draw on the benefits of both, without having to commit [himself] to either as some definitive reading" (1992, 151). The immediate result of Yang's simultaneous engagement with and distance from both interpretive categories is, I would argue, a heightened sense of hybridity in the glocal city. This hybridity is manifest not just in a certain chronological simultaneity of modernity and postmodernity, but also in a multiplicity of urban spaces.

Largely, what Jameson says of *Terrorizer* is also applicable to Yang's two subsequent attempts at remapping Taipei—*A Confucian Confusion* and *Mahjong* (1992, 131):

In our own postmodern world there is no longer a bourgeois or class-specific culture to be indicted, but rather a system-specific phenomenon: the various forms which reification and commodification and the corporate standardizations of media society imprint on human subjectivity and existential experience. This is the sense in which *Terrorizer*'s characters . . . dramatize the maiming of the subject in late capitalism, or . . . indict something like the failure of the subject under the new system to constitute itself in the first place.

Both *A Confucian Confusion* and *Mahjong* seek to dramatize the maiming of the subject and the sheer impossibility of reconstituting subjectivity in the postmodern world. A film intended to "examine the moral poverty of the post-economic boom society" (R. Chen 1994, 36), *A Confucian Confusion* starts playfully. The initial title and credit sequence rolls to the soundtrack of a press conference, in which Birdy, an acclaimed Taiwanese "master" (*dashi*) of the theater, is asked why he is rehearsing a "postmodern comedy" set in Taipei (Yang Dechang 1994). The point Yang wants to make in the film is fairly simple: each character is confused, and each acts out only an assigned role without knowing the meaning and significance of his or her superficial, spontaneous, and often self-contradictory performances. The theme of confusion is carried over to *Mahjong*, in which Alison, a "poor little rich girl" from Taipei who does not know exactly what she wants, is meant to represent every postmodern urbanite: "In a sense we are all like her," so Edward Yang explains in an interview (Chiao 1996a, 26).

As Bérénice Reynaud rightly points out, in *Mahjong*, "Taipei, a city invaded by franchises of the Hard Rock Cafe and pidgin English, has become a playground for transnational greed" (1996, 31). An early scene in the Hard Rock Cafe in Taipei, where guitars reputedly belonging to the Beatles are on display, presents Taipei as a hybridized glocal city. Inside the cafe, the half-drunk Jay uses English to introduce "Hong Kong," a handsome employee in his high-fashion hair salon, to his "friend" Ginger, a white women and former owner of a shady escort service. Markus comes in with Alison, his new Taiwanese girlfriend, but their meeting with Ginger is cut short by the unexpected arrival of Marthe (Virginie Ledoyen), a naive yet stubborn young Frenchwoman who chases Markus all the way from Paris. "Everybody here speaks English!" exclaims Markus, who tries to explain to Marthe why he had to leave London when he had lost his job there. Near the end of the film,

Markus further explains to Marthe why he enjoys working in Taipei: "These people have so much money. . . . In ten years the city will be the center of the world. The future of Western civilization lies right here." Yet Marthe chooses Luen Luen, a kind-hearted local interpreter who has helped her from the beginning, over "the foreign devils [who] are simply too obnoxious, nasty, greedy, ridiculous or surreal" (Reynaud 1996, 31). In the final scene, Marthe and Luen Luen embrace and kiss for the first time, in the middle of a busy street in a night market, thus conveying the director's hopeful endorsement of cultural hybridity in Taipei.[33]

"Cultural hybridization," Pieterse writes, "refers to the mixing of Asian, African, American, European cultures: hybridization is the making of global culture as a global mélange" (1995, 60). *Mahjong* constructs Taipei precisely as a glocal city of such global mélange, where the global languages—English and French—are intermingled with the local tongues—Taiwanese (a dialect denoting the speaker's lower-class identity) and Mandarin (spoken, respectively, with a heavy Taiwan or Hong Kong accent or with a standard Northern Chinese accent, subtly suggesting the origin of each speaker). Parallel to the Hard Rock Cafe in *Mahjong*, there is also a pub scene in *A Confucian Confusion*, but this time Yang's mise-en-scène features two government employees talking to each other against a wall-size screen showing a television broadcast of a women's basketball game in the U.S. Apart from such verbal and visual displays of a global mélange in Taipei, Yang's films often emphasize rock music and popular songs from the West. For example, in his epic film *A Brighter Summer Day* (Gulingjie shaonian sharen shijian, 1991), a group of rebellious Taipei youngsters listen to and imitate the music of Elvis Presley. As Yang recalls, in the 1960s, rock signified anti-communism and functioned as a pro-government instrument that reinforced the alliance with America, but it was the subversive side of rock that affected his generation.

As in the case of global mélange generally and rock music specifically, cultural hybridization may function in the same way as Bakhtin's carnival does, staging a chaotic show of simultaneity and multiplicity, and in the process effecting "a blurring, destabilization or

---

[33] Yang's own interpretation is worth quoting: "The film has a hopeful ending, rather than a 'happy ending' . . . . The subject of *Mahjong* is the next generation, its outlook on the future. A hopeful future, that's not confused or polluted by the present trends of advertising and commercialism" (Kraicer and Roosen-Runge 1998, 53–4).

subversion of that hierarchical relationship" between center and margin, global and local, hegemony and minority, political establishment and counter- or sub-culture (Pieterse 1995, 56). In *Mahjong* the blurring or destabilization of the power relationship in Taipei has not escaped the observation of European cosmopolitans like Markus, who consider it extremely ironic that, given the nineteenth-century Western imperialist conquests around the world, the center of "Western" civilization would be relocated to the East (the formerly marginal or peripheral) in the twenty-first century.

Yang's consistent use of blurring, destabilizing, at times even contestatory hybridity in his remapping of Taipei should be self-evident by now. From *That Day* to *Mahjong*, he maintains a critical stance toward the hegemonic discourse of capitalism. "Taiwanese society has changed for the worse in the last ten years," he asserted in a 1997 interview. "On the outside, it's all money, all wealth; everyone is putting on new costumes, new clothes, new fashion, whatever. It shows we are well off. But on the inside we are going the other way" (Kraicer and Roosen-Runge 1998, 53). Yang has made his subversive intent extremely vocal by holding Taiwan's government responsible for outrageous religious scams and widespread underground criminal operations. "The Taiwanese economy is about 40% an underground economy," he claims. "If this situation isn't corrected, then I would say the government is similar to a mob" (Kraicer and Roosen-Runge 1998, 53). Yang's suspicion of the government is most pronounced when he declares that he has abandoned efforts to show his films commercially in Taiwan. Instead, the audience he has in mind is "just cinema-going people wherever they are," especially those in Japan, Europe, and North America (Kraicer and Roosen-Runge 1998, 55).[34] Indeed, Yang has very much positioned himself as a "hybridized" and globe-trotting cosmopolitan (living at least part-time in the U.S.), keeping a close eye on the local situation in

---

[34] The occasion of Yang's interview was a retrospective of his work organized by the Film Center of the School of the Art Institute of Chicago in November 1997. A year earlier, a similar retrospective was held at Brown University (Chiao 1996a, 24). Yang's disillusionment with Taiwan is such that, despite repeated invitations in 2000, he refused to enter his latest, much-acclaimed film, *A One and a Two* (Yiyi, 2000), into either the Golden Horse Film Festival or the Taipei Film Festival. Yet, he allowed the film to be shown commercially across the U.S. after he had won the Best Director award at the Cannes Film Festival in 2000.

Taiwan while forging a transnational cinephilic affinity with his audiences around the world. Given the transnational pattern of the financing, distribution, and exhibition of Yang's latest films and his unfailing attention to the global/local, Taipei, projected as a site of global mélange in his recent films, can be best studied as a glocal city, as much as Hong Kong and Shanghai can.

Farewell, "South" (*Nanguo*): Taipei, Heterotopias, Postmodernity

There is yet a further connection between cultural hybridization and recent configurations of Taipei in Taiwan cinema. From the perspective of Homi Bhabha's work on postcolonial studies, Pieterse suggests that hybridity can be a condition tantamount to alienation, a state of homelessness. Indeed, due to specific cultural and political situations in Taiwan, alienation and homelessness have been two recurring themes in urban films set in Taipei. *Our Neighbors* (Jietou xiangwei, 1963), for example, features a group of "homeless" mainlanders who interact with native Taiwanese to build a new communal life in Taipei. Both *Early Train from Taipei* (Taibei fade zaobanche, 1964) and *Kang-Ting's Tour of Taipei* (Kang Ding you Taibei, 1969) dramatize the sense of alienation felt by men and women from rural Taiwan who arrive in Taipei and literally lose themselves in the big city. *Papa, Can You Hear Me Sing?* (Da cuoche, 1983) and *Two Sign-Painters* (Liangge youqi jiang, 1990) further explore the impact of Taiwan's urbanization and economic boom on marginal characters (a mute veteran and an aboriginal youth) in the metropolises. To varying degrees, Taipei films like these reflect on the process of hybridization in Taiwan's ethnoscapes and ideoscapes over the last half century (P. Cheng 1995, 130–6; Lin Wenchi 1995).

In the 1970s, Taiwan filmmakers were obsessed with images of Taiwan as a legitimate nation-state with a long history of Chinese (read "mainland") culture (Lin Wenchi 1998). The deep anxiety over homelessness and rootlessness that troubles many hybrid characters in *Home, Sweet Home* (Jia zai Taibei, 1970) is therefore diagnosed as "curable" through the voluntary abandonment of their otherwise promising careers in the U.S. and their whole-hearted participation in the rebuilding of Taiwan. In the 1980s, New Taiwan Cinema sought to reinstate the values of nature and the native soil in opposition to urban alienation and disillusionment, thus projecting a series of conceptual binaries, such as rural and urban, tradition and modernity, innocence and corruption, stability and disorder. The images of Taipei that emerge from New Taiwan Cinema are chaotic, kaleidoscopic, though at times energetic and visually enticing. Whereas *Home, Sweet Home* features an initial montage sequence of the dragon dance, Peking opera masks, and traditional variety shows, all encoding Taipei as a city saturated in Chinese culture, in *Super Citizens* (Chaoji shimin, 1985), the initial montage sequence of monumental structures in Taipei (among them the Yuanshan Hotel, Sun Yat-sen Memorial, Chiang Kai-shek Memorial, and Chung-hwa Shopping Center, as well as temples, mosques, and churches) conveys a sense of disorientation and alienation on the one hand—enhanced by a scene of a madman directing traffic outside the Taipei Railway Station—and to preserve public memory on the other. In the 1990s, nevertheless, urban cinema in Taiwan increasingly configured Taipei as a globalized city, its space hardly recognizable, its identity hybridized and dubious, and its history swept away by the incessant flow of transnational capital.[35] In brief, Lin Wenchi (Lin Wenqi) concludes, if New Taiwan Cinema attempts, by way of emphasizing the experience of Taiwan's native soil and its people's (often repressed) memory of the past, to prove that Taiwan is no longer the imagined "China" of the 1970s, Taiwan cinema of the 1990s informs its audience, by means of the manifestation of "postmodern urban spaces," that Taiwan is no longer the imagined "Taiwan" of the past decade (1998, 110).

What Lin calls "postmodern urban spaces"—not all of them necessarily "postmodern," though, as should become clear below—covers a wide range of new images and perceptions of the city. First, moving from rural Taiwan to urban Taipei, one is said to experience a transition from the "bird's space" to the "worm's space" (*chong de kongjian*) (Zhan Hongzhi 1996, 20). The former is typically captured by Hou Hsiao-hsien's long-take landscape from a static camera, whereas the latter is characterized by claustrophobia engendered by the loss of the horizontal

---

[35] In his study of the historical transformation of Taipei's images in Taiwan cinema, Ching Chih Lee (Li Qingzhi) goes further than Lin Wenchi and offers this periodization: (1) the reconstruction period of the 1950s; (2) the sealing-off period of the 1960s; (3) the void period of the 1970s; (4) the breakaway period of the 1980s; and (5) the puzzle period of the 1990s. Each period is dominated by certain urban images and architectural styles: (1) Japanese colonial architecture and shanty-town structures; (2) palatial architecture and national construction methods; (3) mansions and orphanages; (4) diverse city and garbage mountain; and (5) fringe spaces and overpasses. See C. C. Lee 1995.

view of the countryside. Examples of the worm's space—or what Jameson terms "space of confinement" in connection with *Terrorizer*—abound in *A Confucian Confusion* and *Mahjong*, as well as in *Vive l'amour* (Aiqing wansui, 1994). In *Vive l'amour*, three Taipei loners find a temporary "home" in an empty apartment for sale without understanding one another or securing any stable relationship (Berry 1995a; Cai Mingliang 1994; Stephens 1996a).

Second, home, which was earlier imagined as a self-stabilizing entity, for instance in *Osmanthus Alley* and *Passion in Late Spring*, both analyzed in chapter 6, is transfigured as an alienated, dystopian space, even a "schizo-space," in which one no longer feels emotionally attached to anyone or anything, not to mention feeling psychologically "at home" (Keith and Pile 1993, 2–3). In *Mahjong*, Red Fish's father twice disappeared from home, hiding from his wife and his creditors, and eventually commits a double suicide with his new mistress. In *Rebel of the Neon God* (Qingshaonian Nezha, 1992), Hsiao Kang would rather stay away from home and seek excitement in a hotel room, a video game arcade, or a skating rink. In *The River* (Heliu, 1997), the gay father and his gay son seek sexual pleasure outside their home and other socially sanctioned places, thereby collapsing the traditional spatial demarcation of inside and outside (see also H. Chang and Wang 1995). In *Tonight Nobody Goes Home* (Jintian bu huijia, 1996), practically everyone in the family has left home: father, mother, daughter, and son all pursue their sexual interests elsewhere.

Third, urban adventurers can create a new kind of space when riding a scooter or driving a car at high speed. In films like *Goodbye, South, Goodbye* (Nanguo zaijian, nanguo, 1996), Taipei youngsters experience a rare sense of freedom when they race their cars through the urban landscape, which appears from inside the car as distorted, flattened, compressed, eerie—indeed devoid of any traces of human value (Lin Wenchi 1998, 114; Li Zhenya 1998, 131). The space thus experienced is, understandably, linked to the motifs of rebellion and transgression, as in the case of *Rebel of the Neon God*. Furthermore, this new sense of fluid time-space is visualized by thoroughfares and bridges that cover the city like a giant web and transform it—especially at night—into an unfathomable labyrinth. In *Treasure Island* (Zhiyao weini huo yitian, 1993), a myriad of flashing neon signs and the shining headlights of speeding cars foreground Taipei in an MTV-like fashion (R. Chen and Liao 1995, 151).

Fourth, unlike the street-level view favored by New Taiwan Cinema, which at least facilitates a sense of proximity, legibility, and therefore subjectivity, as in *Taipei Story* and *Daughter of the Nile* (Niluo he de nüer, 1987), the 1990s saw the emergence of a new sense of space associated with the aerial view. In *The Red Lotus Society* (Feixia A Da, 1994) and *Super Citizen Kuo* (Chaoji da guomin, 1995), the aerial view surveys the Taipei landscape from above, at once rendering a breathtaking feeling of superiority, a titillating *jouissance* of voyeurism, and the effect of complete distanciation and defamiliarization between the viewer and the city. The visual and psychological effect in question here resembles what de Certeau theorizes about what once was the view from the summit of the World Trade Center in Manhattan. Once on top, one feels that the "bewitching world" below has been "processed" into a text that lies before one's eyes, but this readable "panorama-city" is but a representation, an optical artifact, a visual simulacrum (1984, 92–3).

Fifth, the digital space, equally imaginary if no less surreal than the aerial view, is produced through the characters' constant use of telephones, mobile phones, pagers, fax machines, KTV, video games, and the like. In *Good Men, Good Women*, a fax machine keeps sending the female protagonist, from an unknown source, pages of her diary written three years before, thus blurring her perception of time-space and merging her own private memories with the historical drama she rehearses on stage. Jean Baudrillard's words seem a fitting description here: "Reality itself founders in hyperrealism, the meticulous reduplication of the real, preferably through another, reproductive medium. . . . From medium to medium, the real is volatilized . . . [and] becomes *reality for its own sake*" (1988, 144–5). In fact, a reproductive medium like the telephone or photography has already been used to produce such hyperreality in urban experience in films such as *Terrorizer*. In both *Terrorizer* and *Good Men, Good Women*, simulacra and the hyperreal created by modern technology combine to weave together a postmodern text.

Sixth, a "postmodern liminal space" may be obtained from the interstices between public and private, old and new, demolished and reconstructed, natural and artificial. The best examples of this include the construction sites of the city park and the fast-rail system (MRT) captured or alluded to in *Vive l'amour* and *Mahjong*. Unlike public spaces of consumption (such as hotels, restaurants, shopping centers, and street markets), the liminal space simultaneously symbolizes despair and hope, destruction and regeneration, disappearance and reinscription—in short, a space beyond good and evil, beyond hatred and love, beyond any fixed meaning or signification.[36]

It is worth noting that Lin Wenchi's elaborate catalogue of post-modern urban spaces—to which I have added my own examples and interpretations above—serves to drive home this argument: namely, in its new representation of Taipei, Taiwan cinema of the 1990s documents the disappearance of what Henri Lefebvre calls the "absolute space," a space that has acquired fixed social and political meaning over a long period of historical accumulation, a space manufactured for the express purpose of legitimation of and identification with the nation-state (Lin Wenchi 1998, 112). Along with the disappearance of the absolute space, Lin continues, the clearly articulated sense of totality (history) and belonging (identity) has also vanished in recent Taiwan cinema. Not surprisingly, all this sounds postmodern. Indeed, if we follow Frederick Buell and envision "a postmodern world of disaggregated production, global population flows, and heightened international circulation of a smorgasbord of cultural simulacra" (1994), then Taipei (or Hong Kong for that matter) will definitely appear to be a postmodern city.

However, what concerns me in this chapter is not merely cinematic documentation of disappearance in the postmodern world; rather, I am more interested in what Chinese filmmakers in different regions have done in response to the process of such disappearance in different geopolitical and geocultural contexts. As far as Edward Yang is concerned, hybridization is surely a tactic of reinscription with which he repositions himself vis-à-vis the discourses of the nation-state, global-ization, and postmodernity. What I would recommend here is that we envision hybridity not simply as a transnational aesthetic (in the Jamesonian sense) but as part and parcel of a new global politics at work. To quote Pieterse, "hybridity when thought of as a politics may be subversive of essentialism and homogeneity, disruptive of static spatial and political categories of centre and periphery, high and low, class and

---

[36] See Lin Wenchi 1998, 113. The phrase "postmodern liminal space" is taken from Zukin 1992, 222. For a brief discussion of Zukin's concept, see Keith and Pile 1993, 7–9. For more discussion of postmodernism and the city, see E. Wilson 1991, 135–59.

ethnos, and in recognizing multiple identities, widen the space for critical engagement" (1995, 58). All this is precisely what Edward Yang and many of his fellow filmmakers have sought to accomplish in their cinematic remapping of Taipei in the 1990s.

V

In conclusion, I would like to contemplate the consequences of examining Chinese urban cinema from the perspective of globalization and transnational imaginaries. Many questions Anthony King raised in 1989 are still pertinent today: "Does [globalization] imply cultural homogenization, cultural synchronization or cultural proliferation? What does it say about the direction of cultural flows? Is it the interaction of the local and the global, with the emphasis on the former, or vice versa?" (1997, 12) For King, "the questions demonstrate that, on a global scale, culture has to be thought spatially, politically, economically, socially and historically and also very specifically" (1997, 12). An insistence on *specificity* is therefore crucial to our investigation of the glocal city as projected and problematized in contemporary Chinese cinema.

Stuart Hall has drawn our attention to two characteristics of a new form of global mass culture: (1) it is centered in the West and in its languages; (2) it is a homogenizing form of cultural representation. Nevertheless, Hall reminds us, "the homogenization is never absolutely complete, and it does not work for completeness" (1997a, 28). The reason why cultural homogenization on a global scale will never be complete can be explained by "the twofold process of the parti-cularization of the universal and the universalization of the particular" that Robertson formulates as the dynamic of globalization (1992, 177–8). This twofold process may appear structurally balanced at first sight, but their relations are far from complimentary or mutually beneficiary. For Jameson, such "binary or point-to-point relations . . . are first and foremost ones of tension or antagonism, when not outright exclusion: in them each term struggles to define itself against the binary other" (Jameson and Miyoshi 1998, xii). Furthermore, "such binary relationships (between a state claiming universality, for example . . . the United States or the West, and another claiming local particularity; or between particulars; or between universals) are necessarily symbolic ones, which express themselves in a range of collective Imaginaries" (Jameson and Miyoshi 1998, xii).

As evident throughout this chapter, the "glocal" or "global/local" is mapped out against, through, or alongside a diverse set of transnational imaginaries in Chinese urban cinema. Cultural hybridization is consistent in most films, and "postmodern" seems to be an appropriate label for many images, sequences, and situations, even if the film in question may not be postmodern in its entirety. As with globalization, we may envision postmodernism not simply as a project working for completeness. To quote Featherstone, "With postmodernism, there is a re-emergence of the vernacular, of representational forms, with the use of pastiche and playful collage of styles and traditions. In short, there is a return to local cultures, and the emphasis should be placed upon local cultures in the plural, the fact that they can be placed alongside each other without hierarchical distinction" (1995, 96). The end of *Autumn Moon*, for instance, places Chinese and Japanese cultures side by side without hierarchical distinction, although one may detect from the poem Wai recites that Clara Law is emotionally more attached to Chinese culture.

Autumn Moon also inscribes another typical experience in the era of globalization. Namely, it is Tokio's travel to Hong Kong that opens up an intermediate space in the glocal city, for himself as well as for Wai. Featherstone's observation proves illuminating again: "Travel can be understood as paradigmatic of experience, and we should remember that the root of the word 'experience' is *per*, which means to try, to test, to risk. . . . Travel, then, thrusts the new into the middle of life, it opens up life to contingency and creates 'exotica' (matter out of place)" (1995, 152). Indeed, the cinematic glocal cities examined here—Hong Kong, Shanghai, and Taipei—are populated by travelers, tourists, and immigrants who move often between cities, regions, nations, and continents.

With constant transnational flows in the ethnoscapes, mediascapes, technoscapes, financescapes, and ideoscapes, globalization has created new possibilities, among them "de-localization," "re-localization," and "re-nationalization" (King 1997, 12). Given these and other possibilities, it is important that we pay attention to "the *terms* under which cultural interplay and crossover take place" and be fully cognizant of "the actual unevenness, asymmetry and inequality in global relations" (Pieterse 1995, 54). Moreover, we must go beyond a mere catalogue of transnational flows and conscientiously confront the question of human agency. Geeta Kapur articulates this position most forcefully: "I would argue for a greater holding power of the historical paradigm where differences are recognized to have real and material consequences, where agency is not ghost-driven nor collapsed into a series of metonymically disposed identities that are but fragments spinning their way to entropy" (1998, 201).

The multiple possibilities—some of them contradictory to one another—that globalization has engendered remind us that disappearance (as conceived by Abbas) is only one aspect of the process. Reinscription, as demonstrated in this chapter, is an effective means of re-localization, reconstituting subjectivity, and reclaiming historical agency. In conclusion, I would contend that, even if a postnational, "borderless world" may be theoretically imaginable (Miyoshi 1993; Yau 2001), the local will inevitably find ways to reinscribe itself—by asserting its difference in the face of its predicted disappearance, if not already its pronounced death—in the transnational, transregional spaces within the hegemonic discourse of the global. Precisely for this reason, the persistence of the glocal city in cinematic representation is worth continued deliberation.

Eight

Conclusion: Entering the New Millennium

> [I]n late capitalism and in its world system even the center is marginalized
> [so] that powerful expressions . . . of the unevenly developed [countries] . . .
> are often more intense and powerful, more expressive, and above all more
> deeply symptomatic and meaningful than anything the enfeebled center still
> finds itself able to say.
>
> Fredric Jameson, *The Geopolitical Aesthetic*

Throughout this book I have examined multifarious forms of "screening China" that surfaced on both sides of the Pacific in the final decades of the twentieth century, with particular attention devoted to critical discourse and the films themselves. In this concluding chapter I further expand my study by investigating a number of developments that seem to propel the transition from the turn of the twentieth century to the new millennium. Among other things, travel is squarely a crucial transnational experience; new alliances are being formed to integrate art, market, and politics (Section I); "the new mainstream film" (*xin zhuliu dianying*) is proposed as a theoretically viable new alternative for mainland China in the new century (Section II); and postmodernism as a contested term continues to fascinate, perplex, and provoke scholars of varied theoretical persuasions in the field of China studies (Section III). All in all, this concluding survey is not meant to bring closure to the project of screening China, but to call for renewed and continued attention to its ongoing transformation.

I

Traveling Heavy

A cultural anthropologist working on interdisciplinary research, James Clifford has discerned a noticeable paradigm shift in the humanities and social sciences over the past decades—a shift of critical attention from

313

"roots" to "routes," from the fixed space of "home" to the open space of travel. As he envisions it, in the era of globalization, "*Travel* emerged as an increasingly complex range of experiences: practices of crossing and interaction that troubled the localism of many common assumptions about culture. In these assumptions authentic social existence is, or should be, centered in circumscribed places. . . . Dwelling was understood to be the local ground of collective life, travel a supplement; roots always precede routes" (1997, 3). What would happen, Clifford asks, if we look the other way around and perceive travel as "a complex and pervasive spectrum of human experience?" (1997, 3) To say the least, "Practices of displacement might emerge as *constitutive* of cultural meanings rather than their simple transfer or extension" (1997, 3). And this is exactly what has happened in the case of both ethnographic cinema and urban cinema I examined in the previous two chapters. Replete with the seemingly timeless images of dwelling and roots, the cultural meanings of Chinese ethnographic cinema have changed considerably and will most likely be reconstituted when they travel to the West. On the other hand, by means of showcasing travel, routes, and transit ports, urban cinema in contemporary China challenges the territorial concept of culture and encourages the audience to rethink issues of identity, nationhood, and cultural tradition.

Experiences of travel have come to dominate Chinese cinema both on and off the screen. Not only do ideas and images travel, but filmmakers are increasingly caught in translocal, transregional, and transnational movements in pursuit of creative input, government approval, investment capital, technical innovation, and distribution and exhibition deals—most often all of these at the same time. In short, Chinese cinema is "traveling heavy," to borrow an apt phrase Geremie Barmé uses to describe the scene of Chinese politics in the immediate post-Tiananmen era (1999, 38–61). As with political culture, film culture in contemporary China appears to be flowing in multiple, often unpredictable directions, and Chinese filmmakers everywhere are engaged in travel through all scales between the local and the global. They no longer look in one direction only: proudly "marching to the world" (*zouxiang shijie*), as the slogan went in the early 1980s. Since the mid-1990s, the flow from the other direction has inundated the Chinese film market as the annual import of mega films from abroad has literally brought the "world" to China.

Between the Global and the Local

Still, signs of this marching to the world have persisted up to the turn of the new millennium. As an international film festival laureate, Zhang Yimou was given yet another round of applause for *Not One Less* (Yige dou buneng shao, 1999), which won the Best Film award at Venice in 1999 and was screened in the U.S. in 2000. Zhang's Venice success was followed by a Silver Bear (Jury Grand Prix) for *The Road Home* (Wode fuqin muqin, 1999) at the Berlin Film Festival in 2000. Back in 1999, Zhang Yuan, a new international film-festival favorite, was honored with a special director's award at the Venice Film Festival for *Seventeen Years* (Guonian huijia, 1999). A year before, a surprise recognition was accorded to a brand-new name, Jia Zhangke, as his *Pickpocket* (Xiao Wu, 1998), a small-budget production funded by Hong Kong investment, went on to win a series of top film-festival awards at Berlin (two prizes), Nantes, Vancouver, Pusan (South Korea), the Belgium Film Archive, and San Francisco (Jintian 1999, 39). Also in 1998, Lü Yue's *Mr. Zhao* (Zhao xiansheng, 1998) earned critical acclaim on both sides of the Atlantic.

In contrast to euphoric media fanfare over award-winning Chinese films in the West, Dai Jinhua sarcastically describes travel—or officially sanctioned, commercially motivated film trafficking—in the opposite direction as "the Titanic enters Zhongnanhai," a phenomenon that has resulted in a disastrous "shipwreck in the icy sea" (*binghai chenchuan*) (1999a, 134–6). By evoking a politically ironic picture of Zhongnanhai (the "forbidden city" of the Communist headquarters situated behind Tiananmen Square in Beijing) as being deluged under the tidal wave brought by *Titanic* (Taitannike hao, 1997), which set the all-time highest box-office record in China, grossing 500 to 600 million yuan nationwide in 1998, Dai aims to convey a sober, indeed apocalyptic vision with her ominous "shipwreck" metaphor. The metaphor is intended not only to place in ironic light the Chinese "success" in marching to and integrating (or submerging?) itself in the world, but also to highlight the dismal statistics regarding the Chinese film industry at the turn of the new millennium. In 1998, only 37 domestic feature films (including two by Sil-Metropole of Hong Kong) were released in China, and this is so far the lowest figure for a film industry capable of producing 130 to 150 films a year and once proud of its remarkable record of maintaining an average of over 100 films per year since 1980 (Dai Jinhua 1999a, 133–4).

Indeed, as recently as 1994, 1995, and 1996, the official figures for the total annual feature productions were 148, 146, and 110, respectively, although the number plunged to 88 in 1997. To Dai, the dismal figure of 37 in 1998 can be interpreted as a sign of the imminent bankruptcy of the film industry in mainland China.

Equally dismal are film statistics from Taiwan. As mentioned in chapter 2, Taiwan feature film output nose-dived from 215 in 1981 to 18 in 1996, and sank further to 11 in 1998, although that year saw two new films by internationally renowned auteurs, Hou Hsiao-hsien's *Flowers of Shanghai* (Haishang hua, 1998) and Tsai Ming-liang's *The Hole* (Dong, 1998). Throughout the 1990s, the Taiwan film industry relied heavily on government subsidies—in the form of increasing "domestic film grants"—to sustain its feature film production. However, the government did very little to improve the distribution and exhibition system or to revive the audience's interest in domestic films. Each year, the Government Information Office (Xinwen ju), the agency overseeing the grant competition, was under attack from all sides, including the media, academia, and the industry. In 1998, one indignant local critic declared that the subsidy system was completely bankrupt, for the government had failed to fulfill its 1997 promise to support nine feature films each with N.T. $10 million and to allocate an additional fund of $15 million to theaters committed to showing domestic films. After a series of criticisms and compromises in 1998, six films were eventually awarded $10 million each, and six others $5 million each (R. Chen 1999). The annual Golden Horse Awards also lost its once prestigious status, not just in Asia, but in Taiwan itself. In 1998 alone, two major international film festivals—the annual Taipei Film Festival and the biannual Taiwan International Documentary Film Festival—were successfully launched, thereby posing a serious challenge to the monopoly, if not legitimacy, of the Golden Horse operations.[1]

In Hong Kong, the years 1998–99 were a transition period in which filmmakers tested the changing market in the wake of the 1997 handover to China. By far still the best performer (with eighty-four feature films in 1998) of the three regions, Hong Kong faces many problems that have also plagued the industry in mainland China and Taiwan, such as the

---

[1] The two new Taiwan film festivals were also supported by government funds. Like the Golden Horse Awards, their operation budgets each exceeded N.T. $20 million in 1998 (Huang Wulan 1999, 220–31).

sharp decline in film attendance and feature film output, the dramatic increase of production costs and ticket prices, and the widespread piracy market (especially in the form of inexpensive VCDs).[2] In addition to the impact of the Asian financial crisis, Hong Kong had to deal with the low morale caused in part by the emigration of leading directors such as John Woo and Tsui Hark, and film stars such as Chow Yun-Fat and Michelle Yeoh to Hollywood earlier in the 1990s. Anxiety and uncertainty continue to permeate the Hong Kong screen in the post-1997 era, and nostalgic or romantic titles compete with gangster and martial arts films in confronting issues of colonial history, geopolitical relations, personal memory, migration, and identity. For some local critics, the Hong Kong "film empire" has finally collapsed, physically symbolized by the relocation of the Golden Harvest studios, which used to play a dominant role in the industry (Huang Wulan 1999, 64–130).[3]

New Year Pictures, New Filmmaking Alliances, New Market Strategies

Against this dismal *fin de siècle* backdrop of Chinese filmmaking, several noteworthy strategies of surviving—and sometimes even thriving on—the moments of crises have emerged, and all of them heavily depend on the travel or traffic of ideas, capital, labor, and technology. Among them, three developments in mainland China merit special attention. First, the unexpected popularity of "New Year Pictures" (*hesui pian*) since 1998; second, new alliances among filmmakers, government, and the market as reflected in recent film production and exhibition; third, the proposal for "the New Mainstream Film" by a group of young Shanghai filmmakers who are endeavoring to forge a middle route between government-sponsored leitmotif films and Hollywood mega imports.

---

[2] In the late 1990s, ticket prices ranged from 10 to 20 yuan (but might be as high as 70 for Hollywood blockbusters) in mainland China, H.K. $30 to 50 in Hong Kong, and N.T. $150 to 250 in Taiwan. During the period, U.S. $1 roughly equaled 8.3 yuan, N.T. $30, and H.K. $7.7.

[3] Representative Hong Kong titles during this transition period include Jackie Chan's *Who Am I?* (Wo shi shui, 1998), Mable Cheung's *City of Glass* (Boli zhicheng, 1998), Stanley Kwan's *Hold You Tight* (Yu kuaile yu duoluo, 1998), as well as Fruit Chan's (Chen Guo) *Made in Hong Kong* (Xianggang zhizao, 1997) and *The Longest Summer* (Qunian yanhua tebie duo, 1998).

For Huang Shixian, Feng Xiaogang's *Dreams Come True* (Jiafang yifang, 1998) was a "black horse" in the lunar year of the tiger. Released in the holiday season between New Year's Day and the Chinese New Year, this comedy of the *nouveaux riches* paying an extra price to literally "live" their fantasies in various situations (such as hunger and torture) grossed 11.8 million yuan in Beijing alone (and 30 million nationwide). With an investment of under 4 million, *Dreams Come True* was highly profitable, with box-office returns second only to *Titanic* (1999, 149–50). The unprecedented success of this first-ever "Chinese New Year Picture" was quickly followed by Feng's *Be There or Be Square* (Bujian busan, 1999), released later in the year during the Christmas season, which did better than its predecessor by raking in 40 million yuan. Feng continued his New Year Picture genre with *Sorry, Baby* (Meiwan meiliao, 2000), a 10 million yuan production that was heavily advertised on CCTV and other local TV channels in December 1999. What is more, Feng's distributor teamed up with Sinal.com and offered huge discounts to internet ticket buyers, a move that proved to be quite successful (Lin Gu 2000). Concurring with Huang that Feng's new films are nothing but "cultural fast food," Dai Jinhua likens Feng's New Year Pictures to small life-boats: "In a shipwreck on the icy sea, there are usually not enough lifeboats to salvage the giant ship of Chinese cinema. Several small boats have started to sail off from the parent ship. Does this suggest some sort of sorrow? Or some slim hope?" (1999a, 145–6).

While no one ventures to predict the outcome of changes in the Chinese film market, we may still track its developments and investigate some of its new characteristics. One distinguishing feature of Feng's films, as hinted above, is their all-too-apparent reliance on transnational cultural imaginaries (see also chapter 7). If, with *Dreams Come True*, Feng was cautious and devoted just one of its several interrelated narratives to the experiment of a private Chinese entrepreneur who wanted to realize his dream of impersonating an American army general in World War II (staged in a battlefield with real army tanks), by the time he worked on *Be There or Be Square* a few months later Feng was confident enough to fly his crew to California and shoot the entire film on location in Los Angeles, the exotic "land of angels" in the Chinese imagination. Transnationalism in recent Chinese productions is further evidenced by the increasing use of dialogue in a foreign language (most often English). An earlier example of this practice is *Red Cherry*, a coproduction with

Russia discussed in chapter 5. The success of *Red Cherry* led to Ye Daying's second "red" film, *A Time to Remember* (Hongse lianren, 1998; the Chinese title literally meaning "red lovers"). To enhance the film's transnational appeal, Ye recruited a Hong Kong superstar (Leslie Cheung) to play the tormented underground Communist leader, employed two Hollywood screenwriters (Mark Kaplan and Andee Nathanson) to finalize the screenplay, and added an unmistakably Western perspective by making a foreign doctor the one who "remembers" the past revolutionary activities and who raises, single-handedly, the orphaned daughter of the fated Communist couple. The transnationalism in question also finds a strong voice in Feng Xiaoning's planned trilogy, "China Through the Eyes of a Foreigner," the first two of which, *Red River Valley* and *Grief Over the Yellow River*, were released to enthusiastic audiences at home and overseas (see chapter 5). More than any time before, at the turn of the millennium, Chinese films and filmmakers were traveling heavy, dashing in multiple directions across a vast stretch of geographic and imaginary space.

It is no coincidence that Feng Xiaogang's films and *A Time to Remember* are all products of a newly established "private" (*minying*) film company in Beijing called the Forbidden City (Zijincheng). Upon closer inspection, however, the company is actually backed by three powerful government units in China's capital city: the Cultural Affairs Department of the Beijing Municipality, the Beijing Film Distribution and Exhibition Company, and the Beijing Television Station. The triple political-financial-commercial protection provided by these three government units has secured strong investments and a near monopoly of the exhibition channel for the Forbidden City's titles in Beijing. For instance, in the summer of 1998, hundreds of lighted advertising boxes along several major Beijing streets that used to carry the slogan "Building Socialism with Chinese Characteristics" were mysteriously replaced by advertisements for *A Time to Remember*. Sure enough, the film opened in Beijing with strong box-office returns, topping the anticipated 6 million yuan (Dai Jinhua 1999a, 142–3).[4] The aggressive marketing practice of the Forbidden City foregrounds a new form of alliance in Chinese filmmaking, which is "established on the basis of sharing the market, capital, and profits," and which furnishes "a clear example of how

---

[4] *A Time to Remember* eventually proved to be a financial disaster, for its nationwide return of 25 million failed to recoup its investment of 30 million (Huang Shixian 1999, 156–9).

political power is quickly transformed into investment capital" (Dai Jinhua 1999a, 142). Given such new alliances of power, money, and "art," new market strategies are invented, and Chinese filmmaking enters a new stage of interdependence.

The new developments in mainland China thus compel us to rethink some of the positions surveyed in earlier chapters. For example, Rey Chow's theory of self-exoticization and autoethnography, which touches only part of the overall picture of Chinese cinema from the mid-1980s to the mid-1990s (see chapter 2), is inadequate when it comes to the recent craze for "low-brow" New Year Pictures in the domestic market. Rather than exhibiting "authentic" samples of ethnic Chinese culture to the West, Feng Xiaogang's films work the other way around, exhibiting the globalized Western styles and spoon-feeding them to the domestic Chinese audience. Feng's transnational imaginary, therefore, is set to play more intensely at the *local* level (particularly in Beijing) than at the global one (say, at international film festivals, which have so far shown scant interest in Feng). Contrary to self-writing in Chinese ethnographic cinema, Feng is more interested in writing the "others" within the self. These "others" are easily classifiable—and, in fact, stereotyped—as *nouveaux riches* (like movie stars and private entrepreneurs in *Dreams Come True*) and transnational cosmopolitans (like new Chinese immigrants in *Be There or Be Square*), among others. In hilariously comic form, desires for fame, money, sex, pursuit of a green card and the American dream, as well as nostalgia for bygone years of hardship, are performed as if live on stage to the audience, at once giving them a taste of the glamorous life and a sense of relief because troubles associated with fame and money belong to "others" rather than to the audience. In short, instead of catering to the global, recent New Year Pictures function first and foremost to satisfy the fantasies of the local.

Chen Kaige: Performance of Patricide-cum-Suicide

Nevertheless, autoethnography (as defined in chapter 6) simply refuses to go away in contemporary Chinese film. At least three types of such autoethnographic images continue to fascinate Western media: China as an impoverished landscape, China as a savage empire, and China as a repressive Communist regime. While *Not One Less* falls easily into the first category, *The Emperor and the Assassin* (Jingke ci Qinwang, 1998; hereafter *The Emperor*) satisfies the expectations of the second. A period piece of epic proportion directed by Chen Kaige, *The Emperor* reinvents the legend of the First Emperor's unification of China by all means, including the massacre of children. When this costliest Asian film ever (U.S. $20 million) opened in the U.S. in late 1999, an allegorical reading of the third category was emphasized in a *New York Times* article: "[Emperor] Ying's desire to unify China at all costs has contemporary relevance, given recent tensions between the mainland and Taiwan" (Brunette 1999). Ingenious remarks such as this notwithstanding, Chen is reportedly very angry about what is going on in China today, but exactly what he is angry about needs to be spelled out in more detail.

Is Chen really angry with those Chinese people who "believe that the most important thing is making money"? (Brunette 1999). Maybe, but Chen himself is equally obsessed with market values. After the fiasco of his *Temptress Moon*, Chen deliberately postponed the release of *The Emperor*. (In part, I would surmise, his aim was to create a cooling-off period in which the audience would forget *The Emperor's Shadow*, a high-budget epic film [39 million yuan] from Zhou Xiaowen that deals with the First Emperor's unification of China.) Is Chen angry about the Communist regime? Not exactly, at least not in the same way as the *New York Times* sees it. After an unusually long period of suspense (three years to be exact) that had heightened the public's curiosity, Chen orchestrated in October 1998 an unprecedented event—the official premiere of *The Emperor* to a packed house of 3,800 inside the Great Hall of the People in Tiananmen Square. In spite of Chen's meticulous attention to this promotional extravaganza (complete simultaneous interpretation in Chinese, English, and Japanese, as well as projection of English and Japanese subtitles), media critics in Beijing unanimously denounced the film, a rare event itself in contemporary China (Dai Jinhua 1999a, 137–8). What is more, a month later, Chen announced that he was willing to make major cuts to the original 160-minute version. This announcement is interpreted as a sign of his submission to market pressure, because a private company prior to the premiere had purchased the domestic distribution rights (Huang Shixiang 1999, 152–4). The new filmmaking alliances and new market strategies as showcased in the premiere of Chen's film thus expose what gets lost or screened out in the simplified political reading preferred by the Western media: namely, the *complicit* relationship Chen Kaige has worked so hard in recent years to establish with the state apparatus on the one hand and the transnational market economy on the other.

As a measure of damage control, Chen postponed the commercial release of *The Emperor* for one more year, but Chinese audiences in all three regions still showed little enthusiasm when his film entered the market in late 1999.[5] Given the success of *Not One Less* at Venice and in China (where Zhang Yimou won the Best Director at the 1999 Golden Rooster Awards), it is not surprising that Chen would direct his anger at a new target. In an interview published on January 21, 2000, Chen accused his rival of selling out to the censors in Beijing: "I'm a little bit angry with Zhang Yimou. He's sort of become part of the government now" (Johnson 2000). However, not only is Chen's accusation of Zhang largely unwarranted, it may even be potentially self-damaging because Chen himself attempted to curry official favor with his 1998 premiere inside the Great Hall of People in Beijing.

Chen might be angry at himself above anyone or anything else, so much so that he has performed a symbolic patricide-cum-suicide in *The Emperor*. According to the *New York Times*, "In what he now realizes was an unconscious homage to his father, who died five years ago, Mr. Chen decided to play the role of Lü Buwei, the prime minister of the Qin kingdom, who is actually the emperor's father" (Brunette 1999). Even though it is rather a cliché by now to refer to Chen's confessed guilt over his denunciation of his father during the Cultural Revolution (Chen Kaige 1991), I suggest that we might push the reading a little further. Just as the First Emperor has to resort to patricide in order to legitimize his rule in *The Emperor*, Chen's on-screen "suicide" (since he directed himself in the fated role) works to (re)establish himself as a self-sacrificing "father" of New Chinese Cinema. From the patricide of the revolutionary generation around the mid-1980s (see chapter 5), we are now given the rationale for another patricidal act. Only this time the patricidal son has chosen to purge his long-lasting guilt by offering himself up as the "murdered" father at a critical moment when a new generation of young directors are entering the scene, as we shall see more clearly below.

---

[5] When I visited Taipei in October 1999, *The Emperor* was shown in local theaters at the same time as *Tempting Heart* (Xindong, 1999), a transnational romance set in contemporary Hong Kong that entirely eclipsed Chen's epic feature in terms of popularity.

Tracking Media

It should be evident by now that the convenient political reading in the Western media, best exemplified in its relentless pursuit of censorship issues, is not enough to explain the complicit new filmmaking alliances and marketing strategies in contemporary China. To cite one more example, it came as a total surprise to many China watchers when the mainland government decided to lift its decade-long ban on Zhang Yuan in late 1999. Zhang's *Seventeen Years*, reputedly the first Chinese film ever shot inside a state prison, was released commercially to considerable media attention in Beijing in January 2000. Earlier, this film was allowed to tour the U.S. East Coast together with Zhang's documentary, *Crazy English* (Fengkuang Yingyu, 1999).[6] The same surprise also applies in the case of Wang Xiaoshuai, another controversial independent filmmaker, whose *So Close to Paradise* (Biandan, guniang, 1998) was approved for commercial release three years after its initial production. Whether this latest "thaw" signified a compromise between the government and the younger filmmakers is a topic worthy of further investigation.

In addition to the domestic front, new filmmaking alliances are sometimes made in transnational terms. *Xiu Xiu: The Sent Down Girl*, the directorial debut of Joan Chen (Chen Chong), a Chinese-American actress, is "banned" in China because Chen shot it without having acquired an official permit.[7] After the film had gathered favorable reviews in the West, Chen was able to proceed with her next feature, *Autumn in New York* (2000), a United Artists production. If Chen thrives on controversy, as Chen Kaige and Zhang Yuan did before her, Ann Hu (Hu An), another Chinese-American director, prefers cooperation with her *Shadow Magic* (2000), a coproduction of the U.S., Germany, China, and Taiwan that features a multinational cast and crew. The film began production in 1998 with government approval and was released in Beijing in January 2000. In fact, if we count *The Sun Has Ears* (Taiyang you er, 1995), a film produced by Zhang Yu, another Chinese-American who has been active in the three regions and who helped Yim Ho, a

---

[6] Zhang Yuan's films were screened at the National Gallery of Art in Washington, D. C. and at a three-day retrospective at the Harvard Film Archive in November 1999 (Eckholm 1999).

[7] Joan Chen's film, however, won almost all the important prizes at the 1998 Golden Horse Awards in Taipei, leaving only the Jury's Prize to *Flowers of Shanghai* (Huang Wulan 1999, 229–31).

Hong Kong director, capture the Best Director award and the Fipresci Prize at the 1996 Berlin Film Festival, there is a minor trend in Chinese women emigrée directors or producers who have returned to make films in China—another sign of "traveling heavy" in the age of globalization.

II

"The New Mainstream Film"

Other than the New Year Pictures and the new marketing strategies mentioned above, one of the most significant new filmmaking alliances to emerge at the turn of the millennium is embodied in the proposal for "the New Mainstream Film." From October 1998 to February 1999, a group of young Shanghai filmmakers gathered regularly to explore new film concepts and market strategies, and the outcome was a manifesto, "The New Mainstream Film: A Proposal for Domestic Films." The article first appeared in *Wenhui Film* (Wenhui dianying shibao) on April 2, 1999, and was republished later in the year under Ma Ning's name in *Contemporary Cinema* (Dangdai dianying), one of China's leading film journals based in Beijing. In spite of its excessive redundancy, ambiguity, and empty rhetoric, the new proposal attracted the Shanghai municipal government's attention. A series of events were organized in Shanghai during March 1999 to discuss and publicize the new concept, and "The New Mainstream Film Workshop" was established under the Shanghai Film Corporation by the end of the month. It was understood that the new workshop would become the center of planning, administration, and "independent" filmmaking, responsible for all kinds of activities, including fund raising, contract negotiation, and publicity work.

But what exactly does the New Mainstream Film mean? According to the Shanghai manifesto, the New Mainstream Film pays close attention to the relationship between film's power of imagination and the audience's level of reception. Budgeted in the range of 1.5 to 3 million yuan per film (U.S. $180,000 to $360,000), New Mainstream Film draws on the legacy of art film but works to return film to the masses. The New Mainstream Film is "fashionable and sensual," for "fashion makes the audience feel in sync with the time, and sensuality satisfies the audience's internal sensitivity" (Ma Ning 1999, 7). It promotes young filmmakers and encourages them to study the impact of new media, computer, video games, and cartoons. Defined as a branch of the mainstream film, it is envisioned as a discovery, not a revolution or a brand new invention. Finally, it is proposed not merely as a theory but as a set of concrete procedures for commercial filmmaking.

As Ma Ning admits, some characteristics—especially the comic, farcical, and satirical—described by the Shanghai manifesto have already emerged in Chinese film production since the late 1980s. Specifically mentioned as potential forerunners of the New Mainstream Film are *The Troubleshooters, Stand Up, Don't Bend Over, Falling in Love, Keep Cool*, as well as *San Mao Joins the Army* (San Mao congjun ji, 1992), in which brief cartoon sequences are inserted into the film narrative. Although none of them quite lives up to all expectations of the new proposal, these films are singled out for praise because of their fascination with cinematic "rules of the game" (*youxi guize*) and their preference for comedy over tragedy in terms of genre and theme. Considering the manifesto's emphasis on the "plebeian consciousness" (*pingmin yishi*), it is little wonder that three popular 1998 titles are also cited as examples in the appendix: *Dreams Come True, Be There or Be Square* (both discussed above), and *Spicy Love Soup* (Aiqing malatang).

The Emergence of Imar Productions

In many ways, *Spicy Love Soup* captures the new vision of successful low-budget commercial filmmaking in China at the turn of the millennium. Composed of five narrative segments targeting different age groups (from retirees to high school students) but unified by the common theme of love and marriage, this light-hearted, at times sentimental urban film performs several functions across multiple levels simultaneously (Yin Hong 1999, 27–8). In terms of ideological positioning, it makes no attempt to question the official views of Chinese history and culture as the early films from the Fifth Generation did around the mid-1980s, nor does it allow itself to be obsessed with alienation and self-exile typical of some younger directors of the early 1990s. In Ni Zhen's judgement, *Spicy Love Soup* and its follow-up, *A Beautiful New World* (Meili xin shijie, 1999), announce the arrival of a New-Born Generation who happily embrace the mainstream and, in a sense, have returned to the forgotten tradition of Shanghai urban cinema of the 1930s.[8] In terms of stylistic features, the new filmmakers prefer conventional camera work, smooth cuts, bright colors, glossy images, a brisk pace, upbeat music, light humor, child-like curiosity, and easy-to-follow story lines. All this, combined with an optimistic outlook on life, points to "the demand for entertainment film as cultural consumption and to the tendency to merge with the gradually improving market economy and civil society" (Ni Zhen 1999, 72). In terms of marketing strategy, *Spicy Love Soup* made a number of unprecedented moves. First, it recruited popular singers from Hong Kong and Taiwan—on top of a cast of well-known actors and actresses in mainland China—and released the soundtrack a month before the film hit the market; the soundtrack sold 500,000 copies and generated advance publicity for the film. Second, the film's Valentine's Day release in Shanghai and a promotional tie-in with Cadbury Chocolate proved immensely successful. All told, the film grossed over U.S. $2.8 million nationwide on its U.S. $350,000 (less than 3 million yuan) production budget (*Beijing Scene* 1999, 1).

As head of Imar (Yima) Productions, Peter Loehr—known as Luo Yi in China—deserves full credit for engineering something new and refreshing that helped revive the public's interest in the "sinking" Chinese film industry (to echo Dai Jinhua's "shipwreck" metaphor) in the late 1990s. An enterprising American in his early thirties, Loehr had acquired experience in the media industries of Japan and Taiwan before traveling to China in 1997 and establishing Imar, a joint venture with the Xi'an Film Studio and Taiwan's Rock Records. It would soon change the landscape of commercial filmmaking in China. Although *A Beautiful New World* did not do well at the box office, it was screened at the Berlin Film Festival in 1999 and paved the way for Imar's third hit, *Shower* (Xizao, 1999). According to one source, by November 1999, "*Shower* won the International Film Critics Award at the Toronto International Film Festival and Zhang Yang nabbed the Best Director Award at the San Sebastian Film Festival. In addition to speedy invitations to eight more major festivals, including Sundance and Rotterdam, *Shower* sold distribution rights to an astonishing 56 countries including the United States (via the prestigious, promotion-savvy Sony Classics) and has already

---

[8] Two early Shanghai titles, *Street Angel* and *Twin Sisters* (Zimei hua, 1933), are cited by Ni Zhen (1999, 72). For an overview of recent urban cinema in mainland China, see Wang Qun 1999.

recouped double its U.S. $350,000 budget in advances alone" (*Beijing Scene* 1999, 3).[9]

Despite the fact that his first three films have definitely fulfilled many requirements of the category of New Mainstream Film (for example, low budget, first-time director, producer-centered operations, urban theme, comic elements, sensual quality, and mass appeal), Loehr himself resisted the new label. For one thing, he does not share the nationalistic sentiments of the young Shanghai filmmakers, who dream of "participating in the project of new mainstream films in the world so as to secure identity and status for Chinese cinema through entertaining creations" (Ma Ning 1999, 16). For another, as much as he values Shanghai as a huge film market, Loehr is essentially a transnational cosmopolitan who pledges no allegiance to any particular geographic region. For this reason, while Imar is registered as a film technology company in Xi'an (evocative of China's West), Loehr bases his operations in Beijing and frequently travels to provincial capitals to negotiate distribution deals. The impact of Imar's mode of commercial filmmaking, however, was felt immediately in *fin de siècle* China. Like its Shanghai counterpart, Beijing Film Studio has started allocating special film funds to aid young directors like Lu Xuechang and Wang Xiaoshuai or even first-timers in their production of small-budget films (averaging 2.2 million yuan).

Art, Politics, and Commercial Filmmaking

To attract critical attention to the new generation and their low-budget films, the *Film Art* editorial office organized a timely critical forum in late November 1999, an event cosponsored by the China Film Association, the Beijing-based China Film Group (Zhongguo dianying jituan), and the Beijing Film Studio. Several young directors identified earlier (some in chapter 2) and a few first-time directors brought their latest (or debut) films to the forum: Ah Nian with *Call Me* (Huwo, 1999), Huo Jianqi with *Postmen in the Mountains* (Nashan naren nagou, 1998; winner of the Best Film at the 1999 Golden Rooster Awards), Li

---

[9] A film about a Shenzhen businessman's reconciliation with his tradition-bound father in Beijing, *Shower* accomplishes several objectives at once: a negative judgement on the rebellion of the previous young directors, willing integration (with a charming smile) to mainstream culture, and an ample view of the harmonious Oriental family to satisfy the new demand from the West (Yin Hong 2000, 13).

Hong with *Soaring High with You* (Banni gaofei, 1998), Lu Xuechang
with *In Broad Daylight* (Guangtian huari, 1999), later renamed *A Lingering
Face* (Feichang xiari), Mao Xiaorui with *Heroes Real and Fake* (Zhengjia
yingxiong xiongdi qing, 1998), Tian Xi with *Soldier* (Bing, 1999), Wang
Quanan with *Lunar Eclipse* (Yueshi, 1999), Wang Rui with *Sky Leopards*
(Chongtian feibao, 1999), Wang Xiaoshuai with *Suburban Dream* (Menghuan tianyuan, 1999), Wu Tiange with *Women's Sky* (Nüren de
tiankong, 1999), and Zhang Yang with *Shower*.[10] By using the generic
term "young directors," the organizer of the Beijing forum avoided the
presumptuousness of the Shanghai manifesto on the one hand, and the
slippery—indeed, unnecessary—distinction between the so-called "Sixth
Generation" and the "New Born Generation" on the other.

The issue we face here is not that at the forum Beijing was better
represented than Shanghai but rather that many propositions in the
Shanghai manifesto do not withstand critical scrutiny. Han Xiaolei, an
outspoken supporter of the young filmmakers, has articulated the urgent
need to expose the ambiguity and misconception in the New Mainstream
Film. For instance, what kind of "imagination" would appeal to mass
audience is never defined in the manifesto, and the proposed New
Mainstream Film is by no means "independent" because it is by
definition subservient to the mainstream both financially and politically.
Furthermore, Han argues that the very concept of low-budget
production misses the point, for a low budget does not automatically
translate into handsome box-office returns, nor does it insure the
"artistic" quality of its product or the "excellence" sought after by the
promoters. Han cites the case of *Love in the Internet Generation*, an
acclaimed Xi'an title produced on a meager budget of 1.2 million yuan
(*Contemporary Cinema* 1999b). Even after Guo Xiaolu (the screenwriter)
and Jin Chen (the director) had forfeited all monetary compensation, the
film returned only around 800,000 yuan to the studio, not enough to
recoup its production cost. For Han, the current low-budget strategy

---

[10] Other films by the young directors who were not represented at the 1999 *Film Art*
forum include Ding Jiancheng's *Paper* (Zhi, 2000; shot in 1997), Hu Xueyang's *Ice and
Fire* (Bing yu huo, 1999), Jia Zhangke's *Platform* (Zhantai, 2000), Li Xin's *Gun with Love*
(Woxue woqing, 1998), Lou Ye's *The Suzhou River* (Suzhou he, 2000), Shen Yue's *The
Taste of the Sun* (Taiyang de weidao, 1998), and Zhang Qian and Ma Weijun's *Pier Heaven*
(Tianzi matou, 1998). For further discussions of this group of young directors, see Han
Xiaolei 1999; Ni Zhen 1999; Yin Hong 1998b.

reflects a more worrisome trend in commercial filmmaking: namely, to cater to the vulgar (*meisu*) and eventually to degrade the cultural status of Chinese cinema (1999, 62–5).

For me, what is most troubling is not so much the commercial reorientation demanded by the New Mainstream Film as its ideological implications. Let us examine how the promoters imagine the battle against the imminent Hollywood invasion after China joins the World Trade Organization. The New Mainstream Film "insists on continuing innovations, fighting shoulder to shoulder with the mainstream films while providing, by way of quality films and complimentary strategies, the best assistance to the mainstream films on the front battleground. Meanwhile, it also functions as a site of experimentation for the gradual transformation of the mainstream films along the line of genre films" (Ma Ning 1999, 9). In other words, the commercialization of small-budget "art" films as envisioned by the Shanghai manifesto works not only to legitimate its own existence within the political establishment but ultimately to bring the mainstream (that is, leitmotif films as discussed in chapter 5) on route to full-scale commercial operations. For these considerations, after the art film is pronounced *passé* once and for all, cinematic "art" itself is re-imagined as related to, if not dependent on, new technologies such as digital production, computer graphics, and video games. In unambiguous terms, the manifesto asserts that the New Mainstream Film "does not want to become an abnormal creature (*guaiwu*) in the ivory tower or to destroy its nature as games by shouting [political slogans]; instead, its attitude is to treat all players as common people rather than saints, as self-gratifying children rather than self-indulging narcissists" (Ma Ning 1999, 15). A key image thus emerges to define the nature of the New Mainstream Film: children playing games. Presumably, as long as the child-like players enjoy the fun of the game, who cares about its outcome?

In reality, however, the young Shanghai filmmakers have not succeeded in convincing anyone that they care nothing about the outcome of their "game" of independent filmmaking, because some of them experienced bitter defeat after similar attempts in 1998.[11] The image

---

[11] According to Huang Shixian (1999, 162–5), in February 1998, ten "Sixth Generation" directors purchased the official license from the Shanghai Film Studio (identified as producer but not investor) and embarked on an ambitious project of a ten-title film-and-TV series, *Super City* (Chaoji chengshi), under the general supervision of Lou Ye. Each

of innocent children at play, therefore, is conjured up strategically as a mask, a pretext, a means of securing both political and financial support in their new filmmaking ventures. Turning away from their earlier, unsuccessful search for a space for their "auteur films" in an industry dominated by repressive political control and unpredictable market fluctuations, they are now willing to pay a high political price: voluntary subjection to the mainstream in exchange for low-budget filmmaking. Such a problematic move thus distinguishes this group of Shanghai promoters—who by no means represent all young filmmakers in Shanghai or mainland China—from their counterparts in Hong Kong and Taiwan.[12]

The troubling ideological repositioning imposed by the New Mainstream Film is actually more apparent if we examine the reference

---

title would consist of two parts, and each part would last 47.5 minutes (designed to fit TV broadcast schedules). By May 1998, they had completed six titles, all of them set in Shanghai: Tang Danian's *Jade* (Yu), Guan Hu's *Walking at Night* (Yexing ren), Li Hong's *I Love Huazi* (Wo ai "Huazi"), Hua Zhongkai's *Mona Lisa* (Mengnalisha), Ruan Hao's *Pirated Pulp Fiction* (Daoban diji xiaoshuo), and Lou Ye's *The Rushing City* (Benpao de chengshi). After showcasing some of these titles at a Hong Kong film exhibition in June 1998, funds ran out and the remaining four titles were never completed. Lou Ye's *The Rushing City*, a 16mm production, was later converted to 35mm and renamed *The Suzhou River* (2000); it won critical acclaim at the 2000 Rotterdam Film Festival and was invited to enter other festivals in the West. Except for Lou's work, it is not clear that other titles in this series were ever aired by television stations in China or elsewhere.

[12] Steve Fore locates a minor "trend" in post-1997 Hong Kong in the production of low-budget, "small-scale, non-mainstream," or "off-centered films" (1999, 7). Two recent films demonstrate that this trend is still running strong: *Little Cheung* (Xilu Xiang, 1999) and *Spacked Out* (Wuren jiashi, 2000). A parallel development occurred earlier in Taiwan, where a group of young directors have similarly been engaged in small-budget productions (from N.T. $4 to $10 million, roughly U.S. $160,000 to $400,000) since the mid-1990s. Like their mainland counterparts, Chang Tso-chi (Zhang Zuoji), Chen Yu-hsun (Chen Yuxun), Hsu Hsiao-ming (Xu Xiaoming), Lin Cheng-sheng (Lin Zhengsheng), Tsai Ming-liang, Wang Shau-di, Wu Nien-chen, Yee Chihyan (Yi Zhiyan), and a few others—sometimes known as the "Second Wave" from Taiwan—have also suffered poor box-office returns and have struggled with the grim production environment (see Chiao 1996b; Teng 1995). But they do not resort to the arrogance and presumptuousness that characterize the Shanghai filmmakers in their manifesto. What is more, in spite of the fact that some of them are the beneficiaries of the government's film grants, these Taiwan directors have conscientiously kept a distance from the political establishment, and some (like Tsai Ming-liang) may even venture to be openly critical of certain government policies and operations (see Huang Wulan 1999, 240).

titles listed in an appendix to the Shanghai manifesto. Apart from ten mainland Chinese titles (some mentioned above), we see eight films from Hong Kong, five from Taiwan, numerous others from Japan, France, Spain, Australia, England, Italy, former Yugoslavia, and Latin America, as well as thirty-five American films, such as *Annie Hall* (1977), *Reservoir Dogs* (1992), *Forrest Gump*, and *Toy Story* (1995).[13] To be sure, the huge list of disparate films might demonstrate the Shanghai promoters' knowledge of the latest film developments in various parts of the world. Nevertheless, their disregard of the diversity and apparent incompatibility in ideologies (from counter- or sub-culture to the mainstream), genres (from comedy to gangster, adventure, and fantasy), and styles (from auteurism to high-tech computer animation) embodied by these films reveals the eagerness of these Chinese filmmakers to participate in what they believe to be a movement of New Mainstream Films in the world. What is truly remarkable in this case is that the young Shanghai filmmakers were able to use their technical know-how to convince the Shanghai government and the Shanghai Film Studio of not only the importance of the New Mainstream Film but also the necessity of China's full—though always already "belated"—participation in this imagined global cinematic enterprise, ideally with Shanghai leading the way as it did in the first half of the twentieth century.[14]

---

[13] More specifically, the appendix includes Hong Kong titles such as *Chungking Express*, *Ashes of Time, A Chinese Ghost Story: The Tsui Hark Animation* (Xiaoqian, 1998), and *Sleepless Town* (Buye cheng, 1997, actually a Japanese production); Taiwan titles include *The Peach Blossom Land, The Red Lotus Society, Daddy's Lover* (A ba de qingren, 1995), *Tropical Fish* (Redai yu, 1995), and *The Personals* (Zhenghun qishi, 1999); as well as *Shall We Dance?* (1996) from Japan, *Crocodile Dundee* (1986) and *Babe* (1995) from Australia, and *Life Is Beautiful* (1997) from Italy. In the original order and excluding those already mentioned in my discussion, the list of thirty-five miscellaneous American films covers *Pulp Fiction* (1994), the *Back to the Future* series (1985, 1989, 1990), *Ice Storm* (1997), *Look Who Is Talking Now* (1993), the *Home Alone* series (1990, 1992), *Groundhog Day* (1993), *Flubber* (1997), and *A Bug's Life* (1998). See Ma Ning 1999, 16.

[14] As Ma Ning later admits (2000, 18), 1999 saw no release of the much anticipated New Mainstream Films from Shanghai, but Shanghai directors are reportedly at work on a series of ten films under the general rubric of "moral tales" (*Daode gushi*).

III

Postpolitics and Postmodernism

New developments in mainland China, such as New Year Pictures, new filmmaking alliances, and the proposed New Mainstream Film, may be further examined in light of this observation by Chen Xiaoming: "The multifarious functions of political codes constitute a peculiar narratological ambience in which Chinese film is produced, circulated, watched, and interpreted. Such a manipulation of political codes can be labeled 'postpolitics' in Chinese film, where everything is political and nothing is political at once and the same time. Politics is everywhere, and yet it subverts itself at any moment" (1997, 124). Sure enough, the omnipresence and occasional subversion of politics in the contemporary Chinese film scene are clearly demonstrated in the operations of the Forbidden City Film Company, the premiere of *The Emperor* in the Great Hall of the People, and the ideological reorientation of the New Mainstream Film. According to Chen, "postpolitics in Chinese film not only animates native cultural production but also manages to dance to the tunes set forth by the Western cultural imaginary about China" (1997, 124). The complexity and ambiguity of power relationships on the global, national, regional, and local levels thus contribute to the formation of what Chen describes as "a strange social and cultural ecosystem" in contemporary China:

> Under such an ecosystem, noble idealism and heroism are completely replaced by a real sense of comedy, manifested in a rhetoric of parody-travesty, irony, and black humor. Postmodernism thus emerges in Chinese social life as well as in cultural and cinematic productions and artistic experiments, not so much as a cultural construct of the artists, critics, and theorists, as is the case in the West, but as an enormous social text produced by the historical process of Chinese modernity in the age of globalization. (1997, 140)

Three key notions in this passage from a leading postmodern critic in mainland China demand more attention: postmodernism as cultural construct, as social text, and as response to modernity. First, as cultural construct, postmodernism may be located in new narrative strategies and new conceptions of time and space in avant-garde fiction and political pop art since the late 1980s (Zhang Yiwu 1997; Yang Xiaobin 1995; S.

Lu 1997a and 1997b). In film production, the recurring uses of parody and self-parody in *San Mao Joins the Army* and *Mr. Wang: Flames of Desire* (Wang xiansheng zhi yuhuo fenshen, 1993) may also be read as postmodern in nature.[15] Secondly, as social text, postmodernity may have manifested itself beyond the confines of cinematic, literary, or other artistic texts, and may have found expression in mass culture of the fast-evolving consumer society in the post-Tiananmen era. Notable recent highlights of this enormous social text certainly include the Mao Zedong craze, nostalgia for the Cultural Revolution, and the emergence of what Dai Jinhua calls the *"guangchang* complex," which tends to displace the political (as symbolized by Tiananmen Square) with the commercial (as embodied in countless new shopping plazas across the country) (Dai Jinhua 1996, 1997, and 1999b). Finally, as a response to modernity, postmodernism in China finds itself in an unsettled and highly contested space because there is no critical consensus as to which type of modernity it should or must respond to. In the field of modern Chinese literature, for instance, a Chinese postmodernism may be conceived in relation, in reverse chronological order, to a series of vastly different—oftentimes diametrically opposing—cultural dominants: (1) high modernism of the 1980s or "New Era"; (2) socialist modernity of the 1950s–1970s; (3) bourgeois modernity of the 1930s Shanghai; (4) May Fourth enlightenment or translated modernity; and (5) repressed or incipient modernities of the late Qing period.[16] In Chinese film studies, postmodern tendencies

---

[15] For a discussion of *San Mao Joins the Army* as a postmodern film, see Meng Xianli 1994, 251–3. *Mr. Wang* contains a parody of the famous love-making scene involving Grandpa and Grandma in *Red Sorghum* (see chapter 6). Instead of the solemnity of the original, the parodied version creates a dream sequence where Mr. Wang tries desperately to unbutton his old-fashioned long gown in front of a reclining, alluring Shanghai sing-song girl (Zhang Yu) in a sorghum field outside the modern metropolis. Among other parodies, *Mr. Wang* features a sequence where the massacre in Sergei Eisenstein's *Battleship Potemkin* (1925) is restaged in Shanghai's Japanese settlement, complete with dead bodies and an infant cart coming down the steps from nowhere. Right after the sequence, Mr. Wang pokes his head into the frame and comments tongue-in-cheek: "So you don't understand, right? Me neither!"

[16] Chinese scholarship on literary and cultural modernity in China is too extensive to be adequately sampled here, and the following are just some representative English publications. For the New Era, see Larson and Wedell-Wedellsborg 1993; J. Wang 1996; X. Zhang 1997. For the socialist period, see Dirlik and Zhang 1997; Link 1999. For bourgeois modernity, see L. Lee 1999c; Shih 1996; Y. Zhang 1996, 117–259. For the May Fourth era, see L. Lee 1991a; L. Liu 1995; Schwarcz 1986. For late Qing literature,

are also discussed in close relation to cinematic modernism (Meng Xianli 1994, 164–260).

Proceeding from Chen Xiaoming's three key notions, we may now differentiate three levels of the postmodern in contemporary China. The first are postmodern narrative strategies, as exemplified in the dissolution of themes, the dismantling of depths, and the use of heteroglossia in avant-garde fiction by writers such as Ge Fei and Yu Hua. The second are popular culture and mass media, as reflected in television soap operas and advertisements that champion a new market ideology. And the third is theoretical postmodernism, as represented by Western thinkers like Jacques Derrida, Michel Foucault, Julia Kristeva, and others.[17] Two salient characteristics of postmodernism, according to its proponents in China, are spatialization and dislocation. Indeed, a number of commercially successful recent films mentioned above, such as *Be There or Be Square* and *Spicy Love Soup*, may very well illustrate an argument Chen Xiaoming made in 1994: "Now people can describe the current situation from multiple, interconnected levels. This is a space like the television screen, where everything from the world can be collaged. In China, things traditional or modern, hegemonic or plebeian, Eastern or Western can all be piled up in this space. This is a dislocated space" (p. 66).

It is appropriate here to revisit the original context in which postmodernism was introduced to modern China. Significantly, Jameson's famous two-month lecture series on postmodernism and cultural theory at Beijing University in 1985 did not immediately produce a postmodern craze in Chinese academic circles (X. Tang 1993). As Zhang Yiwu recalls, it is not until the emergence of experimental or avant-garde fiction after 1987 (see Goldblatt 1995; J. Wang 1998) that Chinese critics had recognized the utter inadequacy of their existing critical tools and methodologies. For Chen Xiaoming, postmodern theory provided an ideal escape route from hegemonic discourse for a generation of young

see D. Wang 1997; Y. Zhang 1998, 133–72. For a collection of primary materials in English translation, see Denton 1996. The history of conceptualizations of literary modernity in China deserves a separate study.

[17] This tripartite division of the postmodern is actually articulated in Wang Yichuan's response to Chen Xiaoming's two levels of Chinese postmodernism—avant-garde fiction and mass culture (see Chen Xiaoming 1994, 65). For a list of Chinese books (including translations of Western theory), journal issues, and conferences on postmodernism during the early and mid-1990s, see Meng Xianli 1994, 10–5; Wang Yuechuan 1996, 181–2.

scholars who were searching for their own discursive space in the late 1980s, a time when consumer culture started to transform Chinese society. As Wang Yichuan puts it, the "accidental" introduction of postmodernism in China actually points to a historical necessity: "The disintegration of Chinese modernity constructed since the Opium War and the May Fourth Movement coincided with the bankruptcy of modernity in the West, so the postmodern discourse as a sign has been transplanted to China" (Chen Xiaoming 1994, 63–5).

Resisting the Postmodern

It is no exaggeration to state that postmodern discourse in China has encountered strong resistance since the early 1990s. We can distinguish this resistance as coming from three fronts—moral, ideological, and historicist. The moral resistance arises from an outrage against the strategic repositioning by several leading postmodern proponents. As early as 1994, Chen Xiaoming evoked the concept of play (*youxi*) to define—indeed, to defend—postmodern discourse in China: "Such a posture of play is to demonstrate that people no longer adopt an authoritative, biased, judgmental, or absolutist attitude toward our theoretical discourse, our life, and our real problems. On the contrary, we adopt a relatively random, ambivalent, neutral, and distantiated method. Postmodernism provides a protective coat for our discourse" (1994, 65). The result of such a strategic repositioning is what Chen calls "a post-critical attitude": "For this era, we no longer issue biased refutations or condescending criticisms, nor do we assume any judgmental posture on the prospects of civilization. Instead, we only interpret, and as interpreters in the era of cultural expansion, we are able to do this alone: attempt to encode and label this era through our discourse" (1994, 69). Concurring with Chen, Wang Yichuan envisions himself as a wanderer or drifter in the field of discourse, looking around as he wanders and making comments along the way: "I refuse to talk about the sense of mission, for intellectuals have been professionalized by now" (Chen Xiaoming 1994, 69).

Ironically, the postmodern critics' repositioning of themselves by way of *self-marginalization* vis-à-vis official discourse has occasioned severe criticism from all sides. Speaking from the point of view of the cultural establishment, Wang Yuechuan detects several problems in Chinese postmodern discourse. Among them are the absence of critical object or thematic substance beyond the rhetorical surface, and the mode of guerilla warfare manifested in chasing moving targets with ever-renewed labels, such as "postmodern fiction," "new realism," "new wave fiction," "post-new wave fiction," "avant-garde fiction," "poetry of the third, the fourth, and the fifth generation," "new situations" (*xin zhuangtai*), "new experiences" (*xin tiyan*), "avant-garde drama," and "the sixth generation directors" (see also Wang Ning 1997, 29–36). Due to its inherent problems, Wang Yuechuan concludes, "Postmodern criticism can only constitute a trend of 'marginal criticism' and never aspire to a mainstream status in cultural and literary criticism in China" (1996, 184–5).

Contrary to Wang's view, Henry Zhao (Zhao Yiheng) and Ben Xu, two vocal overseas Chinese critics, would rather include Chinese postmodernism as part of a larger "conservative" movement that is threatening to take over the center in mainland China. The debate over what Zhao sarcastically terms "post-isms" (*houxue*) erupted in February 1995 when the Hong Kong-based journal *Twenty-First Century* (Ershiyi shiji) published Zhao's controversial essay, which treats postmodernism together with numerous other diverse, sometimes overlapping, even conflicting trends in the Chinese cultural scene of the 1990s, such as the critique of May Fourth modernity and the project of rewriting literary history.[18] What provoked Zhao above all are what he takes to be distinctive trademarks of the new conservatism: the renunciation of the high cultural spirit of the 1980s, the return to traditional culture, and the intellectuals' abandonment of their elite (*jingying*) status and, along with it, their responsibility. After his accusation that the post-isms work to issue apologias for the downfall of elite culture under the pretext of multi-centered cultures and to clear the way for American-style popular culture, Zhao reiterates his conviction that intellectuals by definition must not renounce their concerns for the nation-state, the nation-people, and—most important of all—human destiny (1995 and 1997).

Ostensibly, moral resistance to postmodernism has quickly changed into ideological resistance in Zhao's alarming depiction of a conspiracy among the new conservative cultural coalition in contemporary China. Sharing the same ideological stance as does Zhao, whose loosely structured essay has been subject to critical scrutiny in its own turn in

---

[18] For the rewriting of literary history in the 1980s, see Y. Zhang 1994c.

Twenty-First Century and other academic journals,[19] Ben Xu manages to supplement Zhao's impressionistic commentaries with a series of critical essays. Although he initially described it as "Third World criticism" in 1995, Xu favored the term "nativist cultural theory" in 1998 with reference to what he sees as the outcome of a "prima facie unlikely union of Western theories and Chinese concerns" (1998, 204; see also his 1995). Like Zhao, Xu launches an all-out attack on Chinese postmodern discourse: "Nativist theory appropriates postmodern theory and the notion of postmodernism for a rather specific purpose, and that is to denigrate China's attempts at modernity, especially democratization" (1998, 212). As if this charge is not serious enough, Xu goes on to assert that the nativist theory "obscures the imminent reality of oppression, cruelty, corruption, and gross inequality in China, leaving intellectual critics without the vision or the will to act upon their world as citizen-agents, unable to function as a vital force in China's incomplete project of modernization and democratization" (1998, 227).

Perhaps unintentionally, the authoritative voice with which Xu announces his verdict on Chinese postmodern critics and their "accomplices" reveals the problematic nature of his own critical practice. To an alarming degree, Xu's denunciation of new conservatives' alleged denigration of modernity and democracy has exposed his own intolerance for intellectual freedom and democratic choice. By insisting that "[t]he anti-radical rhetoric of new cultural conservatism is bound, from the beginning, by a disillusion with and fear of a politically engaged and oppositional cultural criticism that has become virtually impossible in China after 1989" (1999a, 185), Xu has single-handedly restricted Chinese intellectuals to one choice alone: be oppositional critics (read "political dissidents") and hold on to the remnants of what Henry Zhao perceives as their elite status.

What is more troubling than mere intolerance, however, is the *binary* logic behind Xu's absolutist criticism: either you believe in modernity and democracy or you are implicated in "the rivalry-complicity relationship" with state ideology (1999a, 184); either you take

---

[19] Critical interventions in Chinese, which tend to spill over to personal attacks, are represented by Liu Kang, Zhang Yiwu, Zhang Longxi, and Zhao Yiheng. For publications in English that favor Zhao's and Xu's positions, see Guo 1999; Zhang Longxi 1998. For more or less neutral surveys, see Saussy 1999; M. Yeh 1998. For those in support of Chinese postmodernism, see Liu Kang 1998; X. Zhang 1999.

an oppositional stance vis-à-vis consumer culture and the repressive political regime or you are guilty of "hypocritical complicity in maintaining the status quo" (1998, 224). Propelled by such binary logic and paranoid in the face of what he perceives as "a broad united front in divergent academic areas," Xu is quick to pass this political judgement: "Post-ist theorists in China, by positing the 1990s as post-New Era and by avoiding commenting on the post-New Era's relations to . . . June 4, 1989, acquiesce to the official definition of this event as 'counterrevolutionary turmoil'" (1999b, 129, 217). In cases like these, Xu's criticism has in effect reproduced the rhetoric of official ideology (here exemplified vividly by his use of the Communist term "united front"). Ironically, therefore, Xu might have implicated himself in a complicit relation with official ideology, and this ideology is precisely what Chinese postmodernists have all along sought to escape by means of renouncing the socially imposed "sense of mission" (although, emphatically, not their own "professional ethics").[20]

On closer analysis of Xu's rhetoric, however, one notices another instance of its resemblance to official discourse. Specifically, Xu's indiscriminate use of the misleading term "nativist cultural theory"—for the theory in question is imported from the West rather than home-grown in China—frames a large number of intellectuals and scholars of incompatible ideological persuasions and methodological preferences in an imaginary conspiracy case. By 1999, Xu seems to have abandoned his two previous labels ("Third-World criticism" and "nativist cultural theory")—a sign of the slippage, inadequacy, and confusion of his project of naming a vast span of discursive positions with a single term. Returning to Henry Zhao's "new conservatism," Xu concentrates his criticism on three such groups in 1990s China: scholars who are influenced by cultural traditionalists and who subscribe to a "parochial view of Chinese learning and values"; post-ist theorists who "employ postmodern and postcolonial theory to defend Chinese identity and authenticity"; and old-generation intellectuals like Li Zehou and Wang Yuanhua who have modified their more "radical" positions of the 1980s

---

[20] As if he had anticipated criticism like Xu's, Zhang Yiwu thus defends his repositioning against the elite status: "As Roland Barthes once said, 'I don't know what a bomb is, but I know my articles are bombs, too'" (see Chen Xiaoming 1994, 69). In other words, Zhang suggests that Chinese postmodernists can exert an impact on society even if they have renounced the traditionally defined "moral" responsibilities of the intellectual.

(1999a, 168–9). As typical of official rhetoric, Xu classifies all these people under a single category on the basis of their alleged denigration of modernity and democracy. However, he fails to specify what kind of modernity and democracy this diverse group of scholars has tried to denigrate in the first place. And Xu's failure to achieve—or deliberate avoidance of—specificity makes his own discursive move similar to and thus complicit with the denunciatory rhetoric of official discourse, which otherwise seems to be his ultimate target.[21]

In a less polemical fashion, Wang Hui deals with the culture-specific context surrounding the issue of modernity in contemporary Chinese thought (1998a). Yet Wang is equally critical of Chinese postmodernism. But unlike Xu and Zhao, Wang's sober reasoning enables him to pinpoint exactly what is missing in Chinese postmodern discourse: "While undertaking the deconstruction of all values, postmodernist critics have yet to come up with an analysis of the activities of capital that constitute an important feature of modern life, nor have they undertaken an appraisal of the relationship between this activity of capital and the Chinese reform movement" (1998b, 249). In other words, Wang sees Chinese postmodernists as helplessly caught in a dilemma in post-1989 China, where "mass culture and ideology actually permeate one another and together occupy the dominant position in contemporary Chinese ideology" (1998b, 249). As with Xu and Zhao, Wang finds the post-modernists' repositioning highly problematic: "In their adopting a posture of embracing mass culture (that is, fabricated mass desire and culture in its marketized condition) and rejecting and denouncing elite culture, what is returned to the center is market 'socialism' with Chinese characteristics" (1998b, 250).

If Wang Hui interrogates Chinese postmodernism from an implicit "modern" standpoint, Paul Pickowicz articulates another kind of historicist resistance that questions the modernist framework as well. The

---

[21] After denouncing a large number of Chinese scholars as conservative and complicit with the status quo, Xu himself cannot suggest any specific political alternative. The best he can do is to propose a vaguely conceived "democratic postcolonial criticism" or "Third-World critical theory in China," which exposes the interstructuration of domination and violence around the world. "A theory of international and intranational domination and violence," he recommends, "is a first step toward involving China's Third-World cultural critique in the emerging framework of globalizing democracy" (1999b, 128). But what that emerging democracy will be is beyond anyone's (including Xu's) guess, at least for now.

historicism in Pickowicz's case is exemplified by his conception of "modern" as referring to "postfeudal, bourgeois culture that developed in capitalist societies in eighteenth- and nineteenth-century Europe," and of the "modernist" as referring to "avant-garde . . . culture that arose in the West in the late nineteenth and early twentieth centuries" (1994, 58–9). From this historicist perspective, Pickowicz asserts that the modernist framework is neither useful nor productive but simply misleading for a study of post-Mao China, especially if one remembers the long history of delegitimizing modernism in socialist China. In a similar way, Pickowicz strongly resists the postmodernist framework, and his historicist rationale is most pronounced in this statement: "The postmodern framework refers primarily to postindustrial contexts. Postmodernism, that is, presupposes advanced capitalism" (1994, 60). For this reason, Pickowicz endorses the use of postsocialism as "the ideological counterpart of postmodernism" (1994, 80). For him, since "postsocialism presupposes socialism," this new framework will illuminate Chinese culture in the 1980s, which "contained the vestiges of late imperial culture, the remnants of the modern or bourgeois culture of the Republican era, the residue of traditional socialist culture, and elements of both modernism and postmodernism" (1994, 83, 60).

Postmodernism and Postsocialism

As should be apparent by now, many critics would interpret the coexistence of disparate, seemingly incongruent temporalities and cultural modes described by Pickowicz as precisely the signs of the postmodern in contemporary China. Even though Chris Berry and Mary Ann Farquhar have followed Pickowicz and expanded his notion of postsocialism to include cinematic styles (see chapter 3), they are perceptive enough to remind us of several unresolved questions. "What remains to be fully explored is the homology between this term [postsocialism] and 'postmodernism,' from which it is clearly derived. Can postsocialism be seen as a complement to postmodernism? Is its pastiche of other styles, its ambiguity and play, part of an aesthetic parallel to postmodernism?" (Berry and Farquhar 1994, 84).

For Arif Dirlik and Xudong Zhang, the answer to Berry and Farquhar's questions is definitely positive. In fact, Dirlik was the first to use the term "postsocialism" (1989). Contrary to Pickowicz, who modifies Dirlick's postsocialism to refer "in large part to a negative, dystopian cultural condition that prevails in late socialist societies," and who believes that, as "popular perception" and "an alienated . . . mode of thought and behavior," postsocialism certainly predates the death of Mao (Pickowicz 1994, 61–2), Dirlik and Zhang squarely situate postmodernism in the post-Mao era and attach positive meanings to the term. In their introduction to the 1997 special issue of *Boundary 2* on postmodernism and China, they propose this parallel conceptualization of postmodernism and postsocialism: "What we need to keep in mind, especially with reference to the PRC [mainland China], is that postmodernity is not just what comes after the modern but rather what comes after particular manifestations of the modern in China's historical circumstances, that the postmodern is also the postrevolutionary and the postsocialist" (1997, 4). From their committed Marxian stance, they argue that the "coexistence of the precapitalist, the capitalist, and the postsocialist economic, political, and social forms represents a significant departure from the assumptions of a Chinese modernity, embodied above all in the socialist revolutionary project" (1997, 3).

Nevertheless, their argument that Chinese modernity is above all embodied in Chinese socialism begs the immediate question of evidence, and their facile reliance for proof on the periodizing concepts in official historiography in mainland China is mechanical at best and self-defeating at worst. In an elaborate footnote, they reason that since *xiandai* (I would say "modern," rather than "contemporary" as in their sentence) refers to the period starting from 1919 (the May Fourth Movement)—or more specifically from 1921 (the birth of the Communist Party)—and stretching all the way through the Communist Revolution, the Chinese term *hou xiandai* (postmodernism) must therefore mean "post*modern*," which is to say "post*revolutionary*," and hence "postsocialist" (1997, 10). On the surface, all this sounds logical. Yet, one may wonder why Dirlik and Zhang deliberately avoid "post-Communist," a term that is already implied in the chain of their mechanical equations. If their avoidance is to distinguish the reform-era China from post-Communist Russia and other East European countries, then Dirlik and Zhang might have shared with their postmodern counterparts in China a desire to endow Chinese postmodernism with specific "Chinese" characteristics.

Obviously unsatisfied with his 1997 formulation with Dirlik, Xudong Zhang revisited the concepts of postmodernism and post-socialism in 1999. Rather than their earlier recourse to the periodizing concepts in Chinese historiography, Zhang contends this time that "the 'post' in Chinese postmodernism refers not so much to a sense that something is over, but that something is finally ready to begin along with the breaking of all kinds of rigid epistemological paradigms, aesthetic canons, historical periodizations, geographical hierarchies, and institutional reifications" (1999, 78). What makes this refreshing is Zhang's reversal of the previous cause-and-effect type of questions. Instead of asking whether or not Chinese postmodernism reflects or corresponds to a changing reality, he contends "that the naming of Chinese postmodernism itself must be regarded as a cultural and political event made possible, even called for, by the socio-economic changes and ideological imperatives of post-socialist China" (1999, 87). A better understanding of postsocialism in China, therefore, is indispensable to any formulation of Chinese postmodernism. For this purpose, Zhang analyzes a vast array of issues, such as the ambiguity of reforms, overproduction crises, concepts of "flexible production" and "institutional fetishism" (both articulated by Zhiyuan Cui), the utopian impulse of Sino-Marxism (especially Maoism), the "shared space" between the state and civil society (Zhang Yiwu's term), market madness and plebeian excess, as well as political anxieties of the "Old Left" (the Party conservatives denouncing all things new), the "New Left" (the liberals defending modernity), and the "New Right" (the critics of postmodernism).[22]

Through his analysis, Xudong Zhang exposes tensions and contradictions in postsocialist China. For him, Chinese postmodernism is "symbiotic with 'socialist market economy,'" where the state now "functions as an agent of international capital and special interest groups at home." Therefore, "Chinese postmodernism, as a Chinese vision of the new at the end of the twentieth century, unwittingly becomes a breathing space between an emergent Chinese lifeworld and the

---

[22] It is significant that all three forces have mounted resistance, each in its own way, to Chinese postmodernism in the 1990s. Although Xudong Zhang is right to expose the "conservative" core of Henry Zhao's elitist position, I would caution against Zhang's labeling of Wang Hui as a New Left (1999, 103), and Zhao (or Ben Xu, for that matter) as a New Right who embraces "global post-cold-war ideology" (1999, 85), for the simple reason that these terms are loaded in Western politics and might misfire when used in the Chinese context. On the other hand, however, Zhang's labels of the New Left and the New Right are appropriate to the current Western intellectual context, where his extensive discussion of Zhiyuan Cui's theory contributes to an ongoing search for alternatives to global capitalism.

unrelenting universal claim of the absolute market as a negation of the historical experience of Chinese modernity" (1999, 103–5). Two possibilities may thus be contemplated. On the one hand, Chinese postmodernism may end up as "nothing more than a manipulated playground creating a cultural illusion for a society in crisis," a charge that has been leveled against postmodernism from several fronts as I outlined above. On the other hand, "if China is to explore a way out of the closing of historical possibilities," as Zhang apparently wishes it would, Chinese postmodernism will then become "a utopian space for reconfigurations of social and class relations, for the imagination of community, nation, and democracy" (1999, 105, 79). As Zhang concedes at the beginning of his new project, Chinese postmodernism is indeed a "nebulous yet productive discourse," and it follows that "the empty signifier of Chinese postmodernism can only be filled with the phenomenological richness of Chinese post-socialism" (1999, 78, 104).

Of Postmodernity and Modernity: Palimpsestic Times of the New Millennium

In his survey of national culture and the new global system, Frederick Buell offers a comment relevant to the Chinese context: "Peripheral cultures either have used or could use postmodernism as a means of claiming new kinds of centrality by claiming that they have in some way been 'always already' postmodern. . . . Peripheral postmodernism is best analyzed . . . from the perspective of globalization" (1994, 327). Although it is debatable whether or not China—given its strategic importance in the global balance of powers, its enormous population, and its long history as a civilization—could qualify as a "peripheral" culture, few would dispute the fact that postmodernism has provided a discursive means through which "China" (an entity itself under contestation) can speak to the "center" of multinational capitalism in the West. The urge to claim—or at least to mimic—some kind of centrality is eloquently articulated in Wang Ning's 1997 remapping of eight forms of postmodernism in accordance with what he admits to be "Jameson's and [Douwe] Fokkema's descriptions of the actual situation in China": (1) a fundamental cultural phenomenon; (2) a kind of worldview privileging plurality, fragmentation, and decentralization; (3) a main current of literature and art after the fall of modernism; (4) a narrative style characterized by suspicion of the "master narrative"; (5) a strategy of reading earlier or non-Western texts from the perspective of postmodernity; (6) a philosophical trend contrary to the elite preoccupation with the Enlightenment; (7) a cultural strategy adopted by Asian and Third World critics in the face of cultural colonialism and linguistic hegemony; and (8) a critical mode marked by poststructuralist approaches to literary texts (1997, 23; also 1993). After enumerating these eight forms of postmodernism, Wang confesses, somewhat unexpectedly, that he has "recently come to understand postmodernism in the current global context . . . as a sort of extended modernism, but one that needs to be distinguished from modernism" (1997, 22).

Ample evidence suggests that the emergence of postmodernism in China has not automatically brought about the "death" of modernity. In fact, several active proponents of Chinese postmodernism have stated a position similar to Wang Ning's: "The project of modernity in China is obviously incomplete" (1997, 38). Chen Xiaoming, as quoted above, conceives of Chinese postmodernism as an enormous social text produced by the historical process of Chinese modernity in the age of globalization. Dirlik and Xudong Zhang also attest to the staying power of modernity in China: "Having experienced modernity as colonialism from the outside and as a coercive state project from the inside, postmodernity may allow for the emergence of alternative social and cultural formations that do not so much signal the end of modernity as mark the beginning of imagining an alternative to it" (1997, 17). Whatever happens, it seems that modernity still occupies a conceptually central position, alongside which various forms of postmodernism articulate their alternatives.

Furthermore, we must come to terms with the fact that not all these alternatives imagined and expressed in literary and cultural production, or improvised and tried out in the everyday world, fall into a neatly defined category of the postmodern. Leo Lee, for instance, would rather believe in the persistence of "true feelings" (*zhenqing*) in the postmodern era, although he concedes that such feelings might have been disembodied or fragmented as demonstrated in *Happy Together*. From his conviction that postmodern theory could never solve every individual's problems, Lee raises the question of attitude, mentality, or feelings: "I believe that only through feelings could we recover our subjectivity, even though postmodernity claims to have dismantled and deconstructed subjectivity" (1999a, 138–9). As proof for his conviction, Lee cites Japanese television drama series such as *Long Vacation, Love Generation,* and *Proposing Marriage for the 101th Time.* These shows typically feature an overwhelmingly "sentimental" (*wenqing zhuyi*) denouement and express a "lingering feeling of nostalgia." And, Lee claims, they "were watched by almost every young viewer in Hong Kong," or "almost all women in Hong Kong,"—not to mention those in Japan and South Korea (1999a 139).[23]

Upon closer scrutiny, however, what Lee proposed in his 1999 lecture at Beijing University is not so much a grand project of reclaiming subjectivity as a mere strategy for survival. "Theoretically speaking, we can never escape the influence of global capitalism, as we are all caught in the so-called postmodern society. Nevertheless, in everyday life, we can still experience certain feelings of the real (*zhenshi gan*), no matter how petty, fragmented, or fleeting they are. I think, perhaps due to our experience of such feelings, we will be able to survive eventually" (1999a, 139). Indeed, Lee's proposal for the attitude of true feelings as a survival strategy finds echoes in Chinese films of the late 1990s. Several recent films, such as *Be There or Be Square* and *Spicy Love Soup,* function precisely to capture moments of such "true feelings" as experienced by non-heroic characters in their everyday life, be it in transnational or local space. From *Tempting Heart* to *The Personals,* numerous other recent titles from Hong Kong and Taiwan can also be used to support Lee's proposal. However, a fundamental question remains to upset or even tease Lee's nostalgic propensity for true feelings (see chapter 7); that is, how can we ignore the obvious fact that these "sentimental" texts may have exposed the hollowness and emptiness, if not hypocrisy and pretentiousness, of the very "true" feelings that are enacted or reenacted on the large or small screen for the purpose of mass consumption in a hyperreal world? In other words, the true feelings in question may function as nothing more than what Jean Baudrillard conceives of as "a kind of simulacrum of a 'nature'"—as mere signs in "the serial and technical age of reproduction" where the notions of origin and authenticity in mass-mediated texts are increasingly problematic if not altogether untenable (1988, 137).

Lee's reference to Taiwan and Hong Kong in his lecture on modernity and postmodernity in contemporary Chinese culture brings us

---

[23] Lacking statistical support, Lee's view of the female Hong Kong viewership of these Japanese soap operas borders on sheer exaggeration. To say the least, one wonders if his unspecified term "women" (*nüxing*) includes, for example, old, illiterate women of working-class background.

to another set of unresolved questions. If the postmodern corresponds, historically, to the postsocialist in mainland China, what has happened to the postmodern in Hong Kong and Taiwan? Could we replace the "postsocialist" with the "postcolonial" in theorizing the postmodern in Hong Kong or Taiwan? If so, how do we account for the manifestations of postmodernity in Hong Kong years before the onset of its postcolonial era in 1997? One may be reminded that, in the early 1990s, Lee had already posed "the inevitable theoretical query: can we regard Hong Kong films as in some way products of a Chinese postmodern culture?" (1994, 212) Rather than Lee's adherence to the term "Chinese," Stephen Teo prefers something like "Hong Kong postmodern," as he demonstrates that "there is a postmodernism unique to Hong Kong in the last decade of the century" by citing examples from Tsui Hark's creative output, Stephen Chow's comic performances, and the time-space compression in nostalgia cinema (1997, 244–50).

In Taiwan, the year 1987 is regarded as pivotal not only because it was the year in which the forty-year-old martial law was lifted by the Nationalist government but also because it was the year postmodernism was systematically introduced to academic circles (as signified by Jameson's first visit to Taipei). Contrary to what occurred in mainland China, "if the postmodern craze in Taiwan sprang up like 'bamboo shoots after the rain,' it soon declined and virtually disappeared" by the early 1990s (Liao 1997, 44; see also K. Chen 1994; Liao 1996). According to Ping-hui Liao, what happened is that Taiwan scholars have shifted their attention to other issues, such as postcolonial criticism, identity politics, and transnational studies. However, from his survey of developments in these and other fronts, Liao concludes that "the postmodern condition in Taiwan is far from over . . . [for] Taiwanese people are only beginning to put together an alternative postmodern puzzle" (1997, 63).

The foregoing discussion of postmodernism—or, more precisely, alternative postmodernisms—in mainland China, Hong Kong, and Taiwan may confirm Jameson's observation that "in late capitalism and in its world system . . . expressions of the marginally uneven and the unevenly developed . . . are often more intense and powerful, more expressive, and above all more deeply symptomatic and meaningful than anything the enfeebled center still finds itself able to say" (1992, 155). As a leading critic of multinational capitalism, Jameson tends to endorse new expressions from the "periphery" in his cognitive mapping of the First and Third Worlds. Still, as we enter the new millennium, the center in question is by no means "enfeebled" or "marginalized" as Jameson claims, and capitalism has not yet exhausted itself in its reputedly final stage of development (as implied by the term "late capitalism").

In *Unthinking Eurocentrism*, Ella Shohat and Robert Stam offer a powerful critique of the epistemological model of center and periphery, a critique that greatly illuminates our remapping of the alternative postmodern conditions in the three regions of China at the turn of the millennium (1995, 293):

> In Jameson's prose the Third World always seems to lag behind . . . condemned to a perpetual game of catch-up in which it can only repeat on another register the history of the "advanced" world. When the First World reaches the stage of late capitalism and postmodernism, the Third World hobbles along toward modernism and the beginnings of capitalism. Jameson thus ignores the world systems theory that sees First and Third Worlds as living the same historical moment although the Third World lives that moment under the mode of oppression. . . . For us, "postmodern" is not a[n] honorific [term], nor are Third World postmodernisms necessarily identical to those of the First World. A more adequate formulation would see time as scrambled and palimpsestic in all the Worlds, with the premodern, the modern, the postmodern and the paramodern coexisting globally, although the "dominant" might vary from region to region.

Indeed, as we enter the new millennium, time appears much more "scrambled and palimpsestic" than ever before. The coexistence of the premodern, the modern, the postmodern, and the paramodern in the vast but geographically dispersed spaces of China and the Chinese diaspora bears witness to the complexities and contradictions in the ever-evolving project of screening China in the era of globalization. Herein lie both the urgent necessity and the crucial importance of our continuous efforts to track the developments of how China will be screened in the new millennium.

Character List

This list includes all directors, films, as well as selected names, studios, and special terms mentioned in the book. Entries are alphabetized letter by letter, ignoring word and syllable breaks.

A ba de qingren　阿爸的情人
A Fei zhengzhuan　阿飛正傳
A Gan zhengzhuan　阿甘正傳
Ah Nian (b. 1965)　阿年
Ai le zhongnian　哀樂中年
Aiqing malatang　愛情麻辣燙
Ai zai biexiang de jijie
　愛在別鄉的季節
A jihua　A計劃
Alishan fengyun　阿里山風雲
Anlian taohuayuan
暗戀桃花源
Aozhan Lu xinan　鏖戰魯西南

Babai zhuangshi　八百壯士
Bai　白
Baihua jiang　百花獎
Bai Jingrui (Pai Ching-jui, b. 1931)
　白景瑞
Baimao nü　白毛女
Ba Jin (b. 1904)　巴金
Banbian ren　半邊人
Banni dao liming　伴你到黎明
Banni gaofei　伴你高飛
Bansheng yuan　半生緣
Baochou　報仇

Baqianli lu yun he yue
　八千里路雲和月
Bashi niandai　八十年代
Bawang bieji　霸王別姬
Bayi　八一
Bei Dao (b. 1949)　北島
Beijing　北京
Beijing dianying xueyuan
　北京電影學院
Beijing nizao　北京你早
Beijing ren zai Niuyue
　北京人在紐約
Beijing zazhong　北京雜種
Bei kao bei, lian dui lian
　背靠背, 臉對臉
Beilie paibang　悲烈排幫
Beiqing chengshi　悲情城市
Benming nian　本命年
Benpao de chengshi
　奔跑的城市
Biancheng　邊城
Biandan, guniang　扁擔姑娘
Bianzou bianchang　邊走邊唱
Bing　兵
binghai chenchuan　冰海沉船
Bingshan shangde laike
　冰山上的來客

Bing yu huo　冰與火
Bohao　跛豪
Boli zhicheng　玻璃之城
Bujian busan　不見不散
Buliao qing　不了情
Bu Wancang (b. 1903–74)
　卜萬倉
Buye cheng　不夜城

Cai Chusheng (1906–68)
　蔡楚生
Cai Jiwei (b. 1929)　蔡繼渭
Cai Mingliang (Tsai Ming-liang,
　b. 1958)　蔡明亮
Cai Yuanyuan　蔡元元
Cao Pi (187–226)　曹丕
Cao Yu (b. 1910)　曹禺
Changchun　長春
Chaoji da guomin　超級大國民
Chaoji shimin　超級市民
Chen Chong (Joan Chen,
　b. 1961)　陳沖
chenfu zitai　臣服姿態
Cheng Bugao (1898–1966)
　程步高
Cheng Jihua (b. 1921)　程季華
Cheng Long (Jackie Chan,
　b. 1954)　成龍
Chengshi aiqing　城市愛情
chengren shi　成人式
Chen Guo (Fruit Chan, b. 1959)
　陳果
Cheng Xiaodong (Ching Siu
　Tung, b. 1953)　程小東
Cheng Yin (1917–84)　成蔭
Chen Huaiai (1920–94)　陳懷皚
Chen Jiashang (Gordon Chan, b.
　1960)　陳嘉上
Chen Kaige (b. 1952)　陳凱歌

Chen Kexin (Peter Chan, b. 1962)
　陳可辛
Chen Kun-hou (b. 1939)
　陳坤厚
Chen Kuo-Fu (Chen Guofu, b.
　1958)　陳國富
Chen Mei (b. 1939)　陳梅
Chen Ruxiu (Robert Ru-shou
　Chen)　陳儒修
Chen Shanzhi　陳善之
Chen Weiwen　陳偉文
Chen Xihe (1912–83)　陳西禾
Chen Yanyan (b. 1916)　陳燕燕
Chen Yaocheng (Evan Chan)
　陳耀成
Chen Yaoxin (b. 1938)　陳耀忻
Chen Yuxun (Chen Yu-hsun)
　陳玉勳
chong de kongjian　虫的空間
Chongqing senlin　重慶森林
Chongtian feibao　沖天飛豹
Chuangye　創業
Chuanwai　窗外
Chuilian tingzheng　垂簾聽政
Chujian nü　出嫁女
Chuncan　春蠶
Chunguang zhaxie　春光乍洩
Chuntao　春桃
Chu Yuan (Chor Yuen, b. 1934)
　楚原
ci　詞
Cui Wei (1912–79)　崔嵬
Cuoai　錯愛
Cuowei　錯位

Da bianzi de youhuo
　大辮子的誘惑
Da chuanqi　大喘氣
Dacuo che　搭錯車
Da dongya gongrong quan

大東亞共榮圈
Daguan　大觀
Da hong denglong gaogao gua
　大紅燈籠高高掛
Dai　傣
Dai Sijie　戴泗杰
Da jinjun: dazhan Ning Hu Hang
　大進軍: 大戰寧滬杭
Da jinjun: nanxian da zhuijian
　大進軍: 南線大追殲
Da jinjun: xijuan da xinan
　大進軍: 席卷大西南
Da juezhan: Huaihai zhanyi
　大決戰: 淮海戰役
Da juezhan: Liao-Shen zhanyi
　大決戰: 遼沈戰役
Da juezhan: Ping-Jin zhanyi
　大決戰: 平津戰役
Dalu　大路
Da mofang　大磨坊
Dangdai dianying　當代電影
Daoban diji xiaoshuo
　盜版低級小說
Daode gushi　道德故事
Daoma dan　刀馬旦
Daoma zei　盜馬賊
Daotian　稻田
Da saba　大撒把
dashi　大師
Da taijian Li Lianying
　大太監李連英
Dayang　大洋
Da youxi　大遊戲
Da yuebing　大閱兵
da Zhongyuan xintai　大中原心態
Da zhuanzhe　大轉折
Debao　德寶
Dengdai liming　等待黎明
Deng Lijun (Teresa Teng, 1953–95)
　鄧麗君

Deng Xiaoping　鄧小平
Dianmao　電懋
Diantong　電通
dianying　電影
Dianying chaodai　電影朝代
dianying nian　電影年
Dianying yishu　電影藝術
Didao zhan　地道戰
Diexue heigu　喋血黑谷
Diexue shuangxiong　喋血雙雄
Dilei zhan　地雷戰
Ding Jiancheng (b. 1963)　丁建城
Ding Junshan　定軍山
Ding Yinnan (b. 1938)　丁蔭楠
Diyi　第一
Dochakuka　土著化
Dong　洞
Dongbei　東北
Dong Chun de rizi　冬春的日子
Dong Cunrui　董存瑞
Dongfang bubai　東方不敗
Dong furen　董夫人
Donggong xigong　東宮西宮
Dong Kena (b. 1930)　董克娜
Dongxie xidu　東邪西毒
Duanjian xingdong　斷箭行動
duanqiao　斷橋
Dubi dao　獨臂刀
Duizhao ji　對照記
Dujiang zhencha ji　渡江偵察記
Dujuan shan　杜鵑山
Duli shidai　獨立時代
Duoluo tianshi　墮落天使
Duomian shuangxiong　奪面雙雄
Duosang　多桑
Dusheng　睹聖
Dushi fengguang　都市風光

dushi lide cunzhuang
　都市里的村莊
Emei　峨嵋
Er Dongsheng (Derek Yee, b.
　1957) 爾東陞
Ermo　二嫫
Erzi　兒子
Erzi de da wan'ou　兒子的大玩偶

Fang Lingzheng (Eddie Fong, b.
　1954) 方令正
Fang Peilin (?–1949) 方沛霖
Fang Yuping (Allan Fong, b. 1947)
　方育平
Fan jiwang　反擊王
Fei Mu (1906–51) 費穆
Feitian　飛天
Feixia A Da　飛俠阿達
Feng Bailu　馮白魯
Feng Baobao (Fung Bobo, b. 1953)
　馮寶寶
Fengkuang de daijia　瘋狂的代價
Fengkuan Yingyu　瘋狂英語
Fengtai　豐泰
Feng Xiaogang (b. 1959) 馮小剛
Feng Xiaoning (b. 1954) 馮小寧
Fengyue　風月
Fengyun ernü　風雲兒女
Fengyun zaiqi　風雲再起
Fujian　福建
Furong zhen　芙蓉鎮
Fusheng　浮生
Fuyi　富藝

Ganglong　港龍
Gangtie shi zheyang liancheng de
　鋼鐵是這樣煉成的
Gaoshan xiade huahuan
　高山下的花環

Ge Fei (b. 1964) 格非
Gei kafei jiadian tang
　給咖啡加點糖
geming yangban xi　革命樣板戲
Ge Xin　葛忻
Ge You (b. 1957) 葛優
Gezi shu　鴿子樹
gongfu　功夫
Gong Li (b. 1966) 鞏俐
Gongtong ti　共同體
Guanfu cun　寡婦村
guaiwu　怪物
Guangbo xueyuan　廣播學院
guangchang　廣場
Guanghua　光華
Guangtian huari　光天化日
Guangxi　廣西
Guangyin de gushi　光陰的故事
Guan Hu (b. 1967) 管虎
Guan Jinpeng (Stanley Kwan, b.
　1957) 關錦鵬
Guanyu jiang zhengzhi
　關於講政治
Gu Changwei (b. 1957) 顧長衛
Gucheng tonghua　古城童話
Gufeng　股瘋
guguo　故國
Guihua xiang　桂花巷
Guixin sijian　歸心似箭
Guling jie shaonian sharen shijian
　牯嶺街少年殺人事件
Gungun hongchen　滾滾紅塵
guofang dianying　國防電影
Guoge　國歌
guojia　國家
Guojia de diren　國家的敵人
Guolian　國聯
Guonian huijia　過年回家
guopian　國片

guopian fudao jin　國片輔導金
Guo Xiaolu　郭小櫓
Guo Wei (b. 1922)　郭維
guoyouhua　國有化
guoyu　國語
Guozhe langbei bukan de shenghuo
　過著狼狽不堪的生活
Gushi hunlian　股市婚戀
Gushu yiren　鼓書藝人
guxiang　故鄉

Haishang hua　海上花
Haitang de yitian　海灘的一天
Haixia　海霞
Haizi wang　孩子王
Han　漢
hanhua　漢化
Han Suyin　韓素音
Hao Dazheng　郝大錚
Haomeng　好夢
Haonan haonü　好南好女
Hei junma　黑駿馬
Hei meigui dui hei meigui
　黑玫瑰對黑玫瑰
Heipao shijian　黑砲事件
Heishan lu　黑山路
He Jianjun (He Yi, b. 1960)
　何建軍(何一)
Heliu　河流
Hengtong　恆通
He Ping (b. 1957)　何平
hesui pian　賀歲片
Hongdeng ting, lüdeng xing
　紅燈停, 綠燈行
Hongfan qu　紅番區
Hongfen　紅粉
Hong gaoliang　紅高粱
Hong haizi　紅孩子
Honghe gu　紅河谷

Hong meigui, bai meigui
　紅玫瑰, 白玫瑰
Hongse niangzi jun　紅色娘子軍
Hong yingtao　紅櫻桃
Hong yu　紅雨
hou xiandai　後現代
Hou Xiaoxian (Hou Hsiao-hsien,
　b. 1947)　侯孝賢
houxue　後學
Hou Yao (1903–42)　侯曜
Huabiao jiang　華表獎
huaijiu dianying　懷舊電影
huaju　話劇
Hualuo shuijia　花落誰家
Huamei　華美
Hu An (Ann Hu, b. 1956)　胡安
Huanghe juelian　黃河絕戀
Huanghe yao　黃河謠
Huang Jianxin (b. 1954)　黃建新
Huang Jianzhong (b. 1943)
　黃建中
Huang jinyu　黃金魚
Huang Liushuang (Anna May
　Wong, 1907–61)　黃柳霜
Huang Shaofen (b. 1911)　黃紹芬
Huang Shixian (b. 1935)　黃式憲
Huang Jun (b. 1958)　黃軍
Huang Sha　黃沙
Huang Shuqin (b. 1940)　黃蜀芹
Huang tudi　黃土地
Huanle yingxiong　歡樂英雄
Hua Zhongkai　華仲愷
Hu Bingliu (b. 1940)　胡炳榴
Hu Dieying (Wu Tip Ying)
　胡蝶影
Hu Jinquan (King Hu, b. 1931–97)
　胡金銓
Hu Lancheng (b. 1906)　胡蘭成
Hu Mei (b. 1956)　胡玫

Hu Lancheng (b. 1906)　胡蘭成
Hu Mei (b. 1956)　胡玫
Huohu　火狐
Huo Jianqi　霍建起
Huoniao　火鳥
Huaoshao Yuanmingyuan
　火燒圓明園
hutong　胡同
Huwo　呼我
Hu Xueyang (b. 1963)　胡雪陽

Jia　家
Jiachou　家丑
Jiafang yifang　甲方乙方
Jiahe　嘉禾
Jiang Qing　江青
Jiang Wen (b. 1963)　姜文
Jiangxi　江西
Jiang Zemin　江澤明
Jiaoliang: kang Mei yuan Chao
　zhanzheng shilu
　較量: 抗美援朝戰爭實錄
Jiao Xiongping (Chiao Hsiung-
　Ping, b. 1953)　焦雄屏
Jiawu fengyun　甲午風雲
Jia zai Taibei　家在台北
Jia Zhangke (b. 1970)　賈樟柯
Jiefang da xibei　解放大西北
Jietou xiangwei　街頭巷尾
Ji Hongchang　吉鴻昌
Jimao xin　雞毛信
Jinding　金鼎
jinbu　進步
Jin Chen (b. 1970)　金琛
jing　精
jingpin　精品
Jingwu men　精武門
jingying　精英
Jinji jiang　金雞獎

Jinma jiang　金馬獎
Jintian bu huijia　今天不回家
Jinzhi yuye　金枝玉葉
Ju Dou　菊豆
Juexiang　絕響
Juelie　決裂
Juxing　巨星

Kaiguo dadian　開國大典
Kang Ding you Taibei
　康丁遊台北
Ke Yizheng (Ko Yi-cheng, b. 1946)
　柯一正
Kongbu fenzi　恐怖分子
Kong Fansen　孔繁森
Kongque　孔雀
Kuangliu　狂流
Kuangwen Eluosi　狂吻俄羅斯
Kunlun　昆侖

Lai Shengchuan (Stan Lai, b. 1954)
　賴聲川
Lan fengzheng　藍風箏
Langman jietou　浪漫街頭
Laogong zhi aiqing　勞工之愛情
Laojing　老井
li　禮
Li An (Ang Lee, b. 1954)　李安
Lianbang　聯邦
liang'an dianying bai Xiyan
　兩岸電影擺喜宴
liang'an sandi　兩岸三地
Liang Chaowei (Tony Leung Chiu-
　Wai)　梁朝偉
Liangge youqi jiang　兩個油漆匠
Liang Jiahui (Tony Leung Ka Fai,
　b. 1958)　梁家輝
Liangjia funü　良家婦女

Liang Puzhi (Leong Po-chi, b. 1939) 梁普智

Liang Shanbo yu Zhu Yingtai 梁山泊與祝英台

Liang Shaopo (Leung Siu-bo) 梁少坡

Liang Chen (Leong Sum) 梁琛

Liang Zhefu (Liang Che-fu, 1920– 92) 梁哲夫

Lianhua 聯華

Lianlian fengchen 戀戀風塵

Li Bai (701–62) 李白

Li Baotian (b. 1946) 李保田

Li Beihai (Lai Buk-hyuok, 1889– 1950) 黎北海

Li Bin (Lai Ban) 黎斌

Liechang zhasa 獵場扎撒

liegu 裂谷

Liehuo zhong yongsheng 烈火中永生

Li Guanghui 李光惠

Li Guoli 李國立

Li Hanxiang (1926–96) 李翰祥

Li Hong (b. 1975) 李虹

Lihun le, jiu bie zailai zhaowo 離婚了，就別再來找我

Li Jun (b. 1922) 李俊

Li Lili (b. 1915) 黎莉莉

Li Ming (Leon Lai) 黎明

Li Minwei (Lai Man-wei, 1893– 1953) 黎民偉

Ling Zi (b. 1941) 凌子

Ling Zifeng (1917–99) 凌子風

Lin Lingdong (Lingo Lam, b. 1955) 林嶺東

Lin Niantong (b. 1944–90) 林年同

Lin Nong (b. 1918) 林農

lilong 里弄

Lin Qingxia (Brigitte Lin, b. 1954) 林青霞

Lin Shan (1914–92) 林杉

Lin Wenqi 林文琪

Lin Yutang (1895–1976) 林語堂

Lin Zhengsheng (Lin Cheng-sheng) 林正盛

Li Pingqian (1902–84) 李萍倩

Li Qiankuan (b. 1941) 李前寬

Li Shaobai (b. 1931) 李少白

Li Shaohong (b. 1955) 李少紅

Li Tie (Lee Tit, b. 1913) 李鐵

Li Tianlu (Li Tien-lu, 1909–99) 李天祿

Li Tuo 李陀

Liu Chenghan (Lau Shing Hon, b. 1945) 劉成漢

Liu Guochang (Lawrence Ah Mon, b. 1949) 劉國昌

Liu Hulan 劉胡蘭

Liu Jialiang (Law Kar-leung, b. 1935) 劉家良

liumang 流氓

Liu Miaomiao (b. 1962) 劉苗苗

Liu Na'ou (1900–40) 劉吶鷗

Liu Qingyun (Lau Ching-wan) 劉青雲

Liu Qiong (b. 1913) 劉瓊

Liu sanjie 劉三姐

Liushou nüshi 留守女士

Liu Xiaoqing (b. 1951) 劉曉慶

Liuyue xinniang 六月新娘

Liu Zhenwei (Jeff Lau) 劉鎮偉

Li Wenhua (b. 1912) 李文化

Li Xianglan (Yamaguchi Yoshiko, b. 1920) 李香蘭(山口淑子)

Li Xiaolong (Bruce Lee, 1940–73) 李小龍

Li Xin (b. 1969) 李欣

Li Xing (Lee Hsing, b. 1930) 李行
Li Yu (937–78) 李煜
Li Zehou 李澤厚
Li Zhiyi (Lee Chi-gnai) 李志藝
Li Zhuotao (Le Cheuk-to, b. 1956) 李焯桃
Longmen kezhan 龍門客棧
Longxiang 龍祥
Lou Ye (b. 1965) 婁燁
Luding ji 鹿鼎記
Luo Feng (Natalia Chan) 洛楓
Luo Ka (Law Kar, b. 1941) 羅卡
Luo Mingyou (1900–67) 羅明佑
Luo Wei (Lo Wei, b. 1918) 羅維
Luo Yi (Peter Loehr, b. 1967) 羅異
Luo Zhuoyao (Clara Law, b. 1957) 羅卓瑤
Lunhui 輪回
Lu Xiaofen (b. 1956) 陸小芬
Lu Xuechang (b. 1964) 路學長
Lu Xun (1881–1936) 魯迅
Lü Yue 呂樂

Mai Dangxiong (Johnny Mak, b. 1949) 麥當雄
Majiang 麻將
Malu tianshi 馬路天使
Mama 媽媽
Manyi bu manyi 滿意不滿意
Manying 滿映
Mao Xiaorui 毛小睿
Mao Zedong 毛澤東
Meili xin shijie 美麗新世界
meisu 媚俗
Meiwan meiliao 沒完沒了
Mei Yanfang (Anita Mui, b. 1963) 梅艷芳
Menggu 蒙古

Menghuan tianyuan 夢幻田園
Mengnalisha 蒙娜麗莎
Mi 米
Miao 苗
Mi Jiashan 米家山
min 民
Mingxing 明星
Minjing gushi 民警故事
Minxin 民新
minying 民營
Minzhu nüshen 民主女神
minzu 民族
minzu fengge 民族風格
minzuhua 民族化
minzu xingshi 民族形式
minzu tedian 民族特點
minzu zhuyi 民族主義
minzu zijiu 民族自救
Modeng baobiao 摩登保鏢
Mo Yan (b. 1957) 莫言

Nanbei xi xiangfeng 南北喜相逢
Nanbei yijia qin 南北一家親
nanguo 南國
Nanguo zimei hua 南國姊妹花
Nanjing da tusha 南京大屠殺
Nanxiong nandi 難兄難弟
Nanyang 南洋
Nanzheng beizhan 南征北戰
nanzong 南宗
Nashan naren nagou 那山那人那狗
Nei Menggu 內蒙古
Niandai 年代
Nie Er (1912–35) 聶爾
Nihongdeng xiade shaobing 霓虹燈下的哨兵
Niluohe de nüer 尼羅河的女兒
Ning Ying 寧瀛

Niupeng　牛棚

Ni Zhen (b. 1938)　倪震

Ni zhenshi! You jiao ren teng! You
re ren ai! Suoyi na Xiao Luo lian
fan dou buxiang chi na!　你真是!
又叫人疼! 又惹人愛!
所以那小羅連飯都不想吃那!

nongcai hua　濃彩畫

Nongnu　農奴

Nongye jiaoyu dianying gongsi
　農業教育電影公司

Nüer lou　女兒樓

Nüren de gushi　女人的故事

Nüren de tiankong　女人的天空

Nüren hua　女人花

nüxing dianying　女性電影

Ouyang Hongying　歐陽紅纓

Pan Hong (b. 1954)　潘虹

Pan Jinlian zhi qianshi jinsheng
　潘金蓮之前世今生

Pan Wenjie (Poon Man-kit)
　潘文杰

Paoda shuangdeng　炮打雙燈

Peng Xiaolian (b. 1953)　彭小蓮

pingshi　平視

Pingyuan youji dui　平原遊擊隊

pingmin yishi　貧民意識

pizi　痞子

Pudong　浦東

qi　氣

Qiancheng wanli　前程萬里

Qiangshen　槍神

Qian Jiang (B. 1919)　錢江

qing　情

Qingchang ru zhanchang
　情場如戰場

Qingcheng zhi lian　傾城之戀

Qingchun ji　青春祭

Qingchun wuhui　青春無悔

Qingchun zhi ge　青春之歌

Qingmei zhuma　青梅竹馬

Qingnian　青年

Qingniao　青鳥

Qingshaonian Nezha　青少年哪吒

Qinsong　秦頌

Qiong Yao (b. 1938)　瓊瑤

Qishier jia fangke　七十二家房客

Qiu Ju da guansi　秋菊打官司

Qiutian de tonghua　秋天的童話

Qiuyue　秋月

Qi Xingjia　齊興家

qiye jia　企業家

Qunian yanhua tebie duo
　去年煙花特別多

Qu Yuan (339–278 B.C.)　屈原

Redai yu　熱帶魚

ren　人

Ren qui qing　人鬼情

Ren Fengtai (1850–1932)　任豐泰

Ren Xudong (b. 1925)　任旭東

Ren zai Niuyue　人在紐約

renzhong　人種

Ruan Hao　阮浩

Ruan Lingyu (1910–35)　阮玲玉

ruanxing dianying　軟性電影

Saishang fengyun　塞上風雲

San'ge modeng nüxing
　三個摩登女性

San'ge nüren de gushi
　三個女人的故事

Sang Hu (b. 1916)　桑弧

sangzhong　喪鐘

San Mao (1943–?)　三毛

San Mao conjun ji　三毛從軍記

Sanyi　三一

Sato Tadao　佐籐忠男

Senxin　森信

Shaanxi　陝西

Sha Meng (1907–64)　沙蒙

Shanggan ling　上甘嶺

Shanghai　上海

Shanghai ershisi xiaoshi
　上海二十四小時

Shanghai jiaqi　上海假期

Shanghai zhi ye　上海之夜

Shangrao jizhong ying
　上饒集中營

Shanjian lingxiang mabang lai
　山間鈴響馬幫來

Shanxi　山西

Shanzhong chuanqi　山中傳奇

Shao Mujun (b. 1928)　紹牧君

Shaonian fan　少年犯

Shaoshi　邵氏

shaoshu minzu　少數民族

shaoshu minzu dianying
　少數民族電影

shemian shi　赦免式

Shen Congwen (1902–88)　沈從文

Shen Danping (b. 1960)　沈丹萍

Shen Fu (1905–94)　沈浮

Shenggang qibing　省港旗兵

Shengming ruge　生命如歌

shengui　神鬼

Shennü　神女

shensi　神思

Shen Xiling (1904–40)　沈西苓

Shen Yaoting　沈耀庭

Shen Yue　沈悅

Shiba chun　十八春

Shidai de ernü　時代的兒女

Shi Dongshan (1902–55)　史東山

Shi Hui (1915–57)　石揮

Shijia　事佳

shijie dianying　世界電影

Shi Runjiu (b. 1969)　施潤玖

Shi Shujun (b. 1939)　史蜀君

Shi Wenzhi　史文幟

Shizi wang　獅子王

Shuangcheng gushi　雙城故事

Shui Hua (1916–95)　水華

shuimo　水墨

Siqin Gaowa (b. 1950)　斯琴高娃

Sishui liunian　似水流年

Situ Huimin (1919–87)　司徒慧敏

Song Chong　宋崇

Song Cunshou (b. 1930)　宋存壽

Songjia san jiemei　宋家三姐妹

Song Qiang　宋強

Su Li (b. 1919)　蘇里

Sun Yu (1900–90)　孫瑜

Sun Zhou (b. 1954)　孫周

suona　嗩吶

Su Tong (b. 1963)　蘇童

Suzhou he　蘇州河

Taibei fade zaoban che
　台北發的早班車

Tailian　台聯

Taitai wansui　太太萬歲

Taitannike hao　泰坦尼克號

Taiyang de weidao　太陽的味道

Taiyang yu　太陽雨

Taiying xuan　泰影軒

Tamen zheng nianqing
　他們正年輕

Tangchen　湯臣

Tang Danian　唐大年

Tang Guoqiang (b. 1952)　唐國強

Tang Jili (Stanley Tong)　唐季禮

Tangshan daxiong　唐山大兄

Tang Shuxuan (b. 1941)　唐書璇

tangtang de Zhongguo ren
　堂堂的中國人

Tang Xiaodan (b. 1910)　湯曉丹

Tang Yingqi (b. 1917)　唐英琦

Tanqing shuoai　談情說愛

Tan Xinpei (1847–1917)　譚鑫培

Tao Dechen (Jim Tao, b. 1952)
　陶德辰

Taoli jie　桃李劫

Tao Qin (To Chun, 1915–69)
　陶秦

Taoxue weilong　逃學威龍

Tao Zeru (b. 1953)　陶澤如

Teng Wenji (b. 1944)　滕文驥

Tian Fang (1911–74)　田方

Tian Han (1898–1968)　田漢

Tianjin　天津

Tian mimi　甜蜜蜜

Tianshan　天山

Tiantang chunmeng　天堂春夢

Tian Xi　田曦

Tianyu　天浴

Tianyunshan chuanqi　天雲山傳奇

Tian Zhuangzhuang (b. 1952)
　田壯壯

Tianzi matou　天字碼頭

Tiedao youji dui　鐵道遊擊隊

Tingjin Dabieshan　挺進大別山

Tingyuan shenshen　庭院深深

Tongdang　童黨

Tongnian wangshi　童年往事

Tongnian zai Ruijin　童年在瑞金

Toufa luanle　頭髮亂了

Tou shaoya　偷燒鴨

Tuishou　推手

Tuoluopucaifu (Toroptsev)
　托洛普采夫

Wanbaolu　萬寶路

Wan Chaochen (1906–92)　萬超塵

Wanchun qingshi　晚春情事

Wan Dihuan　萬滌寰

Wang Bin (1912–60)　王濱

Wang Binglin (1926–70)　王秉林

Wang Cilong (1907–41)　王次龍

Wang Haowei (b. 1940)　王好爲

Wang Hui　汪暉

Wangjiao kamen　旺角卡門

Wang Jiawei (Wong Kar-Wai, b.
　1958)　王家衛

Wang Jiayi (1919–88)　王家乙

Wang Jin (b. 1941)　王進

Wang Jinduo　王金鐸

Wang Jing (Wong Jing, b. 1956)
　王晶

Wang Junzheng (b. 1945)　王君正

Wangluo shidai de aiqing
　網絡時代的愛情

Wangming tianya　亡命天涯

Wang Ping (1916–90)　王蘋

Wang Quanan (b. 1965)　王全安

Wang Rui (b. 1962)　王瑞

Wang Shuo (b. 1958)　王朔

Wang Tong (Wang Tung, b. 1942)
　王童

Wan Guchan (1900–1995)
　萬古蟾

Wang Weiyi (b. 1912)　王爲一

Wang Xianchi　王獻箎

Wang xiansheng zhi yuhuo fenshen
　王先生之欲火焚身

Wang Xiaodi (Wang Shau-di)
　王小棣

Wang Xiaoshuai (b. 1966)　王小帥

Wang Yan (b. 1923)　王炎

Wang Yin (1900–88)　王引

Wang Ying (Wayne Wang, b. 1949)　王穎

Wang Yuanhua　王元化

Wang Zuxian (Joey Wong, b. 1967)　王祖賢

Wan Jen (Wan Ren, b. 1950)　萬仁

Wanjia denghuo　萬家燈火

Wanke　萬科

Wan Laiming (b. 1900)　萬籟鳴

Wannianqing　萬年青

Wanxiang　萬象

Wanzhong　晚鐘

Wanzhu　頑主

Wei Lian (b. 1945)　韋廉

Wei Linyu　韋林玉

Weilou chunxiao　危樓春曉

Weiwuer　維吾爾

Wengshi　翁氏

Wenhua　文華

Wenhui dianying shibao　文匯電影時報

wenqing zhuyi　溫情主義

Wenyi bao　文藝報

Wo ai "Huazi"　我愛"花子"

Wo ai taikong ren　我愛太空人

Wode fuqin muqin　我的父親母親

Wo shi ni baba　我是你爸爸

Wo shi shui　我是誰

Woxue woqing　我血我情

Wo zheyang guole yisheng　我這樣過了一生

wu　無

Wu Chufan (Ng Cho-fan, 1911–93)　吳楚帆

Wu Di　鄔迪

Wuduo jinhua　五朵金花

Wu Feijian (Wu Fei-chien)　吳飛劍

wufu zhi zi　無父之子

Wuge nüzi he yigen shengzi　五個女子和一根繩子

wuge yi gongcheng　五個一工程

Wu Jianhai　吳健海

Wu Kui　五魁

Wu Nianzhen (Wu Nien-chen, b. 1952)　吳念真

Wuren hecai　無人喝采

Wuren jiashi　無人駕駛

Wushan yunyu　巫山雲雨

Wutai jiemei　舞台姐妹

Wu Tiange　吳天戈

Wu Tianming (b. 1939)　吳天明

Wu Wenguang (b. 1956)　吳文光

wuxia　武俠

Wu Xun zhuan　武訓傳

Wuyan de shanqiu　無言的山丘

Wuya yu maque　烏鴉與麻雀

Wu Yigong (b. 1938)　吳貽弓

Wu Yin (1909–91)　吳茵

Wuyi tanzhang Lei Luo　五億探長雷洛

Wu Yonggang (1907–82)　吳永剛

Wu Yusen (John Woo, b. 1946)　吳宇森

Wu Zhaodi (1920–92)　武兆堤

Wu Ziniu (b. 1952)　吳子牛

Xia Gang (b. 1953)　夏鋼

Xi'an　西安

xiandai　現代

Xianggang zhizao　香港制造

Xianghun nü　香魂女

Xiangnü Xiaoxiao　湘女瀟瀟

xiangtu　鄉土

xiangtu wenxue　鄉土文學

Xiangyin　鄉音

Xi'an shibian　西安事變

Xianü　俠女
Xiao baba de tiankong
　小爸爸的天空
Xiao Bi de gushi　小畢的故事
Xiaobing Zhang Ga　小兵張嘎
Xiaocheng zhi chun　小城之春
Xiao ernü　小兒女
Xiao Fangfang (b. 1947)　蕭芳芳
Xiao Guiyun (b. 1941)　蕭桂雲
Xiaojie　小街
Xiao tianshi　小天使
Xiaoqian　小倩
Xiao wanyi　小玩藝
Xiao Wu　小武
Xiaoxiang　瀟湘
Xia Yan (1900–95)　夏衍
Xie Fei (b. 1942)　謝飛
Xiehe　協和
Xie Jin (b. 1923)　謝晉
Xie Tieli (b. 1925)　謝鐵驪
Xie Yuan (b. 1959)　謝園
Xilu Xiang　細路祥
Ximending　西門町
Ximeng rensheng　戲夢人生
Xi Mi (Michelle Yeh)　悉密
Xinchao　新潮
Xin buliao qing　新不了情
Xindong　心動
Xin Kunlun　新昆侖
Xin nanxiong nandi　新難兄難弟
Xin nüxing　新女性
xinsheng dai　新生代
Xinshenghuo yundong
　新生活運動
xinshiqi　新時期
xintiyan　新體驗
Xintu　新土
Xinwen ju　新聞局

Xinxiang　心香
Xinyicheng　新藝城
xin zhuangtai　新狀態
Xixiang ji　西廂記
Xiyan　喜宴
Xiyang jing　西洋鏡
xiyang yingxi　西洋影戲
Xi yingmen　喜盈門
Xizao　洗澡
Xu Anhuan (Ann Hui, b. 1947)
　許鞍華
Xuanlian　懸戀
Xu Ben　徐賁
Xu Da　徐達
Xu Dishan (1893–1941)　許地山
Xuefu　學甫
Xuese qingchen　血色清晨
Xuezhan Taierzhuang
　血戰台兒莊
Xuezhe　學者
Xu Feng (b. 1950)　徐楓
Xu Guanwen (Michael Hui, b.
　1942)　許冠文
Xu Ke (Tsui Hark, b. 1951)　徐克
xungen　尋根
Xu Qingdong　徐慶東
xushi　虛實
Xu Xiaoming (Hsu Hsiao-ming, b.
　1955)　徐小明
Xu Xinfu (1897–1965)　徐欣夫
Xu Xingzhi (1904–91)　許幸之

Yamaha yudang　雅馬哈魚檔
yang　陽
Yang Dechang (Edward Yang,
　b. 1947)　楊德昌
Yangguang canlan de rizi
　陽光燦爛的日子

Yang Guangyuan (b. 1942)
楊光遠

Yangniu zai Beijing　洋妞在北京

Yang Likun (b. 1942)　楊麗坤

Yan Gong (b. 1914)　嚴恭

Yang Xiaozhong (1899–1969)
楊小仲

Yang Yanjin (b. 1945)　楊延晉

Yang Zaibao (b. 1935)　楊在葆

Yang Ziqiong (Michelle Yeoh, b.
1962)　楊紫瓊

Yan Hao (Yim Ho, b. 1952)　嚴浩

Yanmo de qingchun　湮沒的青春

Yanshen　驗身

Yan Xueshu　顏學恕

Yanzhi kou　胭脂扣

Yao a yao, yao dao waipo qiao
搖阿搖, 搖到外婆橋

Yaogun qingnian　搖滾青年

Yapian zhanzheng　鴉片戰爭

Yaqi　啞妻

Yaxiya　亞細亞

Yecao xianhua　野草閑花

Ye Daying (Ye Ying)
葉大鷹(葉纓)

Ye Hongwei (Heh Hong-wei, b.
1963)　葉鴻偉

Ye Ming (b. 1919)　葉明

Yeshan　野山

Ye Weilin　葉蔚林

Yexing ren　夜行人

Yi　彝

Yiban shi huoyan, yiban shi haishui
一半是火燄, 一半是海水

Yige dou buneng shao
一個都不能少

Yige he bage　一個和八個

Yijiang chunshui xiangdong liu
一江春水向東流

Yima (Imar)　藝瑪

yin　陰

Yinchuang weixian　硬闖危險

Yindu　銀都

Yi'neng　藝能

yingxi　影戲

Yingxiong bense　英雄本色

Yingxiong ernü　英雄兒女

Ying Yunwei (1904–67)　應雲衛

Yinzhi jie　影之杰

Yin Li (b. 1957)　尹力

Yinshi nannü　飲食男女

Yinyang jie　陰陽界

Yiyi　一一

Yi Zhyiyan (Yee Chihyan)
易智言

Yongsheng　永盛

you　遊

Youchai　郵差

Youhua haohao shuo　有話好好說

Youji jinxing qu　游擊進行曲

Youma caizi　油麻菜籽

Youseng　誘僧

youxi　遊戲

youxi guize　遊戲規則

Yu　玉

Yuanli zhanzheng de niandai
遠離戰爭的年代

Yuan Kui (Corey Yuen)　元奎

Yuan Muzhi (1908–78)　袁牧之

Yuanye　原野

Yuanzi　原子

Yue Feng (b. 1910)　岳楓

Yueshi　月蝕

Yu Hua (b. 1960)　余華

Yu Kan-ping (b. 1950)　虞戡平

Yu kuaile yu duoluo
愈快樂愈墮落

Yu Lan (b. 1921)　于蘭

Yu meiren　虞美人
Yu Min (b. 1914)　于敏
Yuni tongzhu　與你同住
Yunnan gushi　雲南故事
Yu wangshi ganbei
　與往事干杯
Yu Yanfu (b. 1924)　于彥夫

Zaijian Zhongguo　再見中國
Zai Junjie　翟俊杰
Zang　藏
Zaochun eryue　早春二月
Zaoyu jiqing　遭遇激情
Zedong　澤東
Zeng Zhuangxiang (Tseng
　Chuang-hsiang, b. 1947)
　曾壯祥
zhandao　斬刀
Zhang Aijia (Sylvia Chang, b. 1953)
　張艾嘉
Zhang Ailing (Eileen Chang, 1920–
　96)　張愛玲
Zhang Che (b. 1923)　張徹
Zhangda chengren　長大成人
Zhang Guorong (Leslie Cheung, b.
　1956)　張國榮
Zhang Jianya (b. 1951)　張建亞
Zhang Junxiang (b. 1910)　張駿祥
Zhang Junzhao (b. 1952)　張軍釗
Zhang Ke (1915–89)　張客
Zhang Liang (b. 1933)　張良
Zhang Ming (b. 1961)　章明
Zhang Manyu (Maggie Cheung, b.
　1964)　張曼玉
Zhang mi　張迷
Zhang Nuanxin (1940–95)
　張暖忻
Zhang Qian　張前
Zhang Shankun (1905–57)
　張善琨

Zhang Shichuan (1889–1953)
　張石川
Zhang Wanting (Mabel Cheung, b.
　1950)　張婉婷
Zhang Yang (b. 1967)　張揚
Zhang Yi (Chang Yi, b. 1951)
　張毅
Zhang Yimou (b. 1950)　張藝謀
Zhang Yiwu　張頤武
Zhang Yu (b. 1957)　張瑜
Zhang Yuan (b. 1963)　張元
Zhang Zeming (b. 1951)　張澤鳴
Zhang Zuoji (Chang Tso-chi)
　張作驥
Zhan Shanghai　戰上海
Zhanzheng ziwu xian
　戰爭子午線
Zhanzhi luo, bie paxia
　站直囉，別趴下
Zhao Dan (1915–80)　趙丹
Zhao Huanzhang (b. 1930)
　趙煥章
Zhao Jilie　趙繼烈
Zhaole　找樂
Zhao Ming (b. 1915)　趙明
Zhao Shusen (Chiu Shu-sen, b.
　1904)　趙樹燊
Zhao xiansheng　趙先生
Zhao Xinshui (1930–89)　趙心水
Zhao Yiheng (Henry Zhao)
　趙毅衡
Zhao Yiman　趙一曼
Zheng Dongtian (b. 1944)　鄭洞天
Zhenghun qishi　徵婚啓示
Zhengjiu dabing Leien
　拯救大兵雷恩
Zheng Junli (1911–69)　鄭君里
Zhengqi ge　正氣歌
Zheng Zhengqiu (1888–1935)
　鄭正秋

Zhenjia yingxiong　真假英雄

Zhenjie paifang　貞節牌坊

Zhennü　貞女

zhenqing　真情

zhenshi gan　真實感

Zhi　紙

Zhifen shichang　脂粉市場

zhiqing　知青

Zhiqu Huashan　智取華山

Zhiyao weini huo yitian
　只要爲你活一天

Zhong Dafeng　鍾大豐

Zhong Dianfei (1919–87)　鍾惦棐

Zhonghua ernü　中華兒女

Zhongguo　中國

Zhongguo dianying chubanshe
　中國電影出版社

Zhongguo dianying hezuo zhipian
　gongsi　中國電影合作制片公司

Zhongguo dianyingjia xiehui
　中國電影家協會

Zhongguo dianying jituan
　中國電影集團

Zhongguo dianying nianjian she
　中國電影年鑒社

Zhongguo dianying yishu yanjiu
　zhongxin
　中國電影藝術研究中心

Zhongguo dianying zhipianchang
　中國電影制片廠

Zhongguo dianying ziliaoguan
　中國電影資料館

Zhongguo lianhe yingye gongsi
　中國聯合影業公司

Zhongguo ren jintian shuo bu
　中國人今天說不

Zhongguo ren keyi shuo bu
　中國人可以說不

Zhongguo yinmu　中國銀幕

Zhongji biaoba　終極標靶

Zhonglian　中聯

Zhongyang dianshi tai
　中央電視台

Zhongyang dianying qiye gongsi
　中央電影企業公司

Zhongyang dianying shiye gongsi
　中央電影事業公司

zhongyuan wenhua　中原文化

zhongzu　種族

Zhou Enlai　周恩來

Zhoumo qingren　周末情人

Zhou Runfa (Chow Yun-Fat, b.
　1955)　周潤發

Zhou Xiaowen (b. 1954)　周曉文

Zhou Xingchi (Stephen Chow,
　Stephen Chiau)　周星馳

Zhuang　壯

Zhuang dao zheng　撞到正

Zhuangzi shiqi　莊子試妻

Zhufu　祝福

Zhujiang　珠江

zhuliu dianying　主流電影

Zhu Tianwen (Chu Tien-wen, b.
　1956)　朱天文

zhuxuanlü　主旋律

Zijincheng　紫禁城

Zili　自立

Zimei hua　姊妹花

zishunü　自梳女

ziwo mingming　自我命名

Ziyou nüshen　自由女神

Zongheng　縱橫

zouxiang shijie　走向世界

zouyi dianying　左翼電影

zu　族

Zuihou de fengkuang
　最後的瘋狂

Zuiquan　醉拳

Filmography

All films and television dramas cited in the book are listed below in chronological order by year of release. For Chinese films, the English title is followed by the Chinese title in pinyin, the director, the location, and the studio. Films are also listed in English in the index. Banned films are listed together at the end.

1905
Conquering Jun Mountain (Ding Junshan). Beijing: Fengtai Photography Shop.

1909
Stealing a Roast Duck (Tou shaoya). Leung Siu-bo (Liang Shaopo). Hong Kong: Asia (Yaxiya).

1913
Zhuangzi Tests His Wife (Zhuangzi shiqi). Li Beihai. Hong Kong: Huamei.

1920
Way Down East. D. W. Griffith. U.S.: D. W. Griffith Productions.

1922
Laborer's Love (Laogong zhi aiqing), aka *Cheng the Fruit Seller* (Zhiguo yuan). Zhang Shichuan. Shanghai: Mingxing.

1923
The Ten Commandments. Cecil B. DeMille. U.S.: Famous Players-Lasky.

1924
The Thief of Bagdad. Raoul Walsh. U.S.: United Artists / Douglas Fairbanks Pictures.

1925
Battleship Potemkin. Sergei Eisenstein. Russia: First Studio of Goskino.

1927

Romance of the Western Chamber (Xixiang ji), aka *Way Down West, La Rose de Pu-shui, The Rose of Pushui.* Hou Yao. Shanghai: Minxin.

1929

Welcome Danger. Clyde Bruckman. U.S.: Harold Lloyd Corp.

1930

Wild Flower (Yecao xianhua). Sun Yu. Shanghai: Lianhua.

1933

The Bitter Tea of General Yen. Frank Capra. U.S.: Columbia.
Children of Our Time (Shidai de ernü). Li Pingqian. Shanghai: Mingxing.
King Kong. Merian Cooper and Ernest Schoedsack. U.S.: RKO Pictures.
Little Toys (Xiao wanyi). Sun Yu. Shanghai: Lianhua.
The Market of Beauty (Zhifen shichang). Zhang Shichuan. Shanghai: Mingxing.
Spring Silkworms (Chuncan). Cheng Bugao. Shanghai: Mingxing.
Three Modern Women (San' ge modeng nüxing). Bu Wancang. Shanghai: Lianhua.
Twenty-Four Hours in Shanghai (Shanghai ershisi xiaoshi). Shen Xiling. Shanghai: Mingxing.
Twin Sisters (Zimei hua). Zheng Zhengqiu. Shanghai: Mingxing.
Wild Torrents (Kuangliu). Cheng Bugao. Shanghai: Mingxing.

1934

Big Road (Dalu). Sun Yu. Shanghai: Lianhua.
Brothers (Nanxiong nandi). Chiu Shu-sen (Zhao Shusen). Hong Kong: Overseas Lianhua.
Goddess (Shengnü). Wu Yonggang. Shanghai: Lianhua.
New Woman (Xin nüxing). Cai Chusheng. Shanghai: Lianhua.
Plunder of Peach and Plum (Taoli jie). Yuan Muzhi. Shanghai: Diantong.

1935

Children of a Troubled Time (Fengyun ernü). Xu Xingzhi. Shanghai: Diantong.
Cityscape (Dushi fengguan). Yuan Muzhi. Shanghai: Diantong.
The Little Angel (Xiao tianshi). Wu Yonggang. Shanghai: Lianhua.
Top Hat. Mark Sandrich. U.S.: RKO Radio.

1937

The Good Earth. Sidney Franklin. U.S.: MGM.
The New Land (Xintu). Arnold Frank. Germany / Japan.
Street Angel (Malu tianshi). Yuan Muzhi. Shanghai: Mingxing.

1938

Defending Our Land (Baowei women de tudi). Shi Dongshan. Wuhan: China (Zhongguo dianying zhipianchang).
Eight Hundred Heroic Soldiers (Babai zhuangshi). Ying Yunwei. Wuhan: China.

The March of the Guerrillas (Youji jixing qu). Situ Huimin. Released as *Song of Retribution* (Zhengqi ge) in 1941. Hong Kong: Xinchao.

1940

Storm on the Border (Saishang fengyun). Ying Yunwei. Chongqing: China.

Ten Thousand Li Ahead (Qiancheng wanli). Cai Chusheng. Hong Kong: Xinsheng.

Two Southern Sisters (Nanguo jiemei hua). Lai Ban (Li Bin) and Leong Sum (Liang Chen). Hong Kong: Wu Tip Ying Production.

1941

Family (Jia). Bu Wancang, Xu Xinfu, Yang Xiaozhong, Li Pingqian, Wang Cilong, Fang Peilin, Yue Feng, and Wu Yonggang. Shanghai: Zhongguo lianhe yingye gongsi.

1944

Dragon Seed. Jack Conway and Harold S. Bucquet. U.S.: MGM.

Thirty Seconds Over Tokyo. Marvyn LeRoy. U.S.: MGM.

1947

Dream in Paradise (Tiantang chunmeng). Tang Xiaodan. Shanghai: Central (Zhongyang dianying qiye gongsi) Studio 2.

Eight Thousand Li of Clouds and Moon (Baqianli lu yun he yue). Shi Dongshan. Shanghai: Kunlun.

Lingering Passion (Buliao qing). Sang Hu. Shanghai: Wenhua.

Long Live the Mistress! (Taitai wansui). Sang Hu. Shanghai: Wenhua.

Spring River Flows East (Yijiang chushui xiangdong liu). Cai Chusheng and Zheng Junli. Shanghai: Kunlun.

1948

Myriad of Lights (Wanjia denghuo). Shen Fu. Shanghai: Kunlun.

Spring in a Small Town (Xiaocheng zhi chun). Fei Mu. Shanghai: Wenhua.

1949

Crows and Sparrows (Wuya yu maque). Zheng Junli. Shanghai: Kunlun.

Daughters of China (Zhonghua ernü). Ling Zifeng. Changchun: Northeast (Dongbei).

Sorrows and Joys of a Middle-Aged Man (Aile zhongnian). Sang Hu. Shanghai: Wenhua.

Wind and Cloud on Ali Mountain (Alishan fengyun). Zhang Che. Taipei: Taiwan Agricultural Education (Nongye jiaoyu dianying gongsi).

1950

The Life of Wu Xun (Wu Xun zhuan). Sun Yu. Shanghai: Kunlun.

Liu Hulan (Liu Hulan). Feng Balu. Changchun: Northeast.

The White-Haired Girl (Baimao nü). Wang Bin and Shui Hua. Changchun: Northeast.

Zhao Yiman (Zhao Yiman). Sha Meng. Changchun: Northeast.

1951

Commander Guan (Guan Lianzhang). Shui Hua. Shanghai: Wenhua.

Shangrao Concentration Camp (Shangrao jizhong ying). Sha Meng and Zhang Ke. Shanghai: Shanghai.

1952

From Victory to Victory (Nanzheng beizhan). Cheng Yin and Tang Xiaodan. Shanghai: Shanghai.

1953

Capture Mount Hua by Stratagem (Zhiqu Huashan). Guo Wei. Beijing: Beijing.

Family (Jia). Hong Kong.

In the Face of Demolition (Wulou chunxiao). Lee Tit (Li Tie). Hong Kong: Union (Zhonglian).

1954

Horseback Merchants Arrive in the Frontier Mountains (Shanjian lingxiang mabang lai). Wang Weiyi. Shanghai: Shanghai.

Letter with Feather (Jimao xin). Shi Hui. Shanghai: Shanghai.

Liang Shanbo and Zhu Yingtai (Liang Shanbo yu Zhu Yingtai). Sang Hu and Huang Sha. Shanghai: Shanghai.

Scouting Across the Yangtze River (Dujiang zhencha ji). Tang Xiaodan. Shanghai: Shanghai.

1955

Dong Cunrui (Dong Cunrui). Guo Wei. Changchun: Changchun.

Guerrillas on the Plain (Pingyuan youji dui). Su Li and Wu Zhaodi. Changchun: Changchun.

Love Is a Many-Splendored Thing. Henry King. U.S.: Twentieth Century Fox.

1956

Family (Jia). Chen Xihe and Ye Ming. Shanghai: Shanghai.

New Year's Sacrifice (Zhufu). Sang Hu. Beijing: Beijing.

Railroad Guerrillas (Tiedao youji dui). Zhao Ming. Shanghai: Shanghai.

Shanggan Ridges (Shangganling). Sha Meng and Lin Shan. Changchun: Changchun.

1957

City Without Night (Buye cheng). Tang Xiaodan. Shanghai: Jiangnan.

1958

The Inn of the Sixth Happiness. Mark Robson. U.S.: Twentieth Century Fox.

Five Martyrs of Wolf-Teeth Mountain (Langyashan wu zhuangshi). Shi Wenzhi. Beijing: August First (Bayi).

Red Children (Hong haizi). Su Li. Changchun: Changchun.

1959

Five Golden Flowers (Wuduo jinhua). Wang Jiayi. Changchun: Changchun.
Nie Er (Nie Er). Zheng Junli. Shanghai: Haiyan.
The Shanghai Battle (Zhan Shanghai). Wang Bing. Beijing: August First.
Song of Youth (Qingchun zhi ge). Cui Wei and Chen Huaiai. Beijing: Beijing.

1960

Third Sister Liu (Liu sanjie). Su Li. Changchun: Changchun.
The World of Suzie Wong. Richard Quine. London: Paramount British Pictures.

1961

Love Without End (Buliao qing). To Chun (Tao Qin). Hong Kong: Shaw Brothers
    (Shaoshi).
The Red Detachment of Women (Hongse niangzijun). Xie Jin. Shanghai: Tianma.

1962

Land Mine Warfare (Dilei zhan). Tang Yingqi, Xu Da, and Wu Jianhai. Beijing: August
    First.
Li Shuangshuang (Li Shuangshuang). Lu Ren. Shanghai: Haiyan.
Naval Battle of 1894 (Jiawu fengyun). Lin Nong. Changchun: Changchun.

1963

Early Spring in February (Zaochun eryue). Xie Tieli. Beijing: Beijing.
Our Neighbors (Jietou xiangwei). Lee Hsing (Li Xing). Taipei: Zili.
Satisfied or Not? (Manyi bu manyi). Yan Gong. Changchun: Changchun.
Serfs (Nongnu). Li Jun. Beijing: August First.
Visitor on Ice Mountain (Bingshan shangde laike). Zhao Xinshui. Changchun: Changchun.
Zhang Ga, a Boy Soldier (Xiaobing Zhang Ga). Cui Wei and Ouyang Hongying. Beijing:
    Beijing.

1964

Early Train from Taipei (Taibei fade zaobanche). Liang Che-fu (Liang Zhefu). Taipei:
    Tailian.
Heroic Sons and Daughters (Yingxiong ernü). Wu Zhaodi. Changchun: Changchun.
Sentinels Under the Neon Lights (Nihongdeng xiade shaobing). Wang Ping and Ge Xin.
    Shanghai: Tianma.

1965

Red Crag (Liehuo zhong yongsheng). Shui Hua. Beijing: Beijing.
The Silent Wife (Yaqi). Lee Hsing. Taipei.
Stage Sisters (Wutai jiemei). Xie Jin. Shanghai: Tianma.
Tunnel Warfare (Didao zhan). Ren Xudong. Beijing: August First.

1966

The Arch of Virtues (Zhenjie paifang). Lee Hsing. Taipei: CMPC.

The Sand Pebbles. Robert Wise. U.S.: Twentieth Century Fox.
Whose Belongings? (Hualuo shuijia). Wang Yin. Taipei.

1967

Dragon Gate Inn (Longmen kezhan). King Hu. Taiwan: Union (Lianban).
One-Armed Swordsman (Dubi dao). Zhang Che. Hong Kong: Shaw Brothers.

1969

Kang-Ting' s Tour of Taipei (Kang Ding you Taibei). Wu Fei-chien (Wu Feijian). Taipei:
Wanxiang.

1970

The Arch (Dong furen). Tang Shuxuan. Hong Kong: Film Dynasty (Dianying chaodai).
Deserted Courtyard (Tingyuan shenshen). Song Cunshou. Hong Kong: Fengming.
Home, Sweet Home (Jia zai Taibei). Bai Jingrui. Taipei: CMPC.
Red Detachment of Women (Hongse niangzijun). Opera movie. Cheng Yin. Beijing: August
First.
A Touch of Zen (Xianü). King Hu. Taiwan: Union.
Vengeance (Baochou). Zhang Che. Hong Kong: Shaw Brothers.

1971

Fists of Fury, aka *The Big Boss* (Tangshan daxiong). Lo Wei (Luo Wei). Hong Kong:
Golden Harvest (Jiahe).

1972

The Chinese Connection (Jingwu men). Lo Wei. Hong Kong: Golden Harvest.
The White-Haired Girl (Baimao nü). Ballet movie. Sang Hu. Shanghai: Shanghai.

1973

Outside the Window (Chuanwai). Song Cunshou. Taipei: Eighties (Baishi niandai).
The House of Seventy-Two Tenants (Qishier jia fangke). Chor Yuen (Chu Yuan). Hong
Kong: Shaw Brothers.

1974

Azalea Mountain (Dujuan shan). Opera movie. Beijing: Beijing.
China Behind (Zaijian Zhongguo). Tang Shuxuan. Hong Kong: Film Dynasty.
From Victory to Victory (Nanzheng beizhan). Cheng Yin and Wang Yan. Beijing: Beijing.
Guerrillas on the Plain (Pingyuan youji dui). Wu Zhaodi and Chang Zhenhua. Changchun:
Changchun.
The Pioneers (Chuangye). Yu Yanfu. Changchun: Changchun.
Scouting Across the Yangtze River (Dujiang zhencha ji). Tang Huada and Tang Xiaodan.
Shanghai: Shanghai.

1975

Breaking with Old Ideas (Juelie). Li Wenhua. Beijing: Beijing.

Hai Xia (Haixia). Qian Jiang, Chen Huaiai, and Wang Haowei. Bejing: Beijing.
Hong Yu (Hong yu). Cui Wei. Beijing: Beijing.

1976
Jumping Ash (Tiaohui). Leong Po-chi (Liang Puzhi) and Josephine Siao (Xiao Fangfang).
Hong Kong: Bang Bang.

1977
Annie Hall. Woody Allen. U.S.: United Artists.

1979
Anxious to Return (Guixin sijian). Li Jun. Beijing: August First.
Ji Hongchang (Ji Hongchang). Li Guanghui and Qi Xingjia. Changchun: Changchun.
Legend of the Mountain (Shanzhong chuanqi). King Hu. Taiwan: King Hu Productions.

1980
The Legend of Tianyun Mountain (Tianyunshan chuanqi). Xie Jin. Shanghai: Shanghai.
The Spooky Bunch (Zhuang dao zheng). Ann Hui (Xu Anhua). Hong Kong: High Pitch.

1981
The In-Laws (Xi yingmen). Zhao Huanzhang. Shanghai: Shanghai.
Narrow Street (Xiaojie). Yang Yanjin. Shanghai: Shanghai.
Savage Land (Yuanye). Ling Zi. Beijing: Nanhai.
Security Unlimited (Modeng baobiao). Michael Hui. Hong Kong: Golden Harvest.
Xi'an Incident (Xi'an shibian). Cheng Yin. Xi'an: Xi'an.

1982
The Herdsman (Muma ren). Xie Jin. Shanghai: Shanghai.
In Our Time (Guangyin de gushi). Four parts. Jim Tao (Tao Dechen), Edward Yang
(Yang Dechang), Ko Yi-cheng (Ke Yizheng), and Chang Yi (Zhang Yi). Taipei:
CMPC.

1983
Ah Ying (Banbian ren). Allen Fong (Fang Yuping). Hong Kong: Sil-Metropole (Yindu).
Burning of the Imperial Palace (Huoshao Yuanmingyuan). Li Hanxiang. Beijing: China Joint
Production (Zhongguo dianying hezuo zhipian gongsi) / Hong Kong: Xin kunlun.
Country Couple (Xiangyin). Hu Bingliu. Guangzhou: Pearl River (Zhujiang).
Growing Up (Xiao Bi de gushi). Chen Kun-hou. Taipei: CMPC.
Papa, Can You Hear Me Sing? (Da cuoche). Yu Kan-ping. Taipei: Cinema City (Xin
yicheng).
Rapeseed Woman (Youma caizi). Wan Jen (Wan Ren). Taipei: Wanbaolu / Ming Yi.
Reign Behind a Curtain (Chuilian tingzheng). Li Hanxiang. Beijing: China Joint
Production / Hong Kong: Xin kunlun.
That Day on the Beach (Haitan de yitian). Edward Yang. Taipei: CMPC.

Sandwich Man (Erzi de da wan'ou). Three parts. Hou Hsiao-hsien (Hou Xiaoxian), Tseng Chuang-hsiang (Zeng Zhuangxiang), and Wan Jen (Wan Ren). Taipei: Sanyi Entertainment.

1984

Border Town (Biancheng). Ling Zifeng. Beijing: Beijing.
Garlands at the Foot of the Mountain (Gaoshan xiade huahuan). Xie Jin. Shanghai: Shanghai.
Homecoming (Sishui liunian). Yim Ho (Yan Hao). Hong Kong: Blue Bird (Qingniao).
Hong Kong 1941 (Dengdai liming). Leong Po-chi. Hong Kong: D&B (Debao).
Little Daddy's Sky (Xiao baba de tiankong). Chen Kun-hou. Taipei: Sanyi Entertainment.
Long Arm of the Law (Shenggang qibing). Johnny Mak (Mai Dangxiong). Hong Kong: Johnny Mak Workshop / Bo Ho.
Love in a Fallen City (Qingcheng zhi ian). Ann Hui. Hong Kong: Shaw Brothers.
One and Eight (Yige he bage). Zhang Junzhao. Nanning: Guangxi.
Project A (A jihua). Jackie Chan (Cheng Long). Hong Kong: Golden Harvest.
Secret Decree (Diexue heigu). Wu Ziniu. Changsha: Xiaoxiang.
Shanghai Blues (Shanghai zhi ye). Tsui Hark (Xu Ke). Hong Kong: Cinema City.
Yamaha Fish Stall (Yamaha yudang). Zhang Liang. Guangzhou: Pearl River.
Yellow Earth (Huang tudi). Chen Kaige. Nanning: Guangxi.

1985

Army Nurse (Nüer lou). Hu Mei. Beijing: August First.
Back to the Future. Robert Zemeckis. U.S.: Universal.
Black Cannon Incident (Heipao shijian). Huang Jianxin. Xi'an: Xi'an.
A Girl from Hunan (Xiangnü Xiaoxiao). Xie Fei. Beijing: Youth (Qingnian).
A Good Woman (Liangjia funü). Huang Jianzhong. Beijing: Beijing.
Juvenile Delinquents (Shaonian fan). Zhang Liang. Shenzhen: Shenzhen.
Kuei-mei, a Woman (Wo zheyang guole yisheng). Chang Yi. Taipei: CMPC.
On the Hunting Ground (Liechang zhasa). Tian Zhuangzhuang. Hohhot: Inner Mongolia (Nei Menggu).
Sacrificed Youth (Qingchun ji). Zhang Nuanxin. Beijing: Youth.
Super Citizens (Chaoji shimin). Wan Jen. Taipei: Wanbaolu.
Swan Song (Juexiang). Zhang Zeming. Guangzhou: Pearl River.
Taipei Story (Qingmei zhuma). Edward Yang. Taipei: Wannianqing.
A Time to Live and a Time to Die (Tongnian wangshi). Hou Hsiao-hsien. Taipei: CMPC.

1986

The Battle of Taierzhuang (Xuezhan Taierzhuang). Yang Guangyuan and Zai Junjie. Nanning: Guangxi.
A Better Tomorrow (Yingxiong bense). John Woo (Wu Yusen). Hong Kong: Cinema City.
The Big Parade (Da yuebing). Chen Kaige. Nanning: Guangxi.
Crocodile Dundee. Peter Faiman. Australia: Rimfire / U.S.: Paramount.
Dislocation (Cuowei). Huang Jianxin. Xi'an: Xi'an.
Hibiscus Town (Furong zhen). Xie Jin. Shanghai: Shanghai.
Horse Thief (Daoma zei). Tian Zhuangzhuang. Xi'an: Xi'an.

Terrorizer (Kongbu fenzi). Edward Yang. Taipei: CMPC.

1987

An Autumn' s Tale (Qiutian de tonghua). Mabel Cheung (Zhang Wanting). Hong Kong: D&B.

A Better Tomorrow, II (Yingxiong bense). John Woo. Hong Kong: Cinema City.

Daughter of the Nile (Niluo he de nüer). Hou Hsiao-hsien. Taipei: Scholar (Xuezhe).

Desperation (Zuihou de fengkuang). Zhou Xiaowen. Xi'an: Xi'an.

Drum Singers (Gushu yiren). Tian Zhuangzhuang. Beijing: Beijing.

Dust in the Wind (Lianlian fengchen). Hou Hsiao-hsien. Taipei: CMPC.

Far From the War (Yuanli zhangzhen de niandai). Hu Mei. Beijing: August First.

In the Wild Mountains (Yeshan). Yan Xueshu. Xi'an: Xi'an.

King of the Children (Haizi wang). Chen Kaige. Xi'an: Xi'an.

The Last Emperor. Bernardo Bertolucci. U.S.: Columbia / Hemdale.

Old Well (Laojing). Wu Tianming. Xi'an: Xi'an.

Osmanthus Alley (Guihua xiang). Chen Kun-hou. Hong Kong: Golden Harvest / Taipei: CMPC / Scholar.

Peking Opera Blues (Daoma dan). Tsui Hark. Hong Kong: Cinema City.

Put Some Sugar in the Coffee (Gei kafei jiadian tang). Sun Zhou. Guangzhou: Pearl River.

Red Sorghum (Hong gaoliang). Zhang Yimou. Xi'an: Xi'an.

Rouge (Yanzhi kou). Stanley Kwan (Guan Jinpeng). Hong Kong: Golden Harvest.

Two Virtuous Women (Zhennü). Huang Jianzhong. Beijing: Beijing.

Women' s Story (Nüren de gushi). Peng Xiaolian. Shanghai: Shanghai.

Sunshine and Showers (Taiyang yu). Zhang Zeming. Guangzhou: Pearl River.

Woman, Demon, Human (Ren gui qing). Huang Shuqin. Shanghai: Shanghai.

1988

As Tears Go By (Wangjiao kamen). Wong Kar-Wai (Wang Jiawei). Hong Kong: In-Gear (Yingzhijie).

Between Life and Death (Yinyang jie). Wu Ziniu. Fuzhou: Fujian.

Evening Bell (Wanzhong). Wu Ziniu. Beijing: August First.

Gangs (Tongdang). Lawrence Ah Mon (Liu Guochang). Hong Kong: Sil-Metropole.

Gorillas in the Mist. Michael Apted. U.S.: Guber / Peters.

Joyous Heroes (Huanle yingxiong). Wu Ziniu. Fuzhou: Fujian.

New Chinese Cinema. Television documentary. Tony Rayns. London: Channel 4 Production.

The Other Half and the Other Half (Wo ai taikong ren). Clara Law (Luo Zhuoyao). Hong Kong: Alan and Eric Productions.

The Price of Frenzy, aka *Obsession* (Fengkuang de daijia). Zhou Xiaowen. Xi'an: Xi'an.

Rock 'n' Roll Kids (Yaogun qingnian). Tian Zhuangzhuang. Beijing: Youth.

The Troubleshooters (Wanzhu). Mi Jiashan. Chengdu: Emei.

Widow Village (Guafu cun). Wang Jin. Guangzhou: Pearl River / Hong Kong: Sil-Metropole.

A Woman for Two (Chuntao). Ling Zifeng. Beijing: Nanhai / Shenyang: Liaoning.

1989

Back to the Future, II. Robert Zemeckis. U.S.: Universal.

Ballad of the Yellow River (Huanghe yao). Teng Wenji. Xi'an: Xi'an.

The Birth of New China (Kaiguo dadian). Li Qiankuan and Xiao Guiyun. Changchun: Changchun.

Black Snow (Benming nian). Xie Fei. Beijing: Youth.

China, My Sorrow (Niupeng). Dai Sijie. France: Titane Production / Flach Film.

City of Sadness (Beiqing chengshi). Hou Hsiao-hsien. Taipei: ERA (Niandai).

Deserted Courtyard (Tingyuan shenshen). Shi Shujun. Shanghai: Shanghai.

Full Moon in New York (San' ge nüren de gushi, aka Ren zai Niuyue). Stanley Kwan. Hong Kong: Shoibu (Xuefu).

Half Flame, Half Brine (Yiban shi huoyan, yiban shi haishui). Xia Gang. Beijing: Beijing.

Ju Dou (Ju Dou). Zhang Yimou. Japan: Tokuma Shoten Publishing Co.

The Killer (Diexue shuangxiong). John Woo. Hong Kong: Cinema City.

Out of Breath (Da chuanqi). Ye Daying. Shenzhen: Shenzhen.

Passion in Late Spring (Wanchun qingshi). Chen Yaoxin. Taipei: CMPC / Hong Kong: Golden Harvest.

The Reincarnation of Golden Lotus (Pan Jinlian zhi qianshi jinsheng). Clara Law. Hong Kong: Teopoly (Taiyang xuan).

Transmigration, aka *Samsara* (Lunhui). Huang Jianxin. Xi'an: Xi'an.

1990

All for the Winner (Dusheng). Correy Yuen (Yuan Kui) and Jeff Lau (Liu Zhenwei). Hong Kong: Golden Harvest.

Back to the Future, III. Robert Zemeckis. U.S.: Universal.

The Big Mill (Da mofang). Wu Ziniu. Changhsha: Xiaoxiang / Hong Kong: Sil-Metropole.

The Black Mountain Road (Heishan lu). Zhou Xiaowen. Xi'an: Xi'an.

Bloody Morning (Xuese qingchen). Li Shaohong. Beijing: Beijing.

Childhood in Ruijin (Tongnian zai Ruijin). Huang Jun. Nanchang: Jiangxi.

Farewell, China (Aizai biexiang de jijie). Clara Law. Hong Kong: Golden Harvest.

Good Morning, Beijing! (Beijing nizao). Zhang Nuanxin. Beijing: Youth.

Home Alone. Chris Columbus. U.S.: Twentieth Century Fox.

The Medium of War (Zhanzhen ziwu xian). Feng Xiaoning. Beijing: Youth.

Red Dust (Gungun hongchen). Yim Ho. Hong Kong: Tomson (Tangchen) / Beijing: China Joint Production / Changchun: Changchun.

Song of the Exile (Ketu qiuhen). Ann Hui. Hong Kong: Gaoshi / Taipei: CMPC.

Two Sign-Painters (Liangge youqi jiang). Yu Kan-ping. Taipei: Long Shong (Longxiang).

1991

Alan and Eric: Between Hello and Goodbye (Shuangcheng gushi). Peter Chan (Chen Kexin). Hong Kong: Golden Harvest.

A Brighter Summer Day (Gulingjie shaonian sharen shijian). Edward Yang. Taipei: CMPC / Edward Yang.

Days of Being Wild (A Fei zhengzhuan). Wong Kar-Wai. Hong Kong: In-Gear.

The Decisive Engagements, I: The Liaoning-Shenyang Campaign (Da juezhan: Liao-Shen zhanyi). Li Jun, Yang Guangyuan, et al. Beijing: August First.

The Decisive Engagements, II: The Huaihai Campaign (Da juezhan: Huaihai zhanyi). Li Jun, Cai Jiwei, et al. Beijing: August First.

Fight Back to School (Taoxue weilong). Gordon Chan (Chen Jiashang). Hong Kong: Win's (Yongsheng).

Five Girls and a Rope (Wuge nüzi he yigen shengzi). Yeh Hong-wei (Ye Hongwei). Taipei: Tomson.

A Lady Left Behind (Liushou nüshi). Hu Xueyang. Shanghai: Shanghai.

Lee Rock (Wuyi tanzhang Lei Luo). Lawrence Ah Mon. Hong Kong: Win's.

Li Lianying, the Imperial Eunuch (Da taijian Li Lianying). Tian Zhuangzhuang. Beijing: Beijing / Hong Kong: Skai (Shijia).

Life on a String (Bianzou bianchang). Chen Kaige. Germany: Serenity Productions.

Mama (Mama). Zhang Yuan. Xi'an: Xi'an.

My American Grandson (Shanghai jiaqi). Ann Hui. Shanghai: Shanghai / Taipei: Golden Tripot (Jinding).

No Regrets (Qingchun wuhui). Zhou Xiaowen. Xi'an: Xi'an.

Pushing Hands (Tuishou). Ang Lee (Li An). Taipei: CMPC.

Raise the Red Lantern (Dahong denglong gaogao gua). Zhang Yimou. Hong Kong: ERA.

Ripples Across Stagnant Water (Kuang). Ling Zifeng. Hong Kong: Skai / Chengdu: Emei.

Shanghai 1920 (Shanghai jiaofu). Leong Po-chi. Hong Kong: Fu Gnai (Fuyi).

To Be Number One (Bohao). Poon Man-kit (Pan Wenjie). Hong Kong: Golden Harvest.

Unexpected Passion (Zaoyu jiqing). Xia Gang. Beijing: Beijing.

The Wedding Maidens (Chujia nü). Wang Jin. Guangzhou: Pearl River / Hong Kong: Sil-Metropole.

1992

After Separation (Da saba). Xia Gang. Beijing: Beijing.

Autumn Moon (Qiuyue). Clara Law. Hong Kong / Japan: Trix (Gongtongti).

Centre Stage, aka *The Actress* (Ruan Lingyu). Stanley Kwan. Hong Kong: Golden Harvest / Golden Way.

The Decisive Engagements, III: The Beiping-Tianjin Campaign (Da juezhan: Ping-Jin zhanyi). Li Jun, Wei Lian, et al. Beijing: August First.

For Fun (Zhaole). Ning Ying. Beijing: Beijing / Hong Kong: Vanke (Wanke).

Hard Boiled (Qiangshen). John Woo. Hong Kong: Golden Princess.

The Hills of No Return (Wuyan de shanqiu). Wang Tung (Wang Tong). Taipei: CMPC / Jiacheng.

Home Alone, II. Chris Columbus. U.S.: Twentieth Century Fox.

92 Legendary La Rose Noire (92 hei meigui dui hei meigui). Chen Shanzhi. Hong Kong: Yintao.

Rebel of the Neon God (Qingshaonian Nezha). Tsai Ming-liang (Cai Mingliang). Taipei: CMPC.

Reservoir Dogs. Quentin Tarantino. U.S.: Live Entertainment.

Royal Tramp, I-II (Luding ji). Wong Jing (Wang Jing). Hong Kong: Win's.

San Mao Joins the Army (San Mao congjun ji). Zhang Jianya. Shanghai: Shanghai.

Stand Up, Don't Bend Over (Zhanzhi luo, bie paxia). Huang Jianxin. Xi'an: Xi'an.

The Story of Qiu Ju (Qiu Ju da guansi). Zhang Yimou. Hong Kong: Sil-Metropole.

Swordsman, II (Dongfang bubai). Ching Siu Tung (Chen Xiaodong). Hong Kong: Cinema City.

The True Hearted (Xinxiang). Sun Zhou. Guangzhou: Pearl River.

The Wedding Banquet (Xiyan). Ang Lee. Taipei: CMPC.

Women from the Lake of Scented Souls (Xianghun nü). Xie Fei. Tianjin: Tianjin / Changchun: Changchun.

1993

Beijing Bastards (Beijing zazhong). Zhang Yuan. Beijing.

Beijing Sojourners in New York (Beijing ren zai Niuyue). Television serial. Feng Xiaogang and Zheng Xiaolong. Beijing: CCTV.

The Blue Kite (Lan fengzheng). Tian Zhuangzhuang. Hong Kong: Longwick / Beijing: Beijing.

A Borrowed Life (Duosan). Wu Nien-chen (Wu Nianzhen). Taipei: Long Shong.

C' est la vie, mon chéri (Xin buliao qing). Derek Yee (Er Dongsheng). Hong Kong: Film United.

The Days (Dong Chun de rizi). Wang Xiaoshuai. Beijing: Yinxiang.

Farewell My Concubine (Bawang bieji). Chen Kaige. Hong Kong: Tomson.

The Fugitive. Andrew Davis. U.S.: Warner Brothers.

Groundhog Day. Harold Ramis. U.S.: Columbia.

Hard Target (Zhongji biaoba). John Woo. Hong Kong: Cinema City / U.S.: Universal.

He Ain't Heavy, He's My Father (Xin nanxiong nandi). Peter Chan and Lee Chi-gnai (Li Zhiyi). Hong Kong: United Filmmakers Organization.

The Joy Luck Club. Wayne Wang. U.S.: Buena Vista / Hollywood.

M. Butterfly. David Cronenberg. U.S.: Miranda Productions / Feffen Pictures.

Look Who Is Talking Now. Tom Ropelewski. U.S.: Tri Star.

Mr. Wang: Flames of Desire (Wang xiansheng zhi yuhuo fenshen). Zhang Jianya. Shanghai: Shanghai.

No One Cheers (Wuren hecai). Xia Gang. Beijing: Beijing.

The Peach Blossom Land (Anlian taohua yuan). Stan Lai (Lai Shengchuan). Taipei: CMPC.

The Prostitute and the Raftsmen (Beilie paibang). Huang Jun. Nanchang: Jiangxi / Changchun: Changchun.

The Puppet Master (Ximeng rensheng). Hou Hsiao-hsien. Taipei: ERA.

Red Beads (Xuanlian). He Jianjun (He Yi). Beijing.

Romance of the Stock Exchange (Gushi hunlian). Song Chong. Ürumüqi: Tianshan / Nanchang: Nanchang Institute of Film & Television.

Shanghai Fever (Gufeng). Li Guoli. Changsha: Xiaoxiang / Hong Kong: Yi'neng.

Sparkling Fox (Huohu). Wu Ziniu. Hong Kong: Senxin.

The Story of Xinghua, aka *Apricot Blossom* (Xinghua sanyue tian). Yin Li. Beijing: Youth.

Swordsman III: The East Is Red (Fengyun zaiji). Ching Siu Tung. Hong Kong: Cinema City.

The Temptation of a Monk (Youseng). Clara Law. Hong Kong: Teopoly.

The Woodenman' s Bride (Yanshen), aka *The Porter* (Wu Kui). Huang Jianxin. Xi'an: Xi'an / Taipei: Long Shong.

A Yunnan Story (Yunnan gushi). Zhang Nuanxin. Beijing: Beijing / Taipei: Golden
   Tripot / Zhongsheng.
1994
Ashes of Time (Dongxie xidu). Wong Kar-Wai. Hong Kong: Jet Tone (Zedong) / Beijing:
   Beijing.
Back to Back, Face to Face (Bei kao bei, lian dui lian). Huang Jianxin. Xi'an: Xi'an / Hong
   Kong: Senxin.
Blush (Hongfen). Li Shaohong. Hong Kong: Ocean (Dayang) / Beijing: Beijing.
Chungking Express (Chongqing senlin). Wong Kar-Wai. Hong Kong: Jet Tone.
Crossings (Cuoai). Evans Chan (Chen Yaocheng). Hong Kong: Riverdrive Productions.
Dirt (Toufa luanle). Guan Hu. Hohhot: Inner Mongolia.
The Drowned Youth (Yanmo de qingchun). Hu Xueyang. Shanghai: Shanghai.
Drunken Master, II (Zuiquan). Law Kar-leung (Liu Jialiang). Beijing: China Joint
   Production / Hong Kong: Martial Arts Production.
Eat Drink Man Woman (Yinshi nannü). Ang Lee. Taipei: CMPC.
Ermo (Ermo). Zhou Xiaowen. Shanghai: Shanghai / Hong Kong: Ocean.
Erotique. 4-part film. Lizzie Borden, Clara Law, Ana Maria Magalhaes, Monika Treut.
   U.S.: Group 1 Films.
Family Scandal (Jiachou). Liu Miaomiao. Beijing: Youth / Xining: Ningxia.
Forrest Gump. Robert Zemeckis. U.S.: Paramount.
He's a Woman, She's a Man (Jinzhi yuye). Peter Chan. Hong Kong: Golden Harvest.
Lion King. Roger Allers and Rob Minkoff. U.S.: Disney.
Living with You (Yuni tongzhu). Huang Jun. Fuzhou: Fujian.
Pulp Fiction. Quentin Tarantino. U.S.: Jersey Films / Miramax.
Red Firecracker, Green Firecracker (Paoda shuangdeng). He Ping. Hong Kong: Wengshi.
The Red Lotus Society (Feixia A Da). Stan Lai. Taipei: Long Shong.
Red Rose, White Rose (Hong meigui, bai meigui). Stanley Kwan. Ürümqi: Tianshan /
   Taipei: Taiwan First (Diyi).
Rumble in the Bronx (Hongfan qu). Stanley Tong (Tang Jili). Hong Kong: Golden Harvest.
Suicide (Da youxi). Wang Xiaoshuai. Beijing.
To Live (Huozhe). Zhang Yimou. Shanghai: Shanghai / Taipei: ERA.
Women Flowers (Nüren hua). Wang Jin. Guangzhou: Pearl River.
"Wonton Soup." Clara Law. See *Erotique*.

1995
Accidental Legend (Feitian). Wang Shau-di (Wang Xiaodi). Taipei: Daotian.
Babe. Chris Noonan. Australia: Kennedy Miller Productions / U.S.: Universal.
A Confucian Confusion (Duli shidai). Edward Yang. Taipei: Atom (Yuanzi).
Enchanted by Her Long Braid (Da bianzi de youhuo). Cai Yuanyuan. Macau: Cai Brothers /
   Guangzhou: Pearl River.
Daddy's Lover (A ba de qingren). Wang Xianchi. Taipei: Nengneng.
Falling in Love (Tanqing shuai). Li Xin. Shanghai: Shanghai.
The Gate of Heavenly Peace. Carma Hinton and Richard Gordon. U.S.: Long Bow Group.
Good Men, Good Women (Haonan haonü). Hou Hsiao-hsien. Tokyo: Team Okuyama /
   Taipei: Liandeng.

In the Heat of the Sun (Yangguang canlan de rizi). Jiang Wen. Beijing: China Joint Production / Hong Kong: Ganglong / Taipei: Xiehe.

The King of Masks (Bianlian). Wu Tianming. Beijing: Youth / Hong Kong: Shaw Brothers.

A Mongolian Tale (Hei junma). Xie Fei. Beijing: Youth / Hong Kong: Media Asia (Huanya).

Nanjing Massacre (Nanjing da tusha), aka *Nanjing 1937*. Wu Ziniu. Beijing: China Joint Production / Taipei: Long Shong.

On the Beat (Minjing gushi). Ning Ying. Beijing: Beijing / U.K.: Euro-Asia Exchange Co.

Postman (Youchai). He Jianjun. Beijing: United Frontline.

Rainclouds Over Wushan (Wushan yunyu). Zhang Ming. Beijing: Beijing.

Red Cherry (Hong yingtao). Ye Daying. Beijing: Youth / Moscow: Gorky.

Sense and Sensibility. Ang Lee. U.S.: Columbia.

Shanghai Triad (Yao a yao, yaodao waipo qiao). Zhang Yimou. Hong Kong: Alpha / UGC-Images / La Sept Cinéma / Shanghai: Shanghai.

Signal Left, Turn Right (Hongdeng ting, lüdeng xing). Huang Jianxin. Xi'an: Xi'an.

The Square (Guangchang). Zhang Yuan. Beijing.

The Sun Has Ears (Taiyang you er). Yim Ho. Channgchun: Changchun.

Super Citizen Kuo (Chaoji da guomin). Wan Jen. Taipei: Wan Jen.

Temptress Moon (Fengyue). Chen Kaige. Hong Kong: Tomson.

Toy Story. John Lasserter. U.S.: Disney / Pixar Animation.

Tropical Fish (Redai yu). Chen Yu-hsun (Chen Yuxun). Taipei: Daotian.

Weekend Lovers (Zhoumo qingren). Lou Ye. Fuzhou: Fujian.

Wild Kiss to Russia (Kuangwen Eluosi). Xu Qingdong. Beijing: Beijing.

Yellow Goldfish (Huang jinyu). Wu Di. Hohhot: Inner Mongolia.

Yesterday's Wine (Yu wangshi ganbei). Xia Gang. Hainan: Nanyang / Beijing: Beijing.

1996

Accompany You to the Dawn (Banni dao liming). Xia Gang. Beijing: Beijing.

Broken Arrow (Duanjian xingdong). John Woo. U.S.: Twentieth Century Fox.

Comrades, Almost a Love Story (Tian mimi). Peter Chan. Hong Kong: Golden Harvest.

The Emperor's Shadow (Qinsong). Zhou Xiaowen. Hong Kong: Ocean / Xi'an: Xi'an.

The Decisive Further Advances, I: Liberating the Great Northwest (Da jinjun: jiefang da xibei). Wei Linyu. Beijing: August First.

The Decisive Turning Point, I: Battling in Southeast Shandong (Da zhuanzhe: aozhan Lu xinan). Wei Lian. Beijing: August First.

The Decisive Turning Point, II: Charging to the Dabie Mountains (Da zhuanzhe: tingjin Dabie shan). Wei Lian. Beijing: August First.

Fallen Angels (Duoluo tianshi). Wong Kar-Wai. Hong Kong: Jet Tone.

Fierce Battles: True Records of the Korean War (Jiaoliang: kang Mei yuan Chao zhanzheng shilu). Wang Jinduo. Beijing: August First.

Floating Life (Fusheng). Clara Law. Australia: Hibiscus.

Foreign Babes in Beijing (Yangniu'er zai Beijing). Television serial. Wang Binglin and Li Jianxin. Beijing: Beijing.

Foreign Moon (Yueman yinglun). Zhang Zeming. Hong Kong: Media Asia.

Goodbye, South, Goodbye (Nanguo, zaijian, nanguo). Hou Hsiao-hsien. Tokyo: Team Okuyama / Taipei: Liandeng.

Kong Fansen (Kong Fansen). Chen Guoxing and Wang Ping. Beijing: Beijing / Ji'nan: Shandong.

Liu Hulan (Liu Hulan). Shen Yaoting. Taiyuan: Shanxi.

Mahjong (Majiang). Edward Yang. Taipei: Atom.

Maximun Risk. Ringo Lam (Lin Lingdong). U.S.: Columbia.

Shall We Dance? Masayuki Suo. Japan: Altamira.

Sons (Erzi). Zhang Yuan. Beijing: Beijing Expression Culture Communication Center.

Tonight Nobody Goes Home (Jintian bu huijia). Sylvia Chang (Zhang Aijia). Taipei: Unique.

Who's the Woman, Who's the Man (Jinzhi yuye 2). Peter Chan. Hong Kong: Golden Harvest.

1997

Cello in a Cab (Langman jietou). Guan Hu. Beijing: Beijing.

The Decisive Further Advances, II: Pursuing Down to the South (Da jinjun: nanxian da zhuijian). Zhao Jilie. Beijing: August First.

Double Team. Tsui Hark. U.S.: Columbia.

East Palace, West Palace (Donggong xigong). Zhang Yuan. Hong Kong: Ocean / Amazon Entertainment / France: Quelqu' un d' Autre Productions.

Eighteen Springs (Bansheng yuan, aka Shiba chun). Ann Hui. Hong Kong: Guotai/ Ürumüqi: Tianshan / Shanghai: An' s Visual Communications.

Face/Off. John Woo. U.S.: Paramount / Touchstone.

Flubber. Les Mayfield. U.S.: Disney.

Happy Together (Chunguang zhaxie). Wong Kar-Wai. Hong Kong: Jet Tone.

Ice Storm. Ang Lee. U.S.: Fox Searchlight / Good Machine.

Keep Cool (Youhua haohao shuo). Zhang Yimou. Nanning: Guangxi.

Kundun. Martin Scrosese. U.S.: Disney.

Life Is Beautiful. Roberto Benigni. Italy: Melam Cinematografica.

Life on a Tune (Shengming ruge). Xia Gang. Beijing: Beijing.

Made in Hong Kong (Xianggang zhizao). Fruit Chan (Chen Guo). Hong Kong: Team Work.

The Making of Steel (Zhangda chengren), aka *How Steel Is Forged* (Gangtie shi zheyang liancheng de). Lu Xuechang. Beijing: Beijing / Great Wall Advertising.

No Visit After Divorce (Lihun le, jiu bie zailai zhaowo). Wang Rui. Beijing: Youth.

The Opium War (Yapian zhanzheng). Xie Jin. Chengdu: Emei.

Red River Valley (Honghe gu). Feng Xiaoning. Shanghai: Shanghai.

The River (Heliu). Tsai Ming-liang. Taipei: CMPC.

Seven Years in Tibet. Jaques Aunaud. U.S.: TriStar.

Sleepless Town (Buye cheng). Lee Chi-gnai. Japan: Asmik Ace Entertainment.

The Soong Sisters (Songjia san jiemei). Mabel Cheung. Hong Kong: Golden Harvest.

Titanic. James Cameron. U.S.: Twentieth Century Fox / Paramount.

Tomorrow Never Dies. Roger Spottiswoode. U.S.: United Artists.

Urban Love Affair (Chengshi aiqing). Ah Nian. Beijing: Beijing.

1998

A Bug's Life. John Lasseter and Andrew Stanton. U.S.: Disney / Pixar Animation.

A Chinese Ghost Story: The Tsui Hark Animation (Xiaoqian). Chen Weiwen. Hong Kong: Film Workshop / Polygram K.K. / Win' s / Cathay.

City of Glass (Boli zhicheng). Mabel Cheung. Hong Kong: Golden Harvest.

The Decisive Further Advances, III: Conquering the Great Southwest (Da jinjun: xijuan da xinan). Yang Guangyuan. Beijing: August First.

Dreams Come True (Jiafang yifang). Feng Xiaogang. Beijing: Beijing / Forbidden City (Zijincheng).

The Emperor and the Assassin (Jingke ci Qinwang). Chen Kaige. Beijing: Beijing / Japan: New Waves.

Flowers of Shanghai (Haishang hua). Hou Hsiao-hsien. Taipei: 3 H / Shochiku.

The Gingerbread Man. Robert Altman. U.S.: Island Pictures.

Gun with Love (Woxue woqing). Li Xin. Shanghai: Shanghai.

Heroes Real and Fake (Zhenjia yingxiong xiongdi qing). Mao Xiaorui. Shanghai: Shanghai.

Hold You Tight (Yu kuaile yu duoluo). Stanley Kwan. Hong Kong: Golden Harvest.

The Hole (Dong). Tsai Ming-liang. Taipei: CMPC / Arc Light / France: Haut et Court.

I Love Huazi (Wo ai "Huazi"). Short Feature. Li Hong. Shanghai: Shanghai.

Jade (Yu). Short Feature. Tang Danian. Shanghai: Shanghai.

The Longest Summer (Qunian yanhua tebie duo). Fruit Chan. Hong Kong: Team Work / Nicetop Independent.

Mona Lisa (Mengnalisha). Short Feature. Hua Zhongkai. Shanghai: Shanghai.

Mr. Zhao (Zhao xiansheng). Lü Yue. Hong Kong: Nam Kwong Development.

Pickpocket (Xiao Wu). Jia Zhangke. Hong Kong: Hu Tong Communications.

Pier Heaven (Tianzi matou). Zhang Qian and Ma Weijun. Guangzhou: Pearl River.

Pirated Pulp Fiction (Daoban diji xiaoshuo). Short Feature. Ruan Hao. Shanghai: Shanghai.

Postmen in the Mountains (Nashan naren nagou). Huo Jianqi. Changsha: Xiaoxiang / Beijing: Beijing.

Replacement Killer. Antoine Fuqua. U.S.: Columbia.

The Rushing City (Benpao de chengshi). Short Feature. Lou Ye. Shanghai: Shanghai.

Saving Private Ryan. Steven Spielberg. U.S.: Dream Works.

So Close to Paradise (Biandan, guniang). Wang Xiaoshuai. Beijing: Beijing / Jindie Film & TV.

Soaring High with You (Banni gaofei). Li Hong. Shanghai: Shanghai.

Spicy Love Soup (Aiqing malatang). Zhang Yang. Xi'an: Xi'an / Xi'an: Imar (Yima).

The Taste of the Sun (Taiyang de weidao). Shen Yue. Changsha: Xiaoxiang.

A Time to Remember (Hongse lianren). Ye Daying. Beijing / Forbidden City.

Walking at Night (Yexing ren). Short Feature. Guan Hu. Shanghai: Shanghai.

Who Am I? (Wo shi shui). Jackie Chan. Hong Kong: Golden Harvest.

1999

Anna and the King. Andy Tennant. U.S.: Fox 2000.

Be There or Be Square (Bujian busan). Feng Xiaogang. Beijing: Beijing / Forbidden City.

A Beautiful New World (Meili xin shijie). Shi Runjiu. Xi'an: Xi'an / Xi'an: Imar.

Call Me (Huwo). Ah Nian. Beijing: Beijing.

Crazy English (Fengkuang Yingyu). Documentary. Zhang Yuan. Beijing: Keetman Limited.

The Decisive Further Advances, IV: Battles of Nanjing, Shanghai, and Hangzhou (Da jinjun: dazhan Ning, Hu, Hang). Wei Lian. Beijing: August First.

Grief Over the Yellow River (Huanghe juelian). Feng Xiaoning. Shanghai: Yongle Corp.

Ice and Fire (Bing yu huo). Hu Xueyang. Shanghai: Shanghai.

A Lingering Face (Feichang xiari), aka *In Broad Daylight* (Guangtian huari). Lu Xuechang. Beijing: Beijing.

Little Chueng (Xilu Xiang). Fruit Chan. Hong Kong: Nicetop Independent.

Love in the Internet Generation (Wangluo shidai de aiqing). Jin Chen. Xi'an: Xi'an.

The Love Letter. Peter Chan. U.S.: Dream Works.

Lunar Eclipse (Yueshi). Wang Quanan. Beijing: Beijing.

The National Anthem (Guoge). Wu Ziniu. Changsha: Xiaoxiang.

Not One Less (Yige dou buneng shao). Zhang Yimou. Nanning: Guangxi / Beijing: Xinhuamian yingshi.

The Personals (Zhenghun qishi). Chen Guofu. Taipei: CMPC / Zoom Hunt (Zongheng) International.

The Road Home (Wode fuqin muqin). Zhang Yimou. Nanning: Guangxi / Columbia Asia

Seventeen Years (Guonian huijia). Zhang Yuan. Italy: Fondazione Mondecinemaverita / Fabrica / Keetman Limited.

Shower (Xizao). Zhang Yang. Xi'an: Xi'an / Xi'an: Imar.

Sky Leopards (Chongtian feibao). Wang Rui. Beijing: Youth.

Soldier (Bing). Tian Xi. Xi'an: Xi'an.

Suburban Dream (Menghuan tianyuan). Wang Xiaoshuai. Beijing: Beijing.

Tempting Heart (Xindong). Sylvia Chang. Hong Kong: Media Asia.

Women's Sky (Nüren de tiankong). Wu Tiange. Shanghai: Shanghai.

Xiu Xiu: The Sent Down Girl (Tianyu). Joan Chen (Chen Chong). U.S.: Good Machine.

2000

Autumn in New York. Joan Chen. U.S.: United Artists.

A One and a Two (Yiyi). Edward Yang. Taipei: Atom Films / Japan: Pony Canyon.

Platform (Zhantai). Jia Zhangke. France: Artcam / Japan: Bandai Entertainment / Hong Kong: Hu Tong Communications.

Paper (Zhi). Ding Jiancheng. Beijing: Youth.

Shadow Magic (Xiyang jing). Ann Hu (Hu An). U.S.: C&A Productions, Schulberg / Berlin: Road Movies / Beijing: Beijing / Taipei: CMPC.

Sorry, Baby (Meiwan meiliao). Feng Xiaogang. Beijing: Forbidden City.

Spacked Out (Wuren jiashi). Lawrence Ah Mon. Hong Kong: Milkyway Image.

The Suzhou River (Suzhou he). Lou Ye. Beijing: China Joint Production / Germany: Essential Filmproduktion.

★

Banned films (followed by the year made)

An Awkward Life, aka *A Life under Pressure* (Guozhe langbei bukan de shenghuo). Feng
   Xiaogang. Beijing: Haomeng, unfinished.
The Dove Tree (Gezi shu). Wu Ziniu. Changsha: Xiaoxiang, 1985.
In Their Prime (Tamen zheng nianqing). Zhou Xiaowen. Xi'an: Xi'an, 1986.
Papa (Wo shi ni baba). Feng Xiaogang and Wang Shuo. Beijing: Haomeng, 1996.
Rice (Mi). Huang Jianzhong. Beijing: Beijing, 1996.

Bibliography

Chinese characters for recurring periodical titles are listed below and will not be repeated in individual citations.

Dangdai dianying 當代電影 (Contemporary cinema)
Dianying yishu 電影藝術 (Film art)
Ershiyi shiji 二十一世紀 (Twenty-first century)
Jintian 今天 (Today)
Wenxue pinglun 文學評論 (Literary review)

Abbas, Ackbar. 1997a. *Hong Kong: Culture and the Politics of Disappearance.* Minneapolis: University of Minnesota Press.

———. 1997b. "Hong Kong: Other Histories, Other Politics." *Public Culture* 9.3 (Spring): 293–313.

Adams, Hazard, ed. 1971. *Critical Theory Since Plato.* New York: Harcourt Brace Jovanovich.

Ahmad, Aijaz. 1987. "Jameson's Rhetoric of Otherness and the National Allegory." *Social Texts* 17 (Fall): 3–25.

Allen, Tom. 1981. "China Film Week." *Film Comment* 17.6: 10.

Althusser, Louis. 1971. *Lenin and Philosophy and Other Essays.* Translated by Ben Brewster. New York: Monthly Review.

Amin, Samir. 1989. *Eurocentrism.* Translated by Russell Moore. New York: Monthly Review.

An Jingfu. 1994. "The Pain of a Half Taoist: Taoist Principles, Chinese Landscape Painting, and *King of the Children.*" In *Cinematic Landscapes: Observations on the Visual Arts and Cinema of China and Japan,* edited by Linda Erlich and David Desser. Austin: University of Texas Press.

Anderson, Benedict. 1991. *Imaged Communities: Reflections on the Origin and Spread of Nationalism.* Revised edition. London: Verso.

Andrew, Dudley. 1995. *Mists of Regret: Culture and Sensibility in Classical French Film.* Princeton: Princeton University Press.

———. 1998. "Film and History." In *The Oxford Guide to Film Studies,* edited by John Hill and Pamela Church Gibson. New York: Oxford University Press.

Ang Ien. 1994. "On Not Speaking Chinese: Postmodern Ethnicity and the Politics of Diaspora." *New Formations* 24 (Winter): 1–18.

———. 1998. "Can One Say No to Chineseness? Pushing the Limits of the Diasporic Paradigm." *Boundary 2* 25.3 (Fall): 223–42.

Appadurai, Arjun. 1996. *Modernity at Large: Cultural Dimensions of Globalization.* Minneapolis: University of Minnesota Press.

Arac, Jonathan. 1997. "Postmodernism and Postmodernity in China: An Agenda for Inquiry." *New Literary History* 28.1 (Winter): 135–45.

Armes, Roy. 1987. *Third World Film Making and the West.* Berkeley: University of California Press.

Ashcroft, Bill, Gareth Griffiths, and Helen Tiffin, eds. 1989. *The Empire Writes Back: Theory and Practice in Post-Colonial Literature.* London: Routledge.

Asian Women United of California, ed. 1989. *Making Waves: An Anthology of Writing by and about Asian American Women.* Boston: Beacon.

Asiaweek, ed. 1994. "Box-Office Boom: Asian Films and Themes Light Up the World's Movie Screens." *Asiaweek* (Feb. 16): 27.

Aufderheide, Pat. 1987. "Oriental Insurgents." *Film Comment* 23.6: 73–6.

Baker, Rick, and Toby Russell. 1994. *The Essential Guide to Hong Kong Movies.* London: Eastern Heroes Publications.

Bakhtin, Mikhail. 1981. *The Dialogic Imagination: Four Essays.* Edited by Michael Holquist. Translated by Caryl Emerson and Michael Holquist. Austin: University of Texas Press.

———. 1984. *Rabelais and His World.* Translated by Hélène Iswolsky. Bloomington: Indiana University Press.

Bamyeh, Mohammed A. 1993. "Trend Report: Transnationalism." *Current Sociology* 41.3 (Winter): 1–96.

Barlow, Tani, ed. 1993. *Gender Politics in Modern China: Writing and Feminism.* Durham, N.C.: Duke University Press.

Barmé, Geremie R. 1999. *In the Red: On Contemporary Chinese Culture.* New York: Columbia University Press.

Barthes, Roland. 1972. *Mythologies.* Translated by Annette Lavers. New York: Hill and Wang.

———. 1982. *A Barthes Reader.* Edited by Susan Sontag. London: Jonathan Cape.

———. 1987. *Criticism and Truth.* Translated by K. P. Kuneman. London: Athlone.

Baudrillard, Jean. 1988. *Selected Writings.* Edited by Mark Poster. Translated by Jacques Mourrain. Stanford, Calif.: Stanford University Press.

Befu, Harumi, ed. 1993. *Cultural Nationalism in East Asia: Representation and Identity.* Berkeley: University of California, Institute of East Asian Studies.

Beijing daxue 北京大學, Beijing shifan daxue 北京師範大學, and Beijing shifan xueyuan 北京師範學院, eds. 1979. *Wenxue yundong shiliao xuan* 文學運動史料選 (Selected readings in literary movements). Multiple vols. Shanghai: Shanghai jiaoyu chubanshe.

Beijing Scene. 1999. "Men in Towels." *Beijing Scene* 6.4 (Nov. 5–11): 1–3. [http://www.beijingscene.com/V06i004/feature/feature.html]

Benjamin, Walter. 1969. *Illuminations: Essays and Reflections.* Edited by Hannah Arendt. Translated by Harry Zohn. New York: Schocken.

Bergeron, Régis. 1977. *Le cinéma chinois, 1905–1949* (Chinese cinema, 1905–1949). Lausanne: Alfred Eibel.

———. 1984. *Le cinéma chinois, 1949–1983* (Chinese cinema, 1949–1983). 3 vols. Paris: L'Harmattan.

————. 1996–97. "The Making of a Passion: 40 Years of Living with the World of Chinese Films." *Asian Cinema* 8.2 (Winter): 116–25.

Bernardi, Daniel, ed. 1996. *The Birth of Whiteness: Race and the Emergence of U.S. Cinema.* Brunswick, N.J.: Rutgers University Press.

Bernstein, Matthew, and Gaylyn Studlar, eds. 1997. *Visions of the East: Orientalism in Film.* New Brunswick, N.J.: Rutgers University Press.

Berry, Chris. 1988a. "Chinese Urban Cinema: Hyper-realism Versus Absurdism." *East-West Film Journal* 3.1: 76–87.

————. 1988b. "Chinese 'Women's Cinema.'" *Camera Obscura* 18: 5–41.

————. 1988c. "The Sublimative Text: Sex and Revolution in *Big Road*." *East-West Film Journal* 2.2: 66–86.

————. 1989. "Poisonous Weeds or National Treasures: Chinese Left Films in the 1930s." *Jump Cut* 34 (March): 87–94.

————. 1991a. "Market Forces: China's 'Fifth Generation' Faces the Bottom Line." In *Perspectives on Chinese Cinema*, second and expanded edition, edited by Chris Berry. London: British Film Institute.

————, ed. 1991b. *Perspectives on Chinese Cinema.* Second and expanded edition. London: British Film Institute.

————. 1991c. "Sexual Difference and the Viewing Subject in *Li Shuangshuang* and *The In-laws*." In *Perspectives on Chinese Cinema*, second and expanded edition, edited by Chris Berry. London: British Film Institute.

————. 1992. "Race (*minzu* 民族): Chinese Film and the Politics of Nationalism." *Cinema Journal* 31.2 (Winter): 45–58.

————. 1993. "Interview with Peng Xiaolian." *Modern Chinese Literature* 7.2 (Fall): 103–8.

————. 1994a. "A Nation T(w/o)o: Chinese Cinema(s) and Nationhood(s)." In *Colonialism and Nationalism in Asian Cinema*, edited by Wimal Dissanayake. Bloomington: Indiana University Press.

————. 1994b. "Neither One Thing Nor Another: Toward a Study of the Viewing Subject and Chinese Cinema in the 1980s." In *New Chinese Cinemas: Forms, Identities, Politics*, edited by Nick Browne, Paul G. Pickowicz, Vivian Sobchack, and Esther Yau. New York: Cambridge University Press.

————. 1995a. "Tsai Ming-liang: Look at All the Lonely People." *Cinemaya* 30 (Autumn): 18–20.

————. 1995b. "A Turn for the Better?—Genre and Gender in *Girl from Hunan* and Other Recent Mainland Chinese Films." *Post Script* 14: 81–103.

————. 1996a. "Outrageous Fortune: China's Film Industry Takes a Roller-Coaster Ride." *Cinemaya* 33 (Summer): 17–9.

————. 1996b. "Sexual DisOrientations: Homosexual Rights, East Asian Films, and Postmodern Postnationalism." In *In Pursuit of Contemporary East Asian Culture*, edited by Xiaobing Tang and Stephen Snyder. Boulder: Westview.

————. 1996c. "Zhang Yuan: Thriving in the Face of Adversity." *Cinemaya* 32 (Spring): 40–4.

————. 1998a. "If China Can Say No, Can China Make Movies? Or, Do Movies Make China? Rethinking National Cinema and National Agency." *Boundary 2* 25.3 (Fall): 129–50.

————. 1998b. "Staging Gay Life in China: *East Palace, West Palace.*" *Jump Cut* 42: 84–9.

Berry, Chris, ed. 1985. *Perspectives on Chinese Cinema.* East Asian Papers 39. Ithaca, N.Y.: Cornell University, China-Japan Program.

Berry, Chris, and Mary Ann Farquhar. 1994. "Post-Socialist Strategies: An Analysis of *Yellow Earth* and *Black Cannon Incident.*" In *Cinematic Landscapes: Observations on the Visual Arts and Cinema of China and Japan,* edited by Linda Erlich and David Desser. Austin: University of Texas Press.

Bhabha, Homi. 1994. *Location of Culture.* London: Routledge.

Bhabha, Homi, ed. 1990. *Nation and Narration.* London: Routledge.

Bordwell, David. 2000a. *The Planet Hong Kong: Popular Cinema and the Art of Entertainment.* Cambridge, Mass.: Harvard University Press.

————. 2000b. "Richness through Imperfection: King Hu and the Glimpse." In *The Cinema of Hong Kong: History, Arts, Identity,* edited by Poshek Fu and David Desser. New York: Cambridge University Press.

Browne, Nick. 1994a. "Introduction." In *New Chinese Cinemas: Forms, Identities, Politics,* edited by Nick Browne, Paul G. Pickowicz, Vivian Sobchack, and Esther Yau. New York: Cambridge University Press.

————. 1994b. "Society and Subjectivity: On the Political Economy of Chinese Melodrama." In *New Chinese Cinemas: Forms, Identities, Politics,* edited by Nick Browne, Paul G. Pickowicz, Vivian Sobchack, and Esther Yau. New York: Cambridge University Press.

————. 1996. "Hou Hsiao-hsien's *Puppetmaster:* The Poetics of Landscape." *Asian Cinema* 8.1: 28–37.

Browne, Nick, Beverle Houston, and Robert Rosen. 1985. "China Is Near: A Visit to the People's Republic." *On Film* 14: 11–7.

Browne, Nick, Paul G. Pickowicz, Vivian Sobchack, and Esther Yau, eds. 1994. *New Chinese Cinemas: Forms, Identities, Politics.* New York: Cambridge University Press.

Brownlow, Kevin. 1989. "Sidney Franklin and 'The Good Earth' (MGM, 1937)." *Historical Journal of Film, Radio and Television* 9.1: 79–89.

————. 1990. *Behind the Mask of Innocence—Sex, Violence, Prejudice, Crime: Films of Social Conscience in the Silent Era.* New York: Knopf.

Brunette, Peter. 1999. "From His Act of Betrayal Comes the Stuff of a Career." *New York Times,* Dec. 12, Arts & Leisure, p. 37.

Buck, David D. 1994. "Introduction to Dimensions of Ethnic and Cultural Nationalism in Asia—A Symposium." *Journal of Asian Studies* 53.1 (Feb.): 3–9.

Buck, Pearl. 1951. *My Several Worlds: A Personal Record.* New York: John Day.

Buell, Frederick. 1994. *National Culture and the New Global System.* Baltimore: Johns Hopkins University Press.

Burgwinkle, William, Glenn Man, and Valerie Wayne, eds. 1993. *Significant Others: Gender and Culture in Film and Literature East and West.* Honolulu: University of Hawaii, College of Languages, Linguistics and Literature.

Butler, Judith. 1990. *Gender Trouble: Feminism and the Subversion of Identity.* London: Routledge.

Cai Mingliang (Tsai Ming-liang 蔡明亮). 1994. *Aiqing wansui: Cai Mingliang de dianying* (愛情萬歲): 蔡明亮的電影 (*Vive l'amour:* Tsai Ming-liang's film). Taipei: Wanxiang.

Callahan, W. A. 1993. "Gender, Ideology, Nation: *Ju Dou* in the Cultural Politics of China." *East-West Film Journal* 7.1: 52–80.

Calvino, Italo. 1972. *Invisible Cities.* Translated by William Weaver. New York: Harcourt Brace Jovanovich.

Canby, Vincent. 1988. "Socialist Realist Fable of 1930's China." *New York Times*, Oct. 9, sec. 1, p. 74.

Carson, Diane, Linda Dittmar, and Janice R. Welsch, eds. 1994. *Multiple Voices in Feminist Film Criticism.* Minneapolis: University of Minnesota Press.

Cavell, Stanley. 1981. *Pursuits of Happiness: The Hollywood Comedy of Remarriage.* Cambridge, Mass.: Harvard University Press.

Center for Documentation, Paris, ed. 1982. *Ombres électriques: Panorama du cinéma chinois, 1925–1982* (Electric shadows: a panoramic view of Chinese cinema). Paris: Centre de Documentation sur le Cinéma Chinois.

Chan, Natalia Sui Hung. 2000. "Rewriting History: Hong Kong Nostalgia Cinema and Its Social Practice." In *The Cinema of Hong Kong: History, Arts, Identity*, edited by Poshek Fu and David Desser. New York: Cambridge University Press.

Chang, Eileen 張愛玲. 1994. *Duizhao ji: kan lao zhaoxiangbu* 對照記：看老照相簿 (An album of mutual reflections: reading old photographs). Taipei: Huangguan.

———. 1996. "Love in a Fallen City." Translated by Karen Kingsbury. *Renditions* 45 (Spring): 61–92.

Chang Hsiao-Hung 張小虹, and Chih-Hung Wang 王志弘. 1995. "Taibei qingyu dijing—jia/gongyuan de yingxiang zhiyi" 台北情慾地景—家/公園的影像置移 (Mapping Taipei's landscape of desire: deterritorialization and reterritorialization of the family/park). In *Xunzhao dianying zhongde Taibei, 1950–1990* 尋找電影中的台北 (Focus on Taipei through cinema), edited by Ru-Shou Robert Chen 陳儒修 and Gene-Fon Liao 廖金鳳. Taipei: Wanxiang.

Chang, Michael G. 1999. "The Good, the Bad, and the Beautiful: Movie Actresses and Public Discourse in Shanghai, 1920s–1930s." In *Cinema and Urban Culture in Shanghai, 1922–1943*, edited by Yingjin Zhang. Stanford: Stanford University Press.

Chang Sung-sheng Yvonne. 1993. *Modernism and the Nativist Resistance: Contemporary Chinese Fiction from Taiwan.* Durham, N.C.: Duke University Press.

Chen Bo 陳播, ed. 1993. *Zhongguo zuoyi dianying yundong* 中國左翼電影運動 (The leftist film movement in China). Beijing: Zhongguo dianying chubanshe.

Chen Huangmei 陳荒煤, ed. 1989. *Dangdai Zhongguo dianying* 當代中國電影 (Contemporary Chinese cinema). 2 vols. Beijing: Zhongguo shehui kexue chubanshe.

Chen Kaige 陳凱歌. 1991. *Shaonian Kaige* 少年凱歌 (Young Kaige). Taipei: Yuanliu.

Chen, Kaige, and Tony Rayns. 1989. *"King of the Children" and the New Chinese Cinema.* London: Faber and Faber.

Chen Kuan-hsing. 1994. "Positioning Positions: A New Internationalist Localism of Cultural Studies." *Positions* 2.3 (Winter): 680–710.

Chen Mo 陳墨. 1995. *Zhang Yimou dianying lun* 張藝謀電影論 (Zhang Yimou's films). Beijing: Zhongguo dianying chubanshe.

Chen Ru-Shou Robert 陳儒修. 1993a. "Dispersion, Ambivalence and Hybridity: A Cultural-Historical Investigation of Film Experience in Taiwan in the 1980s." Ph.D. diss., University of Southern California.

————. 1993b. *Taiwan xindianying de lishi wenhua jingyan* 台灣新電影的歷史文化經驗 (Historical and cultural experiences in new Taiwan cinema). Taipei: Wanxiang.

————. 1994. "Review of *A Confucian Confusion.*" *Cinemaya* 24 (Summer): 36–7.

————. 1999. "Fudao jin quanmian pochan" 輔導金全面破產 (Film grants completely bankrupt). In *Dangdai Zhongguo dianying: 1998* 當代中國電影: 1998 (Contemporary Chinese cinema: 1998), edited by Huang Wulan. Taipei: Shibao wenhua.

Chen Ru-Shou Robert, and Gene-Fon Liao 廖金鳳, eds. 1995. *Xunzhao dianying zhongde Taibei, 1950–1990* 尋找電影中的台北 (Focus on Taipei through cinema). Taipei: Wanxiang.

Chen Xiaomei. 1995. *Occidentalism: A Theory of Counter-Discourse in Post-Mao China.* New York: Oxford University Press.

Chen Xiaoming 陳曉明. 1994. "Hou xiandai: wenhua de kuozhang yu cuowei" 後現代: 文化的擴張與錯位 (Postmodernity: the expansion and dislocation of culture). *Shanghai wenxue* 上海文學 3: 62–9.

————. 1997. "The Mysterious Other: Postpolitics in Chinese Film." *Boundary 2* 24.3 (Fall): 123–41.

Chen Xiaoxin 陳孝信. 1989. "Lun *Honggaoliang* de wenhua jiazhi" 論(紅高粱)的文化價值 (On *Red Sorghum*'s cultural values). *Dianying yishu* 2: 29–35.

Chen Xihe. 1990. "Shadowplay: Chinese Film Aesthetics and Their Philosophical and Cultural Fundamentals." In *Chinese Film Theory: A Guide to the New Era*, edited by George S. Semsel, Xia Hong, and Hou Jianping. New York: Praeger.

Chen Zhikuan 陳志寬, ed. 1997. *Zhonghua minguo dianying shiye gaiguan* 中華民國電影事業 概觀 (An overview of film industries in the Republic of China). Taipei: Xingzhengyuan xinwen ju.

Cheng Jihua 程季華, Li Shaobai 李少白, and Xing Zuwen 邢祖文, eds. 1981. *Zhongguo dianying fazhan shi* 中國電影發展史 (History of the development of Chinese cinema). 2 vols. Beijing: Zhongguo dianying chubanshe. 1963. Second edition.

Cheng Pei-Kai 鄭培凱. 1994. "Haohua luojin jian chunzhen: Zhang Yimou de yingpian *Houzhe*" 豪華落盡見真純: 張藝謀的影片(活著)(Truth and simplicity revealed after glamorous shows: Zhang Yimou's *To Live*). *Dangdai* 當代 (Con-Temporary) 99 (July): 72–99.

————. 1995. "Zhongguo dianying shikong zuobiao de zhuanyi: cong Shanghai dao Taibei 1930–1990" 中國電影時空座標的轉移: 從上海到台北 1930–1990 (From Shanghai to Taipei: Metropolis in spatial, cultural, and existential consciousness in Chinese cinema, 1930–1990). In *Xunzhao dianying zhongde Taibei, 1950–1990* 尋找 電影中的台北 (Focus on Taipei through cinema), edited by Ru-Shou Robert Chen 陳儒修 and Gene-Fon Liao 廖金鳳. Taipei: Wanxiang.

Cheshire, Godfrey. 1993. "Time Span: The Cinema of Hou Hsiao-hsien." *Film Comment* 29.6: 56–63.

Cheuk Pak-Tong. 1999. "The Beginning of the Hong Kong New Wave: The Interactive Relationship Between Television and the Film Industry." *Post Script* 19.1 (Fall): 10–27.

Chiao (Peggy) Hsiung-Ping. 1991a. "The Distinct Taiwanese and Hong Kong Cinemas." In *Perspectives on Chinese Cinema*, second and expanded edition, edited by Chris Berry. London: British Film Institute.

———. 1991b. *Tai Gang dianying zhongde zuozhe yu liexing* 台港電影中的作者與類型 (Auteurs and genres in Taiwan and Hong Kong cinemas). Taipei: Yuanliu.

———. 1993a. *Gaibian lishi de wunian: Guolian dianying yanjiu* 改變歷史的五年: 國聯電影研究 (Five years that changed history: studies of Guolian studio). Taipei: Wanxiang.

———. 1993b. "Reel Contact Across the Taiwan Straits: A History of Separation and Reunion." In *New Chinese Cinema*, Dossier 11, edited by Klaus Eder and Deac Rossell. London: National Film Theatre.

———. 1993c. "'Trafficking' in Chinese Films." *Modern Chinese Literature* 7.2 (Fall): 97–101.

———. 1996a. "*Mahjong*: Urban Travails—An Interview with Edward Yang." *Cinemaya* 33 (Summer): 24–27.

———. 1996b. "Second Wave from Taiwan: Three Interviews." *Cinemaya* 34 (Autumn): 4–13.

Chiao (Peggy) Hsiung-Ping 焦雄屏, ed. 1987. *Xianggang dianying fengmao, 1975–1986* 香港電影風貌 (Aspects of Hong Kong cinema, 1975–1986). Taipei: shibao chuban gongsi.

———, ed. 1988. *Taiwan xindianying* 台灣新電影 (New Taiwan cinema). Taipei: Shibao chuban gongsi.

China Screen, ed. 1994. "Western Wonders and Chinese Film Myth." A symposium. *China Screen* 2: 28–9.

Chow, Rey. 1991a. "Violence in Other Country: China as Crisis, Spectacle, and Woman." In *Third World Women and the Politics of Feminism*, edited by Chandra Talpade Mohanty, Ann Russo, and Lourdes Torres. Bloomington: Indiana University Press.

———. 1991b. *Woman and Chinese Modernity: The Politics of Reading Between West and East*. Minneapolis: University of Minnesota Press.

———. 1993. *Writing Diaspora: Tactics of Intervention in Contemporary Cultural Studies*. Bloomington: Indiana University Press.

———. 1995. *Primitive Passions: Visuality, Sexuality, Ethnography, and Contemporary Chinese Cinema*. New York: Columbia University Press.

———. 1997. "Can One Say No to China?" *New Literary History* 28.1 (Winter): 147–51.

———. 1998a. *Ethics after Idealism: Theory-Culture-Ethnicity-Reading*. Bloomington: Indiana University Press.

———. 1998b. "Film and Cultural Identity." In *The Oxford Guide to Film Studies*, edited by John Hill and Pamela Church Gibson. New York: Oxford University Press.

———. 1998c. "Introduction: On Chineseness as a Theoretical Problem." *Boundary 2* 25.3 (Fall): 1–24.

———. 1998d. "King Kong in Hong Kong: Watching the 'Handover' from the U.S.A." *Social Text* 16.2 (Summer): 93–108.

———. 1998f. "The Seductions of Homecoming: Place, Authenticity, and Chen Kaige's *Temptress Moon*." *Narrative* 6.1: 3–17.

———, ed. 1998e. "Modern Chinese Literary and Cultural Studies in the Age of Theory: Reimagining a Field." A special issue. *Boundary 2* 25.3 (Fall).

Choy, Christine. 1978. "Images of Asian-Americans in Film and Television." In *Ethnic Images in American Film and Television*, edited by Randall Miller. Philadelphia: Balch Institute.

Chu, Blanche. 1998. "The Ambivalence of History: Nostalgia Films Understood in the Post-Colonial Context." *Hong Kong Cultural Studies Bulletin* 8–9 (Spring/Summer): 41–54.

Chun, Allen. 1996. "Fuck Chineseness: On the Ambiguities of Ethnicity as Culture as Identity." *Boundary 2* 23.2 (Summer): 111–38.

Ciecko, Anne T. 1997. "Transnational Action: John Woo, Hong Kong, Hollywood." In *Transnational Chinese Cinema: Identity, Nationhood, Gender*, edited by Sheldon Hsiao-peng Lu. Honolulu: University of Hawaii Press.

Ciecko, Anne T., and Sheldon Lu. 1998. "Televisuality, Capital, and the Global Village: *Ermo.*" *Jump Cut* 42: 77–83.

Cinemaya, ed. 1995. "A Tribute to Zhang Yimou." A special forum. *Cinemaya* 30 (Autumn): n.p.

Clark, Paul. 1984. "The Film Industry in the 1970s." In *Popular Chinese Literature and Performing Arts in the People's Republic of China, 1949–1979*, edited by Bonnie S. McDougall. Berkeley: University of California Press.

———. 1987a. *Chinese Cinema: Culture and Politics Since 1949*. New York: Cambridge University Press.

———. 1987b. "Ethnic Minorities in Chinese Films: Cinema and the Exotic." *East-West Film Journal* 1.2 (June): 15–31.

———. 1988. "The Sinification of Cinema: The Foreignness of Film in China." In *Cinema and Cultural Identity: Reflections on Films from Japan, India, and China*, edited by Wimal Dissanayake. Lanham, Md.: University Press of America.

———. 1989. "Reinventing China: The Fifth-Generation Filmmakers." *Modern Chinese Literature* 5: 121–36.

———. 1991. "Two Hundred Flowers on China's Screens." In *Perspectives on Chinese Cinema*, second and expanded edition, edited by Chris Berry. London: British Film Institute.

Clarke, Dave, ed. 1997. *The Cinematic City*. London: Routledge.

Clausen, Soren, Roy Starrs, and Anne Wedell-Wedellsborg, eds. 1995. *Cultural Encounters—China, Japan, and the West: Essays Commemorating 25 Years of East Asian Studies at the University of Aarhus*. Aarhus, Denmark: Aarhus University Press.

Clifford, James. 1986. "Introduction." In *Writing Culture: The Poetics and Politics of Ethnography*, edited by James Clifford and George E. Marcus. Berkeley: University of California Press.

———. 1988. *The Predicament of Culture*. Cambridge, Mass.: Harvard University Press.

———. 1992. "Traveling Cultures." In *Cultural Studies*, edited by Lawrence Grossberg, Cary Nelson, and Paula Treichler. London: Routledge.

———. 1997. *Routes: Travel and Translation in the Late Twentieth Century*. Cambridge, Mass.: Harvard University Press.

Clifford, James, and George E. Marcus, eds. 1986. *Writing Culture: The Poetics and Politics of Ethnography*. Berkeley: University of California Press.

Cohen, Paul A. 1984. *Discovering History in China: American Historical Writing on the Recent Chinese Past.* New York: Columbia University Press.

Conn, Peter. 1996. *Pearl S. Buck: A Cultural Biography.* New York: Cambridge University Press.

Crossley, Pamela Kyle. 1990. "Thinking About Ethnicity in Early Modern China." *Late Imperial China* 11.1 (June): 1–35.

Cui Shuqin. 1997. "Gendered Perspective: The Construction and Representation of Subjectivity and Sexuality in *Ju Dou.*" In *Transnational Chinese Cinema: Identity, Nationhood, Gender,* edited by Sheldon Hsiao-peng Lu. Honolulu: University of Hawaii Press.

———. 2000. "Stanley Kwan's *Center Stage*: The (Im)possible Engagement between Feminism and Postmodernism." *Cinema Journal* 39.4 (Summer): 60–80.

Curtin, Michael. 1999. "Industry on Fire: The Cultural Economy of Hong Kong Media." *Post Script* 19.1 (Fall): 28–51.

Dai Jinhua 戴錦華. 1993. *Dianying lilun yu piping shouce* 電影理論與批評手冊 (Film theory and criticism). Beijing: Kexue jishu wenxian chubanshe.

———. 1995a. "Invisible Women: Contemporary Chinese Cinema and Women's Film." *Positions* 3.1 (Spring): 255–80.

———. 1995b. *Jing yu shisu shenhua: yingpian jingdu shiba li* 鏡與世俗神話: 影片精讀十八例 (The mirror and secular myth: close readings of 18 films). Beijing: Zhongguo guangbo dianshi chubanshe.

———. 1996. "Redemption and Consumption: Depicting Culture in the 1990s." *Positions* 4.1 (Spring): 127–43.

———. 1997. "Imagined Nostalgia." *Boundary 2* 24.3 (Fall): 143–61.

———. 1999a. "Binghai chenchuan—1998 nian Zhongguo dianying beiwang" 冰海沉船: 1998 年中國電影備忘 (Shipwreck in the icy sea—a memo on 1998 Chinese films). In *Dangdai Zhongguo dianying: 1998* 當代中國電影: 1998 (Contemporary Chinese cinema: 1998), edited by Huang Wulan 黃寤蘭. Taipei: Shibao wenhua.

———. 1999b. "Invisible Writing: The Politics of Chinese Mass Culture in the 1990s." *Modern Chinese Literature and Culture* 11.1 (Spring): 31–60.

Dai Jinhua, and Mayfair Yang. 1995. "A Conversation with Huang Shuqin." *Positions* 3.3 (Winter): 790–805.

Dai Qing. 1993. "Raised Eyebrows for *Raise the Red Lantern.*" *Public Culture* 5: 333–7.

Dai Xiaolan 戴小蘭, ed. 1996. *Zhongguo wusheng dianying* 中國無聲電影 (Chinese silent cinema). Beijing: Zhongguo dianying chubanshe.

Dangdai dianying, ed. 1999a. "*Guoge* yingpian pingxi" (國歌)影片評析 (Case study of *The National Anthem*). *Dangdai dianying* 5: 4–24.

———, ed. 1999b. "*Wangluo shidai de aiqing* yingpian pingxi" (網絡時代的愛情)影片評析 (Case study of *Love in the Internet Generation*). *Dangdai dianying* 3: 4–26.

Dannen, Fredric, and Barry Long. 1997. *Hong Kong Babylon: An Insider's Guide to the Hollywood of the East.* London: Faber and Faber.

Dariotis, Wei Ming, and Eileen Fung. 1997. "Breaking the Soy Sauce Jar: Diasporas and Displacement in the Films of Ang Lee." In *Transnational Chinese Cinema: Identity, Nationhood, Gender,* edited by Sheldon Hsiao-peng Lu. Honolulu: University of Hawaii Press.

Davis, Deborah, Richard Kraus, Barry Naughton, and Elizabeth Perry, eds. 1995. *Urban Spaces in Contemporary China: The Potential for Autonomy and Community in Post-Mao China*. New York: Cambridge University Press.

Davis, Fred. 1979. *Yearning for Yesterday: A Sociology of Nostalgia*. London: Macmillan.

de Certeau, Michel. 1984. *The Practice of Everyday Life*. Translated by Steven Rendall. Berkeley: University of California Press.

de Lauretis, Teresa. 1984. *Alice Doesn't: Feminism, Semiotics, Cinema*. Bloomington: Indiana University Press.

Delmar, Rosalind, and Mark Nash. 1976–77. "Breaking with Old Ideas: Recent Chinese Films." *Screen* 17.4: 67–84.

Denton, Kirk , ed. 1996. *Modern Chinese Literary Thought: Writings on Literature, 1893–1945*. Stanford: Stanford University Press.

Desser, David. 2000. "The Kung Fu Craze: Hong Kong Cinema's First American Reception." In *The Cinema of Hong Kong: History, Arts, Identity*, edited by Poshek Fu and David Desser. New York: Cambridge University Press.

Dianying yishu, ed. 1996a. "*Hong yingtao* pindu" (紅櫻桃) 品讀 (Analysis of *Red Cherry*). *Dianying yishu* 1: 43–7.

———, ed. 1996b. "1995 nian guochan maizuo yingpian paihang bang ('qian shiming')" 1995 年國產賣座影片排行榜(前十名) (1995 top ten grossing domestic films). *Dianying yishu* 3: 4–5.

———, ed. 1998. "1997 nian guochan yingpian piaofang shouru paihang bang" 1997 國產影片票房收入排行榜 (1997 top grossing domestic films). *Dianying yishu* 3: 4–5.

Dick, Bernard F. 1995. "Columbia's Dark Ladies and the Femmes-Fatales of Film Noir." *Literature-Film Quarterly* 23.3: 155–62.

Dikötter, Frank. 1992. *The Discourse of Race in Modern China*. Stanford: Stanford University Press.

———. 1994. "Racial Identities in China: Context and Meaning." *China Quarterly* 138 (June): 404–12.

Dirlik, Arif. 1989. "Post-socialism? Reflections on 'Socialism with Chinese Characteristics.'" In *Marxism and the Chinese Experience*, edited by Arif Dirlik and Maurice Meisner. Armonk, N.Y.: M. E. Sharpe.

———. 1994. "The Postcolonial Aura: Third World Criticism in the Age of Global Capitalism." *Critical Inquiry* 20 (Winter): 328–56.

——— 1995. "Confucius in the Borderlands: Global Capitalism and the Reinvention of Confucianism." *Boundary 2* 22.3 (Fall): 229–73.

Dirlik, Arif, and Maurice Meisner, eds. 1989. *Marxism and the Chinese Experience*. Armonk, N.Y.: M. E. Sharpe.

Dirlik, Arif, and Xudong Zhang. 1997. "Introduction: Postmodernism and China." *Boundary 2* 24.3 (Fall): 1–18.

Dissanayake, Wimal. 1996a. "Asian Cinema and the American Cultural Imaginary." *Theory, Culture & Society* 13.4: 102–22.

———, ed. 1988. *Cinema and Cultural Identity: Reflections on Films from Japan, India, and China*. Lanham, Md.: University Press of America.

———, ed. 1993. *Melodrama and Asian Cinema*. New York: Cambridge University Press.

————, ed. 1994. *Colonialism and Nationalism in Asian Cinema.* Bloomington: Indiana University Press.

————, ed. 1996b. *Narratives of Agency: Self-Making in China, India, and Japan.* Minneapolis: University of Minnesota Press.

Donald, Stephanie. 1995. "Women Reading Chinese Films: Between Orientalism and Silence." *Screen* 36.4: 325–40.

————. 1997. "Landscape and Agency: *Yellow Earth* and the Demon Lover." *Theory, Culture & Society* 141: 97–112.

————. 1998. "Symptoms of Alienation: The Female Body in Recent Chinese Film." *Continuum* 12.1: 91–103.

————. 2000. *Public Secrets, Public Spaces: Cinema and Civility in China.* Lanham, Md.: Rowman and Littlefield.

Duara, Prasenjit. 1993. "De-constructing the Chinese Nation." *Australian Journal of Chinese Affairs* 30 (July): 1–26.

————. 1995. *Rescuing History from the Nation: Questioning Narratives of Modern China.* Chicago: University of Chicago Press.

Duke, Michael. 1993. "Past, Present, and Future in Mo Yan's Fiction of the 1980s." In *From May Fourth to June Fourth: Fiction and Film in Twentieth-Century China*, edited by Ellen Widmer and David Der-wei Wang. Cambridge, Mass.: Harvard University Press.

During, Simon. 1997. "Popular Culture on a Global Scale: A Challenge for Cultural Studies?" *Critical Inquiry* 23 (Summer): 808–33.

Dussel, Enrique. 1998. "Beyond Eurocentrism: The World-System and the Limits of Modernity." In *The Cultures of Globalization*, edited by Fredric Jameson and Masao Miyoshi. Durham, N.C.: Duke University Press.

Eberhard, Wolfram. 1972. *The Chinese Silver Screen: Hong Kong and Taiwan Motion Pictures.* Taipei: Orient Cultural Service.

Eckholm, Eric. 1999. "Feted Abroad, and No Longer Banned in Beijing." *New York Times*, Dec. 16, Arts & Leisure.

Eder, Klaus, and Deac Rossell, eds. 1993. *New Chinese Cinema.* Dossier 11. London: National Film Theatre.

Electa, Milan, ed. 1982. *Ombre elettriche: Saggi e ricerche sul cinema cinese* (Electric shadows: essays and studies on Chinese cinema). Milan: Electa.

Elley, Derek. 1993. "Tiananmen and the 5th Generation." In *New Chinese Cinema*, Dossier 11, edited by Klaus Eder and Deac Rossell. London: National Film Theatre.

Ellis, John. 1982. "Electric Shadows in Italy." *Screen* 23.2: 79–83.

Erens, Patricia Brett. 2000. "The Film Work of Ann Hui." In *The Cinema of Hong Kong: History, Arts, Identity*, edited by Poshek Fu and David Desser. New York: Cambridge University Press.

Erhlich, Linda, and David Desser, eds. 1994. *Cinematic Landscapes: Observations on the Visual Arts and Cinema of China and Japan.* Austin: University of Texas Press.

Farquhar, Mary Ann. 1992. "The 'Hidden' Gender in *Yellow Earth.*" *Screen* 33.2: 154–64.

Featherstone, Mike. 1995. *Undoing Culture: Globalization, Postmodernism and Identity.* London: Sage.

Featherstone, Mike, Scott Lash, and Roland Robertson, eds. 1995. *Global Modernities*. London: Sage.

Feng Xiaoning 馮小寧. 1997. "Wo qiangdiao liangge zi jiushi shijian" 我強調兩個字就是 實踐 (I emphasize the word practice). *Dianying yishu* 4: 66–71.

Field, Andrew D. 1999. "Selling Souls in Sin City: Shanghai Singing and Dancing Hostesses in Print, Film, and Politics, 1920–1949." In *Cinema and Urban Culture in Shanghai, 1922–1943*, edited by Yingjin Zhang. Stanford: Stanford University Press, 1999.

Fiske, John. 1987. *Television Culture*. New York: Methuen.

Fong, Suzie Young-Sau. 1995. "The Voice of Feminine Madness in Zhang Yimou's *Raise the Red Lantern*." *Asian Cinema* 7.1: 12–23.

Fonoroff, Paul. 1997. *Silver Light: A Pictorial History of Hong Kong Cinema, 1920–1970*. Hong Kong: Joint.

———. 1998. *At the Hong Kong Movies*. Hong Kong: Film Biweekly.

Fore, Steve. 1993. "Tales of Recombinant Femininity: *The Reincarnation of Golden Lotus*, the *Chin P'ing Mei*, and the Politics of Melodrama in Hong Kong." *Journal of Film and Video* 45.4: 57–70.

———. 1994. "Golden Harvest Films and the Hong Kong Movie Industry in the Realm of Globalization." *Velvet Light Trap* 34: 40–58.

———. 1997. "Jackie Chan and the Cultural Dynamics of Global Entertainment." In *Transnational Chinese Cinema: Identity, Nationhood, Gender*, edited by Sheldon Hsiao-peng Lu. Honolulu: University of Hawaii Press.

———. 1998. "Time-Traveling Under an *Autumn Moon*." *Post Script* 17.3 (Summer): 34–46.

———. 1999. "Introduction: Hong Kong Movies, Critical Time Warps, and Shapes of Things to Come." *Post Script* 19.1 (Fall): 2–9.

Foucault, Michel. 1979. *Discipline and Punish: The Birth of the Prison*. Translated by Alan Sheridan. New York: Vintage Books.

Friedman, Lester D., ed. 1991. *Unspeakable Images: Ethnicity and the American Cinema*. Urbana: University of Illinois Press.

Fu Poshek. 1997. "The Ambiguity of Entertainment: Chinese Cinema in Japanese-Occupied Shanghai, 1942 to 1945." *Cinema Journal* 37.1 (Fall): 66–84.

———. 2000a. "Between Nationalism and Colonialism: Mainland Emigres, Marginal Culture, and Hong Kong Cinema 1937–1941." In *The Cinema of Hong Kong: History, Arts, Identity*, edited by Poshek Fu and David Desser. New York: Cambridge University Press.

———. 2000b. "The 1960s: Modernity, Youth Culture, and Hong Kong Cantonese Cinema." In *The Cinema of Hong Kong: History, Arts, Identity*, edited by Poshek Fu and David Desser. New York: Cambridge University Press.

Fu Poshek, and David Desser, eds. 2000. *The Cinema of Hong Kong: History, Arts, Identity*. New York: Cambridge University Press.

Fukuyama, Francis. 1992. *The End of History and the Last Man*. New York: Free Press.

Fu Jen University 輔仁大學. 1993. *Zhongguo dianying, dianying Zhongguo* 中國電影, 電影中 國 (Chinese Film, China in Films). Taipei: Furen daxue dazhong chuanbo xi.

Gabriel, Teshome H. 1982. *Third Cinema in the Third World: The Aesthetics of Liberation.* Ann Arbor, Mich.: UMI Research Press.

Gaines, Jane, and Thomas Lahusen, eds. 1995. "Views from the Post-Future: Soviet and Eastern European Cinema." *Discourse* 17.3 (Spring): 3–125.

Gallagher, Mark. 1997. "Masculinity in Translation: Jackie Chan's Translated-cultural Star Text." *Velvet Light Trap* 39: 23–41.

Gates, Henry Louis, Jr., ed. 1985. *"Race," Writing, and Difference.* Chicago: University of Chicago Press.

Giddens, Anthony. 1990. *The Consequences of Modernity.* Stanford, Calif.: Stanford University Press.

Gladney, Dru C. 1994. "Representing Nationality in China: Refiguring Majority/Minority Identities." *Journal of Asian Studies* 53.1 (Feb.): 92–123.

———. 1995. "Tian Zhuangzhuang, the Fifth Generation, and Minorities Film in China." *Public Culture* 8.1 (Fall): 161–75.

Glaessner, Verina. 1974. *Kung Fu: The Cinema of Vengeance.* London: Lorrimer.

Gold, Thomas. 1993. "Go with Your Feelings: Hong Kong and Taiwan Popular Culture in Greater China." *China Quarterly* 136: 907–25.

Goldblatt, Howard, ed. 1995. *Chairman Mao Would Not Be Amused: Fiction from Today's China.* New York: Grove.

Golden Horse Film Festival, ed. 1994. *A Perspective of Chinese Cinemas of the 90's.* A special program. Taipei: Golden Horse Film Festival.

Gongsun Lu 公孫魯. 1977. *Zhongguo dianying shihua* (A history of Chinese cinema). 2 vols. Hong Kong: Nantian.

Government Information Office, ed. 1997. *The Republic of China Yearbook, 1997.* Taipei: Government Information Office.

Grossberg, Lawrence, Cary Nelson, and Paula Treichler, eds. 1992. *Cultural Studies.* London: Routledge.

Gunn, Edward. 1980. *Unwelcome Muse: Chinese Literature in Shanghai and Peking, 1937–1945.* New York: Columbia University Press.

Guo Jian. 1999. "Resisting Modernity in Contemporary China: The Cultural Revolution and Postmodernism." *Modern China* 25.3 (July): 343–76.

Hall, Stuart. 1987. "Minimal Selves." In *Identity.* London: ICA Document 6.

———. 1997a. "The Local and the Global: Globalization and Ethnicity." In *Culture, Globalization and the World-System: Contemporary Conditions for the Representation of Identity,* revised edition, edited by Anthony D. King. Minneapolis: University of Minnesota Press.

———. 1997b. "Old and New Identities, Old and New Ethnicities." In *Culture, Globalization and the World-System: Contemporary Conditions for the Representation of Identity,* revised edition, edited by Anthony D. King. Minneapolis: University of Minnesota Press.

Hammond, Stefan, and Mike Wilkins. 1996. *Sex and Zen and a Bullet in the Head: The Essential Guide to Hong Kong's Mind-Bending Films.* New York: Fireside-Simon and Schuster.

Han Xiaolei 韓小磊. 1995. "Dui diwudai de wenhua tuwei: houwudai de geren dianying xianxiang" 對第五代的文化突圍: 後五代的個人電影現象 (A cultural breakaway from the Fifth Generation: the phenomenon of individualist film in the post-Fifth Generation). *Dianying yishu* 2: 58–63.

———. 1999. "Tuwei hou de wenhua piaoyi" 突圍後的文化漂移 (Cultural driftings after the breakaway). *Dianying yishu* 5: 58–65.

Hao Dazheng. 1994. "Chinese Visual Representation: Painting and Cinema." In *Cinematic Landscapes: Observations on the Visual Arts and Cinema of China and Japan*, edited by Linda Erhlich and David Desser. Austin: University of Texas Press.

Harding, Harry. 1993. "The Concept of 'Greater China': Themes, Variations and Reservations." *China Quarterly* 136 (Dec.): 660–86.

Harris, Kristine. 1997a. "*The New Woman* Incident: Cinema, Scandal, and Spectacle in 1935 Shanghai." In *Transnational Chinese Cinema: Identity, Nationhood, Gender*, edited by Sheldon Hsiao-peng Lu. Honolulu: University of Hawaii Press.

———. 1997b. "Silent Speech: Envisioning the Nation in Early Chinese Cinema." Ph.D. diss., Columbia University.

———. 1999. "*The Romance of the Western Chamber* and the Classical Subject Film in 1920s Shanghai." In *Cinema and Urban Culture in Shanghai, 1922–1943*, edited by Yingjin Zhang. Stanford: Stanford University Press.

Hay, James. 1997. "Piecing Together What Remains of the Cinematic City." In *The Cinematic City*, edited by Dave Clarke. London: Routledge.

Hayford, Charles. 1998. "What's So Bad About *The Good Earth?*" *Education About Asia* 3.3 (Winter): 4–7.

Hayles, Katherine. 1999. *How We Became Posthuman: Virtual Bodies in Cybernetics, Literature, and Informatics*. Chicago: University of Chicago Press.

Hayot, Eric. 1999. "Book Review of Rey Chow, *Ethics after Idealism: Theory-Culture-Ethnicity-Reading*." *Modern Chinese Literature and Culture* 11.1 (Spring): 219–25.

Herberer, Thomas. 1989. *China and Its Minorities: Autonomy or Assimilation?* Armonk, N.Y.: M. E. Sharpe.

Hill, John, and Pamela Church Gibson, eds. 1998. *The Oxford Guide to Film Studies*. New York: Oxford University Press.

Hitchcock, Peter. 1992. "The Aesthetics of Alienation, or China's 'Fifth Generation.'" *Cultural Studies* 6.1: 116–41.

Ho, Elaine Yee Lin. 1999. "Women on the Edges of Hong Kong Modernity: The Films of An Hui." In *Spaces of Their Own: Women's Public Sphere in Transnational China*, edited by Mayfair Mei-hui Yang. Minneapolis: University of Minnesota Press.

Hoare, Stephanie. 1993. "Innovation through Adaptation: The Use of Literature in New Taiwan Film and Its Consequences." *Modern Chinese Literature* 7.2 (Fall): 33–58.

Hockx, Michel, ed. 1999. *The Literary Field of Twentieth-Century China*. London: Curzon.

Holden, Stephen. 1995. "Erotic Energy and Social Disorder." *New York Times*, March 17.

Hollinger, David. 1995. *Postethnic America: Beyond Multiculturalism*. New York: Basic Books.

Hong Junhao. 1998. "The Evolution of China's War Movie in Five Decades: Factors Contributing to Changes, Limits, and Implications." *Asian Cinema* 10.1 (Fall): 93–106.

Hong Kong Film Archive, ed. 1997a. *50 Years of the Hong Kong Film Production and Distribution Industries: An Exhibition*. Hong Kong: Urban Council.

———, ed. 1997b. *Hong Kong Filmography*, Vol. I, 1913–1941, Vol. II, 1942–1949. Hong Kong: Urban Council.

hooks, bell. 1992. *Black Looks: Race and Representation*. Boston, Mass.: South End Press.

Hou Yao 侯曜. 1926. *Yingxi juben zuofa* 影戲劇本作法 (The making of a shadowplay script). Shanghai: Taidong.

Hu Ke 胡克. 1995. "Xiandai dianying lilun zai Zhongguo" 現代電影理論在中國 (Contemporary film theory in China). *Dangdai dianying* 2: 65–73.

Huang Jianye 黃建業. 1990. *Renwen dianying de zhuixun* 人文電影的追尋 (In search of humanist film). Taipei: Yuanliu.

———. 1995. *Yang Dechang dianying yanjiu—Taiwan xin dianying de zhixing sibian jia* 楊德昌電影研究: 台灣新電影的知性思辯家 (Films by Edward Yang: a critical thinker in new Taiwan cinema). Taipei: Yuanliu.

Huang Ren 黃仁. 1994. *Dianying yu zhengzhi xuanchuan: zhengce dianying yanjiu* 電影與政治宣傳: 政策電影研究 (Film and political propaganda: a study of policy films). Taipei: Wanxiang.

Huang Shixian 黃式憲. 1992. "Zhongguo dianying daoyan 'xingzuo' jiqi yishu puxi" 中國電影導演 "星座" 及其藝術譜系 (The "galaxy" of Chinese film directors and their artistic genealogy). *Dangdai dianying* 6: 77–85.

———. 1994. "Kua shiji zhichao: Zhongguo dianying san 'huan' jiaohui de xin geju" 跨世紀之潮: 中國電影三 "環" 交會的新格局 (Entering a new century: a new "convergence" of the three branches of Chinese cinema). Golden Horse Film Festival 1994, 31–44.

———. 1999. "Zhongguo 'hunian'" 中國 "虎年" (The year of tiger in China). In *Dangdai Zhongguo dianying: 1998* 當代中國電影: 1998 (Contemporary Chinese cinema: 1998), edited by Huang Wulan 黃寤蘭. Taipei: Shibao wenhua.

Huang Wulan 黃寤蘭, ed. 1999. *Dangdai Zhongguo dianying: 1998* 當代中國電影: 1998 (Contemporary Chinese cinema: 1998). Taipei: Shibao wenhua.

Hulsbus, Monica. 1997. "Oppositional Politics of Chinese Everyday Practices." *Cineaction* 42 (Feb.): 10–14.

Hung Chang-Tai. 1994. *War and Popular Culture: Resistance in Modern China, 1937–1945*. Berkeley: University of California Press.

Hunter, Jane. 1984. *The Gospel of Gentility: American Women Missionaries in Turn-of-the-Century China*. New Haven: Yale University Press.

Huot, Marie-Claire. 1993. "Fuxi Fuxi: What about Nüwa?" In *Gender and Sexuality in Twentieth-Century Chinese Literature and Society*, edited by Tonglin Lu. Albany: State University of New York Press.

Hutcheon, Linda. 1988. *A Poetics of Postmodernism*. London: Routledge.

Hutchinson, John, and Anthony D. Smith, eds. 1994. *Nationalism*. New York: Oxford University Press.

———. 1996. *Ethnicity*. New York: Oxford University Press.

Hwang, Chun-ming. 1980. *The Drowning of an Old Cat and Other Stories*. Translated by Howard Goldblatt. Bloomington: Indiana University Press.

Ing, David. 1993–94. "Love at Last Site: Waiting for Oedipus in Stanley Kwan's *Rouge*." *Camera Obscura* 32: 75–101.

Jaivin, Linda. 1995. "Defying a Ban, Chinese Cameras Roll." *The Wall Street Journal*, Jan. 18, sec. A, p. 12.

James, David, and Rick Berg, eds. 1996. *The Hidden Foundation: Cinema and the Question of Class*. Minneapolis: University of Minnesota Press.

Jameson, Fredric. 1984. "Postmodernism, or, The Cultural Logic of Late Capitalism." *New Left Review* 146 (July–Aug.): 59–92.

———. 1986. "Third-World Literature in the Era of Multinational Capitalism." *Social Text* 15 (Fall): 65–88.

———. 1987. "World Literature in an Age of Multinational Capitalism." In *The Current in Criticism: Essays on the Present and Future of Literary Theory*, edited by Clayton Koelb and Virgil Lokke. West Lafayette, Ind.: Purdue University Press.

———. 1991. *Postmodernism, or, The Cultural Logic of Late Capitalism*. Durham, N.C.: Duke University Press.

———. 1992. *Geopolitical Aesthetic: Cinema and Space in the World System*. Bloomington: Indiana University Press.

———. 1994. "Remapping Taipei." In *New Chinese Cinemas: Forms, Identities, Politics*, edited by Nick Browne, Paul G. Pickowicz, Vivian Sobchack, and Esther Yau. New York: Cambridge University Press.

———. 1998. "Notes on Globalization as a Philosophical Issue." In *The Cultures of Globalization*, edited by Fredric Jameson and Masao Miyoshi. Durham, N.C.: Duke University Press.

Jameson, Fredric, and Masao Miyoshi, eds. 1998. *The Cultures of Globalization*. Durham, N.C.: Duke University Press.

JanMohamed, Abdul R., and David Lloyd, eds. 1990. *The Nature and Context of Minority Discourse*. New York: Oxford University Press.

Ji Hongzheng 季紅真. 1989. "Wenhua 'xungen' yu dangdai wenxue" 文化尋根與當代文學 (Searching cultural roots and contemporary literature). *Wenyi yanjiu* 文藝研究 2: 69–74.

Ji Ji 季季, and Guan Hong 關鴻, eds. 1996. *Yongyuan de Zhang Ailing: didi, zhangfu, qinyou bixia de chuanqi* 永遠的張愛玲: 弟弟, 丈夫, 親友筆下的傳奇 (Everlasting Eileen Chang: romances penned by her brother, husband, and relatives). Shanghai: Xuelin chubanshe.

Jia Leilei 賈壘壘, and Yang Yuanying 楊遠嬰. 1994. "Yu Wu Ziniu duihua lu" 與吳子牛對話錄 (Interview with Wu Ziniu). *Dianying yishu* 6: 40–6.

Jintian, ed. 1999. "Jia Zhangke he tade dianying *Xiao Wu*" 賈樟柯和他的電影(小武) (Jian Zhangke and his film *Pickpocket*). *Jintian* 3 (Autumn): 1–39.

Johnson, G. Allen. 2000. "Chinese Director Sets Sights on L.A." *San Francisco Examiner*, Jan. 21.

Kaes, Anton. 1995. "German Cultural History and the Study of Film: Ten Theses and a Postscript." *New German Critique* 65 (Spring–Summer): 47–59.

Kaldis, Nick. 1999. "Huang Jianxin's *Cuowei* and/as Aesthetic Cognition." *Positions* 7.2 (Fall): 421–57.

Kaplan, E. Ann. 1989. "Problematizing Cross-Cultural Analysis: The Case of Women in the Recent Chinese Cinema." *Wide Angle* 11.2: 40–50. Reprinted in *Perspectives on*

Chinese Cinema, second and expanded edition, edited by Chris Berry. London: British Film Institute.

———. 1991. "Melodrama/Subjectivity/Ideology: Western Melodrama Theories and Their Relevance to Recent Chinese Cinema." *East-West Film Journal* 5.1: 6–27.

———. 1993. "Melodrama/Subjectivity/Ideology: Western Melodrama Theories and Their Relevance to Recent Chinese Cinema." In *Melodrama and Asian Cinema*, edited by Wimal Dissanayake. New York: Cambridge University Press.

———. 1997a. *Looking for the Other: Feminism, Film, and the Imperial Gaze*. London: Routledge.

———. 1997b. "Reading Formations and Chen Kaige's *Farewell My Concubine*." In *Transnational Chinese Cinema: Identity, Nationhood, Gender*, edited by Sheldon Hsiao-peng Lu. Honolulu: University of Hawaii Press.

———, ed. 1980. *Women in Film Noir*. London: British Film Institute.

Kapur, Geeta. 1998. "Globalization and Culture: Navigating the Void." In *The Cultures of Globalization*, edited by Fredric Jameson and Masao Miyoshi. Durham, N.C.: Duke University Press.

Keane, Michael, and Tao Dongfeng. 1998. "Interview with Feng Xiaogang." *Positions* 7.1 (Spring): 192–200.

Keith, Michael, and Steve Pile, eds. 1993. *Place and Politics of Identity*. London: Routledge.

Kellner, Douglas. 1998. "New Taiwan Cinema in the 80s." *Jump Cut* 42: 101–15.

Keng, Chua Siew. 1998. "The Politics of 'Home': *Song of the Exile*." *Jump Cut* 42: 90–3.

King, Anthony D. 1990. *Global Cities: Post-Imperialism and the Internationalization of London*. London: Routledge.

———, ed. 1997. *Culture, Globalization and the World-System: Contemporary Conditions for the Representation of Identity*. Revised edition. Minneapolis: University of Minnesota Press.

Koelb, Clayton, and Virgil Lokke, eds. 1987. *The Current in Criticism: Essays on the Present and Future of Literary Theory*. West Lafayette, Ind.: Purdue University Press.

Kong Haili. 1996–97. "Symbolism Through Zhang Yimou's Subversive Lens in His Early Films." *Asian Cinema* 8.2: 98–115.

Kowallis, Jon. 1997. "The Diaspora in Postmodern Taiwan and Hong Kong Films: Framing Stan Lai's *The Peach Blossom Land* with Allen Fong's *Ah Ying*." In *Transnational Chinese Cinema: Identity, Nationhood, Gender*, edited by Sheldon Hsiao-peng Lu. Honolulu: University of Hawaii Press.

Kraicer, Shelly, and Lisa Roosen-Runge. 1998. "Edward Yang: A Taiwanese Independent Filmmaker in Conversation." *Cineaction* 47 (Sept.): 48–55.

Kristeva, Julia. 1977. *About Chinese Women*. Translated by Anita Barrows. London: Marion Boyars.

Kuo, Jason, ed. 2001. *Shanghai Visual Culture, 1850s–1930s*. Seattle: University of Washington Press.

Kuoshu, Harry H. (Xu Haixin). 1999. *Lightness of Being in China: Adaptation and Discursive Figuration in Cinema and Theater*. New York: Peter Lang.

Lao Lin 老林. 1992. "Zhongguo dalu 'diwudai' daoyan chuangzuo nianbiao" 中國大陸'第五代'導演創作年表 (Filmographies of the "Fifth Generation" directors in mainland China). *Jintian* 2: 41–4.

Larson, Wendy. 1995. "Zhang Yimou: Inter/National Aesthetics and Erotics." In *Cultural Encounters—China, Japan, and the West: Essays Commemorating 25 Years of East Asian Studies at the University of Aarhus*, edited by Soren Clausen, Roy Starrs, and Anne Wedell-Wedellsborg. Aarhus, Denmark: Aarhus University Press.

———. 1997. "The Concubine and the Figure of History: Chen Kaige's *Farewell My Concubine*." In *Transnational Chinese Cinema: Identity, Nationhood, Gender*, edited by Sheldon Hsiao-peng Lu. Honolulu: University of Hawaii Press.

———. 1999. "Displacing the Political: Zhang Yimou's *To Live* and the Field of Film." In *The Literary Field of Twentieth-Century China*, edited by Michel Hockx. London: Curzon.

Larson, Wendy, and Anne Wedell-Wedellsborg, eds. 1993. *Inside Out: Modernism and Postmodernism in Chinese Literary Culture*. Aarhus, Denmark: Aarhus University Press.

Lash, Scott, and Jonathan Friedman, eds. 1992. *Modernity and Identity*. Oxford: Blackwell.

Lau, Jenny (Kwok Wah). 1991a. "A Cultural Interpretation of the Popular Cinema of China and Hong Kong." In *Perspectives on Chinese Cinema*, second and expanded edition, edited by Chris Berry. London: British Film Institute,.

———. 1991b. "*Judou*: A Hermeneutical Reading of Cross-Cultural Cinema." *Film Quarterly* 45.2: 2–10.

———. 1994. "*Judou*: An Experiment in Color and Portraiture in Chinese Cinema." In *Cinematic Landscapes: Observations on the Visual Arts and Cinema of China and Japan*, edited by Linda Erhlich and David Desser. Austin: University of Texas Press.

———. 1995. "*Farewell My Concubine*: History, Melodrama, and Ideology in Contemporary Pan-Chinese Cinema." *Film Quarterly* 49.1: 16–27.

———. 1998. "Besides Fists and Blood: Hong Kong Comedy and Its Master of the Eighties." *Cinema Journal* 37.2 (Winter): 18–34.

———. 2000. "Besides Fists and Blood: Michael Hui and Cantonese Comedy." In *The Cinema of Hong Kong: History, Arts, Identity*, edited by Poshek Fu and David Desser. New York: Cambridge University Press.

Lau Shing-hon, ed. 1980. *A Study of the Hong Kong Martial Arts Film*. Hong Kong: Urban Council.

Law, Kar (Luo Ka), ed. 1994. *Cinema of Two Cities: Hong Kong-Shanghai*. The 18th Hong Kong International Film Festival. Hong Kong: Urban Council.

———. 2000. "The American Connection in Early Hong Kong Cinema." In *The Cinema of Hong Kong: History, Arts, Identity*, edited by Poshek Fu and David Desser. New York: Cambridge University Press.

Lee Ching Chih 李清志. 1995. "Guopianzhong dui Taibei dushi yixiang de suzao yu zhuanhuan" 國片中對台北都市意象的塑造與轉換 (The construction and transformation of Taipei images in Chinese-language films). In *Xunzhao dianying zhongde Taibei, 1950–1990* 尋找電影中的台北 (Focus on Taipei through cinema), edited by Ru-Shou Robert Chen 陳儒修 and Gene-Fon Liao 廖金鳳. Taipei: Wanxiang.

Lee, Joann. 1996. "Zhang Yimou's *Raise the Red Lantern*: Contextual Analysis of Film Through a Confucian/Feminist Matrix." *Asian Cinema* 8.1: 120–7.

Lee, Leo Ou-fan 李歐梵. 1991a. "Modernity and Its Discontents: The Cultural Agenda of the May Fourth Movement." In *Perspectives on Modern China: Four Anniversaries*, edited by Kenneth Lieberthal, Joyce Kallgren, Roderick MacFarquhar, and Frederic Wakeman, Jr. Armonk, N.Y.: M. E. Sharpe.

———. 1991b. "The Tradition of Modern Chinese Cinema: Some Preliminary Explorations and Hypotheses." In *Perspectives on Chinese Cinema*, second and expanded edition, edited by Chris Berry. London: British Film Institute.

———. 1994. "Two Films from Hong Kong: Parody and Allegory." In *New Chinese Cinemas: Forms, Identities, Politics*, edited by Nick Browne, Paul G. Pickowicz, Vivian Sobchack, and Esther Yau. New York: Cambridge University Press.

———. 1998–99. "Xianggang: zuowei Shanghai de 'tazhe'" 香港: 作為上海的"他者" (Hong Kong, as the 'other' of Shanghai). *Dushu* 讀書 12: 17–22; 1: 50–7.

———. 1999a. "Dangdai Zhongguo wenhua de xiandai xing he hou xiandai xing" 當代中國文化的現代性和後現代性 (Modernity and postmodernity in contemporary Chinese culture). *Wenxue pinglun* 5: 129–39.

———. 1999b. "Eileen Chang and Cinema." *Journal of Modern Literature in Chinese* 2.2 (Jan.): 37–60.

———. 1999c. *Shanghai Modern: The Flowering of a New Urban Culture in China, 1930–1945*. Cambridge, Mass.: Harvard University Press.

———. 1999d. "The Urban Milieu of Shanghai Cinema, 1930–1940: Some Explorations of Film Audience, Film Culture, and Narrative Conventions." In *Cinema and Urban Culture in Shanghai, 1922–1943*, edited by Yingjin Zhang. Stanford: Stanford University Press.

Lefebvre, Henri. 1991. *The Production of Space*. London: Blackwell.

Lent, John A. 1990. *The Asian Film Industry*. Austin: University of Texas Press.

———. 1996–7. "Teach for a While, Direct for While: An Interview with Xie Fei." *Asian Cinema* 8.2 (Winter): 91–7.

———, ed. 1995. *Asian Popular Culture*. Boulder: Westview.

———, ed. 2001. *Illustrating Asia: Comics, Humor Magazines, and Picture Books*. London: Curzon.

Lentricchia, Frank, and Thomas McLaughlin, eds. 1990. *Critical Terms for Literary Study*. Chicago: University of Chicago Press.

Leung, Noong-kong. 1997. "The Long Goodbye to the China Factor." In *The China Factor in Hong Kong Cinema*, the 14th Hong Kong International Film Festival, revised edition, edited by Li Cheuk-to. Hong Kong: Urban Council, 1990.

Leung Ping-kwan. 2000. "Urban Cinema and the Cultural Identity of Hong Kong." In *The Cinema of Hong Kong: History, Arts, Identity*, edited by Poshek Fu and David Desser. New York: Cambridge University Press.

Lévi-Strauss, Claude. 1971. *The Scope of Anthropology*. Translated by S. Ortner Paul and R. A. Paul. London: Jonathan Cape.

Leyda, Jay. 1972. *Dianying / Electric Shadows: An Account of Films and the Film Audience in China*. Cambridge, Mass.: MIT Press.

Li Cheuk-to 李焯桃. 1993. *Guanni ji: Zhongwai dianying pian* 觀逆集: 中外電影篇 (Watching counter-currents: Chinese and foreign films). Hong Kong: Ciwenhua.

———. 1994. "The Return of the Father: Hong Kong New Wave and Its Chinese Context in the 1980s." In *New Chinese Cinemas: Forms, Identities, Politics*, edited by

Nick Browne, Paul G. Pickowicz, Vivian Sobchack, and Esther Yau. New York: Cambridge University Press.

———. 1997b. "Young and Dangerous and the 1997 Deadline." In *Hong Kong Panorama, 96–97,* the 21st Hong Kong International Film Festival, edited by Jacob Wong (Wang Qingkeng). Hong Kong: Urban Council.

———, ed. 1997a. *The China Factor in Hong Kong Cinema.* The 14th Hong Kong International Film Festival. Hong Kong: Urban Council, 1990. Revised edition.

Li, H. C. 1989. "Color, Character, and Culture: On *Yellow Earth, Black Cannon Incident,* and *Red Sorghum.*" *Modern Chinese Literature* 5: 91–119.

———. 1993. "Chinese Electric Shadows: A Selected Bibliography of Materials in English." *Modern Chinese Literature* 7.2 (Fall): 117–53.

———. 1994. "More Chinese Electric Shadows: A Supplementary List." *Modern Chinese Literature* 8 (Spring/Fall): 237–50.

———. 1998. "Chinese Electric Shadows III: And the Ship Sails On." *Modern Chinese Literature* 10 (Spring/Fall): 207–68.

———. 2000. "Hong Kong Electric Shadows: A Selected Bibliography of Studies in English." In *The Cinema of Hong Kong: History, Arts, Identity,* edited by Poshek Fu and David Desser. New York: Cambridge University Press.

Li Tianduo 李天鐸. 1997. *Taiwan dianying, shehui yu lishi* 台灣電影, 社會與歷史 (Cinema, society, and history in Taiwan). Taipei: Yatai.

Li Youxin 李又新, ed. 1986a. *Dianying, dianyingren, dianying kanwu* 電影, 電影人, 電影刊物 (Film, film people, film publications). Taipei: Zili wanbao she.

———, ed. 1986b. *Gang Tai liu da daoyan* 港台六大導演 (Six major directors in Hong Kong and Taiwan). Taipei: Zili wanbao she.

Li Zhenya 李振亞. 1998. "Cong lishi de huiyi dao kongjian de xiangxiang: Hou Xiaoxian dianying zhong dushi yingxiang de shiluo" 從歷史的回憶到空間的想像: 侯孝賢電影中都市影像的失落 (From historical memory to spatial imagination: images of the city in Hou Hsiao-hsien's films). *Zhongwai wenxue* 中外文學 (Chung-wai Literary Monthly) 27.5 (Oct.): 120–35.

Liao Ping-hui. 1993. "Rewriting Taiwanese National History: The February 28 Incident as Spectacle." *Public Culture* 5: 281–96

———. 1996. "The Case of the Emergent Cultural Criticism Columns in Taiwan's Newspaper Literary Supplements: Global/Local Dialectics in Contemporary Taiwanese Public Culture." In *Global/Local: Cultural Production and the Transnational Imaginary,* edited by Rob Wilson and Wimal Dissanayake. Durham, N.C.: Duke University Press.

———. 1997. "Postmodern Literary Discourse and Contemporary Public Culture in Taiwan." *Boundary 2* 24.3 (Fall): 41–63.

Lieberthal, Kenneth, Joyce Kallgren, Roderick MacFarquhar, and Frederic Wakeman, Jr., eds. 1991. *Perspectives on Modern China: Four Anniversaries.* Armonk, N.Y.: M. E. Sharpe.

Lin Gu. 2000. "Film Rakes in Money, But Faces Criticism." *China Daily,* Jan. 19.

Lin Niantong 林年同. 1985. "A Study of the Theories of Chinese Cinema in Their Relationship to Classical Aesthetics." *Modern Chinese Literature* 1.2 (Fall): 185–200.

————. 1991. *Zhongguo dianying meixue* 中國電影美學 (Chinese film aesthetics). Taipei: Yunchen.

Lin Wenchi (Lin Wenqi 林文淇). 1995. "Taiwan dianying zhongde Taibei chengxian" 台灣電影中的台北呈現 (The representation of Taipei in Taiwanese films.) In *Xunzhao dianying zhongde Taibei, 1950–1990* 尋找電影中的台北 (Focus on Taipei through cinema), edited by Ru-Shou Robert Chen 陳儒修 and Gene-Fon Liao 廖金鳳. Taipei: Wanxiang.

————. 1998. "Jiushi niandai Taiwan dushi dianying zhongde lishi, kongjian yu jia/guo" 九十年代台灣都市電影中的歷史, 空間與家/國 (History, space, and home/nation in Taiwan urban cinema of the 1990s). *Zhongwai wenxue* 中外文學 27.5 (Oct.): 99–119.

Link, E. Perry. 1999. *The Uses of Literature: Life in the Socialist Chinese Literary System.* Princeton: Princeton University Press.

Link, E. Perry, Richard Madsen, and Paul G. Pickowicz, eds. 1989. *Unofficial China: Popular Culture and Thought in the People's Republic.* Boulder: Westview.

Liu Chi-hui 劉紀蕙. 1996. "Bu yiyang de meigui gushi: *Hong meigui/bai meigui* dianfu wenzi de zhengzhi celüe" 不一樣的玫瑰故事: (紅玫瑰/白玫瑰)顛覆文字的政治策略 (An altered story: the political strategy of subverting language in *Red Rose, White Rose*). In *Zhongguo dianying: Lishi, wenhua yu zaixian* 中國電影: 歷史, 文化與再現 (Chinese cinema: history, culture, and representation), edited by Liu Xiancheng 劉現程. Taipei: Dianying shiliao yanjiuhui, Shijue chuanbo yishu xuehui.

Liu Debin 劉德瀕. 1997. "Minsuhua: dui minzu lishi yu xianshi de diangying chanshi" 民俗化: 對民族歷史與現實的電影闡釋 (Ethnography: cinematic elucidation of national history and reality). *Dianying yishu* 3: 23–31.

Liu Kang. 1998. "Is There an Alternative to (Capitalist) Globalization? The Debate about Modernity in China." In *The Cultures of Globalization*, edited by Fredric Jameson and Masao Miyoshi. Durham, N.C.: Duke University Press.

Liu Kang, and Xiaobing Tang, eds. 1993. *Politics, Ideology, and Literary Discourse in Modern China: Theoretical Interventions and Cultural Critique.* Durham, N.C.: Duke University Press.

Liu, Lydia H. 1993. "Translingual Practice: The Discourse of Individualism between China and the West." *Positions* 1.1 (Spring): 160–93.

————. 1995. *Translingual Practice: Literature, National Culture, and Translated Modernity—China, 1900–1937.* Stanford: Stanford University Press.

————. 1999. "*Beijing Sojourners in New York*: Postsocialism and the Question of Ideology in Global Media Culture." *Positions* 7.3 (Winter): 763–97.

Liu Weihong 劉偉宏. 1988. "Yu Wu Ziniu tan Wu Ziniu" 與吳子牛談吳子牛 (A conversation with Wu Ziniu). *Dangdai dianying* 4: 104–13.

Liu Wu-chi, and Irving Yucheng Lo, eds. 1975. *Sunflower Splendor: Three Thousand Years of Chinese Poetry.* Bloomington: Indiana University Press.

Liu Xiancheng 劉現程, ed. 1996. *Zhongguo dianying: Lishi, wenhua yu zaixian* 中國電影: 歷史, 文化與再現 (Chinese cinema: history, culture, and representation). Taipei: Dianying shiliao yanjiuhui, Shijue chuanbo yishu xuehui.

Liu Xiaoqing 劉曉慶. 1995. *Wo de zibai lu: cong dianying mingxing dao yiwan fujie er* 我的自白錄: 從電影明星到億萬富姐兒 (My own confessions: From a film star to a female billionaire). Shanghai: Shanghai wenyi chubanshe.

Liu Zaifu 劉再復. 1985–6. "Lun wenxue de zhutixing" 論文學的主體性 (The subjectivity in literature). *Wenxue pinglun* 6: 11–26; 1: 1–15.

———. 1986. *Xingge zuhe lun* 性格組合論 (On the construction of personalities). Shanghai: Shanghai wenyi chubanshe.

Lo Kwai-Cheung. 1993a. "Feminizing Technology: The *objet à* in *Black Cannon.*" In *Significant Others: Gender and Culture in Film and Literature East and West*, edited by William Burgwinkle, Glenn Man, and Valerie Wayne. Honolulu: University of Hawaii, College of Languages, Linguistics and Literature.

———. 1993b. *"Once Upon A Time*: Technology Comes to Presence in China." *Modern Chinese Literature* 7.2 (Fall): 79–96.

Logan, Bey. 1996. *Hong Kong Action Cinema*. New York: Overlook Press.

Loh Wai-fong. 1984. "From Romantic Love to Class Struggle: Reflections on the Film *Liu Sanjie.*" In *Popular Chinese Literature and Performing Arts in the People's Republic of China, 1949–1979*, edited by Bonnie S. McDougall. Berkeley: University of California Press.

Longxiang gongsi 龍祥公司. 1995. *Wu Ziniu de dianying: Nanjing 1937* 吳子牛的電影(南京 1937) (Wu Ziniu's film: *Nanjing 1937*). Taipei: Wanxiang.

Lopate, Phillip. 1994. "Odd Man Out: Interview with Tian Zhuangzhuang." *Film Comment* 30.4: 60–4.

Lösel, Jörg. 1980. *Die politische funktion des Spielfilms in der Volsrepublik China zwischen 1949 und 1965* (The political function of feature films in the People's Republic of China between 1949 and 1965). München: Minerva Publikation.

Loshitzky, Yosefa, and Raya Meyuhas. 1992. "'Ecstasy of Difference': Bertolucci's *The Last Emperor.*" *Cinema Journal* 31.2: 26–44.

Loukides, Paul, and Linda K. Fuller, eds. 1990. *Beyond the Stars: Stock Characters in American Popular Film*. Bowling Green, Ohio: Bowling Green State University Popular Press.

Lu Feiyi 盧非易. 1998. *Taiwan dianying: zhengzhi, jingji, meixue, 1949–1994* 台灣電影: 政治, 經濟, 美學 (Taiwan cinema: politics, economy, aesthetics). Taipei: Yuanliu.

Lu, Sheldon Hsiao-peng. 1997a. "Art, Culture, and Cultural Criticism in Post-New China." *New Literary History* 28.1 (Winter): 111–33.

———. 1997b. "Global POSTmodernIZATION: The Intellectual, the Artist, and China's Condition." *Boundary 2* 24.3 (Fall): 65–97.

———. 1997c. "Historical Introduction: Chinese Cinemas (1896–1996) and Transnational Film Studies." In *Transnational Chinese Cinema: Identity, Nationhood, Gender*, edited by Sheldon Hsiao-peng Lu. Honolulu: University of Hawaii Press.

———. 1997d. "National Cinema, Cultural Critique, Transnational Capital: The Films of Zhang Yimou." In *Transnational Chinese Cinema: Identity, Nationhood, Gender*, edited by Sheldon Hsiao-peng Lu. Honolulu: University of Hawaii Press.

———. 2000a. "Chinese Soap Opera: The Transnational Politics of Visuality, Sexuality, and Masculinity." *Cinema Journal* 40.1 (Fall 2000): 25–47.

———. 2000b. "Filming Diaspora and Identity: Hong Kong and 1997." In *The Cinema of Hong Kong: History, Arts, Identity*, edited by Poshek Fu and David Desser. New York: Cambridge University Press.

————, ed. 1997e. *Transnational Chinese Cinema: Identity, Nationhood, Gender*. Honolulu: University of Hawaii Press.

Lu Tonglin. 1993b. "How Do You Tell a Girl from a Boy? Uncertain Sexual Boundaries in *The Price of Frenzy*." In *Significant Others: Gender and Culture in Film and Literature East and West*, edited by William Burgwinkle, Glenn Man, and Valerie Wayne. Honolulu: University of Hawaii, College of Languages, Linguistics and Literature.

————. 1995. *Misogyny, Cultural Nihilism, and Oppositional Politics*. Stanford: Stanford University Press.

————, ed. 1993a. *Gender and Sexuality in Twentieth-Century Chinese Literature and Society*. Albany: State University of New York Press.

Lü Xiaoming 呂曉明. 1999. "90 niandai Zhongguo dianying jingguan zhiyi: 'diliudai' jiqi zhiyi" 九十年代中國電影景觀之一: "第六代"及其質疑 (A view in Chinese cinema of the 1990s: the "sixth generation" and its problematic nature). *Dianying yishu* 3: 23–8.

Luo Feng 洛楓. 1995. *Shijimo chengshi* 世紀末城市 (The decadent city). Hong Kong: Oxford University Press.

Luo Yijun 羅藝軍, ed. 1992. *Zhongguo dianying lilun wenxuan, 1920–1989* 中國電影理論文選 (Chinese film theory: an anthology). 2 vols. Beijing: Wenhua yishu chubanshe.

Ma Junxiang 馬軍驤. 1991. "Cong *Hong gaoliang* dao *Ju Dou*" 從(紅高粱)到(菊豆) (From *Red Sorghum* to *Ju Dou*). *Ershiyi shiji* 7 (Oct.): 123–32.

————. 1993. "Minzu zhuyi suo suzao de xiandai Zhongguo dianying" 民族主義所塑造的現代電影中國 (Modern Chinese film as shaped by nationalism). *Ershiyi shiji* 15 (Feb.): 112–9.

Ma Ning 馬寧 1987a. "Notes on the New Filmmakers." In *Chinese Film: The State of the Art in the People's Republic*, edited by George S. Semsel. New York: Praeger.

————. 1987b. "*Satisfied or Not*: Desire and Discourse in the Chinese Comedy of the 1960s." *East-West Film Journal* 2.1: 32–49.

————. 1989. "The Textual and Critical Difference of Being Radical: Reconstructing Chinese Leftist Films of the 1930s." *Wide Angle* 11.2: 22–31.

————. 1993. "Symbolic Representation and Symbolic Violence: Chinese Family Melodrama of the Early 1980s." In *Melodrama and Asian Cinema*, edited by Wimal Dissanayake. New York: Cambridge University Press.

————. 1994. "Spatiality and Subjectivity in Xie Jin's Film Melodrama of the New Period." In *New Chinese Cinemas: Forms, Identities, Politics*, edited by Nick Browne, Paul G. Pickowicz, Vivian Sobchack, and Esther Yau. New York: Cambridge University Press.

————. 1999. "Xin zhuliu dianying: dui guochan dianying de yige jianyi" 新主流電影: 對國產電影的一個建議 (The new mainstream film: a proposal for domestic films). *Dangdai dianying* 4: 4–16.

————. 2000. "2000 nian: xin zhuliu dianying zhenzheng de qidian" 2000 年: 新主流電影的真正起點 (2000: The real starting point of the New Mainstream Film). *Dangdai dianying* 1: 16–8.

Ma Qiang. 1988. "The Chinese Film in the 1980s: Art and Industry." In *Cinema and Cultural Identity: Reflections on Films from Japan, India, and China*, edited by Wimal Dissanayake. Lanham, Md.: University Press of America.

MacDougall, David. 1998. *Transcultural Cinema*. Edited by Lucien Taylor. Princeton: Princeton University Press.

Mackerras, Colin. 1994. *China's Minorities: Integration and Modernization in the Twentieth Century*. New York: Oxford University Press.

Mao Dun 茅盾. 1979. "Wenxue yu rensheng" 文學與人生 (Literature and life). In *Wenxue yundong shiliao xuan* 文學運動史料選 (Selected readings in literary movements), multiple vols, edited by Beijing daxue 北京大學, Beijing shifan daxue 北京師範大學, and Beijing shifan xueyuan 北京師範學院. Shanghai: Shanghai Jiaoyu chubanshe.

Marchetti, Gina. 1993. *Romance and the "Yellow Peril": Race, Sex, and Discursive Strategies in Hollywood Fiction*. Berkeley: University of California Press.

———.1997. "*Two Stage Sisters*: The Blossoming of a Revolutionary Aesthetic." In *Transnational Chinese Cinema: Identity, Nationhood, Gender*, edited by Sheldon Hsiao-peng Lu. Honolulu: University of Hawaii Press.

———. 2000. "Buying American, Consuming Hong Kong: Cultural Commerce, Fantasies of Identity, and the Cinema." In *The Cinema of Hong Kong: History, Arts, Identity*, edited by Poshek Fu and David Desser. New York: Cambridge University Press.

Marcuse, Herbert. 1978. *The Aesthetic Dimension: Toward a Critique of Marxist Aesthetics*. Boston: Beacon.

Marion, Donald. 1997. *The Chinese Filmography: The 2444 Feature Films Produced by Studios in the People's Republic of China From 1949 Through 1995*. Jefferson, N.C.: McFarland.

Massey, Doreen. 1994. *Space, Place and Gender*. Cambridge, England: Polity.

Matthews, Gordon. 1998. "Book Review of Ackbar Abbas, *Hong Kong: Culture and the Politics of Disappearance*." *Journal of Asian Studies* 57.4 (Nov.): 1112–23.

Matustik, Martin J. 1993. *Postnational Identity: Critical Theory and Existential Philosophy in Habermas, Kierkegaard, and Havel*. New York: Guilford.

Maxfield, James F. 1996. *The Fatal Woman: Sources of Male Anxiety in American Film Noir, 1941–1949*. Madison, N.J.: Fairleigh Dickinson University Press.

McDougall, Bonnie S. 1980. *Mao Zedong's Talks at the Yan'an Conference on Literature and Art: A Translation of the 1943 Text with Commentary*. Ann Arbor: University of Michigan, Center for Chinese Studies.

———, ed. 1984. *Popular Chinese Literature and Performing Arts in the People's Republic of China, 1949–1979*. Berkeley: University of California Press.

———. 1991. *The Yellow Earth: A Film by Chen Kaige, with a Complete Translation of the Filmscript*. Hong Kong: Chinese University Press.

———. 1993. "The Anxiety of Out-fluence: Creativity, History and Postmodernity." In *Inside Out: Modernism and Postmodernism in Chinese Literary Culture*, edited by Wendy Larson and Anne Wedell-Wedellsborg. Aarhus, Denmark: Aarhus University Press.

Meng Xianli 孟憲勵. 1994. *Quanxin de qiguan: hou xiandai zhuyi yu dangdai dianying* 全新的奇觀: 後現代主義與當代電影 (Brand new spectacles: postmodernism and contemporary cinema). Beijing: Zhongguo shehui chubanshe.

Meng Yue. 1993. "Female Images and National Myth." In *Gender Politics in Modern China: Writing and Feminism*, edited by Tani Barlow. Durham, N.C.: Duke University Press.

Mi Jiashan. 1998. "Discussing *The Troubleshooters.*" *Chinese Education and Society* 31.1 (Jan.–Feb.): 8–14.

Miller, Randall, ed. 1978. *Ethnic Images in American Film and Television.* Philadelphia: Balch Institute.

———, ed. 1980. *The Kaleidoscopic Lens: How Hollywood Views Ethnic Groups.* Englewood, N.J.: Jerome S. Ozer.

Mintz, Marilyn. 1978. *The Martial Arts Film.* New York: A. S. Barnes.

Miyoshi, Masao. 1993. "A Borderless World? From Colonialism to Transnationalism and the Decline of the Nation-State." *Critical Inquiry* 19 (Summer): 726–51.

———. 1998. "'Globalization,' Culture, and the University." In *The Cultures of Globalization,* edited by Fredric Jameson and Masao Miyoshi. Durham, N.C.: Duke University Press.

Mo Yan. 1993. *Red Sorghum: A Novel of China.* Translated by Howard Goldblatt. New York: Penguin Books.

Mohanty, Chandra Talpade, Ann Russo, and Lourdes Torres, eds. 1991. *Third World Women and the Politics of Feminism.* Bloomington: Indiana University Press.

Naficy, Hamid. 1996. "Phobic Spaces and Liminal Panics: Independent Transnational Film Genre." In *Global/Local: Cultural Production and the Transnational Imaginary,* edited by Rob Wilson and Wimal Dissanayake. Durham, N.C.: Duke University Press.

Nelson, Cary, and Lawrence Grossberg, eds. 1988. *Marxism and the Interpretation of Culture.* Urbana: University of Illinois Press.

New Cinema Festival, Italy, ed. 1978. *Cinema e spettacolo in Cina oggi* (Cinema and performance in today's China). The 14th International Festival of New Cinema. Catalogue 75. Fano, Italy: Publication Office of the Festival.

New Literary History, ed. 1997. "Cultural Studies: China and the West." A special issue. *New Literary History* 28.1 (Winter).

Ng Ho. 1997. "Exile, a Story of Love and Hate." In *The China Factor in Hong Kong Cinema,* the 14th Hong Kong International Film Festival, revised edition, edited by Li Cheuk-to. Hong Kong: Urban Council, 1990.

Ni Zhen 倪震. 1993a. "After *Yellow Earth.*" In *Film in Contemporary China,* edited by George S. Semsel, Chen Xihe, and Xia Hong. New York: Praeger.

———. 1993b. "Chengshi dianying de wenhua maodun" 城市電影的文化矛盾 (Cultural contradiction in urban cinema). In *Zhongguo dianying, dianying Zhongguo* 中國電影,電影中國 (Chinese film, China in films), edited by Fu Jen University 輔仁大學. Taipei: Furen daxue dazhong chuanbo xi.

———. 1994. "Classical Chinese Painting and Cinematographic Signification." In *Cinematic Landscapes: Observations on the Visual Arts and Cinema of China and Japan,* edited by Linda Erhlich and David Desser. Austin: University of Texas Press.

———. 1999. "Shouwang xinsheng dai" 守望新生代 (Expectations for the New-Born Generation). *Dianying yishu* 4: 70–3.

Nichols, Bill. 1994a. "Discovering Form, Inferring Meaning: New Cinemas and the Film Festival Circuit." *Film Quarterly* 47.3 (Spring): 16–30.

———. 1994b. "Global Image Consumption in the Age of Late Capitalism." *East-West Film Journal* 8.1 (Jan.): 68–85.

————, ed. 1976. *Movies and Methods: An Anthology*. Berkeley: University of California Press.

Nietzsche, Friedrich. 1971. "The Birth of Tragedy from the Spirit of Music." In *Critical Theory Since Plato*, edited by Hazard Adams. New York: Harcourt Brace Jovanovich.

Nowell-Smith, Geoffrey, ed. 1996. *The Oxford History of World Cinema*. New York: Oxford University Press.

Oehling, Richard. 1980. "The Yellow Menace: Asian Images in American Film." In *The Kaleidoscopic Lens: How Hollywood Views Ethnic Groups*, edited by Randall Miller. Englewood, N.J.: Jerome S. Ozer.

Ong, Aihwa. 1999. *Flexible Citizenship: The Cultural Logics of Transnationality*. Durham, N.C.: Duke University Press.

Ong, Aihwa, and Donald Nonini, eds. 1997. *Ungrounded Empires: The Cultural Politics of Modern Chinese Transnationalism*. London: Routledge.

Owen, Stephen. 1990. "The Anxiety of Global Influence: What Is World Poetry?" *New Republic* (Nov. 19): 28–32.

————. 1989. *Mi-Lou: Poetry and the Labyrinth of Desire*. Cambridge, Mass.: Harvard University Press.

Palumbo-Liu, David. 1999. *Asian/American: Historical Crossings of a Racial Frontier*. Stanford: Stanford University Press.

Pan Ruojian 潘若簡. 1996. "*Hong yingtao* zai shangye yunzuo zhiwai" 紅櫻桃在商業運作之外 (Red Cherry: Beyond commercial operations). *Dianying yishu* 3: 6–8.

Pickowicz, Paul G. 1984. "Early Chinese Cinema—The Era of Exploration." *Modern Chinese Literature* 1.1 (Sept.): 135–8.

————. 1985. "The Limits of Cultural Thaw: Chinese Cinema in the Early 1960s." In *Perspectives on Chinese Cinema*, East Asian Papers 39, edited by Chris Berry. Ithaca, N.Y.: Cornell University, China-Japan Program.

————. 1989. "Popular Cinema and Political Thought in Post-Mao China: Reflections on Official Pronouncements, Film, and the Film Audience." In *Unofficial China: Popular Culture and Thought in the People's Republic*, edited by Perry E. Link, Richard Madsen, and Paul G. Pickowicz. Boulder: Westview.

————. 1991. "The Theme of Spiritual Pollution in Chinese Films of the 1930s." *Modern China* 17.1 (Jan.): 38–75.

————. 1993a. "Melodramatic Representation and the 'May Fourth' Tradition of Chinese Cinema." In *From May Fourth to June Fourth: Fiction and Film in Twentieth-Century China*, edited by Ellen Widmer and David Der-wei Wang. Cambridge, Mass.: Harvard University Press.

————. 1993b. "Sinifying and Popularizing Foreign Culture: From Maxim Gorky's *The Lower Depths* to Huang Zuolin's *Ye dian*." *Modern Chinese Literature* 7.2: 7–31.

————. 1994. "Huang Jianxin and the Notion of Postsocialism." In *New Chinese Cinemas: Forms, Identities, Politics*, edited by Nick Browne, Paul G. Pickowicz, Vivian Sobchack, and Esther Yau. New York: Cambridge University Press.

————. 1995. "Velvet Prisons and the Political Economy of Chinese Filmmaking." In *Urban Spaces in Contemporary China: The Potential for Autonomy and Community in Post-Mao China*, edited by Deborah Davis, Richard Kraus, Barry Naughton, and Elizabeth Perry. New York: Cambridge University Press.

Pieterse, Jan Nederveen. 1995. "Globalization as Hybridization." In *Global Modernities*, edited by Mike Featherstone, Scott Lash, and Roland Robertson. London: Sage.

Pines, Jim, and Paul Willemen, eds. 1989. *Questions of Third Cinema*. London: British Film Institute.

Pratt, Mary Louise. 1992. *Imperial Eyes: Travel Writing and Transculturation*. London: Routledge.

Qi Hai 祁海. 1997. "Jilu pian chongfan dianying shichang de chanxiao celüe" 紀錄片重返電影市場的產銷策略 (Strategies of production and marketing in returning documentaries to the film market). *Dianying yishu* 1: 83–6.

Quiquemelle, Marie-Claire. 1991. "The Wan Brothers and Sixty Years of Animated Film in China." In *Perspectives on Chinese Cinema*, second and expanded edition, edited by Chris Berry. London: British Film Institute.

Quiquemelle, Marie-Claire, and Jean-Loup Passek, eds. 1985. *Le cinéma chinois*. Paris: Centre Georges Pompidou.

Rashkin, Elissa. 1993. "Rape as Castration as Spectacle: *The Price of Frenzy*'s Politics of Confusion." In *Gender and Sexuality in Twentieth-Century Chinese Literature and Society*, edited by Tonglin Lu. Albany: State University of New York Press.

Rayns, Tony. 1988. "The Position of Women in New Chinese Cinema." In *Cinema and Cultural Identity: Reflections on Films from Japan, India, and China*, edited by Wimal Dissanayake. Lanham, Md.: University Press of America.

———. 1989. "Chinese Vocabulary: An Introduction." In *"King of the Children" and the New Chinese Cinema*, edited by Chen Kaige and Tony Rayns. London: Faber and Faber.

———. 1991. "Breakthroughs and Setbacks: The Origins of the New Chinese Cinema." In *Perspectives on Chinese Cinema*, second and expanded edition, edited by Chris Berry. London: British Film Institute.

———. 1995. "The Ups and Downs of Zhou Xiaowen." *Sight and Sound* (July): 22–4.

———. 1996. "Provoking Desire." *Sight and Sound* (July): 26–9.

Rayns, Tony, and Scott Meek, eds. 1980. *Electric Shadows: 45 Years of Chinese Cinema*. Dossier 3. London: British Film Institute.

Reynaud, Bérénice. 1996. "Review of *Mahjong*." *Cinemaya* 32 (Spring): 31–2.

———. 1997. "Gay Overtures: Zhang Yuan's *Dong Gong, Xi Gong*." *Cinemaya* 36 (Spring): 31–3.

Ricoeur, Paul. 1965. *History and Truth*. Evanston, Ill.: Northwestern University Press.

Roach, Colleen, ed. 1993. *Communication and Culture in War and Peace*. Newbury Park, Calif.: Sage.

———. 1997. "Cultural Imperialism and Resistance in Media Theory and Literary Theory." *Media, Culture & Society* 19: 47–66.

Robertson, Roland. 1992. *Globalization: Social Theory and Global Culture*. London: Sage.

———. 1995. "Glocalization: Time-Space and Homogeneity-Heterogeneity." In *Global Modernities*, edited by Mike Featherstone, Scott Lash, and Roland Robertson. London: Sage.

Robinson, Lewis. 1984. "*Family*: A Study in Genre Adaptation." *Australian Journal of Chinese Affairs* 12: 35–57.

Rodríquez, Héctor. 1995. "The Cinema in Taiwan: Identity and Political Legitimacy." Ph.D. diss., New York University.

———. 1997. "Hong Kong Popular Culture as an Interpretive Arena: The Huang Feihong Film Series." *Screen* 38.1: 1–24.

———. 1998. "Questions of Chinese Aesthetics: Film Form and Narrative Space in the Cinema of King Hu." *Cinema Journal* 38.1 (Fall): 73–97.

Rogers, John D. 1994. "Post-Orientalism and the Interpretation of Premodern and Modern Political Identities: The Case of Sri Lanka." *Journal of Asian Studies* 53.1 (Feb.): 10–23.

Rony, Fatimah Tobing. 1996. *The Third Eye: Race, Cinema, and Ethnographic Spectacle.* Durham, N.C.: Duke University Press.

Rosen, Stanley. 1998. "Editor's Introduction." *Chinese Education and Society* 31.1 (Jan.–Feb.): 3–7.

Rothman, William. 1993a. "*The Goddess*: Reflections on Melodrama East and West." In *Melodrama and Asian Cinema*, edited by Wimal Dissanayake. New York: Cambridge University Press.

———.1993b. "Overview: What Is American About Film Study in America?" In *Melodrama and Asian Cinema*, edited by Wimal Dissanayake. New York: Cambridge University Press.

Ryan, Barbara. 1995. "Blood, Brothers, and Hong Kong Gangster Movies: Pop Culture Commentary on 'One China.'" In *Asian Popular Culture*, edited by John A. Lent. Boulder: Westview.

Ryan, Michael. 1988. "The Politics of Film: Discourse, Psychoanalysis, Ideology." In *Marxism and the Interpretation of Culture*, edited by Cary Nelson and Lawrence Grossberg. Urbana: University of Illinois Press.

Said, Edward. 1979. *Orientalism.* New York: Vintage.

———. 1983. *The World, the Text, and the Critic.* Cambridge, Mass.: Harvard University Press.

———. 1994. *Culture and Imperialism.* New York: Vintage.

Sakai, Naoki. 1997. *Translation and Subjectivity: On "Japan" and Cultural Nationalism.* Minneapolis: University of Minnesota Press.

Sandell, Jillian. 1996. "Reinventing Masculinity: The Spectacle of Male Intimacy in the Films of John Woo." *Film Quarterly* 49.4: 23–34.

Sassen, Saskia. 1991. *The Global City.* Princeton: Princeton University Press.

Saussy, Haun. 1999. "Postmodernism in China: A Sketch and Some Queries." In *Cross-Cultural Readings of Chinese: Narratives, Images, and Interpretations of the 1990s*, edited by Wen-hsin Yeh. Berkeley: University of California, Institute of East Asian Studies.

Schiller, Herbert. 1993. "Not Yet the Post-Imperialist Era." In *Communication and Culture in War and Peace*, edited by Colleen Roach. Newbury Park, Calif.: Sage.

Schwarcz, Vera. 1986. *The Chinese Enlightenment: Intellectuals and the Legacy of the May Fourth Movement of 1919.* Berkeley: University of California Press.

Semsel, George S., ed. 1987. *Chinese Film: The State of the Art in the People's Republic.* New York: Praeger.

Semsel, George S., Chen Xihe, and Xia Hong, eds. 1993. *Film in Contemporary China.* New York: Praeger.

Semsel, George S., Xia Hong, and Hou Jianping, eds. 1990. *Chinese Film Theory: A Guide to the New Era*. New York: Praeger.

Severson, Matt. 1996. "Silent Behind the Great Wall." *Film Comment* 32.3: 47–8.

Shambaugh, David, ed. 1995. *Greater China: The Next Superpower?* New York: Oxford University Press.

Shao Mujun. 1988. "Chinese Films Amidst the Tide of Reform." In *Cinema and Cultural Identity: Reflections on Films from Japan, India, and China*, edited by Wimal Dissanayake. Lanham, Md.: University Press of America.

———. 1993. "On the Ruins of Modern Beliefs." In *New Chinese Cinema*. Dossier 11, edited by Klaus Eder and Deac Rossell. London: National Film Theatre.

Shen Shiao-Ying. 1995a. "Permutations of the Foreign/er: A Study of the Works of Edward Yang, Stan Lai, Chang Yi, and Hou Hsiao-hsien." Ph.D. diss., Cornell University.

———. 1995b. "Where Has All the Capital Gone?: The State of Taiwan's Film Investment." *Cinemaya* 30 (Autumn): 4–12.

Shih Shu-mei. 1996. "Gender, Race, and Semicolonialism: Liu Na'ou's Urban Shanghai Landscape." *Journal of Asian Studies* 55.4 (Nov.): 934–56.

———. 1998. "Gender and a New Geopolitics of Desire: The Seduction of Mainland Women in Taiwan and Hong Kong Media." *Signs* 23.2 (Winter): 287–319.

———. 2000. *The Lure of the Modern: Writing Modernism in Semicolonial China, 1917–1937*. Berkeley: University of California Press.

Shohat, Ella, and Robert Stam. 1995. *Unthinking Eurocentrism: Multiculturalism and the Media*. London: Routledge.

Sklarew, Bruce H., Bonnie S. Kaufman, Ellen Handler Spitz, and Diane Borden, eds. 1998. *Bertolucci's "The Last Emperor": Multiple Takes*. Detroit: Wayne State University Press.

Smith, Anthony D. 1990. "Towards a Global Culture?" *Theory, Culture & Society* 7: 171–93.

Solanas, Fernando, and Octavio Getino. 1976. "Toward a Third Cinema." In *Movies and Methods: An Anthology*, edited by Bill Nichols. Berkeley: University of California Press.

Sollors, Werner. 1986. *Beyond Ethnicity: Consent and Descent in American Culture*. New York: Oxford University Press.

Spivak, Gayatri Chakravorty. 1988. *In Other Worlds: Essays in Cultural Politics*. London: Routledge.

———. 1992. "Teaching for the Times." *Journal of the MMLA* 25.1: 3–21.

Stam, Robert. 1989. *Subversive Pleasures: Bakhtin, Cultural Criticism, and Film*. Baltimore: Johns Hopkins University Press.

Stephens, Chuck. 1996a. "Intersection: Tsai Ming-liang's Yearning Bike Boys and Heartsick Heroines." *Film Comment* 32.5: 20–23.

———. 1996b. "Time Pieces: Wong Kar-Wai and the Persistence of Memory." *Film Comment* 32.1: 12–18.

Stephenson, Shelley. 1999. "'Her Traces Are Found Everywhere': Shanghai, Li Xianglan, and the 'Greater East Asia Film Sphere.'" In *Cinema and Urban Culture in Shanghai, 1922–1943*, edited by Yingjin Zhang. Stanford: Stanford University Press.

Stringer, Julian. 1997a. "*Centre Stage*: Reconstructing the Bio-Pic." *Cineaction* 42 (Feb.): 28–39.

———. 1997b. "'Your Tender Smiles Give Me Strength': Paradigms of Masculinity in John Woo's *A Better Tomorrow* and *The Killer.*" *Screen* 38.1: 25–41.

Stromgren, Dick. 1990. "The Chinese Syndrome: The Evolving Image of Chinese and Chinese-Americans in Hollywood Films." In *Beyond the Stars: Stock Characters in American Popular Film*, edited by Paul Loukides and Linda K. Fuller. Bowling Green, Ohio: Bowling Green State University Popular Press.

Studlar, Gaylyn. 1989. *In the Realm of Pleasure: Von Sternberg, Dietrich, and the Masochistic Aesthetic*. Urbana: University of Illinois Press.

Su Tong. 1993. *Raise the Red Lantern: Three Novellas*. Translated by Michael Duke. New York: William Morrow.

Sutton, Donald S. 1994. "Ritual, History, and the Films of Zhang Yimou." *East-West Film Journal* 8.2: 31–46.

Tajima, Renee. 1989. "Lotus Blossoms Don't Bleed: Images of Asian Women." In *Making Waves: An Anthology of Writing by and about Asian American Women*, edited by Asian Women United of California. Boston: Beacon.

Tam Kwok-kan, and Wimal Dissanayake. 1998. *New Chinese Cinema*. New York: Oxford University Press.

Tan See Kam, Justin Clemens, and Eleanor Hogan. 1994–95. "Clara Law: Seeking an Audience Outside Hong Kong." *Cinemaya* 25–26 (Autumn–Winter): 50–54.

Tang Wenbiao 唐文標. 1976. *Zhang Ailing zasui* 張愛玲雜碎 (Miscellanies on Eileen Chang). Taipei: Lianjing chubanshe.

———, ed. 1982. *Zhang Ailing juan* 張愛玲卷 (A collection on Eileen Chang). Hong Kong: Yiwen.

Tang Xiaobing. 1993. "The Function of New Theory: What Does It Mean to Talk about Postmodernism in China?" In *Politics, Ideology, and Literary Discourse in Modern China: Theoretical Interventions and Cultural Critique*, edited by Liu Kang and Xiaobing Tang. Durham, N.C.: Duke University Press.

———. 1994. "Configuring the Modern Space: Cinematic Representation of Beijing and Its Politics." *East-West Film Journal* 8.2: 47–69.

———. 2000. *China Modern: The Heroic and the Quotidian*. Durham, N.C.: Duke University Press.

Tang, Xiaobing, and Stephen Snyder, eds. 1996. *In Pursuit of Contemporary East Asian Culture*. Boulder: Westview.

Tay, William. 1994. "The Ideology of Initiation: The Films of Hou Hsiao-hsien." In *New Chinese Cinemas: Forms, Identities, Politics*, edited by Nick Browne, Paul G. Pickowicz, Vivian Sobchack, and Esther Yau. New York: Cambridge University Press.

Teng Sue-feng 滕淑芬. 1993. "Liang'an dianying bai *Xiyan*?" 兩岸電影擺喜宴 ("The Wedding Banquet" for Chinese films from both sides of the Taiwan Strait?). *Sinorama* (May): 32–40.

———. 1995. "Xin daoyan, xiang 'zainan' tiaozhan" 新導演向'災難'挑戰 (New directors take on "hell"). *Sinorama* (June): 43–51.

Teo, Stephen. 1997. *Hong Kong Cinema: The Extra Dimensions*. London: British Film Institute.

———. 2000. "The 1970s: Movement and Transition." In *The Cinema of Hong Kong: History, Arts, Identity*, edited by Poshek Fu and David Desser. New York: Cambridge University Press.

Tomlinson, John. 1991. *Cultural Imperialism: A Critical Introduction*. Baltimore: Johns Hopkins University Press.

Toroptsev, Sergei (Tuoluopucaifu). 1982. *Ocherk istorri kitaiskogo kino, 1896–1966* (Essays on the history of Chinese cinema, 1896–1966). Moscow, 1979. Translated as *Zhongguo dianying shi gailun* 中國電影史概 in Chinese. Beijing: Zhongguo dianying jia xiehui ziliao shi.

Townsend, James. 1996. ."Chinese Nationalism." In *Chinese Nationalism*, edited by Jonathan Unger. Armonk, N.Y.: M. E. Sharpe.

Trinh, T. Minh-ha. 1989. *Woman, Native, Other: Writing Postcoloniality*. Bloomington: Indiana University Press.

Tsui, Athena. 1997. "Interview with Peter Chan." In *Hong Kong Panorama, 96–97*, the 21st Hong Kong International Film Festival, edited by Jacob Wong (Wang Qingkeng). Hong Kong: Urban Council.

Tsui, Curtis. 1995. "Subjective Culture and History: The Ethnographic Cinema of Wong Kar-wai." *Asian Cinema* 7.2: 93–124.

Tu Weiming. 1991. "Cultural China: The Periphery as the Center." *Daedalus* 120.2: 1–32.

Tuohy, Sue. 1999. "Metropolitan Sounds: Music in Chinese Films of the 1930s." In *Cinema and Urban Culture in Shanghai, 1922–1943*, edited by Yingjin Zhang. Stanford: Stanford University Press.

Tyler, Patrick E. 1996. "In China, Letting a Hundred Films Wither." *New York Times*, Dec. 1, sec. H2, p. 26.

Unger, Jonathan, ed. 1996. *Chinese Nationalism*. Armonk, N.Y.: M. E. Sharpe.

Wang Ban. 1997. *Sublime Figure of History: Aesthetics and Politics in Twentieth-Century China*. Stanford: Stanford University Press.

———. 1999. "Trauma and History in Chinese Film: Reading *The Blue Kite* against Melodrama." *Modern Chinese Literature and Culture* 11.1 (Spring): 125–55.

Wang, David Der-wei. 1992. *Fictional Realism in Twentieth-Century China: Mao Dun, Lao She, Shen Congwen*. New York: Columbia University Press.

———. 1997. *Fin-de-Siècle Splendor: Repressed Modernities of Late Qing Fiction, 1849–1911*. Stanford: Stanford University Press.

Wang Fei-yun. 1995. "Flowers Blooming in Barren Soil." *Free China Review* 452 (Feb.): 4–33.

Wang Hui 汪暉. 1989. "Dangdai dianying zhongde xiangtu yu dushi: xunzhao lishi de jieshi yu shengming de guisu" 當代電影中的鄉土與都市: 尋找歷史的解釋與生命的歸宿 (The country and the city in contemporary films: searching for historical explanations and the destiny of life). *Dianying yishu* 2: 12–19, 23.

———. 1998a. "Contemporary Chinese Thought and the Question of Modernity." *Social Text* 16.2 (Summer): 9–44.

———. 1998b. "PRC Cultural Studies and Cultural Criticism in the 1990s." *Positions* 6.1 (Spring): 239–51.

Wang Jing. 1996. *High Culture Fever: Politics, Aesthetics, and Ideology in Deng's China.* Berkeley: University of California Press.

———, ed. 1998. *China's Avant-Garde Fiction: An Anthology.* Durham, N.C.: Duke University Press.

Wang Ning 王寧. 1993. "Constructing Postmodernism: The Chinese Case and Its Different Versions." *Canadian Review of Comparative Literature* 20 (March–June): 49–61.

———. 1995. "Hou zhimin yujing yu Zhongguo dangdai dianying" 後殖民語境與中國當代電影 (The postcolonial context and contemporary Chinese cinema). *Dangdai dianying* 5: 32–9.

———. 1997. "The Mapping of Chinese Postmodernity." *Boundary 2* 24.3 (Fall): 19–40.

Wang Qun 王群. 1999. "Miandui xiandai wenming de sikao: xinshiqi dushi dianying chuangzuo tantao" 面對現代文明的思考: 新時期都市電影創作探討 (Thinking in the face of modern civilization: urban cinema of the New Era). *Dangdai dianying* 5: 74–9.

Wang Yuechuan 王岳川. 1996. "Hou xiandai zhuyi yu Zhongguo dangdai wenhua." 後現代主義與中國當代文化 (Postmodernism and contemporary Chinese culture). *Zhongguo shehui kexue* 中國社會科學 3: 175–85.

Wang, (Eugene) Yuejin. 1989. "The Cinematic Other and the Cultural Self? De-centering the Cultural Identity on Cinema." *Wide Angle* 11.2: 32–9.

———. 1991. "*Red Sorghum*: Mixing Memory and Desire." In *Perspectives on Chinese Cinema*, second and expanded edition, edited by Chris Berry. London: British Film Institute.

———. 1993. "Melodrama as Historical Understanding: The Making and Unmaking of Communist History." In *Melodrama and Asian Cinema*, edited by Wimal Dissanayake. New York: Cambridge University Pres.

———. 1996. "*Samsara*: Self and the Crisis of Visual Narrative." In *Narratives of Agency: Self-Making in China, India, and Japan*, edited by Wimal Dissanayake. Minneapolis: University of Minnesota Press.

Waters, Malcolm. 1995. *Globalization.* London: Routledge.

Wei Lian 韋廉. 1997. "Daoyan Wei Lian tan zhanzheng yingpian" 導演韋廉談戰爭影片 (Director Wei Lian talks about war films). *Dianying yishu* 4: 60–5.

Weisser, Thomas. 1997. *Asian Cult Cinema.* New York: Boulevard Books.

White, Jerry. 1997. "The Films of Ning Ying: China Unfolding in Miniature." *Cineaction* 42 (Feb.): 2–9.

Widmer, Ellen, and David Der-wei Wang, eds., 1993. *From May Fourth to June Fourth: Fiction and Film in Twentieth-Century China.* Cambridge, Mass.: Harvard University Press.

Wilkerson, Douglas. 1994a. "Book Review of Wimal Dissanayake, ed., *Melodrama and Asian Cinema.*" *Journal of Asian Studies* 53.2 (May): 509–10.

———. 1994b. "Film and the Visual Arts in China: An Introduction." In *Cinematic Landscapes: Observations on the Visual Arts and Cinema of China and Japan*, edited by Linda Erhlich and David Desser. Austin: University of Texas Press.

Willemen, Paul. 1989. "The Third Cinema Question: Notes and Reflections." In *Questions of Third Cinema*, edited by Jim Pines and Paul Willemen. London: British Film Institute.

Williams, Tony. 1997a. "From Hong Kong to Hollywood: John Woo and His Discontents." *Cineaction* 42 (Feb.): 40–6.

———. 1997b. "Space, Place, and Spectacle: The Crisis Cinema of John Woo." *Cinema Journal* 36.2: 67–84. Reprinted in *The Cinema of Hong Kong: History, Arts, Identity*, edited by Poshek Fu and David Desser. New York: Cambridge University Press, 2000.

———. 1998. "Border-Crossing Melodrama: *Song of the Exile*." *Jump Cut* 42 (Feb.): 94–100.

Wilson, Elizabeth. 1991. *The Sphinx in the City: Urban Life, the Control of Disorder, and Women*. Berkeley: University of California Press.

Wilson, Patricia. 1987. "The Founding of the Northeast Film Studio, 1946–1949." In *Chinese Film: The State of the Art in the People's Republic*, edited by George S. Semsel. New York: Praeger.

Wilson, Rob, and Wimal Dissanayake, eds. 1996. *Global/Local: Cultural Production and the Transnational Imaginary*. Durham, N.C.: Duke University Press.

Wong, Eugene Franklin. 1978. *On Visual Media Racism: Asians in the American Motion Pictures*. New York: Arno Press.

Wong, Jacob (Wang Qingkeng), ed. 1997. *Hong Kong Panorama, 96–97*. The 21st Hong Kong International Film Festival. Hong Kong: Urban Council.

Woo, Catherine Yi-Yu Cho. 1991. "The Chinese Montage: From Poetry and Painting to the Silver Screen." In *Perspectives on Chinese Cinema*, second and expanded edition, edited by Chris Berry. London: British Film Institute.

Wu Hong. 1997. "The Hong Kong Clock—Public Time-Telling and Political Time/Space." *Public Culture* 9.3 (Spring): 329–54.

Wu Xianggui. 1992. "The Chinese Film Industry since 1977." Ph.D. diss., University of Oregon.

Wu Ziniu 吳子牛. 1999a. "Jiqing benyong song guoge" 激情奔涌頌國歌 (A passionate eulogy of the national anthem). *Dianying yishu* 5: 4–9.

———. 1999b. "Pai *Guoge* de chuzong" 拍國歌的初宗 (My original intentions on shooting *The National Anthem*). *Dangdai dianying* 5: 5–6.

Xia Hong. 1987. "Film Theory in the People's Republic of China: The New Era." In *Chinese Film: The State of the Art in the People's Republic*, edited by George S. Semsel. New York: Praeger.

Xianggang Zhongguo dianying xuehui 香港中國電影學會 (Hong Kong Chinese Film Association), ed. 1984. *Tansuo de niandai* 探索的年代 (Early Chinese cinema: the era of exploration). Program for a festival of films of the 1930s, sponsored by Hong Kong Arts Center and Hong Kong Chinese Film Association.

Xiao Nan 蕭南, ed. 1995. *Guizu cainü Zhang Ailing* 貴族才女張愛玲 (Eileen Chang, a talented aristocratic woman). Chengdu: Sichuan wenyi chubanshe.

Xiao Zhiwei. 1994. "Film Censorship in China, 1927–1937." Ph.D. diss., University of California, San Diego.

———. 1997. "Anti-Imperialism and Film Censorship During the Nanjing Decade, 1927–1937." In *Transnational Chinese Cinema: Identity, Nationhood, Gender*, edited by Sheldon Hsiao-peng Lu. Honolulu: University of Hawaii Press.

―――. 1999. "Constructing a New National Culture: Film Censorship and the Issues of Cantonese Dialect, Superstition, and Sex in the Nanjing Decade." In *Cinema and Urban Culture in Shanghai, 1922–1943*, edited by Yingjin Zhang. Stanford: Stanford University Press.

Xie Fei 謝飛. 1990. "'Disidai' de zhengming" "第四代"的證明 (The testimony of the "Fourth Generation"). *Dianying yishu* 3: 17–29.

Xu Ben 徐賁. 1995. "'Disan shijie piping' zai dangjin Zhongguo de chujing" "第三世界批評"在當今中國的處境 ("Third World criticism" in contemporary China). *Ershiyi shiji* 27 (Feb.): 16–27.

―――. 1998. "'From Modernity to Chineseness': The Rise of Nativist Cultural Theory in Post-1989 China." *Positions* 6.1 (Spring): 203–37.

―――. 1999a. "Contesting Memory for Intellectual Self-Positioning: The 1990s' New Cultural Conservatism in China." *Modern Chinese Literature and Culture* 11.1 (Spring): 157–92.

―――. 1999b. *Disenchanted Democracy: Chinese Cultural Criticism after 1989*. Ann Arbor: University of Michigan Press.

Yang Cun 楊村. 1954. *Zhongguo dianying sanshinian* 中國電影三十年 (Thirty years of Chinese film). Hong Kong: Shijie chubanshe.

Yang Dechang 楊德昌 (Edward Yang). 1994. *Duli shidai* 獨立時代 (A Confucian confusion). Taipei: Wanxiang.

Yang, Mayfair Mei-hui. 1993. "Of Gender, State Censorship, and Overseas Capital: An Interview with Chinese Director Zhang Yimou." *Public Culture* 5: 297–313.

―――. 1997. "Mass Media and Transnational Subjectivity in Shanghai: Notes on (Re)Cosmopolitanism in a Chinese Metropolis." In *Ungrounded Empires: The Cultural Politics of Modern Chinese Transnationalism*, edited by Aihwa Ong and Donald Nonini. London: Routledge.

―――, ed. 1999. *Spaces of Their Own: Women's Public Sphere in Transnational China*. Minneapolis: University of Minnesota Press.

Yang Mingyu. 1995. "China: Once Upon A Time/Hong Kong: 1997: A Critical Study of Contemporary Martial Arts Films." Ph.D. diss., University of Maryland.

Yang, Ping. 1991. "A Director Who is Trying to Change the Audience: A Chat with Young Director Tian Zhuangzhuang." In *Perspectives on Chinese Cinema*, second and expanded edition, edited by Chris Berry. London: British Film Institute.

Yang Xiaobin 楊小濱. 1995. "'Hou xiandai' huo 'hou Mao Deng': guanyu Zhongguo xianfeng wenxue jiqi lishi beijing de lilun tigang" "後現代"或著"後毛鄧": 關於中國先鋒文學及其歷史背境的理論提綱 ("Postmodern" or "post-Mao-Deng": A theoretical outline on China's avant-garde literature and its historical background). *Jintian* 2: 188–209.

Yau, Esther C. M. 1987–8. "*Yellow Earth*: Western Analysis and a Non-Western Text." *Film Quarterly* 41.2: 22–33.

―――. 1989a. "Cultural and Economic Dislocations: Filmic Phantasies of Chinese Women in the 1980s." *Wide Angle* 11.2: 6–21.

―――. 1989b. "Is China the End of Hermeneutics? Or, Political and Cultural Usage of Non-Han Women in Mainland Chinese Films." *Discourse* 11.2: 115–36.

———. 1990. "Filmic Discourse on Women in Chinese Cinema (1949–65): Art, Ideology and Social Relations." Ph.D. diss., University of California, Los Angeles.

———. 1993. "International Fantasy and the 'New Chinese Cinema.'" *Quarterly Review of Film and Video* 14.3: 95–107.

———. 1994a. "Border Crossing: Mainland China's Presence in Hong Kong Cinema." In *New Chinese Cinemas: Forms, Identities, Politics*, edited by Nick Browne, Paul G. Pickowicz, Vivian Sobchack, and Esther Yau. New York: Cambridge University Press.

———. 1994b. "Is China the End of Hermeneutics? or, Political and Cultural Usage of Non-Han Women in Mainland Chinese Films." In *Multiple Voices in Feminist Film Criticism*, edited by Diane Carson, Linda Dittmar, and Janice R. Welsch. Minneapolis: University of Minnesota Press.

———. 1996. "Compromised Liberation: The Politics of Class in Chinese Cinema of the Early 1950s." In *The Hidden Foundation: Cinema and the Question of Class*, edited by David James and Rick Berg. Minneapolis: University of Minnesota Press.

———, ed. 2001. *At Full Speed: Hong Kong Cinema in a Borderless World*. Minneapolis: University of Minnesota Press.

Ye Daying 葉大鷹. 1996. "Wo he *Hong yingtao*" 我和紅櫻桃 (*Red Cherry* and me). *Dianying yishu* 1: 48–50.

Ye Tan 葉坦. 1998. "'Dianying shi ganqing xing de dongxi': yu Zhang Yimou de tanhua" "電影是感情性的東西": 與張藝謀的談話 ("Film is emotional stuff": a conversation with Zhang Yimou). *Dianying yishu* 3: 52–9.

Yeh, Michelle (Xi Mi 奚密). 1991. "Chayi de jiaolü: yige huiying" 差異的焦慮: 一個回應 (The anxiety of difference: a rejoinder). *Jintian* 1: 94–6.

———. 1998. "International Theory and the Transnational Critics: China in the Age of Multiculturalism." *Boundary 2* 25.3 (Fall): 193–222.

Yeh Yueh-yu. 1995. "A National Score: Popular Music and Taiwanese Cinema." Ph.D. diss., University of Southern California.

———. 1999. "A Life of Its Own: Musical Discourse in Wong Kar-Wai' s Films." *Post Script* 19.1 (Fall): 120–36.

Yin Hong 尹鴻. 1998a. *Shiji zhuanzhe shiqi de Zhongguo yingshi wenhua* 世紀轉折時期的中國影視文化 (Chinese film and television culture in the transition period of the century). Beijing: Beijing chubanshe.

———. 1998b. "Zai jiafeng zhong zhangda: Zhongguo dalu xinsheng dai de dianying shijie" 在火縫中長大: 中國大陸新生代的電影世界 (Growing up between the fissures: The film world of the new-born generation). *Ershiyi shiji* 49 (Oct.): 88–93.

———. 1999. "98 Zhongguo dianying beiwang" 98 中國電影備忘 (Memoradum on 1998 Chinese films). *Dangdai dianying* 1: 21–30.

———. 2000. "1999 Zhongguo dianying beiwang" 1999 中國電影備忘 (Memorandum on 1999 Chinese films). *Dangdai dianying* 1: 10–5.

Yip, June. 1997. "Constructing a Nation: Taiwanese History and the Films of Hou Hsiao-hsien." In *Transnational Chinese Cinema: Identity, Nationhood, Gender*, edited by Sheldon Hsiao-peng Lu. Honolulu: University of Hawaii Press.

Yoshimoto, Mitsuhiro. 1991. "The Difficulty of Being Radical: The Discipline of Film Studies and the Postcolonial World Order." *Boundary 2* 18.3: 242–57.

Yoshino, Kosaku. 1992. *Cultural Nationalism in Contemporary Japan: A Sociological Enquiry*. London: Routledge.

Yue Ming-Bao. 1996. "Visual Agency and Ideological Fantasy in Three Films by Zhang Yimou." In *Narratives of Agency: Self-Making in China, India, and Japan*, edited by Wimal Dissanayake. Minneapolis: University of Minnesota Press.

Zha Jianying. 1995. *China Pop: How Soap Operas, Tabloids, and Bestsellers Are Transforming a Culture*. New York: New Press.

Zhan Hongzhi 詹宏志. 1996. *Chengshi ren: dushi kongjian de ganjue, fuhao he jieshi* 城市人: 都市空間的感覺, 符號和解釋 (City people: perceptions, signs, and interpretations of urban space). Taipei: Maitian.

Zhang Che 張徹. 1989. *Huigu Xianggang dianying sanshinian* 回顧香港電影三十年 (30 years of Hong Kong cinema in recollection). Hong Kong: Sanlian shudian.

Zhang Junxiang 張駿祥 and Cheng Jihua 程季華, eds. 1995. *Zhongguo dianying da cidian* 中國電影大辭典 (China cinema encyclopedia). Shanghai: Shanghai cishu chubanshe.

Zhang Longxi. 1992. "Western Theory and Chinese Reality." *Critical Inquiry* 19 (Autumn): 105–30.

———. 1998. *Mighty Opposites: From Dichotomies to Differences in the Comparative Study of China*. Stanford: Stanford University Press.

Zhang Xuan 張暄. 1989. "'Yingtan qianfu' Wu Ziniu" "影壇纖夫"吳子牛 (Wu Ziniu, a "boat tracker" in the film circles). *Wenhui dianying shibao* (Feb. 25–March 25).

Zhang Xudong. 1997. *Chinese Modernism in the Era of Reforms: Cultural Fever, Avant-garde Fiction, and the New Chinese Cinema*. Durham, N.C.: Duke University Press.

———. 1998. "Nationalism, Mass Culture, and the Intellectual Strategies in Post-Tiananmen China." *Social Text* 16.2 (Summer): 109–40.

———. 1999. "Postmodernism and Post-Socialist Society: Cultural Politics in China After the 'New Era.'" *New Left Review* 237 (Sept.–Oct.): 77–105.

Zhang, Yingjin. 1990. "Ideology of the Body in *Red Sorghum*: National Allegory, National Roots, and Third Cinema." *East-West Film Journal* 4.2 (June): 38–53. Reprinted in *Colonialism and Nationalism in Asian Cinema*, edited by Wimal Dissanayake. Bloomington: Indiana University Press, 1994.

———. 1993a. "Narrative, Ideology, Subjectivity: Defining a Subversive Discourse in Chinese Reportage." In *Politics, Ideology, and Literary Discourse in Modern China: Theoretical Interventions and Cultural Critique*, edited by Liu Kang and Xiaobing Tang. Durham, N.C.: Duke University Press.

———. 1993b. "Re-envisioning the Institution of Chinese Literary Studies: Strategies of Positionality and Self-Reflexivity." *Positions* 1.3: 816–32.

———. 1994a. "Engendering Chinese Filmic Discourse of the 1930s: Configurations of Modern Women in Shanghai in Three Silent Films." *Positions* 2.3 (Winter): 603–28.

———. 1994b. "The Idyllic Country and the Modern City: Cinematic Configurations of Family in *Osmanthus Alley* and *The Terrorizer*." *Tamkang Review* 25.1 (Autumn): 81–99.

———. 1994c. "The Institutionalization of Modern Literary History in China, 1922–1980." *Modern China* 20.3 (July): 347–77.

———. 1996. *The City in Modern Chinese Literature and Film: Configurations of Space, Time, and Gender*. Stanford: Stanford University Press.

————. 1997. "Building a National Literature in Modern China: Literary Criticism, Gender Ideology, and the Public Sphere." *Journal of Modern Literature in Chinese* 1.1 (July): 47–74.

————, ed. 1998. *China in a Polycentric World: Essays in Chinese Comparative Literature.* Stanford: Stanford University Press.

————. 1999b. "Prostitution and Urban Imagination: Negotiating the Public and the Private in Chinese Films of the 1930s." In *Cinema and Urban Culture in Shanghai, 1922–1943*, edited by Yingjin Zhang. Stanford, Calif.: Stanford University Press.

————. 2000. "A Typography of Chinese Film Historiography." *Asian Cinema* 11.1: 16–32.

————. 2001a. "Artwork, Commodity, Event: Representations of the Female Body in Modern Chinese Pictorials." In *Shanghai Visual Culture, 1850s–1930s*, edited by Jason Kuo. Seattle: University of Washington Press.

————. 2001b. "The Corporeality of Erotic Imagination: A Study of Pictorials and Cartoons in Republican China." In *Illustrating Asia: Comics, Humor Magazines, and Picture Books*, edited by John A. Lent. London: Curzon.

————, ed. 1999a. *Cinema and Urban Culture in Shanghai, 1922–1943.* Stanford: Stanford University Press.

Zhang, Yingjin, and Zhiwei Xiao. 1998. *Encyclopedia of Chinese Film.* London: Routledge.

Zhang Yiwu 張頤武. 1993. "Quanqiu xing hou zhimin yujing zhong de Zhang Yimou" 全球性後殖民語境中的張藝謀 (Zhang Yimou in the context of global postcoloniality). *Dangdai dianying* 3: 18–25.

————. 1997. "Postmodernism and Chinese Novels of the Nineties." *Boundary 2* 24.3 (Fall): 247–59.

Zhang Zhen. 1998a. "An Amorous History of the Silver Screen." Ph.D. diss., University of Chicago.

————. 1998b. "The 'Shanghai Factor' in Hong Kong Cinema: A Tale of Two Cities in Historical Perspectives." *Asian Cinema* 10.1 (Fall): 146–59.

————. 1999. "Teahouse, Shadowplay, Bricolage: *Laborer's Love* and the Question of Early Chinese Cinema." In *Cinema and Urban Culture in Shanghai, 1922–1943*, edited by Yingjin Zhang. Stanford, Calif.: Stanford University Press.

Zhao, (Henry) Yiheng 趙毅衡. 1995. "'Houxue' yu Zhongguo xin baoshou zhuyi" "後學" 與中國新保守主義 ("Post-isms" and Chinese new conservatism). *Ershiyi shiji* 27 (Feb.): 4–15.

————. 1997. "Post-Isms and Chinese New Conservatism." *New Literary History* 28.1 (Winter): 31–44.

Zheng Dongtian. 1990. "No Need to Be Embarrassed." *China Screen* 2: 31.

————. 1993a. "Promote Yourself." *China Screen* 3: 33.

————. 1993b. "Three in One." *China Screen* 1: 32.

Zheng Junli 鄭君里. 1936. "Xiandai Zhongguo dianying shilüe" 現代中國電影史略 (A concise history of modern Chinese film). *Jindai Zhongguo yishu fazhan shi* 近代中國藝術發展史 (A history of the development of art in modern China). Shanghai: Liangyou. Reprinted in *Zhongguo wusheng dianying* 中國無聲電影 (Chinese silent cinema), edited by Dai Xiaolan 戴小蘭. Beijing: Zhongguo dianying chubanshe, 1996.

Zheng Yi. 1997. "Narrative Images of the Historical Passion: Those *Other* Women—On the Alterity in the New Wave of Chinese Cinema." In *Transnational Chinese Cinema: Identity, Nationhood, Gender*, edited by Sheldon Hsiao-peng Lu. Honolulu: University of Hawaii Press.

Zhong Chengxiang 仲呈祥. 1988. "*Honggaoliang*: xinde dianying gaibian guannian" 紅高梁: 新的電影改編觀念 (*Red Sorghum*: a new concept of film adaptation). *Wenxue pinglun* 4: 44–50.

Zhong Dafeng. 1993. "A Historical Survey of Yingxi Theory." In *Film in Contemporary China*, edited by George S. Semsel, Chen Xihe, and Xia Hong. New York: Praeger.

Zhong Dafeng, Zhen Zhang, and Yingjin Zhang. 1997. "From *Wenmingxi* (Civilized Play) to *Yingxi* (Shadowplay): The Foundation of Shanghai Film Industry in the 1920s." *Asian Cinema* 9.1 (Fall): 46–64.

Zhongguo dianying chubanshe 中國電影出版社, ed. 1994. *Lun Zhang Yimou* 論張藝謀 (Zhang Yimou). Beijing: Zhongguo dianying chubanshe.

Zhongguo dianying nianjian she 中國電影年鑑社 (China film yearbook society), ed. 1996. *Zhongguo dianying nianjian 1996* 中國電影年鑑 1996 (China Film Yearbook 1996). Beijing: Zhongguo dianying chubanshe.

Zhongguo dianying yishu yanjiu zhongxin 中國電影藝術研究中心 (China film arts research center), ed. 1984. *Li shi, zhangzhen, dianying mei* 歷史, 戰爭, 電影美 (History, wars, and cinematic beauty). Beijing: Jiefangjun wenyi chubanshe.

Zhongguo shehui kexue yuan wenxue yanjiu suo 中國社會科學院文學研究所, ed. 1982. "*Liangge kouhao*" *lunzheng ziliao xuanbian* "兩個口號"論爭資料選編 (Selected materials on the debate over "two slogans"). 2 vols. Beijing: Renmin wenxue chubanshe.

Zhongguo yinmu 中國銀幕, ed. 1997. "Zhongguo dianying houji ? ren" 中國電影後繼？人 (Who are the new generation of Chinese filmmakers?). *Zhongguo yinmu* 中國銀幕 1: 34–9.

Zhou, Juanita Huan. 1998. "*Ashes of Time*: The Tragedy and Salvation of the Chinese Intelligentsia." *Asian Cinema* 10.1 (Fall): 62–70.

Zhou Zhengbao 周政保 and Zhang Dong 張東. 1995. "Zhanzheng pian yu Zhongguo kangzhan ticai gushi pian" 戰爭片與中國抗戰題材故事片 (War films and Chinese feature films dealing with the Anti-Japanese War). *Wenyi yanjiu* 文藝研究 5: 13–20.

Zhu Ling. 1993. "A Brave New World? On the Construction of 'Masculinity' and 'Femininity' in *The Red Sorghum Family*." In *Gender and Sexuality in Twentieth-Century Chinese Literature and Society*, edited by Tonglin Lu. Albany: State University of New York Press.

Zukin, Sharon. 1992. "Postmodern Urban Landscapes: Mapping Culture and Power." In *Modernity and Identity*, edited by Scott Lash and Jonathan Friedman. Oxford: Blackwell.

Index

The index includes all English titles of films and television dramas, most Chinese directors, as well as selected names and topics mentioned in the book.

421